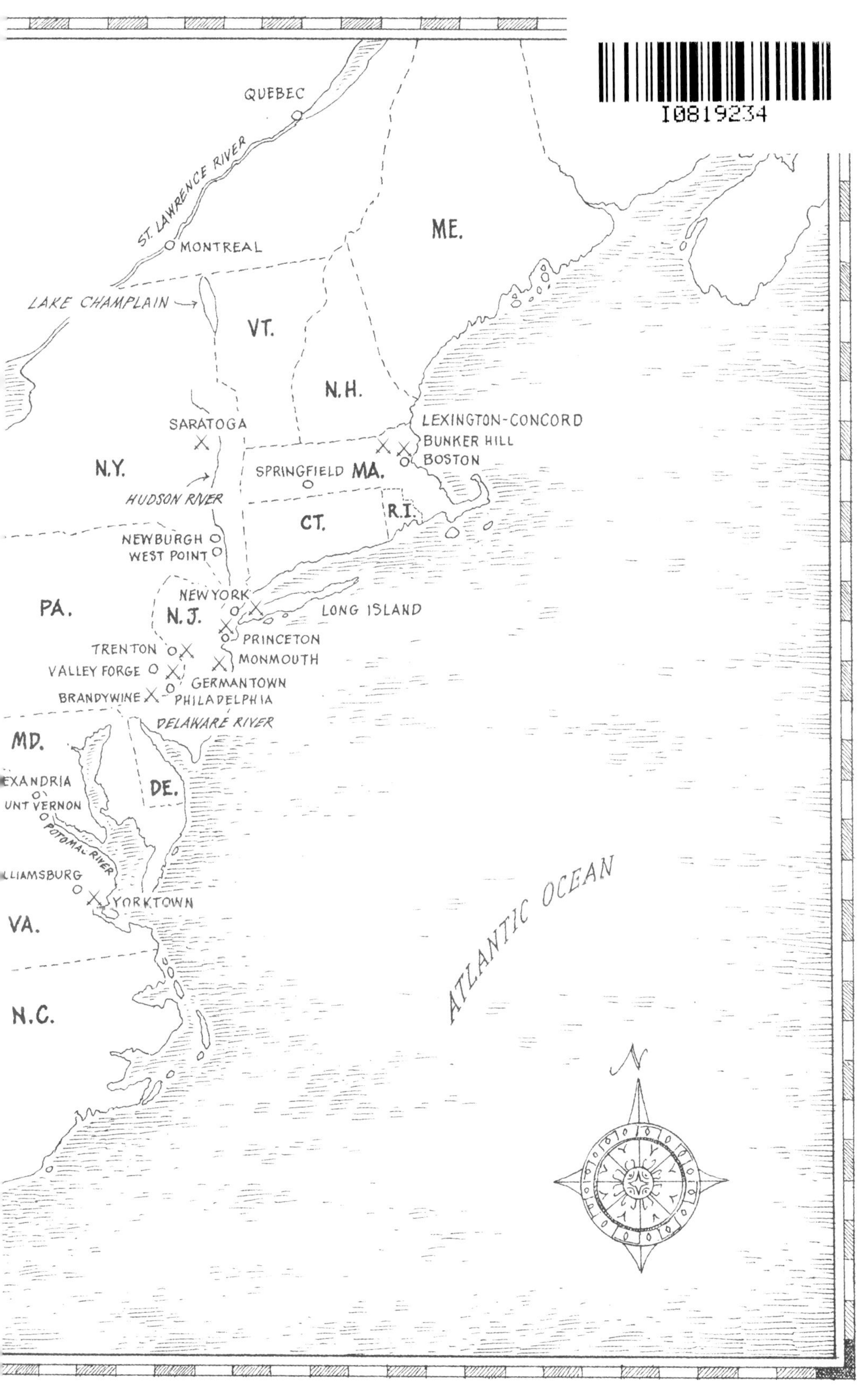
QUEBEC
ST. LAWRENCE RIVER
MONTREAL
LAKE CHAMPLAIN
ME.
VT.
N.H.
SARATOGA
LEXINGTON-CONCORD
BUNKER HILL
BOSTON
N.Y.
SPRINGFIELD
MA.
HUDSON RIVER
R.I.
CT.
NEWBURGH
WEST POINT
NEW YORK
PA.
N.J.
LONG ISLAND
PRINCETON
TRENTON
MONMOUTH
VALLEY FORGE
GERMANTOWN
BRANDYWINE
PHILADELPHIA
DELAWARE RIVER
MD.
EXANDRIA
UNT VERNON
DE.
POTOMAC RIVER
LLIAMSBURG
YORKTOWN
VA.
ATLANTIC OCEAN
N.C.
N

American Patriarch

ALSO BY H. W. BRANDS

T.R.
The First American
The Age of Gold
Lone Star Nation
Andrew Jackson
Traitor to His Class
American Colossus
The Man Who Saved the Union
Reagan
The General vs. the President
Heirs of the Founders
Dreams of El Dorado
The Zealot and the Emancipator
Our First Civil War
The Last Campaign
Founding Partisans
America First

American Patriarch

THE LIFE OF
George Washington

H. W. BRANDS

DOUBLEDAY
New York

FIRST DOUBLEDAY HARDCOVER EDITION 2026

Published by Doubleday, a division of Penguin Random House LLC,
1745 Broadway, New York, NY 10019.

Doubleday and the portrayal of an anchor with a dolphin are registered trademarks of Penguin Random House LLC.

Book design by Cassandra J. Pappas
Endpaper map by John Burgoyne

Cataloging-in-Publication Data has been applied for with the Library of Congress.
ISBN 9780385551557 (hardcover)
ISBN 9780385551564 (ebook)

penguinrandomhouse.com | doubleday.com

Printed in the United States of America
1st Printing

The authorized representative in the EU for product safety and compliance is Penguin Random House Ireland, Morrison Chambers, 32 Nassau Street, Dublin D02 YH68, Ireland, https://eu-contact.penguin.ie.

Contents

Part I

Virginia

1

In 1705, Robert Beverley published *The History and Present State of Virginia*. The colony was almost a century old, and the author thought the world required an account of its origins. He told of the voyage of Walter Raleigh to America in 1584 and the marvelous description the English soldier-statesman-adventurer and his companions brought back to London of what they had seen. The land was portrayed as fertile, the climate sweet and wholesome, the plants and trees abundant and fruitful. The local population was said to be affable, innocent and eager to be instructed. "They represented it as a scene laid open for the good and gracious Queen Elizabeth to propagate the Gospel in and extend her dominions over, as if purposely reserved for her Majesty by a peculiar direction of Providence," wrote Beverley.

Elizabeth was delighted, the more so when Raleigh and his associates proposed to establish a colony in this blessed place. "Her Majesty accordingly took the hint and espoused the project, as far as her present engagements in war with Spain would let her, being so well pleased with the account given that, as the greatest mark of honour she could do the discovery, she called the country by the name of *Virginia,* as well for that it was first discovered in her reign, a Virgin Queen, as that it did still seem to retain the virgin purity and plenty of the first creation and the people their primitive innocence."

THE BLOOM WAS long off the Virginia rose by the time of Beverley's writing. The first colony planted by Raleigh's company, at Roanoke in modern North Carolina, failed, its inhabitants vanishing into the wilderness. A second attempt, at Jamestown, killed nearly half the colonists in the first two years and for a decade barely clung to existence. Only then did the colonists discover their salvation in tobacco. Yet salvation required hard work, by the principals themselves and by the indentured servants and African slaves they imported. The indigenes, of the Powhatan and other tribes, proved less than affable after European diseases ravaged their villages and the Europeans stole their land. The Virginians fell out among themselves, bickering over land rights and other aspects of governance.

The English government occasionally took notice. In 1624 the crown revoked the company charter under which Jamestown had been established and made Virginia a royal colony. But the English government itself was consumed by conflict, most notably a civil war that started in the early 1640s, included the beheading of Charles I and briefly refashioned England into a republic. During the decade of this convulsion, Virginia and the other English colonies that had been established in America were left largely to their own devices. The colonists liked the independence.

Even after the civil war ended with the restoration of the monarchy under Charles II, politics in England remained unsettled. Not until the installation of William of Orange as English king in 1689 did the home country set any kind of model for stability.

The Virginians badly needed it. A rebellion led by Nathaniel Bacon racked the colony in the 1670s. A dispute over Indian policy was the proximate cause of the armed challenge to the authority of Governor William Berkeley. Bacon and his followers wanted Berkeley and the Virginia government to expel the remaining Indian tribes from the colony. But other issues, including taxes and the role of former indentured servants in Virginia politics, added fervor to the dispute. Amid the fighting, Bacon's rebels burned Jamestown. This proved a last gasp for the uprising, for Bacon died of dysentery and the rebels dispersed.

AS DISTURBING AS the Bacon rebellion was to the peace of mind of Virginians, they took comfort that it wasn't nearly as bloody as an almost simultaneous outbreak of violence in New England. The second permanent English colony on the coast of North America was established in 1620 at Plymouth, in modern Massachusetts. The Pilgrim founders hadn't intended to settle so far north, but ill winds blew them off course. Having learned from the Virginia colonists, they came prepared for hard times. Even so, nearly half of them died during the first winter.

The Plymouth colony fell into the shadow of the Massachusetts Bay colony, which drew twenty thousand immigrants from England during the 1630s. Eventually Plymouth was absorbed by its more numerous neighbor. In the meantime, both colonies, plus Connecticut and Rhode Island, had to deal with the Indian tribes they displaced. As in Virginia, indigenes and colonists sometimes got along, but periods of peace simply postponed a larger reckoning. What the Indians had, namely land, the colonists wanted. As the colonial population grew, so did the likelihood the colonists would get it.

In the 1670s a Wampanoag chief named Metacomet, called King Philip by the English, worked to unite other tribes in New England to drive the colonists out. The colonists resisted, and war ensued. The Indians had the better of the early fighting, wiping out dozens of settlements along the frontier and killing hundreds of the English. The English gradually gained the upper hand, burning villages, killing many hundreds of Indians and essentially destroying the Wampanoags and their allies the Narragansetts.

2

John Washington was a child of the English civil war and a survivor, barely, of the Bacon rebellion. Born in the early 1630s in Essex, John was a boy when the civil war forced his father, Lawrence Washington, to take sides in the struggle between the crown and its enemies. Lawrence, an Anglican cleric well positioned at Oxford University, chose the crown. The decision cost him his job and deprived his son of the education the father planned for him. John entered commerce, first as apprentice and then as agent of a trading house that dealt in Virginia tobacco, among other goods.

On a trip to America his ship ran aground in the Potomac River. The delay for repairs gave John time to appreciate Virginia and its people, including a young woman named Anne Pope. Her father, Nathaniel Pope, a planter, liked the English trader and encouraged a match. John and Anne married, and he began to make a name for himself in his new home. He expanded the seven hundred acres the couple received as a wedding gift from her father into holdings of several thousand acres. He became a justice of the peace and joined the militia, rising through the ranks to lieutenant colonel. He was elected to the house of burgesses.

When Bacon's rebellion broke out, John Washington took the side of Governor Berkeley. For his loyalty his estate was attacked and plundered. He died months later, in his early forties. Anne had predeceased him. They left behind three surviving children, including their eldest, Lawrence, named for the child's grandfather.

THIS LAWRENCE WASHINGTON received the formal English education his father missed. Being sent to England for school wasn't unusual for the son of a well-to-do Virginia family, but it nonetheless marked Lawrence as a young man of parts. Another mark came when his father died and bequeathed him two plantations on the Potomac, one at Mattox Creek and the other at Little Hunting Creek.

Lawrence participated in the public life of Westmoreland County and of Virginia. He served as justice of the peace and sheriff. He represented the county in the Virginia house of burgesses. He was elected colonel of the county militia.

He married Mildred Warner, who brought property to the marriage. The couple had three children. The middle child, Augustine, was four years old at the time of his father's death at thirty-eight.

AUGUSTINE WASHINGTON'S MOTHER remarried, to an English merchant. She moved to England and took the three children with her. She died and the children, after a custody battle, returned to Virginia, where they were raised by a Washington cousin.

Upon attaining legal majority, Augustine claimed his inheritance, chiefly a plantation on Bridges Creek. He purchased additional property, including the Hunting Creek plantation from his sister. He married Jane Butler, who brought land to the marriage.

They had four children, of whom two, Lawrence and Augustine Jr., survived to adulthood. Jane died, and Augustine remarried, to Mary Ball. She had six children with him. The oldest, born in 1732 and christened after the patron saint of soldiers and of England, with a name shared by the ruling British monarch, was a boy, George.

3

"I should be glad to hear that you live in harmony and good fellowship with the family at Belvoir, as it is in their power to be very serviceable upon many occasions to us as young beginners," George Washington wrote at twenty-three to his younger brother John Augustine, called Jack. "To that family I am under many obligations, particularly to the old gentleman."

The family was the Fairfaxes, and the obligations George Washington spoke of were those of a young man finding his way forward in Virginia society. The old gentleman was William Fairfax, the master of Belvoir, a plantation on the western bank of the tidewater Potomac. William Fairfax was a cousin of Thomas Fairfax, who became Lord Fairfax upon his father's death. Besides inheriting the title, Thomas Fairfax inherited five million acres of land in Virginia between the Potomac and the Rappahannock Rivers. He didn't get around to visiting his American property for nearly two decades, and he relocated to Virginia only in 1747. Until then William Fairfax acted as his agent and the Virginia representative of the family.

William Fairfax and his wife had a son, George William Fairfax, and two daughters, Anne and Sarah. George Washington's older half brother Lawrence married Anne, giving Washington a reason to spend time at Belvoir. George William Fairfax, eight years older than Washington, became a kind of extra brother. George's wife, Sarah Cary Fairfax, called Sally, was two years older than Washington and became something between a sister and a sweetheart.

THE FAIRFAXES SAT at the apex of Virginia society. No other family boasted a baron in residence. Yet other families did their best to re-create the life of the English aristocracy, adjusted for conditions in America.

The Virginia gentry took time to emerge from the struggles and confusion of the decades after the colony's first settlement. Ambitious men accumulated land via royal grants, treaties with Indians and strategic marriages. This last mode of accumulation proceeded more rapidly in Virginia than in England, due to the high mortality rate. Women often died in childbirth, and men died from illness or accident, giving the surviving spouses new opportunities to pair off and multiply landholdings. It was by this means that George Washington's father and grandfather became land rich. Washington himself married but once, yet to a wealthy widow.

The English practice of primogeniture, by which the eldest son inherited all or most of his father's estate, was adopted by the Virginians, keeping the accumulations from being dissipated. A family once wealthy stayed wealthy, at least the part headed by the eldest son. He became the new patriarch, supporting the others and serving as the public face of the family.

The Virginia gentry differed from the English gentry in distinctive ways. They were more acquisitive, largely because there was more to acquire. The land in England was already claimed, making land transfers a zero-sum game. Much of the land in Virginia was not claimed in any sense the English colonists felt obliged to honor. Where disease hadn't depopulated land occupied by Indians, armed violence did. Land titles were created for the now empty land, tracts were surveyed, and lots were sold, providing cash for the sellers, who often kept the best tracts for themselves.

In England the gentry lived on land rents, payments from the men and women who worked the land. In Virginia land was rented, but much remained under the direct control of the planter, who was so called for operating a plantation. This wasn't entirely by the choice of the planter, instead reflecting a crucial demographic difference between England and America. In England, land was scarce and people plenty. In America, land was plenty and people scarce. In England, the landless had little opportunity to acquire land, which scarcity made expensive. They had no choice but to rent or work for pay. In America, the landless could more easily acquire land, it being cheap. They might rent or work for pay for a time, but many more than in England made the transition to ownership.

This created a labor problem for the gentry. They had far more land than they could work themselves. Anyway, they considered physical labor demeaning. Attempts to enlist Indians were unavailing. Pay meant little to the Indians, and attempts to enslave them failed from the ease of escape to their homes and people.

Indentured service provided an alternative. English men and women who sought to emigrate to America but lacked the price of passage agreed to work for several years in exchange for transport. Indentured service, including apprenticeships, had been practiced in England for centuries and thus was clearly defined in law and custom.

Indentured service worked well in Virginia during the seventeenth century. Most laborers—indeed most immigrants of any kind—arrived by this means. But the system had drawbacks. First, it never satisfied the demand for labor. Not enough English men and women wanted to come. Second, indentured laborers tended to die, which was one reason not enough wanted to come. The same diseases that killed so many of the first colonists in Jamestown still killed newcomers. Third, the limited terms of the indentures meant that laborers had to be replaced regularly.

THE VIRGINIANS TURNED to the age-old practice of slavery. Enslaved Africans had been trafficked for decades to the American colonies of Spain and Portugal, where they proved to be more resistant to disease than Europeans were. In 1619 an English privateer—essentially a pirate licensed by the English crown—arrived in Virginia with two dozen enslaved Africans seized from a Spanish ship. The privateer needed supplies and bartered the slaves for them.

The Africans survived, and Virginia became a regular stop for ships carrying slaves. Their number grew. Virginia took decades to devise a legal code for slavery. Was their servitude time limited, as with the indentured servants? Or for life? Virginia lawmakers said life. What was the status of the children of slaves? Were they also slaves? Virginia said yes, if the mother was enslaved. The status of the father didn't matter. This was an acknowledgment of the doubt that can surround paternity.

Yet it created awkwardness, to say the least, when the father of a child born to an enslaved mother was the owner of that mother, making the father the owner of his own child. In response the Virginia gentry developed a willful blindness about sexual relations between masters and slaves, often pretending that such relations didn't occur, despite the light complexions of certain slave children and the occasional resemblances between owners and owned.

. . .

MEMBERS OF THE GENTRY were the dominant group economically. Their control of land and slaves made them the largest producers of tobacco and other crops. The emphasis on land as the basis of wealth, combined with the geography of Virginia, with tidewater rivers that ran far inland from the sea, worked against the growth of cities. Planters often shipped tobacco straight from their docks to England, rather than through city-based merchants, and they purchased goods direct from England, where they typically had purchasing agents.

The gentry consolidated their dominance by manning government positions. The crown appointed governors, but Virginians elected members of the house of burgesses, which controlled the provincial budget and passed bills the governor either approved or vetoed. A member of the gentry would stand for office—*running* for office was beneath gentry dignity—and would provide refreshments to voters on polling day. The gentry also supplied most of Virginia's professionals, especially the lawyers and physicians.

The Anglican church was the established religion of Virginia, as of England. Anglican ministers were paid from the public purse. Members of the gentry served as vestrymen, who advised the ministers and managed the affairs of the parishes. This involved legislating morality and providing for the poor, among other things.

Though the gentry didn't work physically, they kept busy. They managed their plantations, which could be large operations involving hundreds of people. They corresponded with their English agents, receiving reports of sales and ordering consumer and production goods. They attended sessions of the house of burgesses and meetings of the vestries.

They entertained. A reputation for hospitality was essential to members of the gentry. They built fine houses, ideally on high spots visible from passing roads. These houses had names—Belvoir, Belle Grove, Gunston, Stratford, Shirley—closely associated with the names of the families who owned them. The servants, as domestic slaves were called, had instructions to be prepared to serve meals to guests on a moment's notice. Visiting and receiving visitors filled much of the time of the gentry. The ritual displayed wealth, cemented social ties and circulated news among a scattered people.

For recreation the men of the gentry engaged in hunts. One plantation would be chosen, and the men would come on horseback and spend a morning showing off their horses and hounds and their riding and hunting skills. The finest horseman in a county was held in esteem for that skill, almost regardless of other talents.

The gentry held balls. Men and women danced. The dancing provided exercise, often vigorous, without a descent into physical labor. It allowed young men and women to flirt and touch without incurring social disapproval.

4

In November 1739, the *Pennsylvania Gazette* ran a notice: “Last week the Rev. Mr. Whitefield landed from London at Lewes-Town in Sussex County, where he preached; and arrived in this city on Friday night; on Sunday and every day since, he has preached in the church. And on Monday he designs (God willing) to set out for New-York, and return hither the week after, and then proceed by land through Maryland, Virginia and Carolina to Georgia.”

The Philadelphia newspaper followed the story of George Whitefield, an English preacher. “On Thursday last,” it wrote a week later, “the Rev. Mr. Whitefield began to preach from the court-house-gallery in this city, about six at night, to near 6000 people before him in the street, who stood in an awful silence to hear him; and this continued every night, till Sunday. On Monday he set out for New-York, and was to preach at Burlington in his way going, and in Bucks County coming back. Before he returns to England he designs (God willing) to preach the gospel in every Province in America, belonging to the English. On Monday the 26th he intends to set out for Annapolis.”

Two weeks later: “On Friday last the Rev. Mr. Whitefield, arrived here, with his friends from New-York, where he preached eight times; and on his return hither preached at Elizabethtown, Brunswick, Maidenhead, Trenton, Neshaminy and Abingdon. He has preached twice every day in the church to great crowds, except Tuesday, when he preached at German-Town from a balcony to about 5000 people in the street: And last night the crowd was so great to hear his farewell sermon that the church could not contain one half, whereupon they withdrew to Society Hill, where he preached from a balcony to a multitude, computed at not less than 10,000 people.”

The people of Pennsylvania couldn’t get enough of the tireless preacher. “On Thursday last the Rev. Mr. Whitefield, left this city, and was accompanied to Chester by about 150 horse, and preached there to about 7000 people; on Friday he preached twice at Willingstown to about 5000; on Saturday at Newcastle to about 2500, and the same evening at Christian Bridge to about 3000; on Sunday at Whiteclay Creek he preached twice, resting about half an hour between the sermons, to about 8000, of whom about 3000 'tis computed came on horseback. It rained most of the time and yet they stood in the open air."

The proprietor of the *Pennsylvania Gazette* was Benjamin Franklin, who found the phenomenon of George Whitefield fascinating, besides being good for sales of the paper. Whitefield was the most prominent of a new breed of preachers who conveyed a message of salvation through an emotional connection to Jesus and the gospels. The "new lights," as they were called, challenged the staid institutionalism of the Anglican church and other established denominations, which responded with suspicion, hostility and not a little jealousy. The "old lights" often denied the use of their pulpits to Whitefield and his like, compelling them to preach outdoors. Whitefield turned this to effect, in that outdoors there was almost no limit on how many could hear his message.

The *Gazette*'s reports of the size of Whitefield's audiences must have struck some readers as fanciful. But it had a basis in experiment and geometry. "He had a loud and clear voice, and articulated his words and sentences so perfectly that he might be heard and understood at a great distance, especially as his auditories, however numerous, observed the most exact silence," Franklin wrote in his autobiography. "He preached one evening from the top of the courthouse steps, which are in the middle of Market Street and on the west side of Second Street, which crosses it at right angles. Both streets were filled with his hearers to a considerable distance. Being among the hindmost in Market Street, I had the curiosity to learn how far he could be heard, by retiring backwards down the street towards the river; and I found his voice distinct till I came near Front Street, when some noise in that street obscured it. Imagining then a semicircle, of which my distance should be the radius, and that it were filled with auditors, to each of whom I allowed two square feet, I computed that he might well be heard by more than thirty thousand. This reconciled me to the newspaper accounts of his having preached to twenty-five thousand people in the fields, and to the ancient histories of generals haranguing whole armies, of which I had sometimes doubted."

Franklin also doubted Whitefield's message. Franklin was a skeptic on all religious views, and the more skeptical the more devoutly the views were held. Philadelphia's famous tolerance of all religions, which implied skepticism of each, was much of what made the city congenial to him. Yet Franklin found Whitefield appealing and in certain respects irresistible. Whitefield wanted to build an orphan house in Georgia, which had recently been established as a penal colony for British convicts, many of whom were not well suited to the tasks of building a new community. Many died of the hardships, leaving children behind. "The sight of their miserable situation inspired the benevolent heart of Mr. Whitefield with the idea of building an orphan house there, in which they might be supported and educated. Returning northward, he preached up this charity, and made large collections, for his eloquence had a wonderful power over the hearts and purses of his hearers."

Franklin endorsed Whitefield's purpose but not his plan. "As Georgia was then destitute of materials and workmen, and it was proposed to send them from Philadelphia at a great expense, I thought it would have been better to have built the house here, and brought the children to it." He shared this thought with Whitefield, who rejected it. "I therefore refused to contribute." But not for long. "I happened soon after to attend one of his sermons, in the course of which I perceived he intended to finish with a collection, and I silently resolved he should get nothing from me. I had in my pocket a handful of copper money, three or four silver dollars, and five pistoles in gold. As he proceeded I began to soften, and concluded to give the coppers. Another stroke of his oratory made me ashamed of that, and determined me to give the silver; and he finished so admirably, that I emptied my pocket wholly into the collector's dish, gold and all."

The Great Awakening, the label given to what Whitefield and other itinerant preachers set in motion, challenged received notions of religion, but not of religion only. After his tour of the south, Whitefield chastised the residents of that region for their treatment of their slaves. "I was sensibly touched with a fellow-feeling of the miseries of the poor Negroes," he wrote in an open letter to "the Inhabitants of Maryland, Virginia, North and South Carolina." If he had had more time in the south, he would have shared his thinking in person. But failing that, he put it to paper. "How you will receive it I know not. Whether you will accept it in love, or be offended with me, as the matter of the damsel was with Paul, for calling the evil spirit out of her when he"—the evil spirit—"saw the hope of his gain was gone, I am uncertain." But he had to speak. "I must inform you, in the meekness and gentleness of Christ, that I think God has a quarrel with you for your abuse of and cruelty to the poor Negroes."

Whitefield didn't condemn the institution of slavery per se. "Whether it be lawful for Christians to buy slaves, and thereby encourage the nations from whence they are brought to be at perpetual war with each other, I shall not take upon me to determine." The treatment of slaves was another matter. "Sure I am, it is sinful, when bought, to use them as bad, nay worse than, as though they were brutes, and whatever particular exceptions there may be (as I would charitably hope there are some) I fear the generality of you that own Negroes are liable to such a charge, for your slaves, I believe, work as hard if not harder than the horses whereon you ride. These, after they have done their work, are fed and taken proper care of. But many negroes when wearied with labour in your plantations have been obliged to grind their own corn after they return home. Your dogs are caressed and fondled at your tables. But your slaves who are frequently styled dogs or beasts, have not an equal privilege. They are scarce permitted to pick up the crumbs which fall from their masters' tables. Nay, some, as I have been informed by an eye-witness, have been, upon the most trifling provocation, cut with knives and had forks thrown into their flesh. Not to mention what numbers have been given up to the inhuman usage of cruel task-masters who, by their unrelenting scourges, have ploughed open their backs and made long furrows, and at length."

Whitefield had been told of slaves who killed themselves rather than live under such regimes. "Considering what usage they commonly meet with, I have wondered that we have not more instances of self-murder among the negroes, or that they have not more frequently rose up in arms against their owners," he wrote. "And though I heartily pray they may never be permitted to get the upper hand, yet should such a thing be permitted by Providence, all good men must acknowledge the judgment would be just."

Worse than the violence done the slaves' bodies was the mistreatment of their souls. "Enslaving or misusing their bodies would, comparatively speaking, be an inconsiderable evil was proper care taken of their souls. But I have great reason to believe that most of you, on purpose, keep your negroes ignorant of Christianity, or, otherwise, why are they permitted through your provinces openly to profane the Lord's Day by their dancing, piping and such like? I know the general pretence for this neglect of their souls that teaching them Christianity would make them proud and consequently unwilling to submit to slavery. But what a dreadful reflection is this on your holy religion!"

. . .

WHITEFIELD'S UPBRAIDING OF slaveholders for their mistreatment of slaves echoed among others of the new persuasion. In Virginia the awakening featured attacks by Presbyterians and Baptists against the dominant Anglicans. Samuel Davies was a Presbyterian who held forth in Hanover County, where Patrick Henry was growing up. Henry, no slouch as a speaker himself, remembered Davies as the most compelling orator he ever heard. In his preaching and in his flock-tending, Davies took pains to endorse and promote the spiritual equality of blacks with whites. Like Whitefield, Davies avoided challenging slavery as an institution. This was tactically prudent, given the resistance he already elicited on strictly theological issues. But it probably reflected his belief that slavery was ordained by God—to the extent that God's chosen people, the Hebrews, practiced it and Jesus never spoke against it—and so wasn't something for humans to overturn. Indeed, evidence suggests that Davies himself owned slaves.

Yet slaves should be treated kindly and their souls given the same opportunities as those of white people. Davies brought black people into his congregation, and he helped them learn to read, that they encounter the word of God directly. Much work remained. "There are thousands of Negroes in this colony who still continue in the grossest ignorance and most stupid carelessness about religion, and as rank pagans as when they left the wilds of Africa," he wrote in a letter to a donor to his ministry. "And there are not a few of this unhappy character even in the bounds of my congregation (which, by the by, is about sixty miles in circumference). But I think, sir, my ministry of late has been most successful among them. Two Sundays ago I had the pleasure of seeing forty of their black faces around the table of the Lord, who all make a credible profession of Christianity." Davies especially valued donated books. "When I reflect upon the almost universal neglect of the many thousands of poor slaves in this wide extended country—that they generally continue as heathens in a Christian country, that but few of their masters will furnish them with such means of instructions, and that they are absolutely incapable of furnishing themselves—when I reflect upon the burden of guilt under which my country groans on this account, when the impressions of these things are fresh upon my mind, I am quite insatiable and can never say it is enough."

Baptists in Virginia were more radical than Presbyterian Davies. Some Baptist preachers condemned slavery itself, and most accorded black men and women full equality in their congregations. Blacks were allowed to bring charges against whites in Baptist disciplinary hearings. White slave owners were rebuked for mistreating black slaves.

All of which compounded the alarm felt by adherents of the established order at the challenge of the Great Awakening. What started in theology extrapolated to daily life. Was anything safe? The status of the gentry in Virginia life? The position of Virginia and the other colonies within the British empire?

The Baptists led the way to perdition, in the view of the old lights. "Wives are drawn from their husbands, children from their parents, and slaves from the obedience of their masters," warned the *Virginia Gazette* about the Baptists. "Thus the very heartstrings of those little societies which form the greater are torn in sunder, and all their peace destroyed."

5

George Washington was an eldest son, but of his mother rather than his father. He wasn't first in line of inheritance, but neither would he be left out. He wouldn't become the face of the family. He might become a planter, but first he'd have to do something else.

He would have been sent to England for schooling, as his older half brothers had, if his father hadn't died at forty-eight, when George was eleven. The death threw uncertainty over the family finances, besides making his mother reluctant to send her firstborn across the sea. He stayed home and learned his lessons from tutors.

Mathematics, including geometry and trigonometry, was part of the instruction, and he showed a facility for it. Practical exercises put the math to use in problems of surveying land, first on paper and then in the field. He shone here too, not least because he liked being outdoors, on horse and on foot, in good weather and bad.

"FRIDAY MARCH 11TH. 1747/8. Began my journey in company with George Fairfax Esqr. We travelled this day 40 Miles to Mr. George Neavils in Prince William County."

Thus began the first great adventure of George Washington's young life, as recorded in the first journal he wrote. The "1747/8" characterization of the year reflected the anachronistic calendar of the British empire. The Julian calendar long used in western Europe had been too generous, accounting a year as 365¼ days, and therefore had added a leap day every fourth year. A year is actually several minutes shorter than this, and so the calendar requires fewer leap days to keep the equinox from wandering. Pope Gregory XIII decreed the fix in 1582, which required skipping ten days. Gregory also said each new year would start on January 1, which hadn't been uniform practice. The Church of England, however, having recently broken from Rome on theology, declined to be instructed on chronology. The English stuck with the old system, which for them specified March 25 as the start of the new year. In England, December 1747 was followed by January 1747 rather than January 1748.

Yet the English understood their eccentricity, and they took to labeling January, February and most of March with both the old-style year and the new-style. Consequently Washington's use of March 1747/8. Within a few years more the eccentricity would become unbearable, and London would capitulate to Rome. In 1752, Britain skipped eleven days, with Wednesday, September 2, being followed by Thursday, September 14. New Year's Day became January 1. Some people backdated their own biographies. The calendar read February 11, 1731, on the day Washington was born. By the time he died his birthday would be noted as February 22, 1732.

WASHINGTON WAS ACCOMPANYING George Fairfax to help conduct surveys of land in the holdings of Lord Fairfax. "Saturday March 12th. This morning Mr. James Genn the surveyor came to us," Washington wrote. "We traveled over the Blue Ridge to Capt. Ashby's on Shenandoah. Nothing remarkable happened."The Blue Ridge marked the divide between where Virginia had been and where it was going. The valley of the Shenandoah River on the western side had long served the indigenous peoples of the region as a corridor from northeast to southwest, and it was beginning to serve the newcomers from Europe.

"Sunday March 13th. Rode to his Lordship's quarter about 4 miles higher up the river. We went through most beautiful groves of sugar trees and spent the best part of the day in admiring the trees and richness of the land."

The Shenandoah valley was renowned for its beauty and abundance. One of the attractions of surveying as a trade was that surveyors got an early look at land about to come on market. With their own money or on behalf of investors, they could jump the queue. Washington's journal would help him remember where the best tracts lay.

"Monday 14th. We sent our baggage to Capt. Hite's (near Frederick Town), went ourselves down the river about 16 Miles to Capt. Isaac Pennington's (the land, exceeding rich and fertile all the way, produces abundance of grain, hemp, tobacco etc.) in order to lay off some lands on Cate's Marsh and Long Marsh."

Frederick Town would become Winchester. Jost Hite was a native of Alsace, in the contested region between France and the German-speaking lands to the east. He had come to America and was engaged in the business enterprise that made more people richer than any other in American history: land speculation. He already held title to more than forty thousand acres and would eventually acquire title to nearly a hundred thousand. He bought cheap, far ahead of the frontier of settlement. But with each year, as Virginia's population grew, the closer settlement approached. As it did, his land appreciated in value.

"Tuesday 15th. We set out early with intent to run round the said land, but being taken in a rain and it increasing very fast obliged us to return. It clearing about one o'clock and our time being too precious to lose we a second time ventured out and worked hard till night and then returned to Pennington's. We got our suppers and was lighted in to a room and I not being so good a woodsman as the rest of my company stripped myself very orderly and went in to the bed as they called it, when to my surprize I found it to be nothing but a little straw, matted together without sheets or any thing else but only one threadbare blanket with double its weight of vermin such as lice, fleas etc. I was glad to get up (as soon as the light was carried from us) and put on my clothes and lay as my companions. Had we not have been very tired, I am sure we should not have slept much that night. I made a promise not to sleep so from that time forward, choosing rather to sleep in the open air before a fire."

Likely the senior members of the surveying party, possibly including George Fairfax, got a laugh from Washington's innocence of public houses and their dubious hygiene. He'd had a sheltered upbringing, metaphorically and actually, rarely having slept elsewhere than in his own bed or the beds of people of his social class. To his credit, the experience put him off shared beds, not off the travel that prompted the sharing.

"Wednesday 16th. We set out early and finished about one o'clock and then travelled up to Frederick Town where our baggage came to us. We cleaned ourselves (to get rid of the game we had catched the night before) and took a review of the town and then returned to our lodgings where we had a good dinner prepared for us, wine and rum punch in plenty and a good feather bed with clean sheets which was a very agreeable regale." Likely George Fairfax took pity on Washington and sprang for better lodgings.

. . .

THE EXPEDITION CONTINUED through the late winter rain. When it merely soaked them, they carried on. But at times it stymied their progress. "We travelled up about 35 miles to Thomas Barwick's on Potomack where we found the river so excessively high by reason of the great rains that had fallen up about the Alleghany Mountains as they told us, which was then bringing down the melted snow and that it would not be fordable for several days," Washington wrote on March 18. "It was then above six foot higher than usual and was rising."

They made use of the delay to visit some warm springs long known to the Indians and which were attracting whites to the area. On the second day the head of the party determined to press on. "Finding the river not much abated, we in the evening swam our horses over and carried them to Charles Polk's in Maryland for pasturage till the next morning." They traveled up the Maryland side of the Potomac on what Washington described as "the worst road that ever was trod by man or beast."

They stopped at a trading post run by Thomas Cresap, a Yorkshireman who had emigrated to Maryland as a young man. Cresap was a type specimen of a group Washington would deal closely with during the coming decades: the frontier trader as comfortable with Indians as with whites, as leery of the one as of the other, fluent in the languages and customs of both, and indispensable to both. He built his trading post at the confluence of several Indian trails, which became the confluence of settler roads.

A downpour the next day again kept them from their work. The rain persisted beyond noon the day after that. The surveyors were preparing to leave when a commotion occurred outside the post. "We were agreeably surprised at the sight of thirty odd Indians coming from war with only one scalp." Washington didn't identify the scalp. Presumably it came from another tribe. There hadn't been reports of Indian attacks on whites in the area. The agreeable part of the surprise was probably that the conflict, such as it was, seemed contained.

Nonetheless, it behooved Cresap and his guests to make the visitors feel welcome. "We had some liquor with us, of which we gave them part. It elevating their spirits put them in the humour of dancing." Washington witnessed his first Indian dance. "They clear a large circle and make a great fire in the middle, then seat themselves around it. The speaker makes a grand speech telling them in what manner they are to dance. After he has finished, the best dancer jumps up as one awaked out of a sleep and runs and jumps about the ring in a most comical manner. He is followed by the rest. Then begins their musicians to play. The musick is a pot half of water with a deerskin stretched over it as tight as it can and a gourd with some shot in it to rattle and a piece of an horse's tail tied to it to make it look fine. The one keeps rattling and the other drumming all the while the others is dancing."

The surveyors spent the next day at Cresap's with the Indians. Perhaps, outnumbered as they were, they didn't want to venture forth with the Indians' intentions unknown. But by the day after that they decided to take a chance. They weren't making money sitting still.

They camped on the claim of Solomon Hedges, a Quaker who presided as the local justice of the peace. Squire Hedges, as he was called, offered the hospitality of the place. "When we came to supper there was neither a cloth upon the table nor a knife to eat with, but as good luck would have it we had knives of our own." Perhaps Washington was being facetious. No woodsman traveled anywhere without a knife.

The next several days were all business. "This morning went out and surveyed five hundred acres of land," Washington wrote on March 29. The following day: "We began at the boundary line of the northern 10 miles above Stump's and run off two lots and returned to Stump's." Michael Stump was a recent arrival in the area. The day after that: "Early this morning one of our men went out with the gun and soon returned with two wild turkeys." Working men had to eat. "We then went to our business. Run off three lots and returned to our camping place at Stump's." Three more lots were surveyed on April 1.

On April 2, Washington wrote, "Last night was a blowing and rainy night. Our straw catched a fire that we were laying upon." Most of the men had been sleeping soundly and might have been badly burned. But one awoke and roused the others. The work went on. "We run off four lots this day."

This April was coming in like the proverbial lion. "Last night was a much more blustering night than the former," Washington wrote on April 3. "We had our tent carried quite off with the wind and was obliged to lie the latter part of the night without covering."

The next day they had an audience. "We did two lots and was attended by a great company of people—men, women and children that attended us through the woods as we went, shewing their antic tricks." Washington wasn't impressed, partly because he wasn't able to understand them. "They seem to be as ignorant a set of people as the Indians. They would never speak English but when spoken to they speak all Dutch"—

Deutsch, which was to say German. More wind: "This day our tent was blown down by the violentness of the wind."

The German immigrants followed them the next day as well, when they surveyed four lots. Another bad night followed. "Last night was so intolerably smoky that we were obliged all hands to leave the tent to the mercy of the wind and fire."

The onlookers stayed with them the next morning. At noon the surveyors set off for the next job. "On our journey was catched in a very heavy rain. We got under a straw house until the worst of it was over and then continued our journey."

More rain was followed by one of their larger jobs. "We went and surveyed 15 hundred acres of land." April 8 brought a treat, at least for Washington and George Fairfax, to whom the hospitality of the neighborhood was extended. They visited a man named Van Metris. "We stayed about two hours and walked back again and slept in Cassey's house, which was the first night I had slept in a house since I came to the branch"—the south branch of the Potomac.

The work the next day was complicated. "We rode down below the Trough in order to lay off lots there. We laid off one this day. The Trough is a couple of ledges of mountain impassable running side and side together for above 7 or 8 miles and the river down between them. You must ride round the back of the mountain for to get below them. We camped this night in the woods near a wild meadow where was a large stack of hay. After we had pitched our tent and made a very large fire we pulled out our knapsack in order to recruit ourselves. Every one was his own cook. Our spits was forked sticks. Our plates was a large chip"—of wood. "As for dishes we had none."

Personal affairs called George Fairfax home. Washington decided to leave with him. "We took our farewell of the branch and travelled over hills and mountains to one Coddy's on Great Cacapehon, about 40 miles," Washington wrote on April 10, referring to James Caudy, a modest landowner. The next day: "We travelled from Coddy's down to Frederick Town where we reached about 12 o'clock. We dined in town and then went to Capt. Hite's and lodged." In their eagerness to get home they took a wrong turn. "We set off from Capt. Hite's in order to go over Williams Gap, about 20 miles, and after riding about 20 miles we had 20 to go for we had lost ourselves and got up as high as Ashby's Bent"—also called Ashby's Gap. "We did get over Williams Gap that night and as low as William West's in Fairfax County, 18 miles from the top of the ridge." They had another reason to stay alert. "This day see a rattlesnake, the first we had seen in all our journey," Washington wrote.

"Wednesday the 13th of April 1748. Mr. Fairfax got safe home and I myself safe to my brother's, which concludes my journal."

6

Washington's adventure in surveying hooked him on the profession. And the experience he gained on the trip beyond the Blue Ridge enhanced his credibility. This and the support of the Fairfax clan won him appointment as official surveyor of the newly formed Culpeper County. At seventeen he embarked on a promising career.

For three years he spent each spring and fall in the field, running property lines, establishing markers, recording descriptions of parcels and collecting fees. Winter snows made markers hard to set and harder to find, and the full foliage of summer obscured sight lines through the trees. The occupation played to Washington's strength in mathematics, his taste for the outdoors and the meticulousness that would characterize his keeping of records his whole life.

Surveying sharpened his ability to tell good land from mediocre and poor. It also taught him that others were making a lot more money from buying and selling land than he was from surveying it. Other men might be content with the comfortable life surveying could support. But not Washington, as he gradually realized.

HE OCCASIONALLY DREAMED of a career at sea. His brother Lawrence had been to sea, taking part in a naval campaign during one of Britain's frequent wars. Lawrence brought home stories that beguiled his younger brother. Washington's mother wasn't keen on the plan. The sea sometimes swallowed those who ventured upon it, and a career in the Royal Navy was a slow climb, especially for a provincial.

The maritime fancy still flickered at the time Washington took his first sea voyage. Lawrence had contracted consumption, as tuberculosis was then called, and the illness grew worse. A common prescription, for those who could afford it, was relocation to where the air was thought to be better. Mountains were recommended, as were sea islands. Lawrence chose one of the latter, Barbados, where the Atlantic meets the Caribbean off the coast of South America. Washington joined him on the voyage.

He discovered a world he'd hardly imagined. "Catched a dolphin at 8 p.m.," Washington wrote on October 6, 1751, in a log he kept of the voyage. "A shark at 11 and one of his pilot fish. The dolphin and pilot fish was dressed for dinner." The dolphin in question was the fish, also called mahi-mahi, not the mammal. The next day: "Saw many fish swimming about us, of which a dolphin we catched at noon, but could not entice with a baited hooks two barracudas which played under our stern for some hours."

Ocean weather was daunting. "A disturbed and large sea which eminently endangered our masts," he wrote. "The seamen seemed disheartened, confessing they never had seen such weather before. It was universally surmised there had been a violent hurricane not far distant."

But the captain kept a true course and found what he was looking for. "This morning arose with agreeable assurance of a certain and steady trade wind, which after near five weeks buffeting and being tossed by a fickle and merciless ocean was gladdening news."

The trade winds carried them to their destination, "November 4th 1751. This morning received a card from Major Clarke"—commander of British forces in the Windward Islands, which included Barbados—"welcoming us to Barbadoes, with an invitation to breakfast and dine with him. We went, myself with some reluctance as the smallpox was in his family."

They turned to the matter that had brought them to the island. "Early this morning came Dr. Hilary, an eminent physician recommended by Major Clarke, to pass opinion on my brother's disorder, which he did in a favorable light, giving great assurance that it was not so fixed but that a cure might be effectually made." The cure would begin on the island. "In the cool of the evening we rode out accompanied by Mr. Carter to seek lodgings in the country, as the doctor advised, and were perfectly enraptured with the beautiful prospects, which every side presented to our view the fields of cane, corn, fruit-trees etc. in a delightful green."

Word got out that a rich man needed a place to save his life. "Came Capt. Croftan with his proposals which though extravagantly dear my brother was obliged to give." The house was a mile from Bridgetown, the capital. "The prospect is extensive by land and pleasant by sea, as we command the prospect of Carlisle Bay and all the shipping in such manner that none can go in or out without being open to our view."

Commercial and social connections linked Barbados to Virginia. The locals were happy to host the Washington brothers, to catch up on mutual acquaintances. Fresh produce, especially fruit, was featured on the menus. Pomegranates, guavas, oranges, lemons and apples were items Washington recognized. The two went to a play in Bridgetown. Washington was more interested in the fort that guarded the approach to the town. "It's pretty strongly fortified and mounts about 36 guns within the fortification."

Two weeks after arrival Washington discovered that his reluctance to dine at the Clarkes' was well founded. "Was strongly attacked with the smallpox," he wrote on November 17. "Sent for Dr. Lanahan, whose attendance was very constant." Washington's recovery was slow. Not for nearly a month did he regain his feet. Yet he was one of the lucky. His survival wasn't surprising, in that only a third of people infected died from the disease, and few of these were as young and strong as Washington. But most survivors carried scars Washington didn't. And having survived, he possessed lifetime immunity.

Lawrence's prognosis was bleaker. He didn't contract smallpox, having himself survived an earlier bout. But his pulmonary condition didn't improve. His doctor said Bermuda might suit him better. Lawrence decided to go. He sent Washington home to Virginia. He said that if his condition improved in Bermuda, he'd ask Washington to escort his wife there.

"Took my leave of my brother, Major Clarke, etc.," Washington wrote on December 22. "Weighed anchor and got out of Carlisle Bay about 12." The homeward leg of the journey brought a new experience. "Met with a brisk trade wind and pretty large swell which made the ship roll much and me very sick." The weather calmed for the holiday. "Christmas Day fine, clear and pleasant, with moderate sea." The weather worsened again. "Rain, hail and snow and high and mountainous sea." A dishonest shipmate took advantage of Washington's distress. "Upon searching my chest, discovered I had been robbed of 16 pistoles"—Spanish gold coins. Had he been older, or had Lawrence been with him, he might have insisted that the captain search the passengers and crew. He let it go.

By the time they reached the Chesapeake Bay, Washington couldn't wait to set foot on terra firma. He never again considered a career at sea.

Part II

Ohio

7

The English and the French had been fighting for centuries, at least since the French duke William of Normandy defeated the English king Harold at Hastings and fixed French control and the French language upon the island across the channel from France. The conflict was brutal, including the burning at the stake of Jeanne d'Arc. Generations of English men and women and French men and women grew up fearing and hating each other and believing that conflict between their peoples was much of what made them who they were.

Thus it was only natural that the struggle should follow French and English explorers and settlers to North America. The western continent was large and the number of colonists small at first. During the early decades the newcomers didn't see much of each other. But by the late seventeenth century they met frequently enough to engage militarily. King William's War pitted colonists of New England against those of New France, as what would become Canada was called. It lasted a decade and was part of a contemporaneous European conflict called the War of the League of Augsburg. The eighteenth century opened with Queen Anne's War, the American salient of the War of the Spanish Succession. This conflict lived in the memories of Anglo-Americans for a particular French and allied Indian assault on Deerfield, Massachusetts, in which scores of English colonists were killed and more than a hundred carried into captivity. Many of the captives died on the march to Canada. Others, notably young women, were forcibly adopted into Indian tribes. The worst of it, in the minds of many of the English, was that some of the adoptees refused rescue when it belatedly arrived, having so thoroughly identified with their captors.

The War of Jenkins' Ear was brief but meaningful for the family of George Washington, who was seven when this round of the fighting commenced. Washington's brother Lawrence was of prime military age, in his early twenties, and eager to make his mark among his fellow Virginians. King George II sent an officer across the Atlantic with a sheaf of officer's commissions that required only the names of likely young men. Lawrence Washington stepped forward and was named captain of a Virginia company of infantry.

This war pitted Britain—as it was properly called after the 1707 act of union between England and Scotland—against Spain, often an ally of France. It sent Lawrence Washington and his regiment to the Caribbean, where they took part in an expedition against the Spanish stronghold of Cartagena on the South American coast. The expedition failed as the North Americans were devastated by yellow fever and other tropical diseases. Lawrence Washington was among the few survivors, and he remembered the campaign fondly enough to rename his Virginia home on a hilltop above the Potomac River for his commander, Edward Vernon.

King George's War began when George Washington was twelve, old enough to be impressed by Lawrence's tales of swash and buckle but too young to create such stories for himself. This conflict was part of the War of the Austrian Succession in Europe, and for the English Americans it had the advantage of being fought in the less lethal climate of New England and Canada. The war begot a brilliant success for British colonial arms when a campaign commanded by Massachusetts governor William Shirley captured Louisbourg, a French fortress on Cape Breton Island that had threatened the commerce and fisheries of New England. American elation at the triumph turned to anger against Britain when Louisbourg was returned to France in 1748 as part of the settlement of the European war. New Englanders were the angriest, having done most toward the triumph. A suspicion of the mother country smoldered in the hearts of many in Boston and its hinterland.

"ON WEDNESDAY THE 31ST of October 1753 I was commissioned and appointed by the Honorable Robert Dinwiddie Esq., Governor etc. of Virginia to visit and deliver a letter to the commandant of the French forces on the Ohio," Washington wrote. Robert Dinwiddie was technically the lieutenant governor of Virginia. But in keeping with a practice common in Britain's colonial system, the titular governor, Lord Albemarle, stayed in Britain and had nothing to do with the management of the colony. Dinwiddie had learned of French military activity in the region beyond the Allegheny Mountains and north of the Ohio River.

Virginia claimed the territory. So did Pennsylvania. Yet though the British colonies couldn't agree which had the better claim, they concurred that France had no claim at all. Ohio was British.

Dinwiddie, via Washington, was laying Britain's claim against France, and implicitly Virginia's against Pennsylvania's. "The lands upon the River Ohio, in the western parts of the Colony of Virginia, are so notoriously known to be the property of the Crown of Great Britain that it is a matter of equal concern and surprise to me to hear that a body of French forces are erecting fortresses and making settlements upon that river, within his Majesty's dominions," the governor's letter declared. "The many and repeated complaints I have received of these acts of hostility lay me under the necessity of sending, in the name of the King, my master, the bearer hereof, George Washington, Esq., one of the adjutants-general of the forces of this dominion, to complain to you of the encroachments thus made, and of the injuries done to the subjects of Great Britain, in violation of the law of nations, and the treaties now subsisting between the two Crowns." Dinwiddie welcomed any explanation the French officer had to give, in a letter Washington would carry back. Yet explanation or no, the outcome must be the same. "It becomes my duty to require your peaceable departure."

Neither Dinwiddie nor Washington knew who the French commandant was. They didn't know where he could be found. This was for Washington to discover. It might not be easy. The journey was long. Winter was coming. Washington had authority and resources to hire assistants, including an interpreter, but the party would be too small to defend itself against concerted opposition. They would encounter Indians. Some would be friendly, others not. The latter, if not positively urged by the French to waylay British soldiers or travelers, might infer that the French wouldn't be upset if they did.

Perhaps Washington doubted his ability to carry out the mission assigned to him. If so, he hid his doubts well. With all the authority a twenty-one-year-old could muster, he set out from Williamsburg. Traveling north on horseback, he reached Fredericksburg the next day. There he engaged a Dutchman who spoke French, Jacob Van Braam. With Van Braam he continued north to Alexandria, where he purchased a few provisions for the journey. From Alexandria they struck west through the Blue Ridge and into the Shenandoah valley beyond. At Winchester he purchased more supplies—food, ammunition, presents for Indians—and horses to carry them.

A new road led from Winchester northwest to Wills Creek, where the stream of that name entered the northern branch of the Potomac. This was a staging point where guides and baggage handlers awaited travelers to Ohio. Washington enlisted Christopher Gist as a guide. Gist knew Ohio and its inhabitants as well as anyone in Virginia and had stood the test of many expeditions. He came highly recommended. Washington added to the encomiums after working with Gist himself. "He has had extensive dealings with the Indians, is in great esteem among them; well acquainted with their manners and customs, is indefatigable, and patient: most excellent qualities indeed, where Indians are concerned." Washington additionally hired four other men, including two experienced in trading with the Indians.

By now it was mid-November. A slate sky pelted the travelers with rain and wet snow. Gist directed them to a trading post operated by a man named Frazer at the spot where Turtle Creek entered the Monongahela River, a north-flowing tributary of the Ohio. Here Washington learned that his journey might be longer than he thought. Traders reported that the French commandant in Ohio had recently died and most of his command had been recalled to Canada for the winter. This left Washington wondering who should receive the letter he carried from Governor Dinwiddie and how far north he would have to go to find him.

The traveling got harder. The rain raised the rivers and streams. "The waters were quite impassable without swimming our horses," Washington wrote in his journal of the expedition. At least the current was flowing in the right direction. He borrowed a canoe from Frazer and sent two of the men with most of the baggage down the river to the Forks of the Ohio, where the Monongahela met the Allegheny River to form the Ohio River proper. Washington, Gist and the other two men continued on horseback.

They beat the canoe to the Forks. Washington made use of the wait. "I spent some time in viewing the rivers, and the land in the Fork, which I think extremely well situated for a fort, as it has the absolute command of both rivers," he wrote in his journal. "The land at the point is 20 or 25 feet above the common surface of the water, and a considerable bottom of flat well-timbered land all around it very convenient for building. The rivers are each a quarter of a mile or more across and run here very nigh at right angles, Alleghany bearing NE and Monongahela SE." Washington was looking upstream on both rivers. "The former of these two is a very rapid swift-running water, the other deep and still, with scarce any perceptible fall." Washington subsequently visited a site about two miles west, on the south bank of the Ohio, where the Ohio Company, a band of speculators in western land, intended to erect a fort.

The Ohio Company was an example of something already common in British imperial history: a private company given a royal charter to pursue profit in the service of the empire. The East India Company was one such, the Virginia Company another, the Hudson's Bay Company a third. The charter of the Ohio Company instructed it to promote British settlement in Ohio, and to do so quickly to preempt French efforts in the region. In the bargain the investors were given title to land for sale to loyal subjects of the British crown. Principals in the company included Robert Dinwiddie, Lawrence Washington and Augustine Washington. George Washington too held a stake. Washington's mission to the French commandant promoted the interests of Britain and the Ohio Company both.

Washington thought the previous agents of the company, the ones who had chosen the site for the fort two miles below the Forks, had done badly. "My judgement is to think it greatly inferior, either for defence or advantages, especially the latter," he said. "For a fort at the Forks would be equally well situated on Ohio"—on the Ohio River—"and have the entire command of Monongahela, which runs up to our settlements and is extremely well designed for water carriage, as it is of a deep still nature."

WASHINGTON WAS ALREADY developing a strategic sense. He was right about the defense inferiority of the site chosen by the previous agents. But they had other motives. Their site was the residence of Shingas, the king—or first chief—of the Delaware Indians in the area. The chief was at home, and Washington invited him to accompany the British party to Logstown, a larger Indian village on the north bank of the Ohio about eighteen miles below the Forks. Logstown had been the location of previous parleys between colonists and Indians, and Washington thought it a suitable place to introduce himself and his mission to the Indians of the area.

He most hoped to see Tanacharison, a Seneca chief commonly called the Half King by the British. He was told the Half King was at his hunting lodge fifteen miles from Logstown. Monacatoocha, standing in for the Half King, received Washington and learned of his mission. "I gave him a string of wampum"—ceremonial beads—"and a twist of tobacco, and desired him to send for the Half King, which he promised to do by a runner in the morning, and for other sachems"—chiefs. "I invited him and the other great men present to my tent, where they stayed an hour."

Before the Half King and the others arrived, Washington received intelligence of French activities from four men who said they had deserted a French military unit. Washington listened to their story. "They were sent from New Orleans with 100 men and 8 canoe load of provisions to this place, where they expected to have met the same number of men from the forts this side Lake Erie," he wrote. He wasn't surprised that the French were trying to link their northern and southern possessions in North America: Canada and Louisiana. Any military commander would have made such an attempt. But firm evidence that the plan was afoot was significant. Apparently the connection was slow in forming. The Canadians hadn't arrived at the rendezvous point when the deserters took their leave.

Washington quizzed them further. "They informed me that there were four small forts between New Orleans and the Black Islands"—*Isles Noires,* or Illinois—"garrisoned with about 30 or 40 men and a few small pieces of cannon in each. That at New Orleans, which is near the mouth of the Mississippi, there is 35 companies of 40 men each, with a pretty strong fort mounting 8 large carriage guns, and at the Black Islands there is several companies, and a fort with 6 Guns."

Washington took care to write this information down. Besides being a diplomat and a land scout, he was a spy. Should tensions with France give rise to war, the intelligence he gathered might be invaluable.

8

The Half King arrived. Washington learned that the Seneca leader was being wooed by the French. He had recently visited the French commandant. Washington asked for directions. The Half King was evasive. He said the route he had traveled became impassable during the winter. Washington would have to find an alternative.

Yet the Half King related in detail his reception by the French commandant. He recapitulated their conversation. He said he had spoken sternly to the commandant and through him to the French authorities. "Fathers," he said, "you in former days set a silver bason"—container—"before us wherein there was the leg of a beaver, and desired of all nations to come and eat of it; to eat in peace and plenty, and not to be churlish to one another; and that if any such person should be found to be a disturber, I here lay down by the edge of the dish a rod, which you must scourge them with. And if me your Father should get foolish in my old days, I desire you may use it upon me as well as others."

The Half King paused while this was interpreted for Washington by one of the men Washington had hired.

"Now, Fathers," the Half King continued, relating his speech to the French commandant, "it is you that is the disturber in this land, by coming and building your towns, and taking it away unknown to us and by force. Fathers, we kindled a fire a long time ago at a place called Morail"—Montreal—"where we desired you to stay, and not to come and intrude upon our land. I now desire you may dispatch to that place, for be it known to you Fathers, this is our land and not yours. Fathers, I desire you may hear me in civilness. If not, we must handle that rod which was laid down for the use of the obstreperous. If you had come in a peaceable manner like our brothers the English, we should not have been against your trading with us as they do. But to come, Fathers, and build great houses upon our land, and to take it by force, is what we cannot submit to."

Another pause for interpretation.

"Fathers, both you and the English are white. We live in a country between. Therefore the land does not belong either to one or the other. But the Great Being above allowed it to be a place of residence for us. So, Fathers, I desire you to withdraw, as I have done our brothers the English, for I will keep you at arm's length. I lay this down as a trial for both, to see which will have the greatest regard to it. And that side we will stand by, and make equal sharers with us. Our brothers the English have heard this, and I come now to tell it to you, for I am not afraid to discharge you off this land."

The French commandant was not impressed, according to the Half King, who related the response. "My child, I have heard your speech," the commandant said. "You spoke first, but it is my time to speak now. Where is my wampum that you took away, with the marks of towns in it?" The wampum showed where the French would build forts. "This wampum"—wampum the Half King had just presented—"I do not know, which you have discharged me off the land with. But you need not put yourself to the trouble of speaking, for I will not hear you. I am not afraid of flies or mosquitoes, for Indians are such as those. I tell you down that river I will go, and will build upon it according to my command. If the river was ever so blocked up, I have forces sufficient to burst it open and tread under my feet all that stand in opposition, together with their alliances, for my force is as the sand upon the sea shore. Therefore here is your wampum, I fling it at you. Child, you talk foolish. You say this land belongs to you, but there is not the black of my nail that is yours. I saw that land sooner than you did, before the Shawnees and you were at war. La Salle was the man that went down and took possession of that river. It is my land, and I will have it, let who will stand up for or say against it." The commandant concluded gravely: "If people will be ruled by me, they may expect kindness, but not else."

Washington heard out the Half King and asked questions. He learned that two British traders had been captured by the French and carried off to Canada for questioning, to discover what the British were plotting. He inquired about French forts between the Ohio and Lake Erie. "He informed me that they had built two forts, one on Lake Erie, and another on French Creek near a small lake about 15 miles asunder," Washington recorded of the Half King. The former was Presque Isle and the latter Le

Boeuf. "And a large wagon road between. They are both built after the same model, but different in the size; that on the lake the largest. He gave me a plan of them of his own drawing."

SEVERAL OTHER CHIEFS arrived at Logstown. It became Washington's turn to speak. The young man was a rank novice in elocution, especially of the formal style the Indians employed and expected. He did his best.

"Brothers," Washington said, "I have called you together in council, by order of your brother the governor of Virginia, to acquaint you that I am sent with all possible dispatch to visit and deliver a letter to the French commandant of very great importance to your brothers the English and, I dare say, to you, their friends and allies. I was desired, brothers, by your brother the governor, to call upon you, the sachems of the Six Nations"—the Iroquois confederacy—"to inform you of it, and to ask your advice and assistance to proceed the nearest and best road to the French. You see, brothers, I have got thus far on my journey. His Honour likewise desired me to apply to you for some of your young men to conduct and provide provisions for us on our way and to be a safeguard against those French Indians that have taken up the hatchet against us. I have spoke this particularly to you, brothers, because his Honour our governor treats you as good friends and allies, and holds you in great esteem. To confirm what I have said I give you this string of wampum."

The Half King and the other chiefs spoke among themselves. The Half King gave their reply. "In regard to what my brother the governor has desired of me, I return you this answer," he said. "I rely upon you as a brother ought to do, as you say we are brothers, and one people. We shall put heart in hand and speak to our fathers the French, concerning the speech they made to me, and you may depend that we will endeavour to be your guard."

Washington was encouraged, albeit less so by what the Half King said next. "Brother, as you have asked my advice, I hope you will be ruled by it, and stay till I can provide a company to go with you. The French speech belt is not here. I have to go for it to my hunting cabin. Likewise the people I have ordered are not yet come, nor can till the third night from this, till which time, brother, I must beg you to stay. I intend to send a guard of Mingoes, Shawnees and Delawares, that our brothers may see the love and loyalty we bear them."

Washington couldn't tell what motivated the Half King's desire for delay. It might have been just as he said. But more might be involved. He tried to change the Half King's mind. He thanked him for his pledge of a guard but said the governor had ordered him to proceed with all dispatch. He could not wait for the Indians.

The Half King insisted. "He was not well pleased that I should offer to go before the time he had appointed, and told me that he could not consent to our going without a guard, for fear some accident should befall us and draw a reflection upon him," Washington wrote. "Besides, says he, this is a matter of no small moment, and must not be entered into without due consideration, for I now intend to deliver up the French speech belt, and make the Shawnees and Delawares do the same." This would signify that the Half King and his allies were siding with the British against the French. The Half King did agree to hasten the arrival of the warriors who would accompany Washington's party.

Washington bowed to necessity. "As I found it impossible to get off without affronting them in the most egregious manner, I consented to stay," he wrote.

THE HALF KING APPEARED to make good on his promise. He sent runners to summon the missing chiefs, and he himself went to his cabin to fetch the French speech belt.

Yet the next day, after returning with the belt, he began to waver. He asked Washington what he was going to say to the French commandant when he tracked him down.

Now it was Washington's turn to deflect. "This was a question I all along expected, and provided as satisfactory an answer as I could, which allayed their curiosity a little," he recorded.

Monacatoocha joined the Half King for this conversation. He volunteered that an Indian from Venango, north of Logstown and not far south of Lake Erie, reported that a French officer named Joncaire had called together Indian leaders and announced that the season was too far advanced for the French to march south, as they had intended. Rather, they would go into winter quarters and resume their advance in the spring, with far greater numbers. Joncaire had told the Indians to lie low and not antagonize the British prematurely. "They expected to fight three years (as they supposed there would be some attempts made to stop them), in which time they should conquer," was how Washington paraphrased Monacatoocha's account of Joncaire's message.

The next day was Washington's new departure date. That morning the Half King and Monacatoocha came to his tent and urged him to wait one more day. The Shawnee chiefs, it seemed, had come without their wampum. It was following them and would arrive that night.

"When I found them so pressing in their request, and knew that returning of wampum was the abolishing of agreements," Washington reflected in his journal, "and giving this up was shaking off all dependence upon the French, I consented to stay, as I believed an offence offered at this crisis might have been attended with greater ill consequence than another day's delay."

The next morning brought new delays. One of the chiefs was kept home by his wife's sickness. "I believe by fear of the French," Washington countered parenthetically in his journal. The chiefs gathered in the village council house. They emerged to tell Washington that only three of them, plus one hunter, would join him on his mission to the French. They said that sending more would alarm the French and perhaps provoke violence. "But I rather think they could not get their hunters in," Washington wrote.

At last Washington and his party, and the three chiefs and the hunter, set out for Venango. The road was well marked, and although the weather was cold and wet, they arrived after a journey of seventy miles and four days.

Captain Philippe Thomas Joncaire greeted Washington. He explained that he commanded the fort, but that his commander was at the next fort north. It was to this officer that Washington should deliver his message. Joncaire treated Washington as an equal, though a potential enemy. He invited Washington to dinner. This proved enlightening. "The wine, as they dosed themselves pretty plentifully with it, soon banished the restraint which at first appeared in their conversation, and gave license to their tongues to reveal their sentiments more freely," Washington wrote. "They told me it was their absolute design to take possession of the Ohio, and by G— they would do it, for though they were sensible that the English could raise two men for their one, yet they knew their motions were too slow and dilatory to prevent any undertaking of theirs." The French officers asserted the justice of their cause. "They pretended to have an undoubted right to the river from a discovery made by one La Salle 60 years ago. And the use of this expedition is to prevent our settling on the river or waters of it, as they have heard of some families moving out in order thereto."

At this dinner and in conversations with men around the village, Washington gathered information about the size and disposition of French forces in Ohio. "From the best intelligence I could get, there has been 1,500 men this side Oswego Lake"—Lake Ontario—"but upon the death of the general, all were recalled to about 6 or 7 hundred, which were left to garrison four forts, 150 or thereabouts in each." The forts included one at Niagara Falls and another at Presque Isle on Lake Erie. Washington inquired about communications. "From the fort on Lake Erie to Morail"—Montreal—"is about 600 miles, which they say, if good weather, requires no more than 4 weeks voyage, if they go in barks or large vessels that can cross the lake. But if they come in canoes, it will require five or six weeks for they are obliged to keep under the shore."

Washington was eager to press on to Fort Le Boeuf. But the weather was against him. "Rained successively all day, which prevented our traveling," he noted. His French host wasn't helpful. "Capt. Joncaire sent for the Half King, as he had but just heard that he came with me. He affected to be much concerned that I did not make free to bring him in before. I excused it in the best manner I was capable, and told him I did not think their company agreeable, as I had heard him say a good deal in dispraise of Indians in general."

To his journal Washington admitted another motive. "I knew that he was interpreter and a person of very great influence among the Indians, and had lately used all possible means to draw them over to their interest. Therefore I was desirous of giving no more opportunity than could be avoided." He now yielded to Joncaire's wishes and brought the Half King and the other chiefs to a meeting. "When they came in there was great pleasure expressed at seeing them. He wondered how they could be so near without coming to visit him, made several trifling presents, and applied liquors so fast that they were soon rendered incapable of the business they came about, notwithstanding the caution that was given."

The Half King had sobered up by the next morning. He came to Washington's tent and said Washington mustn't leave before he had heard what he—the Half King—had to say to Joncaire. Washington asked him to save his words for the commandant at Fort Le Boeuf. The Half King refused. "He told me that at this place the council fire was kindled, where all their business with these people were to be transacted, and that the management of the Indian affairs was left solely to Monsieur Joncaire." Washington consented to remain yet another day.

The Half King put on a good show. He repeated to Joncaire what he had earlier told the general who had died. He handed over the speech belt with the marks of the four towns on it. Joncaire refused it, telling the Half King to carry it to Fort Le Boeuf and give it to the commandant there.

Still the Half King delayed. More excuses were given for not being ready.

Unexpectedly the French turned helpful. "Monsieur La Force, commissary of the French stores, and three other soldiers came over to accompany us up," Washington recorded. He had no doubt the French escort was to keep watch on him. There was nothing he could do about that, except be mindful of what he said and did.

Whether on account of the French escort or for some other reason, the Half King finally agreed to leave Venango.

9

Washington was relieved to be moving, despite bad weather. The rain and snow turned the road to mud and swelled rills to torrents. Christopher Gist kept his own journal. "Friday 7"—December 7—"Encamped at Sugar creek, five miles from Venango," Gist wrote. "The creek being very high we were obliged to carry all our baggage over on trees, and swim our horses. The Major"—Washington—"and I went first over, with our boots on. Saturday.—We set out and travelled twenty-five miles to Cussewago, an old Indian town. Sunday 9.—We set out, left one of our horses here that could travel no further. This day we travelled to the big crossing, about fifteen miles, and encamped, our Indians went out to look out logs to make a raft; but as the water was high, and there were other creeks to cross, we concluded to keep up this side the creek. Monday 10.—Set out, travelled about eight miles, and encamped. Our Indians killed a bear. Here we had a creek to cross, very deep; we got over on a tree, and got our goods over."

Washington, as before, observed the countryside with care. "We passed over much good land since we left Venango, and through several extensive and very rich meadows, one of which was near 4 miles in length and considerably wide in some places," he wrote.

On December 11, in the late afternoon, they reached Fort Le Boeuf. Washington readied himself for his big moment, which came the next morning. An adjutant summoned him and escorted him to the fort, where he met Jacques Legardeur de Saint-Pierre. "He is an elderly gentleman and has much the air of a soldier," Washington wrote. "He was sent over to take the command immediately upon the death of the late general, and arrived here about 7 days before me." Washington presented his letter from Governor Dinwiddie.

Saint-Pierre didn't speak or read English. He took the letter and retired to his office with a captain who seemed to know a little English.

The captain translated the letter. Saint-Pierre offered to let Washington's interpreter, Van Braam, make corrections to the translation, which he did.

The next day Saint-Pierre gathered his aides to consider Dinwiddie's demands. Washington took the opportunity to examine the fort. "It is situated on the south or west fork of French Creek, near the water, and is almost surrounded by the creek and a small branch of it which forms a kind of an island," he wrote. He drew a map of the fort and its site. "4 houses compose the sides. The bastions are made of piles drove into the ground and about 12 feet above, sharp at top, with port holes cut for cannon and small arms to fire through. There are eight 6 lb. pieces mounted, two in each bastion, and one of 4 lb. before the gate. In the bastions are a guard house, chapel, doctor's lodgings, and the commander's private store, round which is laid platforms for the cannon and men to stand on. There is several barracks without the fort for the soldiers' dwelling, covered some with bark and some with boards, and made chiefly of logs. There is also several other houses such as stables, smith's shop etc."

Washington watched the comings and goings of the soldiers. "According to the best judgement I could form, there is an hundred, exclusive of officers, which are pretty many." He had his own men count the canoes they saw around the fort. The French traveled by water whenever possible. The total appeared to be about 50 canoes made of birch bark and 170 of pine. Many more canoes were under construction. The French would be on the move come spring. Fort Le Boeuf was within the drainage of the Ohio River, meaning that the journey to the Forks would be downstream and swift.

For now, Washington had to deal with winter. "The snow increased very fast and our horses daily got weaker," he wrote. He feared that the animals might give out. He sent them back to Venango with the four hired men. He would return by canoe.

He might have to return alone, or nearly so. The French at Le Boeuf were doing their best to woo the chiefs who had accompanied Washington and prevent them from handing back their wampum. If they succeeded, they might foil British plans for Ohio. "I endeavoured all in my power to frustrate their schemes," Washington wrote.

It wasn't easy. Saint-Pierre conducted private interviews with the chiefs. Washington quizzed them on what was said. "The Half King told me that he offered the wampum to the commander, who evaded taking it, and made many fair promises of love and friendship, said he wanted to live in peace and trade amicably with them, as a proof of which he would send some goods immediately down to the Logstown for them."

The Half King and the other chiefs were evasive about what they told Saint-Pierre. Washington was still guessing when he received a sealed letter from Saint-Pierre to Dinwiddie, answering the governor's letter.

As Washington prepared to return south, Saint-Pierre continued to work on the Half King and the other Indians. "The commander ordered a plentiful store of liquor, provisions etc., to be put on board our canoe, and appeared to be extremely complaisant, though he was plotting every scheme that the devil and man could invent to set our Indians at variance with us, to prevent their going till after our departure. Presents, rewards, and everything that could be suggested by him or his officers was not neglected to do. I can't say that ever in my life I suffered so much anxiety as I did in this affair. I saw that every stratagem that the most fruitful brain could invent was practised to get the Half King won to their interest." Washington's eagerness to leave was obvious, and Saint-Pierre reckoned that if the Half King could be enticed to remain a bit longer, Washington would leave without him.

"I went to the Half King and pressed him in the strongest terms to go," Washington wrote. The Half King responded that he hadn't completed his business with Saint-Pierre. "I then went to the commander and desired him to do their business, and complained of ill treatment, for keeping them, as they were part of my company, was detaining me, which he promised not to do." Saint-Pierre disclaimed malign intent. "He protested he did not keep them but was innocent of the cause of their stay." Washington learned otherwise. "He had promised them a present of guns, etc. if they would wait till the morning." Washington again concluded he had no choice but to wait. "I consented on a promise that nothing should hinder them in the morning."

Saint-Pierre wasn't finished. He handed over the guns to the Indians the next day, but he also offered liquor.

Washington had had enough. "I taxed the King so close upon his word that he refrained, and set off with us as he had engaged."

"WE SET OUT by water about sixteen miles, and encamped," wrote Christopher Gist. "Our Indians went before us, passed the little lake, and we did not come up with them that night." Washington and Gist overtook the Indians the next morning. Or rather they found the camp of the Indians, who were out hunting. The Indians killed three bears for the travelers' supper.

Overnight the water in the creek they were following fell worrisomely. As the rain turned to snow, and water to ice, it would continue to fall. Washington feared being stranded. One of the Indians hadn't come in from the hunt, but Washington chose to push on without him. The message he was carrying might make the difference between war and peace, and if the water fell much further, canoes would be useless.

As it was, the going was slow. Washington and Gist covered only eight miles in a fatiguing day. The next day went better. They made twenty miles but were stopped in the late afternoon by ice, which thickened overnight. "The ice was so hard we could not break our way through, but were obliged to haul our vessels across a point of land and put them in the creek again," Gist wrote on December 21. They soon had the company of three French canoes, likewise trying to beat the winter south.

The water continued to fall. "The creek began to be very low and we were forced to get out, to keep our canoe from oversetting, several times, the water freezing to our clothes," Gist wrote. "We had the pleasure of seeing the French overset, and the brandy and wine floating in the creek, and run by them and left them to shift for themselves."

That afternoon they reached Venango, where they found their horses and the men who had charge of them. Washington wished to proceed the next day. He asked the Half King if he would join him on horseback or continue by canoe. Washington wasn't surprised to hear the chief make a new excuse for delay. One of the other chiefs had hurt himself and would require a day or two to rest, he said. Washington worried that the French might yet turn the Half King against the British. The Half King offered assurance. "He desired I might not be concerned, for he knew the French too well for anything to engage him in their behalf."

The first day on the horses went slowly. Washington had to make a decision. "Our horses were now so weak and feeble, and the baggage heavy, as we were obliged to provide all the necessaries the journey would require, that we doubted much their performing it," he wrote. They got off the horses and walked beside them, to ease their load. This didn't suffice. "The horses grew less able to travel every day. The cold increased very fast, and the roads were getting much worse by a deep snow continually freezing. And as I was uneasy to get back to make a report of my proceedings to his Honour the Governor, I determined to prosecute my journey the nearest way through the woods on foot."

Gist didn't think this wise. "Indeed, I was unwilling he should undertake such a travel, who had never been used to walking before this time," Gist wrote. But Washington insisted. He put the letter and his journal in a pack, along with some provisions, picked up his gun and set off. Gist had no choice but to follow.

They covered eighteen miles that day. "The major was much fatigued," Gist wrote. "It was very cold. All the small runs were frozen, that we could hardly get water to drink." They spent the night in an Indian cabin.

The next day they reached an Indian village called Murdering Town. "Here we met with an Indian whom I thought I had seen at Joncaire's, at Venango, when on our journey up to the French fort," Gist wrote. "This fellow called me by my Indian name and pretended to be glad to see me. He asked us several questions, as how we came to travel on foot, when we left Venango, where we parted with our horses, and when they would be there, etc."

Washington thought the Indian could be of use in guiding them to the Forks. "We asked the Indian if he could go with us and show us the nearest way," Gist wrote. "The Indian seemed very glad and ready to go with us." The Indian offered to assist Washington, obviously the least experienced of the three in wilderness trekking. "The Indian took the major's pack. We travelled very brisk for eight or ten miles, when the major's feet grew very sore, and he very weary." Washington suggested they pitch camp. The Indian, reluctant to halt, proposed to carry Washington's gun. Washington declined. "The Indian grew churlish and pressed us to keep on, telling us that there were Ottawa Indians in these woods, and they would scalp us if we lay out, but to go to his cabin and we should be safe," Gist recorded.

Gist was growing suspicious. He thought the Indian was steering north of the most direct route to the Forks. Yet he said nothing at first.

The Indian declared they were nearing his cabin. They were within a gunshot's sound of it, he asserted. He led them even farther north of the line Gist would have followed. The Indian said they were within whooping distance. They went two miles more.

Washington said they would camp at the next water. But before they reached water, they came to a meadow, covered with snow. "The Indian made a stop, turned about. The major saw him point his gun toward us and fire. Said the major, 'Are you shot?' 'No,' said I. Upon which the Indian ran forward to a big standing white oak, and set to loading his gun. But we were soon with him. I would have killed him, but the major would not suffer me to kill him."

Gist thought Washington foolish. "I said to the major, 'As you will not have him killed, we must get him away, and then we must travel all night.'" Gist acted as though he thought the Indian's rifle shot an accident. He gave the Indian a piece of bread and told him to go on to his cabin. They would follow in the morning and expect to be fed some meat.

The Indian appeared to accept the story. "He was glad to get away," Gist wrote. "I followed him, and listened until he was fairly out of the way, and then we set out about half a mile, when we made a fire, set our compass, and fixed our course, and travelled all night." They traveled all the next day too, stopping only after dark. "We encamped and thought ourselves safe enough to sleep," wrote Gist.

They started early the next day and reached the Allegheny River. "We expected to have found the river froze," Washington related. "But it was not, only about 50 yards from each shore. The ice, I suppose, had broke up above, for it was driving in vast quantities." They had to cross to continue their journey. "There was no way for us to get over but upon a raft, which we set about with but one poor hatchet." A day's hard labor produced something that might do. "We got it launched, and on board of it, and set off. But before we got half over, we were jammed in the ice in such a manner that we expected every moment our raft would sink and we perish."

Washington was no riverman. "I put out my setting pole, to try to stop the raft, that the ice might pass by, when the rapidity of the stream threw it with so much violence against the pole that it jerked me into 10 feet water. But I fortunately saved myself by catching hold of one of the raft logs."

Their problem remained. "Notwithstanding all our efforts, we could not get the raft to either shore, but were obliged, as we were pretty near an island, to quit our raft and wade to it," Washington wrote. Wet and exposed, they spent a painful night on the island. "The cold was so extreme severe that Mr. Gist got all his fingers and some of his toes froze." Yet the same cold proved their salvation. "The water was shut up so hard that we found no difficulty in getting off the island on the ice in the morning."

The worst was over. They made their way to a trader's post. "We met here with 20 warriors that had been going to the southward to war, but coming to a place upon the head of the Great Cunnaway"—the Kanawha River—"where they found people killed and scalpt, all but one woman with very light hair, they turned about and ran back, for fear of the inhabitants rising and taking them as the authors of the murder," Washington wrote. "They report that the people were lying about the house, and some of them much torn and eat by hogs. By the marks that were left, they say they were French Indians of the Ottawa Nation etc. that did it."

On New Year's Day, Washington and Gist resumed their journey. "We arrived at Wills Creek, after as fatiguing a journey as it is possible to conceive, rendered so by excessive bad weather," Washington wrote on January 6. "From the first day of December till the 15th there was but one day but what it rained or snowed incessantly, and throughout the whole journey we met with nothing but one continued series of cold wet weather, which occasioned very uncomfortable lodgings."

Leaving Gist, Washington took five days to reach Belvoir, the Fairfax home. He rested a day and continued to Williamsburg. On January 16 he delivered Saint-Pierre's letter to Dinwiddie. In it the French officer acknowledged the letter Washington had delivered. He went on, to Dinwiddie: "I should have been glad if you had given him orders, or he had been inclined, to proceed to Canada to see our General"—the governor-general, the Marquis Duquesne—"to whom it belongs, rather than to me, to set forth the evidence and the reality of the rights of the King, my master, to the lands situated along the Belle Rivière"—the Ohio River—"and to contest the pretensions of the King of Great Britain thereto," he wrote. Because Washington had not gone to Canada, Saint-Pierre had forwarded Dinwiddie's letter to Duquesne. "His reply will be a law to me, and, if he should order me to communicate it to you, sir, I can assure you that I shall neglect nothing to have it reach you very promptly."

As to Dinwiddie's demand that Saint-Pierre withdraw his troops from Ohio, this was out of the question. "Whatever may be your instructions, I am here by virtue of the orders of my General, and I entreat you, sir, not to doubt for a moment that I have a firm resolution to follow them with all the exactness and determination which can be expected of the best officer."

Dinwiddie had asserted hostile actions by the French. Saint-Pierre rejected the charge. "I do not know that anything has happened in the course of this campaign which can be construed as an act of hostility, or as contrary to the treaties between the two Crowns, the continuation of which interests and pleases us as much as it does the English. If you had been pleased, sir, to go into detail regarding the deeds which caused your complaints, I should have had the honor of answering you in the most positive manner, and I am sure that you would have had reason to be satisfied."

10

Dinwiddie was disappointed, albeit not surprised, by the French response. Yet he was pleased and impressed that Washington had successfully carried out the difficult mission assigned to him. The governor was the more impressed when he read Washington's journal of the expedition. Dinwiddie immediately ordered that the journal be published. His purpose was to demonstrate his devotion to the interests of the British crown. The published journal did that. It also introduced Washington to a large audience of American readers who had never heard of the young Virginian and couldn't help thinking highly of this doughty and enterprising soldier-diplomat.

Dinwiddie hadn't expected the French to yield Ohio without a fight. He prepared to give them one. He summoned the representatives of the people of Virginia, the house of burgesses. He described the French encroachments on Ohio and requested funds to counter them. While the lawmakers debated the matter, Dinwiddie wrote to his fellow governors in the neighboring colonies urging them to join Virginia's cause in repelling Britain's historic foe. He invited the chiefs of friendly tribes in the region to a council at Winchester to formulate a strategy against the French and French-allied Indians. As enticement to the chiefs he promised gifts worthy of Britain's friends.

And he sent Washington back to Ohio. The major was promoted to lieutenant colonel, second-in-command to Joshua Fry at the head of a regiment of Virginia militia. Washington was actually to take the lead for the regiment, pushing with half the troops to Wills Creek while Fry raised the rest of the force at Alexandria. Washington should push on from there. "You are to use all expedition in proceeding to the Fork of Ohio with the men under command and there you are to finish and complete in the best manner and as soon as you possibly can the fort which I expect is there already begun by the Ohio Company," Dinwiddie told

Washington. "You are to act on the defensive, but in case any attempts are made to obstruct the works or interrupt our settlements by any persons whatsoever you are to restrain all such offenders and in case of resistance to make prisoners of or kill and destroy them. For the rest you are to conduct yourself as the circumstances of the service shall require and to act as you shall find best for the furtherance of His Majesty's service and the good of his dominion."

Washington was flattered by the appointment and eager for the opportunity it provided. "Everything being ready, we began our march according to our orders the 2d of April," he wrote in a new journal. He led two companies of infantry comprising a dozen officers and 125 soldiers, and a train of two wagons guarded by three officers and 25 soldiers. A surgeon, a drummer and a Swedish gentleman volunteer completed the column.

A trader named William Trent had led a band of frontiersmen to the Forks during the winter, to build a post at the site Washington had recommended to Dinwiddie. This was the Ohio Company fort Dinwiddie referred to. The idea was to raise a British flag before the spring thaw unleashed the two hundred canoes at Fort Le Boeuf and let the French arrive there in force. Two weeks into Washington's march from Alexandria, he learned that the French were on the move. "Met an express who had letters from Captain Trent, at the Ohio, demanding a reinforcement with all speed, as he hourly expected a body of eight hundred French," Washington wrote on April 19. Next day the imminent became the accomplished. "News was confirmed by Mr. Wart, the ensign of Captain Trent, who had been obliged to surrender to a body of one thousand French and upwards." The assault force had sixty bateaux—flat-bottomed rivercraft—and three hundred canoes. The bateaux carried eighteen cannons. The French force vastly outnumbered and outgunned that of Trent, who had no choice but to surrender.

This development dramatically changed the nature of Washington's mission. Instead of defending a British fort at the Forks against French assault, Washington and his comrades would be assaulting a French fort there. Speed had been of the essence, but no longer. Now heft mattered more.

Washington called a council of his officers. He was the commander on the spot, but others had greater experience of war and of relations with the Indians. The Indians were crucial, for without them the Virginians had no chance of driving the French from the Forks. And the Indians were understandably alarmed at the sudden shift in France's favor. Washington had received a message from the Half King for the governors of Virginia and Pennsylvania. In the message the chief affirmed his determination to attack the French, but only if the British arrived quickly. "Come as soon as possible," the Half King said. "You will find us as ready to encounter with them as you are yourselves." But this condition couldn't last. "If you do not come to our assistance now, we are entirely undone, and imagine we shall never meet together again."

Washington's council concluded that the best course was to move forward steadily but deliberately. This would encourage the Indians but not expose the troops excessively. "I hope my proceedings in these affairs will be satisfactory to your Honour," Washington wrote to Dinwiddie, "as I have to the utmost of my knowledge consulted the interest of the expedition and good of my country, whose rights, while they are asserted in so just a cause, I will defend to the last remains of life." He elaborated on the strategy the council approved. "I am destined to Monongahela with all the diligent dispatch in my power. We will endeavour to make the road sufficiently good for the heaviest artillery to pass and when we arrive at Red Stone Creek fortify ourselves as strongly as the short time will allow of." Washington presumed to tell Dinwiddie what the governor could contribute. "I hope your Honour will see the absolute necessity there is for having as soon as our forces are collected a number of cannon (some of heavy metal) with mortars, grenadoes etc. to attack the French and put us on an equal footing with them."

The governor should rally friendly Indians. "It may also be thought advisable to invite the Cherokees, Catawbas, and Chickasaws to march to our assistance (as we are informed that six hundred Chippewas and Ottawas are marching down Scioto Creek to join the French that are coming up Ohio)."

Washington informed Dinwiddie that he had written similarly to the governors of Pennsylvania and Maryland—"which I hope your Honour will not think me too forward in doing." The assembly of Pennsylvania was currently sitting, and that of Maryland was about to convene. Dinwiddie should second Washington's appeal. "By giving them timely notice, something might be done which would turn to the advantage of this expedition, which now requires all the force we can muster."

WHILE DINWIDDIE MARVELED at the audacity of his twenty-two-year-old lieutenant colonel, Washington set to work himself on the Half

King and his fellow chiefs. "It gives me great pleasure to learn that you are marching to assist me with your counsels," he declared by a speech sent through an Indian messenger, who also carried a gift. "Be of good courage, my brethren, and march vigorously towards your brethren the English, for fresh forces will soon join them, who will protect you against your treacherous enemy the French." Together the British and their Indian allies would drive the French back to Canada. Peace once more would bless Ohio. The British were true to their word, as the French were not. "For the confirmation of all this, I here give you a belt of wampum."

The Half King responded with a letter addressed to any British officers it might find. "As 'tis reported that the French army is set out to meet M. George Washington, I exhort you, my brethren, to guard against them, for they intend to fall on the first English they meet," the Half King said. "They have been on their march these two days." Britain's Indian allies were coming. "The Half King and the other chiefs will join you within five days, to hold a council, though we know not the number we shall be. I shall say no more, but remember me to my brethren the English."

Washington questioned the two messengers who brought the Half King's message. What did they know about the movements of the French? "They say there are parties of them often out, but they do not know of any considerable number coming this way," Washington wrote in his journal. He asked about French construction of defenses at the Forks. The messengers said the work proceeded in stages. "That part next to the land is very well enclosed, but that next to the water is much neglected, at least without any defence." What artillery had the French? "They have only nine pieces of cannon, and some of them very small, and not one mounted. There are two on the point, and the others some distance from the fort next to the land." The Indian informants told of personnel issues. "They relate that there are many sick among them, that they cannot find any Indians to guide their small parties towards our camp."

This last was encouraging, but the effect didn't persist. That same day Washington's column reached the Great Meadows, an open area beneath Laurel Hill, about sixty miles south of the Forks. He encountered a trader who said he had seen two Frenchmen the previous night. The trader stated with confidence that a large detachment of French troops was moving in Washington's direction.

Washington decided to halt at the Meadows and prepare to meet whatever force the French sent his way. What he called "two natural intrenchments"—the beds of two intermittent creeks—crossed the Meadows. He placed his troops behind these and brought up the wagons. He sent scouts on foot into the woods to the north, and horsemen to range the roads. They were out for hours and went far in the direction from which the French were said to be coming. But returning that night, they said they'd seen nothing.

Washington ordered the soldiers to improve the natural entrenchments into something closer to a military defense. While they were doing so, Christopher Gist arrived with intelligence of French movements. Gist said a company of fifty soldiers had been at his farm the previous day. He wasn't at home, but two Indians were there. They said the French soldiers were bent on destruction and would have wreaked it if the Indians hadn't dissuaded them.

Washington didn't know what to make of the details of the story, but its central point—that a French force had been sighted—required a response. "I immediately detached 65 men under the command of Capt. Hog," he wrote.

Another part of Gist's account afforded motivation for Washington's Indian allies. The French raiding party had inquired of the Indians at Gist's where the Half King could be found. They apparently meant him no good. "I did not fail to let the young Indians who were in our camp know that the French wanted to kill the Half King," Washington recorded. His statement elicited the reaction he wanted. "They thereupon offered to accompany our people to go after the French, and if they found it true that he had been killed or even insulted by them, one of them would presently carry the news thereof to the Mingoes, in order to incite their warriors to fall upon them."

On the night of June 27, Washington received a hurried message from the Half King saying he was coming and that he had seen the tracks of two men he took to be French soldiers. He had followed the tracks to the edge of a low-lying tangle of trees and brush. Not wishing to give himself away, he hadn't gone farther. But he concluded that the French raiding party was hiding there.

Washington responded at once. "That very moment I sent out forty men and ordered my ammunition to be put in a place of safety under a strong guard to defend it," he wrote. "And with the rest of my men set out in a heavy rain, and in a night as dark as pitch, along a patch scarce broad enough for one man." Washington wanted to join forces with the Half King and strike the French before they struck him. The night travel was difficult. "We were sometimes fifteen or twenty minutes out of the path before we could come to it again, and so dark that we would often strike one against another." Yet Washington kept on. "All night long we continued our route, and the 28th, about sunrise, we arrived at the Indian camp."

The Half King agreed on a joint strike against the French. "We sent out two men to discover where they were, as also their posture and what sort of ground was thereabout," Washington wrote. "After which we formed ourselves for an engagement, marching one after the other in the Indian manner."

Washington and the Half King intended to surprise the French. Instead, they were the ones surprised. "We were advanced pretty near to them, as we thought, when they discovered us," Washington recorded. Yet contact was contact. "I ordered my company to fire."

Apparently the French hadn't expected a battle. They returned fire, but not effectively. The engagement was short but sharp. Washington's company was next to that of a lieutenant. "My company and his received the whole fire of the French during the greatest part of the action, which only lasted a quarter of an hour before the enemy was routed."

11

Washington couldn't know that his order to fire on the French started a war that would change the balance of power in North America, not only between Britain and France but also between Britain and the American colonies. What he did know was that he had survived his first battle and had never felt anything so thrilling.

He wrote to his brother Jack recounting the battle. "We had an engagement with the French that is, between a party of theirs and ours," Washington said. "Most of our men were out upon other detachments, so that I had scarcely 40 men under my command and about 10 or a dozen Indians. Nevertheless we obtained a most signal victory. The battle lasted about 10 or 15 minutes, sharp firing on both sides, when the French gave ground and run, but to no great purpose. There were 12 killed, among which was Monsieur De Jumonville, the commander, and taken 21 prisoners." Washington sent the prisoners under guard to Virginia. "We had but one man killed, 2 or 3 wounded and a great many more within an inch of being shot."

The wounded almost included Washington himself. "I fortunately escaped without a wound, though the right wing where I stood was exposed to and received all the enemy's fire and was the part where the man was killed and the rest wounded. I can with truth assure you I heard bullets whistle, and believe me there was something charming in the sound."

ON HEARING OF THIS COMMENT by Washington, King George II responded, "He would not say so, if he had been used to hear many."

George was wrong. The monarch misunderstood Washington. The mistake was natural, for most men recoil from war and the danger it entails. Washington was one who didn't. He was part of the small class who find war invigorating and seductive. These are the natural warriors, few in any society but essential to the conduct of war and especially its mastery. In his first battle, with the bullets whizzing close by, Washington found his calling. He was a soldier.

THE FRENCH HAD THEIR OWN interpretation of Washington's initial performance under fire. They considered the attack on Jumonville's company an ambush and his killing a murder. France and Britain were not at war. Their dispute over Ohio still lay in the realm of diplomacy. Washington hadn't been murdered when he carried the cease-and-desist letter from Dinwiddie to Saint-Pierre. Indeed Jumonville was carrying something similar to Washington and other British officers at the time of Washington's unprovoked attack. Washington had started a war where there needn't have been a war.

There still might not be. But the killing of Jumonville and his troops must be avenged. The larger force of which Jumonville was a part mobilized against Washington's position at the Great Meadows.

Washington made ready. "We expect every hour to be attacked by a superior force, but shall if they stay one day longer be prepared for them," he wrote to brother Jack. "We have already got intrenchments and are about a pallisadoed fort, which will I hope be finished today." Washington called the structure and its works Fort Necessity. His Indian allies were active, and he anticipated reinforcements. "The Mingoes have struck the French and I hope will give a good blow before they have done, I expect 40 odd of them here tonight, which with our fort and some reinforcements from Col. Fry, will enable us to exert our noble courage with spirit."

The French were slower than Washington expected. The fort was completed, and Fry's reinforcements arrived, although without their commanding officer. Fry had fallen from his horse, landed badly and died. Command of the Virginia regiment passed to Washington.

Another contingent consisted of Carolina troops enlisted in the British army. Their commander, Captain James Mackay, was outranked by Major Washington, but Mackay, with a commission from King George, refused to acknowledge Washington's seniority, and his men, following their captain's lead, refused to do Washington's bidding.

Washington handled this first experience of coalition warfare with patience born of lack of alternative. Partly to ease the friction, partly to see what delayed the French, he led an advance in the direction of the Forks. He hadn't gone far when he met Indians from the Ohio who told him the French were advancing in powerful force. He quickly retreated to the Great Meadows and Fort Necessity.

He discovered later that one reason for the French delay was a decision to place the reprisal force under the command of Jumonville's brother Coulon de Villiers, who arrived at Fort Duquesne—the name the French gave to their post at the Forks—in late June. Villiers would avenge his family's honor. The honor of France was no less at stake, as the fort commandant, Claude-Pierre Pécaudy de Contrecoeur, explained to the Indians he summoned there to join the attack on Washington. "The English have murdered my children," the commandant said. "My heart is sick. Tomorrow I shall send my French soldiers to take revenge. And now, men of the Saut St. Louis, men of the Lake of Two Mountains, Hurons, Abenakis, Iroquois of La Présentation, Nipissings, Algonquins and Ottawas—I invite you by this belt of wampum to join your French father and help him to crush the assassins." Contrecoeur presented a hatchet to the warriors as symbol of the wrath they would deliver. He also presented two barrels of wine, to strengthen their courage for the battle to come.

The French column of soldiers and Indian warriors advanced toward Washington's position. In early July they reached the forested glen where Jumonville had been killed. His brother paid respect and his men buried bodies that remained where they had fallen and been scalped by Washington's Indians. They came within sight of Fort Necessity on July 3.

Washington's position had improved in the unexpected month he had to prepare. The fort looked more like a fort than a pile of logs turned on end. The earthworks outside the walls had been extended and deepened. But it still suffered from a grave vulnerability. The fort lay within rifle shot of the forest that surrounded the Meadows. Attackers could fire from the cover of the trees with reasonable chance of hitting the fort's defenders.

The weather worked to Washington's disadvantage, too. Summer rain, intermittent but heavy, had set in. The earthworks reverted to the waterways they often were. Soldiers in the trenches had to choose between lying uncomfortably in the water and standing perilously exposed to enemy fire. To make matters worse, the forest cover curved around the fort, allowing attackers to get Washington's troops in a cross fire.

The battle began in the late morning of July 3. Washington's pickets discovered the French in the woods and fired before retreating. Washington, realizing his jeopardy, ordered an attack to dislodge the French. It went poorly, for the British troops were exposed while the French remained hidden in the trees. Washington changed his mind and pulled his men back to the fort.

VILLIERS LATER DESCRIBED how the battle commenced. "We marched the whole day in the rain, and I sent scouts one after another," he wrote. "I stopped at the place where my brother had been assassinated and saw there yet some dead bodies. When I came within three quarters of a league from the English fort, I ordered my men to march in columns, every officer to his division, that I might the better dispose of them as necessity would require. I sent scouts and gave them orders to go close up to the camp, twenty others to sustain them, and I advanced in order. My scouts soon informed me that we were discovered, and that the English were coming in battle array to attack us, and that they were very near us, upon which I ordered my men in a posture suitable for a bush fight. It was not long before I perceived that my scouts had misled me, and ordered the three troops to advance on that side where we expected them to attack us."

Villiers moved forward carefully. "As we had no knowledge of the place, we presented our flank to the fort." Suddenly they were discovered. "They began to fire upon us, and almost at the same time, I perceived the English on the right, in order of battle, and coming towards us. The Indians, as well as ourselves, set up a great cry, and advanced towards them. But they did not give us time to fire upon them before they sheltered themselves in an entrenchment, which was adjoining to their fort. After which we aimed to invest the fort, which was advantageously enough situated in a meadow within a musket shot from the woods. We drew as near them as possible, that we might not expose his Majesty's subjects to no purpose."

The battle began in earnest. "The fire was very brisk on both sides, and I chose that place which seemed to me the most proper in case we should be exposed to a sally. We fired so smartly as to put out (if I may use the expression) the fire of their cannon with our musket shot."

Yet with the British behind their entrenchments, the French behind the trees, and the rain pouring down, the firing claimed casualties only sporadically. It continued for several hours.

"Towards 6:00 at night, the fire of the enemy increased with more vigor than ever, and lasted until 8:00," Villiers continued. "We briskly returned their fire. We took particular care to secure our posts, to keep the English fast up in their fort all night, and after having fixed ourselves in the best position we could, we let the English know that if they would speak to us, we would stop firing. They accepted the proposal. There came a captain to the place where I was. I sent M. le Mercier to receive him, and I went to the meadow where I told him that as we were not at war, we were very willing to save them from the cruelties to which they exposed themselves on account of the Indians. But if they were stubborn we would take away from them all hopes of escaping." Villiers expected that his threat of unleashing the Indians would get the attention of the British. "We consented to be favorable to them at present, as we were come only to revenge my brother's assassination, and to oblige them to quit the lands of the King our Master."

Washington remembered events differently. In a summary for Dinwiddie that also carried the signature of James Mackay, he started with the morning of the day of the battle. "About 9 o'clock, we received intelligence that the French, having been reinforced with 700 recruits, had left Monongahela and were in full march with 900 men to attack us. Upon this, as our numbers were so unequal (our whole force not exceeding 300), we prepared for our defence in the best manner we could, by throwing up a small entrenchment, which we had not time to perfect before our sentinel gave notice, about 11 o'clock, of their approach, by firing his piece, which he did at the enemy, and as we learned afterwards killed three of their men, on which they began to fire upon us at about 600 yards distance, but without any effect. We immediately called all our men to their arms and drew up in order before our trenches. But as we looked upon this distant fire of the enemy only as an artifice to intimidate or draw our fire from us, we waited their nearer approach before we returned their salute. They then advanced in a very irregular manner to another point of woods, about 60 yards off, and from thence made a second discharge. Upon which, finding they had no intention of attacking us in the open field, we retired into our trenches, and still reserved our fire, as we expected from their great superiority of numbers that they would endeavour to force our trenches. But finding they did not seem to intend this neither, the Colonel"—Washington—"gave orders to fire, which was done with great alacrity and undauntedness."

As commanding officers tend to do when writing reports for their superiors, Washington cast as favorable a light on himself and his men as Villiers did on *himself* and *his* men. "We continued this unequal fight with an enemy sheltered behind the trees, ourselves without shelter, in trenches full of water, in a settled rain, and the enemy galling us on all sides incessantly from the woods, till 8 o'clock at night, when the French called to parley."

Washington was cautious. "From the great improbability that such a vastly superior force, and possessed of such an advantage, would offer a parley first, we suspected a deceit, and therefore refused to consent that they should come among us. On which they desired us to send an officer to them, and engaged their parole for his safety. We then sent Capt. Van Braam, and Mr. Peronie, to receive their proposals, which they did, and about midnight we agreed that each side should retire without molestation, they back to their fort at Monongahela, and we to Wills's Creek: That we should march away with all the honours of war, and with all our stores, effects and baggage."

THE VERSIONS OF VILLIERS and Washington of what happened after the battle differed more strikingly. "We made the English consent to sign that they had assassinated my brother in his own camp," Villiers said. "We had hostages for the security of the French who were in their power. We made them abandon the King's country. We obliged them to leave us their cannon, consisting of nine pieces. We destroyed all their horses and cattle, and made them to sign that the favour we granted them was only to prove how desirous we were to use them as friends. That very night the articles of capitulation were signed, and the two hostages I had demanded were brought to my camp."

Washington claimed ignorance of any admission of assassination. Adam Stephen was an officer present when Van Braam brought back the articles of capitulation. He described the conditions under which the French demands were conveyed. "We were obliged to take the sense of them by word of mouth," Stephen said. "It rained so heavily that he could not give us a written translation of them; we could scarcely keep the candle light to read them. They were wrote in a bad hand, on wet and blotted paper, so that no person could read them but Van Braam, who had heard them from the mouth of the French officer. Every officer then present is willing to declare that there was no such word as assassination mentioned. The terms expressed to us were 'the death of Jumonville.'" Stephen added, "If it had been mentioned, we could have got it altered, as the French seemed very condescending and willing to bring things to a conclusion."

Perhaps the French would have altered the text. Yet Washington was no less eager to end the battle. The rain had soaked his men, fouled their guns and ruined their powder. Food in the fort had dwindled to nothing. The French Indians were eager to fall upon his soldiers and do their bloody worst.

Washington didn't read French, but he must not even have glanced at the text to have missed "L'assasin" in the preamble and "l'assasinat du Sr de Jumonville" in the seventh article. Possibly he did notice, and Van Braam softened the meaning to "death" to make sure Washington signed. Van Braam's native language was Dutch, and he knew French better than English. Perhaps he didn't realize that English had a direct cognate for the French. Maybe things happened just as Adam Stephen said: the text was unreadable and so Washington relied wholly on Van Braam's translation. Conceivably Washington knew what he was signing, or knew not to ask, and chose to spare his command in the moment and deal with the consequences later.

THE TRIAL OF Washington's command wasn't over. "The next morning, with our drums beating and our colours flying, we began our march in good order, with our stores, etc. in convoy, but we were interrupted by the arrival of a reinforcement of 100 Indians among the French, who were hardly restrained from attacking us, and did us considerable damage by pilfering our baggage." Washington wondered if Villiers had double-crossed him.

But the Indians confined themselves to looting. The pickings were easy, because without horses and cattle, killed by the French Indians, the Virginians could take away only what they could carry on their backs.

The journey back to Virginia was slow and painful. Washington's men carried their wounded, who moaned in their agony.

It was an embarrassing defeat. Washington had utterly failed in his mission to drive the French from Fort Duquesne. He had not even been able to hold the fort he had built himself.

Yet he was lucky to get off as lightly as he did. His troops were substantially outnumbered by the French and their Indians. With a bit more patience, Villiers might have destroyed Washington's force completely.

But Villiers didn't have orders to start a war, and he didn't want to take the responsibility on himself. He had succeeded in his mission of establishing and defending Fort Duquesne and driving the British invaders back from the Ohio. He had avenged his brother and gotten his brother's killer to admit to assassination. It was a heartening victory for French arms, and a dubious start to Washington's career as a soldier.

— 12 —

While Washington was fighting the French in Ohio, a meeting took place in Albany addressing the French threat indirectly. The British board of trade, the body responsible for the American colonies, directed the governors of the colonies to appoint commissioners to a congress that would coordinate provincial policies toward the Indians. Even before news of Washington's battles reached London, the government there anticipated war with France, and it wanted to ensure that friendly Indians like the Six Nations of the Iroquois remained friendly.

Some of the commissioners hoped for more. Benjamin Franklin was a member of Pennsylvania's delegation. He and his fellow commissioners set out for Albany. "In our way thither, I projected and drew a plan for the union of all the colonies under one government, so far as might be necessary for defense and other important general purposes," Franklin recalled. The Pennsylvanians paused in New York, allowing Franklin to test his ideas on friends with expertise in matters of government and politics. They liked his plan and encouraged him to lay it before the Albany congress.

Other delegates had been thinking similarly. The shared attitude caused the congress to call a vote on whether a union of the colonies should be created. The verdict was unanimously in favor. A committee was formed, with one delegate from each of the colonies represented at the congress. The committee considered the various plans and deemed Franklin's the best. It became the basis for what was called the Albany plan of union.

The plan proposed an American government consisting of a council chosen by the colonies and a president general appointed by the British crown. The government would have control of treaties with the Indians, answering the original charge of the board of trade. Yet the plan aimed further. It would direct land policies on the frontier to reduce intercolonial competition that often riled the Indians. It would coordinate colonial defense by raising troops for an American army and paying them through import duties and other taxes. A central treasury would apportion and collect the taxes.

Franklin and the other delegates to the congress were pleased with their work and proud to send copies of their plan to the assemblies of the colonies and to the board of trade.

To their disappointment, the plan fell flat. "The assemblies did not adopt it, as they all thought there was too much *prerogative* in it, and in England it was judged to have too much of the *democratic.*" That is, the assemblies thought it granted too much power to the crown, through the royally appointed president general, while the crown thought it gave too much power to the assemblies, by their selection of the members of the council.

Franklin thought both sides myopic. "The different and contrary reasons of dislike to my plan makes me suspect that it was really the true medium," he wrote in his autobiography decades later. "And I am still of opinion it would have been happy for both sides the water if it had been adopted. The colonies, so united, would have been sufficiently strong to have defended themselves; there would then have been no need of troops from England; of course, the subsequent pretence for taxing America, and the bloody contest it occasioned, would have been avoided." Ever the philosopher, especially in his old age, Franklin mused, "But such mistakes are not new; history is full of the errors of states and princes."

13

The essence of empire is the compelled connection of peoples and issues not intrinsically related to one another. Time and again British Americans found their interests sacrificed to those of Britons in the mother country and other parts of the empire. Often they were lucky if the wielders of power in London even knew where on a map of the world they were located. Horace Walpole was characteristically caustic in his description of the manner in which policy regarding America was handled. "What facilitated the enterprises of the French was the extreme ignorance in which the English Court had kept themselves of the affairs of America," Walpole wrote in his diary. "That department is subjected to the Secretary of State for the Southern Province, assisted by the Board of Trade. That Board, during Sir Robert Walpole's administration, had very faultily been suffered to lapse almost into a sinecure." Robert Walpole was Horace Walpole's father. The son didn't spare family from his criticism. "And during all that period the Duke of Newcastle had been Secretary of State. It would not be credited what reams of papers, representations, memorials, petitions, from that quarter of the world lay mouldering and unopened in his office. West Indian Governors could not come within the sphere of his jealousy: nothing else merited or could fix his mercurial inattention. He knew as little of the geography of his province as of the state of it: when General Legonier hinted some defence to him for Annapolis, he replied with his evasive lisping hurry, 'Annapolis, Annapolis! oh! yes, Annapolis must be defended; to be sure, Annapolis should be defended—where is Annapolis?'"

Yet ignorance alone didn't explain decisions in London that often puzzled and dismayed British Americans. In Britain's empire their provinces had to compete for attention and resources with India and the West Indies, and in British thinking they vied with continental Europe. India and the West Indies mattered more than Virginia and Massachusetts to the merchants and investors who had the ear of King George's ministers, and as dangerous as the French were to Britain across the Atlantic in Ohio, they were more dangerous to Britain across the Channel in Europe. Newcastle's inability to locate Annapolis might insult Marylanders, but it didn't threaten core British interests the way a misplacing of Normandy might have. New Englanders never forgave the British for handing Louisbourg back to France, but to London, Madras in India mattered more.

For such reasons British governors in America had to look to the assemblies of their colonies for funding to secure their frontiers against the French and the Indians. Robert Dinwiddie tried to shame the Virginia assembly by relating tales of atrocities committed against the good people of the province. "These depredations were said to be done by the French Indians," he told the Virginia assembly, "but if I be rightly informed, some of the French subjects always go with the Indians on these incursions and are both privy to and instigators of their robberies and murders. How compassionate then must be the distressful situation of that poor, unhappy family, surrounded by a crowd of miscreants dreadfully rushing on to perpetrate the most savage barbarity, insensible to the cries of the tender infant, inexorable to the parents' entreaties, basely determined to destroy without provocation those who could not resist their violence. Think! You see the infant torn from the unavailing struggles of the distracted mother, the daughters ravished before the eyes of their wretched parents, and then, with cruelty and insult, butchered and scalped. Suppose the horrid scene completed and the whole family, man, wife and children (as they were) murdered and scalped by these relentless savages and then torn in pieces and in part devoured by wild beasts, for whom they were left a prey by their more brutal enemies."

There was more of this, leading to the governor's plea to the assembly. "I assure you, gentlemen, these insults on our Sovereign's protection and barbarities on our fellow subjects, make deep impressions on my heart," Dinwiddie said. "And I doubt not, as you must hear them with horror and resentment, but you will enable me by a fully and sufficient supply to exert the most vigorous efforts to secure the rights and assert the honour and dignity of our Sovereign, to drive away these cruel and treacherous invaders of your properties and destroyers of your families, and thereby to gratify my warmest wishes in establishing the security and prosperity of Virginia on the most solid and permanent foundations."

. . .

BUT SOMETIMES EVENTS on the imperial periphery moved the metropole to action. Britain hadn't intended another war with France so soon after the last one. It didn't yet expect a war, not least since it thought France wasn't ready to fight again and wouldn't be for several years. Wars exhausted armies and depleted navies. They also eroded government finances, emptying exchequers and deterring purchasers of government bonds. The endless struggle between Britain and France was endless largely because the most recent losing side, whichever it happened to be, felt obliged to redeem its losses. After a few more rounds of fighting, in the early nineteenth century European statesmen would learn to make a place at the table for the losers, finally crafting a settlement that would last a century. But in the mid-eighteenth century, the game still had a zero sum: what one side won, the other lost. And that other wanted it back.

The fighting on the frontier in America initiated by Washington caused the governments in London and Paris to rethink their timetables. Each thought the other the provocateur and ascribed a grander intent than the facts justified. To the British, the French construction of forts from Louisiana to Canada—the construction Washington reported to Dinwiddie, and Dinwiddie to London—seemed alarmingly aggressive. To the French, the British advance into Ohio, leading to Washington's killing of Jumonville, exemplified the perfidy they had come to expect from the English in centuries past. Each side's defensive measures seemed offensive to the other, prompting more such measures and more such reactions.

TO DEAL WITH the French aggression in America, the British government sent Edward Braddock, a soldier born to the art of war. His father had been major general of the Coldstream Guards, which Braddock joined as an ensign at the age of fifteen. He climbed the ranks of the army, reaching major general about the time Washington headed for Ohio with the Virginia regiment.

When word of the rout at Fort Necessity reached London, Braddock's superiors in the army and *their* superiors in the government concluded he was just the man to take charge of the situation in America. Washington's failure was ascribed to his amateurism, not to mention his youth. An experienced officer in the regular British army would know better than any raw provincial how to reduce a fort such as Duquesne and scatter its garrison. To America Braddock must go.

Two regiments accompanied him, and he expected to raise more troops in America. He landed at Alexandria, to which he invited the governors of the several colonies. William Shirley came all the way from Massachusetts, and he brought the greatest ambition of the group: to drive the French clear out of North America. Braddock and the governors laid a plan to strike against Canada and Ohio simultaneously, with Shirley leading a column into the former and Braddock one to the latter.

Much time was spent talking about financial support. Braddock relayed the views of the government in London that the colonies should levy taxes to contribute to a general war fund, because they and the rest of the empire were in this fight together. The governors expressed doubt that their assemblies, the bodies that would have to approve any taxes, would be willing to contribute to a general fund. They were jealous of their control of money, and they were jealous of one another. Each colony believed it was doing more than its share.

The funding issue wasn't resolved when the meeting broke up. Braddock began preparing for a march inland to the Forks and Fort Duquesne. He would follow the route Washington had blazed. But he would accomplish what Washington had not: he would defeat the French and seize the Forks.

14

A young man seeking a career requires a role model, or at least benefits from one. Washington's father had been a planter and merchant, but Augustine Washington's early death deprived the boy of direct observation during the years when he was becoming a man. Brother Lawrence Washington's military service doubtless turned George's eyes in that direction, yet the temporary nature of Lawrence's service gave George little more than a taste of what a life at arms entailed. And Lawrence's early death, following the failure of the Barbados therapy for his tuberculosis, attenuated even that.

Edward Braddock was different. The general revealed the full flowering of a military career in the British empire. Washington's taste of battle had whetted his appetite for its drama and danger, and his time in command made him think he was good at giving orders and having them obeyed. He wanted more of the soldier's life, and Braddock showed what more looked like. The British army might be his future.

It would have to be the *British* army. Washington had hit a wall in the Virginia militia. He'd been promoted to colonel after the death of Joshua Fry, but that simply meant that all the responsibility for the defeat at Fort Necessity fell on his shoulders. He offered the expected excuses: he was outnumbered, supplies ran low, the rain made defense impossible. He overreported the damage his men had done to the French. "The number killed and wounded of the enemy is uncertain," he wrote, "but by the information given by some Dutch in their service to their countrymen in ours, we learn that it amounted to above three hundred, and we are induced to believe it must be very considerable, by their being busy all night in burying their dead." Villiers doubtless *under*reported the French casualties, but his tally of three dead and seventeen wounded was likely closer to the mark. The French were behind cover all day, and of course they won the battle.

Washington adamantly denied having admitted to assassination. "That we were willfully, or ignorantly, deceived by our interpreter in regard to the word *assassination,* I do aver, and will to my dying moment; so will every officer that was present," he said. "The interpreter was a Dutchman, little acquainted with the English tongue, therefore might not advert to the tone and meaning of the word in English; but, whatever his motives were for so doing, certain it is, he called it the *death,* or the *loss,* of the Sieur Jumonville. So we received and so we understood it, until, to our great surprise and mortification, we found it otherwise in a literal translation."

The defeat at first did him little harm. The Virginia house of burgesses voted to thank him and the militia for their service, with the lawmakers attributing the defeat to the failure of the other colonies to come to Virginia's aid.

The burgesses might have voted differently—or they might not have—had they heard other assessments of Washington's performance. Conrad Weiser was a Pennsylvania German who had roamed the frontier for decades, learning the Indian languages and befriending Indian leaders, including some who encountered Washington in Ohio. One in particular told him about dealing with the young Virginian. Weiser recorded the conversation in his journal. "Tanacharisson, otherwise called the Half King, complained very much of the behaviour of Col. Washington to him (though in a very moderate way, saying the colonel was a good-natured man but had no experience), saying that he took upon him to command the Indians as his slaves and would have them every day upon the out scout and attack the enemy by themselves, and that he would by no means take advice from the Indians; that he lay at one place from one full moon to the other and made no fortifications at all but that little thing upon the Meadow, where he thought the French would come up to him in open field; that had he taken the Half King's advice and made such fortifications as the Half King advised him to make he would certainly have beat the French off; that the French had acted as great cowards, and the English as fools in that engagement."

Another Iroquois chief thought Washington faithless as well as foolish. This warrior spoke to a council of chiefs called by the British in the aftermath of the Fort Necessity fight. His name wasn't recorded, but his sentiments were clear. "We now open our minds to you, and desire that you will not be foolhardy and depend too much on your strength as Col. Washington did," he said. The people the chief represented had counted on the good faith of the British but been disappointed. The disappointment started on Washington's journey to Fort Le Boeuf the previous year. "Col. Washington, whom we convoyed to the French fort, left us there, came through the woods, and never thought it worth his while to come to Logstown or near us and give us any account of the speeches that passed between him and the French at the fort which he promised to do."

Washington continued to ignore them in the recent campaign. "Col. Washington never consulted with us nor yet to take our advice," the Iroquois chief said. He paid for his mistake. "Then happened the battle at the Meadows, before which we gave Col. Washington an account of how strong the French were, and when they were just at hand, he would not believe us."

The ways of the whites puzzled the Indians. "What afterward passed in council between him and the French we never could yet understand. Had it been us, we must have been all killed or taken prisoners without we had run away, for we never council in time of war."

Washington's neglect of his Indian allies continued after the battle. "Then Col. Washington carrying all his people down to the great towns and leaving all this thin settled country to be protected by a few strangers, and never in all this time to return back or come with other men, as there are men enough in all this great province. All which gives us more reason to suspect that what the French had told us had some foundation." The French had said the British were faithless.

Fortunately for Washington, the Indians' opinions weren't heard or heeded in Williamsburg. Yet even while the burgesses commended Washington, they broke up his regiment, as part of imperial retrenchment. The parts that remained were commanded by captains. If Washington wanted to stay in the militia, he'd have to accept a demotion. He didn't and so resigned. He resumed civilian life.

BUT NOT FOR LONG. When he learned Braddock was coming, with force to accomplish what he had failed to, the twenty-three-year-old former colonel wanted back in. Happily for him, Braddock was looking for locals with knowledge of the country he aimed to conquer. Dinwiddie gave him Washington's name. Braddock invited Washington to join his "family," or personal staff, albeit as a volunteer.

Washington said he was honored by the invitation, especially from an officer of such distinction. He avowed his desire to serve king and country. And he confessed to a selfish motive. "I wish earnestly to attain some knowledge in the military profession," he wrote to Braddock's adjutant, Robert Orme.

Washington required time to finish up a few personal matters. Yet he kept in touch with Braddock. "I herewith send you a small map of the back country, which, though imperfect and roughly drawn, for want of proper instruments, may give you a better knowledge of the parts designated, than you have hitherto had an opportunity of acquiring," he wrote to Orme.

Washington tried to convince himself that an unpaid, uncommissioned post with Braddock was just what he wanted. "The sole motive which invites me to the field," he wrote to John Robinson, the speaker of the house of burgesses, "is the laudable desire of serving my country, and not the gratification of any ambitious or lucrative plans. This, I flatter myself, will manifestly appear by my going a volunteer, without expectation of reward or prospect of attaining a command, as I am confidently assured it is not in General Braddock's power to give a commission that I would accept." Yet one never knew: if Washington did well, Braddock might find a commission he *could* accept.

Being part of Braddock's family came with perquisites. The British army would cover most of Washington's expenses. And proximity to power opened doors most useful to a young man of ambition. "I have had the honour to be introduced to the several governors and of being well received by them all," he wrote to William Fairfax after Braddock's conference in Alexandria. Washington thought he'd made a particular impression on Massachusetts governor Shirley, the most intelligent and energetic of the bunch. The admiration was mutual. "I think his every word and action discover in him the gentleman and politician."

15

The campaign commenced for Washington when he caught up with Braddock at Frederick, Maryland, in early May. They marched to Fort Cumberland, as Wills Creek was now called. "We are to halt here till forage can be brought from Philadelphia, which I suppose will introduce the month of June," Washington wrote on May 14. "And then we are to proceed upon our tremendous undertaking of transporting the heavy artillery over the mountains, which, I believe, will compose the greatest difficulty of the campaign." This was what made Braddock's approach to the Forks different from Washington's of the previous year. Braddock's army was larger and better equipped, which made it more ponderous. The cannons would allow Braddock to blast Fort Duquesne, but first he had to get them there.

Yet Washington wasn't worried, certainly not about the French. "As to any apprehensions of the enemy," he continued, "I think they are more to be provided against than regarded, as I fancy the French will be obliged to draw their force from the Ohio to repel the attacks in the north, under the command of Governor Shirley etc." To his brother Jack, Washington declared, "As to any danger from the enemy, I look upon it as trifling."

Washington employed the delay to make himself useful. "The General has appointed me one of his aides-de-camp," he told Jack, "in which character I shall serve this campaign agreeably enough, as I am thereby freed from all commands but his, and give orders to all, which must be implicitly obeyed. I now have a good opportunity, and shall not neglect it, of forming an acquaintance which may be serviceable hereafter if I find it worth while to push my fortune in the military line."

Braddock's confidence in Washington grew. Delays in provisioning set back the timetable. Braddock called a council of his lieutenants to consider their options. "The General (before they met in council) asked my private opinion concerning the expedition," Washington wrote to Jack.

He recommended dividing the force, the better to engage the enemy at once. "I urged it, in the warmest terms I was able, to push forward even if we did it with a small but chosen band, with such artillery and light stores as were absolutely necessary, leaving the heavy artillery, baggage, etc. with the rear division of the army, to follow by slow and easy marches, which they might do safely while we were advanced in front." Washington cited intelligence reports that the French were undermanned at the Forks at present but expected reinforcements.

He was pleased at the response. "This advice prevailed," Washington told Jack. Braddock and twelve hundred troops would hasten forward while the balance of the force would follow.

Whether Washington would be in the advance force was unclear. A summer fever had seized him. "My illness was too violent to suffer me to ride," he wrote. "Therefore I was indebted to a covered wagon for some part of my transportation. But even in this, I could not continue far, for the jolting was so great that I was left upon the road with a guard and necessaries." Washington hated falling behind. Braddock promised he wouldn't miss any battle. "This promise, and the doctor's threats that if I persevered in my attempts to get on, in the condition I was, my life would be endangered, determined me to halt."

Given his own immobility, Washington wasn't wholly displeased that Braddock's flying column was soon crawling. He thought the British engineers were overly fastidious. "Instead of pushing on with vigour, without regarding a little rough road, they were halting to level every molehill and erect bridges over every brook," he wrote. In one four-day stretch, they advanced only twelve miles.

By early July, Washington was almost well and Braddock was nearly at the Forks. The closer the general approached to the enemy, the more cautious he became. He dispatched scouts ahead and put sentries behind them. Intelligence continued to indicate that Fort Duquesne was short-manned. Braddock didn't want a slip to spoil an easy victory.

Washington shared the confidence. Once again with Braddock, he expected to share the victory.

THE FRENCH WERE WATCHING. "Our scouts reported on June 26 that the English had left their fort and that they marched with many wagons and cannons," explained an account of the campaign compiled from the testimony of French participants and addressed to a cousin of the compiler. "On July 7 we learned by Huron scouts that they were no more than ten leagues from the fort, which was confirmed by the return of M. Rigauville, who went out with a party of 120 Hurons and Sauteurs on June 28."

The French commander, Daniel de Beaujeu, gathered his Indian allies. "July 8 was spent assembling all the Indian nations into one body. The same day the Iroquois and Shawnees of the Five Nations who inhabit the area around Fort Duquesne, and who hitherto had remained neutral, came to join themselves to M. de Beaujeu."

They readied for battle. "On July 9 Captain Beaujeu departed at daybreak with a detachment of 891 men, among which there were 2 captains, 4 lieutenants, 6 ensigns, 23 cadets, 72 men of the Regular troops, 146 militia, and 637 Indians." A small garrison remained at Fort Duquesne.

Beaujeu's Indian scouts sighted the British without being seen themselves. "The English had halted in the woods, in a road that they had built the year before, from Fort Necessity up to 3 leagues from Fort Duquesne." This was Washington's work, from which he had fallen back to Fort Necessity to fight. The scouts described the order of the British soldiers. "They were formed in a column, the center of which, from the head to the tail, was filled with their wagons and baggage." The British tried to march in the fashion to which they were trained, in this case fifteen abreast. But the narrow road crowded them, and their cannons and wagons clogged things the more. They made an inviting target.

"Certain of the enemy's position, M. de Beaujeu divided the Indian nations and spread them out on both sides of the road in the woods," the French history said. "He placed at the head of each nation an officer or cadet who spoke the language and ordered them to reveal themselves only when he had attacked the enemy in front." He massed his own soldiers in the line of the British march.

"In this order, he attacked them with intrepid courage." At first the British returned fire effectively. "They received him on their side with a heavy fire, and opened their ranks after every discharge to the right and to the left to leave a free passage to the cannons that they concealed, charged with grapeshot." The French troops were shaken and unable to advance.

But the fire gave the signal to the Indians beside the road. "All at once our Indians, who had advantageously posted themselves behind trees, fired their discharge (a discharge all the more terrible as their fire was continual"—rather than in volleys—"and, as you know, dear cousin, no shot of theirs is ever false)."

The deadly cross fire threw the British into confusion. Those in the front pulled back, allowing the French there to regroup and press forward. Beaujeu had been leading from the front, and had paid for his courage with his life, being killed in an early salvo by the British. His second, Jean-Daniel Dumas, ordered the French soldiers to fix bayonets and charge. The British in the front fell back and collided with the troops behind.

The French Indians poured from the woods onto the road, war clubs raised and scalping knives ready. Their war cries intensified the terror that overtook the trapped British. "The English, unable to withstand this shock, although they had their bayonets fixed, broke ranks and, unable to rally because of the poor disposition of their order of battle, fled in disorder. Half of our detachment pursued them, almost to the banks of the Monongahela, while the other half remained to guard the battlefield."

THE DEBACLE APPEARED even worse to Washington. "We were attacked (very unexpectedly) by about three hundred French and Indians," Washington wrote to Dinwiddie afterward. "Our numbers consisted of about thirteen hundred well armed men, chiefly regulars, who were immediately struck with such an inconceivable panic that nothing but confusion and disobedience of orders prevailed among them."

While the British regulars had acted discreditably, the militia had done much better. "The Virginia companies behaved like men and died like soldiers," Washington wrote. "I believe out of three companies that were on the ground that day scarce thirty were left alive. Captn. Peyroney and all his officers, down to a corporal, were killed; Captn. Polson had almost as hard a fate, for only one of his escaped."

Washington reiterated his disillusionment at the performance of the British troops, which had caused such casualties among the provincials. "The dastardly behaviour of the Regular troops (so-called) exposed those who were inclined to do their duty to almost certain death, and at length, in despite of every effort to the contrary, broke and ran as sheep before hounds, leaving the artillery, ammunition, provisions, baggage, and, in short, everything a prey to the enemy. And when we"—Virginia officers, among whom Washington counted himself in spirit if not by present commission—"endeavoured to rally them, in hopes of regaining the ground and what we had left upon it, it was with as little success as if we had attempted to have stopped the wild bears of the mountains, or rivulets with our feet; for they would break by, in despite of every effort that could be made to prevent it."

The casualties were still being counted. "It is supposed that we had three hundred or more killed; about that number we brought off wounded." The British regulars were responsible for much of the mayhem on the British side. "It is conjectured (I believe with much truth) that two thirds of both received their shot from our own cowardly Regulars, who gathered themselves into a body, contrary to orders, ten or twelve deep, would then level, fire and shoot down the men before them."

Braddock was one of those killed. Washington didn't know which side the fire that felled him came from. "The General was wounded in the shoulder and breast, of which he died three days after," he told Dinwiddie.

The news of the battle was spreading along the frontier, among those who were supposed to feel protected by the British presence. They were now feeling anything but protected. "I tremble at the consequences that this defeat may have upon our back settlers, who, I suppose, will all leave their habitations unless there are proper measures taken for their security."

Braddock's successor, Thomas Dunbar, did nothing to calm the frontier folk. "Colo. Dunbar, who commands at present, intends, as soon as his men are recruited at this place, to continue his march to Philadelphia for winter quarters." This was in July. "Consequently there will be no men left here, unless it is the shattered remains of the Virginia troops, who are totally inadequate to the protection of the frontiers."

In a letter to Jack, Washington reflected more personally. "We have been most scandalously beaten by a trifling body of men," he said, still underestimating the French and Indian numbers. He would give Jack more details when they met in person, which would be soon. With the British bound for Philadelphia, Washington saw no reason not to head home. The campaign was over for the season. "We are done in thus far." He revealed how close he had come to being done in for good. "I had four bullets through my coat, and two horses shot under me, yet escaped unhurt, although death was levelling my companions on every side of me!" Washington concluded that someone or something had been looking out for him. "By the all-powerful dispensations of Providence, I have been protected beyond all human probability and expectation."

16

The defeat caused Washington to reconsider his career options. "I am always ready and always willing to render my country any services that I am capable of," he wrote to brother Augustine in early August, "but *never* upon the terms I have done, having suffered much in my private fortune, besides impairing one of the best constitutions." He still felt effects of the fever that hit him before the battle.

Washington reviewed his recent history in the service of the British empire. "I was employed to go a journey in the winter (when, I believe, few or none would have undertaken it), and what did I get by it? My expenses borne! I then was appointed, with trifling pay, to conduct a handful of men to the Ohio. What did I get by *this*? Why, after putting myself to a considerable expense in equipping and providing necessaries for the campaign, I went out, was soundly beaten, lost them all!—came in and had my commission taken from me, or in other words, my command reduced, under pretence of an order from home!"—from London. "I then went out a volunteer with General Braddock, and lost all my horses and many other things, but this being a *voluntary* act, I ought not to have mentioned *this,* nor should I have done it was it not to show that I have been upon the losing order ever since I entered the service, which is now near two years." Things would have to change for him to reenter the service. "I think I cannot be blamed should I, if I leave my family again, endeavour to do it upon such terms as to prevent my suffering (to *gain* by it being the least of my expectation)."

Two more weeks' distance from the dire event mellowed his tone a bit. Or maybe it was that he was writing to his mother rather than his brother. Mary Ball Washington had expressed the usual maternal concern for her eldest child. "Honored Madam," he addressed her. "If it is in my power to avoid going to the Ohio again, I shall. But if the command is pressed upon me by the general voice of the country, and offered upon such terms as cannot be objected against it, it would reflect dishonour upon me to refuse, and *that,* I am sure, must or ought to give you greater uneasiness than my going in an honourable command, for upon no other terms will I accept it." She needn't worry at all for now. "At present I have no proposals made to me, nor have I any advice of such an intention except from private hands."

Washington wasn't leveling with his mother. He had just received a letter from Warner Lewis, a planter and Washington cousin well connected in Virginia politics. The assembly, flabbergasted by the defeat on the Monongahela and Dunbar's flight from the frontier, was realizing it couldn't count on Britain for defense. It would have to look to itself, and to its own. The one bright spot on the dark horizon was Washington, whose performance in defeat was acknowledged to have been beyond reproach. "I have just come from Williamsburg where your friends are extremely impatient to see you," Lewis wrote. "Every one of my acquaintance profess a fondness for your having the command of the men now to be raised." Lewis explained that the assembly had voted new taxes for provincial defense. The plan was to muster twelve hundred men at once, toward a total of four thousand. "In short they all seem to think it absolutely necessary to raise as many men as will be thought sufficient to repel the enemy." Washington was the one they wanted for command. "Should you incline to proceed on this expedition, 'twould give a general satisfaction to our country."

On the same day he wrote to his mother, Washington replied to Lewis laying out the conditions on which he would accept the command. "I never will quit my family, injure my fortune, and (above all) impair my health to run the risk of such changes and vicissitudes as I have met with, but shall expect, if I am employed again, to have something *certain,*" Washington said. "I should insist upon some things which ignorance and inexperience made me overlook before, particularly that of having the officers appointed, in some measure, with my advice and concurrence." This was crucial. "A commanding officer, not having this liberty, appears to me to be a strange thing, when it is considered how much the conduct and bravery of an officer influence the men, how much a commanding officer is answerable for the behaviour of the inferior officers, and how much his good or ill success, in time of action, depends upon the conduct of each particular one."

Having stated his conditions, Washington still played hard to get. "I had other reasons which withheld me from offering my services," he told

Lewis. "I believe our circumstances are brought to that unhappy dilemma that no man can gain any honour by conducting our forces at this time, but will rather lose reputation if he attempts it." Braddock's defeat had spoiled an opportunity that wouldn't return soon. Horse wranglers and teamsters had lost their animals and vehicles at the Monongahela and not been paid. They and others would be wary of government promises. Without their support, a commander could do nothing. "Whoever undertakes this command will meet with such insurmountable obstacles that he will soon be viewed in the light of an idle, indolent body, have his conduct criticised, and meet perhaps with opprobrious abuse, when it may be as much out of his power to avoid delays as it would be to command the raging seas in a storm."

WASHINGTON GOT WHAT he wanted. His coyness didn't keep Dinwiddie from pushing his appointment on the assembly, or the assembly from approving. The commission that resulted met Washington's essential demands. "I reposing especial trust in your loyalty, courage and good conduct, do by these presents appoint you colonel of the Virginia Regiment and Commander in Chief of all the forces now raised and to be raised for the defence of this His Majesty's colony," the governor declared. Washington's mission was to defend Virginia against the French and their Indian allies. He had full power to act defensively and offensively. Washington's commission didn't explicitly state he would appoint the officers beneath him, but that appeared to come with the rank of commander in chief. At least Washington could interpret it that way, even if Dinwiddie might not always.

The governor doubtless thought he was giving Washington a lot of authority for a twenty-three-year-old. The commission concluded with a reminder of who answered to whom. "You are to regulate your conduct in every respect by the rules and discipline of war," Dinwiddie commanded, "and punctually to observe and follow such orders and directions from time to time as you shall receive from me."

17

Washington's assignment to defend the frontier came too late for many of the settlers living there. The defeat of Braddock and the flight of Dunbar left the frontier at the mercy of the French and their Indian allies. Jean-Daniel Dumas now commanded Fort Duquesne, and he was pleased to report to his French superiors how well the campaign was going. "I have succeeded in setting against the English all the tribes of this region who had been their most faithful allies," he said. His strategy was stern. "If any of them resisted I have always managed to destroy them, so that I have put the Iroquois in fear of the Delawares and Shawnees unless they follow their example, and since the war parties I have intercepted here have taken scalps and prisoners back to their towns, they find themselves engaged in the war, so to speak, in spite of themselves." The results were splendid. "I have succeeded in ruining the three adjacent provinces, Pennsylvania, Maryland, and Virginia, driving off the inhabitants and totally destroying the settlements over a tract of country thirty leagues wide"—about a hundred miles—"reckoning from the line of Fort Cumberland."

What delighted Dumas appalled the settlers. "Two and forty bodies have been buried on Patterson's Creek," a trader reported. "And since, they have killed more and keep on killing." A hundred men, women and children were massacred near Fort Cumberland. "We are in as bad circumstances as ever any poor Christians were ever in, for the cries of widowers, widows, fatherless and motherless children are enough to pierce the most hardest of hearts," wrote a frontiersman. "Likewise it's a very sorrowful spectacle to see those that escaped with their lives with not a mouthful to eat, or bed to lie on, or clothes to cover their nakedness or keep them warm, but all they had consumed into ashes."

The reign of terror spread for hundreds of miles along the frontier. "All burned to ashes," wrote a survivor of one brutal raid. "It is really very shocking to see an husband looking on while these Indians are chopping the head off the wife of his bosom, and children's blood drank by these bloody and cruel savages." What made it worse was that the Indian perpetrators of the atrocities had been friends of their victims. "Most of the Indians which are so cruel are such as were almost daily familiar at their houses: ate, drank and swore together, was even intimate play mates," reported a Pennsylvania Quaker, whose pacifism was sorely tested. "And now without any provocation destroyeth all before them with fire, ball and tomahawk." The tactics of the killers were as cunning as they were ruthless. "If they attack a house that is pretty well manned, they creep up behind some fence or hedge or tree and shoot red hot slugs or punk into the roof, and fires the house over their heads, and if they run out they are sure to be shot at and most or all of them killed. If they come to a house where most of the family is women and children, they break into it, kills them all, plunders the house and burns it with the dead in it or if any escaped out they pursueth them and kills them."

The cries of suffering reached Washington as the new commander in charge of repelling the attacks. "Not an hour, nay scarcely a minute, passes that does not produce fresh alarms and melancholy accounts," he wrote to Dinwiddie. "Three families were murdered the night before last, at the distance of less than twelve miles from this place." Washington was at Winchester, which he had made his headquarters. "Every day we have accounts of such cruelties and barbarities as are shocking to human nature. Nor is it possible to conceive the situation and danger of this miserable country. Such numbers of French and Indians are all around, no road is safe to travel, and *here*"—even in Winchester—"we know not the hour how soon we may be attacked." The French strategy of violent depopulation was working. "The inhabitants are removing daily, and in a short time will leave this country as desolate as Hampshire"—a county closer to the frontier—"where scarce a family lives."

WASHINGTON COMMANDED A regiment that didn't yet exist. On September 1, 1755, he issued instructions for recruiting soldiers. He cast his net broadly but not blindly. "No officer shall list any men under sixteen or above fifty years of age," he said. "Nor are they to list men under five feet four inches high, unless they are well made, strong, and active; then and in that case they will be received. Neither are they to list any men who have old sores upon their legs, or who are subject to fits, which will be inspected into by the surgeons upon their arrival at quarters, and such as are found to come under these articles will be discharged." The officers were given quotas for recruiting: captains, thirty recruits; lieutenants, eighteen; ensigns, twelve. The officers would be paid a bounty of two pistoles for each accepted recruit. Each captain should nominate noncommissioned officers, subject to approval by the colonel—Washington.

The soldiers had to be provided for. Washington issued orders to the man he chose as commissary. "You are to lay in provisions at Winchester, Fredericksburg and Alexandria, as they arrive, and to send up a quantity of salt for curing the beef at Fort Cumberland. Also to procure coopers to make casks for pickling the beef. You are to provide kettles and barracks for the soldiers as they arrive. Likewise fuel etc. upon as reasonable terms as possible, and I will answer the charge."

The officers needed to learn their duties. Washington instructed them. Record-keeping was crucial. "You are to be very careful in having exact returns made every day of each company, by which you are to see no more provisions are drawn for than what is necessary." Good order would make the men good soldiers. "You are to see that the muster-rolls of each company and party are called three times a day, and that the men are as often called out and taught the new platoon way of exercising." This was a drill for delivering volleys of rifle and musket fire. Washington said he would bring in an experienced sergeant or two to show how it was done. "The men are to be regularly practised in shooting at targets, in order that they may acquire a dexterity in that kind of firing." Some of the soldiers would be frontiersmen and therefore hunters, who could be expected to shoot well. But some would be farmers less skilled. "The men are to cook their own provisions in the barracks." Those who hadn't cooked before could catch on from those who had. Finally, each officer must instill proper behavior by modeling it. "In all things, you are to see that good regular discipline is observed, in order to do which you are to govern yourself in every respect by the rules and articles of war."

While giving orders down the chain of command, Washington sent reports up the chain, to Dinwiddie. He explained the regiment's needs. "All the shoes, stockings, shirts and hats may be had here," he wrote from Alexandria. "Also one hundred complete suits at sixty shillings or less, which I think would not be amiss to engage, as no one part of the country can, I believe, furnish the whole." No detail was too small. "A pattern is sent. It would be right to have them differing in size." Timeliness mattered. "Unless there is a proper provision made to supply the soldiers with clothing after they receive their first allowance, great inconveniences will necessarily arise, particularly if shoes, stockings and shirts, are not laid in, for those are the least durable and the most needed." Getting the shoes quickly was crucial. "Otherwise the soldiers will soon be barefooted etc., which always pleads exemption from duty; and, indeed, in the approaching season will render it a very just excuse."

Washington was unhappy to report that the recruiting hadn't gone well. "It was attempted at the general muster in this county, without success," he told Dinwiddie. Though the frontier was in flames, Virginians in the settled regions weren't feeling the danger. They refused to volunteer. Nor would they be compelled even by the officers Washington sent out. "A proof of this is very flagrant in Fredericksburg, where they were obliged to imprison the men"—the individuals conscripted—"who were afterwards rescued by their companions."

If Virginians wouldn't enlist, their neighbors might. "You are hereby ordered to repair as soon as possible to Annapolis and other public places in Maryland and there to use your utmost endeavours in recruiting men for His Majesty's service, under my command," Washington directed one of his captains. "You are to send your subalterns into the back parts of Maryland, Pennsylvania or such other places as you shall think most advisable to expedite the recruiting process." Washington would poach in the other provinces and let Dinwiddie deal with their governors.

The men who did enlist acted as young men do. Washington identified offenses and their consequences. "If any man changes or loses his firelock or other arms, he is to be confined and severely punished," he said. "Any soldier who is guilty of any breach of the articles of war by swearing, getting drunk or using an obscene language shall be severely punished without the benefit of a court martial." The court-martial, which Washington appointed, would deal with more serious offenses, starting with the most common. "If any soldier is absent without leave, he is to be confined immediately and tried by court martial, or punished at the discretion of the Commanding Officer." Washington's would be the final judgment.

He gave warning before pronouncing sentence. "As complaint has been made to me that John Stewart, soldier in Captain Bronaugh's company, keeps a disorderly and riotous assembly constantly about him, I do order that for the future he shall not presume to sell any liquor to any soldier or any other person whatsoever, under pain of the severest punishment."

Adam Stephen was lieutenant colonel of the regiment. At Fort Cumberland, Washington delegated eleven tasks to his supervision. "1st: To complete the stockade round the magazine as soon as possible, and to have that house which contains the empty casks covered with dirt and the ammunition removed into it. 2ly: To have the barracks well cleaned and sweetened as soon as the hospital is removed, and the troops moved into them." After Braddock's defeat the Fort Cumberland barracks had been converted into a hospital. "3ly: To have wood on the other side of the run"—creek—"cut down and burnt, or corded up for firing." Washington wasn't going to be shot at from the woods again. "4ly: To secure all the public horses that may be brought in by the country people, and to use all possible diligence in getting those that are carried off by others. 5ly: To send out a party after the horses John Nickols informs of; also after some that were sold to John Nealand without leave, and to employ hands to look after the whole until I return."

Perhaps Stephen paused in his reading to catch his breath. Washington continued: "6ly: To see that both officers and soldiers are regularly and constantly exercised twice a day, and that the adjutant is very diligent in his duty. 7ly: To be particularly kind etc. to Captain Montour, and to treat the Indians, if any arrive with him, in the most familiar manner." Andrew Montour had married into the Delaware tribe and was thought a likely liaison to that tribe and others. "8ly: To leave instructions with Captain Savage to observe the same directions when you come to Williamsburg. 9ly: When the coopers arrive, to see they are constantly employed and they are to make their casks so small that a horse may carry two of them. If they do not arrive soon, you are to send an express for them. 10ly: To see that the gun smith is as expeditious as possible in repairing the arms, and to order the carpenters to make ramrods for them. 11ly. To send three sergeants to each place of rendezvous as soon as they shall be thought capable of teaching the recruits, and to deliver each of them one of the country's horses, if it is thought advisable—as they are to be answerable for them."

Washington's attention to detail would be a hallmark of his leadership style. Adam Stephen would come to admire it. Three weeks into Washington's command of the regiment, Stephen might have thought it obsessive. It certainly was exhausting.

➝ 18 ⟵

Washington's style of command was exhausting for him, too. Or it would have been had he not been young, strong and apparently possessed of a constitution that tolerated long hours on horseback, riding from post to post on the frontier and back to the settled regions for supplies and mustering; short nights in inns, private houses, tents and under the stars; food of dubious quality and uncertain quantity; exposure to infectious disease, parasites and tainted water; and endless demands on his attention and time. Washington's bout with smallpox in Barbados preserved him from further troubles with that scourge, and the fever that afflicted him on the Braddock campaign possibly inured him to more of whatever that was. Beyond this he simply seems to have been blessed with a robust immune system and a strength of constitution not given to many others.

In some ways his position suited him perfectly. He preferred the out-of-doors to life behind a desk. He sat a horse better than most in a horsey society and considered a long ride a form of enjoyable exercise. His horses, of which he was able to afford an ample supply, wore out before he did. He had learned in his days as a surveyor how to deal with sun, wind, rain and snow, and he rarely let weather interfere with his travel plans.

He wasn't a literary man, but his literary skills were more than adequate for the colonel of the regiment. The logs he kept as a surveyor and the journals of his Ohio mission and campaign accustomed him to expressing himself concisely and accurately. The letters and orders he now drafted reflected the same style. He got plenty of practice, spending almost every hour he wasn't on horseback or asleep communicating up or down the chain of command.

In doing so, he discovered the importance of tone in getting his messages across. To his subordinates he was authoritative but not imperious. To his superior, the governor, he was respectful but not uncertain.

"We are at a loss for want of almost every necessary—tents, kettles, arms, ammunition, cartridge paper etc. etc.," he wrote to Dinwiddie in October. He hoped the governor would bend all effort to filling the wants. Dinwiddie should also get the assembly to rewrite the militia laws. "I must again take the liberty of mentioning to your honour the necessity there is of putting the militia (when they are drawn out into actual service) under better regulations than they are at present." The men seemed to think they weren't under military discipline. Some were merely lax, others mutinous. The former would be "a burthensome charge to the country," Washington warned. "The others will prove its ruin."

To emphasize the danger, Washington sent Adam Stephen to Williamsburg. The lieutenant colonel had just sent a report of the parlous conditions at the front. "Matters are in the most deplorable situation at Fort Cumberland," Stephen wrote. "Our communication with the inhabitants is cut off. By the best judges of Indian affairs, it's thought there are at least 150 Indians about us." They roamed in small parties to do the greatest damage. "They go about and commit their outrages at all hours of the day and nothing is to be seen or heard of but desolation and murders heightened with all barbarous circumstances and unheard of instances of cruelty. They spare the lives of the young women and carry them away to gratify the brutal passions of lawless savages. The smoke of the burning plantations darken the day and hide the neighbouring mountains from our sight." This was the message Washington wanted conveyed to Dinwiddie and the assembly, and Stephen was the man to convey it.

Events outran Stephen's horse. Washington shortly reported to Dinwiddie additional deterioration on the frontier. From Winchester he wrote, "I arrived yesterday about noon and found everything in the greatest hurry and confusion by the back inhabitants flocking in and those of the town removing out." He tried to calm the frightened refugees, to little avail. He attempted to gather militiamen and lead them out against the Indian raiders and their French provocateurs. The local commander said he had tried and failed. Washington had no better luck. The men declared they would rather die at home with their wives and children. Washington resorted to sending riders to neighboring counties to summon help. "Also hired spies to go out and see to discover the numbers of the enemy, and to encourage the rangers who we were told are blocked up by the Indians in small fortresses."

Washington thought the alarm of the locals excessive. "I believe they are more encompassed by fear than by the enemy." Yet the fear had real consequences. His orders fell dead from his hand. "In all things I meet with the greatest opposition," he told Dinwiddie. "No orders are obeyed but what a party of soldiers or my own drawn sword enforces. Without this a single horse for the most urgent occasion cannot be had. To such a pitch has the insolence of these people arrived." Yet Washington vowed that the popular insolence would not prevail against his responsibilities. "I have given up none where His Majesty's service requires the contrary, and where my proceedings are justified by my instructions. Nor will I, unless they execute what they threaten, i.e., 'to blow out my brains.'"

Even so, the cause and his sword could use some help from the assembly. "I would again hint the necessity of putting the militia under better regulation had I not mentioned it twice before, and a third time may seem impertinent," Washington told Dinwiddie, in a construction the governor doubtless did deem impertinent. Washington backed his statement with a threat to resign. The rough men of the frontier had faced down more formidable characters than a twenty-three-year-old colonel, and they would continue to do so unless he received stiffer backing from the government. Shooting one or two mutineers, as was done in the regular army, would have a salutary effect on the others. Anything less than such authority would continue to make his job impossible and would produce the loss of the frontier regions to the French and the Indians. "I see the growing insolence of the soldiers, the indolence and inactivity of the officers, who are all sensible how confined their punishments are, in regard to what they ought to be," Washington said. This had to change. At the very least he had to be able to flog deserters. Under current law he couldn't do even that.

Before Washington could send this letter, he received fresh bad news. "Last night at 8 o'clock arrived an express"—express rider—"just spent with fatigue and fear, reporting that a party of Indians were seen at the plantation of one Isaac Julian about 12 miles off, and that the inhabitants were flying in the most promiscuous manner from their dwellings," Washington told Dinwiddie. Lest the raiders descend on Winchester, he called out the town guards and posted some recently arrived recruits. He sent scouts in the direction of the raid to discover the intentions of the enemy.

The news got worse. "This morning before we could parade the men to march upon the last alarm," Washington continued, "arrived a second express ten times more terrified than the former, with information that the Indians had got within four miles of the town and were killing and destroying all before them, for that he himself"—the rider—"had heard constant firing and the shrieks of the unhappy murdered."

Washington gathered men he thought could be spared from the defense of the town and led them out to the scene of the attack. "When we got there, who should we find occasioning all this disturbance but 3 drunken soldiers of the light horse"—cavalry—"carousing, firing their pistols, and uttering the most unheard off imprecations." Relieved but angry, Washington arrested the drunken soldiers and marched them back to town.

On arriving, he met one of the scouts he'd dispatched the previous night. The scout had comparable news. "The party of Indians discovered by Isaac Julian proved to be a mulatto and negro seen hunting of cattle by his son, who alarmed the father, and the father the neighbourhood."

Washington was glad the enemy wasn't at the gate, but he thought the episodes significant all the same. "These circumstances are related only to shew what a panic prevails among the people, how much they are alarmed at the most usual and customary cries," he wrote to Dinwiddie, "and yet how impossible it is to get them to act in any respect for their common safeties." Washington added the latest instance of the impossibility. George Fairfax, Washington's friend and former surveying partner, now colonel of Fairfax County militia, had arrived at Winchester while Washington was chasing down the false alarm. Fairfax had sent an order to one of his captains to bring his company into Winchester for its defense. "With coolness and moderation, this great captain answered that his wife, family, and corn was at stake. So were those of his soldiers. Therefore it was not possible for him to come." Washington concluded, "Such is the example of the officers! Such the behaviour of the men! And such the unhappy circumstances on which our country depends!"

A delay prevented the regular courier from setting off for Williamsburg, giving Washington time to add a further installment to his letter. His scouts reported that the Indians in the area hadn't all been imagined. Their number appeared to be around 150, a sizable force for raiding. They had done grave damage. "Seventy or near it of our people are killed and missing," Washington informed Dinwiddie. "Several houses and plantations are destroyed."

. . .

WASHINGTON'S WARNINGS HAD the desired effect on the assembly. The members usually felt greater affinity for the militiamen than for him. Many would have answered his call to duty the way the Fairfax captain had, placing greater weight on the welfare of their families and farms than on the good of the province as a whole. The large planters and their representatives in the assembly had a particular reason for not going all in on frontier defense: they feared an uprising of their slaves if too many men were sent from their districts to the frontier. Yet they finally granted Washington power to discipline martial misbehavior. As colonel of the regiment, he was authorized to convene courts-martial that could impose penalties up to death on mutineers, deserters and the merely disobedient.

Encouraged, Washington directed Adam Stephen to put the new measures to work. "You will be particularly careful in seeing that strict order is observed among our soldiers, as that is the life of military discipline," Washington said. "We now have it in our power to enforce obedience, and obedience will be expected from us, the men being subject to death as in the military law." The new measures offered rewards to those who seized deserters and threatened fines and worse against those who sheltered them. Stephen should publicize the changes in the law at once and should do so regularly until the message sank in.

Washington himself addressed the panic of the people. He circulated a notice to the people of Frederick County. Recent events were cause for concern but not for panic, he said. False alarms must be guarded against, in both the airing and the hearing. The Indian raiders recently in the area had departed. The county was calm. It should remain that way until genuine reason for a different attitude emerged. "I do advise all my countrymen not to be alarmed on every false report they may hear," Washington said. They should not flee their farms at the slightest noise but tend to their business, on which the welfare of the county and province depended. "I can venture to assure them that in a short time the frontiers will be so well guarded that no mischief can be done, either to them or their plantations, which must of course be destroyed if they desert them in so shameful a manner."

Washington had words for his own officers as well. "Remember that it is the actions, and not the commission, that make the officer, and that there is more expected from him than the title," Washington advised, in a statement read by Adam Stephen to the officer corps. Washington made a commitment to his subordinates. "I am determined, as far as my small experience in service, my abilities and interest of the service, dictate, to observe the strictest discipline through the whole economy of my behaviour," he said. By the same token: "You may as certainly depend upon having the strictest justice administered to all." He added, "I shall make it the most agreeable part of my duty to study merit and reward the brave and deserving."

— 19 —

Washington's immediate aim was to limit the damage the Indians and the French could do to the frontier settlements. His broader goal was to destroy the ability of the former to wage war upon the settlements. This required driving the latter out of Ohio. Which in turn required completing the mission that had claimed the life of General Braddock: the capture of Fort Duquesne. And which, finally, required a decision made at a much higher level than Washington occupied.

The conflict between Britain and France in North America mattered greatly to the British and French colonists there, but it was a sideshow to the struggle between those two countries in Europe. Eighteen months after the battle of Fort Necessity, and six months after the death of Braddock on the Monongahela, Britain and France remained officially at peace. They did so not from principled nonviolence but because both governments were sizing up potential allies and foes for a resumption of their historic struggle. The treaty that ended the last war had left unfinished business between Austria and Prussia, which failed to finish it before Prussia in the spring of 1756 invaded Saxony, a German state in league with Austria. Thereupon France allied with Austria, and Britain with Prussia. Several additional countries joined one side or the other.

The outbreak of war in Europe at once clarified and obscured the conflict in America. The clarity came from the fact that Britain and France were openly at war. The ambiguity that had given rise to the French charge of assassination against Washington, and that had puzzled the Half King and other Indians about Washington's behavior toward the French, was cleared up. Britain and France were again avowed enemies, and the British and the French, and their respective colonials and allies, would behave as such.

The obscuring reflected the circumstance that North America was now one theater among several, and by no means the most important.

What became known as the Seven Years' War centered on Europe, but India and the West Indies also figured in the thinking of ministers, generals and admirals. Washington and the Virginians suddenly had to compete for British attention and resources with Britain's European allies and its other colonial protégés. And they ran the risk of another Louisbourg: of winning a great victory with colonial arms, only to have it negated at a peace conference afterward.

IN FEBRUARY 1756, Washington journeyed to see the man who remembered Louisbourg better than anyone else. William Shirley had been born in England, had been educated there and had entered and thrived in the legal profession there. But a lavish lifestyle and unlucky speculation left him strapped for cash. Rather than remain in London poor, he emigrated to America hoping for a fresh start. He arrived in Boston at the age of thirty-six in 1731, the year before Washington was born.

Shirley's abilities and his connections to home landed him a position in the colonial government of Massachusetts, as advocate general of the admiralty court. Those abilities and connections meanwhile excited the distrust of the colonial governor of Massachusetts, Jonathan Belcher. Shirley aggravated things by prosecuting friends of Belcher for corrupt practices. The feud animated Massachusetts politics for years before the British government gave Belcher the boot and Shirley his job.

As Massachusetts governor Shirley won the hearts of New Englanders by organizing, during the installment of the Anglo-French military epic then under way, the successful expedition against Louisbourg that relieved Massachusetts and its neighbors from the fear of French depredations launched from the Cape Breton fortress. When the peace treaty returned Louisbourg to France, the fears returned as well, but respect for Shirley lingered.

It persisted among British military men as well. Thus when Edward Braddock summoned the American governors to Annapolis on Braddock's arrival in America, Shirley was the one he heeded the most. To Shirley was given responsibility for an attack on the French fortress at Niagara, to accompany Braddock's campaign against Fort Duquesne at the Forks. Between the two arms of the pincers, the French would be squeezed out of Ohio.

Braddock's part in the plan failed, and as of early 1756 Shirley's hadn't succeeded. He led an army to Lake Ontario, but winter stalled the campaign. Shirley left his army on the shore of the lake to wait for spring while he returned to Boston to do what governors do when not on military campaign. But he now had an additional responsibility, as commander in chief of British forces in America, inherited from Braddock.

It was the general rather than the governor that Washington wanted to see. A problem he had first encountered on his first Ohio campaign had reemerged. An officer inferior in rank refused to take orders from Washington because that officer had his commission from the crown rather than a provincial government. In this case the officer was a Maryland captain, John Dagworthy, with a commission from the previous war, now heading a company at Fort Cumberland. His defiance undermined the authority Washington had struggled so hard to achieve with his own troops. It prevented Washington from gaining access to supplies stored at Fort Cumberland that Virginia had paid for but that Dagworthy refused to release. And it revived the annoyance Washington had felt at British pretensions on the Braddock campaign.

Washington's own governor, Dinwiddie, didn't always take Washington's part in disputes with other officers. The crusty Scot sometimes judged the young colonel too full of himself. But Washington's squabble with Dagworthy endangered Virginia, besides costing those stores at Fort Cumberland that Dinwiddie had had to cajole out of the Virginia assembly.

Dinwiddie proposed a solution. In November 1755 he wrote a letter to Shirley as one royal governor to another, with the latter happening to be commander in chief as well. "Last night Colonel Washington came here from Fort Cumberland, which obliges me to write to you on the following subject," Dinwiddie said. "One Captain John Dagworthy commands a company from Maryland of 36 men and was formerly an officer on the late expedition to Canada with a captain's commission from His Majesty but is not now on the half-pay list. However, he produces his commission, by which he sets up a right to command over the field officers in the pay of this Dominion"—Virginia—"which creates a great uneasiness among our officers and troops. He is a very good officer, but what he insists on, in my opinion, is not only unreasonable but also unjust, having not the least pretention from the regulations from home. The dispute is like to prevent our forces from doing their duty to protect our frontiers and annoy the enemy."

Dinwiddie proposed a simple solution. "I therefore entreat Your

Excellency to grant a private commission of colonel to George Washington, Esquire, and of lieutenant colonel to Mr. Adam Stephen, and one for major to Mr. Andrew Lewis, in order to make our affairs go on in a regular manner."

Dinwiddie anticipated Shirley's immediate objection. "If you grant these commissions, it's not intended that the Crown is to be loaded with any pay to them. They will be properly paid by this country"—Virginia—"and is only intended to settle their rank, which, I observe, often is a great hindrance to expeditions." Dinwiddie emphasized this point. "I am in hopes you will consider it, as our country is left open without any regular troops." He repeated, "I therefore hope you will think it necessary, and for the good of the service, to grant these commissions, for which I send this express, and beg the favor. You will please give him all dispatch."

"LAST WEEK COLONEL WASHINGTON arrived here from Virginia," the *Pennsylvania Gazette* reported on February 12, 1756. Washington's reputation from his exploits in Ohio preceded him, and his appearance in Philadelphia occasioned notice. He didn't stay long and he didn't say much. In particular he didn't reveal that General Shirley hadn't acted on Dinwiddie's urgent recommendation, and that he was going to Boston to second it. Dinwiddie supposed Washington would make a good impression on Shirley and might thereby win him over.

The next week's edition of the *Gazette* offered an update. "Last week Colonel Washington set out from this city for New York." Under Benjamin Franklin's proprietorship, the *Gazette* had become the closest thing to a national paper for the British North American colonies. Franklin's sideline as postmaster general for the colonies assisted his expansion of the paper's reach. The *Gazette* followed Washington's journey north. "New York, February 23. Colonel Washington, of and from Virginia, but last from Philadelphia, left this city for Boston on Friday last, there 'tis thought, to consult with General Shirley measures proper to be taken with several tribes of Indians to the southward, and particularly the Cherokees, some hundreds of whom, from the back parts of the two Carolinas, it is reported, have assured the western governments of their coming in, and firmly adhering to the interest of the English, in opposition to the French."

This wasn't exactly a cover story. Washington would talk to Shirley about Indian matters. But he wouldn't have made the long journey just for that. From the *Gazette* of March 11: "Boston, March 1. Last Friday came to this town, from Virginia, the Hon. Colonel Washington."

Neither Washington nor Shirley wrote a detailed account of their interview. It seems to have been polite and friendly, and it produced an order resolving Washington's problem with Dagworthy, in Washington's favor. "Governor Dinwiddie, at the instance of Colonel Washington, having referred to me concerning the right of command between him and Captain Dagworthy, and desiring that I should determine it," Shirley wrote, "I do therefore give it as my opinion that Captain Dagworthy, who now acts under a commission from the Governor of Maryland, and where there are no regular troops joined, can only take rank as a provincial Captain, and of course is under the command of all provincial field-officers"—including Washington. To make things perfectly clear, Shirley added, "And in case it should happen that Colonel Washington and Captain Dagworthy should join at Fort Cumberland, it is my order that Colonel Washington shall take the command."

Shirley's order resolved the problem of rank but not as Dinwiddie had suggested and not as Washington doubtless wished. Rather than promoting Washington, Shirley demoted Dagworthy. Shirley didn't detail his reasoning. Perhaps he wasn't as impressed with Washington as Dinwiddie thought he would be. Quite possibly he didn't want to confer commissions unnecessarily. Shirley had political enemies, and he didn't want to give them additional ammunition. The simpler solution, the one he provided, seemed the better.

20

Washington arrived back at Winchester on April 6. Winter had brought a lull in the violence on the frontier, but with spring the raiding resumed. "The enemy have returned in greater numbers, committed several murders not far from Winchester, and even are so daring as to attack our forts in open day," Washington informed Dinwiddie. The panic had resurfaced. "Many of the inhabitants are in a miserable situation by their losses, and so apprehensive of danger that, I believe, unless a stop is put to the depredations of the Indians, the Blue Ridge will soon become our frontier." This was the goal of the French: to drive the English out of Ohio and back across the mountains to the seaboard.

For the moment they had pinned Washington to Winchester. "I find it impossible to continue on to Fort Cumberland until a body of men can be raised," he told Dinwiddie. He explained that he had taken measures to encourage enlistments. He would sally forth when the recruits arrived. "I shall, with such men as are ordered from Fort Cumberland to join these, scour the woods and suspected places in all the mountains, valleys, etc. on this part of our frontiers, and doubt not but I shall fall in with the Indians and their more cruel associates"—the French.

The Indians worried Washington more than the French did. "Five hundred Indians have it more in their power to annoy the inhabitants than ten times their number of regulars. For, besides the advantageous way they have of fighting in the woods, their cunning and craft are not to be equalled; neither their activity and indefatigable sufferings: They prowl about like wolves, and like them do their mischief by stealth." They required no resupply, instead living off the land and the people thereon. "They depend upon their dexterity in hunting, and upon the cattle of the inhabitants for provisions." Cattle thefts by Indians caused Washington to advocate new action by the lawmakers in Williamsburg. "I do not think it unworthy the notice of the legislature to compel the inhabitants (if a general war is likely to ensue, and things to continue in this unhappy situation for any time) to live in townships, working at each other's farms by turn: and to drive their cattle into the thick settled parts of the country." During peacetime, remoteness from neighbors signaled independence of mind and heart. During war, it meant danger and more killings than necessary. Washington was willing that the settlers be ordered back from the frontier. Whether the legislature would listen was another matter.

Recruitment went slowly. "I was in high hopes of being by this time at the head of a large party scouring the Allegheny hills," Washington wrote to John Robinson, the speaker of the burgesses, several days later. "But the timidity of the inhabitants of this county is to be equalled by nothing but their perverseness." Washington had announced a rendezvous of all inclined to pursue the enemy. "Only fifteen came, some of whom refused to go but upon such terms as must have rendered their services burthensome to the country. Therefore, I am again reduced to the necessity of waiting the arrival of a party from Fort Cumberland before I can leave this place."

Washington was gratified to learn that the assembly had voted funds to increase the regiment from its present twelve hundred or so to two thousand. He immediately began reckoning how the new men would best be used. He proposed arranging the two thousand into a single regiment of two battalions. Each battalion would have ten companies. Each company would have one captain, two lieutenants, several noncommissioned officers and eighty-seven privates.

To raise the privates, Washington urged conscription. "No other method can be used to raise two thousand men but by drafting," he told Robinson. Yet even with conscription, recruitment should be selective. "Great care should be observed in choosing active marksmen. The manifest inferiority of inactive persons unused to arms, in this kind of service, although equal in numbers to lively persons who have practiced hunting, is inconceivable. The chance against them is more than two to one."

WASHINGTON'S DAYS RAN to weeks, and weeks to months. He traveled from fort to fort tending to matters that arose locally. He responded to Indian raids with sorties that arrived too late to catch the raiders. He continued to write to Dinwiddie and Robinson pleading for provisions and other resources to keep the men from deserting. Courts-martial could do only so much.

The problem, he concluded, was that he was fighting a defensive battle when he should be taking the offensive. He enumerated the difficulties of his task in a letter to Lord Loudoun, a Scottish earl who had replaced William Shirley as commander in chief. "First, erecting of forts at greater distances than fifteen and eighteen miles, or a day's march asunder, and garrisoning them with less than eighty or an hundred men, is not answering the intention; because if they are at greater distances, it is inconvenient for the soldiers to scout between and gives the enemy full scope to make their incursions without being discovered. . . . Secondly, our frontiers are of such immense extent that if the enemy were to make a formidable attack on one side, before our troops on the other could march to oppose them, they might overrun great part of the country; and it is not unlikely if they had a design upon one part, they would make a feint upon the other. . . . Thirdly, building a chain of forts and removing stores and provisions to each must necessarily create very great expence. . . . Fourthly, and lastly—this expence is never to end; for we may be assured if we don't endeavour to remove the cause, we are liable to the same incursions seven years hence as now, and more so; because the French are allowed to possess the lands in peace, and will accumulate Indian interest and grow strong in their alliances, while we, by our defensive schemes and pusillanimous behaviour exhaust our treasury, reduce our strength and become the contempt and derision of these savage nations, who are enriching themselves in the meantime with the plunder and spoil of our people."

Washington's letter produced no effect. More time passed. "I have been posted for twenty months past upon our cold and barren frontiers, to perform I think I may say impossibilities—that is, to protect from the cruel incursions of a crafty savage enemy a line of inhabitants of more than 350 miles extent with a force inadequate to the task," he wrote to an acquaintance in April 1757. He saw no end to his task unless things changed at a level beyond his rank. "Experience, sir, has convinced every thinking man in this colony that we must bid adieu to peace and safety whilst the French are allowed to possess the Ohio, and to practice their hellish arts among the numerous tribes of Indian nations that inhabit those regions. They are also convinced that it must be attended with an expence infinitely greater to defend our possessions (as they ought to be defended) against the skulking enemy than to remove the cause of our groundless fears in the reduction of the place—Fort Duquesne, I mean."

Yet nothing seemed likely to happen. "From what strange causes I know not, no attempt this season will be made, I fear, to destroy this hold of barbarians—for they deserve no better a name who have become a terror to three populous colonies." He didn't blame his own colony. "Virginia may justly say she was always willing to furnish her full proportion of men and money for this desirable end."

The initiative had to come from London. And it ought to come soon. "I think I can venture to affirm that there never was, and verily I believe never will be, a more favourable time than now for an enterprize of this kind." The French were distracted by the British offensives in the north. Fort Duquesne was vulnerable.

21

John Forbes was a Scotsman, born in Edinburgh in the first decade of the eighteenth century. His father was laird of Pittencrieff in Dunfermline, the birthplace a century later of Andrew Carnegie, who would build an industrial empire based at the very spot Forbes would deliver to the British empire. Forbes trained in medicine but wound up in the army. He fought in the War of the Austrian Succession with enough gallantry and skill to warrant repeated promotion. In 1757 he sailed to America with Loudoun, the new commander in chief. As adjutant general to Loudoun, based in New York, he controlled the communications linking the various campaigns against the French and their Indian allies. In early 1758 he put to paper his thoughts on how the war should proceed. These were for Loudoun's benefit but also for the government in London. "I shall enter into no discussion how the French have these several years past outwitted us with our Indian neighbors, have baffled all our projects of compelling them to do us justice, nay have almost everywhere had the advantage over us both in political and military genius," he began, employing the hoary device of saying something by professing not to say it. Those bad things had happened under the old command. The new command would do better.

Britain had crucial advantages over France in America, Forbes said. The British colonies were broad and bountiful, spreading across the temperate zone and supporting agriculture of all kinds. The French colonies were constricted and confined to the northern regions where winter lasted eight months. Agriculture there was negligible, leaving the French colonies dependent on supply from France, which could arrive only during the months when the St. Lawrence River was free of ice. This rendered French forces especially vulnerable at the end of winter, before the ships could get through. The population of the British colonies was ten times that of the French colonies. The French might prosper in a war of raids, but in any extended campaign British numbers must prevail. "I shall not pretend to show the strength of the French settlements either in defending themselves or attacking us," Forbes wrote, "but at present shall only show what strength we have and how and where we may not only attack them but be obliging them to divide their force, rendering them weak and of easy conquest to a zealous, vigorous and active people."

Forbes conceived of the North American conflict as comprising four theaters. In the north was Nova Scotia, which controlled the approach to Canada. Britain had a base at Halifax, which threatened the French position at Louisbourg. That fortress should be attacked as soon as possible. In the south was South Carolina, from which operations could harass the French on the lower Mississippi River. In between was the corridor of the Hudson River and Lake Champlain. Forbes advocated an invasion of Canada by this route.

Forbes's fourth theater, and the key to the whole campaign, was Ohio. "Whatever can be done in those parts to harass and drive the enemy from their settlements is of the utmost consequence," he told Loudoun. He specified a strategy of striking early in the season, when the Indians were hungry from winter. "While their Indians are out upon their hunting, and their defence at home small, one is naturally led to believe that any attempt made upon Fort Duquesne might be attended with success." For such purpose Forbes would assemble a force at Fort Cumberland consisting of two regiments of British regulars and the provincial regiments of Pennsylvania, Maryland and Virginia. The combined army would march the hundred miles to the Forks and destroy the French garrison at Fort Duquesne before it could be reinforced. "There is no doubt of their success, which will secure the whole tribe of the Seneca Indians to our interest and entirely destroy the French trade and communications in those parts."

LOUDOUN LIKED FORBES'S PLAN and gave him command of the Ohio column. There was but one concern: Forbes's health. The adjutant general had been having difficulty with his legs. The ailment might have been circulatory or nerve related. Whatever the cause, it gave him fits. "My infirmities are really no joke, nor are they to be played the fool with," he told Loudoun. "Both legs and thighs are an absolute sight, and the soles of my feet blistered." For days he was confined to his quarters. The symptoms varied over time, which might not be a bad thing. "My damned legs have fallen down to my toes and soles of my feet, so hope by tomorrow it will fly off," he wrote. "But at present can not walk."

Perhaps Loudoun reasoned that a commander needn't walk. He could ride or, if need arose, be carried. Forbes got the job of taking Fort Duquesne.

Forbes wrote to the governors of the nearby provinces. To Pennsylvania's William Denny he expressed confidence that the governor and assembly there were doing everything in their power to support the king's army. "And therefore must beg that the officers and soldiers raised in Pennsylvania for the service are able bodied good men, capable of enduring fatigue, and that their arms be the best that can be found in the province." The American frontiersmen would make good rangers, familiar with the country and able to fight the Indians on their own terms. A spy would be helpful. "If it could possibly be contrived to find some intelligent person who would venture up to the Ohio, either as a merchant or a deserter, and would bring us intelligence what was going on in those parts, I should certainly reward him handsomely."

FORBES CONNECTED WITH Washington indirectly, through John Blair, president of Dinwiddie's governor's council. Forbes had heard positive things about Washington. "He has the character of a good and knowing officer in the back countries," Forbes wrote. Washington was just the kind of man the campaign to Ohio needed.

Blair passed the message to Washington, who responded at once. "Permit me to return you my sincere and hearty thanks for the honour you were pleased to do me in a letter to Mr. President Blair," he wrote to Forbes, "and to assure you that to merit a continuance of the good opinion you seem to entertain of me shall be one of my principal studies, for I have now no ambition that is higher, and it is the greatest reward I expect for my services in the ensuing campaign." Washington gushed further: "It gives me no small pleasure to find we have an officer of your universal good character and consummate prudence to command in this expedition, and it is with equal degree of pleasure I congratulate you on the promising prospect of a glorious campaign."

Washington offered information Forbes could use. The Cherokees were coming. Washington had learned that seven hundred warriors were on their way. Yet they must be handled with care. "There are two things I can find that will contribute greatly to their ease and contentment of mind, namely, an early campaign and plenty of goods." The Indians would fight not from love for King George but from need of British merchandise. And they wouldn't wait forever for the fight and their pay.

Washington added that the Virginia government could use a nudge. "I have received no orders yet to assemble the dispersed companies of the Virginia Regiment, some of whom are two hundred miles distant," he told Forbes. Moreover, they were short of basic provisions. "So that I fear we shall make a very shabby appearance at the general rendezvous"—which Forbes had set for Winchester. "We are in great want of tents, having none to encamp our troops as they arrive, and this place can't yet furnish barracks, nor the town quarters for them."

Washington thought Forbes could use a nudge too. After all the waiting for another chance to take Fort Duquesne, drive the French from Ohio and finally secure the frontier, he didn't want Forbes to fail as Braddock had failed. The new general needed to hear some old lessons, Washington judged. "Pardon the liberty I am going to use, a liberty that nothing but the most disinterested regard for the safety and welfare of these colonies could cause me to take," he wrote to Forbes in June. "How far my ideas on what I am going to observe is compatible with reason, and how far they may correspond with your sentiments on the matter, I shall candidly submit to your Excellency to determine." Washington had warned that the Indian allies would get restive if the campaign were delayed, and now the campaign *had* been delayed, because the governments of the provinces were slow to forward funds. The consequence was what he had predicted. Most of the Indians had gone home. Only a few still lingered. "How long these can be prevailed upon to remain with us, I won't absolutely affirm," Washington told Forbes. "But this I can venture to say, not 6 weeks, if it requires that time to form our magazines and prepare for our march, as Colonel Bouquet seems to think it will." Henry Bouquet was a Swiss-born soldier of fortune who had recently signed on with the British. His experience of previous wars gave his observations on the current one extra weight.

The loss of the Indians was a serious problem, Washington said. "We are left to perform a march of more than 100 miles from our most advanced post before we arrive at Fort Duquesne, a great part of which over mountains and rocks, and through some such defiles as will enable the enemy, with assistance of *their* Indians and irregulars, and their superior knowledge of the country, to render our march extremely arduous, perhaps impracticable, and at best very tedious, unless assisted by a considerable body of Indians, who I conceive to be the only troops fit to cope with Indians in such ground." Washington put the matter succinctly: "Indians to us are of the utmost importance."

The issue was larger than the present campaign. The Cherokees were the leading tribe in the southern colonies, and the tribe most harassed by English settlers. Washington urged Forbes to send an envoy to the Cherokees to emphasize the good feelings of the British government toward them. And he should take measures to curb the settlers. If the settlers' harassment of the Cherokees didn't end, the Indians might defect to the French or simply sit out the war, either of which "may be productive of the most destructive consequences to the British affairs in America and terminate in the ruin of our southern settlements," Washington said. Present trends weren't promising. "The southern Indians of late seem to be in a very wavering situation and have, on several occasions, discovered an inclination to break with us. I think it can admit of no doubt that if we should be unsuccessful in this quarter—which Heaven avert!—the united force of several powerful nations of these Indians could be employed against us." Washington repeated: "Such acquisition to the enemy would enable them to extirpate our southern colonies and make themselves masters of this part of the continent at least."

22

The Forbes campaign proceeded slowly. Persuading one colony to contribute its share was difficult, but persuading several, and then coordinating the contributions, was nearly impossible. The Indians weren't the only ones frustrated by the delays. Provincial militiamen, who like the Indians had wives and children to worry about, abandoned their posts in dismaying numbers. Forbes cast the problem in moral and criminal terms in an advertisement he published in the *Pennsylvania Gazette* on June 1. "Sundry persons have enlisted in the several provincial levies, received the bounty money"—signing bonuses—"and afterward feloniously, treacherously and wickedly, with a view to defraud the public, have absconded themselves. Notice is hereby given to all such that if they do not return to their several companies on or before the twelfth day of June next, they will be proceeded against as deserters and tried without mercy by all the rigour of a court martial."

Forbes's health troubles continued. "I have lately been much out of order by a kind of cholera morbus," he wrote to James Abercrombie, Britain's second-in-command in America. "Cholera morbus" was the term for acute gastroenteritis, typically occurring during the summer. Victims experienced debilitating cramps, vomiting and diarrhea. Forbes could barely write letters, and traveling was out of the question. As luck would have it, there wasn't much traveling to do. Forbes had moved from New York to Philadelphia, but there was little reason to advance farther. "Our proceedings," he reported, "have been so extremely slow that we have lost very near all our Cherokees. And there is no remedying this unhappy situation, for the want of the artillery of the provincials and Montgomery's battalion did not afford us the show of any design to attack the enemy or defend ourselves." Richard Montgomery headed a regiment of British infantry, which hadn't arrived. Pennsylvania's assembly was as recalcitrant as usual. "I need not tell you the unhappiness of this government, nor the difficulties that I daily struggle with from the mutual jealousies of party."

Forbes's mood wasn't improved by news that Jeffery Amherst had been given command of the British forces in America. Amherst was fresh from his capture of Louisbourg and was expected to accomplish similar things against the French in the other theaters of the war, starting with an assault against Fort Ticonderoga, near the south end of Lake Champlain. "Mr. Amherst has come to lick the butter off both our breads," Forbes predicted to James Abercrombie. "No manner of trouble, every thing ready to his hand, a weak garrison to oppose him, and a great name to be acquired by the surrender of the place, and I suppose a speedy passage home. This you will allow is very good luck. I hope when he has performed all this that he will send us back a few regulars, for I do assure you I have not so many as to keep my irregulars in due decency and order."

Forbes managed to advance his headquarters to Carlisle, a third of the way from Philadelphia to the Forks, in July. "I am in hopes of finding a better way over the Allegheny Mountains than that from Fort Cumberland which General Braddock took," he reported to London. "If so, I shall shorten both my march and my labour of cutting the road about 40 miles, which is a great consideration."

To be sure, challenges remained. "The Cherokee Indians, being but bad judges of time, came in too early in the year to our assistance, and therefore had not patience to wait our time, so that from the fickleness of their temper, the greatest part of them went home three weeks ago," Forbes wrote. "No method was left untried to detain them, but they are like sheep. Where one leaps, all the rest must follow." The provincials were worse than the Indians. The Maryland assembly had ignored an order from the crown to increase funding for the war. "So glaring an infraction of His Majesty's royal command at this critical time draws the eye of all upon them, and their refusing all aid and assistance, for their own protection and repelling the enemy, strikes all honest men with a horrible idea of their ingratitude to the best of kings."

Just before the mail went out, Forbes added a gloomy postscript: "I am this moment informed, since writing the above, that 50 of the Catawba Indians have left us and are gone home. Those were the tribe we placed the greatest confidence in."

The news grew worse. "I received some imperfect accounts, rather surmises than particulars, of a repulse which a part of your army had met with near Ticonderoga," Forbes wrote to Abercrombie in late July. "They talk of no less than 97 officers with 1500 men being killed and wounded." Forbes hoped that these reports were exaggerated or entirely wrong. He didn't like any reverse for British arms, but this one, if real, would increase the pressure on his own campaign. "I was extremely unhappy upon receiving this sort of information. I cannot express the uneasiness and anxiety which I have been under."

The reports were about right. The French under the Marquis de Montcalm had repulsed Abercrombie's much larger army of British regulars, provincial militia and Indians. The losses on the British side were heavy, and the French, far from being driven back from Lake Champlain, remained in control, more confident than ever.

Abercrombie's defeat made Forbes's campaign more important than before, yet perhaps more difficult if the French shifted troops from the site of their recent victory to the locale of the next British attack, upon Fort Duquesne. Forbes tried to move faster, but everyone and everything continued to conspire against him.

His maladies made everything harder. "I have been very much out of order by what Dr. Bassett will call the flux, which is a most violent constipation attended with inflammation in the rectum, violent pain and total suppression of the urine," he wrote to Abercrombie. "I have been most miserable."

WASHINGTON HAD HIS OWN PROBLEMS. "My men are very bare of clothes (regimentals I mean) and I have no prospect of a supply," he wrote to Henry Bouquet in early July, referring to uniforms. Bouquet was Washington's immediate superior in Forbes's army. Washington might simply have regretted the want, but instead he hoped to turn it to use. "Left to pursue my own inclinations, I would not only cause the men to adopt the Indian dress but officers also, and set the example myself." He requested clearance from headquarters. "Nothing but the uncertainty of its taking with the General causes me to hesitate a moment at leaving my regimentals at this place and proceeding as light as any Indian in the woods. 'Tis an unbecoming dress I confess for an officer, but convenience rather than shew I think should be consulted."

Bouquet endorsed the idea to Forbes, who had been thinking similarly. "I have been long in your opinion of equipping numbers of our men like the savages," Forbes wrote. "I was resolved upon getting some of the best people in every corps to go out scouting in that style." Unlike some other British officers, Forbes was willing to take instruction. "In this country we must comply and learn the art of war from enemy Indians or anyone else who have seen the country and war carried on in it."

Washington appreciated the response. "It gave me great pleasure to find you approved of the dress I have put my men into," he wrote to Bouquet, who had relayed Forbes's approval. Washington elaborated on the advantages of going native. "Soldiers in such a dress are better able to carry their provisions, are fitter for the active service we are engaged in, and less liable to sink under the fatigues of a long march." An additional advantage was the reduction of horses and wagons required to carry baggage.

Washington's recommendations weren't all so well received. Forbes was drawing men from Pennsylvania and from Virginia. He himself was moving west from Philadelphia. It occurred to him and the Pennsylvanians that the fastest way to the Forks was the most direct: from the east. This was not how Braddock had approached the Forks. He had come from the south, from Fort Cumberland. Braddock's fate by itself seemed reason to Forbes and others not to trace his route. A new road from the east would also be shorter.

Washington spoke vigorously against the eastern approach. In early August he marshaled his arguments in a long letter to Bouquet. He started with history. "Several years ago the Virginians and Pennsylvanians commenced a trade with the Indians settled on the Ohio, and to remove the many inconveniences a bad road subjected them to, they, after reiterated efforts to discover where a good one might be made were found ineffectual, employed several of the most intelligent Indians, who in the course of many years hunting acquired a perfect knowledge of these mountains, to attempt it," Washington wrote. The mountains were the Alleghenies. "But these Indians, after having taken the greatest pains to gain the rewards then offered for this discovery, declared the path leading from Will's Creek"—where Fort Cumberland had been built—"was infinitely preferable to any that could be made at any other place. Time and experience so clearly demonstrated this truth that the Pennsylvania traders"—coming from the same direction Forbes was coming from—"commonly carried their goods thither by Will's Creek. Therefore the Ohio Company in 1753 at a considerable expence opened a road thither. In 1754 the troops I then had the honor to command greatly repaired it as far as Gist's plantation, and in 1755 it was widened and completed by

General Braddock within 6 miles of Fort Duquesne." The needed road existed, Washington summarized, at least all but the last six miles.

But suppose a road from Rays Town, to which Forbes's men had advanced, could be built, Washington continued. And suppose it could be built to the standard of the existing Braddock road. Could it be built in time? "Certainly not," said Washington. "Surmounting the vast difficulties to be encountered in making it over such monstrous mountains covered with woods and rocks would require so much time as to blast our otherwise well grounded hopes of striking the long wished for and important stroke this season." The blow couldn't wait. "Deferring it to another year would, I am morally certain, be productive of the most destructive consequences to the southern and middle colonies." The current season's effort had strained the budgets and politics of the colonies to the breaking point. Supporting the army through the winter and another fighting season would be impossible. Provisions would dwindle, and troops would desert or be disbanded. Holding his regiment together this long had required all of Washington's acumen and resourcefulness. To have to re-create it next spring, after the disappointment of failure this fall, would be impossible.

Regathering the Indians would be harder still. "The southern Indians have from our bad success and inactivity long looked upon us in a despicable light," Washington said. At the least they would refuse to fight on the British side. Not improbably they would join the French—"which would be such an acquisition to the enemy as might terminate in our destruction."

Regardless of which route Forbes traveled, Washington and the Virginians would be coming from Fort Cumberland. As a result the army would be divided until perhaps the very end. Washington cited this as additional cause not to build the new road. "By dividing our army we divide our strength," he said, "and by pursuing quite distinct routes put it entirely out of the power of each division to succour the other." Timing would be thrown off. "If we depart from our advanced posts at the same time, and make no deposits by the way, those troops who go from Rays Town, as they will be light, having carrying horses only"—and not wagons, which would require completion of the new road—"will arrive at Fort Duquesne long before the others, and must, if the enemy are strong there, be exposed possibly to many insults in their entrenchments from the cannon of the enemy." The whole premise of the current campaign was the advantage massed force would provide against the French.

Division would negate the premise. Forbes hoped to surprise the French. Doubling the approaches would double the chance of detection.

Washington assured Bouquet he was speaking disinterestedly. "I have offered nothing but what to me appears beyond a probability. I have nothing to fear but for the general service, and no hopes but the advantages it will derive from the success of our operations, therefore cannot be supposed to have any private interest or sinister views." He hoped the present plan would be scrapped.

IT WASN'T. Bouquet dispatched scouts who told him what he wanted to hear: that a direct route west was feasible and more desirable than the Braddock road Washington recommended.

Washington, almost beside himself, jumped the chain of command. He wrote directly to Forbes's headquarters complaining of Bouquet's obstinacy. "I find him fixed—I think I may say fixed—upon leading you a new way to the Ohio, through a road every inch of it to cut at this advanced season, when we have scarce time left to tread the beaten track, universally confessed to be the best passage through the mountains," Washington told Francis Halkett, Forbes's aide. Washington feared that the British command had learned nothing from the Braddock debacle, remaining as convinced as ever that they knew more than the locals about everything. He refused to yield silently to further British folly.

"If Colonel Bouquet succeeds in this point with the General, all is lost!" said Washington. "All is lost by Heavens!—our enterprize ruined." The campaign would stall, the militia dissolve, the Indians flee to the French, the colonies be threatened with destruction. "These are the consequences of a miscarriage, and a miscarriage the consequence of the attempt"—the attempt Bouquet advocated. "I am uninfluencd by prejudice, having no hope or fears but for the general good," Washington reiterated. "That be assured of."

Forbes trusted Bouquet more than Washington. The latter was alarmist, Forbes concluded, perhaps losing his nerve. He was certainly losing the respect Forbes had begun to feel toward him. Forbes summarized the matter to Abercrombie. "A jealousy arising amongst the Virginians that I was to direct my march by another route than by Fort Cumberland came such a length as to be most singularly impertinent," Forbes said. "Nor could I discover the bottom or cause from whence this sprung until Colonel Washington in a letter to Major Halkett fairly shows the leader and adviser of their foolish suggestions"—Washington himself. Forbes related how he had resolved the fuss. "I believe I have now got the better of the whole by letting them very roundly know that their judging and determining of my actions and intentions before I had communicated my opinion to them was so premature and was taking the lead in so ridiculous a way that I could by no means suffer it."

The new road was being constructed as he wrote. Forbes dismissed Washington's worry about the loss of surprise. "The enemy has as yet given us no disturbance nor do I believe that they suspect my coming this way." By contrast, the Braddock road was exactly what they *did* expect. Forbes didn't propose to be ambushed the way Braddock had been ambushed, and certainly not on the same road.

WASHINGTON DIDN'T THINK he was wrong about the roads. He didn't believe he had been imprudent in pushing his objections so vigorously. But he knew when he had been beaten. "The General's orders, or the orders of any superior officer, will, when once given, be a law to me," he assured Bouquet on learning of Forbes's verdict. "I shall never hesitate in obeying them."

Yet he couldn't leave it at that. "Till this order came out, I thought it incumbent upon me to say what I could to divert you (the commanding officer present) from a resolution of opening a new road, of which I had the most unfavourable reports, and believed from the height of the hills, the steepness of them, the unevenness of the ground in general, and what above all principally weighed with me, the shortness of the season, that it was impossible to open a road in time to answer our purpose. I am still of this opinion, partly from my own observations of the country, and partly from the information of as good judges as any that will be employed"—Washington's Indian allies and scouts, who preferred the Braddock route. "My duty therefore to His Majesty, and the colony whose troops I have the honour to command, obliged me to declare my sentiments upon the occasion with that candour and freedom of which you are witness."

Washington here was creating a record in case things went wrong, as he thought they would. "If I am deceived in my opinion, I shall acknowledge my error as becomes a gentleman," he told Bouquet. "If I unfortunately am right, my conduct will acquit me of having discharged my duty."

23

The summer dragged on. Its heat and humidity made the soldiers' ordinary tasks tiresome and the difficult ones painful. "We are still encamped here, very sickly and quite dispirited at the prospect before us," Washington wrote to John Robinson, the burgess speaker, from Fort Cumberland on September 1. "That appearance of glory once in view, that hope, that laudable ambition of serving our country and meriting its applause, is now no more! 'Tis dwindled into ease, sloth and fatal inactivity. And in a word, all is lost."

Washington had learned that the French at Fort Duquesne were vulnerable. "We have certain intelligence that the French strength at Fort Duquesne the 13th ultimo"—the previous month, August—"did not exceed 800 men, Indians included." The British mustered many more, if only they could get to the Forks. "See therefore how our time has been misspent. Behold the golden opportunity lost."

What accounted for this? "Can General Forbes have orders for this?" It couldn't be so. "Impossible." But if not that, then what?

The least Virginia could do was inform London of the situation on the ground. "Let a full representation of the matter go to His Majesty," Washington urged Robinson. "Let him know how grossly his honor and the public money have been prostituted." Washington volunteered to carry the news himself, perhaps as a military aide to a civilian representative of Virginia. "I think without vanity I could set the conduct of this expedition in its true colours, having taken some pains, perhaps more than any other, to dive into the bottom of it."

Washington had never felt more the Virginian. "It has long been the luckless fate of poor Virginia to fall a victim to the views of her crafty neighbours and yield her honest efforts to promote their common interests at the expence of much blood and treasure." Virginia's sincerity had been its blindness. "We now can only bewail that blindness and wish for happier times, which seem at so remote a distance."

OTHERS WERE AS impatient as Washington. James Grant was a major in the British Seventy-Seventh Regiment. He talked Bouquet into letting him conduct an armed reconnaissance to Fort Duquesne. Grant took 800 men, including 150 of Washington's Virginians, and crept close to the fort. They were detected and set upon by French and Indians, who drove them off with heavy losses.

Washington related the episode to George Fairfax. He said his regiment had lost five officers and more than sixty men killed. "This is a heavy stroke upon the regiment, who only had 8 officers and 166 men there," Washington said. Again he felt proud to be a Virginian. "It is with infinite pleasure I tell you that the Virginians, officers and men, distinguished themselves in the most eminent manner, that the General"—Forbes—"has complimented me publicly on their good behaviour, and that every mouth resounds their praises."

The failed raid seemed another instance of foolish decision. "The troops were divided, which caused the front to give way and put the whole into confusion, except the Virginians," Washington explained to Francis Fauquier, who had replaced Dinwiddie as Virginia's lieutenant governor, at the end of September. "This mistake, I fear, may be productive of bad consequences to the common cause!"

Worse was coming. "The promoters of opening a new road either do believe (or would fain have it thought so) that there is time enough to accomplish our plan this season. But others who judge freer from prejudice are of a quite contrary opinion." The road wasn't half completed, and already the mornings brought frost. "We know there is not more than a month left for enterprize. We know also that a number of horses cannot subsist after that time on a road stripped of its herbage. And very few there are who apprehend that our affairs can be brought to favourable issue by that period. Nor do I see how it is possible, if everything else answered, that men half-naked can live in tents much longer."

Though Washington's advice on the route had been rejected, he didn't cease offering opinions. Forbes consulted his colonels on how to move an army through a forested country without courting ambush. Washington submitted a plan. "This plan supposes 4000 privates, 1000 of which, picked men, are to march in front, in three divisions, each division having a field officer to command it, besides the commander of the whole, and is to be in readiness to oppose the enemy whose attack, if the necessary precautions are observed, must always be in front," he wrote. "The first division is, so soon as the vanguard is attacked (if that gives the first notice of the enemy's approach) to file off to the right and left and take to trees, gaining the enemy's flanks and surrounding them.... The flank guards on the right which belong to the 2d division are immediately to extend to the right followed by that division.... The rear grand division is to follow the left flankers in the same manner in order if possible to encompass the enemy, which being a practice different from anything they have ever yet experienced from us, I think may be accomplished. What Indians we have should be ordered to get round unperceived and fall upon the enemy rear at the same time."

Forbes was still listening to Washington. When the march to Fort Duquesne was finally ordered, it proceeded much as Washington recommended.

But in early October that still seemed far off. Washington had a chance to experience the new road for himself. "My march to this post gave me an opportunity of forming a judgment of the road," he wrote to Fauquier from Loyalhanna, near the western end of the road. "And I can truly say that it is undescribably bad. Had it not been for an accidental discovery of a new passage over the Laurel Hill, the carriages must inevitably have stopped on the other side. This is a fact nobody here takes upon him to deny!"

The campaign appeared to be ending as Washington had forecast. "The General and great part of the troops etc., being yet behind, and the weather growing very inclement, must, I apprehend, terminate our expedition for this year, at this place." Washington declined to mention his prescience. "As our affairs are now drawing to a crisis, and a good or a bad conclusion of them will shortly ensue, I choose to suspend my judgment."

Another week brought no improvement. "The General being arrived, and most of the artillery and troops, we expect to move on in a very few days, encountering every hardship that an advanced season, want of clothes, and indeed no great stock of provisions will expose us to," Washington wrote to Fauquier. "But it is no longer a time for pointing out difficulties. And I hope my next will run in a more agreeable strain."

At Loyalhanna, Forbes gathered his forces. Henry Bouquet paid Washington the compliment of consulting his views on a final push to Fort Duquesne.

Washington answered in questions. "Do you believe our stock of provisions—to say nothing of other matters—will allow you to execute this plan?" he said. "Will it last till we could reduce Fort Duquesne and march back?" If the answer was yes, Bouquet's plan seemed sound. But what if not? "Is it not neglecting the strengthening of this place, consuming the provisions that should support a garrison here?"

What if the French came out to repulse them? What was the best that could be imagined? "Suppose the enemy gives us a meeting in the field and we put them to the rout. What do we gain by it?" The French might suffer large losses, but they would still control the fort—the objective of the campaign. Anyway, Washington was by no means sure British arms would prevail in a meeting in the woods. They hadn't before. If the British side lost, it would have to choose between abandoning the artillery brought over the mountains at such effort and expense and risking total destruction.

Conceivably a British victory outside the fort would frighten the French into abandoning the post. But this was no sure thing. "Therefore to risk an engagement when so much depends upon it, without having the accomplishment of the main point in view, appears in my eye, to be a little imprudent."

The question received a fuller airing in a council of war called by Forbes a few days later. The general reviewed the number of troops present, their stock of food and other provisions and the latest intelligence on the enemy's forces and disposition. He asked his officers, including Bouquet and Washington, to assess the arguments for and against advancing. Bouquet summarized the discussion. "The arguments for advancing are: the hope of driving the enemy from the Ohio, thereby assuring us possession of it; the hope of getting rid of the Indians, who have settled along the river and who continually overrun and ravage our provinces; finally, the hope of justifying the expenses of the expedition and the hopes of our colonies who, ignorant of the difficulties the enterprise involves, regard the Fort as a very easy objective for the body of troops undertaking this expedition," Bouquet wrote.

The arguments against advancing were more numerous. "1st. The lack of clothing to protect the troops from the cold, and the impossibility of obtaining any. 2nd. The scarcity of provisions and the uncertainty of obtaining any by a convoy because bad weather has made the roads almost impassable. The shortage of horses and of grass to feed them makes them so weak that but little use can be expected of them. 3rd. The impossibility of providing this post with provisions for the winter if we and the army consume that on hand. 4th. The reduction of the army to one half its normal strength and the absolute lack of any knowledge about the enemy's forces in spite of all our efforts to obtain it. 5th. The risk of losing the ordnance if bad weather, the lack of provisions, or a defeat forces us to retreat without capturing the place. 6th. The impossibility of maintaining this fort if we should take it, as the provinces have made no provision to sustain it or to keep or replace the troops whose time is about to expire. 7th. The results of a defeat, which would cause us to lose the advantages we had acquired by the extension of our frontiers, would open our provinces to the enemy, and would bring down upon us not only the Indians who are our declared enemies but also those who have made peace at the Treaty of Easton, who from contempt for us and fear of the French would not fail to declare against us." At Easton, Pennsylvania, several tribes that had been undecided threw their support to Britain in exchange for a promise of security for their lands.

The conclusion was clear. "The risks being so obviously greater than the advantages, there is no doubt as to the sole course that prudence dictates," Bouquet wrote for Forbes. There would be no final push to Fort Duquesne.

THE DECISION SAT for all of twenty-four hours. Since the deadly skirmish in September, Forbes had kept his officers on watch for the approach of French raiders against the British supply lines. "You may believe we have frequent skirmishes and alarms," he wrote to Abercrombie. So far none had been of consequence. "Yet we are thereby kept extremely alert, as my numbers do not at all answer to the immense tract of country I must protect, nor to the multiplicity of convoys and escorts that I must have through a barren uninhabited wilderness two or three hundred miles."

One such alarm occurred on the day after the war council. "Two hundred of the enemy came to attack our live cattle and horses on the 12th," Forbes continued. "I sent 500 men to give them chase, with as many more to surround them. There were some killed on both sides, but unfortunately our parties fired upon each other in the dark, by which we lost two officers and 38 privates killed or missing."

Washington was among the five hundred sent out, and he found himself in the cross fire on the British side. The details of the incident were cloudy. "We have had several imperfect accounts of a skirmish between a party of our army, and another of the French, near Loyalhanning, from which the best account we can at present give is as follows," reported the *Pennsylvania Gazette* on November 30. "That on the 12th instant, Colonel Washington being out with a scouting party, fell in with a number of the enemy about three miles from our camp, whom he attacked, killed one, took three prisoners, an Indian man and woman, and one Johnson, an Englishman (who, it is said, was carried off by the Indians some time ago from Lancaster County) and obliged the rest to fly. That on hearing the firing at Loyalhanning, Colonel Mercer, with a party of Virginians, was sent out to the assistance of Colonel Washington, who, coming in sight of our people in the dusk of the evening, and seeing them about a fire the enemy had been drove from, and the two Indians with them, imagined them to be French. And Colonel Washington being under the same mistake, unhappily a few shots were exchanged, by which a lieutenant and thirteen or fourteen Virginians were killed."

Washington neglected to mention the cross-fire casualties in his next letter to Fauquier. He referred to the incident itself only in passing, citing "three prisoners who providentially fell into our hands at Loyal-Hannan at a time when we despaired of proceeding and a council of war had determined that it was not advisable to advance." He remained silent on the subject for many years.

Only in the 1780s, after he assumed that his military career was over, and probably his public service too, did he write an account for a prospective biographer. "During the time the Army lay at Loyalhaning, a circumstance occurred which involved the life of G. W. in as much jeopardy as it had ever been before or since," Washington said of himself. "The enemy sent out a large detachment to reconnoitre our camp and to ascertain our strength. In consequence of intelligence that they were within 2 miles of the camp, a party commanded by Lt. Colo. Mercer of the Virginia line (a gallant and good officer) was sent to dislodge them, between whom a severe conflict and hot firing ensued, which lasting some time and appearing to approach the camp it was conceived that our party was yielding the ground. Upon which G. W. with permission of the General called for dispatch for volunteers and immediately marched at their head to sustain, as was conjectured, the retiring troops. Led on by the firing till he came within less than half a mile, and it ceasing, he detached scouts to investigate the cause and to communicate his approach to his friend Colo. Mercer, advancing slowly in the meantime. But it being near dusk and the intelligence not having been fully disseminated among Colo. Mercer's corps, and they, taking us for the enemy, who had retreated approaching in another direction, commenced a heavy fire upon the relieving party, which drew fire in return in spite of all the exertions of the officers, one of whom and several privates were killed and many wounded before a stop could be put to it. To accomplish which G. W. never was in more imminent danger, by being between two fires, knocking up with his sword the presented pieces."

In this version Washington came to Mercer's rescue rather than the reverse. By the time Washington wrote, Mercer was dead. The earlier version appeared to impute blame for the cross fire to Washington in not recognizing the relief unit coming to his assistance. Washington's version again portrayed things oppositely. Washington presumably wouldn't have forgotten the moment when his life, as he put it, was in the greatest danger he'd ever experienced. But years can blur things. And perhaps Washington, by then the hero of the American Revolution, didn't want to tarnish his reputation.

Washington told substantially the same story to William Findley, a resident of western Pennsylvania, who recalled it decades after Washington died. "He asked me how near I lived to Layalhana old Fort, and if I knew a run from the Laurel Hill that fell into the creek near it," Findley related in a letter to the editor of *Niles' Register* in 1818. "I told him the distance of my residence, and that I knew the run. He told me that at a considerable distance up that run his life was in as great hazard as ever it had been in war. That he had been ordered to march some troops to reinforce a bullock-guard on their way to the camp—that he marched his party in single file with trailed arms, and sent a runner to inform the British officer in what manner he would meet him. The runner arrived and delivered his message, but he did not know how it was that the British officer paid no attention to it, and the parties met in the dark and fired on each other till they killed thirty of their own men; nor could they be stopped till he had to go in between the fires and threw up the muzzles of their guns with his sword."

Yet the initial version survived in the recollections of soldiers present. An account ascribed to Thomas Bullitt, a captain under Washington, was later published by a member of the Bullitt family. "Two detachments from Colonel Washington's regiment (one commanded by himself) were out upon the frontiers endeavoring to surprise a detachment of French troops from Fort Duquesne (now Fort Pitt), but instead of falling in with the French, they met themselves (the day being remarkably dark and foggy); each party mistook the other for the enemy, and a very warm fire was immediately commenced on both sides. Captain Bullitt was one of the first who discovered the mistake, and running between the two parties, waving his hat and calling to them, put a stop to the firing. It was thought and said by several of the officers, and among others by Captain Bullitt, that Colonel Washington did not discover his usual activity and presence of mind upon this occasion. This censure thrown by Captain Bullitt upon his superior officer gave rise to a resentment in the mind of General Washington which never subsided."

THE DISCREPANCIES IN the accounts might have reflected the bigger story by which the friendly-fire incident was overtaken. The prisoners captured that day said that the French garrison at Fort Duquesne was weak in numbers and short of provisions. "Which if true gives me great hopes I shall in spite of every cross perverse accident still be able to give a good account," Forbes wrote to Abercrombie.

Forbes dispatched Washington and his Virginians, as well as a column of Pennsylvanians, to see if the prisoners were telling the truth. Washington began thinking ahead. "The keeping Fort Duquesne (if we should be fortunate enough to take it) in its present situation, will be attended with great advantages to the middle colonies," he wrote to Forbes from the march north. "And I do not know so effectual a way of doing it, as by the communication of Fort Cumberland and General Braddock's road." Washington was still preaching the virtues of Braddock's route, besides lobbying for Virginia against Pennsylvania in the contest for Ohio.

Faulty intelligence threatened Washington's mission. "I fear we have been greatly deceived with regard to the distance from hence to Fort Duquesne," he wrote to Forbes. "Most of the woodsmen that I have conversed with seem to think we are still 30 miles from it. I have sent out one party that way to ascertain the distance, and the kind of ground between; and two others to scout on the right and left, for the discovery of tracks." The woodsmen were right. Getting to the Forks was no quick hop.

But perseverance paid off. "I have the pleasure to inform you, that Fort Duquesne—or the ground rather on which it stood—was possessed by His Majesty's troops on the 25th instant," Washington reported to Fauquier on November 28. "The enemy, after letting us get within a day's march of the place, burned the fort, and ran away (by the light of it) at night, going down the Ohio by water."

Washington was still trying to make sense of such unexpected good fortune. "The possession of this fort has been a matter of great surprise to the whole army, and we cannot attribute it to more probable causes than those of weakness, want of provisions, and desertion of their Indians," he wrote. Subsequent intelligence revealed that the British capture in August of Fort Frontenac on Lake Ontario had severed the French supply line from the St. Lawrence to Ohio. Fort Duquesne had been left dangling.

In the moment, Washington and his comrades could hardly believe their luck. The campaign was suddenly ended with their mission accomplished.

Success had been long in coming. Washington and his men were eager to get home. He hoped Fauquier would arrange a suitable reception for the regiment. "They should have some little recess from fatigue, and time to provide themselves with necessaries, for at present they are destitute of every comfort of life."

Part III

A Young Man's Fancy

24

"Be fruitful and multiply," God commanded in Genesis. The Anglicans who dominated Virginia's religious life took the command seriously. So did the other Christian denominations in the American colonies, and nearly every other religion and culture in that preindustrial era when numbers were essential to a society's chances of survival and most children died before reaching adulthood. Women were expected to have babies, the more the better.

To have babies, women were expected to have husbands. Men were expected to have wives. The pressure to marry was powerful in Virginia society. If a marriage was disrupted early by death, the surviving partner was assumed to be seeking a new spouse.

Economic arrangements reinforced the expectations. Especially among the gentry, women did not work for money. The men in their lives—in girlhood their fathers, in adulthood their husbands, in widowhood their adult sons—provided the material support women needed. The women bore children and managed the young ones and the households. Occasional exceptions—maidens who never married, widows who didn't remarry—proved the rule.

Men were somewhat freer than women not to marry. They certainly were allowed to take longer to marry, without raising eyebrows. Men could sire children further into maturity than women could bear them. The economic imperative was less, given that men controlled most of the resources. But a confirmed bachelor was viewed hardly more sympathetically than a spinster.

MARTHA DANDRIDGE WAS BORN nine months before Washington, to John Dandridge and his wife. Martha was the oldest of eight children. Her father was a planter in southeastern Virginia, albeit not a wealthy one. Her parents sought a good match for her. When she was seventeen, they thought they found one in Daniel Custis. Their concern over Custis's age and long bachelorhood—he was twenty years older than Martha and had never married—was allayed by his wealth. He was the heir of John Custis, one of the richest men in Virginia.

Rather, Daniel *would be* the heir when the cantankerous old man died. Daniel's mother, Frances Parke Custis, had died years earlier, but not before the affairs of the Custis household had become the scandal and secret entertainment of the province, even spilling across the Atlantic to England. Frances's father, Daniel Parke, had failed to deliver a promised marriage payment and then had been murdered in the Leeward Islands, a British-controlled archipelago in the Caribbean, where as governor he was said to have debauched young women, whose kin mobbed the governor's house and slew the debaucher. Not content with blood, Parke's enemies sued his heirs, including his daughter and her husband, John Custis. Custis was already aggrieved at Parke and said he'd be damned before he paid the old lecher's debts. "I would go to law the whole course of my life, spend the last penny I have in the world rather than I will pay one farthing of your unjust and unreasonable demand," he declared. "You may give me some trouble and put me to some charge; but depend upon it, where you put me to one penny worth you will put your self to a pound." He was as good, or bad, as his word. The suits and countersuits supported attorneys on both sides of the Atlantic for decades, ending only amid the rupture of the American Revolution.

Custis's anger at his wife's family did nothing for harmony in his own house. The quarrels got so bad that he had lawyers prepare a contract giving her control of their domestic affairs if she would agree to control her tongue and stop slandering him. Smallpox silenced her more effectively. She died before the deal was formalized.

Custis proceeded to scandalize the neighbors further by siring a child with the wife of a tavern owner and then another with one of his slaves, Alice. The siring with Alice was less the scandal than Custis's acknowledging it. He named the son after himself and freed the young man when he reached majority. He bequeathed to him 250 acres, Alice and her other children, and four slave boys of his choosing. He ordered young John's portrait painted and provided him with a pension. In his will he directed Daniel, his legitimate son, to build his half brother a house and furnish it handsomely.

In his will the old man also decreed that Daniel, on pain of being left with no more than a shilling, erect a tombstone with the deceased's assessment of his life: "*Aged 71 Years and yet lived but Seven Years, which was the space of time He kept A Bachelors Home at Arlington.*"

John Custis didn't approve of Martha Dandridge, thinking she and her family were after his money. But Daniel Custis persisted and illness overtook the father. Daniel and Martha were married five months after he died. As sole heir, Daniel became a very wealthy man.

The couple had four children. The first died at two, the second at three. Then Daniel died, at forty-five, in 1757, leaving a very wealthy widow, aged twenty-six, with a two-year-old boy and a one-year-old girl.

IN LETTERS TO FRIENDS and relatives, Washington had occasionally expressed interest in certain young women. "My place of residence at present is at his Lordship's"—the Fairfax home at Belvoir—"where I might, was my heart disengaged, pass my time very pleasantly, as there's a very agreeable young lady lives in the same house (Colo. George Fairfax's wife's sister)," he wrote at age seventeen or eighteen. "But as that's only adding fuel to fire, it makes me the more uneasy, for by often and unavoidably being in company with her revives my former passion for your Low Land Beauty." Sally Fairfax's sister was probably Mary Cary. The "Low Land Beauty" has never been identified.

He resorted to poetry now and then. "Oh ye gods, why should my poor restless heart / Stand to oppose thy might and power / At last surrender to Cupid's feathered dart / And now lays bleeding every hour." Possibly this was his own composition. Possibly he copied it.

Washington admired Sally Fairfax and evidently had a crush on her. That she was married to George Fairfax made his feelings more poignant. In a letter from Fort Cumberland during the campaign against Fort Duquesne, Washington wrote to Sally, "'Tis true, I profess myself a votary to love. I acknowledge that a lady is in the case, and further I confess that this lady is known to you. Yes, Madam, as well as she is to one who is too sensible of her charms to deny the power whose influence he feels and must ever submit to. I feel the force of her amiable beauties in the recollection of a thousand tender passages that I could wish to obliterate, till I am bid to revive them. But experience—alas!—sadly reminds me how impossible this is. . . . You have drawn me, my dear Madam, or rather have I drawn myself, into an honest confession of a simple fact—misconstrue not my meaning—'tis obvious—doubt it not, nor expose it—the world has no business to know the object of my love, declared in this manner to you, when I want to conceal it. One thing, above all things in this world I wish to know, and only one person of your acquaintance can solve me that, or guess my meaning. But adieu to this, till happier times, if I ever shall see them."

THIS APPEARS TO BE as far as Washington ever took his feelings for Sally Fairfax, and his expression here accompanied an acknowledgment that he was engaged to Martha Custis. Hence his "adieu to this." Martha wouldn't have been pleased to read: "till happier times, if ever I shall see them." But she was practical, and so was he—in actions if not in every word. She needed a husband. Or rather, a husband would make her life easier. A husband would manage her property and let her care for her children. A husband would give her standing in the community she'd lack as an unattached woman. She had never lived on her own, and she displayed no desire to start doing so.

If a husband there must be, George Washington was a likely choice. He was a more suitable companion than Daniel Custis had been, if only because Washington was her own age. He cut an attractively imposing figure. He was accomplished and honored. He had a promising future. What else could a young widow ask in a second husband?

From Washington's perspective, marrying Martha had complementary attractions. She was amiable and seemed kind. Still in her twenties, she retained the attractiveness of youth. Her surviving children were so young they'd grow up almost as his own.

And Martha was very rich. Washington hadn't worried about money, largely because he'd been too busy to spend it. But he'd always been aware that the most prominent people in Virginia had much more than he. The gentry weren't so crass as to accord respect to someone simply for being rich. Instead, they focused on habits and lifestyle, which money made simpler to sustain. Especially now, at the successful end of a tedious military campaign, Washington looked to life beyond the militia. Clearly it wouldn't be in the British army. Being a planter appealed. And being a planter with Martha's money and property appealed still more.

Probably these calculations occurred to friends of Washington and friends of Martha before they dawned on the couple. The first positive record of contact between the two is a note in Washington's account ledger of a gratuity given to the household slaves on a visit to the Custis plantation in New Kent County north of Williamsburg. Washington was visiting the capital on militia business and apparently stopped to see Martha while in the area. His suit proceeded swiftly, and by September 1758, when he wrote to Sally Fairfax, they had agreed to marry. The nuptials were scheduled for the following January.

BEFORE OPENING A new chapter with Martha, he had to close the current one. He resigned his commission as colonel of the Virginia regiment, to the dismay of the junior officers. "We your most obedient and affectionate officers beg leave to express our great concern at the disagreeable news we have received of your determination to resign the command of that corps in which we have under you long served," wrote twenty-seven of his subordinates in a joint letter. "The happiness we have enjoyed and the honor we have acquired, together with the mutual regard that has always subsisted between you and your officers, have implanted so sensible an affection in the minds of us all that we cannot be silent at this critical occasion."

With praise for Washington's sense of justice, his concern for the welfare of his officers and men and his devotion to his country—Virginia—the subordinates' letter mingled a feeling of abandonment. "How rare is it to find those amiable qualifications blended together in one man? How great the loss of such a man?" Indeed, the authors implored Washington not to leave. The war wasn't over. Why resign now? They knew he had his reasons. "Yet we with the greatest deference presume to entreat you to suspend those thoughts for another year, and to lead us on to assist in completing the glorious work of extirpating our enemies, towards which so considerable advances have been already made." The regiment still needed him. "Your presence only will cause a steady firmness and vigor to actuate in every breast, despising the greatest dangers and thinking light of toils and hardships while led on by the man we know and love."

Doubtless Washington felt a twinge on reading this letter. He and the officers had shared toil and danger, defeat and victory. He had asked much of them, and they had delivered. They now asked this of him.

Yet he had made up his mind. The destruction of Fort Duquesne had broken the back of French ambition for Ohio. The Indians allied with the French there would no longer receive the moral and material support that had rendered them a scourge to the English settlements on the frontier. They would have to make peace or depart. The war with France would be won or lost in theaters other than Ohio. Washington could fairly account his mission accomplished. He could in good conscience turn to the next phase of his life.

"To the Officers of the Virginia Regiment," he wrote in reply. "If I had words that could express the deep sense I entertain of your most obliging and affectionate address to me, I should endeavour to shew you that gratitude is not the smallest ingredient of a character you have been pleased to celebrate." Silently ignoring their plea that he reconsider, he declared that it pained him too that their time together was at an end. "If I have acquired any reputation, it is from you I derive it." He thanked them for their love and regard. "It is in this, I am rewarded. It is herein I glory."

— 25 —

William Pitt climbed to the apex of British politics by the improbable strategy of first alienating the king. George II was German by his birth in the city of Hanover. English was his third language. He had to be naturalized by act of Parliament in 1705, when he was already an adult. Pitt never let George forget his foreignness, while emphasizing his own Englishness. When George hired Hanoverian mercenaries with English money, Pitt decried the move as revealing the king's true loyalties. "It is now too apparent that this great, this powerful, this formidable kingdom is considered only as a province to a despicable electorate," Pitt told the House of Commons. "And that in consequence of a scheme formed long ago, and invariably pursued, these troops are hired only to drain this unhappy nation of its money." Pitt cast himself, in contrast to George, as the representative of the soul of England and the conscience of the Commons. By long refusing elevation to the peerage, he won his country's embrace as "the Great Commoner."

George needed a man with the common touch after the reversals of the early phase of the war with France. Pitt played hard to get. Horace Walpole recounted his accession to power. The king's antagonist had not been healthy. "Pitt, it was expected, would take advantage of illness, and not appear," Walpole wrote. "But he refined on that old finesse; and pretending to waive the care of a broken constitution, when his country demanded his service, and as a pledge of his sincerity in the scrutiny, he came to the discussion in all the studied apparatus of a theatric valetudinarian. The weather was unseasonably warm; yet he was dressed in an old coat and waistcoat of beaver laced with gold: over that, a red surtout, the right arm lined with fur, and appendent with many black ribands, to indicate his inability of drawing it over his right arm, which hung in a crape sling, but which, in the warmth of speaking, he drew out with unlucky activity, and brandished as usual. On his legs were riding stockings. In short, no aspiring Cardinal ever coughed for the Tiara with more specious debility."

Pitt exuded confidence if not robust health. "My Lord, I am sure I can save the country and nobody else can," he told the Duke of Devonshire, who asked his qualifications. And he would save the country—that is, the British empire—by winning the war in America. He sent the fleet against Louisbourg, and once more that fortress fell. The Forbes expedition against Fort Duquesne concluded successfully. All that remained was Quebec.

YET QUEBEC HAD SURVIVED this long for a reason. The city took its name from an Algonquin word for "narrows," and it was the place where the estuary of the St. Lawrence narrowed to a river. The city stood on a point above the confluence of the St. Charles River and the St. Lawrence. With a bend in the St. Lawrence protecting the city on the east and south, and the St. Charles guarding the north, the remaining western approach was commanded by the Plains of Abraham, an elevated expanse named for an early settler. Access to the plain from the St. Lawrence was secured by an escarpment thought unclimbable by regular soldiers.

James Wolfe thought differently. Wolfe, a bold major general just thirty-two years old, was given the command by Pitt and ordered to take Quebec by any means available. Pitt passed over senior officers in selecting Wolfe, adopting the startling view—for the politics of the British army—that promotion should reflect merit rather than connection. Some of the seniors groused. One of their friends gossiped to George that Wolfe was mad. "Mad is he?" answered the king. "Then I hope he will bite some others of my generals."

In his own mind Wolfe was merely a patriot. "All that I wish for myself is that I may at all times be ready and firm to meet that fate we cannot shun, and to die gracefully and properly when the hour comes," he wrote to his mother. He had hoped for a command in Europe. "If I had followed my own taste it would lead me to Germany." He had been given America instead. He accepted without complaint. "It is not our part to choose but to obey."

Wolfe gathered a fleet to ascend the St. Lawrence. He had to await the melting of ice, which flowed down from far in the interior. Then the vessels, under the senior command of Admiral Charles Saunders but the tactical direction of Captain James Cook, had to negotiate the islands, shoals and rapids of the turbulent river. Cook's success astonished the French. "The enemy have passed sixty-six ships of war where we dare not risk a vessel of a hundred tons," recorded the governor-general of New France, the Marquis de Vaudreuil. "Notwithstanding all our precautions, the English, without any accident, by night as well as by day, passed through it their ships of seventy and eighty guns, and even many of them together."

Wolfe laid siege to Quebec. The guns of the city constrained the movements of the British but didn't prevent them from planting guns of their own on the opposite shore, from which they returned the French fire. Wolfe made feints and forays designed to lure the French, commanded by the Marquis de Montcalm, out from behind the city's walls. The French general refused to take the bait. Wolfe landed parties on the shore beneath the French guns, but couldn't make headway up the steep cliffs.

Time told on both sides. Ammunition and provisions were running low inside the city, as Wolfe learned from deserters. Montcalm couldn't hold out forever. But Wolfe couldn't remain forever. Cold weather would freeze the river again, and his army wasn't prepared to live off the land.

He tried to force the issue. He unleashed his rangers—provincial woodsmen and friendly Indians—against the civilian society along the St. Lawrence. Reasoning that he was doing no more than the French had done to civilians on the British frontier farther south, Wolfe hoped to shame Montcalm into coming out to protect the men and women assigned to his protection.

Montcalm sent rangers of his own. One of Wolfe's men kept a journal of the campaign, and though the journal survived, the name of the journalist did not. This soldier-historian recorded an early skirmish. "The 8th"—of July—"we landed on Quebec shore, without any interruption, and marched up the river about 2 miles, when the Louisbourg grenadiers were ordered out to get fascines"— bundles of sticks from which to fashion defenses. "They had scarce set down to take a small refreshment, and detached a small party of rangers to guard the skirts of the wood, before a large party of Indians surrounded them, killed and scalped thirteen, wounded the captain, lieutenant and nine privates; they likewise killed and wounded 14 royal Americans, wounded 2 of the 22nd and one of the 40th regiment; we got only 3 prisoners and killed two of the savages."

Clashes continued. "On the 17th we went out a-fascining, and to make oars, with a small party to cover us. Five were killed, of which four were scalped, and we were obliged to quit the wood directly." In early August: "A party of Capt. Dank's rangers went from the Island of Orleans to Quebec side, a little down the river. They were attacked by a party of French and were smartly engaged for the space of half an hour. But the rangers put them to flight, killed several and took one prisoner. The rangers lost the lieutenant, who died of his wounds, and two or three privates. They got a great deal of plunder."

The skirmishes intensified. A Captain Gorham headed a contingent of 150 rangers and assorted others. "They proceeded down to St. Paul's bay, where was a parish containing about 200 men who had been very active in distressing our boats and shipping. At three o'clock in the morning, Capt. Gorham landed and forced two of their guards, of 20 men each, who fired smartly for some time. But in two hours he drove them all from their covering in the wood and cleared the village, which they afterward burnt. It consisted of about 50 fine houses and barns. Destroyed most of their cattle etc. In this they had one man killed and six wounded, but the enemy had two killed and several wounded, who were carried off. From thence they proceeded to Mal Bay, ten leagues to the eastward on the same side, where they destroyed another pretty parish, drove off the inhabitants and stock without any loss. After which they made a descent on the south shore, opposite the Isle of Coudre, destroyed part of the parishes of St. Ann's and St. Roc, where were many handsome houses with good farms, and loaded the vessels with cattle, and then returned from their expedition."

In the last week of July the Louisbourg grenadiers marched along the north bank of the St. Lawrence, intending to destroy all they found there. "They were attacked by a party of French, who had a priest for their commander, but our party killed and scalped thirty-one of them, and likewise the priest, their commander. They did our people no damage. The three companies of Louisbourg grenadiers halted about four miles down the river at a church called the Guardian Angel (Ange Gardien), where they were to fortify themselves till further orders. Our people had several small parties in houses, and the remainder continued in the church. The 25th they began to destroy the country, burning houses, cutting down their corn etc. At night the Indians"—the French Indians—"fired several scattering shots at the houses, which killed one highlander and wounded another. But they were soon repulsed by the heat of our firing. It was said that the number of the enemy consisted of 800 Canadians and Indians. Sept. 1st, they set fire to the enemy's houses and fortifications."

. . .

BY THEN THE GROUND on both sides of the river for miles above and below the city had been thoroughly scorched. Most of the civilians had fled. This episode of destruction would live long in the memory of the French Canadians.

But it didn't accomplish Wolfe's goal, the capture of the city. The French thought the worst was over. "Everything proves that the grand design of the English has failed," Governor Vaudreuil wrote.

Wolfe made one last try. For months he'd scanned the cliffs below the Plains of Abraham, peering for a path to the top. He'd found nothing. But desperation adjusted his vision, and one route rejected earlier began to seem possible. With his telescope he followed it up to a group of French tents at the top. It must be a route, he concluded. Why else put a guard at its head?

He prepared his men and issued his orders. "The officers and men will remember what their country expects from them, and what a determined body of soldiers inured to war is capable of doing," Wolfe admonished.

On the night of September 12, Wolfe sent boats toward the base of the cliff at the bottom of the path. A French sentry, hearing the creak of oars in the darkness below, called out, "*Qui vive?*"

A captain of Scottish Highlanders who had served in Holland and spoke French responded, "*La France.*"

"*À quel regiment?*"

"*De la Reine.*" The sentry was satisfied and didn't call the alarm.

The boats landed. Twenty-four volunteers went first up the path, searching for footholds and handholds in the dark. They kept still and could barely see. Finally they reached the top.

They stole upon the tents, hoping to silence the guards there. They captured several of the French soldiers, but others fled into the city.

MONTCALM HAD BEEN expecting an attack. He didn't think Wolfe would simply sail away. Now that he knew where the attack was being made, he rallied his men. "I remember very well Montcalm's attitude before the fight," one of his men recalled in old age. "He rode a brown or black horse at the front of our lines, holding his sword high as if to excite us to do our duty. He wore a uniform with wide sleeves, one of which, thrown back from the weapon he was holding, revealed the white linen of his cuff."

While Montcalm was marshaling his forces, more British soldiers were mounting the heights. Those behind the first ascenders improved the path from the river to the plain. Simultaneous attacks allowed other landings and opened other routes. By daybreak Wolfe had a respectable army arrayed for battle.

The anonymous journal keeper with the British army was part of the second landing. "The 12th, we received orders to embark on board the transports again and to hold ourselves in readiness to land next morning at day light under the heights of Abraham," he recounted. "Accordingly we landed at break of day and immediately attacked and routed a considerable body of the enemy and took possession of their battery of 24-pounders, and one 13-inch mortar, with but a very inconsiderable loss on our side. We then took post on the plains of Abraham, where M. Montcalm (on hearing that we were landed, for he did not expect us) hasted with his whole army, consisting of cavalry as well as infantry, to give us battle. About nine o'clock we observed the enemy marching toward us in three columns. At ten they formed their line of battle, which was at least six deep, having their flanks covered by a thick wood on each side, into which they threw above 1000 Canadians and Indians, who galled us much. We got two six-pounders to fire against the enemy; very soon six more, besides two royal howitzers came up while the enemy were making haste to attack before our artillery could be got up, as they dreaded our quick firing. Accordingly their regulars then marched briskly up to us and gave us their first fire at about fifty yards distance, which we did not return, as it was General Wolfe's express orders not to fire till they came within twenty yards of us. They continued firing by platoons in a very regular manner till they came close up to us, and then the action became general. Our artillery fired briskly, seconded by the small arms from the regiments, who behaved with the greatest intrepidity, order and regularity, with a cheerfulness which foretold victory on our side. And in about fifteen minutes they gave way, so that we fairly beat them in open field, drove them before us, part into Quebec. The rest ran precipitately cross the St. Charles River, over a bridge of boats, and some through the water."

Both generals led bravely. Both died gallantly, of battle wounds. Wolfe, watching the enemy break and run, said, "Now, God be praised, I will die in peace." Montcalm, bleeding badly, comforted his subordinates, "Don't be troubled for me, my friends."

⤞ 26 ⤝

The battle of the Plains of Abraham was arguably the most decisive single battle in the history of North America. The French lost not merely Quebec but also, before the dust settled, the rest of Canada. The war that began with Washington's ambush of Jumonville near the Forks of the Ohio ended with Britain as the sole European claimant to the lands east of the Mississippi River and north of New Spain.

The consequences didn't stop there. The danger to the British colonies from the French, including from the Indians allied with the French, had long served to hold the colonies close to the mother country. At the same time, the French threat compelled the British government to humor the colonists, at least so far as to gain their support in war against the French. When the French departed Canada, Britain and the colonies needed each other less than before. Necessity had bound British America to Britain. Its absence would cause the bonds to loosen.

"NO BRITISH MONARCH had ascended the throne with so many advantages as George the Third," wrote Horace Walpole. A first advantage was the absence of a father, which accelerated his advancement to the throne. George II's eldest son and heir apparent, Frederick, died at the age of forty-four, making *his* son George the heir apparent and then, when George II died in 1760, the king.

Another advantage of the new king was birth in the country he ruled. "Being the first of his line born in England, the prejudice against his family as foreigners ceased in his person," Walpole continued. "Hanover was no longer the native soil of our princes; consequently, attachment to the electorate"—Hanover, an electorate in the Holy Roman Empire—"was not likely to govern our councils, as it had done in the last two reigns."

The new George spoke English like a native rather than with an off-putting accent.

He came fresh to the throne. "In the flower and bloom of youth"—he was twenty-two—"George had a handsome, open, and honest countenance; and with the favour that attends the outward accomplishments of his age, he had none of the vices that fall under the censure of those who are past enjoying them themselves."

Politics augured well for the new George. The partisanship of the previous reign had eased. "Thus it was not a race of factions running to offer themselves, as is common, to a new prince, bidding for his favour, and ready each to be disgusted if their antagonists were received with more grace, but a natural devolution of duty from all men to the uncontroverted heir of the Crown," said Walpole. "The administration was firm, in good harmony with one another, and headed by the most successful genius that ever presided over our councils." The genius was William Pitt. "Conquest had crowned our arms with wonderful circumstances of glory and fortune, and the young king seemed to have the option of extending our victories and acquisitions, or of giving peace to the world."

Yet fortunate though the new king was, he didn't have everything his way. His mother, Princess Augusta, who had expected to be queen, struggled to make the best of her diminished circumstances. When George III fell in love with a young woman of excessively independent mind—Lady Sarah Lennox—the princess-mother persuaded her son to direct his devotion elsewhere. "So complete was the king's deference to the will of his mother that he blindly accepted the bride she had chosen for him," said Walpole. The new queen was Princess Charlotte of Mecklenburg-Strelitz. The wedding was made awkward by the inclusion of George's first love as one of the bridesmaids. Some at court thought Lady Sarah would become the king's mistress, and they judged this an outcome acceptable to all. But George, from further deference to his mother, from simple prudence, or from his wife's hidden charms, fell in love with Charlotte. They eventually had fifteen children together.

POLITICS GOT HARDER. The king was subordinate to Parliament in theory, yet what this meant in practice was for the king and Parliament to decide, issue by issue. Taxing and spending were clearly prerogatives of Parliament, while foreign policy lent itself to royal influence. George's youth and inexperience left him vulnerable to ambitious ministers, especially Lord Bute, a favorite of the princess-mother. Bute was a Tory, which was reason enough for the Whigs to spread malicious stories about him. One that gained wide currency was that Bute wasn't merely a favorite of Augusta but her lover.

Bute battled with Pitt, the Whig leader, who himself battled chronic illness. Bute became prime minister two years into George's reign, only to be succeeded after ten months by George Grenville, his brother-in-law though a Whig. The political fighting reflected, among other things, divergent views on how the war with France should end. The central question was whether France should be humiliated, at the risk of sowing seeds of a war of revenge, or mollified, toward a lasting peace.

The mollifiers won. In the 1763 Paris treaty that ended the war, France received back islands in the West Indies that had been captured by the British, and which were considered more valuable for their sugar than Canada for its furs. Britain kept Canada, while giving guarantees that French nationals in Canada would be allowed to live under their own laws, religion and customs. French fishermen could continue working the bountiful banks off the Canadian coast.

British hard-liners complained that the screws hadn't been turned tight enough on Albion's historic rival. But the peace faction had a powerful counterargument: that the war had nearly bankrupted Britain. The country couldn't afford to fight much longer. Better to be benevolent by choice than have benevolence imposed by necessity.

"I AM THE MAKER of heaven and earth, the trees, lakes, rivers and all things else. I am the Maker of mankind, and because I love you, you must do my will."

Thus spoke the Master of Life to the Delaware Prophet, as related by Pontiac, an Ottawa chief. Pontiac wasn't the first Indian leader to call for unity among tribes against the European interlopers, and he wouldn't be the last. But he was one of the most violently effective, in part because of his persuasiveness in channeling the will of heaven.

"The land on which you live I have made for you and not for others," the Master of Life continued. "Why do you suffer the white men to dwell among you? My children, you have forgotten the customs and traditions of your forefathers. Why do you not clothe yourselves in skins, as they did, and use the bows and arrows and the stone-pointed lances, which they used? You have bought guns, knives, kettles and blankets from the white men, until you can no longer do without them. And what is worse, you have drunk the poison fire-water, which turns you into fools. Fling all these things away. Live as your wise forefathers lived before you. And as for these English—these dogs dressed in red, who have come to rob you of your hunting grounds and drive away the game—you must lift the hatchet against them. Wipe them from the face of the earth, and then you will win my favor back again, and once more be happy and prosperous."

Pontiac preached the message of a return to Eden by the expulsion of the English just as the English, or British, war against France was ending. He could see that the British were winning, but he didn't know that the French were abandoning Canada entirely. He looked to France to assist his alliance against the English in the way the French had assisted Indians against the English for decades.

In the spring of 1763, Pontiac's allies launched a coordinated attack on British forts—mostly captured from the French—along a wide front stretching from the upper Great Lakes to the Ohio River. The Indians struck by surprise and with terrifying effect.

Alexander Henry was a trader at Fort Michilimackinac, where Lake Huron meets Lake Michigan. The Ojibwas and Sauks who frequented the fort announced that a ball-and-sticks game they called baggataway—the French labeled it lacrosse—would be played in the field outside the gate of the fort. All were invited, Indians and whites. Betting would be lively.

Henry would have gone to the game, but he needed to write some letters to send off with the next departing canoe. He was just finishing when he heard a war cry and a hubbub of general confusion. As he later pieced events together, the Indian players had brought weapons to the game, hiding them under their shirts. At the height of the game's excitement, one player aimed the ball at the open gate of the fort. The players chased it, and surged into the fort before the soldiers could react.

"Going instantly to the window I saw a crowd of Indians within the fort furiously cutting down and scalping every Englishman they found," Henry recalled. "I had in the room in which I was a fowling piece, loaded with swan shot. This I immediately seized and held for a few minutes, waiting to hear the drum beat to arms." The drum would signify that a defense was being mounted. "In this dreadful interval I saw several of my countrymen fall, and more than one struggling between the knees of an Indian, who, holding him in this manner, scalped him while yet living."

Not hearing the drum, Henry concluded that the defenders must all have been killed. He began to consider how he could escape the carnage. One aspect of the violence stuck in his memory. "Amid the slaughter which was raging I observed many of the Canadian inhabitants of the fort calmly looking on, neither opposing the Indians nor suffering injury." The Indians were targeting the English and not the French. Henry hoped that a French family might conceal him. He put the question to a Frenchman he knew well. The man shrugged and said he could do nothing for him.

Luckily an Indian slave woman belonging to the man offered to hide him. She led him to a garret and told him to go up. He thanked her and did as directed.

The garret lacked windows, but through a crack in the wall Henry looked down on the interior of the fort. "I beheld, in shapes the foulest and most terrible, the ferocious triumphs of the barbarian conquerors. The dead were scalped and mangled; the dying were writhing and shrieking under the unsatiated knife and tomahawk; and from the bodies of some, ripped open, their butchers were drinking the blood, scooped up in the hollow of joined hands and quaffed amid shouts of rage and victory."

When there were no more English to kill, the Indians began searching the fort. Henry heard them enter the house where he was hiding. They climbed the stairs to the garret.

"The die appeared to be cast," Henry wrote. He looked desperately around the small room. A pile of birch-bark containers used in making maple syrup lay in one dark corner. He crawled behind the pile.

"I could scarcely breathe, but I thought that the throbbing of my heart occasioned a noise loud enough to betray me. The Indians walked in every direction about the garret, and one of them approached me so closely that at a particular moment, had he put forth his hand, he must have touched me." But the general darkness of the room served Henry well. Seeing no one, the Indians left.

Henry made his escape and told those he met of the Michilimackinac massacre. He discovered that the violence was general. Pontiac's allies attacked a dozen forts, including those at Venango and Le Boeuf that Washington had visited. At most of the forts the soldiers and traders were slaughtered. A lucky few escaped to spread the word of the vengeance Pontiac had unleashed.

One fort that didn't fall at once was at the Forks, where the British had built a new structure on the site of the French-burned Fort Duquesne and called it Fort Pitt, for the prime minister. Fort Pitt was besieged in late June 1763, with hundreds of settlers from the region crowded behind its walls. The crowding contributed to an outbreak of smallpox, which prompted some of those inside to consider taking their chances on flight, to escape the virus if not the tomahawks.

It also prompted British officials to ponder the use of smallpox against the besiegers. Jeffery Amherst, the British commander, wrote to Henry Bouquet, who headed an expedition to lift the Fort Pitt siege: "Could it not be contrived to send the smallpox among those disaffected tribes of Indians? We must on this occasion use every stratagem in our power to reduce them."

Bouquet was willing to oblige. "I will try to inoculate the Indians with some blankets that may fall into their hands, taking care not to get the disease myself," he replied to Amherst. Yet he preferred another approach. "I wish we could make use of the Spanish method, to hunt them with English dogs, supported by rangers and some light horse, who would, I think, effectually extirpate or remove that vermin."

Amherst repeated his smallpox suggestion. "You will do well to try to inoculate the Indians by means of blankets," he said. Setting dogs upon the Indians would have to wait. "I should be very glad your scheme for hunting them down by dogs could take place, but England is at too great a distance to think of that at present."

Whether Bouquet in fact employed the infected blankets is unclear. Smallpox did break out among the Indians, but the timing suggests it might have arrived naturally, in the same way it infected the settlers inside the fort.

The flame Pontiac lit burned fiercely for a while. Hundreds of British soldiers and probably thousands of civilian traders and settlers were killed. Thousands more fled the frontier, as they had during the war against France.

But the flame flickered when French aid didn't materialize. The British gathered sufficient troops to break the siege at Fort Pitt and another at Fort Detroit. As the Indian casualties mounted, the tribes in Pontiac's alliance fell away. Pontiac saw no alternative to suing for peace. He signed a treaty that ended the hostilities. He himself was killed by another Indian three years later.

THE PONTIAC UPRISING confirmed what British leaders already believed about the American frontier: that it was a sinkhole for imperial finance. As Washington had discovered, frontier settlements were impossible to defend preemptively, being too far apart and too far from forts. Indian raiders could swoop down upon a hamlet, kill the men, kidnap the women and children and disappear long before soldiers could arrive. Post hoc defense, in the form of reprisal, was expensive and inaccurate. The soldiers could kill Indians, but they often didn't know if the ones they killed were the right Indians. When they got it wrong, the mistake embittered the Indians all the more.

Further, the frontier yielded little of material worth to the empire. Britain valued the tobacco and other farm produce of the settled regions. But the frontier was useful chiefly as a buffer against the French in Canada. With France gone, that use value plunged.

Consequently, when London's budget experts at the end of the war insisted on retrenchment, lest the war debt drag the country down, the government decided to close the western territories to new settlement. King George declared it his royal will and pleasure that no British governor in America "grant warrants of survey or pass patents for any lands beyond the heads or sources of any of the rivers which fall into the Atlantic Ocean."

This was a legal move rather than a geographic one. London couldn't stop Americans in small groups from crossing the mountains to hunt or even build cabins in the forest. But it could prevent their gaining legal title to land there. Because so much western land was surveyed and partitioned for sale by speculators, and because sale required legal title, the proclamation threatened the system on which many Americans had built dreams of wealth.

➝ 27 ➝

Washington didn't like the proclamation. He wasn't the largest speculator in western lands, but his interest in the Ohio Company made western speculation an important part of his personal business model. After his marriage to Martha, he controlled a great deal of land, but cash flow was a problem. In a typical letter to Robert Cary, his London commercial agent, Washington requested patience regarding his credit line. "It might possibly answer very little purpose were I to enter into a minute detail of the reasons that have caused me to fall so much in arrears to you," he said. Yet he would try. "Mischances rather than misconduct hath been the causes of it. For it was a misfortune that seasons and chance should prevent my making even tolerable crops in this part of the country for three years successively, and it was a misfortune likewise when they were made that I should get little or nothing for them." This was the perennial plight of the farmer: when crops failed, there was nothing to sell, and when crops boomed, their glut collapsed the price.

"It may also be looked upon as unlucky at least that the debts which I thought I had collected, and actually did remit to you, should be paid in bills void of credit," Washington continued. Monetary problems were chronic in the colonies. Lacking cash money, Virginians substituted bills of credit, promissory notes, real estate and slaves. Washington assured Cary that he would get what he was owed, eventually. If he needed to charge interest, Washington wouldn't object.

Sales of tobacco and other crops were Washington's principal source of revenue, as his lament to Cary intimated. But these were unpredictable, depending on the weather not only in Virginia but in other parts of the British empire where the same crops were grown. Proceeds from the sale of land were crucial in smoothing out the fluctuations.

Washington, along with the other speculators, hoped the proscription on western lands would be temporary. It was a response to the Pontiac rising, on one hand, and the debt fears in London, on the other. The effects of these would diminish over time. Washington couldn't imagine that the British government intended to keep Americans fenced up on the eastern side of the mountains forever. This would defy common sense and the obvious needs of the American people.

WASHINGTON THREW HIMSELF into his life as a planter. His journal recorded the activities of a gentleman farmer during a typical winter and spring. "Visited my plantations and received an instance of Mr. French's great love of money in disappointing me of some pork because the price had risen to 22/6"—22 shillings, 6 pence—"after he had engaged to let me have it at 20/. Called at Mr. Posey's in my way home and desired him to engage me 100 barrels of corn upon the best terms he could in Maryland.... Killed and dressed Mr. French's hogs which weighed 751 lbs. neat. Col. West leaving me in doubt about his pork yesterday obliged me to send to him again today, and now no definitive answer was received, he purposing to send his overseer down tomorrow to agree about it.... Passing by my carpenters that were hewing, I found that four of them viz. George, Tom, Mike and young Billy had only hewed 120 foot yesterday from 10 o'clock. Sat down therefore, and observed. Tom and Mike in a less space than 30 minutes cleared the bushes from about a poplar stock, lined it 10 foot long, and hewed each their side 12 inches deep....

"A small fine rain from northeast wet the top of my hay that had been landed last night. It was all carted up however to the barn and the wet and dry separated.... Found one of my best wagon horses (namely Jolly) with his right foreleg mashed to pieces, which I suppose happened in the storm last night by means of a limb of a tree or something of that sort falling upon him. Did it up as well as I could this night.... Southerly wind and remarkable fine clear day. Set my people to carting and carrying rails round the peach orchard. The broken legged horse fell out of his sling and by that means and struggling together, hurt himself so much that I ordered him to be killed.... The vast quantity of rain which had fallen in the last two days had swelled the waters so high that Dogue Run carried off the tumbling dam of my mill and was near carrying off the house also.... In a bed that had been prepared with a mixture of dung on Saturday last, I sowed clover, lucerne and rye grass seeds in the garden, to try their goodness.... Got several composts and laid them to dry in order to mix with the earth brought from the field below to try their several virtues. . . . Planted out 20 young pine trees at the head of my cherry walk. . . . This morning my plows began to work in the clover field, but a hard shower of rain from northeast (where the wind hung all day) about 11 o'clock stopped them for the remainder of the day. I therefore employed the hands in making two or three hauls of the seine, and found that the herrings were come."

Labor in all the colonies was provided by a mix of paid workers, indentured servants and slaves. In the northern colonies the paid workers and indentured servants outnumbered the slaves. In the southern colonies the opposite was true. Washington had foremen and overseers who supervised his workforce on a daily basis, but he interposed at times. "Sir," he wrote to the captain of a merchant ship bound for the West Indies. "With this letter comes a negro (Tom), which I beg the favor of you to sell in any of the islands you may go to, for whatever he will fetch, and bring me in return from him: one hogshead of best molasses, one hogshead of best rum, one barrel of limes if good and cheap, one pot of tamarinds containing about 10 lbs., two small pots of mixed sweetmeats about 5 lbs. each, and the residue, much or little, in good old spirits." Tom had to be watched closely. "That this fellow is both a rogue and a runaway (though he was by no means remarkable for the former, and never practised the latter till of late) I shall not pretend to deny. But that he is exceeding healthy, strong, and good at the hoe, the whole neighborhood can testify, and particularly Mr. Johnson and his son, who have both had him under them as foreman of the gang; which gives me reason to hope he may with your good management sell well, if kept clean and trimmed up a little when offered for sale. I shall very cheerfully allow you the customary commissions on this affair, and must beg the favor of you (lest he should attempt his escape) to keep him handcuffed till you get to sea, or in the bay, after which I doubt not but you may make him very useful to you."

WASHINGTON'S COMMAND OF his and Martha's property would have made him a public figure even if his military reputation had not. Men of means were expected to participate in the life of the community. Becoming a vestryman was natural for Washington. He was a conventional Anglican, steady rather than enthusiastic. He attended church every month but not every week. He was a dutiful member of Truro parish, and he did his duty by serving on the vestry, where he helped administer the finances of the parish, contributing where necessary to cover extraordinary expenses.

He stood for election to the house of burgesses. Elections were festive affairs in Virginia's counties. Votes were given by voice for all at the polling place to hear—and for all at the polling place to boo or cheer. Candidates provided refreshments, meaning liquor, which rendered the voting more raucous still. Washington sought election in 1755 and lost. Perhaps he didn't provide enough booze. He stood again in 1758 and won, and he kept winning for almost two decades, until a new military assignment took him away.

Washington treated politics more as an obligation than an opportunity. Partly this was temperamental. He wasn't gregarious in the way politicians often are. Partly it was a reflection of his experience in the military. Armies have chains of command. Legislatures do not. Washington liked things clearly defined. He also liked giving orders. Partly it was the low ceiling that existed in colonial politics. Above the burgesses there was only the governor, and he was chosen by the king for reasons beyond the ken of provincials. Washington had bumped against the ceiling for Americans in the military. He could see the ceiling in politics. A talented American had to look elsewhere to fulfill his ambitions.

Washington attended the sessions of the burgesses every May. Williamsburg was the center of Virginia's public life during the sessions, which gathered the gentry as nothing else did in a province of scattered landholdings. He met the important men among his elders, his contemporaries and his juniors. He dined with Peyton Randolph and George Wythe. He heard the speeches of Patrick Henry. He conversed with Thomas Jefferson. He hunted foxes in the fields about Williamsburg with the horsier of his colleagues and fished for sturgeon in the James River with the fishier.

He said little in the meetings of the burgesses. He didn't consider himself an orator, and he thought oratory overrated. In another man, silence might have been taken for timidity. In Washington, it was interpreted as gravity. John Robinson, longtime speaker of the house, welcomed Washington at his first session and thanked him, in glowing terms, for his military service to the province. Washington rose to answer but was so confounded he couldn't speak a single word. "Sit down, Mr. Washington," Robinson said, smiling. "Your modesty is equal to your valour, and that surpasses the power of any language I possess."

. . .

YET WASHINGTON DIDN'T dodge the important issues of the day. "Another tempest has arose upon our frontiers, and the alarm spread wider than ever," Washington wrote amid the violence unleashed by Pontiac. "In short, the inhabitants are so apprehensive of danger that no families stand above the Conococheague road"—near the upper Potomac—"and many are gone off below it. Their harvests are in a manner lost, and the distresses of the settlement appear too evident and manifold to need description. In Augusta many people have been killed, and numbers fled, and confusion and despair prevail in every quarter." When Washington heard the news, he anticipated, as a burgess, a journey to Williamsburg. But the assembly had been in a fight with the governor over money, and the governor declined to summon the burgesses. Instead, he took matters into his own hands. "The Governor and Council have directed one thousand militia to be employed for the protection of the frontiers." It was unclear where the money to pay the men would come from. Washington supposed the assembly would hear about it later. For now he awaited further word of the trouble on the frontier. "It is of a melancholy nature indeed and yet we cannot tell how or when it is to end."

After the Pontiac war produced the proclamation closing the west, Washington considered his response. William Crawford had been with Washington on the Forbes campaign against Fort Duquesne. He was a man of resourcefulness and initiative, familiar with the western country. Washington hoped to put Crawford's knowledge to work. He wrote to Crawford with a proposition that required delicacy. The proclamation barred western settlement, but it wouldn't do so forever, Washington said. "I can never look upon that proclamation in any other light (but this I say between ourselves) than as a temporary expedient to quiet the minds of the Indians, and must fall, of course, in a few years, especially when those Indians are consenting to our occupying the lands. Any person, therefore, who neglects the present opportunity of hunting out good lands, and in some measure marking and distinguishing them for his own (in order to keep others from settling them) will never regain it."

Washington couldn't identify the forbidden lands himself, being occupied at Mount Vernon, besides being a distinguished and law-abiding member of the community. He proposed that Crawford act in his place. "If you will be at the trouble of seeking out the lands, I will take upon me the part of securing them so soon as there is a possibility of doing it, and will moreover be at all the cost and charges of surveying, and patenting etc., after which you shall have such a reasonable proportion of the whole as we may fix upon at our first meeting." Washington proposed to make himself and Crawford wealthy by this subtle operation. "My plan is to secure a good deal of land. You will consequently come in for a very handsome quantity."

Washington specified what Crawford should look for. "I would choose, if it were practicable, to get large tracts together, and it might be desirable to have them as near your settlement"—Crawford lived on a tributary of the Monongahela River—"or Fort Pitt as we could get them." Washington was willing to look farther west if necessary. "I should have no objection to a grant of land upon the Ohio, a good way below Pittsburg, but would willingly secure some good tracts nearer hand first."

Washington reemphasized discretion. "I would recommend it to you to keep this whole matter a secret, or trust it only with those in whom you can confide and who can assist you." Washington didn't want to be seen as disloyal to the crown. "I might be censured for the opinion I have given in respect to the King's proclamation."

No less important, if word spread that Washington was scouting western lands, others might get the same idea. "If the scheme I am now proposing to you was known, it might give the alarm to others, and, by putting them upon a plan of the same nature (before we could lay a proper foundation for success ourselves) set the different interests a-clashing and probably in the end overturn the whole."

Washington suggested Crawford portray his land searching as a hunting trip. He should keep notes and relate their substance. Washington would handle the legal side of things. "If there appears but a bare possibility of succeeding any time hence, I will have the lands immediately surveyed, to keep others off, and leave the rest to time and my own assiduity to accomplish."

— 28 —

Government debt reflects an imbalance between government expenditures and government revenues. The British ban on western settlement aimed to reduce expenditures, by preventing another Indian war. Complementing the reductions were attempts to increase revenues. The Sugar Act of 1764 was designed to increase tax revenues by the seemingly paradoxical method of reducing tax rates. The paradox was resolved by a concomitant crackdown on smuggling. The lower rate would reduce the incentive to smuggle, and the firmer enforcement would diminish the chance of success. Between them they would increase the total tax take.

American colonists grumbled, but they couldn't complain too loudly without convicting themselves of smuggling. Moreover, their grounds for complaining lacked constitutional heft. Parliament had long legislated on trade, via navigation laws, to few complaints from America. The new law was new in detail but not in principle.

Another tax law was different. George Grenville, successor to Lord Bute as prime minister, proposed to tax a variety of documents and papers. A stamp signifying payment of the tax would be applied to the materials, and so the tax came to be called a stamp tax. The tax was novel in America and unprecedentedly intrusive. It was to be levied on licenses and titles, newspapers and pamphlets, playing cards and dice. The fact that lawyers, whose licenses had to be stamped; land speculators, who required stamps on their land titles; and editors, whose newspapers needed stamps, were among those most affected guaranteed that the stamp tax would meet loud resistance in America.

Grenville was prepared for that. What he wasn't prepared for was the violence that followed approval of the Stamp Act in early 1765. Boston had a history of roughnecking, with mobs from the North End and South End regularly bashing each other. The Stamp Act had the effect of aligning the mobs' energies, under the direction of a group of shopkeepers and artisans who would call themselves the Sons of Liberty, against the local representatives of the British government. Andrew Oliver, appointed commissioner to collect the stamp tax, was hanged in effigy. The rioters went after Oliver himself, marching to his house and battering down his door. He wasn't at home. They smashed his furniture. He resigned his tax commission the next day.

The mob sought new targets. Most tempting was the home of Thomas Hutchinson, the lieutenant governor (and de facto governor). Hutchinson had one of the finest houses in Boston. Its sturdiness compelled the mob to work all night to dismantle it, board by board and brick by brick. The mob was angry but not crazy. They didn't burn the house, because it might set nearby buildings alight. But by dawn the next day it was a ruined shell, a grim testament to Boston's determination not to pay the new tax.

PATRICK HENRY WAS new to the Virginia assembly when the stamp law took effect. Not yet thirty, he'd made a name as a lawyer challenging the prerogatives of the Anglican clergy in Virginia, on behalf of the people of the province. The people of his county thanked him by electing him to the house of burgesses. Unfazed by his youth and inexperience, Henry proposed a series of resolutions against the Stamp Act. "Resolved, that the first adventurers and settlers of this, his majesty's colony and dominion, brought with them and transmitted to their posterity and all other his majesty's subjects since inhabiting in this, his majesty's said colony, all the privileges, franchises and immunities that have at any time been held, enjoyed and possessed by the people of Great Britain," Henry declared. In other words, Virginians were fully the equals of the British back home.

Henry's second resolution asserted that the British crown itself had confirmed this point. "That by two royal charters granted by King James the First, the colonists aforesaid are declared entitled to all the privileges, liberties and immunities of denizens and natural born subjects, to all intents and purposes as if they had been abiding and born within the realm of England."

Henry's third resolution focused on taxes. "That the taxation of the people by themselves, or by persons chosen by themselves to represent them, who can only know what taxes the people are able to bear and the easiest mode of raising them, and are equally affected by such taxes themselves, is the distinguishing characteristic of British freedom, and without which the ancient constitution cannot subsist."

Virginians heretofore had been the only taxers of themselves. "That his majesty's liege people of this most ancient colony have uninterruptedly enjoyed the right of being thus governed by their own assembly in the article of their taxes and internal police, and that the same hath never been forfeited or any other way given up, but hath constantly been recognized by the king and people of Great Britain."

All leading to Henry's conclusion: "That the general assembly of this colony have the sole right and power to lay taxes and impositions upon the inhabitants of this colony, and that every attempt to vest such power in any person or persons whatsoever, other than the general assembly aforesaid, has a manifest tendency to destroy British as well as American freedom."

Henry's resolutions were seconded, and debate began. The dramatic climax came when Henry warned what would happen if the crown persisted on the illegitimate road it was traveling. "Caesar had his Brutus, Charles the First his Cromwell, and George the Third . . ."

"Treason! Treason!" cried the speaker and certain members of the house.

Henry paused. He coolly eyed the shouters. He completed his sentence: ". . . may well profit by their example." He extemporized a coda: "If this be treason, make the most of it."

The debate was followed by a close vote. Most of the burgesses supported Henry's belief that the taxing power ought to remain as close to the people as possible. But many were unnerved by the categorical nature of his conclusions, and more than a few thought Henry's language would inflame an issue that could be handled more reasonably.

Thomas Jefferson watched from the wings. "I was then but a student"—at William and Mary College—"and was listening at the door of the lobby (for as yet there was no gallery)," he recalled later. The opposition initially had the advantage in the debate. "But torrents of sublime eloquence from Mr. Henry, backed by the solid reasoning of Johnston"—George Johnston, who seconded Henry's resolutions—"prevailed. The last, however, and strongest resolution was carried but by a single vote. The debate on it was most bloody. . . . Peyton Randolph, after the vote, came out of the house, and said, as he entered the lobby, 'By god, I would have given 500 guineas for a single vote.' For as this would have divided the house, the vote of Robinson, the speaker, would have rejected the resolution."

WASHINGTON HAD LEFT Williamsburg before the vote on Henry's resolutions. Spring was a busy time at Mount Vernon, and its business needed tending to. "Peter Green came to me a gardener," Washington wrote in his journal for the day of the vote. "Cut my clover for hay," he recorded the next day.

Yet he didn't ignore the Stamp Act or the turmoil it caused. No one in Virginia or just about anywhere else in America could ignore it. The protests produced boycotts of the stamps, enforced by threats and worse against those so bold as to purchase them. "Government is set at defiance, not having strength enough in her hands to enforce the laws of the community," Virginia governor Fauquier reported to London. "The private distress which every man feels increases the general dissatisfaction at the duties laid by the stamp act, which breaks out and shews itself upon every trifling equation." The stamp boycott led to a boycott of British merchandise imports, intended to punish British merchants, who would seek relief from Parliament by a repeal of the obnoxious measure.

Washington thought the British government had blundered badly. "The Stamp Act imposed on the colonies by the Parliament of Great Britain engrosses the conversation of the speculative part of the colonists, who look upon this unconstitutional method of taxation as a direful attack upon their liberties and loudly exclaim against the violation," he told his wife's uncle, living in London. "What may be the result of this and some other (I think I may add) ill judged measures, I will not undertake to determine. But this I may venture to affirm, that the advantage accruing to the Mother Country will fall greatly short of the expectations of the ministry. For certain it is, our whole substance does already in a manner flow to Great Britain and that whatsoever contributes to lessen our importations must be hurtful to their manufacturers."

The effect might be enduring. "The eyes of our people, already beginning to open, will perceive that many luxuries which we lavish our substance to Great Britain for can well be dispensed with whilst the necessaries of life are (mostly) to be had within ourselves. This consequently will introduce frugality and be a necessary stimulation to industry. If Great Britain therefore loads her manufactures with heavy taxes, will it not facilitate these measures?" Here Washington was extrapolating from the thinking that had produced the stamp tax. It didn't tax manufactures, but the next tax might. That tax wouldn't work either, he said. "They will not compel us, I think, to give our money for their exports, whether we will or no."

Washington described a likely future. "Our courts of judicature must inevitably be shut up," he said. Legal proceedings required stamped papers. Even if Virginians had been willing to pay the tax, they couldn't do so. "We have not money to pay." All would suffer, not least the British merchants, who relied on the courts to collect debts. "If a stop be put to our judicial proceedings, I fancy the merchants of Great Britain trading to the colonies will not be among the last to wish for a repeal of it."

29

Benjamin Franklin had retired from daily participation in the printing business in 1748 to pursue his scientific interests. His research results in electricity brought him to the attention of the leading lights in the field in Britain and continental Europe. His secondary interest in politics grew simultaneously, and it aroused the hostility of the heirs of William Penn, who through the governor of Pennsylvania held a veto over the actions of the provincial assembly. In 1757 the assembly asked Franklin to go to London to represent the interests of the assembly and the people of Pennsylvania to Parliament. He made the journey and soon found himself at the center of a congenial circle of friends and admirers. He extended his stay.

Franklin was in London at the end of the war with France. He watched and occasionally commented as the plan of the British government to pay down its debt unfolded. Franklin, like Washington, had speculated in western lands, and like Washington he had pecuniary reason to regret the closing of those lands to new settlement. He had another reason, more scientific. Franklin had studied the demographics of the American colonies and concluded that the population of British North America was doubling every generation. Because most Americans were farmers, the land available to them would have to double each generation lest they grow successively poorer. If Americans were shut out of the west, their children and grandchildren faced a grim future.

Franklin had as little to say about the Sugar Act as most other Americans not engaged in the smuggling trade. He was skeptical of the Stamp Act, yet he didn't think it as fatal a blow to American liberty as Patrick Henry and the Sons of Liberty made it appear. Franklin had never been a hothead, and, approaching sixty, he grew less excitable by the year. He assumed Parliament and the provinces would work something out.

Consequently he was surprised by the violence that greeted the act in America.

George Grenville, the prime minister behind the Stamp Act, didn't like Franklin, not least because Franklin didn't like Grenville's policies. Yet Grenville's opponents did like Franklin, and they employed him to help make a case for repeal. In February 1766 the House of Commons convened as a committee of the whole to hear Franklin comment on the Stamp Act, the response to it in America and the future of relations between Britain and the colonies.

"What is your name and place of abode?" he was asked.

"Franklin, of Philadelphia."

"Do the Americans pay any considerable taxes among themselves?" This questioner favored repeal.

"Certainly. Many and very heavy taxes."

"What are the present taxes in Pennsylvania laid by the laws of the colony?"

"There are taxes on all estates real and personal; a poll tax; a tax on all offices, professions, trades and business, according to their profits; an excise on all wine, rum and other spirits; and a duty of ten pounds per head on all Negroes imported, with some other duties."

"For what purposes are those taxes laid?"

"For the support of the civil and military establishments of the country, and to discharge the heavy debt contracted in the last war." Grenville's ministry had portrayed the stamp tax as recompense for Britain's protection during the war. Franklin's point was that Pennsylvania had protected itself and incurred a debt in doing so.

There was more, including hostile questions, which Franklin parried. "Are not the colonies, from their circumstances, very able to pay the stamp duty?" a Grenville ally queried.

"There is not gold and silver enough in the colonies to pay the stamp duty for one year," Franklin replied.

"Don't you know that the money arising from the stamps was all to be laid out in America?" It was to be spent provisioning British troops and therefore wouldn't reduce the American money supply.

"I know it is appropriated by the act to the American service, but it will be spent in the conquered colonies"—Canada—"not in the colonies that pay it."

Other colonies besides Virginia had denied the right of Parliament to tax them. "If the Stamp Act should be repealed, would it induce the assemblies of America to acknowledge the rights of Parliament to tax them, and would they erase their resolutions?"

"No, never."

"Is there no means of obliging them to erase those resolutions?"

"None that I know of. They will never do it unless compelled by force of arms."

"Is there a power on earth that can force them to erase them?"

"No power, how great soever, can force men to change their opinions."

"Can anything less than a military force carry the stamp act into execution?"

"I do not see how a military force can be applied to that purpose."

"Why may it not?"

"Suppose a military force sent into America. They will find nobody in arms. What are they then to do? They cannot force a man to take stamps who chooses to do without them. They will not find a rebellion. They may indeed make one."

FRANKLIN'S WORDS AND the falling profits of British merchants persuaded Parliament to repeal the Stamp Act. Lawyers again could litigate, editors opine and gamblers deal and roll without paying the British government for the privilege. The channels of commerce reopened.

Yet Grenville and the ministry, while yielding to prudence, clung to principle. A companion measure to the repeal, titled "An act for the better securing the dependency of his majesty's dominions in America upon the crown and parliament of Great Britain," stated explicitly that the American colonies "have been, are, and of right ought to be subordinate unto and dependent upon the imperial crown and parliament of Great Britain," and that the crown and Parliament had "full power and authority" to make laws for the colonies "in all cases whatsoever."

30

Several years into Washington's marriage with Martha, he and she had no children together. Given the children from her first marriage, the explanation seemed to lie with him. Smallpox was known to reduce fertility in some men, and Washington had contracted smallpox in Barbados. But the question was complicated. No one could know for sure. And no one in those days could do anything about it.

Without children of his own and apparently without prospects, Washington devoted himself to the care of Martha's children. Jack required schooling. "He is a boy of good genius, about 14 years of age, untainted in his morals and of innocent manners," Washington wrote to the Reverend Jonathan Boucher, who conducted a school for young men. "Two years and upwards he has been reading of Virgil and was (at the time Mr. Magowan left him) entered upon the Greek testament." Walter Magowan had tutored Jack at Mount Vernon but now was returning to England. "I presume he has grown not a little rusty in both having had no benefit of his tutor since Christmas, notwithstanding he left the country in March only." Jack would come with a servant—a personal slave—and other necessities. "He will have a boy well acquainted with house business, which may be made as useful as possible in your family to keep him out of idleness, and two horses to furnish him with the means of getting to church and elsewhere, as you may permit; for he will be put entirely and absolutely under your tuition and direction to manage as you think proper in all respects."

Cost was no consideration, within reason. "As to his board and schooling (provender for his horses, he may lay in himself) I do not think it necessary to enquire into and will cheerfully pay ten or twelve pounds a year, extraordinary, to engage your peculiar care of, and a watchful eye to him, as he is a promising boy, the last of his family and will possess a very large fortune. Add to this my anxiety to make him fit for more useful purposes than horse racer." Jack had a fondness for fast horses.

Washington reflected on the peculiar position he held regarding Jack. "A natural parent has only two things principally to consider: the improvement of his son and the finances to do it with," he wrote to Boucher. "If he fails in the first (not through his own neglect) he laments it as a misfortune. If exceeded in the second"—by spending too much on his son—"he endeavors to correct it as an abuse unaccountable to any, and regardless of what the world may say, who do not, cannot suspect him of acting upon any other motive than the good of the party; he is to satisfy himself only." Guardians like Washington were held to a different standard. "They are not only to be actuated by the same motives which govern in the other case but are to consider in what light their conduct may be viewed by those whom the constitution hath placed as a controlling power over them, because a faux pas committed by them often incurs the severest censure and sometimes punishment, when the intention may be strictly laudable."

The question came up when Jack wanted to devote a year of his education to travel. Boucher had proposed the idea, but Washington wasn't sure the cost could be justified. "You may possibly conceive that I am averse to his travelling," Washington wrote to Boucher, "but be assured, sir, I am not. There is nothing, in my opinion, more desirable to form the manners and increase the knowledge of observant youth than such a plan as you have sketched out. And I beg of you to believe that there is no gentleman under whose care Mrs. Washington and myself would so soon entrust Mr. Custis as yourself (after he is sufficiently instructed in classical knowledge here)." Yet Boucher should bear in mind the constraints on such a plan. "Though he is possessed of what is called a good estate, it is not a profitable one. His lands are poor, consequently the crops short; and though he has a number of slaves, slaves in such cases only add to the expence. About 60 and from that to 80 hogsheads of tobacco is as much as he generally makes of a year. And if this is cleared, it is as much as can be expected considering the number of people he has to clothe and the many incident charges attending such an estate."

Washington did approve of one preparation for the trip. "As to his being inoculated for the smallpox previous to such an event, the propriety of it is so striking that it cannot admit of a doubt," he told Boucher. Inoculation as a means of stimulating the body's resistance and fostering immunity had been practiced in America for several decades but remained controversial. Washington was an advocate. "My opinion of this is that it ought to happen whether he travels or not, as this disorder will in the course of a few years be scarce ever out of his own country."

MARTHA'S DAUGHTER MARTHA, called Patsy, had different needs. Education of girls and young women followed a separate track from that of boys and young men. And Patsy had health issues that required attention. She suffered from epileptic fits. Medical science in those days didn't know the cause and fumbled for a remedy. "Joshua Evans, who came here last night, put an iron ring upon Patsy (for fits)," Washington wrote in his diary in February 1769. Evans was a blacksmith, and a ring on the finger was thought by some to ease the convulsions. Patsy's ring appears to have been ordinary iron, but other rings for fits were of other materials. Some were blessed, others anointed superstitiously.

When the ring didn't work, Washington and Martha fell back on the all-purpose cure of medicinal waters. A warm spring in western Virginia had been a healing spot for centuries before Europeans arrived in America. By Washington's day it attracted Virginians rich and poor. "About a fortnight ago I came to this place with Mrs. Washington and her daughter, the latter of whom being troubled with a complaint which the efficacy of these waters it is thought might remove, we resolved to try them, but have found little benefit as yet from the experiment," Washington wrote to a friend in the summer of 1769. "What a week or two more may do, we know not, and therefore are inclined to put them to the test."

A visit to the springs was an education in last resorts. "Many poor miserable objects are now attending here, which I hope will receive the desired benefit, as I dare say they are deprived of the means of obtaining any other relief," Washington said.

THE SQUIRE OF Mount Vernon looked beyond his house and family to others in need. Perhaps reflecting on his own missed opportunities, he tried to ensure that talent not go undeveloped. "Having once or twice of late heard you speak highly in praise of the Jersey College, as if you had a desire of sending your son William there (who, I am told, is a youth fond of study and instruction, and disposed to a sedentary studious life, in following of which he may not only promote his own happiness, but the future welfare of others), I should be glad, if you have no other objection to it than what may arise from the expense, if you would send him there as soon as it is convenient," he wrote to William Ramsay, a former contractor to Washington's Virginia regiment. The College of New Jersey would become Princeton. "And depend on me for twenty-five pounds this currency a year for his support, so long as it may be necessary for the completion of his education." Washington didn't often speak of mortality, but life was uncertain. Young Ramsay's education need not be. "If I live to see the accomplishment of this term, the sum here stipulated shall be annually paid; and if I die in the mean while, this letter shall be obligatory upon my heirs, or executors, to do it according to the true intent and meaning hereof." Washington stipulated that the money was not to be treated as a loan. "No other return is expected, or wished, for this offer than that you will accept it with the same freedom and good will with which it is made, and that you may not even consider it in the light of an obligation or mention it as such; for be assured that from me it will never be known."

Sometimes philanthropy didn't work out. John Posey, a neighbor, encountered financial difficulties and came to Washington for help. Washington lent him seven hundred pounds, a sizable sum. Posey's troubles persisted, to Washington's dismay. "It is difficult for me to tell which was greatest—my surprise or concern at finding by your letter of the 20th that instead of being able with the money I agreed to lie somewhat longer out of to discharge your debts, that you wanted to borrow a further sum of £500 to answer this purpose," he wrote to Posey. "I was in hopes, and you gave me the strongest assurance to believe, that when I lent you (and very inconvenient it was for me to do it) the first sum of £700, you could therewith not only discharge all your creditors, but in two years time sink the principal, which was lent to effect that end. How it comes to pass then, that instead of being prepared in twice two years to discharge my claim, you should require £500 more to satisfy others, is, as I at first said, entirely beyond my comprehension."

Posey required help of a different sort than Washington could provide. "I wish with all my heart you may be strengthened by some able and friendly hand in such a manner as to keep your effects together, provided it may turn to your future good in enabling you to work through the load of debt you seem to be entangled in." Washington explained that ready money was hard to come by. He'd have to sell some of his property. "I have struggled to the utmost of my power for two years past, unsuccessfully, to raise four or five hundred pounds to lend a very particular friend of mine, who I know must sell part of his estate without it." There were numerous other demands on what money he did have available. "How absurd and idle would it be then, under these circumstances, to enter myself security for the payment of your debts, unless I foresaw some prospect of raising the money."

Another plea from Posey caused Washington to compromise. He agreed to co-sign for a Posey note to a third party, on the condition that Posey offer collateral. But just before he sent the letter outlining the agreement, he received new intelligence. "P.S. I have this instant been informed that you have declared you paid me all you owed me except about £20. Does such disingenuity as this deserve any favour at my hands? I think anybody might readily answer for you, no."

A SPECIAL CAUSE FOR Washington was care of soldiers he'd commanded during the war against France. In recruiting officers and men at the start of the war, Governor Dinwiddie had promised 200,000 acres to be divided among the first three hundred to enlist. Fifteen years later, the promise still pended. Washington raised the issue with the current governor, Lord Botetourt, during a session of the assembly. After the governor and assembly continued to do nothing, Washington wrote a letter recounting the history of the pledge and reminding the governor of the obligation to the three hundred covered by it. "The terms were offered, the conditions were embraced," Washington told Botetourt. The agreement amounted to a contract. The honor and reputation of Virginia depended on fulfilling it.

WASHINGTON HAD HIS OWN reputation to uphold. Part of reputation was appearance. "My old chariot, having run its race and gone through as many stages as I could conveniently make it travel, is now rendered incapable of any further service," Washington wrote to Robert Cary, his London agent. It was time to get a new one. "Have the chariot you may now send me made in the newest taste, handsome, genteel and light; yet not slight, and consequently unserviceable; to be made of the best seasoned wood, and by a celebrated workman. The last importation which I have seen, besides the customary steel springs, have others that play in a brass barrel and contribute at one and the same time to the ease and ornament of the carriage. One of this kind, therefore, would be my choice; and green being a color little apt, as I apprehend, to fade, and grateful to the eye, I would give it the preference, unless any other color more in vogue and equally lasting is entitled to precedency. In that case I would be governed by fashion."

Details mattered to Washington. "A light gilding on the mouldings (that is, round the panels) and any other ornaments, that may not have a heavy and tawdry look (together with my arms agreeable to the impression here sent) might be added, by way of decoration. A lining of a handsome, lively colored leather of good quality I should also prefer, such as green, blue, or etc., as may best suit the color of the outside. Let the box that slips under the seat be as large as it conveniently can be made (for the benefit of storage upon a journey), and to have a pole (not shafts) for the wheel horses to draw by; together with a handsome set of harness for four middle sized horses ordered in such a manner as to suit either two postilions (without a box), or a box and a postilion. The box being made to fix on, and take off occasionally, with a hammel cloth &c., suitable to the lining. On the harness let my crest be engraved."

WASHINGTON'S LIFE DEVELOPED a comfortable rhythm. He liked nothing more than riding about his properties to see how the crops were faring. "Rid to Muddy Hole, Doeg Run and the Mill," he wrote in his journal for June 1, 1768. "Upon looking over my wheat, I found all those places which had been injured by the March frosts extremely thin, low and backward, having branched but little and looking puny. Indeed, in many places the ground was entirely naked, and where it was not, there was but too much cause to apprehend that the wheat would be choked with weeds."

On June 4: "At home all day writing."

June 5 was Sunday. "Went to church at Alexandria and dined at Col. Carlyle's. The Maryland hound bitch Lady took Forrester, and was also served by Captain." Dogs were important to the gentry, and the dogs required watching. "Captain Posey's bitch Countess was discovered lined to Dabster and was immediately shut up and none but Sterling suffered to go to her. Musick was also in heat and served promiscuously by all the dogs. Intending to drown her puppies."

Washington constantly improved his holdings. "The carpenters finished getting the frame for the barn at my house," he wrote on June 25.

He rode to Fredericksburg to inspect a property he held there. "Began to cut the upper part of my timothy meadow. Rid round and examined the wheat fields there, which were fine."

July brought the wheat harvest. "Rid to see my wheat at different places," he noted on July 4. "Began to cut my wheat at the mill, but upon examination, finding it too green, desisted." Disease was a constant concern. "Upon looking into my wheat, the rust was observed to be more or less in it all. But except some at Doeg Run, it was thought no great damage would follow, as the wheat was rather too forward." The next day: "Went to Muddy Hole with Dr. Rumney to see the cradlers at work. Jonathan Farmer coming down last night and examining my wheat today was of opinion that some Muddy Hole field was fit, at least might be cut with safety. Accordingly began it with himself, three other white men and negro cradlers, letting the grain lie upon the stubble about two days to dry." On July 8: "I rid to the cradlers cutting my wheat at the mill. Began to cut the wheat at the mill in the field round the overseer's house, which was cut and about four acres in the other this day, by about ten and sometimes eleven cradlers." On July 12: "Rid to Muddy Hole before breakfast, where all hands were harvesting the wheat." More of same until July 25. "Finished the last cut about one o'clock this day."

Washington kept careful records, that he might improve the performance of his properties. "Note: from the most accurate experiments I could make this year upon wheat seized with the rust before it is fully formed and beginning to harden, it appears to be a matter of very little consequence whether it is cut down so soon as it is seized with this distemper (I mean the parts of the field that are so), or suffered to stand, for in either case the grain perishes and has little or no flower in it," he wrote. "Note also, from this year's experiments, it appears certain that wheat may be cut down (suffering it to take a day or two sun) much sooner than it generally is. I took wheat of three different degrees of ripeness, i.e. some whose straw and head was green (but the grain of full size and milky), some whose straw from the upper joint was coloring, and some that the straw from the said joint was cold but the knots (at the joints) green, and observed after they had lain two or three days in the sun that the grain of the first was but little shrunk, the second scarce perceptible, and the last plump and full, by which it evidently appears that to cut wheat knot green is not only safe but the most desirable state it can be cut in."

. . .

WASHINGTON'S ATTENTION TO wheat had significance beyond his own harvests. Tobacco had been the cash crop of Virginia since the early seventeenth century, but tobacco depletes soils, and by Washington's day yields were flagging. Forward-looking planters like Washington were shifting to other crops, including wheat.

The switch had two consequences. First, it made the colonies less dependent on Britain. Tobacco was grown mostly for export, and the trade tied planters to their agents and creditors in London. Most wheat was consumed in America.

Second, where tobacco was a labor-intensive crop that kept the workers who tended it busy most of the year, wheat's demands were fewer and more intermittent. Permanent workers made economic sense for tobacco, less so for wheat. Permanent workers, especially in the southern colonies, were mostly slaves. The decline in tobacco culture portended a shift from enslaved labor to paid labor. At the least, it made such a shift plausible and even appealing.

— 31 —

Parliament didn't take long to act on its declaration of right to legislate for the colonies. In 1767 it approved a measure proposed by Charles Townshend, the chancellor of the exchequer, that levied taxes on such essential items as tea, paper, glass, lead and paint pigments. Companion laws directed that revenues from the duties would pay British officials in America, thus freeing them from dependence on the provincial assemblies; punished New York for failing to quarter British troops, as a previous law required; and favored the British East India Company in the American tea trade.

The American foes of the Stamp Act were expecting something like this. They quickly mobilized against the new affronts. The Massachusetts house of representatives dispatched a circular letter to the other colonies asserting Americans' claim to "the full enjoyment of the fundamental rules of the British constitution," among which the right not to be taxed without representation was central. Americans were not represented in Parliament and never could be, "being separated by an ocean of a thousand leagues." Thus the current tax law was illegitimate, and so would be any other tax laws of Parliament. The Massachusetts assemblymen believed that a united front among the colonies would have the greatest chance of defending American rights. For this reason they were sharing their views, and they solicited the views of the other assemblies.

The Virginia house of burgesses sent a letter to George III confirming their gratitude for his assent to the repeal of the Stamp Act, and segueing at once to a condemnation of the new law as "equally derogatory to those constitutional privileges which they"—the burgesses—"the heirs and descendants of free-born Britons, have ever esteemed their unquestionable and invaluable birth rights." A burgess letter to Parliament declared of the Virginians, "As members of the British Empire, they presume not to claim any other than the common unquestionable rights of British subjects, who, by a fundamental and vital principle of their constitution cannot be subjected to any kind of taxation, or have the smallest portion of their property taken from them by any power on Earth without their consent given by their representatives in Parliament."

THE TOWNSHEND MEASURES engaged Washington's attention fully. "At a time when our lordly masters in Great Britain will be satisfied with nothing less than the deprivation of American freedom, it seems highly necessary that something should be done to avert the stroke and maintain the liberty which we have derived from our ancestors," he wrote to George Mason, a fellow burgess. The question was how to do so effectively.

As a soldier, if a retired one, Washington thought in military terms. "That no man should scruple, or hesitate a moment, to use a—ms in defence of so valuable a blessing, on which all the good and evil of life depends, is clearly my opinion." This was a bold, even shocking statement. Taking arms against Britain would be treason. It was especially significant coming from one who had fought on Britain's behalf not long before. That Washington even considered it at this early stage showed how seriously he took the latest threat to American rights.

He realized he was speaking dangerously, which is probably why he declined to spell out "arms" in his letter to Mason. And why he immediately added, "Yet a—ms, I would beg leave to add, should be the last resource, the *dernier resort*." Things might come to violence, but they hadn't so far.

Washington approved the boycott strategy in principle. "It is a good one, and must be attended with salutary effects, provided it can be carried pretty generally into execution," he told Mason. He wasn't sure it could, especially in the southern colonies, which were more dependent on imports than the northern colonies. Yet for this reason the southern colonies would gain more from a boycott. Southerners too often staggered under debt to British creditors, incurred to maintain an exaggerated style of living. A boycott would teach them to do without. "That many families are reduced almost, if not quite, to penury and want from the low ebb of their fortunes, and estates daily selling for the discharge of debts, the public papers furnish but too many melancholy proofs of," Washington wrote. "A scheme of this sort will contribute more effectually than any other I can devise to emerge the country from the distress it at present labors under."

Washington imagined the southern debtor wrestling with the idea of personal retrenchment. "How can I, says he, who have lived in such and such a manner, change my method? I am ashamed to do it, and, besides, such an alteration in the system of my living will create suspicions of the decay in my fortune, and such a thought the world must not harbour." A boycott, if broadly supported, would give this man social cover to do what needed to be done.

"Upon the whole, therefore," Washington concluded, "I think the scheme a good one, and that it ought to be tried here." If it didn't work, there were always a—ms.

THE TARGETS OF the boycott were British merchants. The idea was that they, feeling the pain at their profit margins, would press Parliament to repeal the Townshend duties. The approach had worked against the Stamp Act. Why not again?

The answer was that American merchants suffered too. The British merchants sold directly to wealthy men like Washington, but ordinary consumers dealt with American merchants, who purchased their stock from Britain. The boycott hurt them as much as it did the British merchants. The American merchants had been caught by surprise at the uproar after the Stamp Act, but now they organized in their own defense. While affirming their devotion to American rights, they explained why exceptions to a boycott were necessary and desirable. In Virginia the merchants allied with consumers who couldn't or wouldn't cut back in the way Washington wished they would, to evade the boycott and call for its loosening.

The burgesses bowed to reality. "A new Association is formed, much upon the old plan, but more relaxed, to which the merchants then in town acceded," Washington reported to George Fairfax after the spring 1770 meeting of the assembly. "Committees in each county are to be chosen to attend to the importations and see if our agreements cannot be more strictly adhered to."

Washington was disappointed but not surprised. "That there should be a dissatisfaction and murmuring at the Virginia Association (by those who are more strictly bound) I do not much wonder at, but it was the best that the friends to the cause could obtain here," he wrote to Jonathan Boucher. He hoped this version would receive wider support.

Washington noted a difference in responses between north and south to the Townshend duties. "Upon the whole I think the people of Virginia have too large latitude and wish that the inhabitants of the North may not have too little." Washington questioned whether the northerners weren't being pressed beyond endurance. Merchants had to do business, and people had to live.

For himself, he would stick with the boycott as long as necessary. In August 1770 he wrote to Robert Cary identifying several items to purchase. But he added a proviso: "You will perceive in looking over the several invoices that some of the goods there required are upon condition that the Act of Parliament imposing a duty upon tea, paper etc. for the purpose of raising a revenue in America is totally repealed. And I beg the favour of you to be governed strictly thereby, as it will not be in my power to receive any articles contrary to our non-importation agreement, to which I have subscribed and shall religiously adhere to, if it was, as I could wish it to be, ten times as strict." The order reminded Cary how much he was profiting by his trade with Washington. The proviso revealed how much he would lose if the duties persisted.

32

In another area, relations between Britain and America were improving. As Washington supposed, the ban on western settlement turned out to be temporary. By a series of treaties with the Iroquois and other tribes, the British government resolved the problem of frontier violence sufficiently to allow renewed westward movement. In the autumn of 1770, Washington undertook a journey to Ohio that recapitulated parts of his first journey west, as an apprentice surveyor. He once more scouted land for himself and others—the others in this case being the war veterans whose case he'd been pleading with Governor Botetourt.

The route to Fort Pitt was familiar from the war, though its aspect was more pleasing in peace. "Set out about sunrise," Washington wrote in his journal for October 13. "Breakfasted at the Great Meadows thirteen miles, and reached Captain Crawford's about five o'clock." William Crawford had been scouting land in secret, per Washington's previous directive. Now he could do so openly. "The lands we travelled over today till we had crossed the Laurel Hill (except in small spots) was very mountainous and indifferent; but when we came down the hill to the plantation of Mr. Thos. Gist"—a lieutenant in the Virginia regiment, also son of Christoper Gist—"the land appeared charming, that which lay level being as rich and black as anything could possibly be. The more hilly kind, though of a different complexion, must be good, as well from the crops it produces as from the beautiful white oaks that grow thereon. Though white oak in general indicates poor land, yet this does not appear to be of that cold kind. The land from Gist's to Crawford's is very broken though not mountainous, in spots exceeding rich and in general free from stone."

Washington felt that his western project was back on track. "Went to view some land which Captain Crawford had taken up for me near the

Youghiogheny, distant about twelve miles," he wrote on October 15. "This tract, which contains about one thousand six hundred acres, includes some as fine land as ever I saw, and a great deal of rich meadow, and in general is leveller than the country about it. This tract is well watered, and has a valuable mill-seat (except that the stream is rather too slight, and, it is said, not constant more than seven or eight months in the year; but on account of the fall, and other conveniences, no place can exceed it)."

The Indians of the region remembered Washington and noted he'd become a big man. "Received a message from Colonel Croghan that the White Mingo and other chiefs of the Six Nations had something to say to me, and desiring that I should be at his house about eleven (where they were to meet), I went up and received a speech, with a string of wampum from the White Mingo," Washington wrote on October 19. George Croghan was an Irishman who had taken up the fur trade and become famous in Ohio. Washington paraphrased the chiefs' speech: "That I was a person whom some of them remember to have seen when I was sent on an embassy to the French, and most of them had heard of. They were come to bid me welcome to this country and to desire that the people of Virginia would consider them as friends and brothers, linked together in one chain. That I would inform the governor that it was their wish to live in peace and harmony with the white people, and that though there had been some unhappy differences between them and the people upon our frontiers, they were all made up, and they hoped forgotten; and concluded with saying that their brothers of Virginia did not come among them and trade as the inhabitants of the other provinces did, from whence they were afraid that we did not look upon them with so friendly an eye as they could wish."

Washington accepted the wampum. "I answered (after thanking them for their friendly welcome) that all the injuries and affronts that had passed on either side were now totally forgotten, and that I was sure nothing was more wished and desired by the people of Virginia than to live in the strictest friendship with them; that the Virginians were a people not so much engaged in trade as the Pennsylvanians etc., which was the reason of their not being so frequently among them; but that it was possible they might for the time to come have stricter connexions with them, and that I would acquaint the governor with their desires."

Peace on the frontier was a comparative concept. West of Pittsburgh, Washington learned of the killing of two traders down the Ohio. He paused his journey, before discovering that the initial report had been garbled. Only one trader had died, and he had drowned trying to ford the big river.

The Ohio was an impressive stream, with formidable denizens. "We threw out some line at night and found a catfish, of the size of our largest river cats, hooked to it in the morning, though it was of the smallest kind here." Washington was comparing the Ohio catfish with the ones in the Potomac.

Farther downstream Washington heard another echo of the past. "Left our encampment about seven o'clock," he wrote on October 28. "Two miles below, a small run comes in on the east side, through a piece of land that has a very good appearance, the bottom beginning above our encampment and continuing in appearance wide for four miles down to a place where there comes in a small run, and to the hills, where we found Kiashuta and his hunting party encamped." Kiashuta was one of the Iroquois chiefs who had accompanied Washington to Fort Le Boeuf. "He expressed a satisfaction at seeing me, and treated us with great kindness, giving us a quarter of very fine buffalo." In Washington's day, buffalo, or bison, ranged as far east as the Appalachians. "He insisted upon our spending that night with him, and, in order to retard us as little as possible, moved his camp down the river about six miles."

Word got out among chiefs in the area that Washington was there. "After much counselling over night, they all came to my fire the next morning with great formality; when Kiashuta, rehearsing what had passed between me and the sachems at Colonel Croghan's, thanked me for saying that peace and friendship were the wish of the people of Virginia, and for recommending it to the traders to deal with them upon a fair and equitable footing; and then again expressed their desire of having a trade opened with Virginia, and that the governor thereof might not only be made acquainted therewith, but of their friendly disposition towards the white people. This I promised to do."

Washington reached the Great Bend in the Ohio, where the river doubles back on itself in a large oxbow that then included a short stretch of rapids. Over ages the river had deposited silt on the inside of the bend, yielding "about three or four thousand acres of exceeding valuable land," Washington wrote.

At the Kanawha River they turned their canoes up that stream, to the south. "In many places very rich, in others somewhat wet and pondy, fit for meadow, but upon the whole exceeding valuable, as the land after you get out of the rich bottom is very good for grain."

"Went a hunting," he recorded on November 2. "Killed five buffaloes and wounded some others, three deer, etc. This country abounds in buffaloes and wild game of all kinds; as also in all kinds of wild fowl, there being in the bottoms a great many small, grassy ponds or lakes, which are full of swans, geese, and ducks of different kinds."

The Kanawha was where Washington's soldiers were supposed to receive their land. "Above the junction of the rivers, and at the mouth of a branch on the east side, I marked two maples, an elm, and hoop-wood tree, as a corner of the soldiers' land (if we can get it), intending to take all the bottom from hence to the rapids in the Great Bend into one survey." He similarly marked a second tract, to supplement the first.

He turned toward home. From residence at Mount Vernon, with its commanding view up and down the Potomac, Washington had become fascinated by rivers and their prospects for opening the American interior. Now finding himself on America's great river of the west, as the west was then conceived, he took careful notes. "There is very little difference in the general width of the river from Fort Pitt to the Kanawha," he recorded. "But in the depth I believe the odds are considerably in favor of the lower parts, as we found no shallows below the Mingo Town, except in one or two places where the river was broad, and there, I do not know but there might have been a deep channel in some part of it. Every here and there are islands, some larger and some smaller, which, operating in the nature of locks, or steps, occasion pretty still water above, but for the most part strong and rapid water alongside of them. However there is none of these so swift but that a vessel may be rowed or set up with poles."

The question of transit was crucial to Washington. He imagined farmers growing crops on the rich soil near the river and its tributaries, and employing the river as their highway to market. The Indians showed the way. "When the river is in its natural state, large canoes that will carry five or six thousand weight or more may be worked against stream by four hands, twenty or twenty-five miles a day; and down, a good deal more. The Indians, who are very dexterous (even their women) in the management of canoes, have their hunting-camps and cabins all along the river, for the convenience of transporting their skins by water to market. In the fall, so soon as the hunting season comes on, they set out with their families for this purpose; and in hunting will move their camps from place to place, till by the spring they get two or three hundred or more miles from their towns; then beaver catch it in their way up."

The Indians would have to be dealt with—fairly, Washington hoped, though he had doubts fairness would rule. Many of them were wary of the English. "The Indians who reside upon the Ohio (the upper parts of it at least) are composed of Shawnees, Delawares, and some of the Mingoes, who, getting but little part of the consideration that was given for the lands eastward of the Ohio, view the settlement of the people upon this river with an uneasy and jealous eye, and do not scruple to say that they must be compensated for their right if the people settle thereon, notwithstanding the cession of the Six Nations thereto." Washington wasn't confident this would happen. "People from Virginia and elsewhere are exploring and marking all the lands that are valuable, not only on Redstone and other waters of the Monongahela, but along down the Ohio as low as the Little Kanawha, and by next summer I suppose will get to the Great Kanawha at least. How difficult it may be to contend with these people afterwards is easy to be judged from every day's experience of lands actually settled." The frontiersmen Washington was familiar with weren't easily dissuaded—by Indians or the British government—from occupying whatever lands looked good to them. Once in occupation, they were hard to dislodge.

Washington interviewed men who had gone farther down the Ohio than he. From his own calculations and from what he learned, he listed distances from Fort Pitt: 18 miles to Logstown, 73 to Mingo Town, 94 to Wheeling, 272 to the mouth of the Kanawha, 682 to the Falls of the Ohio, 1,164 to the mouth at the Mississippi River.

He reached Fort Pitt on the return on November 21. He invited the officers at the fort and other gentlemen to dinner and from them gleaned further information about the Ohio country. John Connolly, a nephew of George Croghan, was eager to found a new colony west of the mountains. He especially liked the Shawnee River. "Dr. Connolly is so much delighted with the lands and climate on that river that he seems to wish for nothing more than to induce one hundred families to go there and live, that he might be among them. A new and most desirable government might be established there."

Washington settled accounts with the Indians and others who had guided and assisted him. In late November he hit snow in the Alleghenies east of Pittsburgh. High rivers forced him to swim his horse. He arrived home on December 1, nine weeks and a day after departing.

33

Since the Albany congress of 1754, various people in America had promoted cooperation among the colonies. Their avowed aim was greater security, especially against the French and the Indians on the frontier. Their tacit goal was greater leverage against London. The British caught on, which was why Benjamin Franklin's Albany plan was rejected by the crown and its American governors. A congress called in 1765 to protest the Stamp Act was openly anti-British, in the sense of defying the law just passed by Parliament. It was more effective, not least because it didn't seek British approval. Previously the colonies had communicated with each other primarily through London. Now they communicated directly.

The British tried to suppress this development. After the Massachusetts assembly issued its circular letter to the other colonies against the Townshend duties, London ordered the governors in America to block efforts by the colonial assemblies to act on the Massachusetts call for unity. The effort backfired. In Virginia, when the house of burgesses proposed to consider the Massachusetts letter, the governor dismissed the burgesses. They didn't go far, reconvening at Williamsburg's Raleigh Tavern, where they compared complaints against British heavy-handedness and paid more attention to the Massachusetts unity call than they might have in regular session.

Yet differences remained between Massachusetts and Virginia regarding the degree of oppression ascribed to Parliament and the crown. In Boston, radicals like Samuel Adams and James Otis made agitation against Britain a regular job. The Sons of Liberty acted as an informal militia enforcing the boycott of British goods. Virginia lacked an urban center to facilitate such focus. It also lacked the popular politics that brought out people to protest British mistreatment of America. When the burgesses were in Williamsburg, they spoke out. But most of the time they weren't in Williamsburg. That town fell quiet, and so did Virginia.

For this reason the British government treated Massachusetts differently than it did Virginia. In 1768 the government ordered a regiment of soldiers to Boston to give the radicals second thoughts about causing trouble. But much as Benjamin Franklin had predicted to Parliament, rather than finding a rebellion, they created one.

With British warships in the harbor and British soldiers patrolling the streets, Bostonians felt they were under enemy occupation. The soldiers had little to do and, being poorly paid, not much money to do it with. Some applied for work in the city. Even when their applications weren't spurned by the shopkeepers and other employers, they were resented by Bostonians who needed jobs themselves. Young men formed most of both groups, and they acted toward each other as young men do. Posturing, provoking and punching became a nightly ritual.

Things escalated in March 1770. Not all Bostonians bought into the Adams-Otis interpretation of British malevolence. Merchants chafed under the boycott. One merchant was accused of consorting with the enemy by breaking the boycott. "IMPORTER," proclaimed a sign affixed before his shop. One of the merchant's friends, Ebenezer Richardson, removed the sign and was branded a traitor himself. Richardson was trailed to his house, where the jeers of the mob rang about him. One taunter dared, "Come out, you damn son of a bitch. I'll have your heart out!"

Richardson emerged from his house with a gun loaded with swan shot. As rocks rained upon him, he fired. The discharge killed a boy of eleven, Christopher Seider. Richardson narrowly escaped dismemberment at the hands of the mob. Seider became a martyr to British oppression. His funeral brought thousands into the streets.

Boston grew tenser. A rope maker in league with the Sons of Liberty asked a British soldier if he wanted a job. The soldier said he did and asked what he would do. "Clean my shithouse!" the rope maker sneered.

On the night of March 5 the mob was larger and more belligerent than usual. A Boston apprentice mocked a soldier. The soldier struck the apprentice, who shouted for help. Scores of Bostonians materialized out of the dark. They surrounded several British soldiers and began hurling rocks and shards of ice at them. Members of the crowd dared the soldiers to shoot. "Damn you, you sons of bitches, fire!" yelled one. "You can't kill us all."

Credibly fearing for their lives, the soldiers did what the darer demanded. One fired, then another and another. Five in the crowd were wounded lethally, others less so.

The alacrity with which the Boston press responded to the affair suggested that something like this had been expected, perhaps intended. "Horrid Massacre," was Sam Adams's label. "Bloody Massacre," read a print by Paul Revere.

IF THE VIOLENCE in Boston was indeed intended, it accomplished what Adams and the Boston radicals hoped for. News of the killings spread through the colonies and intensified the feeling that American liberties, and now American lives, were in danger.

Yet the feeling would have become stronger had Parliament not voted to repeal the Townshend duties, save the one on tea, even as the news from Boston was crossing the Atlantic. Their author, Charles Townshend, had died, and Britain had a new prime minister, Lord North, who preferred to reset relations with the colonies. The remaining tea tax was a signal to the Americans that Parliament still governed them.

IN THE CALM that followed the repeal, Washington renewed his commitment to the affairs of Mount Vernon. He meticulously recorded the weather, for future reference. "Feb. 1st. Ground hard froze and day cool, wind being fresh from the northwest," he wrote in the second month of 1771. "2. Ground froze but not so cool, nor the wind so fresh as yesterday. The morning cloudy after a white frost but the evening clear and wind south. 3. Ground a little froze. Day clear and pleasant with but little wind. 4. Wind pretty fresh and somewhat raw from the southward." And so on, day by day. At the end of the month: "28. Wind hard from the northwest, and growing very cold."

A Virginia gentleman should have his portrait painted. Washington sat for one, with ambivalence. "Inclination having yielded to importunity, I am now contrary to all expectation under the hands of Mr. Peale, but in so grave—so sullen—a mood, and now and then under the influence of Morpheus, when some critical strokes are making, that I fancy the skill of this gentleman's pencil will be put to it in describing to the world what manner of man I am," he wrote to Jonathan Boucher. Peale was Charles Willson Peale, who was touring Virginia and painting its gentry. Morpheus was sleep.

Washington instructed an Alexandria merchant on how to run his business. The fellow had raised his prices from a low introductory level. Washington took this amiss. "You may believe me sincere when I assure you that no man wishes to see your company prosper in trade more than I do," he said. "And self-interest apart, I have always thought the way to do this was to import largely and sell low provided you could get a ready vend and quick payments for your goods." This was what the merchant had promised. But he interpreted early sales as indicative of great demand and raised prices. Washington chided him for his mistake. "The mind of man is fond of novelty; curiosity led many to your store," he wrote. "But, my good sir, this is but the work of a day, and like the evening of it, will sink into obscurity, unless by a steady adherence to your plan you convince the judgment as well as satisfy the curiosity of your customers."

HE WAS SADDENED by the death of his stepdaughter, Patsy. "It is an easier matter to conceive than to describe the distress of this family, especially that of the unhappy parent of our dear Patsy Custis, when I inform you that yesterday removed the sweet innocent girl into a more happy and peaceful abode than any she has met with in the afflicted path she hitherto has trod," Washington wrote to a friend. Death had come quickly. "She rose from dinner about four o'clock, in better health and spirits than she appeared to have been in for some time; soon after which she was seized with one of her usual fits, and expired in it, in less than two minutes without uttering a word, a groan, or scarce a sigh."

Martha was understandably distraught. "This sudden and unexpected blow, I scarce need add, has almost reduced my poor wife to the lowest ebb of misery."

HE WAS FLUMMOXED to learn that Jack Custis had become engaged. "I am now set down to write to you on a subject of importance and of no small embarrassment to me," he explained awkwardly to the father of the bride-to-be. Her name was Eleanor Calvert. "My son-in-law"—a term for stepson—"and ward, Mr. Custis, has, as I have been informed, paid his addresses to your second daughter, and, having made some progress in her affections, has solicited her in marriage. How far a union of this sort may be agreeable to you, you best can tell, but I should think myself wanting in candor were I not to confess that Miss Nellie's amiable qualities are acknowledged on all hands, and that an alliance with your family will be pleasing to his."

Yet he had to reveal his reservations. "You must permit me to add, sir, that at this, or in any short time, his youth, inexperience, and unripened education are, and will be, insuperable obstacles, in my opinion, to the completion of the marriage. As his guardian, I conceive it my indispensable duty to endeavor to carry him through a regular course of education (many branches of which, I am sorry to add, he is totally deficient in), and to guard his youth to a more advanced age before an event on which his own peace and the happiness of another are to depend takes place. Not that I have any doubt of the warmth of his affections, nor, I hope I may add, any fears of a change in them, but at present I do not conceive that he is capable of bestowing that attention to the important consequences of the married state which is necessary to be given by those who are about to enter into it." Jack and Nellie should wait. "If the affection which they have avowed for each other is fixed upon a solid basis, it will receive no diminution in the course of two or three years, in which time he may prosecute his studies and thereby render himself more deserving of the lady and useful to society. If, unfortunately, as they are both young, there should be an abatement of affection on either side, or both, it had better precede than follow marriage."

Washington supposed Mr. Calvert would want to know what Jack would bring to the marriage. He preferred not to discuss details prematurely. But he could speak in general. "Mr. Custis's estate consists of about fifteen thousand acres of land, a good part of it adjoining the city of Williamsburg, and none of it forty miles from that place; several lots in the said city; between two and three hundred negroes; and about eight or ten thousand pounds upon bond and in the hands of his merchants. This estate he now holds independent of his mother's dower, which will be an addition to it at her death."

Whether from Washington's admonition, Martha's or perhaps Nellie's, Jack agreed to postpone the wedding in favor of enrollment at King's College, the forerunner of Columbia University, in New York. To ensure his safe arrival, Washington accompanied him north. On the journey Washington renewed acquaintance with Thomas Gage, now a general stationed in New York, and other officers from the war. He dined in Burlington, New Jersey, with Governor William Franklin, the son of Benjamin Franklin. He dined and stayed in Annapolis with the governor of Maryland, and he dined in Philadelphia with the governor of Pennsylvania. He observed a session of the Pennsylvania assembly. He attended a play in New York and a ball in Philadelphia. He frequented taverns and clubs.

He had a fine time. Those he met had a chance to size up the celebrated Virginia soldier.

IN THE SUMMER of 1773 an advertisement appeared in the *Virginia Gazette* and the *Maryland Gazette.* It was also printed as a broadside, or poster, and affixed in prominent places. "The subscriber having obtained patents for upwards of 20,000 acres of land on the Ohio and great Kanhawa, being part of 200,000 acres granted by proclamation in 1754 (10,000 of which are situated on the banks of the first mentioned river, between the mouths of the two Kanhawas; the remainder on the Great Kanhawa or New River, from the mouth, or near it, upwards in one continued survey) proposes to divide the same into any sized tenements that may be desired, and lease them upon moderate terms," the announcement said. Tenants would pay no rent at first, provided they cleared and improved a portion of the lands. Afterward, at a time to be negotiated, they would pay an annual quitrent of two shillings per hundred acres.

The advertisement didn't mention the fact, but knowledgeable readers realized that the Virginia government had finally come through on the land it had promised to the soldiers of the Virginia regiment. The author of the advertisement was offering his portion for sale.

"As these lands are among the first which have been surveyed in the part of the country where they lie," the notice continued, "it is almost needless to premise that none can exceed them in luxuriancy of soil or convenience of situation, all of them lying upon the banks either of the Ohio or Kanhawa and abounding in fine fish and wild fowl of various kinds, as also in most excellent meadows, many of which (by the bountiful hand of nature) are in their present state almost fit for the scythe. From every part of these lands water carriage is now had to Fort Pitt by an easy communication; and from Fort Pitt up the Monongahela to Redstone, vessels of convenient burthen may and do pass continually; from whence, by means of Cheat River and other navigable branches of Monongahela, it is thought the portage to Potomac may and will be reduced within the compass of a few miles, to the great ease and convenience of the settlers in transporting the produce of their lands to market."

A new colony beyond the mountains was being discussed. "If the scheme for establishing a new government on the Ohio in the manner talked of should ever be effected, these must be among the most valuable lands in it, not only on account of the goodness of the soil and the other advantages above enumerated, but from their contiguity to the seat of government, which more than probable will be fixed at the mouth of the Great Kanhawa."

This early version of a genre that would become a staple in American history—the real-estate promotional flyer—identified the seller: George Washington of Mount Vernon, near Alexandria. Those knowledgeable readers correctly inferred that his part of the land bounty, though slow in coming, had been quite generous.

Part IV

Recalled to Arms

→ 34 ←

In December 1773 the Sons of Liberty kept watch on three ships in the Boston harbor. The vessels carried tea of the East India Company for sale in the colonies at a special low price, by the terms of a new tea act. The cheap tea was intended to undercut smuggled Dutch tea, thereby benefiting the well-connected but poorly managed East India Company, while also enticing American tea drinkers to swallow the Townshend duty that remained on tea. Lord North, the prime minister and chancellor of the exchequer, smiled at his cleverness in solving two problems with one cup.

What North judged clever the Boston radicals deemed diabolical. They refused to let the tea be landed. The ships' captains grew impatient, for time was money in the maritime trade. The captains didn't want to leave Boston without delivering the tea and getting paid, but they couldn't wait forever. Thomas Hutchinson, the royal governor, was no less reluctant for them to leave, for their departure would grant a victory to the radicals. Hutchinson let it be known that his patience was running out. The tea would be landed, even if the guns of the British warships in the harbor had to blow protesters to bits.

George Hewes mended shoes during the day and caused trouble at night. He joined a meeting of tea resisters at a Boston church. The governor had lately hinted at compromise. The meeting sent a committee to hear what Hutchinson was thinking. They learned only that he had left town and couldn't be reached. His absence might be a precursor to a forcible landing of the tea. "When the committee returned and informed the meeting of the absence of the governor, there was a confused murmur among the members," Hewes recalled. "The meeting was immediately dissolved, many of them crying out, 'Let every man do his duty, and be true to his country'; and there was a general huzza for Griffin's wharf"—where the tea ships were moored.

The men at the meeting had received instructions. "I immediately dressed myself in the costume of an Indian, equipped with a small hatchet, which I and my associates denominated the tomahawk, with which, and a club, after having painted my face and hands with coal dust in the shop of a blacksmith, I repaired to Griffin's wharf." By ones and in small groups, the faux Indians fell into a silent march. "When we arrived at the wharf, there were three of our number who assumed an authority to direct our operations, to which we readily submitted. They divided us into three parties, for the purpose of boarding the three ships which contained the tea at the same time. The name of him who commanded the division to which I was assigned was Leonard Pitt." Hewes never learned the names of the other commanders.

"We were immediately ordered by the respective commanders to board all the ships at the same time, which we promptly obeyed. The commander of the division to which I belonged, as soon as we were on board the ship, appointed me boatswain and ordered me to go to the captain and demand of him the keys to the hatches and a dozen candles. I made the demand accordingly, and the captain promptly replied, and delivered the articles; but requested me at the same time to do no damage to the ship or rigging." The captains could explain the loss of the tea but not of the ships.

"We then were ordered by our commander to open the hatches and take out all the chests of tea and throw them overboard, and we immediately proceeded to execute his orders, first cutting and splitting the chests with our tomahawks, so as thoroughly to expose them to the effects of the water. In about three hours from the time we went on board, we had thus broken and thrown overboard every tea chest to be found in the ship, while those in the other ships were disposing of the tea in the same way, at the same time. We were surrounded by British armed ships, but no attempt was made to resist us." Caught off guard, the naval commanders didn't want to repeat the fiasco of the Boston massacre, perhaps destroying the merchant ships besides.

"We then quietly retired to our several places of residence, without having any conversation with each other, or taking any measures to discover who were our associates," Hewes recalled. "Nor do I recollect of our having had the knowledge of the name of a single individual concerned in that affair, except that of Leonard Pitt, the commander of my division, whom I have mentioned. There appeared to be an understanding that each individual should volunteer his services, keep his own secret, and risk the consequence for himself. No disorder took place during that transaction, and it was observed at that time that the stillest night ensued that Boston had enjoyed for many months."

Hewes and the others took pains to distinguish protest from looting. "During the time we were throwing the tea overboard, there were several attempts made by some of the citizens of Boston and its vicinity to carry off small quantities of it for their family use," Hewes said. "To effect that object, they would watch their opportunity to snatch up a handful from the deck, where it became plentifully scattered, and put it into their pockets. One Captain O'Connor, whom I well knew, came on board for that purpose, and when he supposed he was not noticed, filled his pockets, and also the lining of his coat. But I had detected him and gave information to the captain of what he was doing. We were ordered to take him into custody, and just as he was stepping from the vessel, I seized him by the skirt of his coat, and in attempting to pull him back, I tore it off; but, springing forward, by a rapid effort he made his escape." Yet he paid for his tea in the currency of blows. He passed through the crowd as through a gauntlet, receiving buffets and kicks as he ran.

"Another attempt was made to save a little tea from the ruins of the cargo by a tall, aged man who wore a large cocked hat and white wig, which was fashionable at that time. He had sleightly"—by sleight of hand—"slipped a little into his pocket, but being detected, they seized him and, taking his hat and wig from his head, threw them, together with the tea, of which they had emptied his pockets, into the water. In consideration of his advanced age, he was permitted to escape, with now and then a slight kick."

Hewes and some of the others returned to the scene the next morning. Tea littered the harbor. "It was discovered that very considerable quantities of it were floating upon the surface of the water, and to prevent the possibility of any of its being saved for use, a number of small boats were manned by sailors and citizens, who rowed them into those parts of the harbor wherever the tea was visible, and by beating it with oars and paddles so thoroughly drenched it as to render its entire destruction inevitable."

WHAT BECAME KNOWN as the Boston Tea Party infuriated the government in London. Parliament determined to put the Bostonians in their place. One bill centralized authority in Massachusetts in the hands of the royal governor. A second closed the port of Boston. A third transferred trials for certain offenses from courts in Massachusetts to courts in Britain. A fourth required all the colonies to make provisions for quartering British troops.

The laws weren't uniformly popular even in Britain. Merchants winced at the thought of another boycott. Persons familiar with America warned that the crackdown would strengthen the radicals there.

North defended the measures as the least his government could do in the face of the insurrectionary violence in Boston. Referring specifically to the bill expanding the powers of the governor, he told Parliament, "Are we, sir, seeing all this, to be silent, and give the governor no support? Gentlemen say, let the colony come to your bar and be heard in their defence; though it is not likely that they will come, when they deny your authority in every instance. Can we remain in this situation long? We must effectually take some measure to correct and amend the defects of that government." The Americans grew more reckless and violent by the month. They must be taught to obey. "So clement and so long forbearing has our conduct been that it is incumbent on us now to take a different course. Whatever may be the consequence, we must risk something; if we do not, all is over."

35

The British called the punitive measures the Coercive Acts. The Americans called them the Intolerable Acts. The Americans moved to show the acts wouldn't be tolerated.

Washington learned of the new laws at Williamsburg, where the burgesses were meeting. Thomas Jefferson, by now a burgess, and some other young members drafted a resolution making Boston's cause Virginia's by calling for a day of prayer and fasting, to coincide with the June 1 closing of Boston's port. After the burgesses adopted the resolution, Governor Dunmore, under instructions to forestall such solidarity, dismissed the assembly. The burgesses again repaired to the Raleigh Tavern, where they agreed to issue a call to the other colonies for a continental congress. "Things seem to be hurrying to an alarming crisis and demand the speedy, united councils of all those who have a regard for the common cause," their summons said.

UNTIL NOW WASHINGTON'S DISSATISFACTION with Britain had been intermittent. He had concluded during the Braddock campaign that the British army was run by fools. He had been disappointed and insulted when those fools denied him a royal commission despite his demonstrated talent and courage. He had been frustrated when London closed the west to settlement. Yet to this point he'd been willing to ascribe Britain's failings to incompetence.

Something more was required to explain London's latest moves. The Intolerable Acts were not incompetent but malevolent. The British government knew exactly what it was doing in depriving the people of Boston of their rights, including, by closing Boston's port, the right to make a living. The punishment of Boston didn't touch Washington personally, yet it awakened him—and many other Americans—to a larger threat against all of them. "The cause of Boston—the despotic measures in respect to it, I mean—now is and ever will be considered as the cause of America," he wrote to George William Fairfax. Washington endorsed the call for a continental congress, for unity was crucial. "We shall not suffer ourselves to be sacrificed by piecemeal."

This was a big step, fraught with dangers of its own. "God only knows what is to become of us, threatened as we are with so many hovering evils as hang over us at present, having a cruel and bloodthirsty enemy upon our backs—the Indians—between whom and our frontier inhabitants many skirmishes have happened, and with whom a general war is inevitable, whilst those from whom we have a right to seek protection are endeavouring by every piece of art and despotism to fix the shackles of slavery upon us," Washington wrote to Fairfax. The memory of Pontiac's war stuck in his head. "From the best accounts we have been able to get, there is a confederacy of the western and southern Indians formed against us." Virginians were as anxious as anyone in Boston, with reason. "Since the first settlement of this colony, the minds of people in it never were more disturbed or our situation so critical as at present."

Bryan Fairfax was a brother of George Fairfax and, as might have been expected of one who would become Lord Fairfax, less enamored of Americans' claims to rights than other Virginians. Washington carried on a running conversation with him on this subject. "As to your political sentiments," Washington wrote, "I would heartily join you in them so far as relates to a humble and dutiful petition to the throne, provided there was the most distant hope of success." But previous such efforts by the Americans had been spurned. Stronger action was required.

Washington normally took pride in his dispassionate judgment. But now he grew hot. "Does it not appear, as clear as the sun in its meridian brightness, that there is a regular, systematic plan formed to fix the right and practice of taxation upon us?" he asked Bryan Fairfax. "Does not the uniform conduct of Parliament for some years past confirm this?" Washington recited the assaults on American rights in the separate acts. These were undeniable evidence that petitions didn't work. "Ought we not, then, to put our virtue and fortitude to the severest test?"

Fairfax cautioned against trying too much. Washington didn't disagree. "With you I think it a folly to attempt more than we can execute, as that will not only bring disgrace upon us but weaken our cause," he said. Some had suggested a debt strike, with Virginians refusing to pay their

British creditors. "I have my doubts on several accounts but principally on that of justice, for I think whilst we are accusing others of injustice, we should be just ourselves."

WASHINGTON CHAIRED A MEETING in Fairfax County devoted to the new British laws and the proper response. The meeting approved a series of resolutions. "That this Colony and Dominion of Virginia cannot be considered as a conquered country, and, if it was, that the present inhabitants are the descendants not of the conquered but of the conquerors," the Fairfax resolutions declared. "That the same was not settled at the national expense of England but at the private expense of the adventurers, our ancestors." Hence Britain's claim to a right to tax the Americans to recoup expenses was unfounded. "That our ancestors, when they left their native land and settled in America, brought with them, even if the same had not been confirmed by charters, the civil constitution and form of government of the country they came from." English rights applied as fully to Englishmen in the provinces of America as to Englishmen in the shires of England. The most fundamental English right was to be free of taxes levied without consent of elected representatives in Parliament. The colonies were not represented and, given the distance, could not be represented. Consequently the regime of tax laws and laws to enforce them was "totally incompatible with the privileges of a free people and the natural rights of mankind" and was "calculated to reduce us from a state of freedom and happiness to slavery and misery."

A final Fairfax resolution said that Washington should represent the county at a province-wide meeting in Williamsburg.

THE WILLIAMSBURG GATHERING proposed putting theory to practice. Starting November 1, 1774, Virginians would import nothing from Britain save medicines, the delegates declared. They would refuse imports of slaves from Africa or the West Indies. Virginians would refuse not merely to import tea but to use it or suffer it to be used in the province. If the Bostonians were compelled to reimburse the East India Company for the lost tea, Virginia would boycott the company. If the current grievances were not remedied by August 1, 1775, Virginia would embargo tobacco to Britain. Virginians would increase their flocks of sheep, to free themselves from dependence on Britain for wool. Merchants who raised prices on account of boycott-induced shortages would themselves be boycotted. Virginians would be encouraged to contribute money to a fund for the relief of Boston. Finally, the delegates stated their intention to be guided by "the united wisdom of the general congress" to be held in Philadelphia.

36

"On Friday, September 16th, the honourable delegates, now met in general congress, were elegantly entertained by the gentlemen of Philadelphia," recorded the proceedings of the Continental Congress. "Having met at the City Tavern about three o'clock, they were conducted from thence to the State House by the managers of the entertainment, where they were received by a very large company, composed of the clergy, such genteel strangers as happened to be in town, and a number of respectable citizens, making in the whole near five hundred."

The dinner gave way to toasts: to the king, to the queen, to the Duke of Gloucester, to the Prince of Wales and the royal family, to perpetual union of the colonies, to the faithful execution by the colonies of what the Congress resolved, to beleaguered Boston and Massachusetts, to a just Great Britain and a free America, to no standing armies, to the hope that the cloud over Britain and the colonies should burst upon the present ministry, to the genius of liberty finding asylum in America, to the freedom of the press, to conciliation between Britain and America on constitutional ground, to the virtuous few in Parliament. The recorder of the toasts added a comment: "The acclamations with which several of them were received not only testified the sense of honour conferred by such worthy guests but the fullest confidence in their wisdom and integrity, and a firm resolution to adopt and support such measures as they shall direct for the public good at this alarming crisis."

"COLONEL WASHINGTON IS nearly as tall a man as Colonel Fitch, and almost as hard a countenance, yet with a very young look, and an easy, soldier-like air and gesture," Silas Deane wrote to his wife. Deane was a delegate from Connecticut. Thomas Fitch was a veteran of the French and Indian War noted for his height.

Deane had been a lawyer before turning merchant. He had married almost as well as Washington and done so twice. He made himself a student of men, and he practiced his study on the delegates to the Congress. "He does not appear above forty-five," Deane continued of Washington, "yet was in the first actions in 1753 and 1754, on the Ohio, and in 1755 was with Braddock, and was the means of saving the remains of that unfortunate army. It is said that in the house of burgesses in Virginia, on hearing of the Boston port bill, he offered to raise and arm and lead one thousand men himself at his own expense, for the defense of the country, were there need of it. His fortune is said to be equal to such an undertaking."

Other evidence that Washington said such a thing in the house of burgesses is lacking. He typically spared his words in public, and he never boasted of his wealth. But that Deane credited the story revealed the impression of importance Washington conveyed.

Patrick Henry was similarly taken. Asked after the Congress adjourned who was the greatest man there, Henry replied, "If you speak of eloquence, Mr. Rutledge of South Carolina is by far the greatest orator. But if you speak of solid information and sound judgment, Colonel Washington is unquestionably the greatest man on that floor."

John Adams was a lawyer from Boston, where until now he had moved in the shadow of his cousin Samuel Adams. "He never spoke in public," John Adams recalled of Washington at the Congress. "In private he advocated a non-exportation as well as a non-importation agreement. With both, he thought we should prevail. Without either, he thought it doubtful."

WASHINGTON ATTENDED THE SESSIONS of the Congress faithfully, though his dinner engagements made a greater impression in his diary. It was at those dinners that he advocated the positions Adams identified. He signed the manifesto the Congress produced. "The present unhappy situation of our affairs is occasioned by a ruinous system of colony administration, adopted by the British ministry about the year 1763, evidently calculated for enslaving these colonies and, with them, the British empire," the manifesto declared. It delineated the crimes of Parliament, culminating in the Intolerable Acts and the Quebec Act, a companion measure transferring Ohio from Virginia and Pennsylvania to Canada and giving special protection to French Catholics in that province.

The manifesto asserted that these grievances threatened destruction to the lives, liberty and property of Americans and hence required a stout response, to wit a "non-importation, non-consumption and non-exportation agreement faithfully adhered to." Non-importation would begin on December 1, 1774, and would apply to all goods from Britain and all slaves. Non-consumption would follow from this. Non-exportation would be delayed until September 10, 1775, giving the British government time to come to its senses.

WHILE IN PHILADELPHIA, Washington received a letter from an old comrade. Robert McKenzie had been a captain in Washington's Virginia regiment. Near the end of the war he received a commission in the British regular army and proceeded up the ranks. He wrote to Washington from the British army camp at Boston, warning against the designs of the Massachusetts radicals. "Mr. Atchison"—a mutual friend from Virginia who had been in Boston—"can sufficiently inform you of the state of this unhappy province, of their tyrannical oppression over one another, of their fixed aim at total independence, of the weakness and temper of the main springs that set the whole in motion, and how necessary it is that abler heads and better hearts should draw a line for their guidance," McKenzie wrote. "Even when this is done 'tis much to be feared they will follow it no further than where it coincides with their present sentiments." Boston was peaceful at the moment. "But the rebellious and numerous meetings of men in arms, their scandalous and ungenerous attacks upon the best characters in the province, obliging them to save their lives by flight, and their repeated but feeble threats to dispossess the troops have furnished sufficient reasons to General Gage to put the town in a formidable state of defence, about which we are now fully employed, and which will be shortly accomplished to their great mortification."

Prompted by McKenzie's letter, Washington made a point of meeting with the Massachusetts delegates: John Adams, Samuel Adams, Thomas Cushing and Robert Treat Paine. "Spent the afternoon with the Boston gentlemen," Washington wrote in his diary on September 28. What he heard at the meeting allayed such concerns as he might have felt. If anything, it convinced him more than ever that Britain was bent on depriving Americans of their freedom and that the British army was its agent of oppression.

"Permit me with the freedom of a friend (for you know I always esteemed you) to express my sorrow that fortune should place you in a service that must fix curses to the latest posterity upon the contrivers, and, if success (which, by the by, is impossible) accompanies it, execrations upon all those who have been instrumental in the execution," he replied to McKenzie. Washington understood that a soldier must do his duty. But he didn't have to do it cheerfully, or in this case ignorantly. McKenzie wasn't hearing the whole story about Massachusetts. "Otherwise you would not wonder at a people who are every day receiving fresh proofs of a systematic assertion of an arbitrary power, deeply planned to overturn the laws and constitution of their country, and to violate the most essential and valuable rights of mankind, being irritated, and with difficulty restrained from acts of the greatest violence and intemperance." Washington had it on the authority of the Massachusetts men that they were not rebels but reformers. "It is not the wish or interest of that government"—Massachusetts—"or any other upon this continent, separately or collectively, to set up for independence," he told McKenzie. Yet Americans were determined. "None of them will ever submit to the loss of those valuable rights and privileges which are essential to the happiness of every free state and without which, life, liberty, and property are rendered totally insecure."

Washington didn't blame McKenzie for the actions of the British, but he thought McKenzie should know with whom he had consorted and should prepare for the consequences. The punitive laws aimed at Massachusetts were a blow against American rights, and America would respond in kind. "More blood will be spilled on this occasion, if the ministry are determined to push matters to extremity, than history has ever yet furnished instances of in the annals of North America," Washington warned. "And such a vital wound will be given to the peace of this great country as time itself cannot cure or eradicate the remembrance of."

37

Washington's warnings were confined to his correspondence, at this point. But they were no less chilling for that. When America's most accomplished soldier, a veteran of the brutal fighting on the frontier, foretold a bloodier war than North America had ever experienced, the recipients of his letters had to take note. Whether Robert McKenzie shared Washington's words with his superiors is unclear. If he did, they didn't conspicuously heed them.

Patrick Henry, by contrast to Washington, aired his warnings for all to hear. By the time the Continental Congress met, Henry's reputation for oratory had been building for a decade. He solidified it in Philadelphia. Silas Deane called Henry "the completest speaker I ever heard." Deane added, in a letter to his wife, "I can give you no idea of the music of his voice or the high-wrought yet natural elegance of his style and manner." Charles Thomson, a Philadelphian who served as secretary of the Congress, later recalled the tentative opening session. "As soon as the body had organized by choosing Peyton Randolph president, all seemed impressed with a sense of the high responsibility they had assumed, and a most profound silence ensued, as if to say, *what next?* None seemed willing to break the eventful silence until a grave-looking member, in a plain dark suit of minister's gray and unpowdered wig arose." The delegates wondered who this country parson could be. Thomson felt embarrassed for him. "But as he proceeded he evinced such unusual force of argument and such novel and impassioned eloquence as soon electrified the whole house. Then the excited inquiry passed from man to man. Who is it? Who is it? The answer from the few who knew him was, it is *Patrick Henry!*"

HENRY WAS NEVER in finer voice than several months later. Henry, Washington and the other Virginia delegates carried the resolutions of the Continental Congress back to Virginia for the consideration of the convention that had effectively replaced the provincial assembly. The convention met a second time, in Richmond, beyond the reach and hearing of Governor Dunmore. At their first gathering the delegates had avowed their loyalty to King George and their desire to remain part of the British empire. Nine months later they adopted a different tone.

Henry spoke the most powerfully. He proposed summoning a militia. This wasn't new. The Virginia assembly had summoned militias many times in the past. But the convention wasn't the assembly. It operated outside the colonial government. And—here was the striking part—it might have to operate *against* the colonial government. "Resolved," proposed Henry, "That this colony be immediately put into a state of defence, and that"—a blank space here to be filled in with names—"be a committee to prepare a plan for embodying, arming and disciplining such a number of men as may be sufficient for that purpose."

Henry's resolution provoked an uproar. The cautious among the delegates said more time was required to give America's friends in Britain a chance to change the policies of the imprudent administration. More time was needed for the non-importation agreement to bite among British manufacturers. Besides, what could Virginia do against the British empire? It might muster a militia, but it could never raise an army to match what Britain could send against it. Britain's navy would have the run of the Virginia coast and of the bays and rivers that cut deep into Virginia's heartland. Virginia's rights might one day require the armed force Henry described. But that day hadn't come. And it couldn't effectively come without the cooperation of the other colonies.

"No man thinks more highly than I do of the patriotism, as well as abilities, of the very worthy gentlemen who have just addressed the house," Henry said in reply. "But different men often see the same subject in different lights; and, therefore, I hope it will not be thought disrespectful to those gentlemen if, entertaining as I do opinions of a character very opposite to theirs, I shall speak forth my sentiments freely and without reserve."

Henry typically worked gradually into a speech, gaining momentum as he went. On this day he bolted from the gate. "This is no time for ceremony. The question before the house is one of awful moment to this country. For my own part, I consider it as nothing less than a question of freedom or slavery." Men must speak fully and frankly. "Should I keep back my opinions at such a time, through fear of giving offense, I should consider myself as guilty of treason towards my country, and of an act of disloyalty toward the Majesty of Heaven, which I revere above all earthly kings."

The gentlemen who had spoken hoped for better days to come. "It is natural to man to indulge in the illusions of hope," Henry said. "We are apt to shut our eyes against a painful truth, and listen to the song of that siren till she transforms us into beasts. Is this the part of wise men, engaged in a great and arduous struggle for liberty? Are we disposed to be of the number of those who, having eyes, see not, and, having ears, hear not, the things which so nearly concern their temporal salvation? For my part, whatever anguish of spirit it may cost, I am willing to know the whole truth—to know the worst, and to provide for it."

Henry paused for breath and emphasis before proceeding.

"I have but one lamp by which my feet are guided, and that is the lamp of experience. I know of no way of judging of the future but by the past. And judging by the past, I wish to know what there has been in the conduct of the British ministry for the last ten years to justify those hopes with which gentlemen have been pleased to solace themselves and the house. Is it that insidious smile with which our petition has been lately received? Trust it not, sir; it will prove a snare to your feet. Suffer not yourselves to be betrayed with a kiss. Ask yourselves how this gracious reception of our petition comports with those warlike preparations which cover our waters and darken our land. Are fleets and armies necessary to a work of love and reconciliation? Have we shown ourselves so unwilling to be reconciled that force must be called in to win back our love?

"Let us not deceive ourselves, sir. These are the implements of war and subjugation; the last arguments to which kings resort. I ask gentlemen, sir, what means this martial array, if its purpose be not to force us to submission? Can gentlemen assign any other possible motive for it? Has Great Britain any enemy, in this quarter of the world, to call for all this accumulation of navies and armies? No, sir, she has none. They are meant for us: they can be meant for no other. They are sent over to bind and rivet upon us those chains which the British ministry have been so long forging."

Another pause, to let the image of chains sink in.

"And what have we to oppose to them? Shall we try argument? Sir, we have been trying that for the last ten years. Have we anything new to offer upon the subject? Nothing. We have held the subject up in every light of which it is capable; but it has been all in vain. Shall we resort to entreaty and humble supplication? What terms shall we find which have not been already exhausted? Let us not, I beseech you, sir, deceive ourselves. Sir, we have done everything that could be done to avert the storm which is now coming on. We have petitioned; we have remonstrated; we have supplicated; we have prostrated ourselves before the throne, and have implored its interposition to arrest the tyrannical hands of the ministry and Parliament.

"Our petitions have been slighted; our remonstrances have produced additional violence and insult; our supplications have been disregarded; and we have been spurned, with contempt, from the foot of the throne! In vain, after these things, may we indulge the fond hope of peace and reconciliation. There is no longer any room for hope.

"If we wish to be free—if we mean to preserve inviolate those inestimable privileges for which we have been so long contending—if we mean not basely to abandon the noble struggle in which we have been so long engaged, and which we have pledged ourselves never to abandon until the glorious object of our contest shall be obtained—we must fight! I repeat it, sir, we must fight! An appeal to arms and to the God of hosts is all that is left us!"

The delegates were stunned by Henry's call to battle. Some murmured among themselves. Others were still as stone.

"They tell us, sir, that we are weak, unable to cope with so formidable an adversary. But when shall we be stronger? Will it be the next week, or the next year? Will it be when we are totally disarmed, and when a British guard shall be stationed in every house? Shall we gather strength by irresolution and inaction? Shall we acquire the means of effectual resistance by lying supinely on our backs and hugging the delusive phantom of hope, until our enemies shall have bound us hand and foot?

"Sir, we are not weak if we make a proper use of those means which the God of nature hath placed in our power. The millions of people, armed in the holy cause of liberty, and in such a country as that which we possess, are invincible by any force which our enemy can send against us. Besides, sir, we shall not fight our battles alone. There is a just God who presides over the destinies of nations, and who will raise up friends to fight our battles for us.

"The battle, sir, is not to the strong alone; it is to the vigilant, the active, the brave. Besides, sir, we have no election. If we were base enough to desire it, it is now too late to retire from the contest. There is no retreat but in submission and slavery! Our chains are forged! Their clanking may be heard on the plains of Boston! The war is inevitable—and let it come! I repeat it, sir, let it come.

"It is in vain, sir, to extenuate the matter. Gentlemen may cry, Peace, peace—but there is no peace. The war is actually begun! The next gale that sweeps from the north will bring to our ears the clash of resounding arms! Our brethren are already in the field! Why stand we here idle? What is it that gentlemen wish? What would they have? Is life so dear, or peace so sweet, as to be purchased at the price of chains and slavery? Forbid it, Almighty God! I know not what course others may take; but as for me, give me liberty or give me death!"

THE EFFECT ON Henry's listeners was profound. One delegate recalled his reaction to the declaration that America must fight. "Imagine to yourself this sentence delivered with all the calm dignity of Cato of Utica. Imagine to yourself the Roman senate, assembled in the capitol, when it was entered by the profane Gauls, who at first were awed by their presence as if they had entered an assembly of the gods! Imagine that you heard Cato addressing such a senate. Imagine that you saw the handwriting on the wall of Belshazzar's palace. Imagine you heard a voice as from heaven uttering the words *'We must fight'* as the doom of fate, and you may have some idea of the speaker, the assembly to whom he addressed himself, and auditory, of which I was one."

Henry's speech carried the day. The convention approved his resolution. When the committee the resolution specified was formed, Washington's name was one of those filling the blank. The committee recommended that Virginia's counties form companies of infantry and troops of cavalry. Each infantryman should have a rifle or musket, a tomahawk and a hunting shirt. The counties should tax themselves to provide arms and ammunition for their militiamen.

Washington took particular care with these recommendations. He assumed he'd be leading Virginia soldiers into battle, should things with Britain come to that. "I have promised to review the independent company of Richmond some time this summer, they having made me a tender of the command of it," he wrote to his brother Jack. This might be merely the start. "It is my full intention to devote my life and fortune in the cause we are engaged in, if needful."

⟶ 38 ⟵

"The winter has passed over without any great bickerings between the inhabitants of this town and His Majesty's troops," Thomas Gage wrote to Lord Dartmouth, the colonial secretary, from Boston in late March 1775. Gage had commanded British forces in America since the end of the war with France. Recently he had replaced Thomas Hutchinson as governor of Massachusetts. He had counseled the British government on the drafting of the Coercive Acts, and in his dual position he was well placed to enforce them. He was pleased at how smoothly things were going. "Some quarrels now and then happened, though of no very great consequence."

Yet he couldn't be too careful. "Reports are various of the temper and disposition of the people in the different townships," Gage told Dartmouth. "Government is so totally unhinged, and the people so possessed with the notions instilled into them that all authority is derived from them, that it may be doubted whether Government can ever revert again into its old channel without some convulsion."

Transatlantic mail was slow, and before Dartmouth received his letter, Gage filed an update. It required some background. "Having received intelligence of a large quantity of military stores being collected at Concord, for the avowed purpose of supplying a body of troops to act in opposition to His Majesty's Government, I got the grenadiers and light infantry out of town under the command of Lieutenant Colonel Smith of the 10th Regiment and Major Pitcairne of the Marines with as much secrecy as possible on the 18th"—of April—"at night and with orders to destroy the said military stores." The next morning Gage sent reinforcements under Lord Percy to help in case of trouble.

"It appears from the firing of alarm guns and ringing of bells that the march of Lieutenant Colonel Smith was discovered," Gage continued. "And he was opposed by a body of men within six miles of Concord, some few of whom first began to fire upon his advanced companies which brought on a fire from the troops that dispersed the body opposed to them. And they proceeded to Concord, where they destroyed all the military stores they could find."

The fighting had merely begun. "On the return of the troops they were attacked from all quarters where any cover was to be found, from whence it was practicable to annoy them, and they were so fatigued with their march that it was with difficulty they could keep out their flanking parties to remove the enemy to a distance, so that they were at length a good deal pressed." The reinforcements proved crucial. "Lord Percy then arrived opportunely to their assistance with his brigade and two pieces of cannon, and notwithstanding a continual skirmish for the space of fifteen miles, receiving fire from every hill, fence, house, barn, etc., His Lordship kept the enemy off, and brought the troops to Charlestown, from whence they were ferried to Boston."

Gage praised the performance of his soldiers and condemned the colonials. "The whole country was assembled in arms with surprising expedition, and several thousand are now assembled about this town, threatening an attack and getting up artillery. And we are very busy making preparations to oppose them."

THE NEWS REACHED Mount Vernon as Washington was preparing to leave for Philadelphia. The Richmond convention had chosen delegates to a second continental congress, due to meet in May, and Washington was one.

"You must undoubtedly have received an account of the engagement in the Massachusetts Bay," Washington wrote to George William Fairfax, "between the ministerial troops (for we do not, nor can we yet prevail upon ourselves to call them the King's troops), and the provincials of that government. But as you may not have heard how that affair began, I enclose you the several affidavits, which were taken after the action." The accounts showed that Gage acknowledged giving orders to destroy the military stores at Concord—"to destroy private property," Washington glossed, "or, in other words, to destroy a magazine which self-preservation obliged the inhabitants to establish." A clearer violation of English rights was hard to imagine. "And he also confesses, in effect at least, that his men made a very precipitate retreat from Concord, notwithstanding the reinforcement under Lord Percy."

Washington was proud of how the Massachusetts militia acquitted themselves. "If the retreat had not been as precipitate as it was, and God knows it could not well have been more so, the ministerial troops must have surrendered or been totally cut off."

He checked himself. "Unhappy it is, though, that a brother's sword has been sheathed in a brother's breast, and that the once happy and peaceful plains of America are either to be drenched with blood or inhabited by slaves. Sad alternative!"

Yet he knew what must be done. "Can a virtuous man hesitate?"

39

"Colonel Washington appears at Congress in his uniform," John Adams wrote to his wife, Abigail, from Philadelphia.

Washington always cut an impressive figure, but especially in uniform, and still more when America throbbed with martial ardor. "The military spirit which runs through the continent is truly amazing," Adams continued. "This city turns out 2000 men every day. Mr. Dickinson is a colonel. Mr. Reed a lieutenant colonel. Mr. Mifflin a major." Adams wondered if he himself had chosen the wrong profession. "Oh that I was a soldier! I will be. I am reading military books. Everybody must and will and shall be a soldier."

Yet only one would be the commander. Adams later recalled the events that led to the choice of a general for the American army. He grew frustrated by the slowness of the Congress to take substantive action. Some delegates insisted on another petition to the crown. Adams thought petitioning useless. "This measure of imbecility, the second petition to the King, embarrassed every exertion of Congress," he recalled. "It occasioned motions and debates without end for appointing committees to draw up a declaration of the causes, motives and objects of taking arms." Meanwhile, reports from Boston described the militias surrounding Gage and the British in Boston as lacking arms, ammunition and other essentials. Adams felt the matter almost personally. "Every post brought me letters from my friends Dr. Winthrop, Dr. Cooper, General James Warren, and sometimes from General Ward and his aides and General Heath and many others, urging in pathetic terms the impossibility of keeping their men together without the assistance of Congress."

Adams and others wanted the Congress to adopt the army at Boston—to take responsibility for the pay and provision of the militias investing the city. But an army funded by the Continental Congress must have a general appointed by the Continental Congress. Agreeing on that man was no small task. New Englanders wanted a New England man and thought they had a strong case. Boston for years had been the target of British attack, and New Englanders had done all the fighting so far.

But Virginians wanted a southern man, one in particular. Their argument was that a continental army must be continental and not merely regional. Pragmatically they pointed out that though all Americans might be united at present against the British outrages, unity might fray without southern skin in the game.

Adams was a pragmatist himself on this point. "The intention was very visible to me, that Colonel Washington was their object, and so many of our staunchest men"—delegates to the Congress—"were in the plan that we could carry nothing without conceding to it." Yet the northerners didn't yield easily. The favorite of some of them was John Hancock, a wealthy merchant turned radical who had been president of the provisional assembly of Massachusetts and was currently president of the Congress. Hancock didn't conceal his desire to don a general's uniform, or at least be asked to. "Mr. Hancock himself had an ambition to be appointed commander in chief," Adams said. "Whether he thought an election a compliment due to him and intended to have the honor of declining it, or whether he would have accepted, I know not. To the compliment he had some pretensions, for at that time his exertions, sacrifices and general merit in the cause of his country had been incomparably greater than those of Colonel Washington." Hancock had been an able militia officer, mustering and training troops. But he entirely lacked experience of battle. To Adams, this made Washington the only acceptable candidate.

Adams decided to force the issue. "Apprehending daily that we should hear very distressing news from Boston, I walked with Mr. Samuel Adams in the State House yard for a little exercise and fresh air before the hour of Congress, and there represented to him the various dangers that surrounded us. He agreed to them all, but said what shall we do? I answered him that he knew I had taken great pains to get our colleagues to agree upon some plan that we might be unanimous. But he knew that they would pledge themselves to nothing. But I was determined to take a step which should compel them and all the other members of Congress to declare themselves for or against something. I am determined this morning to make a direct motion that Congress should adopt the army before Boston and appoint Colonel Washington commander of it." Samuel Adams said nothing.

"Accordingly when Congress had assembled, I rose in my place and in as short a speech as the subject would admit represented the state of the colonies, the uncertainty in the minds of the people, their great expectations and anxiety, the distresses of the army, the danger of its dissolution, the difficulty of collecting another, and the probability that the British army would take advantage of our delays, march out of Boston and spread desolation as far as they could go. I concluded with a motion in form that Congress would adopt the army at Cambridge and appoint a general, that though this was not the proper time to nominate a general, yet as I had reason to believe this was a point of the greatest difficulty, I had no hesitation to declare that I had but one gentleman in my mind for that important command, and that was a gentleman from Virginia who was among us and very well known to all of us, a gentleman whose skill and experience as an officer, whose independent fortune, great talents and excellent universal character, would command the approbation of all America and unite the cordial exertions of all the colonies better than any other person."

While Adams was speaking, Washington sensed where he was going. "Mr. Washington, who happened to sit near the door, as soon as he heard me allude to him, from his usual modesty darted into the library room," Adams remembered.

The reaction of John Hancock was quite different. "Mr. Hancock, who was our president, which gave me an opportunity to observe his countenance while I was speaking on the state of the colonies, the army at Cambridge and the enemy, heard me with visible pleasure. But when I came to describe Washington for the commander, I never remarked a more sudden and sinking change of countenance. Mortification and resentment were expressed as forcibly as his face could exhibit them."

Adams's motion carried, although not without debate along the lines he'd already encountered. Most of the dissenters would eventually conclude that Washington had been an inspired choice. "Mr. Hancock, however, never loved me so well after this event as he had done before, and he made me feel at times the effects of his resentment and of his jealousy in many ways and at diverse times, as long as he lived."

"TO GEORGE WASHINGTON ESQUIRE," read Washington's commission. "We reposing especial trust and confidence in your patriotism, conduct and fidelity, do by these presents constitute and appoint you to be General and Commander in Chief of the army of the United Colonies and of all the forces raised or to be raised by them and of all others who shall voluntarily offer their service and join the said army for the defence of American liberty and for repelling every hostile invasion thereof. And you are hereby vested with full power and authority to act as you shall think for the good and welfare of the service."

Washington was the highest authority in the army, but he answered to one higher. "You are to regulate your conduct in every respect by the rules and discipline of war (as herewith given you) and punctually to observe and follow such orders and directions from time to time as you shall receive from this or a future Congress of the said United Colonies or a committee of Congress for that purpose appointed."

Washington responded with sober humility. "Mr. President," he said, addressing Hancock but speaking to the Congress as a whole, "Though I am truly sensible of the high honor done me in this appointment, yet I feel great distress from a consciousness that my abilities and military experience may not be equal to the extensive and important trust." But Congress had called him to service, and he would answer. "I will enter upon the momentous duty and exert every power I possess in the service and for support of the glorious cause."

Still, he couldn't resist a disclaimer. "Lest some unlucky event should happen unfavourable to my reputation, I beg it may be remembered by every gentleman in the room that I this day declare with the utmost sincerity I do not think myself equal to the command I am honored with."

The commission included compensation of five hundred dollars per month for pay and expenses. Washington, perhaps recalling his earlier complaints about pay in the service of Virginia, declined the salary. "I beg leave to assure the Congress that as no pecuniary consideration could have tempted me to accept this arduous employment at the expense of my domestic ease and happiness, I do not wish to make any profit from it. I will keep an exact account of my expenses. Those I doubt not they will discharge, and that is all I desire."

Part V

Boston

40

Washington's protest that he wasn't equal to the task before him wasn't merely for the benefit of the delegates. He said the same in a letter to Martha. "My dearest," he wrote, "I am now set down to write to you on a subject which fills me with inexpressible concern. And this concern is greatly aggravated and increased when I reflect on the uneasiness I know it will give you. It has been determined in Congress that the whole army raised for the defence of the American cause shall be put under my care, and that it is necessary for me to proceed immediately to Boston to take upon me the command of it. You may believe me, my dear Patsy, when I assure you in the most solemn manner that, so far from seeking this appointment, I have used every endeavour in my power to avoid it, not only from my unwillingness to part with you and the family, but from a consciousness of its being a trust too great for my capacity."

Washington wasn't one to sell himself short. But the duty before him would have daunted anyone. He would command a continental army, if such a thing could be called into existence. Each colony had its militia, over which each colony's assembly had been jealous about relinquishing control. Washington would have to overcome these jealousies. A continental army would have to be provisioned. Washington had no provisioning authority. He would depend on the Continental Congress and the colonies. The provisioning authority of the former was nil. The authority of the latter was hardly greater. Their assemblies either had been prorogued by the governors or would be prorogued at the slightest hint of rebellion. The conventions that met in lieu of the assemblies had no standing in law and little in practice.

As challenging as the political part of his assignment was, the military part was worse. Washington would be taking on the army of the British empire. As ponderous as that army had sometimes proved in the war against France, it had weight and solidity Washington's so-far-notional force wouldn't come close to matching. Britain's soldiers were trained and disciplined. They had fought on many battlefields and defeated many foes.

They were backed by the greatest navy in the world. The British navy owned the ocean between Britain and America. It could bring provisions and fresh troops. It could land troops wherever it chose and do so without warning. It could evacuate armies from tight spots and set them down elsewhere before Washington could respond.

Washington had ample reason for thinking he wasn't up to the task before him. No one was. Yet no one was *better* qualified than he. During the last twenty-two years—of his forty-three years on earth—no American had gained more experience of war and military command. He'd been in the thick of battle and displayed courage and resourcefulness. His men responded to his example and his concern for their welfare.

At times Washington sensed that heaven watched out for him. He'd had that feeling in his first battle and in difficult moments since. He had it now. "As it has been a kind of destiny that has thrown me upon this service," he told Martha, "I shall hope that my undertaking of it is designed to answer some good purpose." He supposed the campaign at Boston would last the summer. "I shall rely, therefore, confidently on that Providence which has heretofore preserved and been bountiful to me, not doubting but that I shall return safe to you in the fall."

"THE SKIRMISH THAT HAPPENED on the 19th of April has shewn the general disposition of the provinces in a manner not to be mistaken," Thomas Gage wrote to Dartmouth shortly before Washington's appointment. "All have armed, and though there are people no doubt in all"—the provinces—"who disapprove of violent measures, and some who would join government had they opportunities, they are now borne down by force and numbers. The Congress is sitting at Philadelphia, and though nothing of great moment has yet transpired toward their resolutions, people here"—in Boston—"despair of their disposition towards works of peace." To make himself clear: "War therefore is likely to become general."

This being so, Gage urged a rapid increase in British forces in America. "Not less than fifteen thousand men should be employed on this side"—in Massachusetts. These could include regular troops, loyal Americans, Canadians and Indians. "Another body of ten thousand men should act on the side of New York, and a third corps of seven thousand, composed of some regular troops with a large corps of Canadians and Indians, on the side of Lake Champlain."

This wasn't what Dartmouth and the North ministry in London wanted to hear. The war against France was scarcely a decade in the past, and now Gage was speaking of a war against the Americans. Where did he think the troops he called for would come from? With what would they be paid?

Gage's letter was en route when he penned another, which reinforced the first. The general described the opening pitched battle of the war he predicted. At daybreak on June 17 lookouts on a British ship in the harbor spied activity on the heights above Charlestown, across the bay from Boston. The Americans appeared to be developing earthworks, presumably for cannons to fire down on Gage and his troops. Gage ordered his own guns to bombard the rebel position and dispatched troops to cross the water to Charlestown and engage the rebels directly. He was pleased to report success in the operation. "This action has shewn the superiority of the King's troops, who under every disadvantage attacked and defeated above three times their own number, strongly posted and covered by breastworks. The conduct of Major General Howe was conspicuous on this occasion, and his example spirited the troops, in which Major General Clinton assisted."

Yet though the removal of the rebels from the Charlestown peninsula, including Bunker Hill and Breed's Hill, had been accomplished, there was a catch. "I wish most sincerely that it had not cost us so dear," Gage told Dartmouth. "The number of the killed and wounded is greater than our force can afford to lose. The officers who were obliged to exert themselves have suffered very much, and we have lost some extraordinary good officers. The trials we have had shew that the rebels are not the despicable rabble too many have supposed them to be."

This was the lesson of the battle of Bunker Hill: the rebels could fight. "I find it owing to a military spirit encouraged amongst them for a few years past, joined with an uncommon degree of zeal and enthusiasm," Gage explained. "Wherever they find cover they make a good stand, and the country, naturally strong, affords it them, and they are taught to assist its natural strength by art, for they entrench and raise batteries. They have engineers to instruct them, one by the name of Gridley who served at the two sieges of Louisbourg." Gage noted the irony that what the rebels had learned fighting on behalf of Britain was now being turned against Britain.

Gage told Dartmouth to expect a long war. "The conquest of this country is not easy and can be effected only by time and perseverance, and strong armies attacking it in various quarters."

Robert Dinwiddie was the senior official of the British government in Virginia during the 1750s and gave George Washington his first military assignment.

THE

JOURNAL

OF

MAJOR *George Waſhington,*

SENT BY THE

Hon. ROBERT DINWIDDIE, Eſq;
His Majeſty's Lieutenant-Governor, and Commander in Chief of *Virginia,*

TO THE

COMMANDANT of the *French* Forces

ON

OHIO.

To which are added, the

GOVERNOR'S LETTER:

AND A

TRANSLATION of the *French* Officer's Anſwer.

WITH

A New MAP of the Country as far as the *MISSISSIPPI.*

WILLIAMSBURGH Printed,
LONDON, Reprinted for *T. Jefferys*, the Corner of St. *Martin's Lane.*

MDCCLIV.

[Price One Shilling.]

Washington's mission to Ohio put the French on notice of Britain's intent to contest the territory. His account of the mission introduced the twenty-two-year-old militia major to his fellow Americans.

Skirmishes led to a larger British campaign that ended disastrously near the Forks of the Ohio River. Washington's reputation survived, but his respect for British competence did not.

Amid the French and Indian War, George III took the throne in London. Six years younger than Washington, he inherited greater responsibilities but possessed fewer talents.

Though the war ended in a British victory, postwar retrenchment riled the Americans. New taxes and regulations provoked protests, including the mass vandalism of the Boston Tea Party.

A former comrade in arms of Washington, Thomas Gage, was ordered to teach the Americans to obey British law.

Instead of producing calm, Gage's efforts triggered armed rebellion, which began at Lexington.

To bolster the American cause, the Continental Congress created a Continental army. Washington was named commanding general.

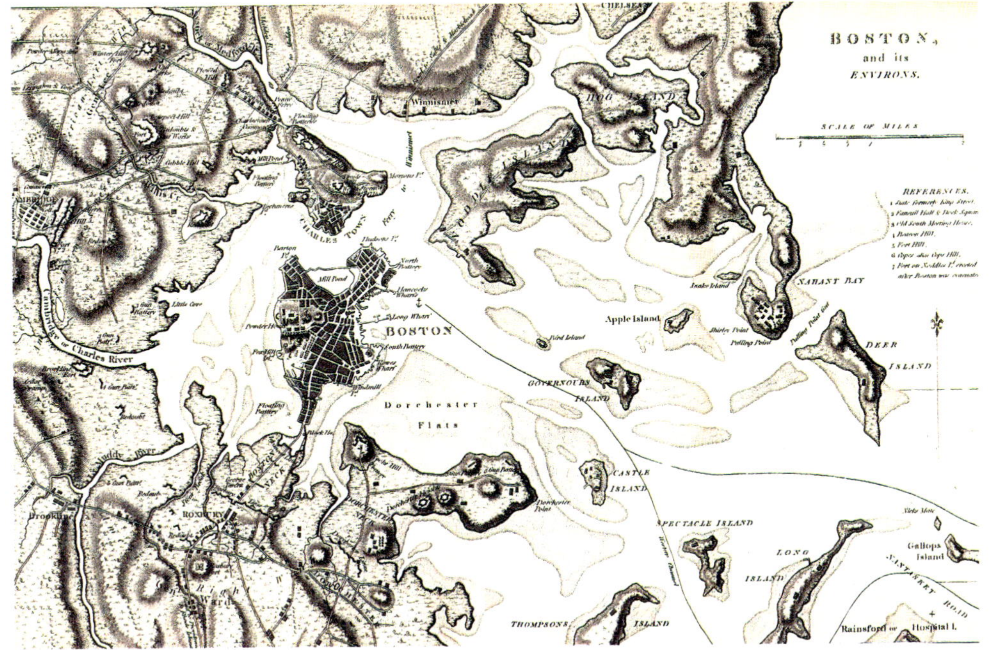

Washington joined the army outside Boston, where his soldiers besieged the British.

Washington's counterpart was William Howe. Three years older than Washington, Howe had the advantages of broader military experience and the vast resources of the British empire.

Howe gave up Boston in the spring of 1776, evacuating by ship. Washington hastened to New York to defend that strategic port. Howe outmaneuvered Washington and forced a harrowing American retreat from Long Island.

Washington's retreat didn't halt until Howe had driven him out of New York and through New Jersey into Pennsylvania. But at the end of 1776, Washington recrossed the Delaware River to land a stunning blow at Trenton.

Washington's good fortune didn't last. Howe kept him guessing before launching a campaign against Philadelphia, the seat of the Continental Congress. Washington resisted but lost the pivotal battle at Brandywine.

The British took Philadelphia, and Washington observed from outside the city. The Valley Forge winter of 1777–78 sorely tested his leadership, and though the army suffered, the experience confirmed the men's faith in their commander.

Washington's fear at this time was that British forces would seize the corridor of the Hudson River and Lake Champlain and sever New England from the rest of America. His hopes rested with Horatio Gates.

Gates came through, defeating the British army of John Burgoyne at Saratoga. This first major American victory of the war eased Washington's military problems but complicated his political position by causing many Americans to conclude that Gates should replace him.

Washington's troubles were compounded by the defection of Benedict Arnold to the British. Washington had praised and promoted Arnold, and the shocking news of Arnold's betrayal cast doubt on Washington's judgment.

Arnold was beyond Washington's reach, but John André, Arnold's British handler, was not. When Howe refused to exchange Arnold for André, Washington gave the grim order to have the young officer executed.

The victory at Saratoga having persuaded the French to ally with America, the Comte de Rochambeau (pointing) and Washington laid plans to trap the British in Virginia.

More crucial than French troops were French ships, which bested the British in the battle of the Capes at the mouth of Chesapeake Bay.

Pinned to landward by Washington and Rochambeau, and to seaward by the French fleet, the British army of Lord Cornwallis surrendered at Yorktown in October 1781.

Peace talks brought a treaty confirming American independence. Americans hailed their heroes, Washington above all.

While Washington withdrew from public life, James Madison worried that the Articles of Confederation, the national government crafted during the war, would fail the trials of peace.

Madison and Alexander Hamilton arranged a meeting of reformers in Philadelphia in 1787. Washington rebuffed invitations but changed his mind after unrest in Massachusetts threatened to unravel the union of the states.

Washington presided over the Constitutional Convention, lending credibility to its deliberations and supervising the signing at the end.

To no one's surprise, Washington was elected first president under the Constitution. He was inaugurated at Federal Hall in New York in April 1789.

Two oppositely opinionated men dominated Washington's cabinet. Thomas Jefferson was one.

Alexander Hamilton was the other.

A tax on whiskey sparked a rebellion in western Pennsylvania. Washington summoned militias and saddled up. His resolve dispersed the rebels and affirmed the authority of the government.

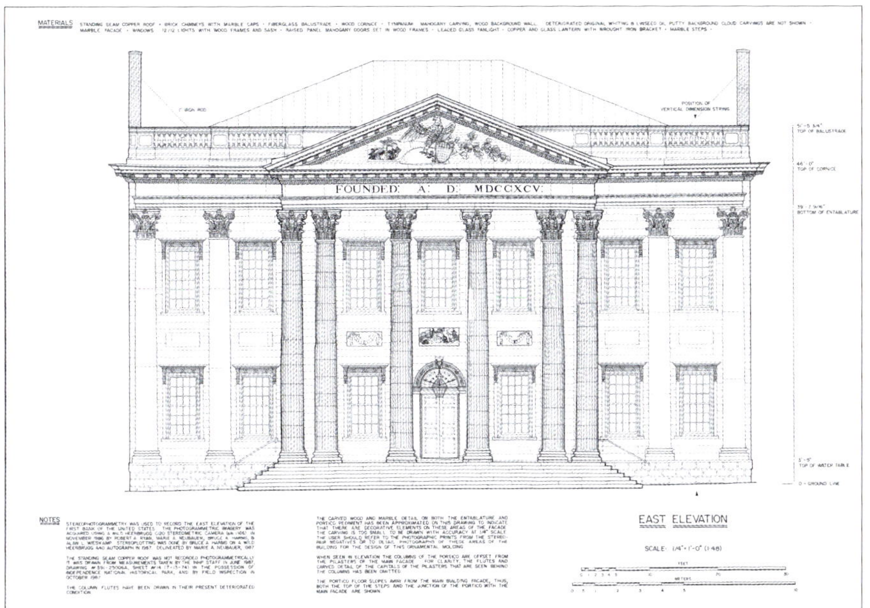

An early test of strength between Hamilton and Jefferson occurred over the Bank of the United States. Hamilton's big-government philosophy won.

Residual difficulties with Britain led Washington to send John Jay, the chief justice, to London. The resulting treaty split American politics and aggravated partisanship.

After two terms as president, Washington retired to Mount Vernon, happy to be out of politics and back to farming.

A sudden infection carried Washington off in December 1799. He lies beside Martha Washington in a tomb beside his fruit garden.

— 41 —

I have this morning been out of town to accompany our Generals Washington, Lee, and Schuyler a little way on their journey to the American camp before Boston," John Adams wrote to Abigail from Philadelphia on June 23. Lee was Charles Lee, native of England, veteran of the British army in the Seven Years' War and subsequently soldier of fortune. He moved to America in 1773, purchasing land in Virginia. The outbreak of fighting in Massachusetts prompted him to volunteer his services to the Americans against the land of his birth. Schuyler was Philip Schuyler of New York, who had fought in the French and Indian War. The Congress had commissioned Lee and Schuyler as major generals, a rank below Washington.

"The three generals were all mounted on horseback," Adams continued. "All the delegates from Massachusetts with their servants and carriages attended. Many others of the delegates from the Congress, a large troop of light horse in their uniforms, many officers of militia besides in theirs. Music playing etc. etc. Such is the pride and pomp of war. I, poor creature, worn out with scribbling for my bread and my liberty, low in spirits and weak in health, must leave others to wear the laurels which I have sown, others to eat the bread which I have earned—a common case."

The interest in Washington's departure was heightened by word of the battle of Bunker Hill. What to Gage appeared a worrisome victory seemed to most Americans a heartening defeat. They had yielded the positions around Charlestown, to be sure, but they had done so in good order and at cost to the British, whom they still besieged in Boston. They had convinced themselves, as much as they convinced Gage, that they could fight.

Washington, Lee and Schuyler rode through New Jersey. As they approached the Hudson River, they were warned to take care. A British warship lay off the Battery at the southern end of Manhattan. Its guns might be trained on ferries crossing nearby. Better to proceed north beyond range and take a ferry there. Washington and the others followed the advice.

They received a rousing welcome—to the disgust of those who disliked their cause. Thomas Jones was a native New Yorker who in 1775 served on the provincial supreme court. He blamed malcontents like Samuel Adams for the troubles with Britain and prideful gentry like George Washington for making things worse. "Washington, Lee and Schuyler, three of the first rebel generals appointed by Congress to the command of their army," wrote Jones later, "arrived from Philadelphia and were entertained at the house of Leonard Lispenard, Esq., about two miles out of town. Upon this occasion the volunteer companies raised for the express purpose of rebellion, the members of the provincial congress, those of the city committee, the parsons of the dissenting meeting-houses, with all the leaders and partisans of faction and rebellion, including"—here Jones identified several individuals he especially didn't like—"waited upon the beach to receive them upon their landing from the Jersey shore and conducted them up to Lispenard's, amidst the repeated shouts and huzzas of the seditious and rebellious multitude, where they dined and towards evening were escorted to town, attended and conducted in the same tumultuous and ridiculous manner."

It was in New York that Washington received the first detailed account of the battle of Bunker Hill. He did so only by taking liberties with his new commission. The provincial congress of Massachusetts had sent a letter addressed to the Continental Congress. The path of the letter crossed Washington's in New York, and he decided to open and read it. Naturally curious about the caliber of soldiers he would be commanding, Washington doubtless paid particular attention to the details of the battle proper. "The fire was general by twelve o'clock," the letter said of the events of June 17. "About two the enemy began to land at a point which leads out toward Noddle's Island and immediately marched up to our intrenchments, from which they were twice repulsed; but in the third attack, forced them. Our forces which were in the lines, as well as those sent for their support, were greatly annoyed on every side by balls and bombs from Copp's Hill, the ships, scows, etc. At this time the buildings in Charlestown appeared in flames in almost every quarter, kindled by hot balls, and are since laid in ashes. Though this scene was most horrible and altogether new to most of our men, yet many stood and received wounds by swords and bayonets before they quitted their lines."

The letter added that the army at Boston was badly in need of gunpowder. The provincial congress hoped the Continental Congress would remedy the lack. The Boston force also needed a commander. "We beg leave humbly to suggest that if a commander in chief over the army of the United Colonies should be appointed, it must be plain to your honors that no part of this continent can so much require his immediate presence and exertions as this colony."

Washington, in forwarding the opened letter to John Hancock and the Continental Congress, underlined the need for powder—"which I sincerely hope the Congress will supply as speedily and effectually as in their power." He added he would do his part to meet the plea of the Massachusetts men. "I propose to set off for the provincial camp tomorrow and will use all possible dispatch to join the forces there."

Before he departed, Washington provided instructions to Philip Schuyler, who would be remaining in New York. "You are to take upon you the command of all the forces destined for the New York department, and see that the orders of the Continental Congress are carried into execution with as much precision and exactness as possible," Washington wrote. Schuyler should keep close watch on William Tryon, a British army officer who was currently governor of New York. "If you find him attempting directly or indirectly any measures inimical to the common cause, use every means in your power to frustrate his designs." Washington realized he was speaking vaguely, but he couldn't help it. "It is not in my power at this time to point out the mode by which this end is to be accomplished. But if forceable measures are adjudged necessary respecting the person of the governor, I should have no difficulty in ordering of it, if the Continental Congress were not sitting. But as this is the case, and seizing of governors quite a new thing and of exceeding great importance, I must refer you to that body for direction in case his excellency the governor should make any move towards increasing the strength of the Tory party or in arming them against the cause we are embarked in." Washington recognized that Schuyler knew New York better than he did. "Your own good sense must govern in all matters not particularly pointed out."

"THE GREATEST CIVILITY and attention was paid to the generals on their arrival at the camp, which was on Sunday about noon," reported a letter to the *Pennsylvania Gazette* from Cambridge, outside Boston, dated Monday, July 3. "When they were within 20 miles of the camp, they received an express that the Parliamentary troops"—the British troops—"had, on Saturday morning about 6 o'clock, begun a very heavy cannonading on the town of Roxbury, which continued better than 2 hours without intermission, though with little or no loss on the side of the Provincials." The cannon fire was thought to be a prelude to a general attack on Sunday, which would probably take place in the early afternoon when high tide allowed British boats greatest room for maneuver. But no attack occurred, probably on account of the heavy rain that began at noon and continued until night.

Washington and Lee put the time to use. "The generals have spent this whole day in reviewing the troops, lines, fortifications, etc. They find the troops to be 15,000 strong and the works to be in as good order as could be expected." The *Gazette*'s correspondent added his own assessment of morale: "Our men are all in good spirits."

Washington introduced himself to his new army via general orders. "The Continental Congress having now taken all the troops of the several colonies which have been raised or which may be hereafter raised for the support and defence of the liberties of America into their pay and service, they are now the troops of the United Provinces of North America," he declared on July 4. "And it is hoped that all distinctions of colonies will be laid aside, so that one and the same spirit may animate the whole, and the only contest be who shall render on this great and trying occasion the most essential service to the great and common cause in which we are all engaged."

What came next reflected what Washington had learned from his command in Virginia. "It is required and expected that exact discipline be observed and due subordination prevail through the whole army, as a failure in these most essential points must necessarily produce extreme hazard, disorder and confusion, and end in shameful disappointment and disgrace. The General most earnestly requires and expects a due observance of those articles of war, established for the government of the army which forbid profane cursing, swearing and drunkenness, and in like manner requires and expects of all officers and soldiers not engaged on actual duty a punctual attendance on divine service, to implore the blessings of heaven upon the means used for our safety and defence."

The officers would set the tone. "All officers are required and expected to pay diligent attention to keep their men neat and clean—to visit them often at their quarters and inculcate upon them the necessity of cleanliness, as essential to their health and service. They are particularly to see that they have straw to lay on, if to be had, and to make it known if they are destitute of this article. They are also to take care that necessaries"—latrines—"be provided in the camps and frequently filled up to prevent their being offensive and unhealthy."

Ammunition must be husbanded. "It is strictly required and commanded that there be no firing of cannon or small arms from any of the lines or elsewhere, except in case of necessary, immediate defence, or special order given for that purpose." Intelligence about the enemy was crucial. "All prisoners taken, deserters coming in, persons coming out of Boston who can give any intelligence, any captures of any kind from the enemy are to be immediately reported and brought up to headquarters in Cambridge."

Discipline would be enforced fairly but firmly. "A general court martial is ordered to sit tomorrow at 10 o'clock A.M. for the trial of William Patten charged with 'leaving his post on guard'; David Wells and Gideon Cole for 'sleeping on their posts as sentinels'; John Scott for 'insulting the sentry and attempting to pass the guard at Boston'; and James Foster for 'theft.'"

Other offenses were more serious. "It is with inexpressible concern that the General upon his first arrival in the army should find an officer sentenced by a general court martial to be cashiered for cowardice—a crime of all others the most infamous in a soldier, the most injurious to an army, and the last to be forgiven, inasmuch as it may and often does happen that the cowardice of a single officer may prove the destruction of the whole army." Washington had reviewed the case and endorsed its verdict.

"He now therefore most earnestly exhorts officers of all ranks to shew an example of bravery and courage to their men," he continued, referring to himself, "assuring them that such as do their duty in the day of battle as brave and good officers shall be honored with every mark of distinction and regard, their names and merits made known to the general Congress and all America; while on the other hand, he positively declares that every officer, be his rank what it may, who shall betray his country, dishonour the army and his General by basely keeping back and shrinking from his duty in any engagement, shall be held up as an infamous coward and punished as such with the utmost martial severity."

42

As commanding general, Washington naturally thought of the British army before him as the enemy. Their soldiers were trying to kill his soldiers. How else could he describe them?

The Continental Congress wasn't sure how to think of Britain. The British army was fighting the army of the Congress. But what were the two armies fighting for?

The heart of the question for the Congress was whether it wanted to restore the British colonial government in America to something like what it was before the Stamp Act, or to create a new government for a new country. The delegates all endorsed American liberty, but did American liberty require American independence?

The Congress did what congresses do in such cases: it formed a committee. Thomas Jefferson was on the committee, and with the encouragement of the other members he drafted a statement of purpose. "It was too strong for Mr. Dickinson," Jefferson recalled, speaking of John Dickinson of Delaware, who had written the petition to the king the previous year. "He still retained the hope of reconciliation with the mother country, and was unwilling it should be lessened by offensive statements. He was so honest a man, and so able a one that he was greatly indulged even by those who could not feel his scruples. We therefore requested him to take the paper and put it into a form he could approve. He did so, preparing an entire new statement, and preserving of the former only the last paragraphs and half of the preceding one. We approved and reported it to Congress, who accepted it. Congress gave a signal proof of their indulgence to Mr. Dickinson, and of their great desire not to go too fast for any respectable part of our body, in permitting him to draw their second petition to the King according to his own ideas, and passing it with scarcely any amendment. The disgust against this humility was general; and Mr. Dickinson's delight at its passage was the only circumstance which reconciled them to it. The vote being passed, although further observation on it was out of order, he could not refrain from rising and expressing his satisfaction and concluded by saying 'there is but one word, Mr. President, in the paper which I disapprove, and that is the word "Congress,"' on which Ben Harrison rose and said 'there is but one word in the paper, Mr. President, of which I approve, and that is the word "Congress."'"

"A Declaration by the Representatives of the United Colonies of North America, now met in Congress at Philadelphia, setting forth the causes and necessity of their taking up Arms," was the title the Congress affixed to Dickinson's statement, which wasn't as milquetoast as Benjamin Harrison, a fellow Virginian to Jefferson, suggested. Parliament, it said, "stimulated by an inordinate passion for a power," had adopted the "cruel and impolitic purpose of enslaving these colonies by violence." After the last war, "these devoted colonies were judged to be in such a state as to present victories without bloodshed and all the easy emoluments of statutable plunder." One new tax after another had been levied to pick the pockets of the Americans. When the Americans complained, new laws abridged ancient rights. Parliament audaciously asserted the right to make laws to bind the colonies in all cases whatsoever. "What is to defend us against so enormous, so unlimited a power?"

Nothing but American arms, the declaration of Congress averred. Petitions and entreaties were ignored. Nay, they were answered with armed force. General Gage, unprovoked, had descended on Lexington and Concord to deprive the residents of their property and thereby their means to defend their liberties. They responded as free men must.

The Congress was coming to their aid. The perfidious ministry in London had better take note. "Our cause is just," the declaration asserted. "Our union is perfect. Our internal resources are great, and, if necessary, foreign assistance is undoubtedly attainable." Dickinson and the Congress must have realized this last clause would explode like a bombshell in London, for it threatened an alliance between America and France. A clearer statement of treasonous intent was harder to imagine.

Yet for now it was merely a warning. "Lest this declaration should disquiet the minds of our friends and fellow-subjects in any part of the Empire, we assure them that we mean not to dissolve that union which has so long and so happily subsisted between us, and which we sincerely wish to see restored. Necessity has not yet driven us into that desperate measure, or induced us to excite any other nation to war against them. We have not raised armies with ambitious designs of separating from

Great Britain and establishing independent states. We fight not for glory or for conquest." Americans fought only for their liberty and their rights under the English constitution. "In our own native land, in defence of the freedom that is our birth-right, and which we ever enjoyed till the late violation of it; for the protection of our property, acquired solely by the honest industry of our forefathers and ourselves, against violence actually offered, we have taken up arms. We shall lay them down when hostilities shall cease on the part of the aggressors and all danger of their being renewed shall be removed, and not before."

BRANDISHING A SWORD in one hand, the Congress offered an olive branch with the other. A second document, also drafted by Dickinson and in fact soon dubbed the Olive Branch Petition, accompanied the declaration of the causes of taking arms. Addressed to America's "Most Gracious Sovereign," it cast the current troubles as the work of evil ministers and invited George to turn back the calendar between Britain and the colonies. "We solemnly assure your Majesty that we not only most ardently desire the former harmony between her and these colonies may be restored, but that a concord may be established between them upon so firm a basis as to perpetuate its blessings, uninterrupted by any future dissensions, to succeeding generations in both countries." Americans were willing to forgive and forget. "Notwithstanding the sufferings of your loyal colonists during the course of the present controversy, our breasts retain too tender a regard for the kingdom from which we derive our origin to request such a reconciliation as might in any manner be inconsistent with her dignity or her welfare." The future of the empire lay in George's hands. "The apprehensions that now oppress our hearts with unspeakable grief, being once removed, your Majesty will find your faithful subjects on this continent ready and willing at all times, as they ever have been, with their lives and fortunes to assert and maintain the rights and interests of your Majesty, and of our Mother country." The petition closed on another affectionate note: "That your Majesty may enjoy a long and prosperous reign, and that your descendants may govern your dominions with honor to themselves and happiness to their subjects, is our sincere and fervent prayer."

43

"Dear Brother," Washington wrote to Jack Washington in late July, summarizing his first three weeks on the new job. "I found a mixed multitude of people here, under very little discipline, order, or government. I found the enemy in possession of a place called Bunker's Hill, on Charlestown Neck, strongly intrenched and fortifying themselves. I found part of our army on two hills (called Winter and Prospect Hills) about a mile and a quarter from the enemy on Bunker's Hill, in a very insecure state. I found another part of the army at this village"—Cambridge—"and a third part at Roxbury, guarding the entrance in and out of Boston. My whole time since I came here has been employed in throwing up lines of defence at these three several places, to secure, in the first instance, our own troops from any attempts of the enemy, and, in the next place, to cut off all communication between their troops and the country. To do this, and to prevent them from penetrating into the country with fire and sword, and to harass them if they do, is all that is expected of me, and if effected, must totally overthrow the designs of administration, as the whole force of Great Britain in the town and harbor of Boston can answer no other end than to sink her under the disgrace and weight of the expense."

This was Washington's strategy: to parry Britain's military efforts and thereby to outlast Britain's political will. Simple enough to articulate, it might be hard to accomplish. Washington reckoned the British force under Gage at twelve thousand men and his own at sixteen thousand. Yet this advantage was hardly decisive. "We have a semicircle of eight or nine miles to guard, to every part of which we are obliged to be equally attentive, whilst they, situated as it were in the center of the semicircle, can bend their whole force (having the entire command of the water) against any one part of it with equal facility."

Gage had to deal with the difficulties of a siege. "The enemy are sickly and scarce of fresh provisions," Washington wrote. He had this information from Bostonians who had crossed the siege lines. "Beef, which is chiefly got by slaughtering their milch cows in Boston, sells from one shilling to eighteen pence sterling per pound, and that it may not get cheaper or more plenty, I have drove all the stock, within a considerable distance of this place, back into the country, out of the way of the men-of-war's boats. In short, I have done and shall continue to do everything in my power to distress them."

Washington expected further action from Gage. "The transports are all arrived, and their whole reinforcement is landed, so that I can see no reason why they should not, if they ever attempt it, come boldly out, and put the matter to issue at once." But maybe Gage was too cautious for a direct attack. "If they think themselves not strong enough to do this, they surely will carry their arms (having ships of war and transports ready) to some other part of the continent."

Washington wanted Gage to come out and fight. If the British decided to skip away, all Washington's work around Boston would have been wasted, and he wouldn't know where they were going to land until they arrived. A war like that could go on forever.

OR AT LEAST UNTIL the next year. In early August, Washington's informants revealed that Gage was stockpiling coal. This could mean but one thing: he was planning to spend the winter in Boston. Which meant Washington must spend the winter outside Boston. "I have directed that such huts as have been lately made of boards should be done in such a manner that if necessary they may serve for covering during the winter," he reported to John Hancock and the Continental Congress. Washington added that much else would be needed for a winter siege: food, clothing, fuel. Congress must provide these. Otherwise he wouldn't be able to hold the army together. Hungry and shivering soldiers would head for their homes.

Doubtless this was part of Gage's plan. His soldiers couldn't easily desert, for their homes were thousands of miles away. But for many of Washington's men, a welcoming hearth was within walking distance.

Some were already taking unauthorized leave. Washington complained of the matter to James Otis Sr., president of the Massachusetts provisional council. "I find there are a great number of soldiers and non-commissioned officers who absent themselves from duty, the greatest part of which I have reason to believe are at their respective homes in different parts of the country"—province—"some employed by their officers on their farms and others drawing pay from the public while they are working on their own plantations, or for hire." Washington pleaded for help. "My utmost exertions have not been able to prevent this base and pernicious conduct. I must therefore beg the assistance of the general court to cooperate with me in such measures as may remedy this mischief." People in the communities to which the deserters had gone knew they had come. These people should report the slackers so that Washington could make examples of a few as warning to the rest. "I need not enlarge upon the ruinous consequences of suffering such infamous deserters and defrauders of the public to go unnoticed or unpunished."

WASHINGTON COMMUNICATED WITH Gage as well. By the late eighteenth century, customs of warfare had been well established in Europe. Among these were the proper treatment of prisoners, often leading to exchanges. But war supposed belligerents to be sovereign nations. By no stretch of the British imagination did America constitute a sovereign nation. Few Americans as yet considered it such, and no provisional or presumptive American government had declared it to be. By the most reasonable interpretation, Washington headed an insurrectionary force against the army of the established government of Britain.

Yet Washington wanted the rules of war to apply to his army, in particular to prisoners held by the British. "I understand that the officers engaged in the cause of liberty and their country, who by the fortune of war have fallen into your hands, have been thrown indiscriminately, into a common gaol appropriated for felons," Washington wrote to Gage. "That no consideration has been had for those of the most respectable rank when languishing with wounds and sickness. That some have been even amputated in this unworthy situation." Washington didn't expect Gage to honor the principle for which the prisoners fought—"a love of freedom and their country"—but he expected better from a fellow soldier. "The obligations arising from the rights of humanity and claims of rank are universally binding and extensive, except in case of retaliation. These I should have hoped would have dictated a more tender treatment of those individuals whom chance or war had put in your power."

Washington had mentioned retaliation advisedly. "My duty now makes it necessary to apprize you that for the future I shall regulate my conduct towards those gentlemen who are or may be in our possession exactly by the rule which you shall observe towards those of ours who may be in your custody. If severity and hardship mark the line of your conduct, painful as it may be to me your prisoners will feel its effects. But if kindness and humanity are shewn to ours, I shall with pleasure consider those in our hands only as unfortunate, and they shall receive the treatment to which the unfortunate are ever entitled."

Gage declined to be instructed by an insurrectionist provincial. "To the glory of civilized nations, humanity and war have been compatible, and compassion to the subdued is become almost a general system," he replied to Washington. "Britons, ever preeminent in mercy, have outgone common examples and overlooked the criminal in the captive." Gage, too, chose his words carefully, in his case the reference to crime. "Your prisoners, whose lives by the laws of the land are destined to the cord"—death by hanging—"have hitherto been treated with care and kindness and more comfortably lodged than the King's troops in the hospitals." Gage granted that he didn't distinguish between officers and men. "I acknowledge no rank that is not derived from the King."

Washington had claimed principle for the actions of his army, Gage observed. Did he not acknowledge that the British were motivated by principle, too? Gage relied on it, and would continue to rely on it. "I trust that British soldiers asserting the rights of the state, the laws of the land, the being of the constitution, will meet all events with becoming fortitude. They will court victory with the spirit their cause inspires, and from the same motive will find the patience of martyrs under misfortune."

Washington realized he wouldn't get Gage to admit the rectitude of the Americans' actions. Yet he wouldn't let his old comrade have the last word. "You affect, sir, to despise all rank not derived from the same source with your own," he wrote. "I cannot conceive any more honourable than that which flows from the uncorrupted choice of a brave and free people, the purest source and original fountain of all power." There was no more to be said. "I shall now, sir, close my correspondence with you, perhaps forever."

44

Indeed this was the last of the correspondence between Washington and Gage. The British government, unable to decide whether Gage was more culpable for having provoked the fighting in America by his bumbling raid on Lexington and Concord or for heartening the rebels by his Pyrrhic victory at Bunker Hill, relieved him of his command. In his place London chose William Howe.

Washington meanwhile worked to widen the theater of conflict. Weeks after Lexington and Concord, New England militia under Ethan Allen and Benedict Arnold rowed across Lake Champlain and surprised a British garrison at Ticonderoga, at the southern end of the lake and athwart the ancient path between the valley of the Hudson River and that of the St. Lawrence. Washington weighed how the victory could be exploited. In August his thoughts came together. "The design of this express is to communicate to you a plan of an expedition which has engrossed my thoughts for several days," he wrote to Philip Schuyler, the major general he had dropped off in New York. "It is to penetrate into Canada by way of Kennebec River"—in Maine, then part of Massachusetts—"and so to Quebec, by a route 90 miles below Montreal. I can very well spare a detachment of 1000 or 1200 men, and the land carriage by the route proposed is too inconsiderable to make an objection." Washington's estimate of the ease of the Kennebec route was wrong, but Benedict Arnold, whom Washington chose to lead the mission, discovered this only later.

Washington wanted Schuyler to lead a second column into Canada. "It would make a diversion that would distract Carlton"—Guy Carleton, the governor-general of Canada. Carleton would have to choose between Arnold and Schuyler in making his defense. A victory in Canada would have a "decisive effect on the public interests," Washington said. Realizing that Canada was at risk might bring the British to their senses. At the least, it would give them more to think about.

Washington asked Schuyler for intelligence: "what late accounts you have had from Canada, your opinion of the temper of the inhabitants as well as Indians upon a penetration into their country, what number of troops are at Quebec and whether any men of war, and all other circumstances which may be material in the consideration of a measure of such importance."

Schuyler should move as quickly as possible. "Not a moment's time is to be lost in the preparation for this enterprize," Washington said.

"YOU ARE ENTRUSTED with a command of the utmost consequence to the interest and liberties of America," Washington wrote to Benedict Arnold three weeks later. "Upon your conduct and courage and that of the officers and soldiers detached on this expedition not only the success of the present enterprize and your own honour but the safety and welfare of the whole continent may depend."

This was a lot of responsibility to be given to someone with little experience of war. Arnold had been a merchant in Connecticut before the fighting broke out. He joined the Connecticut militia and marched to the siege of Boston, but inaction there prompted him to propose a dash to Ticonderoga, where his company joined the force of Ethan Allen for the victory, which included the capture of scores of cannons. Arnold oversaw the transport of the guns to Boston, where they substantially augmented Washington's batteries. Washington perceived Arnold as a man who got things done.

The Canada mission was delicate. The Canadians hadn't rallied to the cause of the English-speaking colonies, but neither had they hastened to defend the British crown. Arnold should encourage the former action but at all costs prevent the latter. "I charge you therefore, and the officers and soldiers under your command, as you value your own safety and honour, and the favour and esteem of your country, that you consider yourselves as marching not through an enemy's country but that of our friends and brethren," Washington told Arnold.

This wouldn't be easy. Some of those with Arnold knew the Canadians and their Indian allies only as foes from the war with France. Arnold must restrain his troops. "Check by every motive of duty and fear of punishment every attempt to plunder or insult any of the inhabitants of Canada. Should any American soldier be so base and infamous as to injure any Canadian or Indian in his person or property, I do most earnestly enjoin you to bring him to such severe and exemplary punishment as the enormity of the crime may require. Should it extend to death itself, it will not be disproportionate to its guilt at such a time and in such a cause." Arnold's care should extend to matters of faith. "Avoid all disrespect or contempt of the religion of the country and its ceremonies," Washington said. "While we are contending for our own liberty, we should be very cautious of violating the rights of conscience in others, ever considering that God alone is the judge of the hearts of men, and to him only in this case they are answerable."

The stakes couldn't be higher. This was the message Arnold must convey to his men. "Represent to them the shame and disgrace and ruin to themselves and country if they should by their conduct turn the hearts of our brethren in Canada against us. And on the other hand the honour and rewards which await them if by their prudence and good behaviour they conciliate the affections of the Canadians and Indians to the great interests of America."

WASHINGTON HAD A MESSAGE for the Canadians too. He wasn't a preacher or a pamphleteer, but on this occasion he drafted a sermon that was printed in English and French on broadsides for Arnold to distribute in Canada. "Friends and Brethren," Washington proclaimed, "The unnatural contest between the English colonies and Great Britain has now risen to such a height that arms alone must decide it. The colonies, confiding in the justice of their cause and the purity of their intentions, have reluctantly appealed to that Being in whose hands are all human events. He has hitherto smiled upon their virtuous efforts. The hand of tyranny has been arrested in its ravages, and the British arms which have shone with so much splendor in every part of the globe are now tarnished with disgrace and disappointment."

The British had underestimated the English colonies, and they underestimated Canada as well. "They have persuaded themselves, they have even dared to say, that the Canadians were not capable of distinguishing between the blessings of liberty and the wretchedness of slavery, that gratifying the vanity of a little circle of nobility would blind the eyes of the people of Canada." Washington knew better. The fire of liberty burned as bright in the hearts of Canadians as in their brothers to the south. "Come then, my brethren, unite with us in an indissoluble union, let us run together to the same goal."

The Canadians should take not alarm but courage from the approach of two American armies. "The grand American Congress have sent an army into your province under the command of General Schuyler, not to plunder but to protect you," Washington said. "To cooperate with this design, and to frustrate those cruel and perfidious schemes which would deluge our frontiers with the blood of women and children, I have detached Colonel Arnold into your country with a part of the army under my command." Canadians had nothing to fear. "Let no man desert his habitation. Let no one flee as before an enemy."

Canadians instead should rally to the side of their American defenders. "The cause of America, and of liberty, is the cause of every virtuous American citizen, whatever may be his religion or his descent," Washington said, sweeping Canadians into the category of Americans. "Come then, ye generous citizens, range yourselves under the standard of general liberty, against which all the force and artifice of tyranny will never be able to prevail."

45

Washington was willing to send soldiers to Canada not least because he wasn't sure he could sustain them at Boston. The excitement of April and the drama of June had worn off by September, abraded by the static nature of the conflict. Soldiers in camp had time to grouse about the army and their officers and to worry about their wives and children. If they weren't going to be fighting, many reasoned, they ought to be farming or smithing or whatever kept the home front secure.

Some things Washington couldn't control. But others he might, with the help of the Continental Congress. Washington's soldiers had enlisted in their home colonies under various conditions. Pay scales differed from colony to colony, as did the length of terms of service. The discrepancies complicated Washington's efforts to forge a single army out of the colonial militias. In fact they imperiled the existence of the army itself. "The Connecticut and Rhode Island troops stand engaged to the first of December only," he wrote to John Hancock and the Congress in mid-September. Other troops would be discharged on January 1. "A dissolution of the present army therefore will take place unless some early provision is made against such an event." Washington requested authority and resources to reenlist the men. He intended to do so according to a uniform standard, regardless of the province the soldiers came from.

Washington specified the needs of his army for the coming winter. "So far as regards the preservation of the army from cold, they may be deemed in a state of nakedness," he told Hancock. "Many of the men have been without blankets the whole campaign, and those which have been in use during the summer are so much worn as to be of little service." Blankets, uniforms and shoes were essential if the army were to hold together. Housing was crucial. "The season advances so fast that I have given orders to prepare barracks and other accommodations for the winter."

Washington disliked having to supplicate. "It gives me great pain to be obliged to solicit the attention of the honorable Congress to the state of this army in terms which imply the slightest apprehension of being neglected," he told Hancock. "But my situation is inexpressibly distressing, to see the winter fast approaching upon a naked army, the time of their service within a few weeks of expiring, and no provision yet made for such important events."

Moreover, he was broke. "The military chest is totally exhausted. The paymaster has not a single dollar in hand. The commissary general assures me he has strained his credit for the subsistence of the army to the utmost. The quartermaster general is precisely in the same situation. And the greater part of the troops are in a state not far from mutiny upon the deduction from their stated allowance." The soldiers' pay had had to be cut due to insufficient funds. Washington couldn't morally fault the men, who relied on this pay to feed their families back home.

"I know not to whom I am to impute this failure," he told Hancock. "But I am of opinion if the evil is not immediately remedied and more punctuality observed in future, the army must absolutely break up."

TACT ALONE DIDN'T cause Washington to claim ignorance regarding blame. The Continental Congress had taken a blind leap in nationalizing the militia into a single Continental army. The Congress had no taxing authority to raise funds to support the army, and no reasonable prospect of acquiring such authority. Hancock and the Congress could ask the colonies to contribute, but the provisional congresses that had replaced the assemblies in the colonies had no taxing authority either. For the time being, the existence of Washington's army relied on voluntary contributions from persons committed to the anti-Parliament resistance.

The Congress responded to Washington's plea by forming a committee to confer with him. Benjamin Franklin, Benjamin Harrison and Thomas Lynch were the members, and they traveled to Cambridge in October. Franklin was as observant as he always was, and being a Boston native, he took particular note of the appearance of the Bostonians he encountered near Washington's camp at Cambridge. He was pleased by what he saw. "There are as many cheerful countenances among those who are driven from house and home at Boston or lost their all at Charlestown as among other people," he remarked to his son-in-law, Richard

Bache. "Not a murmur has yet been heard that if they had been less zealous in the cause of liberty they might still have enjoyed their possessions."

Franklin hoped morale would remain high, and that it would prompt the sacrifices needed to sustain the fight against Britain. "Though I am for the most prudent parsimony of the public treasure, I am not terrified by the expence of this war, should it continue ever so long," Franklin told Bache. "A little more frugality or a little more industry in individuals will with ease defray it. Suppose it £100,000 a month or £1,200,000 a year. If 500,000 families will each spend a shilling a week less, or earn a shilling a week more, or if they will spend 6 pence a week less and earn 6 pence a week more, they may pay the whole sum without otherwise feeling it. Forbearing to drink tea saves three fourths of the money, and 500,000 women doing each threepence worth of spinning or knitting in a week will pay the rest. How much more then may be done by the superior frugality and industry of the men?" Franklin hoped for peace, but not at the sacrifice of American liberty. "We have nothing to expect from submission but slavery and contempt."

Franklin, Harrison and Lynch met with Washington over several days. He enumerated the army he considered necessary and appropriate to the task at hand. Each regiment should consist of 728 men, including officers. Each regiment should be divided into eight companies. Each company should consist of 1 captain, 2 lieutenants, 1 ensign, 4 sergeants, 4 corporals, 2 drums or fifes and 76 privates. The army should total 20,372 officers and men.

Each soldier's rations should consist of one pound of beef, three-quarters pound of pork or one pound of salt fish per day. Also one pound of bread or flour per day, three pints of beans per week, one pint of milk per day, one-half pint of rice or one pint of cornmeal per week, one quart of spruce beer or cider per day (or nine gallons of molasses per company per week, to make rum), three pounds of candles per one hundred men per week, twenty-four pounds of soft soap or eight pounds of hard soap per one hundred men per week.

Firearms should be standardized: "good firelocks with bayonets, each firelock to be made with a good bridle lock, ¾ of an inch in the bore and of good substance at the breech, the barrel to be 3 feet 8 inches in length and a bayonet of 18 inches in the blade," in the words of the report Franklin's committee filed with the Continental Congress.

Washington recommended and the committee concurred that pay

should be standardized within ranks. Existing, or rather promised, pay mustn't be cut. "The proposition of lowering the pay of the troops would be attended with dangerous consequences," the committee said.

Washington recommended and the committee agreed that he must be given explicit authority to deal with deserters, mutineers and other misbehavers. The most serious violations should be punishable by death.

Captured prisoners should be treated "as prisoners of war but with humanity." On the question of whether Negroes, slave or free, should be enlisted: "Agreed that they be rejected altogether." Indian allies should be cultivated.

Certain questions with broad ramifications were referred to the Congress. That body should establish a policy for interdicting British supply ships, which until this point sailed unopposed. Washington especially sought guidance on how to deal with Boston and the British garrison there. "The General wishes to know how far it may be deemed proper and advisable to avail himself of the season to destroy the troops who propose to winter in Boston by a bombardment, when the harbour is blocked up." There was no point bombarding the garrison in the town now, for British ships could carry the troops away. This escape route would close when the harbor froze. Anyway, Washington didn't yet have the cannons.

But bombarding the garrison risked destroying the town. Was the benefit worth the cost? "The committee are of opinion this is a matter of too much consequence to be determined by them and therefore refer it to the honorable Congress."

46

"We have had a very fatiguing time," Benedict Arnold wrote to Washington from the march to Canada. "The men, in general not understanding batteaus, have been obliged to wade and haul them more than half way up the river." Yet Arnold was hopeful. "As the men are in high spirits, I make no doubt of reaching the River Chaudiere in eight or ten days, the greatest difficulty being, I hope, already past." The Chaudière would carry Arnold's column down to the St. Lawrence, entering that stream opposite the city of Quebec. Arnold acknowledged his slow progress. "But when you consider the badness and weight of the batteaus and large quantity of provisions etc. we have been obliged to force up against a very rapid stream"—the Kennebec—"where you would have taken the men for amphibious animals, as they were a great part of the time under water, add to this the great fatigue in portage, you will think I have pushed the men as fast as they could possibly bear. The officers, volunteers and privates in general have acted with the greatest spirit and industry."

The difficulties multiplied. "I have been much deceived in every account of our route, which is longer and has been attended with a thousand difficulties I never apprehended," Arnold wrote two weeks later. But he remained hopeful. "If crowned with success and conducive to the public good, I shall think it but trifling," he said of the effort being required of his men.

Another two weeks brought additional challenges. Illness from the fatigue and exposure, compounded by short rations, reduced the strength of Arnold's column. Yet after reaching the Chaudière, he pressed on. "I accordingly set out the 28th"—October 28—"early in the morning and descended the river, amazingly rapid and rocky for about twenty miles, where we had the misfortune to stave three of our batteaus, and lose their provisions etc. but happily no lives." They reached the St. Lawrence two days later, minus one man who had drowned.

Per the original plan, Arnold had hoped to rendezvous with Philip Schuyler. But Schuyler had fallen sick and his command devolved to Richard Montgomery, who reached Montreal and subdued the city. Montgomery then headed down the St. Lawrence to meet Arnold. Quebec was still as formidable geographically as it had been in the days of Montcalm and Wolfe, and this time the defenders rather than the attackers had naval superiority. Believing delay worked against them, Montgomery and Arnold assaulted Quebec in a December snowstorm. They failed miserably, with Montgomery decapitated by a load of grapeshot from a cannon, Arnold's leg shattered by a musket ball, and nearly half the American force killed, captured or wounded.

"I received the melancholy account of the unfortunate attack on the City of Quebec, attended with the fall of General Montgomery and other brave officers and men, and your being wounded," Washington wrote to Arnold in January 1776. "This unhappy affair affects me in a very sensible manner, and I sincerely condole with you upon the occasion."

Yet he wanted Arnold to try again. "I need not mention to you the great importance of this place and the consequent possession of all Canada in the scale of American affairs," Washington said. "To whomsoever it belongs, in their favour probably will the balance turn. If it is in ours, success I think will most certainly crown our virtuous struggles. If it is in theirs, the contest at best will be doubtful, hazardous and bloody. The glorious work must be accomplished in the course of this winter, otherwise it will become difficult, most probably impracticable." London would send reinforcements that would overwhelm what Washington could provide.

Washington had a high opinion of Arnold's valor and constancy. If anyone could take Quebec, Arnold could. "I already view the approaching day when you and your brave followers will enter this important fortress with every honor and triumph attendant on victory and conquest. Then will you have added the only link wanting in the great chain of continental union and render the freedom of your country secure."

Arnold promised to do what he could. "You may be assured my utmost exertions will not be wanting to effect your wishes in adding it"—Canada—"to the United Colonies," he replied to Washington. Victory wouldn't come easily. "Notwithstanding every precaution that could be used, the smallpox has crept in among the troops. We have near one hundred men in the hospital." The winter was harsh, provisions were short, the soldiers chafed at late pay, and the locals rejected Washington's invitation to join the American cause. "I have often been at a loss how to conduct matters," Arnold told Washington.

47

Fresh eyes see things withheld from the weary. Standing too close to events induces myopia. Newcomers, lacking a stake in the status quo, have less reason to defend it.

Thomas Paine was a newcomer to America, having emigrated from England only at the end of 1774. He landed in Philadelphia on the recommendation of Benjamin Franklin, whom he had met in London while Franklin served as agent for Pennsylvania and other states. Paine was drawn to political controversy, and he reveled in the debates of the Continental Congress in his adopted city. He weighed the arguments and drew his own conclusions. By the end of 1775 he had decided that the fighting between the Americans and the British must lead to independence for America.

"In the following pages I offer nothing more than simple facts, plain arguments, and common sense," Paine declared at the start of a pamphlet called *Common Sense,* which appeared in January 1776. America had been at arms against Britain for most of a year, yet most Americans clung to hope of reconciliation. This was fatuous, said Paine. "I challenge the warmest advocate for reconciliation to show a single advantage that this continent can reap by being connected with Great Britain. I repeat the challenge; not a single advantage is derived. Our corn will fetch its price in any market in Europe, and our imported goods must be paid for buy them where we will."

In contrast, reasons for severing the connection were many and strong. "The injuries and disadvantages which we sustain by that connection are without number," Paine said. "Any submission to or dependance on Great Britain tends directly to involve this continent in European wars and quarrels and set us at variance with nations who would otherwise seek our friendship and against whom we have neither anger nor complaint. As Europe is our market for trade, we ought to form no partial connection with any part of it. It is the true interest of America to steer clear of

European contentions, which she never can do while, by her dependance on Britain, she is made the make-weight in the scale of British politics."

Some cited America's English heritage as cause to stay connected to Britain. Paine, noting the Scots and Germans in Pennsylvania and other colonies, thought this Englishness exaggerated. "But admitting that we were all of English descent, what does it amount to? Nothing. Britain, being now an open enemy, extinguishes every other name and title, and to say that reconciliation is our duty is truly farcical. The first king of England, of the present line (William the Conqueror) was a Frenchman, and half the peers of England are descendants from the same country; wherefore, by the same method of reasoning, England ought to be governed by France."

Some Americans felt a debt for the protection Britain had provided against the French. This was foolish, too. "Her motive was *interest* not *attachment*," said Paine. "She did not protect us from *our enemies* on *our account*, but from *her enemies* on *her own account*, from those who had no quarrel with us on any *other account*, and who will always be our enemies on the *same account*." Americans had required protection from France because they were connected to Britain. Were the connection severed, France would have no quarrel with America, nor America with France.

Paine expanded this point. "Europe is too thickly planted with kingdoms to be long at peace, and whenever a war breaks out between England and any foreign power, the trade of America goes to ruin, *because of her connection with Britain*. The next war may not turn out like the last, and should it not, the advocates for reconciliation now will be wishing for separation then, because neutrality in that case would be a safer convoy than a man of war."

Paine generalized: "America is only a secondary object in the system of British politics. England consults the good of this country no further than it answers her own purpose." This had always been so, and it would remain so as long as America remained an appendage of England.

America must separate from England not for America's sake alone. The freedom of all men was at stake. "O! ye that love mankind! Ye that dare oppose not only the tyranny but the tyrant, stand forth! Every spot of the old world is overrun with oppression. Freedom hath been hunted round the globe. Asia and Africa have long expelled her. Europe regards her like a stranger, and England hath given her warning to depart." Speaking directly to his new compatriots, Paine pleaded, "O! receive the fugitive, and prepare in time an asylum for mankind."

Reason required one conclusion. "Nothing can settle our affairs so expeditiously as an open and determined declaration for independence." Morality and nine months of war said the same thing. "Everything that is right or reasonable pleads for separation. The blood of the slain, the weeping voice of nature cries, 'TIS TIME TO PART."

48

"The small pox is a terrible enemy," John Adams wrote to Samuel Cooper, a Boston friend. "Cruel small pox! worse than the sword!" he declared to his wife, Abigail. "The small pox! The small pox! What shall we do with it?" he expostulated to Abigail in another letter.

Smallpox was on everyone's mind during the first six months of 1776. It finally killed the hopes of Benedict Arnold of capturing Quebec. "Our army consists of few more than two thousand effective men, and twelve hundred sick and unfit for duty chiefly with the small pox, which is universal in the country," Arnold wrote to Washington in May. Arnold was lucky to lead his army out of Canada in the months that followed.

No one worried more about smallpox than Washington. He learned that the disease had infected Boston, and he feared it would infect his army outside the city. "It will appear that some of the people who came out of Boston were infected with the small pox," he wrote to James Otis Sr. "This disorder, should it spread, may prove very disastrous and fatal to our army and the country around it." To John Hancock, he declared, "The small pox is in every part of Boston. The soldiers there who have never had it are, we are told, under inoculation and considered as a security against any attempt of ours."

Inoculation consisted of scraping a sore of an infected person and applying the pus to a scratch in the skin of a healthy person. The usual result was a mild infection, which produced resistance against a more virulent one. But inoculation made recipients contagious, and unless they were quarantined, they could become transmitters of the disease. Washington's interpretation was that Howe and the British believed Washington wouldn't expose his army to the contagion that would likely follow contact with the inoculated—that is, infected—troops.

Howe did more than inoculate his troops. He expelled from Boston individuals infected with smallpox. Doing so relieved the strain on the city's resources and reduced the chance of further spread there. It also increased the chances the disease would spread outside the city, wherever the stricken landed. "About 150 more of the poor inhabitants are come out of Boston," Washington informed Hancock. "The small pox rages all over the town. Such of the military as had it not before are now under inoculation. This I apprehend is a weapon of defence they are using against us." The next day he noted that another group had been expelled from Boston. "If we escape the small pox in this camp and the country round about, it will be miraculous. Every precaution that can be, is taken to guard against this evil."

The first precaution was isolation. Soldiers were hospitalized and quarantined at the least sign of infection. Refugees from the city were kept away from the camps. By this stage of medical knowledge it was understood that smallpox spread by contact. Isolation worked—except that soldiers were sometimes hard to keep in camp, and individuals could become contagious before they were symptomatic.

The second precaution, inoculation, was more controversial. Occasionally the cases induced by inoculation were lethal, and all the cases were contagious. An inoculation campaign could produce outbreaks where none had existed before. Among the devoutly religious were those who believed that inoculation usurped God's oversight of humans.

Resistance to inoculation policy ran both ways. When inoculation was ordered, some people would refuse it. When inoculation was forbidden, some people inoculated themselves on the sly.

Smallpox was a greater problem for Washington than for Howe. Smallpox was endemic in Britain in this era, meaning that nearly every child was exposed at an early age. Some died, but those who survived to military age had at least some resistance. In America, given its lesser density of population, smallpox was episodic. Especially in rural parts of the colonies, many children were never exposed. Thus Washington's army included many young men at full risk of falling badly ill when exposed in the crowded conditions of camp.

At Boston, Washington relied on isolation. It worked well enough that he chose not to incur the opposition a campaign of inoculation would entail.

Yet the lesson he took from that winter was that smallpox might decimate an army. Thus the following winter, amid another outbreak, he ordered inoculation for all his troops. "Should the disorder infect the army in the natural way and rage with its usual virulence," he said, "we should have more to dread from it than from the sword of the enemy."

➛ 49 ➛

William Howe recalled getting instructions to evacuate Boston. "On the 9th of November, 1775, I received the Secretary of State's order to abandon that town before winter and to move the army to New York or to some other place to the southward," the British general told a committee of the House of Commons. But the evacuation couldn't happen at once. "The late arrival of the order and the deficiency of transport tonnage rendered the removal of troops impracticable." By the time the ships would have arrived, the gales of winter would have set in and ice would have closed the harbor. Howe decided to wait until spring.

He waited almost too long. Winter ice clogged harbors, but it facilitated some land transport, especially of heavy loads on sledges over frozen roads. Henry Knox and a brawny band of teamsters dragged the cannons captured at Ticonderoga and Crown Point the three hundred miles to Boston, arriving in late January. Finding powder for the guns took longer, but by late March enough had been secured to give Washington the option of using the guns against Boston. The Congress had kicked the matter back to him, letting him decide what military necessity allowed. He put it to his war council, and they told him to bomb away.

He initially did so to conceal a larger scheme. He sought to place a battery on Dorchester Heights, across the water south of Boston, from which he could fire down upon the town and on any ships that didn't keep clear. "To harass the enemy and divert their attention from that quarter"—Dorchester Heights—"on Saturday, Sunday and Monday nights last, we carried them"—bombardments—"on from our posts at Cobble Hill, Letchmores Point and Lams Dam," Washington wrote to John Hancock on Thursday, March 7. "Whether they did the enemy any considerable and what injury, I have not yet heard, but have the pleasure to acquaint you that they greatly facilitated our schemes." The British hunkered down in Boston while Washington's engineers and artillerists planted their guns on the heights.

"When the enemy first discovered our works in the morning, they seemed to be in great confusion, and from their movements to have intended an attack," Washington continued. "It is much to be wished that it had been made." He was tired of the siege and wanted to force Howe to fight. He thought he was going to get his wish. "On Tuesday evening a considerable number of their troops embarked on board of their transports and fell down to the Castle, where part of them landed before dark." Washington readied his own men for battle.

But a violent storm set in, and Howe suspended the operation. Washington fidgeted, trying to glean intelligence from any sources that came to hand. An escapee from Boston told of life under Washington's fire. "Our bombardment and cannonade caused a good deal of surprise and alarm in town, as many of the soldiery said they never heard or thought we had mortars or shells," Washington paraphrased to Hancock. "Several of the officers acknowledged they were well and properly directed. They made much distress and confusion. The cannon shot for the greatest part went through the houses, and he"—the refugee from Boston—"was told that one took off the legs and arms of six men lying in the barracks on the neck."

Washington's fire forced Howe to try to end it. "Preparations were directly made for that purpose," Washington's informant continued. "From twelve to two o'clock about 3,000 men embarked on board the transports which fell down to the Castle with a design of landing on that part of Dorchester next to it and attacking the works on the heights at 5 o'clock next morning."

The British rank and file weren't thrilled. "He heard several of the privates and one or two sergeants say as they were embarking that it would be another Bunker Hill."

The storm spared them the repetition. Howe changed his mind about engaging Washington. Having been ordered months before to abandon Boston, he now decided to obey. "The army is preparing to leave Boston and they will do it in a day or two," Washington's informant explained, as Washington recounted to Hancock.

The terms of Howe's departure occasioned discussion. On March 8, Washington received a letter signed by four of Boston's selectmen. They and other Bostonians had approached Howe, asking what they could do to prevent the destruction of their city. They feared he would burn it to the ground as he departed. He responded that the matter was up to Washington. "He has no intention of destroying the town unless the troops under his command are molested during their embarkation or at their departure," the selectmen said of Howe. "If such an opposition should take place, we have the greatest reason to expect the town will be exposed to entire destruction." The selectmen sought Washington's promise to let Howe go. "We beg we may have some assurances that so dreadful a calamity may not be brought on."

Washington gave no promise to the selectmen. But he realized he couldn't prevent Howe's escape. His guns didn't command the whole harbor. Howe's ships could depart almost unmolested.

Nor did Washington want to give Howe an excuse to burn Boston. "There is no possibility of stopping them in case they determine to go," Washington explained to Hancock. He would hold his fire and watch. "I shall order lookouts to be kept upon all the headlands to discover their movements and course." Washington added that he would direct the small naval squadron at his disposal to tail Howe, in hopes of discovering where he was bound.

Howe made his getaway, in haste and no little confusion regarding the transports and who should be allowed on them.

WASHINGTON ENTERED THE CITY. Whether he was capturing or liberating it depended on one's point of view. The purpose of the rebellion Washington led hadn't been defined. Some of those who had stayed in Boston sympathized with Howe and the British government more than with Washington and the rebels. Others didn't. Washington couldn't readily tell who was on which side.

He didn't propose to try. There would be no score settling. "All officers and soldiers are hereby ordered to live in the strictest peace and amity with the inhabitants," he proclaimed. "And no inhabitant or other person employed in his lawful business in the town is to be molested in his person or property on any pretence whatever. If any officer or soldier shall presume to strike, imprison or otherwise ill-treat any of the inhabitants, they may depend on being punished with the utmost severity. And if any officer or soldier shall receive any insult from any of the inhabitants, he is to seek redress in a legal way and no other."

At the same time, the Bostonians must cooperate with Washington and his army. "The inhabitants and others are called upon to make known to the quarter-master general or any of his deputies all stores belonging to the ministerial army that may be remaining or secreted in the town. Any person or persons whatever that shall be known to conceal any of the said stores or appropriate them to his or their own use will be considered as an enemy of America and treated accordingly." This was audacious language, Washington presuming to declare who was an American and who not.

There was more. "The selectmen and other magistrates of the town are desired to return to the commander in chief the names of all or any person or persons they may suspect of being employed as spies upon the Continental Army, that they may be dealt with accordingly." Bostonians were being asked to report on one another.

Washington took particular care about the smallpox. The first troops he sent into Boston consisted solely of men who had had the disease. He told the rest of the army to be wary. "As the enemy with a malicious assiduity have spread the infection of the smallpox through all parts of the town, nothing but the utmost caution on our part can prevent that fatal disease from spreading through the army and country, to the infinite detriment of both," he declared. Washington's medics were placed on high alert. "The hospital and regimental surgeons are to examine carefully the state of their sick and whenever they discover the smallest symptom of the small-pox, they are without delay to send the patient to the small-pox hospital in Cambridge."

Washington didn't know what to expect when he entered the town. He wondered how much damage his cannon fire had done. Part of him hoped not much. Boston, after all, was the cradle of the current resistance movement. On the other hand, he didn't like to think his cannoneers had wasted powder and shells. What he found favored Boston. "The town has shared a much better fate than was expected, the damage done to the houses being nothing equal to report," Washington wrote to brother Jack. More harm had been done by the British. "The inhabitants have suffered a good deal by being plundered by the soldiery at their departure."

Washington had nothing but scorn for the Bostonians who had opposed his cause. Luckily for them, most had fled with the British. "All those who took upon themselves the style and title of government men in Boston—in short all those who have acted an unfriendly part in this great contest—have shipped themselves off in the same hurry but under still greater disadvantages than the king's troops have done, being obliged to man their own vessels," he told Jack. Such foes of liberty deserved their fate. "One or two have done what a great many ought to have done long ago: committed suicide."

This sounded harsh, but the tories deserved no better. "There never existed a more miserable set of beings than these wretched creatures now are, taught to believe that the power of Great Britain was superior to all opposition," Washington wrote. To the end they had looked to Howe to protect them. "When the order issued, therefore, for embarking the troops in Boston, no electric shock, no sudden clap of thunder, in a word the last trump, could have struck them with greater consternation." They had no choice but to flee Boston—or kill themselves—rather than face their patriot countrymen.

Driving the British from Boston was no mean feat, but Washington wanted more. He had hoped for a full battle with Howe. "Much blood was saved," he acknowledged to Jack. But the point of war was decision. Howe's flight postponed the day of reckoning. "I can scarce forbear lamenting the disappointment," Washington said.

Part VI

New York

50

Though smallpox was the proximate cause of the failure of Benedict Arnold and his comrades to conquer Canada, the deeper reason was the refusal of the Canadians to join the rebel cause. Washington's summons to a defense of American liberty stirred few of the French inhabitants of Canada and even fewer of the Indians there. Both groups were as suspicious of the Americans as of the British. The British lived far away, while the Americans were the pushy neighbors next door.

Similar sentiments gave many New Yorkers concern about the patriot cause. The colony had been founded by the Dutch and become British only decades later, in the same sort of diplomatic cession that made Canada British. The Dutch influence remained strong in New York and caused many New Yorkers to want to have nothing to do with the quarrel among the English. The Dutch merchants minded business rather than politics. They resented what spoiled their trade. They followed the counsel of pragmatism. If the winds of war blew toward Washington and his American army, they'd support Washington. If toward Howe and the British, they'd support Howe.

They expected their city to be fought over. They knew it occupied the single most important location in British North America, where the Hudson River met the sea. The Hudson afforded access by ship far into the interior, almost severing New England from the colonies to the south. In the hands of the British, New York would threaten to cut the rebellion in half. Washington couldn't relinquish New York without a fight.

THOMAS JONES, the skeptical judge in New York, was English by descent rather than Dutch, but he shared the distrust of his Dutch neighbors for the rebel cause. The return of the rebel generals didn't improve his opinion of them. "Early in February 1776, General Lee arrived at New York with a detachment of the grand rebel army from Boston, under orders from General Washington to fortify the city, swear the tories, and take their property; which orders were as punctually as they were rigorously, wantonly and cruelly carried into execution," Jones remembered later. Lee was Charles Lee, the soldier of fortune who brought out the skeptic in many people. "Upon his arrival in New York he took up his lodgings at a Mrs. De La Montaine's, who kept a public house upon the Common. Here he was supplied with his provisions and liquor, here his headquarters were established, here his friends, his suite, and his principal officers were all entertained and feasted; the whole was at the poor woman's expense." Lee and his entourage remained for months. When he left, his host presented her bill. He rejected it angrily. "He damned her for a tory, cursed her for a bitch, and left the house without paying her a sixpence."

Lee mistreated others. "While this immaculate general had the command in New York, about 200 pieces of heavy cannon, which were mounted in Fort George and upon the Battery, were forcibly taken away by his orders and lodged upon the Common," Jones recounted. "But lest, upon the arrival of the British army, they should be retaken, he ordered them carried up to King's Bridge, about 14 miles from New York. The persons employed in this service, wanting horses, applied to the general to supply the defect. An honest, a virtuous man, and a Christian, will shudder at the answer: 'Chain 20 damned tories to each gun and let them draw them out and be cursed. It is a proper employment for such villains, and a punishment they deserve for the eternal loyalty that they boast so much of.'"

The behavior of Lee was prelude to what followed, Jones said. "In the beginning of the April following, General Washington entered New York with the main body of the rebel army from Boston, took possession of the city, converted it into a garrison, pulled down houses, dug up streets, built fortifications, and threatened, robbed, confined, imprisoned, and banished his Majesty's loyal subjects without mercy." The residents of the city did their best to get clear. "New York being now taken and reduced to a rebel garrison, the loyalists, as also the republicans"—the patriots—"moved with their effects into the country. They had different motives. The loyalists that they might be ready to join the British army whenever it arrived. The republicans to be out of harm's way in case the royal army should attack the city, and because they knew (which was then a secret to the loyalists) that a resolution had been entered into the preceding year by a committee from Congress and a committee of the New

York provincial convention, and solemnly ratified by both, to burn the city of New York if the rebel army should be obliged to abandon it. The town being thus forsaken, the inhabitants took refuge, some in one place, and some in another."

Washington was as vindictive as Lee, Jones said. He let republicans terrorize the loyalists who hadn't fled. "A republican mob was raised in the middle of the day, headed by a number of staunch Presbyterians"—unlike the largely loyalist Anglicans in the city—"among whom the principal was one Lasher, a shoemaker and then a colonel in the rebel army." Jones named other republicans who marched beside Lasher. "This mob, thus led on, searched the whole town in pursuit of tories (his Majesty's loyal subjects, meaning) and found and dragged several from their lurking holes, where they had taken refuge to avoid the undeserved vengeance of an ungovernable rabble. When they had taken several of these unhappy victims, destined to the will, the sport, and the caprice of a banditti, and the diversion of republicans and rebels, they placed them upon sharp rails with one leg on each side. Each rail was carried upon the shoulders of two tall men, with a man on each side to keep the poor wretch straight and fixed in his seat. In this manner were numbers of these poor people, in danger of their lives from the extremity of pain occasioned by this cruel contrivance, paraded through the most public and conspicuous streets in the town, and at every corner a crier made proclamation declaring the offenders to be such and such (mentioning their names) and notorious tories (loyal subjects, meaning). The mob then gave three huzzas and the procession went on. The like proclamations were made before the city hall, where the provincial convention was then sitting forming laws for the civil government of the province; before the exchange where the committee were sitting making rules and regulations for preserving the good order, the peace and quiet of the city; and before the door of General Washington, who pretended the army under his command was raised for the defense of *American liberty,* for the preservation of the *rights of mankind,* and for the protection of America against the unjust usurpation of the British ministry.

"Notwithstanding which, so far did this humane general, and the two public bodies aforesaid, approve of this unjustifiable mob that it received the sanction of them all. They appeared at the windows, raised their hats, returned the huzzas and joined in the acclamations of the multitude. Nay, so far did General Washington give his sanction of and approbation to this inhuman barbarous proceeding that he gave a very severe reprimand to General Putnam, who accidentally meeting one of the processions in the street, and shocked with its barbarity, attempted to put a stop to it, Washington declaring that to discourage such proceedings was to injure the cause of liberty in which they were then engaged, and that nobody would attempt it but an enemy to his country."

Washington, according to Jones, didn't spare the dignity of womanhood. "A lady of the first rank, character, and family, happened to be upon a visit to some of her relations upon New York Island, attended by her postilion only, at the time that General Howe landed upon Staten Island with the army from Halifax. Upon this event General Washington issued orders that no person should pass the ferries without a written order from the commandant of the city. Not knowing who the commandant was, and the lady desirous of returning to her family upon Long Island, nearly 30 miles from the city, she wrote a polite note to General Washington, begging the favor of a permit to pass the ferry. This note was delivered to General Washington by a gentleman of character, fortune, and reputation, a near relation of the lady. Washington read the note, whispered to McDougal, turned around, tossed the paper towards the gentleman, and insultingly said, 'Carry the note back to your tory relation, I have nothing to do with it.'"

JONES LIKELY EXAGGERATED Washington's intolerance. Losers in war, as Jones proved to be, often carry grudges. Yet Washington had reason to be suspicious. He knew his cause was less popular in New York than in Boston, and he supposed some New Yorkers were spies for the British. The lady whose ferry passage he opposed might have been a spy, for all he knew, carrying intelligence to Howe regarding Washington's preparations to defend the city. "Congress, I doubt not, will have heard of the plot that was forming among many disaffected persons in this city and government for aiding the King's troops upon their arrival," Washington wrote to John Hancock in late June. "No regular plan seems to have been digested, but several persons have been enlisted and sworn to join them." Washington was relieved to have caught it in time. "Many citizens and others, among whom is the mayor, are now in confinement. The matter has been traced up to Governor Tryon, and the mayor appears to have been a principal agent or go-between him and the persons concerned in it. The plot had been communicated to some of the army, and part of my guard engaged in it." Washington treated the matter with the rigor he thought it required. "Thomas Hickey, one of them, has been tried, and, by the unanimous opinion of a court-martial, is sentenced to die, having enlisted himself and engaged others. The sentence, by the advice of the whole council of general officers, will be put in execution to-day at eleven o'clock."

Washington proposed to fight fire with fire. He received reports that reinforcements dispatched to assist Howe included German Hessians. "May it not be advisable and good policy to raise some companies of our Germans to send among them when they arrive, for exciting a spirit of disaffection and desertion?" he asked Hancock. "If a few sensible and trusty fellows could get with them, I should think they would have great weight and influence with the common soldiery, who certainly have no enmity towards us, having received no injury nor cause of quarrel from us."

The balance of battle might rest on the loyalties of the populace. Washington heard of a pocket of loyalism around Perth Amboy, New Jersey, across a narrow channel from Staten Island. "The disaffection of the people at that place and others not far off is exceedingly great, and unless it is checked and overawed it may become more general and be very alarming," he told Hancock. "The arrival of the enemy will encourage it." Washington and the Congress had to devise methods to *dis*courage it, lest the American cause be stymied from within.

WASHINGTON WROTE THESE WORDS on July 4, just as the Congress was clarifying what the American cause was. Five days later he passed the news to the troops, via a general order. "The honorable the Continental Congress, impelled by the dictates of duty, policy and necessity, having been pleased to dissolve the connection which subsisted between this country and Great Britain, and to declare the United Colonies of North America, free and independent STATES: The several brigades are to be drawn up this evening on their respective parades at six o'clock, when the declaration of Congress, shewing the grounds and reasons of this measure, is to be read with an audible voice."

Samuel Webb was a soldier in Washington's army, having joined a Connecticut militia that hastened to Boston after the battles of Lexington and Concord. He served bravely at Bunker Hill and afterward came to the attention of Washington, who valued his literary skills and made him an aide. Webb found time to keep a journal of his own. "Agreeable to this day's orders," he recorded on July 9, "the Declaration of Independence was read at the head of each brigade, and was received by three huzzas from the troops. Every one seeming highly pleased that we were separated from a king who was endeavouring to enslave his once loyal subjects. God grant us success in this our new character."

The troops did more than cheer. "Last night the statue of George the third was tumbled down and beheaded," Webb wrote the next day. The equestrian statue of the king had been commissioned by the New York assembly several years earlier and erected on Bowling Green near the southern tip of Manhattan. "The troops, having long had an inclination so to do, thought this time of publishing a Declaration of Independence to be a favorable opportunity."

Washington felt obliged to comment. "Though the General doubts not the persons who pulled down and mutilated the statue in the Broadway last night were actuated by zeal in the public cause, yet it has so much the appearance of riot and want of order in the Army that he disapproves the manner and directs that in future these things shall be avoided by the soldiery and left to be executed by proper authority."

THE DECISION FOR independence simplified Washington's task. For a year he had thought of the British army before him as the enemy, but it had been the enemy in no actual or legal sense. He and his soldiers remained subjects of the same king as Thomas Gage, William Howe and their soldiers. Washington had looked upon Americans who opposed him as traitors to the cause of American liberty, but they weren't traitors to any duly constituted government. If anything, he and his men were the traitors, making war against the government under which they lived.

By proclaiming a new country, the Declaration of Independence made honest soldiers, so to speak, of the Continental army. No longer a rebel force, they were the official army of the United States of America. Washington had never shrunk before Gage and Howe, but now he could more credibly demand their respect in the fraternity of arms. And his condemnation of Americans who remained loyal to King George as traitors gained weight from the fact that they were now traitors to the United States. That they didn't see things that way—that they, like Howe, refused to recognize the existence of the United States—didn't diminish the value in Washington's mind of having not merely a cause to fight for but a country.

⤞ 51 ⤝

More than ever Washington wanted to fight Howe. But Howe wasn't eager to fight him. The British general appeared but kept his distance from Manhattan. "General Howe's fleet from Halifax has arrived, in number about 130 sail," Washington wrote to Philip Schuyler. "His army is between 9 and 10 thousand, being joined by some of the regiments from the West Indies, and having fallen in with part of the Highland troops in his passage. He has landed his men on Staten Island, which they mean to secure, and is in daily expectation of the arrival of Lord Howe, with one hundred and fifty ships, with a large and powerful reinforcement." Lord Howe was Admiral Richard Howe, General William Howe's older brother. Washington had his information from prisoners and deserters. "They add that nothing will be attempted till his arrival. Their intelligence I have no doubt is well founded; indeed the enemy's having done nothing yet affords proof beyond question that they are waiting for more troops."

Washington made use of the delay. "We are strengthening ourselves as much as possible and deem their staying out so long a fortunate circumstance, as it not only gives us an opportunity of advancing our works, but of getting some relief from the neighbouring provinces," he told Schuyler. Washington expected a decisive contest. "From every appearance, they mean to make a most vigorous push to subdue us this campaign, and for this purpose to possess themselves of this colony, if possible, as a step leading to it."

Weeks passed. Washington tightened the noose on tories behind his lines. "As this city is hourly threatened with an attack from a powerful enemy," he wrote to the New York committee of safety, "and as there is too much reason to apprehend from their vicinity to this city, and from the number of suspicious characters still in it that they may receive intelligence which may counteract all my operations for its defence, I strongly recommend it to you to remove for some time all equivocal and suspicious characters." He supplied a list and demanded action. "If through an ill-timed lenity my attempts to secure this province should be baffled, the blame of it may not be imputed to my want of vigilance."

Washington found time to write to brother Jack. "As I expect every hour to be engaged in too busy a scene to allow time for writing private letters, I will take an opportunity by this day's post to address you a few lines giving a brief account of the situation of affairs in this quarter. To begin then: we have a powerful fleet within full view of us, distant about 8 miles. We have General Howe's present army, consisting by good report of about eight or nine thousand men upon Staten Island, covered by their ships. We have Lord Howe just arrived (that is about 10 days ago), and we have ships now popping in which we suppose but don't know to be part of the fleet with the expected reinforcement. When this arrives, if the report of deserters, prisoners and tories are to be depended upon, the enemy's numbers will amount at least to 25,000 men. Ours to about 15,000. More indeed are expected, but there is no certainty of their arrival as harvest and a thousand other excuses are urged for the reasons of delay. What kind of opposition we shall be able to make time only can shew. I can only say that the men appear to be in good spirits, and if they will stand by me the place shall not be carried without some loss, notwithstanding we are not yet in such a posture of defence as I could wish."

Perhaps his brother wondered why Washington didn't attack Howe before the additional British reinforcements arrived. He had given thought to doing so. But it was too risky. "Our situation at present, both with respect to men and other matters is such as not to make it advisable to attempt anything against them, surrounded as they are by water and covered with ships, lest a miscarriage should be productive of unhappy and fatal consequences." Reason told Washington to wait. He generally listened to reason and did so now. "It is provoking nevertheless to have them so near without being able in their weakest part to give them any disturbance."

August brought the day of trial closer. It also tilted the odds further against Washington. "By two deserters this day we have the following intelligence," he wrote to Jonathan Trumbull. "That General Clinton and Lord Cornwallis with the whole southern army have arrived from South Carolina and landed on Staten Island, in number between 3 and 4,000." The British had attempted to outflank Washington and rally southern loyalists by an attack on Charleston. Washington had sent Charles Lee to defend the city. Patriot spirit and British blunders produced a surprising American victory, and the British assault force under Henry Clinton and Charles Cornwallis sailed north to join the Howes at New York.

"The fleet which came in a few days since are the Hessians and Scotch Highlanders, part of 12,000 who were left off Newfoundland, and the whole making about 30,000 men," Washington continued. "It is said by both the officers of the navy and army they are to attack New York, Long Island etc. in the course of a week." Perhaps sooner. "The uncommon movements of the fleet this day together with this intelligence convinces us that, in all human probability, there can but a very few days pass before a general engagement takes place."

HE ADMONISHED THE MEN on what their country expected of them. "The enemy's whole reinforcement is now arrived, so that an attack must and will soon be made," Washington declared. "The General therefore again repeats his earnest request that every officer and soldier will have his arms and ammunition in good order; keep within their quarters and encampment, as much as possible; be ready for action at a moment's call; and when called to it, remember that liberty, property, life and honor are all at stake; that upon their courage and conduct rest the hopes of their bleeding and insulted country; that their wives, children and parents expect safety from them only, and that we have every reason to expect Heaven will crown with success so just a cause."

The enemy had no such principled purpose. "Their cause is bad; their men are conscious of it, and if opposed with firmness and coolness at their first onset, with our advantage of works and knowledge of the ground, victory is most assuredly ours."

Obedience was imperative. "Every good soldier will be silent and attentive, wait for orders and reserve his fire 'till he is sure of doing execution: the officers to be particularly careful of this." Washington encouraged, but he also warned. "If any infamous rascal, in time of action, shall attempt to skulk, hide himself or retreat from the enemy without orders of his commanding officer, he will instantly be shot down as an example of cowardice."

He expected the opposite, and he would act accordingly. "The General solemnly promises that he will reward those who shall distinguish themselves by brave and noble actions; and he desires every officer to be attentive to this particular, that such men may be afterwards suitably noticed."

"IT WAS ABOUT two o'clock on the morning of the 27th of August that I was awakened by seeing a soldier at the side of my bed," William Howard remembered. William was fourteen years old and the son of a Brooklyn barkeeper of the same name. "I got up and dressed, and went down into the bar room, where I saw my father standing in one corner, with three British soldiers before him with muskets and bayonets fixed. The army was then lying in the field in front of the house. I remember that the market men had nearly all gone by before the troops made their appearance. General Howe and another officer were standing in the bar room. General Howe wore a camlet cloak over his regimentals.

"After asking for a glass of liquor from the bar, which was given him, he entered into familiar conversation with my father, and among other things said, 'I must have some one of you to show me over the Rockaway Path around the pass.' My father replied, 'We belong to the other side, General, and can't serve you against our duty.' General Howe replied, 'That is all right, stick to your country, or stick to your principles. But, Howard, you are my prisoner and must guide my men over the hill.' My father made some further objection but was silenced by the general, who said, 'You have no alternative. If you refuse, I shall have you shot through the head.'"

Possibly the exchange between Howe and the elder Howard took place just as the son remembered. But after the war it was hard to find Americans who admitted to aiding the British voluntarily. These were the ones Washington wanted to hunt down as spies. Perhaps significantly—but perhaps not—William Jr. remembered almost charitably the British soldiers who invaded his home. "The British guards were apparently without the slightest feeling of hatred or embittered feeling in their position as enemies, and we experienced nothing disagreeable during their stay. In fact most of the plundering during the war was perpetrated by the inhabitants upon each other, the Whig robbing the Tory and the latter retaliating whenever opportunity offered."

The path Howe was seeking was one that had been reported to him by local tories. On August 22 he had dispatched Clinton and Cornwallis from Staten Island to Long Island, where they landed unopposed at

Gravesend Bay. Washington suspected a feint and refused to fall for it. By the time he learned otherwise, the British had fifteen thousand troops ashore.

Washington hurried troops of his own to the area, under command of Israel Putnam. They established a defensive line on Brooklyn Heights, a line of hills between the British landing area and the town of Brooklyn. Putnam's men patrolled the main routes leading through the heights, the ones most directly in the path of a British advance. There were other paths less frequented and more out of the way. Howe's informants had told him of one such. This was the path he demanded William Howard's father show him, on pain of death.

"My father, thus compelled to serve the cause of the enemy, was marched out under a guard, who had orders to shoot him if he attempted to desert, and I was taken along with him. The Rockaway Path was a wood road which led around to the east of the Kings Highway, under the brow of the hill (now Evergreen Cemetery), at the back of Mr. Furman's garden, to a place on the Bushwick Lane, about a quarter of a mile from the turn in the Kings Highway, where it runs straight to Brooklyn. The place where the British came out into the cleared fields is now near the north gate of the Evergreen Cemetery."

The British moved as quietly as an army column could. "The pioneers"—woodsmen—"came just behind us and sawed down the trees which came in the way of the cannon, as the noise made by felling them with axes, it was expected, would alarm the American guard," young William recalled. "Everything in the march was conducted in the most silent manner possible, and the movements were performed with such caution against surprise as showed that the enemy expected momentarily to be attacked by the Americans. By this maneuver they had completely flanked the position in the hills, supposed to be guarded, coming upon the road which passed through them more than a mile below the pass."

HOWE CAUGHT WASHINGTON out of position. When fighting began after sunrise on August 27, the British inflicted heavy casualties on the Americans, driving them back toward the East River. The retreat might have become a rout if not for the gallant efforts of a Maryland regiment led by Mordecai Gist, nephew of Washington's Ohio comrade Christopher Gist. The Marylanders fought a stubborn rearguard action that bought time for others to escape, at the cost of nearly all their own lives.

Washington rushed across from Manhattan. Realizing he had been outflanked and outgeneraled, he faced a crucial choice. Should he throw more troops into the present battle, or husband his resources for another day's fight? Possibly at this moment he realized what Howe had divined at Boston: the war wouldn't be won in a single battle, but it might be lost in one. At Boston, Howe had frustrated Washington's hope to have things out, opting for retreat and for resumption under more favorable circumstances. Now Washington faced a similar choice. Throwing all his forces into the battle for Brooklyn risked losing them all. He would face William Howe's army in front and Richard Howe's navy behind.

He couldn't take the chance. He watched the battle unfold. He observed the Marylanders' heroics and was reported to have said, "Good God, what brave fellows I must this day lose!" He made the decision not to lose more than he had to.

These were dauntingly many. Washington lost more than two thousand killed, captured or wounded, against a fifth that number on the British side.

HE WOULD HAVE LOST more if Howe hadn't stopped short of the American redoubts. "Had the troops been permitted to go on, it is my opinion they would have carried the redoubts," Howe wrote to London a few days later. "But as it was apparent the lines must have been ours at a cheap rate by regular approaches, I would not risk the loss that might have been sustained in the assault, and ordered them back to a hollow in the front of the works, out of the reach of musquetry."

At the time, Howe's decision wasn't controversial in Britain, where confidence remained high that the American rebellion would be crushed. But three years later, with the rebels still in the field, Howe's decision at Brooklyn was increasingly second-guessed. He was summoned before Parliament to explain why he hadn't pressed his advantage and defeated Washington when he had the chance.

Howe denied the premise. "I am at a loss to know from whence it has been supposed that carrying the lines would have been followed by the defeat of the rebel army," he said. Washington had been too canny, or too cautious, to bring his whole army to Brooklyn. "The remainder of the corps was posted behind the lines, the main army being then on York Island"—Manhattan. "So that, admitting the works to have been forced on the day of action, the only advantage we should have gained would have been the destruction of a few more men." He had his own army to consider. "The most essential duty I had to observe was not wantonly to commit his Majesty's troops where the object was inadequate. I knew well that any considerable loss sustained by the army could not speedily nor easily be repaired. I also knew that one great point towards gaining the confidence of the army (and a general without it is upon the most dangerous ground) is never to expose the troops where, as I said before, the object is inadequate." The object was inadequate at Brooklyn. "To have permitted the attack in question would have been inconsiderate and even criminal."

THE LESSON WASHINGTON TOOK from Long Island was that he could lose ground but mustn't lose the army. The British could never occupy all of America. He could retreat and retreat, so long as he had an army to retreat with.

His challenge became how to extract his remaining force from Brooklyn. Benjamin Tallmadge was a New Yorker whose baptism by fire came at Brooklyn. "This was the first time in my life that I had witnessed the awful scene of a battle, when man was engaged to destroy his fellow man," he recalled later. He described the difficulties confronting Washington in the evacuation that followed the battle. "To move so large a body of troops, with all their necessary appendages, across a river full a mile wide, with a rapid current, in face of a victorious, well-disciplined army nearly three times as numerous as his own, and a fleet capable of stopping the navigation so that not one boat could have passed over, seemed to present most formidable obstacles. But, in the face of these difficulties, the Commander-in-Chief so arranged his business that on the evening of the 29th, by 10 o'clock, the troops began to retire from the lines in such a manner that no chasm was made in the lines, but as one regiment left their station on guard, the remaining troops moved to the right and left and filled up the vacancies, while General Washington took his station at the ferry, and superintended the embarkation of the troops."

Under cover of night the evacuation proceeded, nerve-rackingly. "It was one of the most anxious, busy nights that I ever recollect, and being the third in which hardly any of us had closed our eyes to sleep, we were all greatly fatigued," Tallmadge said. But the oar-powered boats could accommodate only so many troops at a time, and dawn broke with several regiments still on the Brooklyn side.

Washington often credited a higher power for his successes. Providence appeared to intervene now. "A very dense fog began to rise, and it seemed to settle in a peculiar manner over both encampments," Benjamin Tallmadge said. "I recollect this peculiar providential occurrence perfectly well; and so very dense was the atmosphere that I could scarcely discern a man at six yards' distance." The British remained oblivious to the American departure.

A miscommunication threatened to foul things. "We had just received orders to leave the lines, but before we reached the ferry, the Commander-in-Chief sent one of his aides to order the regiment to repair again to their former station on the lines." Tallmadge and his men were among the last remaining, and they couldn't tell what had gone wrong. They did as ordered.

The sun came up, with its prospect of burning off the fog. Their luck—Washington's luck—seemed to be running out. Then the countermand was countermanded. "The second order arrived for the regiment to retire, and we very joyfully bid those trenches a long adieu. When we reached the Brooklyn ferry, the boats had not returned from their last trip, but they very soon appeared and took the whole regiment over to New York." Tallmadge looked back. "I saw General Washington on the ferry stairs."

Washington stayed until the last of the troops had boarded. On the final boat he crossed to safety under the lingering cover of the lifting fog.

52

Richard Howe wasn't disappointed that his brother had declined to storm the American defenses in Brooklyn. Neither Howe was an ardent supporter of his government's policy toward America, with each thinking a war over taxes a blunder. They did their work as professionals rather than advocates. They had another assignment too. Both men had been appointed peace commissioners to the colonies, with authority to grant pardons to rebels who put down their weapons and renewed allegiance to the crown. Richard Howe took this part of his assignment especially seriously. He sent a letter to Benjamin Franklin, whom he knew from Franklin's time in London, explaining his authority and expressing hope an accommodation could be reached.

Franklin showed the letter to John Hancock, who had it read before the Congress, which instructed Franklin to respond. Franklin told Howe the offer came too late. "Long did I endeavour with unfeigned and unwearied zeal to preserve from breaking that fine and noble China vase, the British empire. For I knew that being once broken, the separate parts could not retain even their share of the strength or value that existed in the whole, and that a perfect reunion of those parts could scarce even be hoped for."

Franklin's reply had come before the battle of Brooklyn. Richard Howe hoped the setback Washington suffered there—serious enough to sober but not so humiliating as to embitter—had caused a change of mind. He renewed the offer of amnesty, paroling the senior American captured in the battle, General John Sullivan, to deliver the offer to the Congress.

This time the Congress responded by appointing Franklin, John Adams and Edward Rutledge of South Carolina to meet with Howe on Staten Island. "We walked up to the house between lines of guards of grenadiers looking as fierce as ten furies and making all the grimaces and gestures and motions of their musquets with bayonets fixed which I suppose military etiquette requires but which we neither understood nor regarded," Adams recalled afterward. "The house had been the habitation of military guards and was as dirty as a stable, but his lordship had prepared a large handsome room by spreading a carpet of moss and green sprigs from bushes and shrubs in the neighbourhood till he had made it not only wholesome but romantically elegant, and he entertained us with good claret, good bread, cold ham, tongues and mutton."

Richard Howe was the soul of friendly regard. If the matter had been up to him, the meeting might have ended happily for all. But he'd been denied authority to recognize American independence. A return to the status quo as of 1765, when the American troubles started, yes. Independence, no.

For their part, Franklin, Adams and Rutledge weren't authorized to accept anything short of independence. Neither were they inclined to do so. The American appetite had grown with the eating. Had Britain made a credible offer before July 1776, the moderates in the Congress might have deprived the radicals of a majority for independence. But the offer wasn't made then. And when it was made, it came too late.

Howe and his American guests finished their lunch. Howe said he wished things had turned out differently. He said he had respect and affection for America, not least because Massachusetts—here he nodded to Adams—had honored his elder brother, who had been killed in the war against France, by paying for a statue in Westminster Abbey. Howe said he thought of America as a brother and that if America fell, he'd lament the fall like the loss of a brother.

"Dr. Franklin," wrote Adams, concluding his account of the meeting, "with an easy air and a collected countenance, a bow, a smile and all that naivetee which sometimes appeared in his conversation and is often observed in his writings, replied, 'My lord, we will do our utmost endeavours to save your lordship that mortification.'"

THE FLIGHT FROM BROOKLYN had bought Washington time, but the experience on Long Island left him chastened. "Our situation is truly distressing," he wrote to John Hancock on September 2. "The check our detachment sustained on the 27th ultimo has dispirited too great a proportion of our troops and filled their minds with apprehension and despair. The militia, instead of calling forth their utmost efforts to a brave and manly opposition in order to repair our losses, are dismayed, intractable and impatient to return"—to go home. "Great numbers of them have gone off, in some instances almost by whole regiments, by half ones, and by companies at a time."

The mood of the men caused Washington to reconsider the defensibility of New York city. "Till of late I had no doubt in my own mind of defending this place," he told Hancock. "Nor should I have yet if the men would do their duty. But this I despair of. It is painful and extremely grating to me to give such unfavourable accounts, but it would be criminal to conceal the truth at so critical a juncture."

Removal from New York appeared the only alternative to losing the whole army, either by British capture or by desertion. This was a decision Washington made on military grounds. But he needed guidance on a corollary decision. "If we should be obliged to abandon this town, ought it to stand as winter quarters for the enemy?" he asked Hancock. Or should it be burned before the British occupied it? "They would derive great conveniences from it on the one hand, and much property would be destroyed on the other." He thought he knew what General Howe preferred. "I dare say the enemy mean to preserve it if they can."

He needed an answer at once. Confidentiality was key. "If Congress therefore should resolve upon the destruction of it, the resolution should be a profound secret."

Washington got his answer. "Congress, having taken your letter of the 2d inst. into consideration, came to a resolution in a committee of the whole house that no damage should be done to the city of New York," Hancock informed Washington.

MOVING WASHINGTON'S HEADQUARTERS was simple. He got on his horse and rode to a house his staff had located in Harlem Heights near the north end of Manhattan Island, well beyond the city. Moving the army was a bigger job, and it was still under way on September 15 when the British crossed from Brooklyn to Kips Bay on the eastern side of Manhattan.

The British operation began with a bombardment from the guns of five ships in the East River. "It is hardly possible to conceive what a tremendous fire was kept up by those five ships for fifty-nine minutes, in which time we fired away, in the *Orpheus* alone, five thousand three hundred and seventy-six pounds of powder," recalled a midshipman on the

Orpheus who would eventually become an admiral. "The first broadside made a considerable breach in their works, and the enemy fled on all sides, confused and calling for quarter, while the army landed, but, as usual, did not pursue the victory, though the rebels in general had left their arms in the entrenchment." Richard Howe's seamen were as scornful of William Howe's soldiers as navy men often are of their terrestrial counterparts. "The havoc was by no means so great as it would have been had we not been obliged to cease firing on the landing of the troops; however, the ground in some places was filled with the slain."

What seemed propitious to the British sounded ominous to Washington. "As soon as I heard the firing," he reported to Hancock, "I road with all possible dispatch towards the place of landing, when to my great surprize and mortification I found the troops that had been posted in the lines retreating with the utmost precipitation and those ordered to support them, Parsons's and Fellows's brigades, flying in every direction and in the greatest confusion, notwithstanding the exertions of their generals to form them. I used every means in my power to rally and get them into some order but my attempts were fruitless and ineffectual, and on the appearance of a small party of the enemy, not more than sixty or seventy, their disorder increased and they ran away in the greatest confusion without firing a single shot."

Realizing that preventing the British landings was impossible, and fearing that the enemy would cross the island to the Hudson and cut off the northern end, he ordered a swift retreat to Harlem Heights. "The retreat was effected with but little or no loss of men, though of a considerable part of our baggage occasioned by this disgraceful and dastardly conduct," Washington told Hancock. "Most of our heavy cannon and a part of our stores and provisions which we were about removing was unavoidably left in the city."

Matters had calmed by the time of Washington's writing, but he remained on edge. "We are now encamped with the main body of the army on the heights of Harlem, where I should hope the enemy would meet with a defeat in case of an attack, if the generality of our troops would behave with tolerable bravery, but experience to my extreme affliction has convinced me that this is rather to be wished for than expected." He hoped for better. "I trust that there are many who will act like men and shew themselves worthy of the blessings of freedom."

. . .

ALMOST AT ONCE he got his hope. "About the time of the post's departure with my letter," he wrote to Hancock in his next report, "the enemy appeared in several large bodies upon the plains about two and a half miles from hence. I rode down to our advanced posts to put matters in a proper situation if they should attempt to come on." William Howe, having landed all his troops, had decided to give chase, albeit half-heartedly. "When I arrived there, I heard a firing which I was informed was between a party of our rangers under the command of Lieutenant Colonel Knowlton and an advanced party of the enemy," Washington continued. "Our men came in and told me that the body of the enemy, who kept themselves concealed, consisted of about three hundred as near as they could guess."

Washington tried to lure the British into a trap. "I immediately ordered three companies of Colonel Weedon's regiment from Virginia under the command of Major Leitch, and Colonel Knowlton with his rangers, composed of volunteers from different New England regiments, to try to get in their rear, while a disposition was making as if to attack them in front and thereby draw their whole attention that way." The British fell for it. "On the appearance of our party in front, they immediately ran down the hill, took possession of some fences and bushes, and a smart firing began, but at too great a distance to do much execution." The timing was a bit off, though. "The parties under Colonel Knowlton and Major Leitch unluckily began their attack too soon, as it was rather in flank than in rear." Andrew Leitch was badly wounded and Thomas Knowlton gravely so. Both died of their wounds. "Their men, however, persevered and continued the engagement with the greatest resolution."

Washington threw more soldiers into the battle. "These troops charged the enemy with great intrepidity and drove them from the wood into the plain, and were pushing them from thence (having silenced their fire in a great measure) when I judged it prudent to order a retreat, fearing the enemy (as I have since found was really the case) were sending a large body to support their party."

The battle of Harlem Heights wasn't a major engagement. Washington lost slightly more killed and wounded than Howe. But for the first time, his men made him proud. They fought the British on equal terms. "This affair I am in hopes will be attended with many salutary consequences, as it seems to have greatly inspirited the whole of our troops," he told Hancock.

. . .

FOUR DAYS LATER, in the middle of the night, a fire broke out on the west side of New York city. The flames rapidly spread. "The fire raged with inconceivable violence," an eyewitness reported, "and in its destructive progress swept away all the buildings between Broad street and the North River"—the Hudson—"almost as high as the City Hall, and from thence all the houses between Broadway and the North River as far as King's College, a few only excepted. Long before the main fire reached Trinity church, that large, ancient and venerable edifice was in flame, which baffled every effort to suppress them. The steeple, which was one hundred and forty feet high, the upper part wood, and placed on an elevated situation, resembled a vast pyramid of fire, exhibiting a most grand and awful spectacle. Several women and children perished in the fire. Their shrieks, joined to the roaring of the flames, the crush of falling houses, and the widespread ruin which everywhere appeared, formed a scene of horror great beyond description, which was still heightened by the darkness of the night."

As many as a quarter of the city's structures were destroyed or damaged before the flames were brought under control by city residents and British soldiers, aided by a shift in the wind. Fire wasn't unusual in American cities, but the timing of this conflagration, when New York was no longer of use to Washington and was about to become useful to Howe, appeared suspicious.

Washington denied complicity in the fire even as he acknowledged its convenience. To John Hancock he wrote, "I have not been informed how the accident happened." To his cousin Lund Washington he said of the fire, "Providence—or some good honest fellow—has done more for us than we were disposed to do for ourselves." Indeed Washington regretted that more damage hadn't been done to what he left the British. "Near one fourth of the city is supposed to be consumed. However, enough of it remains to answer their purposes."

Washington added, "Had I been left to the dictates of my own judgment, New York should have been laid in ashes before I quitted it. To this end I applied to Congress, but was absolutely forbid. That they will have cause to repent the order, I have not a moment's doubt of, nor never had, as it was obvious to me (covered as it may be by their ships) that it will be next to impossible for us to dispossess them of it again as all their supplies come by water, whilst ours were derived by land. Besides this, by leaving it standing, the enemy are furnished with warm and comfortable barracks in which their whole force may be concentred, the place secured by a small garrison (if they choose it) having their ships round it, and only a narrow neck of land to defend, and their principal force left at large to act against us or to remove to any other place for the purpose of harassing us. This in my judgment may be set down among one of the capitol errors of Congress."

No one admitted setting the fire. The British interrogated scores of people but found none to prosecute. The fire might have been accidental. It might have been lit by friends of American independence thinking they were doing Washington a favor. Or it might have been set by criminal types who understood that a city between military regimes was an easy target for arson and the opportunities a fire provided for plunder. Larcenous arson had plagued cities for centuries and would do so in America for decades more.

53

Washington's pleasure at the modest victory on Harlem Heights didn't last. Washington's intelligence brought reports that William Howe was moving troops across the neck between Long Island Sound and the Hudson. Washington risked being cut off from his supplies, which came mostly from New England. "If the enemy advance from the Sound, so must we," he told Connecticut's Jonathan Trumbull. "They must never be allowed to get above us and possess themselves of the upper country if it is possible to avoid."

White Plains was a crossroads in the middle of the neck between the sound and the river. It was also one of Washington's supply depots. To secure the junction and the supplies before Howe did, Washington sent most of his troops marching in that direction.

Joseph Martin had joined the Connecticut militia at sixteen and come under Washington's command during the summer of 1776. He evacuated New York with Washington, and now he evacuated Harlem Heights. "We crossed Kings Bridge"—linking upper Manhattan Island to the mainland—"and directed our course toward the White Plains," Martin recounted. "We saw parties of the enemy foraging in the country, but they were generally too alert for us. We encamped on the heights called Valentine's Hill, where we continued some days, keeping up the old system of starving." Short rations in Washington's army gave rise to grim humor. "A sheep's head which I begged of the butchers, who were killing some for the 'gentleman officers,' was all the provisions I had for two or three days."

The troops were ordered to proceed carefully. "We marched from Valentine's Hill for the White Plains in the night. There were but three of our men"—from Martin's company—"present. We had our cooking utensils, at that time the most useless things in the army, to carry in our hands. They were made of cast iron and consequently heavy. I was so beat out before morning, with hunger and fatigue, that I could hardly move one foot before the other. I told my messmates that I *could not* carry our kettle any further; they said they *would not* carry it any further. Of what use was it? They had nothing to cook."

They reached White Plains at dawn. No battle seemed imminent and so they went foraging. They found a field of turnips, but the owner was there protecting it against the likes of Martin and his hungry mates. Lacking money, they worked out an agreement by which they would pick the farmer's turnips in exchange for a portion of the harvest.

When they arrived back at the camp, it was abuzz. "Upon inquiry, we found that the British were advancing upon us. We flung our turnip plunder into the tent, packed up our things, which was easily done for we had but a trifle to pack, and fell into the ranks." Their regiment marched in the direction of the British and took shelter behind a stone wall to await the enemy's approach. "They were not far distant, at least that part of them with which we were quickly after engaged," Martin recalled. "There was in our front, about ten rods distant"—some fifty yards—"an orchard of apple trees. The ground on which the orchard stood was lower than the ground that we occupied but was level from our post to the verge of the orchard, when it fell off so abruptly that we could not see the lower parts of the trees. A party of Hessian troops, and some English, soon took possession of this ground. They would advance so far as just to show themselves above the rising ground, fire, and fall back and reload their muskets. Our chance upon them was, as soon as they showed themselves above the level around, or when they fired, to aim at the flashes of their guns." Neither side did much damage to the other.

"We were engaged in this manner for some time, when finding ourselves flanked and in danger of being surrounded, we were compelled to make a hasty retreat from the stone wall," Martin said. This exposed them to the enemy fire. "We lost, comparatively speaking, very few at the fence, but when forced to retreat, we lost, in killed and wounded, a considerable number."

They didn't retreat far. "We fell back a little distance and made a stand, detached parties engaging in almost every direction." In time the shooting died down. "We did not come in contact with the enemy again that day, and just at night we fell back to our encampment."

Martin and his comrades discovered what the enemy had been up to. "In the course of the afternoon the British took possession of a hill on the right of our encampment, which had in the early part of the day been occupied by some of the New York troops. This hill overlooked the one upon which we were, and was not more than half or three-fourths of a mile distant. The enemy had several pieces of field artillery upon this hill and, as might be expected, entertained us with their music all the evening."

Howe's troops outnumbered Washington's, and more were on the way. Washington decided to disengage and retreat farther north. Howe declined to pursue.

HOWE HAD SOME WORK on Manhattan to finish. Washington, upon departing the island, had left a garrison at Fort Washington, on a high point on the east bank of the Hudson, from which its cannons, in conjunction with those of Fort Lee on the New Jersey side, could challenge British ships plying the channel. Washington felt misgivings about his decision, for the post would soon be surrounded by British troops on the east and ships on the west. But Congress didn't want to surrender the Hudson to the British, and Nathanael Greene, whom Washington had left in charge of the area, thought the position could be held.

When reports revealed that British warships were sailing past Fort Washington and Fort Lee with impunity, Washington's misgivings increased. "If we cannot prevent vessels passing up, and the enemy are possessed of the surrounding country, what valuable purpose can it answer to attempt to hold a post from which the expected benefit cannot be had?" he wrote to Greene. But he made clear he was giving an opinion rather than an order. "I am therefore inclined to think it will not be prudent to hazard the men and stores at Mount Washington"—Fort Washington—"but as you are on the spot, leave it to you to give such orders as to evacuating Mount Washington as you judge best."

Greene judged best to hold Fort Washington, or at least try. It was a bad choice. Fort Washington became a trap for its garrison. William Howe's soldiers closed in by land, and Richard Howe's sailors prevented relief or escape by water. Washington belatedly visited the area, having crossed the Hudson to New Jersey upstream and then slipping back across from Fort Lee. But by then the fort was surrounded.

Robert Magaw, the garrison's commandant, led a spirited defense but was outmanned and outgunned. Realizing the futility of continued resistance, he surrendered the fort and its nearly three thousand surviving defenders.

"This is a most unfortunate affair and has given me great mortification," Washington wrote to brother Jack. And it was his fault. He had heeded Congress and his subordinate when he should have followed his own counsel. "I did not care to give an absolute order for withdrawing the garrison till I could get round and see the situation of things, and then it became too late as the fort was invested." He told Jack about advising Greene to abandon the fort. "But as the order was discretionary, and his opinion differed from mine, it unhappily was delayed too long, to my great grief."

Washington confessed deep discouragement. "I am wearied almost to death with the retrograde motions of things," he told Jack.

54

Two weeks later Washington opened a letter delivered to his temporary headquarters. The retrograde motion had continued as Howe trailed him and most of the American army across New Jersey. Confident of that army's demise, Howe took his time in pursuit, establishing a chain of posts to secure New Jersey against rebel recidivism.

Washington had reached Brunswick when the letter arrived. It was from Charles Lee, whom Washington had left with a small force in northern New Jersey, and was addressed to Joseph Reed, Washington's adjutant general. Correspondence intended for Washington was often addressed to Reed, who happened to be away from camp. "Having no idea of its being a private letter, much less suspecting the tendency of the correspondence, I opened it, as I had done all other letters to you from the same place," Washington informed Reed by a letter of his own. "This, as it is the truth, must be my excuse for seeing the contents of a letter which neither inclination or intention would have prompted me to."

Lee's letter was not meant for Washington's eyes. It was clearly a response to a letter from Reed to Lee on a subject that became apparent as Washington read. "I received your most obliging flattering letter—lament with you that fatal indecision of mind which in war is a much greater disqualification than stupidity or even want of personal courage," Lee wrote to Reed. "Accident may put a decisive blunderer in the right, but eternal defeat and miscarriage must attend the man of the best parts if cursed with indecision." Washington had heard criticism of his indecision at Fort Washington. He realized Lee and Reed were talking about him.

Lee offered a more recent example. "The General recommends in so pressing a manner as almost to amount to an order to bring over the Continental troops under my command, which recommendation or order throws me into the greatest dilemma from several considerations," he wrote. "Part of the troops are so ill furnished with shoes and stockings, blankets etc. that they must inevitably perish in this wretched weather. Part of 'em are to be dismissed on Saturday next"—November 30, the end of their term of enlistment—"and this part is the best accoutred for service." If Washington gave an actual order, Lee would move the troops. But Washington refused to take responsibility for making the decision.

Washington never liked criticism. He especially didn't like overhearing it from his subordinates. Washington had thought Reed talented and loyal. He had great hopes for him. But now he began to have doubts. He didn't know exactly what Reed had written that Lee was responding to. He wasn't going to ask.

If he had, he would have become more upset. "I do not mean to flatter nor praise you at the expense of any other," Reed had written to Lee, "but I confess I do think that it is entirely owing to you that this army and the liberties of America so far as they are dependent on it are not totally cut off. You have decision, a quality often wanting in minds otherwise valuable and I ascribe to this our escape from York Island, from Kingsbridge and the Plains"—White Plains—"and I have no doubt had you been here the garrison at Mount Washington would now have composed a part of this army. Under all these circumstances I confess I ardently wish to see you removed from a place where I think there will be little call for your judgment and experience to the place where they are like to be so necessary. Nor am I singular in my opinion. Every gentleman of the family, the officers and soldiers generally have a confidence in you. The enemy constantly inquire where you are, and seem to me to be less confident when you are present."

Reed's sources told him that Howe and the British were laughing at Washington. "They hold us very cheap in consequence of the late affair at Mount Washington, where both the plan of defence and execution were contemptible. If a real defence of the lines was intended, the number was too few. If the fort only, the garrison was too numerous by half. General Washington's own judgment, seconded by representations from us, would, I believe, have saved the men and their arms, but, unluckily, General Greene's judgment was contrary. This kept the General's mind in a state of suspense till the stroke was struck." It was a fateful stroke, and it was Washington's fault. "An indecisive mind is one of the greatest misfortunes that can befall an army. How often have I lamented it this campaign."

Someone had to act, Reed said. "All circumstances considered, we are in a very awful and alarming state, one that requires the utmost wisdom and firmness of mind. As soon as the season will admit, I think yourself and some others should go to Congress and form the plan of the new army." Reorganization was afoot. It should start at the top. "If they will not or cannot do this, I fear all our exertions will be vain."

HOW MUCH OF THIS Washington surmised is unclear. He chose to say nothing more for the time being. And then Lee was captured by a British scouting party and made a prisoner.

This unexpected development threw Reed back on Washington as the one who must save the army and the cause. The reason Reed wasn't in camp with Washington when Lee's letter arrived was that he was nosing around New Jersey and Pennsylvania to discover what Howe was up to and what the people of those states were thinking about the war. Reed was a New Jersey native and had been a Pennsylvania resident, with contacts throughout both states. He was serving as Washington's eyes and ears at what seemed a critical moment for the American cause.

From what Reed discovered, the end was near unless things changed. He had spoken with other officers and with civilians sympathetic to the cause of independence. "We are all of opinion, my dear General, that something must be attempted to revive our expiring credit, give our cause some degree of reputation and prevent a total depreciation of the Continental money, which is coming on very fast," he wrote to Washington from Bristol, Pennsylvania. The Continental Congress had been paying its bills with paper money that depreciated with each issue from the printing press. "Even a failure cannot be more fatal than to remain in our present situation. In short, some enterprize must be undertaken in our present circumstances or we must give up the cause." The soldiers were dispirited. "In a little time the Continental Army is dissolved," Reed predicted. "The militia must be taken before their spirits and patience are exhausted."

The Howe brothers in their capacity as peace commissioners had published a new offer of amnesty to rebels who would put down their arms and swear allegiance to the crown. The offer was good for two months. "Something must be attempted before the 60 days expires which the commissioners have allowed," Reed said to Washington, "for however many affect to despise it, it is very evident that a very serious attention is paid to it, and I am confident that unless some more favourable appearance attends our arms and cause before that time a very great number of the militia officers here will follow the example of those of Jersey and take benefit from it."

Reed suggested that Howe had overextended his army. He was trying to occupy too much territory with too few troops. "The scattered, divided state of the enemy affords us a fair opportunity of trying what our men will do when called to an offensive attack." Howe seemed to be settling in for the winter. He supposed Washington was too. So Washington should do the opposite. "Will it not be possible, my dear General, for your troops or such part of them as can act with advantage to make a diversion or something more at or about Trenton? The greater the alarm the more likely success will attend the attacks. If we could possess ourselves again of New Jersey or any considerable part of it, the effects would be greater than if we had never left it."

Reed likely thought that if Washington was already angry for feeling betrayed, he couldn't get much angrier at being told how to do his job. "Pardon the freedom I have used," he said. "The love of my country, a wife and four children in the enemy's hands, the respect and attachment I have to you, the ruin and poverty that must attend me and thousands of others"—in the event of defeat—"will plead my excuse."

He stressed again the need for decisive action. "Our cause is desperate and hopeless if we do not take the opportunity of the collection of troops at present to strike some stroke. Our affairs are hasting fast to ruin if we do not retrieve them by some happy event. Delay with us is now equal to a total defeat."

REED WAS RIGHT about Howe's deciding to wind down the campaign. "The weather having become too severe to keep the field, and the winter cantonments being arranged, the troops marched from both places to their respective stations," Howe wrote to George Germain in London. He had gathered two parts of his army and distributed the soldiers across New Jersey. "The chain"—of defensive positions—"I own, is rather too extensive, but I was induced to occupy Burlington to cover the county of Monmouth, in which there are many loyal inhabitants; and trusting to the almost general submission of the country to the southward of this chain, and to the strength of the corps placed in the advanced posts, I conclude the troops will be in perfect security."

. . .

SUCH COMPLACENCY WAS what Washington was counting on. If the commanding general's ears burned more from Reed's admonition to take the offensive than from Lee's lament about his refusal to make decisions, he rose above it—almost. He replied to Reed saying that such an attack as he suggested was already in the works. Reed wasn't the only one who could think offensively. "Christmas day at night, one hour before day, is the time fixed upon for our attempt on Trenton," he wrote to Reed on December 23. He added, in what Reed must have taken as deserved criticism for careless unconfidentiality, "For heaven's sake, keep this to yourself."

Washington was writing from the west bank of the Delaware River, above Trenton on the east side. Most of the army had crossed over with him. The attack on Trenton would come from several directions at once. "The more we can attack at the same instant, the more confusion we shall spread and greater good will result from it," he told Reed. Washington hoped for a moral and political victory rather than anything strategic. But who knew? "I have ordered our men to be provided with three days provisions ready cooked, with which and their blankets they are to march. For if we are successful, which heaven grant and other circumstances favour, we may push on."

— 55 —

Each brigade to be furnished with two good guides," ordered Washington on Christmas Day. "General Stevens's brigade to form the advanced party and to have with them a detachment of the artillery without cannon, provided with spikes and hammers to spike up the enemy's cannon in case of necessity or to bring them off if it can be effected. The party to be provided with drag ropes for the purpose of dragging off the cannon. General Stevens is to attack and force the enemy's guards and seize such posts as may prevent them from forming in the streets, and in case they are annoyed from the houses to set them on fire." Other brigades had other assignments.

"Four pieces of artillery to march at the head of each column, three pieces at the head of the second brigade of each division, and two pieces with each of the reserves," he continued. "The troops to be assembled one mile back of McKonkey's ferry, and as soon as it begins to grow dark, the troops to be marched to McKonkey's ferry and embark onboard the boats."

Surprise was essential to success. Discipline was all-important. "A profound silence to be enjoined, and no man to quit his ranks on the pain of death." Nor should civilians be allowed to spread the alarm. "Captain Washington and Captain Flahaven with a party of 40 men each to march before the divisions and post themselves on the road about three miles from Trenton and make prisoners of all going in or coming out of town."

Punctuality was vital. "The heads of the columns to be appointed to arrive at Trenton at five o'clock."

"TRENTON IS AN OPEN TOWN, situated nearly on the banks of the Delaware, accessible on all sides," Henry Knox wrote to his wife. "Our army was scattered along the river for nearly twenty-five miles. Our intelligence agreed that the force of the enemy in Trenton was from two to three thousand, with about six field cannon, and that they were pretty secure in their situation, and that they were Hessians—no British troops. A hardy design was formed of attacking the town by storm. Accordingly a part of the army, consisting of about 2,500 or 3,000, passed the river on Christmas night, with almost infinite difficulty, with eighteen field pieces. The floating ice in the river made the labor almost incredible." Lack of ice on the river had protected Washington's army from the British, who otherwise could have marched over the Delaware. But the weather was getting colder, and now the forming ice impeded Washington's crossing by boat. "However, perseverance accomplished what at first seemed impossible," Knox said.

Yet it put the operation behind schedule. Washington wanted the attacking columns to converge on the town in the dark. They wouldn't get there until after daylight. "About two o'clock the troops were all on the Jersey side," Knox continued. "We then were about nine miles from the object. The night was cold and stormy. It hailed with great violence. The troops marched with the most profound silence and good order. They arrived by two routes at the same time, about half an hour after daylight, within one mile of the town. The storm continued with great violence, but was in our backs, and consequently in the faces of our enemy." Washington's force had lost the cover of darkness but partly compensated with the cover of the storm.

"About half a mile from the town was an advanced guard on each road, consisting of a captain's guard," said Knox. Washington expected the guard to be light and inattentive. The Germans weren't anticipating an attack, and they would probably be hungover from their Christmas celebration. He wasn't wrong.

"These we forced, and entered the town," Knox said of the guards. The surprise of the Hessians was almost complete. They staggered around disoriented. Knox couldn't believe the good luck. "Here succeeded a scene of war of which I had often conceived but never saw before. The hurry, fright and confusion of the enemy was not unlike that which will be when the last trump shall sound." American cannons and howitzers had been placed strategically around the town. "These, in the twinkling of an eye, cleared the streets." The Hessians sought shelter in houses. "The musketry soon dislodged them."

The Hessians were soldiers for hire. Every battle entailed a weighing of risk against reward. A quick reckoning convinced them that this fight was too risky. Fleeing the cannons and the muskets, the Hessians converged in the one place Washington had left open to them, a plain at the edge of town surrounded by his soldiers. "The poor fellows after they were formed on the plain saw themselves completely surrounded," Knox said. They put down their weapons and surrendered.

ELISHA BOSTWICK REMEMBERED Washington on the march from the Delaware landing to Trenton. This son of Connecticut had besieged Boston with Washington, evacuated New York with him and trudged across New Jersey with him. Bostwick recalled the ice-clogged river and the driving snow, hail and rain. "About daylight a halt was made at which time his Excellency"—Washington—"and aides came near to front on the side of the path where the soldiers stood. I heard his Excellency as he was coming on speaking to and encouraging the soldiers. The words he spoke as he passed by where I stood and in my hearing were these: 'Soldiers, keep by your officers. For God's sake, keep by your officers'—spoke in a deep and solemn voice. While passing a slanting slippery bank, his Excellency's horse's hind feet both slipped from under him and he seized his horse's mane and the horse recovered."

Bostwick and the other soldiers had heard scary stories of the Hessians. He was curious to see what they looked like up close. They didn't appear to be monsters or devils, certainly not after being taken prisoner. "They are of a moderate stature," he wrote, "rather broad shoulders, their limbs not of equal proportion, light complexion with a bluish tinge hair queued as tight to the head as possible sticking straight back like the handle of an iron skillet. Their uniform blue with black facings, brass drums which made a timbling sound, their flag or standard of the richest black silk and the devices upon it and the lettering in gold leaf. When crossing the Delaware with the prisoners in flat bottom boats, the ice continually stuck to the boats driving them downstream. The boatman endeavoring to clear off the ice pounded the boat, and stamping with their feet beckoned to the prisoners to do the same and they all set to jumping at once with their queues flying up and down. Soon shook off the ice from the boats."

FOR THE FIRST TIME in months, Washington had good news for John Hancock. "I have the pleasure of congratulating you upon the success of an enterprize which I had formed against a detachment of the enemy lying in Trenton, and which was executed yesterday morning," he wrote on December 27. He described the danger and delay of the Delaware crossing. "This made me despair of surprizing the town, as I well knew we could not reach it before the day was fairly broke," he said. But he pressed on. "I formed my detachment into two divisions, one to march by the lower or river road, the other by the upper or Pennington road." The latter reached Trenton at eight o'clock, the former a few minutes after.

Amid the confusion occasioned by the attack, some of the Hessians formed into a column and tried to escape by the road to Princeton. "But perceiving their intention, I threw a body of troops in their way, which immediately checked them," Washington said. "Finding from our disposition that they were surrounded, and that they must inevitably be cut to pieces if they made any further resistance, they agreed to lay down their arms." Nine hundred had been taken. "Our loss is very trifling indeed, only two officers and one or two privates wounded."

Yet the victory had been less than complete. The ice and storm had kept two of Washington's commanders from reaching Trenton. "I am fully confident that could the troops under Generals Ewing and Cadwallader have passed the river, I should have been able with their assistance to have driven the enemy from all their posts below Trenton. But the numbers I had with me, being inferior to theirs below me, and a strong battalion of light infantry being at Princeton above me, I thought it most prudent to return"—across the river to Pennsylvania—"the same evening with the prisoners and the artillery we had taken."

Washington had criticized his soldiers for their shortcomings following defeats. Now he praised them for their strengths. "Their behaviour upon this occasion reflects the highest honor upon them," he told Hancock. "The difficulty of passing the river in a very severe night, and their march through a violent storm of snow and hail did not in the least abate their ardour." So uniform was the gallant performance that he wouldn't identify any by name. "Were I to give a preference to any particular corps, I should do great injustice to the others."

56

As pleased as Washington was with the attack on Trenton, the more he thought about the enemy who had gotten away, the more their escape galled him. He decided to finish the job. "I am just setting out to attempt a second passage over the Delaware," he wrote to Hancock on December 29. "I am determined to effect it, if possible, but know that it will be attended with much fatigue and difficulty on account of the ice, which will neither allow us to cross on foot or give us an easy passage with boats."

Perhaps he sought to preempt criticism that he hadn't been sufficiently decisive in following up the victory at Trenton. He explained, "The peculiar distresses to which the troops who were with me were reduced by the severities of cold, rain, snow and storm; the charge of the prisoners they had taken; and another reason that might be mentioned"—apparently drunkenness among soldiers who got into the Hessians' liquor supply—"and the little prospect of receiving succours on account of the season and situation of the river would not authorize a further pursuit at that time."

On this second crossing, Washington was better prepared and more determined than ever.

He had a particular reason for making his second crossing so soon after the first. "Three or four days after the victory at Trenton, the American army recrossed the Delaware into New Jersey," recalled a sergeant in Washington's army whose name was lost to history. "At this time our troops were in a destitute and deplorable condition. The horses attached to our cannon were without shoes and when passing over the ice they would slide in every direction and could advance only by the assistance of the soldiers. Our men too were without shoes or other comfortable clothing, and as traces of our march toward Princeton, the ground was literally marked with the blood of the soldiers' feet. Though my own feet did not bleed, they were so sore that their condition was little better."

The sergeant discovered what Washington's hurry was, if he hadn't discerned it already. "While we were at Trenton, on the last of December, 1776, the time for which I and most of my regiment had enlisted expired. At this trying time General Washington, having now but a little handful of men and many of them new recruits in which he could place but little confidence, ordered our regiment to be paraded and personally addressed us, urging that we stay a month longer. He alluded to our recent victory at Trenton, told us that our services were greatly needed and that we could now do more for our country than we ever could at any future, and in the most affectionate manner entreated us to stay." Washington likely reasoned that his soldiers would be more willing to reenlist when in enemy territory and dependent on him for their safety.

"The drums beat for volunteers, but not a man turned out," the sergeant said. "The soldiers, worn down with fatigue and privations, had their hearts fixed on home and the comforts of the domestic circle, and it was hard to forego the anticipated pleasures of the society of our dearest friends."

Washington wouldn't give up. "The general wheeled his horse about, rode in front of the regiment and, addressing us again, said, 'My brave fellows, you have done all I asked you to do, and more than could be reasonably expected. But your country is at stake—your wives, your houses, and all that you hold dear. You have worn yourselves out with fatigues and hardships, but we know not how to spare you. If you will consent to stay only one month longer, you will render that service to the cause of liberty and to your country which you probably never can do under any other circumstances. The present is emphatically the crisis, which is to decide our destiny.' The drums beat the second time. The soldiers felt the force of the appeal. One said to another, 'I will remain if you will.' Others remarked, 'We cannot go home under such circumstances.' A few stepped forth, and their example was immediately followed by nearly all who were fit for duty in the regiment, amounting to about two hundred volunteers."

WASHINGTON HAD ANOTHER PURPOSE for returning to Trenton, aside from shaming his soldiers into staying. He wanted to win a second victory in New Jersey before going into winter quarters, to show that the first wasn't a fluke.

Howe had been embarrassed by Washington's rout of the Hessians, and he was eager to smite him back. Howe dispatched Charles Cornwallis from New York to attack Washington. Cornwallis chose Princeton as a gathering spot.

"Cornwallis left that place"—Princeton—"with the intention of attacking and at one blow cutting off the rebel army," the anonymous American sergeant said. A creek separated Cornwallis's army from Washington's smaller force. A bridge spanned the creek. Cornwallis tried the bridge once, twice, thrice. The Americans repelled the British each time. Cornwallis pulled his troops back, content to delay the decisive stroke until the morrow.

Washington decided not to wait around. "Leaving our fires kindled to deceive the enemy, we decamped that night and by a circuitous route took up our line of march for Princeton," the sergeant recalled. Washington put mile after mile between him and Cornwallis and arrived at Princeton at sunrise. "As we were descending a hill through an orchard, a party of the enemy who were entrenched behind a bank and fence rose and fired upon us," the sergeant said. "Their first shot passed over our heads, cutting the limbs of the trees under which we were marching. At this moment we were ordered to wheel. As the platoon which I commanded were obeying the order, the corporal who stood at my left shoulder received a ball and fell dead on the spot. He seemed to bend forward to receive the ball, which might otherwise have ended my life.

"We formed, advanced and fired upon the enemy. They retreated eight rods to their packs, which were laid in a line. I advanced to the fence on the opposite side of the ditch which the enemy had just left, fell on one knee and loaded my musket with ball and buckshot. Our fire was most destructive. Their ranks grew thin and the victory seemed nearly complete, when the British were reinforced. Many of our brave men had fallen, and we were unable to withstand such superior numbers of fresh troops.

"I soon heard General Mercer command, in a tone of distress, 'Retreat!' He was mortally wounded and died shortly after. I looked about for the main body of the army which I could not discover, discharged my musket at part of the enemy, and ran for a piece of wood at a little distance where I thought I might shelter.

"At this moment Washington appeared in front of the American army, riding towards those of us who were retreating, and exclaimed, 'Parade with us, my brave fellows! There is but a handful of the enemy, and we will have them directly.' I immediately joined the main body and marched over the ground again."

The Americans' new energy made itself felt. "The British were unable to resist this attack and retreated into the college where they thought themselves safe. Our army was there in an instant, and cannon were planted before the door, and after two or three discharges, a white flag appeared at the window and the British surrendered. They were a haughty, crabbed set of men, as they fully exhibited while prisoners, on their march to the country. In this battle my pack, which was made fast by leather strings, was shot from my back, and with it went what little clothing I had. It was, however, soon replaced by one which had belonged to a British officer and was well furnished. It was not mine long, for it was stolen shortly afterwards."

One scene from the battle remained with the sergeant for the rest of his life. "Oh, the barbarity of man! On our retreat we had left a comrade of ours whose name was Loomis, from Lebanon, Connecticut, whose leg was broken by a musket ball, under a cart in a yard. But on our return he was dead, having received several wounds from a British bayonet. My old associates were scattered about groaning, dying and dead. One officer who was shot from his horse lay in a hollow place in the ground rolling and writhing in his blood, unconscious of anything around him. The ground was frozen and all the blood which was shed remained on the surface, which added to the horror of this scene of carnage."

Washington's men carried the day. Their victory at Princeton was less complete than the one at Trenton had been, but it had the merit of being fought against a prepared enemy. Trenton had shown that the Americans were capable of surprise, Princeton that they were capable of fighting.

Part VII

Valley Forge

57

"My Lord, it is with much concern that I am to inform your lordship the unfortunate and untimely defeat at Trenton has thrown us farther back than was at first apprehended, from the great encouragement it has given to the rebels," Howe wrote to Germain. "I do not now see a prospect of terminating the war but by a general action, and I am aware of the difficulties in our way to obtain it as the enemy moves with so much more celerity than we possibly can with our foreign troops, who are too much attached to their baggage which they have in amazing quantities in the field. Nor can we hazard a march at this unfavourable season with any hope of making a stroke upon the enemy in his present situation that might turn the scale in our favour."

Given that another campaign would be necessary, Howe requested reinforcements. "Twenty thousand men would by no means exceed our wants," he said. "Yet fifteen thousand will give us a superiority that I should hope may be materially experienced in the course of the campaign." Howe explained his strategy. "Philadelphia being now the principal object, by the greatest number"—the twenty thousand—"we should be enabled to detach a corps to enter the Delaware by sea and the main body to penetrate into Pennsylvania by way of Jersey. There would also in that case be a sufficient corps to act from Rhode Island." If he got the smaller number of reinforcements or none at all, he could not expect to expand British control beyond New York and New Jersey.

Germain let Howe know he'd get nothing near the twenty thousand he wanted. The general would have to make do or revise his strategy.

"In these circumstances," Howe rejoined, "I find myself under the necessity of relinquishing a principal part of the plan." Rhode Island was out of the question, as was the overland march through New Jersey. The central objective—Philadelphia—remained. "I propose to invade Pennsylvania by sea," said Howe. This would probably take all summer, given the absence of the land army that would have pinned Washington down. The whole timetable of the war would have to be readjusted. "My hopes of terminating the war this year are vanished."

Yet taking Philadelphia would speed subsequent action. "I have reason to expect in the case of success in Pennsylvania there will be found a considerable part of the inhabitants who may be embodied as militia, and some as provincial troops for the interior defence of the province, which must be a great aid in the further progress of the war."

The long-term prognosis was good. "I think it probable that by the latter end of the campaign we shall be in possession of the provinces of New York, the Jerseys"—New Jersey—"and Pennsylvania."

Howe added a disclaimer: "This in some measure must depend upon the successes of the northern army."

HOWE'S NORTHERN ARMY, commanded by John Burgoyne and based in Canada, was what kept Washington awake nights. Its existence made him regret again the failure of the campaign against Quebec. If Arnold and Richard Montgomery had captured Quebec, they would have deprived the British of the St. Lawrence and secured America's northern frontier. But they hadn't, and now Burgoyne was prepared to drive south along the Lake Champlain–Hudson River corridor. If he succeeded in linking with the British troops holding the lower Hudson, America would be cut in two. Washington was struggling to keep his army intact with the resources of all America. Without New England and New York, his fate would be sealed.

Washington assumed Howe reckoned similarly. The British general would be tempted to send troops north to meet Burgoyne. Between Burgoyne and Howe stood Horatio Gates with a northern army of Washington's own. Gates, the former British officer, thought he knew better than Washington how to beat his old comrades in arms. Even more did he think he knew better than Philip Schuyler, his senior in the Continental army's northern department. Washington and the Congress came to agree with the latter part of Gates's judgment, giving him Schuyler's job.

Washington had to decide whether to reinforce Gates. Washington had few troops to spare. And as important as the New York corridor was, Philadelphia was important too. It was the new nation's seat of government. For Howe to capture Philadelphia would signal to Americans and the world that Washington was feckless and the independence cause hopeless.

Washington couldn't afford to lose either the New York corridor or Philadelphia. But he couldn't afford to strengthen both. Which way should he go: north or south?

FROM NEW JERSEY AND through spies and other informants he kept a close watch on Howe and the British forces in New York. "As yet they have made no movement," Washington reported to Jonathan Trumbull in April. "But from our advices of their preparations, there are strong reasons to believe that they are upon the eve of doing it, and from a variety of combining circumstances, it appears that Philadelphia will be the first object of their attention."

Yet Washington wasn't ready to commit. "The stratagems of war are various and may be easily changed, especially when they have the entire command of the water," he wrote to John Hancock about Howe and the British. Hancock wanted Washington to hasten to Philadelphia to defend the government. Washington demurred. "In the present divided, separated state of the army, we are weak at all points." To strengthen Philadelphia would weaken the New York corridor, perhaps irretrievably.

Washington assured Hancock his army was nimbler than Howe's. "If the enemy pushed for Philadelphia, we should have notice of it and could hang upon their flank and rear," he said. "Nor is it likely they would undertake such an expedition without attempting the destruction or dispersion of the army first. If they embarked and should go by sea, we should have information of it and could be there in time. On the other hand, should all they have done prove a feint, and they should turn their views to the North River"—the Hudson—"we should be in a much better situation to counteract their designs and to check the progress of their arms in that quarter."

Washington's refusal to commit revived the old charges of indecisiveness. Connecticut's Trumbull complained that he was writing off New England. Washington responded that he was doing the best he could. "I should be happy, were it in my power, to station guards of Continental troops at every place subject to the depredations of the enemy," he said. "But this cannot be done. If we divide and detach our forces to every part where the enemy may possibly attempt an impression, we shall effect no one good purpose, in the end destroy ourselves and subjugate our country." Reacting to diversionary attacks was just what Howe wanted Washington to do. Washington wouldn't play that game. "The enemy have certainly some capital object in view, either Philadelphia or Hudson's River. Till their designs are unfolded, all the troops from this and the more southern states must assemble in this quarter to prevent their possessing the former."

WHILE WAITING FOR Howe to move, Washington had to quiet what seemed a minor ruckus in his own ranks. Benedict Arnold had been passed over for promotion and was threatening to resign. Washington tried to talk him back. "I was surprized when I did not see your name in the list of major generals," he wrote to Arnold. He had inquired about the reason. "The members from each state seemed to insist upon having a proportion of general officers adequate to the number of men which they furnish." Connecticut, Arnold's state, already had its quota. "I confess this is a strange mode of reasoning, but it may serve to shew you that the promotion which was due to your seniority was not overlooked for want of merit in you."

Washington wrote to Hancock on Arnold's behalf. Arnold's record on the battlefield spoke for itself. As to his moral rectitude and other intangibles: "It is needless to say anything of this gentleman's military character. It is universally known that he has always distinguished himself as a judicious, brave officer, of great activity, enterprise and perseverance."

WASHINGTON'S GENERAL ORDERS often included announcements of personnel changes. The orders for March 1, 1777, introduced a new member of the headquarters staff. "Alexander Hamilton Esquire is appointed Aide-De-Camp to the Commander in Chief, and is to be respected and obeyed as such."

Hamilton had been born on Nevis in the British Leeward Islands. His father and mother never married. His father abandoned the family when Hamilton was a boy, and his mother died of disease, leaving him a de facto orphan. Yet he had gifts. He was smart. He had received the beginnings of a good education. He possessed a desire to advance himself. "My ambition is prevalent," he wrote to a friend when he was twelve years old and working for a merchant in St. Croix. "I contemn the groveling and condition of a clerk or the like, to which my fortune etc. condemns me and would willingly risk my life, though not my character, to exalt my station." He had a talent for impressing people who could help him get ahead. Among the impressed were a group of locals who sent him to British North America for further education.

Hamilton entered King's College in New York in 1773. He was sixteen, but he seemed older than his years. Indeed, questions later arose about his date of birth, suggesting he might have *been* older than his stated years. Whatever the case, he blazed a trail of distinction in the college. As the troubles with Britain intensified, Hamilton ardently embraced the American cause in speech and writing. Understanding that war offered unusual opportunities for advancement, he studied the military arts in books and began drilling with fellow college students. After fighting broke out at Lexington, he helped raise a company of artillery and got himself elected captain. His company joined Washington's army when Washington arrived in New York from Boston. Hamilton took part in the battles of Harlem Heights and White Plains. He crossed the Delaware with Washington for the attack on Trenton, and at Princeton he commanded some of the cannons that flushed British soldiers out of the college's Nassau Hall.

He made a good impression on Washington, who invited him to join his military family, as a general's staff was called. Perhaps Washington, recalling his time with Edward Braddock, saw something of himself in Hamilton. Perhaps he thought of Hamilton as the son he never had.

Perhaps Hamilton saw Washington as a substitute for his missing father. He certainly perceived in Washington someone who could advance his career.

Within days of his arrival at headquarters, Hamilton was speaking in Washington's name. "Your letter of the 7th instant to his Excellency fell into my hands," he wrote to Brigadier General Alexander McDougall on March 10. "He has been very much indisposed for three or four days past, insomuch that his attention to business is pronounced by the doctor to be very improper; and we have made a point of keeping all from him which was not indispensably necessary. I detained your express a day in hopes of a convenient opportunity to communicate your letter to him; but though he has grown considerably better than he was, I find he is so much pestered with matters which cannot be avoided that I am obliged to refrain from troubling him on the occasion; especially as I conceive the only answer he would give may be given by myself."

McDougall had asked for more troops for his command at Peekskill, New York. He worried that the British might attack him. Hamilton told him to make do with what he had. "It is greatly to be lamented that the present state of things does not admit of having the requisite number of troops at every post," he said. "On the contrary the most important are deficient, and we are under the necessity of calling all that can be gotten together to those places where the danger is the most pressing and imminent. 'Till matters get into a better train, it is impossible but those posts must suffer which from their situation ought only to be the objects of a secondary attention."

After telling McDougall that the position he held wasn't important, the nineteen-year-old aide explained that McDougall wouldn't be worried if he knew what Hamilton knew. The British were heading south, he said. "To this end they are drawing all their forces into the Jerseys, and as soon as the weather will permit 'tis expected they will move towards Philadelphia. Not being very numerous, 'tis unlikely they should attempt such an object without collecting their whole force, and for that reason 'tis not much to be apprehended they should make any stroke of the kind you mention, which would require a number of men they could not spare and would probably delay the execution of what clearly appears to be their principal intention."

ARNOLD AND HAMILTON WERE worth promoting, Washington judged. Others were not. The Congress had sent Benjamin Franklin to Paris to secure French aid against Britain. Ideally this would take the form of a French alliance. Until then French money would suffice. Franklin deployed his charm and wit against King Louis XVI and the French foreign minister, the Comte de Vergennes. Vergennes was dubious, while Louis was opposed. Vergennes's doubts had to do with America's chances of beating the British. If France linked arms with America, it would find itself at war with Britain. Vergennes was willing for his country to fight Britain but not to do it alone. The Americans needed to show staying power and credibility. An important battlefield victory would go far in that direction. Louis's opposition reflected his royal dislike for republicanism. The Americans' effort to overthrow their king might give dangerous ideas to the French people about *their* king.

Awaiting the victory that would bring the French government around, Franklin recruited wealthy and influential French individuals. Some were willing to enlist their money, in the form of loans to America. More than a few wanted to enlist themselves. Some of these were experienced soldiers but currently underemployed. Others were dreamers who fancied playing soldier against the historic foe of France. Both sorts asked Franklin to recommend them to the American commander in chief. Franklin frequently did so, especially when the requesters had powerful patrons.

Washington humored them and Franklin at first. In time, though, their numbers grew unmanageable. "I have been honored with your favor of the 2d of April by Monsieur de Cenis, written in behalf of that gentleman on the credit of Monsieur Turgot's recommendation," Washington wrote to Franklin in the summer of 1777. "I should have been happy had it been in my power, in deference to your recommendation, founded upon that of so respectable a character as Monsieur Turgot, to afford Monsieur de Cenis the encouragement to which his zeal and trouble in coming to America to offer his services give him a claim to." But the supply had outstripped the demand. "Our troops being already formed and fully officered, and the number of foreign gentlemen already commissioned and continually arriving with fresh applications throw such obstacles in the way of any future appointments that every new arrival is only a new source of embarrassment to Congress and myself, and of disappointment and chagrin to the gentlemen who come over."

Washington urged Franklin to spare him any more volunteers. "It would be both prudent and just to discourage their coming over by candidly opening the difficulties they have to encounter," Washington told Franklin. "If, after that, they will persist in it, they can only blame themselves." Washington didn't want to make Franklin's diplomatic work more difficult. "I am sensible, sir, that it is a delicate and perplexing task to refuse applications of persons patronized (as I suppose often happens) by some of the first characters in the kingdom where you are, and whose favor it is of importance to conciliate." But enough was enough.

Franklin cut back. Yet he still asked favors of Washington. One involved "a young nobleman of great expectations and exceedingly beloved here," as Franklin explained to Washington. The nobleman was the Marquis de Lafayette, a teenager of vast inherited wealth and growing ardor for liberty. Lafayette had defied the expectations of his class and the discouragement of the king to travel to America. Franklin liked Lafayette but thought him naive. He asked Washington to look after him. "His friends here have sent him over about £500 sterling and have proposed sending him more. But on reflection, knowing the extreme generosity of his disposition, and fearing that some of his necessitous and artful countrymen may impose on his goodness, they wish to put his money into the hands of some discreet friend who may supply him from time to time." Franklin hoped Washington would be that person. Lafayette might or might not become a good officer, but his money would certainly be useful. And Washington's care for Lafayette would be "gratefully remembered and acknowledged by a number of very worthy persons here."

Washington was skeptical. Lafayette's wealth and connections dazzled Congress, which on his arrival made him a major general in Washington's army. Many in Congress thought the young man would be satisfied with an honorary post, but he had other ideas, as Washington discovered. "He has misconceived the design of his appointment, or Congress did not understand the extent of his views," Washington wrote to Benjamin Harrison, a Virginia member of Congress. "For certain it is, if I understood *him,* that he does not conceive his commission is merely honorary but given with a view to command a division of this army. It is true he has said that he is young and inexperienced, but at the same time has always accompanied it with a hint that, so soon as *I* shall think *him* fit for the command of a division, he shall be ready to enter upon the duties of it, and in the meantime has offered his service for a smaller command." Washington was skeptical that Lafayette's appointment would turn out any better than the others he'd been complaining of.

WASHINGTON HAD COME to expect deliberation from Howe. For the most part the British commander's slowness worked to Washington's benefit. Yet during the summer of 1777 it kept him on edge. Howe, in his headquarters in New York, must be planning a campaign. But toward what objective?

"By the motions among their shipping, they appear to be preparing for some expedition by water; it is impossible to determine where," Washington observed to John Rutledge of South Carolina in early July. Rutledge was the chief executive of South Carolina at a time when the states considered themselves sovereign, and so his title was president, although he and the other chief executives were often called governor. Howe's expedition might be to the south, which was why Washington was informing Rutledge.

On the other hand, it might be to the north. "We have lately received intelligence from General Schuyler that the enemy are beginning to operate against Ticonderoga. If this proves to be anything more than a diversion, there is no doubt General Howe will proceed up Hudson's River, for if they have any rational end in view, it must be a junction of the two armies to intercept the communication between the eastern and southern states." Washington couldn't let the joining happen. He'd have to move his own army to prevent it.

"But this may be nothing more than a diversion," he acknowledged. Howe's main objective might be elsewhere. "Our situation is truly delicate and perplexing."

Fresh intelligence suggested the Hudson was *not* Howe's objective. Mentioning reports from deserters and spies, Washington wrote to Jonathan Trumbull, "We are told by these that accommodations for horses are filling up in the transports, that they are taking in large supplies of provisions, water, and provender, and that officers' baggage is continually transporting on board of them from New York, marked with their names and the corps they belong to. These representations, if true, seem to denote an expedition that would take longer time than would be necessary for one up the North River. But where, is all matter of conjecture, and cannot be determined with any degree of certainty. Prudence dictates that we should be as much upon our guard as possible everywhere."

Two weeks later Washington knew no more. "General Howe still lays entirely quiet on board the fleet at Staten Island," Washington wrote to William Heath, one of his major generals. "Very few troops remain on shore, and the destination a profound secret." To John Hancock he professed chagrin. "We have been under great embarrassments respecting the intended operations of General Howe, and still are, notwithstanding the utmost pains to obtain intelligence of the same. At present it would appear that he is going out to sea. By authentic information, there are only forty ships at New York; the rest are gone elsewhere and have fallen down between the Narrows and the Hook"—Sandy Hook, the New Jersey spit at the lower end of the Hudson estuary. "Between these two places the number, from the most accurate observation, was about one hundred and twenty yesterday. As I observed before, their destination is uncertain and unknown."

Again as before, Washington was wary of tricks. "The enemy will probably make many feints," he told Hancock. He had to be vigilant but not gullible. "Our situation is already critical and may be rendered still more so by inaccurate and ill-grounded intelligence."

He caught one trick in late July, or thought he did. A young man arrived at Washington's camp with a letter from Howe to the British general Burgoyne. The fellow said he'd been a prisoner of the British and was offered a reward to deliver the letter to Burgoyne. He said he'd accepted the assignment with the intention of delivering the letter instead to Washington. The letter told Burgoyne there had been a change of plans. "The expedition to B——n"—Boston, presumably—"will take place of that up the North River. If, according to my expectations, we may succeed rapidly in the possession of B, the enemy having no force of consequence there, I shall, without loss of time, proceed to cooperate with you in the defeat of the rebel army opposed to you." Howe added, "I am now making demonstration to the southward, which I think will have the full effect in carrying our plan into execution."

The letter seemed bogus to Washington. "The complexion of it, the circumstances attending it, etc. evinces this beyond a doubt in my mind." Howe was not going to Boston, he concluded.

So where *was* Howe going? "If it was not too dangerous to hazard their shipping to sea, merely to perform a maneuver to deceive, I should think it not unlikely that the North River might yet be the object, and that they had run out with a view of returning when our troops should be drawn off," Washington continued. "But the possibility of a dispersion of their fleet makes so much against this that I am persuaded more than ever that Philadelphia is the place of destination."

YET THERE WAS MORE than one route to Philadelphia, even by sea. The direct approach was up the Delaware River, which fronted the city. More circuitous was via the Chesapeake Bay, with an overland march from the northern end of that estuary, likely at Head of Elk, the farthest point of navigation up the Elk River, a Chesapeake tributary in northeastern Maryland. The different possible approaches required Washington to prepare very different plans of defense.

His frustrations were getting the better of him. "Since General Howe's remove from the Jerseys, the troops under my command have been more harassed by marching and countermarching than by anything that has happened to them in the course of the campaign," Washington wrote to brother Jack in early August. "After General Howe had embarked his troops, the presumption that he would operate upon the North River to form a junction with General Burgoyne was so strong that I removed from

Middle Brook to Morristown, and from Morristown to the Clove, (a narrow pass leading through the Highlands,) about eighteen miles from the river. Indeed, upon some pretty strong presumptive evidence, I threw two divisions over the North River. In this situation we lay till about the 24th ult., when receiving certain information that the fleet had actually sailed from Sandy Hook (the outer point of New York Harbor) and the concurring sentiment of every one (though I acknowledge my doubts of it were strong) that Philadelphia was the object, we countermarched and got to Coryell's Ferry on the Delaware, (about thirty-three miles above the city) on the 27th, where I lay till I received information from Congress that the enemy were actually at the Capes of Delaware. This brought us in great haste to this place for defence of the city." Washington was writing from Germantown, Pennsylvania, north of Philadelphia.

"But in less than twenty-four hours after our arrival," Washington continued, "we got accounts of the disappearance of the fleet on the 31st, since which, nothing having been heard of them, we remain here in a very irksome state of suspense, some imagining that they are gone to the southward, whilst a majority (in whose opinion upon this occasion I concur) are satisfied they are gone to the eastward. The fatigue, however, and injury, which men must sustain by long marches in such extreme heat, as we have felt for the last five days, must keep us quiet till we hear something of the destination of the enemy."

The longer Howe stayed at sea, the less Washington knew about where he might ultimately land. "I am now of opinion that Charlestown is the present object of General Howe's attention, though for what sufficient reason, unless he expected to drag this army after him by appearing at different places, and thereby leave the country open for General Clinton to march out and endeavor to form a junction with General Burgoyne, I am at a loss to determine," Washington wrote to Horatio Gates on August 20.

IT WAS PHILADELPHIA after all. On August 22, Washington informed Hancock that Howe's fleet had been spotted entering Chesapeake Bay. Washington at once mobilized to get his army between Philadelphia and Head of Elk, where the British indeed landed. "I this morning returned from the Head of Elk, which I left last night," he wrote to Hancock on August 27. Though Howe had finally brought his soldiers to shore again, he continued to take his time. "They remain where they debarked at first. I could not find out from inquiry what number is landed, nor form an estimate of it from the distant view I had of their encampment."

Two weeks later Howe still hadn't made serious contact. "The enemy advanced yesterday with a seeming intention of attacking us upon our post near Newport," Washington wrote on September 9. Newport, Delaware, lay between Head of Elk and Philadelphia. "We waited for them the whole day, but in the evening they halted at a place called Milltown, about two miles from us. Upon reconnoitring their situation, it appeared probable that they only meant to amuse us in front, while their real intent was to march by our right, and by suddenly passing the Brandywine and gaining the heights upon the north side of that river get between us and Philadelphia and cut us off from it."

Washington couldn't let that happen. "The army accordingly marched at two o'clock this morning and will take post this evening on the high grounds near Chadds Ford"—the main crossing over Brandywine Creek, or River. He added, "We have heard nothing circumstantial of the enemy today."

58

William Howe wasn't just being tricky in keeping Washington in the dark about his attack plans. Like Washington, he had priorities to juggle and political masters to appease. Almost as often as Washington wrote to John Hancock and the state governors for more men and provisions, Howe pleaded with George Germain and the British ministry. "The war is now upon a far different scale with respect to the increased powers and strength of the enemy than it was the last campaign, their officers being much better and the addition of several from the French service and a very respectable train of field artillery," Howe wrote to Germain in July. "I must therefore urge the completing the British regiments here with drafts and good British recruits, or we shall soon lose our consequence by the current casualties of a campaign exclusive of a general action." Howe valued the Hessians who fought on his side, and he thought the principle behind their recruitment could be gainfully extended. "A corps of Russians of 10,000 effective fighting I think would ensure the success of the war to Great Britain in another campaign." Failing this, Howe said, he'd be hard pressed to sustain control of any territory his troops conquered.

Just as Washington tried to guess where Howe would go, Howe did the same with Washington. After his informants told of Washington's movement toward the Hudson when he thought Howe was going north, Howe wrote to Germain, "He seems to point at preventing a junction between this and the northern army." Howe *wasn't* going north, but he still laid plans to deal with what Washington did. "If the enemy should cross the North River before I sail from hence"—New York—"or should approach it so near as to give me a prospect of reaching Philadelphia before him, I shall in either case strengthen Sir Henry Clinton still more than by the reserve which is already ordered to remain here." Clinton was going to secure New York while Howe went to Philadelphia. "He will then have a sufficient force to act against the whole rebel army." But if Washington instead marched toward Philadelphia, Howe would need the extra troops there.

King George expressed concern that Howe's thrust toward Philadelphia would jeopardize Burgoyne's attack down the Champlain-Hudson corridor. Through Germain, George said he hoped Howe would be able to take Philadelphia and return north in time to assist Burgoyne. Howe thought his contingency plan with Clinton had covered this scenario. Tactfully he told George, through Germain, that he wasn't planning on returning north at once. He couldn't simply take Philadelphia and leave. The victory wouldn't stick. "I cannot flatter myself I shall be able to act up to the King's expectations in this particular," Howe said. "My progress independent from the enemy's principal army must be greatly impeded by the prevailing disposition of the inhabitants, who I am sorry to observe seem to be, excepting a few individuals, strongly in enmity against us, many having taken up arms and by far the greater numbers deserted their dwellings, driving off at the same time their stock of cattle and horses." Howe reminded Germain that he hadn't received the troops he needed. Germain had better tell the king not to hold his breath awaiting victory in America. Howe said that without those troops he had "not the smallest hope" of winning the war during the present fighting season.

"LAST NIGHT GENERAL HOWE received the reliable information that General Washington has retreated somewhat, that he now has 3,000 men on this side of the Brandywine, in the hills before Chads Ford, and that the main army is positioned also in the region of Chads Ford and higher up in the hills that come close to the Brandywine," wrote Friedrich von Muenchhausen, an aide to Howe, in his diary for September 11. "At five o'clock in the morning General Howe marched off to his left, up the Brandywine." Charles Cornwallis had tactical command of this column, with Howe accompanying. "Our column consisted of two battalions of English light infantry, two battalions of English grenadiers, two battalions of English guards, two brigades of English infantry, two squadrons of dragoons, the Hessian jaegers and the Hessian grenadiers." Howe sent a second column more directly toward Washington's army. "At six o'clock in the morning General Knyphausen set out to march with his column, which consisted of four regiments of Hessians, two brigades of Englishmen under General Grant, the 71st regiment of Highland Scots, one squadron of dragoons, the Hessian mounted jaegers, and 350 Provincials, as well as the English riflemen, plus all the baggage, including cattle," wrote Muenchhausen. "His route was toward Chads Ford by way of Welch's tavern."

Howe's plan was for Knyphausen's column to engage Washington's front, while Cornwallis's column circled to his rear. Washington would either stand and fight on two fronts or break and run.

"Since our column had no baggage but did have a number of sappers in the van, we moved forward quickly in spite of the great heat," Muenchhausen continued. Sappers were adept in clearing roads, among other things. "During the march, we heard some small arms fire about 10 o'clock in the morning, and later cannon shot, which continued almost during the whole march. At noon our vanguard came upon 200 rebel dragoons, who wounded some of our men by their fire, but they soon retreated. We crossed the Brandywine seven miles up from Chads Ford, where the river is divided into two branches; the bridges were destroyed." Washington had burned the bridges trying to prevent the British from doing what Howe was now doing. "The men had to cross these two branches in up to three feet of water. We then continued our march a short distance straight ahead, and then suddenly to the right down along the Brandywine toward the region of Chads Ford. After a march of 17 miles we finally arrived on a steep, barren height, where we formed into two lines by brigades. We were now on the other side of Chads Ford, although it was still three miles to the left." Howe called a halt to give the men an hour to rest and to let stragglers catch up.

The cannon fire Muenchhausen had heard came from the guns of Knyphausen, who had engaged Washington's front at mid-morning and kept him busy all day, while Cornwallis was circling to his rear. In the late afternoon, Cornwallis attacked.

"Now the rebels found themselves between two fires," Muenchhausen explained. He gave the enemy credit. "The rebels fought very bravely." Their commander had done well too. "Washington executed a masterpiece of strategy today by sending columns from his right to his left wing in the beginning, without attempting to veil these movements. This was to give us the impression that his strength was there"—when it wasn't. Moreover, Washington maneuvered his troops to slow Howe's advance. "The battle lasted longer than it should have. This delay benefited Washington, who in case he should be defeated could not be pursued by us because of darkness."

Which was what happened. Pinned between Cornwallis and Knyphausen, Washington had to give way. The one thing that allowed him to escape with his army was that Howe's roundabout march had taken so long to accomplish. "If daylight had lasted a few hours longer, I dare say that this day would have brought an end to the war," Muenchhausen remarked. "Without doubt we would have taken half of Washington's army and all of his cannon."

WASHINGTON'S ACCOUNT OF the battle of Brandywine was more succinct. "I am sorry to inform you that in this day's engagement we have been obliged to leave the enemy masters of the field," he wrote to Hancock late on September 11. "Unfortunately the intelligence received of the enemy's advancing up the Brandywine and crossing at a ford about six miles above us was uncertain and contradictory, notwithstanding all my pains to get the best. This prevented my making a disposition adequate to the force with which the enemy attacked us on our right, in consequence of which the troops first engaged were obliged to retire before they could be reinforced. In the midst of the attack on the right, that body of the enemy which remained on the other side of Chad's Ford crossed it and attacked the division there under the command of General Wayne and the light troops under General Maxwell, who after a severe conflict also retired."

Things could have been worse. "Though we fought under many disadvantages and were from the causes above mentioned obliged to retire, yet our loss of men is not, I am persuaded, very considerable—I believe much less than the enemy's. We have also lost seven or eight pieces of cannon, according to the best information I can at present obtain."

When daylight allowed a closer tally, Washington discovered that his first estimate was quite wrong. His casualties numbered more than a thousand, or twice Howe's. The cannons lost were eleven out of fourteen.

Even so, the army was intact. "Notwithstanding the misfortune of the day, I am happy to find the troops in good spirits," Washington told Hancock. "And I hope another time we shall compensate for the losses now sustained."

⤞ 59 ⤝

In early October, Washington received a packet from John Hancock that contained good news but nonetheless irked him. Washington's retreat after Brandywine left Philadelphia open to Howe and the British. Congress had fled the city ahead of the enemy, in search of a new seat of government. The members stopped at Lancaster, Pennsylvania, before moving on to York. The hasty movements disrupted communications, delaying letters from Washington to Hancock and from Hancock to Washington, along with most other messages to and from Congress.

On September 30, Hancock wrote to Washington from York, saying that the Congress would be meeting there until further notice. Hancock continued, "I have just now received by General Gates's aide de camp (Major Troup) sundry letters, copies of which I have the honour to inclose you, by which it appears that our affairs in the northern department wear a favourable aspect."

One of Gates's letters was dated September 22, and was written at Bemis Heights, New York, near Saratoga. "Friday morning"—September 19—"I was informed by my reconnoitring parties that the enemy had struck their camp and were moving towards our left," Gates wrote. The enemy was the British northern army led by Burgoyne. "I immediately detached Colonel Morgan's corps, consisting of the rifle regiment and the light infantry of the army to observe their direction and harass their advance. This party at half after twelve fell in with a picquet of the enemy which they drove, but the enemy being reinforced after a brisk conflict, they were in turn obliged to retire. This skirmish drew the main body of the enemy, and a brigade from my left to support the action, which, after a short cessation was renewed with great warmth and violence. At this instant, hearing from prisoners that the whole British force and a division of foreigners had engaged our party, I reinforced with four more regiments. This continued the action till the close of day, when both armies retired from the field."

Not only had Gates fought Burgoyne to a standstill. He had hurt him personally and done great damage to his army. "I am well assured by the concurrent testimony of prisoners and deserters of various characters that General Burgoyne, who commanded in person, received a wound in his left shoulder, that the 62d Regiment was cut to pieces, and that the enemy suffered extremely in every quarter where they were engaged."

Gates's success at arms gave pleasure to Washington. The fact that Gates had bypassed him—his commanding officer—in reporting it did not. The timing could hardly have put Washington in a worse light. Washington had just been routed by Howe, losing Philadelphia in the process, as every member of Congress was painfully aware. Meanwhile, Gates had delivered a telling blow against Burgoyne, likely saving the United States from being split in two. And he had boasted of that fact to those same discomfited members of Congress, while leaving his own superior in the dark.

Washington's state of mind didn't improve when he suffered another setback at Howe's hands. After the defeat at Brandywine, Washington had retreated to a position west of Philadelphia. Howe pursued him, and Washington turned to engage. But as the battle began, the autumn skies opened and soaked the two armies. The downpour dampened Washington's powder and with it his ardor for battle against the more numerous foe. He left the field to Howe, who permitted him to escape again.

Howe stationed a few thousand troops in Philadelphia but encamped most of his soldiers at Germantown, to the north. Washington let Howe get settled and distracted by the business—and pleasures—of holding and administering America's principal city. Washington laid plans for a multipronged surprise attack against the British force at Germantown, like the one that had taken Trenton, only bigger and more momentous.

"The divisions of Sullivan and Wayne, flanked by Conway's brigade, were to enter the town by the way of Chestnut Hill, while General Armstrong with the Pennsylvania militia should fall down the Manatawny road by Vandeering's Mill, and get upon the enemy's left and rear," Washington explained to Hancock after the fact. "The divisions of Greene and Stephen, flanked by McDougall's brigade, were to enter by taking a circuit by way of the Lime-kiln road, at the Market-house, and to attack their right wing. And the militia of Maryland and Jersey, under Generals Smallwood and Forman, were to march by the old York road and fall upon the rear of their right. Lord Stirling, with Nash's and Maxwell's brigades, was to form a *corps de reserve*."

Washington's troops approached the enemy camp on the night of October 3 and rested on their arms. "General Sullivan's advanced party, drawn from Conway's brigade, attacked their picket at Mount Airy, or Mr. Allen's house, about sunrise the next morning, which presently gave way," Washington continued. "And his main body, consisting of the right wing, following soon, engaged the light infantry and other troops encamped near the picket, which they forced from their ground." The British retreated, leaving their baggage behind. "The attack from our left column, under General Greene, began about three quarters of an hour after that from the right, and was for some time equally successful."

But things became confused. "I cannot enter upon the particulars of what happened in that quarter, as I am not yet informed of them with sufficient certainty and precision," Washington said. "The morning was extremely foggy, which prevented our improving the advantages we gained, so well as we should otherwise have done. This circumstance, by concealing from us the true situation of the enemy, obliged us to act with more caution and less expedition than we could have wished; and gave the enemy time to recover from the effects of our first impression. And what was still more unfortunate, it served to keep our different parties in ignorance of each other's movements and hinder their acting in concert. It also occasioned them to mistake one another for the enemy, which I believe more than anything else contributed to the misfortune that ensued. In the midst of the most promising appearances, when everything gave the most flattering hopes of victory, the troops began suddenly to retreat, and entirely left the field, in spite of every effort that could be made to rally them."

Washington tried to put the best face on things. "Upon the whole, it may be said the day was rather unfortunate than injurious. We sustained no material loss of men, and brought off all our artillery, except one piece which was dismounted. The enemy are nothing the better by the event, and our troops, who are not in the least dispirited by it, have gained what all young troops gain by being in actions."

Additional intelligence again forced Washington to revise his initial battle assessment. "Since I had the honor of addressing you on the 5th," he wrote to Hancock on October 7, "I have obtained a return of our loss in the action on Saturday, by which it appears to be much more considerable than I first apprehended." Washington's casualties exceeded a thousand in killed, wounded, captured and missing, or about twice Howe's.

He remained as mystified as before at the sudden turn of the battle. "Every account confirms the opinion I first entertained that our troops retreated at the instant when victory was declaring herself in our favor. The tumult, disorder and even despair which, it seems, had taken place in the British army, were scarcely to be paralleled. And, it is said, so strongly did the ideas of a retreat prevail, that Chester"—a village on the far side of Philadelphia—"was fixed on as their rendezvous. I can discover no other cause for not improving this happy opportunity than the extreme haziness of the weather."

Washington said he would regroup and reconsider. "My intention is to encamp the army at some suitable place to rest and refresh the men, and recover them from the still remaining effects of that disorder naturally attendant on a retreat. We shall here wait for the reinforcements coming on and shall then act according to circumstances."

WASHINGTON WAS STILL BLAMING the weather as he recounted the Germantown defeat to Jack two weeks later. "But for a thick fog, which rendered so infinitely dark at times as not to distinguish friend from foe at the distance of thirty yards, we should, I believe, have made a decisive and glorious day of it," he said. "But Providence or some unaccountable something designed it otherwise, for after we had driven the enemy a mile or two, after they were in the utmost confusion and flying before us in most places, after we were upon the point (as it appeared to everybody) of grasping a complete victory, our own troops took fright and fled with precipitation and disorder."

Washington was sealing his letter to Jack when a messenger arrived. Washington added a postscript. "I had scarce finished this letter when by express from the state of New York I received the important and glorious news which follows: 'Last night at 8 o'clock the capitulation whereby General Burgoyne and whole army surrendered themselves prisoners of war, was signed and this morning they have to march out towards the river' "—the Hudson—" 'above Fish Creek with the honours of war (and there ground their arms). They are from thence to be marched to Massachusetts Bay. We congratulate you on this happy event.' " The message was signed by George Clinton, governor of New York, who added, "I most devoutly congratulate you, my country, and every well-wisher to the cause on this signal stroke of Providence."

Washington didn't comment to Jack that this was the second time he'd learned about a Gates victory only indirectly.

MUCH AS WASHINGTON BLAMED his defeat at Germantown on the fog—which Howe didn't notice, or at least didn't mention in the account of his victory there—Burgoyne blamed the surrender at Saratoga on the auxiliaries he was compelled to employ. In a letter to Germain from his detention after the surrender, Burgoyne bemoaned the "total defection of the Indians" and the "desertion or timidity of the Canadians and provincials"—American loyalists. His own British troops were sturdier. "The British have persevered in a strenuous and bloody progress. Had the force been *all* British, perhaps the perseverance had been longer." The outnumbered British troops had stood up to a wearing campaign conducted with short supplies for as long as could be reasonably asked. Burgoyne went on to suggest that the outcome wasn't as bad as it seemed. "Will it be said, my lord, that in the exhausted situation described and in the jaws of famine and invested by quadruple numbers, a treaty which saves the army to the state for the next campaign was not more than could be expected? I call it saving the army because if sent home, the state is thereby enabled to send forth the troops now destined to her internal defense; if exchanged, they become a force to Sir William Howe as effectually as if any other junction had been made."

Burgoyne had to say something about the American rebels. "The standing corps I have seen are disciplined. I do not hazard the term but apply it to the great fundamental points of military institution, sobriety, subordination, regularity and courage. The militia are inferior in method and movement but not a jot less serviceable in woods." Occasionally the Americans could be spooked, but not for long. "The panic of the rebel troops is confined and of short duration, the enthusiasm is extensive and permanent."

William Howe had his own interpretation of Saratoga, as devaluing his capture of Philadelphia. The effects were both immediate and longer lasting. "My lord," he wrote to Germain, "in consequence of the misfortune that has fallen upon the troops under Lieutenant General Burgoyne's command, a considerable reinforcement from General Gates's corps has joined General Washington." This was the immediate effect, making more difficult Howe's present pursuit of Washington.

The longer effect was on American morale. "The hopes of the people at large as well as of the rebel army are greatly raised from this event," Howe said. Victory over the rebellion receded still further into the future. "I do not apprehend the successful termination to the war from any advantages His Majesty's troops can gain while the enemy is able to avoid or unwilling to hazard a decisive action which might reduce the leaders in rebellion to make an overture for peace; or that this is to be expected unless a respectable addition to the army is sent from Europe."

Howe knew that Germain and the government wanted good news. They wouldn't be getting any until policy changed. "As a duty I owe to your lordship and in obedience to His Majesty's commands, I candidly declare my opinion that in the apparent temper of the Americans a considerable addition to the present force will be requisite for effecting any essential change in their disposition and the reestablishment of the king's authority, and that this army acting on the defensive will be fully employed to maintain its present possessions."

60

Washington's annoyance at Gates grew further when he learned that other officers were casting aspersions on his leadership. The victories at Trenton and Princeton had silenced the mutterings of Charles Lee and Joseph Reed, but Brandywine, Germantown and the loss of Philadelphia raised the old questions about his leadership. In early November he received a letter recounting what Thomas Conway, a native of Ireland who had become a brigadier general in the Continental army, had written to Gates. The offending line, said to have been written by Conway, was, "Heaven has been determined to save your country, or a weak general and bad counsellors would have ruined it."

Conway, at least in the part of the letter Washington heard about, hadn't recommended Washington's removal from command. But the fact that the letter was to Gates, who had recently shown himself strikingly more successful than Washington, and who on that account was the obvious candidate to replace him, appeared significant. Washington tersely copied the line in a letter to Conway, to let him know he was aware some thing was afoot.

Conway denied having written the line ascribed to him. "I wrote to General Gates by Major Troop the 9th or 10th of last month," he replied to Washington. "I spoke my mind freely. I found fault with several measures pursued in this army. But I will venture to say that in my whole letter the paragraph of which you are pleased to send me a copy cannot be found."

Lest Washington think Conway had something to hide, Conway stated directly what he thought of him. "My opinion of you, sir, without flattery or envy is as follows: you are a brave man, an honest man, a patriot, and a man of great sense. Your modesty is such that although your advice in council is commonly sound and proper, you have often been influenced by men who were not equal to you in point of experience, knowledge or judgment."

Conway said he had expressed these sentiments in private conversations. "I think they will be found such in my letter to General Gates. I believe I can attest that the expression *weak general* has not slipped from my pen. However, if it has, this weakness by my very letter cannot be explained otherwise even by the most malicious people than an excess of modesty on your side and a confidence in men who are much inferior to you in point of judgment and knowledge. I defy the most keen and inveterate detractors to make it appear that I levelled at your bravery, honesty, honour, patriotism or judgment, of which I have the highest sense."

Conway didn't like the whispering campaign being conducted against him. He had served in the French army before relocating to America to join the fight against Britain, the historic oppressor of Ireland, and he now gave Washington a short course in comparative military cultures. "Correspondence between general officers in all armies is encouraged rather than discountenanced, because from this intercourse of ideas something useful might arise." He chided Washington for conducting an "inquisition in letters" unbecoming a commander in a republican army. Yet he offered to show Washington the full letter he wrote to Gates, "in order that the least suspicion should not remain in your Excellency's mind about my way of thinking."

A short while later Conway offered to resign. The American victory at Saratoga seemed to increase the chances of a French alliance with America against Britain. "The hopes and appearance of a French war, along with some other reasons, have induced me to send my resignation to Congress," he informed Washington. "I hope your Excellency will permit me to depart the army in order to return to France as soon as possible." He would leave with nothing but goodwill in his heart. "I return thanks to your Excellency for the civilities you have shewed me while I had the honour of being under your orders, and beg you will accept my warm and sincere wishes for the liberty of America and the success of your arms."

Not so fast, said Washington. "It remains with Congress alone to accept your resignation," he replied. "This being the case, I cannot permit you to leave the army till you have obtained their consent. When that is done, I shall not object to your departure, since it is your inclination."

Congress did not consent. Rather, it promoted Conway to major general and made him inspector general of Washington's army. Some members wanted him to apply to America's army what he'd learned of professional military practices in France. Others reckoned that if a

French alliance did happen, Conway would be a good liaison. Still others, themselves disappointed with Washington's performance, wanted to keep him around as a witness for the prosecution should they decide to replace Washington.

Washington chose not to fight this battle. He dismissed the notion that he might be uncomfortable on account of Conway's new posting. "Your appointment of Inspector General to the Army I believe has not given the least uneasiness to any officer in it," he told Conway. Washington included himself among the non-uneasy. Anyway, what Congress did was the business of Congress. "I have nothing to do in the appointment of general officers and shall always afford every countenance and due respect to those appointed by Congress, taking it for granted that prior to any resolve of that nature they take a dispassionate view of the merits of the officer to be promoted."

WASHINGTON MIGHT HAVE let the matter drop, but others weren't willing. Henry Laurens, the new president of the Continental Congress, passed along an unsigned essay urging Congress to switch commanders, citing the success of the Saratoga campaign as indication where to look for Washington's replacement.

"I cannot sufficiently express the obligation I feel to you for your friendship and politeness upon an occasion in which I am so deeply interested," Washington answered Laurens. "I was not unapprized that a malignant faction had been for some time forming to my prejudice, which, conscious as I am of having ever done all in my power to answer the important purposes of the trust reposed in me, could not but give me some pain on a personal account." He had chosen not to answer in public. "My chief concern arises from an apprehension of the dangerous consequences which intestine dissentions may produce to the common cause."

Washington said he welcomed an investigation into his conduct, if Laurens and Congress thought the accusations merited looking into. "My enemies take an ungenerous advantage of me. They know the delicacy of my situation and that motives of policy deprive me of the defence I might otherwise make against their insidious attacks. They know I cannot combat their insinuations, however injurious, without disclosing secrets it is of the utmost moment to conceal."

Patrick Henry, now serving as the first governor of the independent state of Virginia, sent Washington a copy of an anonymous letter that cast additional aspersions on his leadership. Washington thanked Henry for the information, again explaining his public silence in the matter. "My caution to avoid anything that could injure the service prevented me from communicating but to very few of my friends the intrigues of a faction which I know was formed against me, since it might serve to publish our internal dissentions," he said. "But their own restless zeal to advance their views has too clearly betrayed them and made concealment on my part fruitless. I cannot precisely mark the extent of their views, but it appeared in general that General Gates was to be exalted on the ruin of my reputation and influence. This I am authorised to say from undeniable facts in my own possession, from publications the evident scope of which could not be mistaken, and from private detractions industriously circulated. General Mifflin, it is commonly supposed, bore the second part in the cabal." Thomas Mifflin had been quartermaster general until recently. "And General Conway, I know, was a very active and malignant partizan. But I have good reasons to believe that their machinations have recoiled most sensibly upon themselves."

Washington's use of "cabal" in proximity to "Conway" gave rise to the term by which the episode lived in history. "Conway cabal" ascribed more coherence to the criticisms of Washington than they deserved. Why wouldn't people question whether Washington was the best general the country possessed, given his losing record against Howe? The label was misleading in other ways. Conway never proposed himself for Washington's replacement. Neither did anyone else propose Conway. Horatio Gates was the one the dissatisfied, including Gates himself, had in mind. But the support for Gates never amounted to enough to make a change. The affair fizzled out.

Washington chided Gates merely for failure to communicate. "I do myself the pleasure to congratulate you on the signal success of the army under your command in compelling General Burgoyne and his whole force to surrender themselves prisoners of war," he wrote to Gates. The victory did honor to American arms. "At the same time, I cannot but regret that a matter of such magnitude and so interesting to our general operations should have reached me by report only, or through the channel of letters not bearing that authenticity which the importance of it required and which it would have received by a line under your signature, stating the simple fact."

Yet Washington let Gates know he was being watched. "I have, by the advice of my general officers, sent Colonel Hamilton, one of my aides, to lay before you a full state of our situation and that of the enemy in this quarter. He is well informed upon the subject and will deliver my sentiments upon the plan of operations that is now necessary to be pursued." Washington didn't have to add that Hamilton would report back his assessment of Gates. "From Colonel Hamilton you will have a clear and comprehensive view of things, and I persuade myself you will do everything in your power to facilitate the objects I have in contemplation."

HAMILTON MIGHT NOT have been the best person to send to Gates. He was one with an incentive to keep the "cabal" idea alive. Hamilton rarely missed an opportunity to ingratiate himself with those who might further his career. He wrote to Governor Clinton of New York, Hamilton's adopted state, lamenting what he called the "degeneracy of representation in the great council of America." The twenty-year-old proposed a thorough restructuring of Congress, a project that for Hamilton would last a decade. In this letter he employed gossip as cement in his relationship with Clinton and as a sign of his insider status with Washington. "You and I had some conversation when I had the pleasure of seeing you last with respect to the existence of a certain faction," Hamilton said. "Since I saw you, I have discovered such convincing traits of the monster that I cannot doubt its reality in the most extensive sense. I dare say you have seen and heard enough to settle the matter in your own mind. I believe it unmasked its batteries too soon and begins to hide its head; but as I imagine it will only change the storm to a sap"—change a frontal assault to an undermining—"all the true and sensible friends to their country, and of course to a certain great man, ought to be upon the watch to counterplot the secret machinations of his enemies. Have you heard anything of Conway's history? He is one of the vermin bred in the entrails of this chimera dire, and there does not exist a more villainous calumniator and incendiary."

61

Albigence Waldo was a doctor with a Connecticut regiment that joined Washington's army in Pennsylvania in time for the battle of Germantown. The weeks after that engagement saw sporadic fighting with the British as Howe calculated whether to try one more blow against Washington or simply call it a season. For his part Washington had to keep one eye on Howe and the other looking for a place to winter. Soldiers on both sides showed the symptoms of a long campaign. "Prisoners and deserters are continually coming in," Waldo wrote in his diary on December 14. "The army, which has been surprisingly healthy hitherto, now begins to grow sickly from the continued fatigues they have suffered this campaign." Conditions in camp didn't help. "Poor food, hard lodging, cold weather, fatigue, nasty clothes, nasty cookery." Waldo longed for the familiar. "What sweet felicities have I left at home: a charming wife, pretty children, good beds, good food, good cookery, all agreeable, all harmonious. Here all confusion, smoke and cold, hunger and filthiness. A pox on my bad luck. There comes a bowl of beef soup, full of burnt leaves and dirt, sickish enough to make a Hector spew."

Thin humor prevailed in camp. "Cold rainy day," Waldo wrote on December 16. "Good morning, Brother Soldier (says one to another). How are you? All wet, I thank ye, hope you are so (says the other)."

Washington found the wintering spot he wanted, and on December 19 the army marched to Valley Forge, twenty-five miles northwest of Philadelphia. "Preparations made for huts," Waldo recorded. "Provisions scarce. Mr. Ellis"—a Connecticut neighbor—"went homeward; sent a letter to my wife. Heartily wish myself at home. My skin and eyes are almost spoiled with continual smoke. A general cry through the camp this evening among the soldiers: 'No meat! No meat!' The distant vales echoed back the melancholy sound: 'No meat! No meat!' . . . What have you for your dinners, boys? 'Nothing but fire cake and water, sir.' At night,

'Gentlemen, the supper is ready.' What is your supper, lads? 'Fire cake and water, sir.'" Fire cake was flour mixed with water and cooked in the ashes of a campfire.

"Lay excessive cold and uncomfortable last night," Waldo wrote on December 22. "My eyes are started out from their orbits like a rabbit's eyes, occasioned by a great cold and smoke. What have you got for breakfast, lads? Fire cake and water, sir."

Waldo's regiment was sent to forage. Washington ordered the soldiers to maintain strict discipline lest the locals become alienated. Waldo wasn't sure he could comply. "I am ashamed to say it, but I am tempted to steal fowls if I could find them, or even a whole hog, for I feel as if I could eat one." He needn't have worried. "The impoverished country about us affords but little matter to employ a thief."

Christmas Eve brought no respite. "Huts go on slowly," Waldo wrote. "Cold and smoke make us fret." He turned philosopher. "Mankind are always fretting, even if they have more than their proportion of the blessings of life. We are never easy, always repining at the providence of an all-wise and benevolent being, blaming our country or faulting our friends." A gust brought him back to the present. "But I don't know of anything that vexes a man's soul more than hot smoke continually blowing into his eyes, and when he attempts to avoid it, is met by a cold and piercing wind."

Christmas Day elicited a sigh. "We are still in tents when we ought to be in huts. The poor sick"—Waldo's responsibility—"suffer much in tents this cold weather."

He heard soldiers grumbling against Washington. "Why don't his Excellency rush in and retake the city?" he summarized their complaint. He answered, "Because he knows better than to leave his post and be catched like a d——d fool cooped up in the city. He has always acted wisely hitherto. His conduct when closely scrutinized is uncensurable." The carpers overestimated the troops available to Washington and underestimated those of Howe. And Washington raised new troops only with great difficulty. "If this army is cut off, where should we get another as good? General Washington has doubtless considered these matters, and his conduct this campaign has certainly demonstrated his prudence and wisdom."

Yet the grumbling couldn't be ignored. "Yesterday upwards of fifty officers in General Greene's division resigned their commissions," Waldo wrote on December 28. "Six or seven of our regiment are doing the like today. All this is occasioned by officers' families being so much neglected at home on account of provisions. Their wages will not buy considerable, purchase a few trifling comfortables here in camp, and maintain their families at home, while such extravagant prices are demanded for the common necessaries of life." Careless issue of paper money by Congress had caused the value of the currency to plunge and prices to soar. "What then have they to purchase clothes and other necessaries with?"

Waldo didn't blame the officers for resigning. "When the officer has been fatiguing through wet and cold and returns to his tent where he finds a letter directed to him from his wife filled with the most heart-aching tender complaints a woman is capable of writing, and finally concluding with expressions bordering on despair of procuring a sufficiency of food to keep soul and body together through the winter, that her money is of very little consequence to her, that she begs of him to consider that charity begins at home, and not suffer his family to perish with want in the midst of plenty—when such, I say, is the tidings they constantly hear from their families, what man is there, who has the least regard for his family, whose soul would not shrink within him? Who would not be disheartened from persevering in the best of causes, the cause of his country, when such discouragements as these lie in his way?"

Waldo gained a bit of comfort from learning that life was hard in the enemy camp. "Eleven deserters came in today, some Hessians and some English," he wrote on December 30. "One of the Hessians took an ax in his hand and cut away the ice of the Schuylkill which was 1½ inches thick and 40 rod wide and waded through to our camp. He was half an hour in the water. They had a promise when they were engaged that the war would be ended in one year. They were now tired of the service."

In the first week of 1778, Waldo was called to the side of a dying soldier. He was too late. The soldier expired. "He was an Indian, an excellent soldier and an obedient good-natured fellow." Waldo didn't say what tribe the man was from. Some tribes had sided with the British, others with the Americans. Oneidas and Tuscaroras arrived at Valley Forge later. The sick man might have anticipated them. Or he might have come from a different tribe on his own. "He engaged for money doubtless as others do," Waldo continued, "but he has served his country faithfully. He has fought for those very people who disinherited his forefathers. Having finished his pilgrimage, he was discharged from the War of Life and Death. His memory ought to be respected more than those rich ones who supply the world with nothing better than money and vice."

Waldo had occasion to size up the officers in Washington's army. The foreigners were the most interesting. "The Marquis de la Fayette, a volunteer in our army, and he who gave three ships to Congress, is very agreeable in his person and great in his character, being made a major general. Brigadier Conway, an Irish colonel from France, took umbrage thereat"—at Lafayette's receiving higher rank than Conway—"and resigned, but now is made Inspector General of the army. . . . Major General Lord Stirling is a man of very noble presence and the most martial appearance of any general in the service. . . . Count Pulaski, general of the horse, is a man of hardly middling stature, sharp countenance and lively air. . . . Baron de Kalb, a major general, is another very remarkable character and a gentleman much esteemed."

WALDO DIDN'T MENTION the foreigner who contributed the most at Valley Forge to the American war effort. His diary ended before the arrival of Friedrich Wilhelm von Steuben, a Prussian born into a military family. Steuben fought in the Seven Years' War in the Prussian army and served on the general staff of Frederick II. He won sufficient favor that after the war he was made a baron. But he subsequently fell out of favor, and upon learning that the American colonies had gone to war against Britain and that American diplomats in France were handing out military commissions to experienced officers, he traveled to Paris to tender his services. Benjamin Franklin and Silas Deane misunderstood him, or he misrepresented himself, and they described him in a reference letter as a lieutenant general in the Prussian army, when he had been only a lieutenant to the general. Congress liked his looks and résumé when he arrived in America and made him a major general. After Conway lost favor as inspector general, Steuben took his place.

Washington found Steuben as impressive as the others did. He set him to work creating an American approximation of the Prussian army. The task was complicated by Steuben's lack of English. But he spoke French, and through a translator from French to English he made himself understood.

He emphasized simplicity in commands and celerity in following them. His Prussian background and bearing, and the rank he was thought to have held under Frederick, gave him a military stature no one at Valley Forge except Washington could match. During the winter he wrote a book on military discipline, *Regulations for the Order and Discipline of the*

Troops of the United States, that became a second bible to the Continental army. He created a staff modeled on the Prussian staff.

Washington expressed pleasure with the discipline Steuben and his aides instilled in the troops. "I am perfectly satisfied with the conduct of the officers who have acted as your assistants, and think that the army has derived every advantage from the institution under you that could be expected in so short a time," he wrote to Steuben.

MARTHA WASHINGTON SPENT the winter at Valley Forge with her husband. She hadn't expected to be an army wife when she married Washington, whose military career seemed to be over. Even when he was appointed commanding general of the Continental army in the summer of 1775, she accepted his prediction that he'd be home in the fall. But when he didn't come home, she decided to join him in Cambridge for the winter. They parted in the spring of 1776 when he moved the army to New York. She returned to Mount Vernon. When the war persisted into the following winter, which he and the army spent at Morristown, New Jersey, she rejoined him. By the third winter of the war, her presence during the season between campaigns had come to be expected.

Compared with her life at Mount Vernon, her winters with her husband were cramped and uncomfortable. To be sure, he and she occupied large houses commandeered for the purpose. But these were shared with members of Washington's staff—the domestic arrangement that gave rise to the use of "family" to refer to the group. The commanding couple had servants, but these were few compared with what they were used to at home.

Martha had less to do in camp than at home. Yet she kept busy. As the general's wife, she was hostess to visiting notables. Her husband had become a father figure to many of the troops, and she became a second mother. She visited the hospitals and encouraged the sick and wounded.

She wasn't the only woman in camp, by any means. Other wives joined their husbands. Children weren't unknown. Especially for the common soldiers, having wives and children with them could be a matter of necessity. Army rations, short and monotonous though they were, were better than nothing, which might be the dependents' alternative when the breadwinner was far away.

Unattached women lived around the army, and not only in winter.

Women worked as cooks, nurses, laundresses, seamstresses, provisioners and prostitutes. Where the army went, they went.

War offered opportunities for advancement to some women. Hannah Till was a slave early in the war, hired out to cook for Washington. She received what amounted to hazard pay and saved enough to purchase her freedom. She continued to cook for Washington, on salary. She was with him at Valley Forge. "She could speak, in a good strong voice, of all the things she saw in her long life, with better recollection and readier utterance than any other narrator with whom I have had occasion to so converse," wrote a reporter who met Hannah Till in her old age. The reporter asked about Washington's domestic habits. "She said he was very positive in requiring compliance with his orders, but he was a moderate and indulgent master. He was sometimes familiar among his equals and guests, and would indulge a moderate laugh. He always had his lady with him in the winter campaigns, and on such occasions was pleased when freed from mixed company to be alone in his family. He was moderate in eating and drinking."

The reporter asked if Washington ever prayed. Stories had circulated from Valley Forge of the general on his knees imploring God for help. "She answered that she expected he did, but she did not know that he practiced it." Did he ever swear? "She answered that ideas then about religion were not very strict, and that she thought he did not strictly guard against it in times of high excitements, and she well remembered that on one provocation with her he called her a c——d"—cursed or cussed, presumably—"fool."

Martha Washington mingled with the wives of her husband's senior subordinates. She was younger than Sarah Alexander, the wife of Lord Stirling, but substantially older than Catharine Greene, the wife of Nathanael Greene, and Lucy Knox, the wife of Henry Knox. In dealing with the stresses of camp life, she acted as an older sister to the younger women.

She deflected petitioners from her husband. Four Quaker women arrived at Valley Forge seeking Washington's assistance in obtaining the return of their husbands and several other Quakers who had been exiled from Pennsylvania to Winchester, Virginia, for refusing to swear a loyalty oath to the revolutionary government. "We arrived at about half past one," recorded Elizabeth Drinker, one of the four. "Requested an audience with the General. Set with his wife (a sociable pretty kind of woman) until he came in." Eventually Washington arrived. He chatted with the visitors and invited them to dinner. "There was fifteen of the officers besides the General and his wife, General Green and General Lee. We had an elegant dinner, which was soon over, when we went out with the General's wife up to her chamber, and saw no more of him." Martha amused the women for a time. They then departed, with nothing more from Washington than a pass to get them through the American lines.

WASHINGTON WAS PLEASED to have Martha with him whenever possible, and not simply for her companionship. He worried about her safety amid the turmoil the war had unleashed. Support for independence was by no means universal, with neighbors becoming enemies and each side deeming the other traitors. Patriot militias roamed the countryside looking for loyalists, and loyalist militias looking for patriots. Property was seized and destroyed. Civilians were often collateral damage, sometimes targets.

In a state like Virginia, and for a planter like Washington, concern for wife and home had an additional aspect. Servile insurrections—slave revolts—were a constant worry where enslaved populations outnumbered free. In coastal parts of the Carolinas, the imbalance could be ten to one. In Virginia the ratio was less, but even there the thought of slaves taking arms against their masters and the masters' families kept the planters awake nights. During times of peace, the planters organized patrols to prevent trouble. During the war, most of the young men who typically did the patrolling were off fighting the British.

The British inflamed fears of slave revolts. In November 1775, Governor Dunmore of Virginia issued a proclamation offering freedom to slaves of rebel masters who took up arms on behalf of the British king in the struggle against their masters. It was this offer that motivated Thomas Jefferson to say of King George in the Declaration of Independence that "he has excited domestic insurrections amongst us."

And it was this offer that caused Washington to fear especially for Martha's safety at home. Washington considered himself a responsible master. Like other members of the gentry, he fancied himself above the brutality that characterized slavery when practiced by the lower classes. Yet he didn't expect his slaves to love him, especially not those who worked his fields and rarely even saw him. When they ran away, he paid bounties for their capture and return. He had them punished for trying to escape. He understood that the British offer of freedom would be attractive to some of his slaves. Not to all, for it required military service, in which a man might get killed. And less attractive to men with wives and children who would be left behind if their husbands and fathers went off to join the British army. But to single young men, precisely the ones best suited to military service, the British army might seem an improvement over Washington's army of labor.

Several of Washington's slaves accepted Dunmore's offer. Harry—named Harry Washington after he reached British lines—had been born in West Africa around 1740. He was stolen from his home by slavers, transported to the coast and shipped to America. Washington purchased him in the 1760s. Harry fled Mount Vernon in 1771 but was captured and returned. When he fled again following Dunmore's offer of freedom, he never came back. He crossed British lines and joined the British army, serving first in New York and later in the Carolinas. At the conclusion of the war, he joined the large loyalist evacuation and sailed off to Nova Scotia.

Long before then, Washington changed his mind about permitting the enlistment of black soldiers in the Continental army. Indeed, soon after Dunmore's offer, Washington, with the approval of Congress, began accepting black soldiers, both enslaved and free. This put the former in the position of fighting in bondage for the freedom of their masters from British tyranny. They noticed the irony. "Alas!" wrote Jeffrey Brace, an Africa-born slave dragged to war by his Connecticut master. "Poor African slave to liberate freemen, *my* tyrants."

THE WINTER THE ARMY spent at Valley Forge wasn't especially cold by Pennsylvania standards. But it seemed colder because the troops lacked adequate food to keep their internal fires burning. "Three or four days bad weather would prove our destruction," Washington wrote in late December to Henry Laurens. "What then is to become of the army this winter? And if we are as often without provisions now as with them, what is to become of us in the spring, when our force will be collected, with the aid perhaps of militia, to take advantage of an early campaign before the enemy can be reinforced?"

Washington lamented the opportunities already lost from lack of provisions. And he resented bearing the blame. "It is time to speak plain in exculpation of myself," he told Laurens. "With truth then I can declare that no man, in my opinion, ever had his measures more impeded than I have by every department"—of the government. He had repeatedly requested a minimal store of two days' rations on hand so that the army could strike when a weakness in the enemy appeared. He had been consistently ignored. "No opportunity has scarcely ever offered of taking advantage of the enemy that has not been either totally obstructed or greatly impeded on this account."

He wasn't asking for more than the basic items essential to life and health. "Soap, vinegar and other articles allowed by Congress we see none of, nor have we seen them, I believe, since the battle of Brandywine. The first indeed we have now little occasion for, few men having more than one shirt, many only the moiety of one, and some none at all." The army was disintegrating from want. "Besides a number of men confined to hospitals for want of shoes, and others in farmers' houses on the same account, we have, by a field return this day made, no less than 2898 men now in camp unfit for duty because they are barefoot and otherwise naked." The men couldn't get a decent night's sleep, on account of lacking blankets. To keep from freezing, they had to sit up by fires.

Washington normally treated his political superiors—the members of Congress—with respect. Yet respect came hard now. "I can assure those gentlemen that it is a much easier and less distressing thing to draw remonstrances in a comfortable room by a good fireside than to occupy a cold, bleak hill and sleep under frost and snow without clothes or blankets," he said to Laurens.

Washington's demands received little response. By late January the men were in huts and mostly out of the wind, but they were also out of food. "The present situation of the army is the most melancholy that can be conceived," he wrote. "Our supplies in provisions of the flesh kind for some time past have been very deficient and irregular. A prospect now opens of absolute want such as will make it impossible to keep the army much longer from dissolving unless the most vigorous and effectual measures be pursued to prevent it." Foraging parties had done all they could. "Jersey, Pennsylvania and Maryland are now entirely exhausted. All the beef and pork already collected in them or that can be collected will not by any means support the army one month longer." Washington had heard of provisions in the southern states, but getting the goods to Valley Forge might be impossible. "The distance will not allow it to be effected by land carriage, and the navigation up Chesapeake Bay is interrupted by the enemy's vessels." He was nearly cut off. "To the eastward only"—New England—"can we turn our eyes with any reasonable hope of timely and adequate succour." Washington was writing in this letter to Congress's purchasing agent in Connecticut. "If every possible exertion is not made use of there to send us immediate and ample supplies of cattle, with pain I speak the alarming truth, no human efforts can keep the army from speedily disbanding."

He tried George Clinton. "It is with great reluctance I trouble you on a subject which does not properly fall within your province," he wrote to the New York governor. "But it is a subject that occasions me more distress than I have felt since the commencement of the war and which loudly demands the most zealous exertions of every person of weight and authority who is interested in the success of our affairs. I mean the present dreadful situation of the army for want of provisions, and the miserable prospects before us with respect to futurity. It is more alarming than you will probably conceive, for to form a just idea it were necessary to be on the spot. For some days past, there has been little less than a famine in camp. A part of the army has been a week without any kind of flesh, and the rest three or four days."

The men deserved better from their government. "Naked and starving as they are, we cannot enough admire the incomparable patience and fidelity of the soldiery, that they have not been, ere this, excited by their sufferings to a general mutiny and dispersion," Washington said. But their patience couldn't last forever.

He appealed to the public at large, even at the risk of alerting the British to the dire condition in his camp and of tipping his hand about a future campaign. "To the inhabitants of New Jersey, Pennsylvania, Delaware, Maryland and Virginia," he wrote. "Friends, countrymen and fellow citizens! After three campaigns during which the brave subjects of these states have contended, not unsuccessfully, with one of the most powerful kingdoms upon earth, we now find ourselves at least upon a level with our opponents. And there is the best reason to believe that efforts adequate to the abilities of this country would enable us speedily to conclude the war and to secure the invaluable blessings of peace, liberty and safety." Washington promised a spring offensive to drive back the British oppressors.

But he needed the help of citizens. "Unless the virtuous yeomanry of the states of New Jersey, Pennsylvania, Delaware, Maryland and Virginia will exert themselves to prepare cattle for the use of the army during the months of May, June and July next, great difficulties may arise in the course of the campaign. It is therefore recommended to the inhabitants of those states to put up and feed, immediately, as many of their stock cattle as they can spare, so as that they may be driven to this army within that period."

They weren't being asked to do this gratis. "A bountiful price will be given." Yet it was the right thing to do regardless of money. "The proprietors may assure themselves that they will render a most essential service to the illustrious cause of their country and contribute in a great degree to shorten this bloody contest."

62

Against all odds, the army held together. "By death and desertion, we have lost a good many men since we came to this ground, and have encountered every species of hardship that cold, wet and hunger, and want of clothes were capable of producing," Washington wrote in March. But more stayed than left. "Contrary to my expectations, we have been able to keep the soldiers from mutiny or dispersion, although in the single article of provisions they have encountered enough to have occasioned one or the other of these in most other armies."

Spirits in the camp lifted as the weather warmed. "Last evening May poles were erected in every regiment in the camp," George Ewing wrote in his diary for May 1. Ewing was a junior officer in the Third New Jersey regiment. He had fought at Brandywine and Germantown. "At the reveille I was awoke by three cheers in honor of King Tamany." King Tammany was a revered chief of the Lenape Indians who became a symbol of America. "The day was spent in mirth and jollity, the soldiers parading, marching with fife and drum and huzzaing as they passed the poles, their hats adorned with white blossoms." The troops paraded according to regiment. One regiment featured a sergeant dressed as King Tammany, thirteen sergeants—one per state—each with a bow in his left hand and thirteen arrows in his right, thirteen fife-and-drum pairs and thirteen platoons of thirteen men each. The paraders gave three cheers at the Maypole and then headed off toward Washington's headquarters house. "But just as they were descending the hill to the house, an aide met them and informed them that the general was indisposed and desired them to retire, which they did with the greatest decency and regularity.

"They then returned and marched from right to left of Lord Stirling's division huzzaing at every pole they passed and then retired to their regimental parade, taking a drink of whiskey which a generous contribution of their officers had procured for them." To Ewing's amazement, no one got hurt. "Each man retired to his own hut without any accident happening throughout the whole day."

They weren't done. "In the evening the officers of the aforesaid regiment assembled and had a song and dance in honour of King Tamany."

Finally it ended. "About 12 o'clock we dismissed and retired to rest."

The good feeling spilled over to the next day. "In the afternoon played a game at wicket with a number of gentlemen of the artillery," Ewing wrote on May 2. Wicket, a version of cricket, was popular in the camp. "His Excellency"—Washington—"dined with General Knox and after dinner did us the honor to play at wicket with us."

A FEW DAYS LATER the camp really had something to celebrate. The news all had been waiting for, the word that would mean that everything they had endured might not be in vain, arrived in the saddlebags of a galloping horse.

"This day we fired a grand feu de joie"—celebratory discharge of guns—"on account of the news brought by Mr. Silas Deane in the La Sensible from our plenipotentiary at the court of France," George Ewing wrote. "The courts of France and Spain had declared the United States of America to be free and independent states and had ceded to us all the territories on the continent of America which formerly belonged to the crown of Great Britain, and also the island of Bermuda, and also to assist us in carrying on this just and necessary war with no other conditions on our part but that we should not in any treaty of peace with England give up our independency." The alliance with France, the more important part of the diplomatic breakthrough, had been made possible by the American victory at Saratoga, but it still required lengthy negotiations in Paris by Benjamin Franklin, Silas Deane and Arthur Lee. Washington declared a day of celebration.

Cannon after cannon saluted the alliance and the deliverance it appeared to augur. Muskets were fired in triumphal volleys. Three cheers were given, followed by "Long live the king of France!" More cheers, and "God save the friendly powers of Europe!" More cheers, and "God save the American states!"

"After the feu de joir was over and the troops dismissed," Ewing recounted, "his Excellency invited the officers of the army to assemble under a booth that was prepared for the purpose and partake of a cold collation which was prepared for them, where he did us the honour to eat and drink with us, where many patriotic toasts were drank."

IN PROPORTION AS the French alliance elevated American spirits, it cast down those in Britain. The shadow had first fallen in the wake of the British defeat at Saratoga, and it fell most darkly across George Germain and the other architects of policy in the American war. Critics of the war and of the government's policy were emboldened. They called the policy misguided and its execution abysmal. For the policy they blamed Germain, for the execution William Howe.

Howe refused to be made scapegoat and resigned. He sailed home to England and was given a hearing in Parliament at the behest of the government's critics. In a long session before a committee of the House of Commons he explained how he had been asked to do the impossible, to suppress a rebellion in a country many times larger than England with an army utterly insufficient in size to the task. He took particular umbrage at those who from the safe distance of London had second-guessed his decisions to conserve the troops he had lest he be forced to make do with still fewer. It was in this session that he explained not pursuing Washington's army into Brooklyn at the battle of Long Island. More recent criticism was that he had abandoned Burgoyne in the wilds of upper New York in order to capture Philadelphia. Germain had allowed the impression to take hold that this idea was Howe's alone, and a bad one at that.

Howe refuted this impression chapter and verse, showing to the committee his correspondence with Germain, in which he had taken pains to temper unrealistic expectations. Citing a letter of January 1777, Howe told the committee, "I there assure him that there must be another campaign"—that is, the following summer—"for I found that upon the good news from Quebec, in 1776, he had hoped that a prospect was open for ending the war in one campaign. I pressed for more troops. I told him that a reinforcement of 20,000 was requisite, but that 15,000 would give us a superiority." Howe said to Germain that his primary objective would be Philadelphia, whose capture would deal a heavy blow to rebel morale. Germain had responded favorably, in a letter of March 3, 1777. "I had now the secretary of state's entire approbation," Howe emphasized to the committee. Howe had laid out the Philadelphia plan in another letter, and again received endorsement. "The noble Lord's answer to this letter, dated the 18th of May, 1777, contains a repeated approbation of the expedition to Pennsylvania."

Yet Germain had denied him the troops he needed. Howe thought he had been set up. "These expressions, sir, require observation," Howe said, referring to Germain's statements in the May letter. "They seem eager to catch me in the confession that my force was suitable to the operations of the last campaign"—against New York—"and would from thence imply that my force was equally suitable to the operations of any other campaign. Now, sir, even if I had not explained my idea upon the point (which however I clearly did), I think it might have been obvious to any man less acquainted than his lordship with military reasoning that the force which had been sufficient to take possession of New York and other strongholds of the enemy could not, after the necessary divisions for preserving the variety of posts we had gained"—starting with New York itself—"be equally suitable to the making of new conquests."

As for the defeat of Burgoyne, that had been a direct consequence of the decision by Germain and the government in London to deny Howe the troops he needed. He couldn't take Philadelphia—as repeatedly approved by Germain—and send an army to rescue Burgoyne too.

There was much more in the same vein. Howe recounted his whole tenure as commanding general in America. The moral of his story was that victory in the war would take longer than the government had let on and would require more resources than the government had been willing to provide.

Part VIII

Yorktown

63

"The favorable issue of our negotiation with France is matter for heartfelt joy, big with important events, and it must, I should think, chalk out a plain and easy road to independence," Washington wrote to Richard Henry Lee in late May. But though the path was clear, America still had to travel it. Britain would surely declare war on France. How the British would conduct the new war remained to be seen. They couldn't defend everything. "That they will be under a necessity of giving up the continent or their islands seems obvious to me." Should they try to retain the continent rather than the islands—that is, North America rather than the West Indies—they still would have to make choices. "If they can afford a garrison sufficient, they may attempt to hold New York." More than that would be impossible.

Washington drew conclusions and made more conjectures. "That the enemy in Philadelphia are bound to New York, I have no doubt," he wrote to Gouverneur Morris, a member of Congress from New York who took special interest in the army. "Whether as a place of rendezvous, or to facilitate any operations up the North River, time—and less of it than you have taken to arrange the business of this army—will unfold." How the British would get from Philadelphia to New York was unclear. "Whether they will go thence by land or water, or whether they may not pay their compliments to us before they go, is not yet certain. My own opinion is that they will march the flower of their army, unencumbered with baggage, through the Jerseys."

Washington was ready when they did. He sent a thousand men under Lafayette to pursue and harass the British. "You are to use the most effectual means for gaining the enemy's left flank and rear, and giving them every degree of annoyance," Washington instructed the marquis. "You will take such measures, in concert with General Dickinson, as will cause the enemy the greatest impediment and loss in their march." Philemon

Dickinson was a New Jersey man on whom Washington relied for local knowledge.

Daniel Morgan would head another column. "Take the most effectual means for gaining the enemy's right flank with all possible expedition, and give them every degree of annoyance in that quarter," Washington wrote to Morgan. To Charles Scott: "You are immediately to march with the detachment under your command towards Allen Town, in order to fall in with the enemy's left flank and rear, and give them all the annoyance in your power." To William Maxwell: "I have directed Colonel Morgan to keep on the right flank of the enemy, and General Scott who has a very respectable body of troops to hang on their rear and left flank. You yourself will give them all the annoyance you can on their left also."

"THE ENEMY EVACUATED Philadelphia on the 18th," Washington wrote to Jack, summarizing events of the last part of June. "At ten o'clock that day I got intelligence of it, and by two o'clock, or soon after, had six brigades on their march for the Jerseys, and followed with the whole army next morning. On the 21st we completed our passage over the Delaware at Coryell's Ferry (about thirty-three miles above Philadelphia) and distant from Valley Forge near forty miles. From this ferry we moved down towards the enemy, and on the 27th got within six miles of them." The nearest town was Monmouth, New Jersey.

Charles Lee marched in front. Washington had just about forgotten the flap with Lee from the previous fall. He sought to land a blow before the British got to New York. "General Lee, having the command of the van of the army, consisting of full five thousand chosen men, was ordered to begin the attack next morning, so soon as the enemy began their march, to be supported by me." Washington counted on Lee's battlefield experience.

"But, strange to tell! when he came up with the enemy, a retreat commenced," Washington told Jack. "Whether by his order or from other causes is now the subject of inquiry and consequently improper to be descanted upon, as he is in arrest, and a court-martial sitting for trial of him. A retreat, however, was the fact, be the causes as they may, and the disorder arising from it would have proved fatal to the army had not that bountiful Providence, which has never failed us in the hour of distress, enabled me to form a regiment or two (of those that were retreating) in the face of the enemy and under their fire, by which means a stand was made long enough (the place through which the enemy were pursuing being narrow) to form the troops, that were advancing upon an advantageous piece of ground in the rear."

Washington's action stemmed the retreat and reversed the momentum of battle. "From being pursued, we drove the enemy back over the ground they had followed, and recovered the field of battle, and possessed ourselves of their dead."

Washington was tempted to pursue. "But as they retreated behind a morass very difficult to pass, and had both flanks secured with thick woods, it was found impracticable with our men fainting with fatigue, heat, and want of water to do anything more that night."

He hoped to resume the battle the next day. Henry Clinton, who succeeded William Howe as commander for North America, had other ideas, as Washington discovered in the morning. "Behold, the enemy had stole off as silent as the grave in the night, after having sent away their wounded. Getting a night's march of us, and having but ten miles to a strong post, it was judged inexpedient to follow them any further."

Washington's strategy had served its purpose of signaling to the British that the American army had plenty of fight left in it, whatever the involvement of France portended. "Without exaggeration, their trip through the Jerseys, in killed, wounded, prisoners, and deserters, has cost them at least 2000 men of their best troops," he told Jack. "We had 60 men killed, 132 wounded, and about 130 missing, some of whom I suppose may yet come in."

THE BATTLE OF MONMOUTH wasn't as one-sided as Washington first thought. The casualties were about even, and Clinton wasn't prevented from getting to New York. But given that the last big battles of the previous season, at Brandywine and Germantown, had been American defeats, a draw was an improvement.

What it would lead to was anyone's guess. Both sides in the war wondered what French entry meant. Would the French come to America to fight? Would they simply employ their ships against the British navy? Even the latter would be a boon to Washington, who had been pinned to the earth in his campaigns while the British enjoyed the additional dimension of the sea. If he had had a navy at Boston, his siege there might have ended quite differently, with a British surrender rather than escape.

At the least, French entry would limit the reinforcements London could send to America. A war against France might be fought in the Caribbean, in Canada, even in Europe. France was an older and more dangerous foe than the fledgling United States. It would become Britain's priority.

If the French sent troops to fight alongside Washington's, that would be even better. He'd have to figure out how to coordinate with their generals. He'd have to adjust his strategy to suit theirs. But following a winter when he thought his army might melt away, the problem of accommodating new, fresh troops was one he'd welcome.

THE CHEERS OF WASHINGTON'S SOLDIERS on learning of the French alliance reflected the common belief that the alliance augured a rapid end to the war. But for many months it seemed to have the opposite effect. Just as the French and Indian War had dragged on after that Anglo-French conflict broadened into a general European war, so the Anglo-American war that had started in 1775 slowed down as it broadened into an Anglo-American-French struggle. Indeed, a clause of the American treaty with France specified that neither would quit fighting until the other was ready to do so. Spain subsequently entered the war, as an ally of France but not of America. The Franco-Spanish pact had a similar no-quit provision. Consequently America found itself bound by the ambitions not only of the French but of the Spanish.

At first blush a longer war seemed to favor America, which was fighting on its own territory with interior lines of communication. The British, by contrast, had to support an army thousands of miles from home. Providing such support required maintaining a political majority in favor of the war. As the appearance of William Howe before Parliament revealed, that majority was looking precarious.

Yet Washington faced similar imperatives. Unlike the British army, manned by military careerists and troops with long terms of enlistment, Washington's force was an army of citizens on short enlistments. Some enrolled from patriotism, but bonuses for enlistment and promised salaries attracted others. The families of nearly all the soldiers depended on their pay. If the pay was late or not forthcoming at all, they couldn't afford to remain at arms. And if, as increasingly happened, the profligate printing of currency by Congress eroded the value of their pay, their financial straits grew even worse. The excitement of an active campaign of battles would keep some on task, but the tedium of watchful waiting elicited grumbles and threatened worse.

After Monmouth, Washington took up a position in New Jersey from which he could monitor Henry Clinton in New York. Washington was tempted to strike at Clinton and bring the war to a decision. But until the French revealed their plans, he'd be wasting his time. Clinton would skip away from New York as Howe had skipped from Boston. Washington needed the French navy to prevent a British escape. If he could get French troops to help with a strike at the British, all the better.

CLINTON MEANWHILE WATCHED Washington and likewise waited for the French. The experience of the British in occupying Philadelphia had cured them of any belief they could end the American rebellion by seizing American territory. They had taken the American capital, and the Americans continued to fight.

That left Clinton with two options. One was meeting Washington in open battle, to crush his army. But Washington so far had avoided such a definitive contest. At Long Island, White Plains, Brandywine and Germantown, he'd taken flight rather than be destroyed. There was no reason to think he'd grown more reckless since then.

The other option was to build a backfire against Washington among American loyalists. The British crown still had friends in America. If they could be encouraged to take on the rebels, they might weaken Washington both militarily and politically. He would have to send troops to fight the loyalists, and those troops would be unavailable to fight Clinton. Additionally, a war in the countryside might antagonize the populace, who would call for an end to the fighting, on Britain's terms if necessary.

Such was the thinking that prompted Clinton to open a new front in the south. Loyalists in Philadelphia during the British occupation had told William Howe that Georgia and the Carolinas were rife with loyalists and were a promising ground for a British campaign. After Howe's departure Clinton acted on the tip and in the latter part of 1778 prepared an expedition against Savannah. It succeeded by the end of the year and triggered a series of battles in Georgia and South Carolina between British troops and loyalist militia on one side and Continental troops and patriot militia on the other. An American attempt to retake Savannah in

1779 failed, as did the American defense of Charleston, which fell to the British in 1780. The loss of Charleston was a disaster to American arms, because it included the surrender of some five thousand American troops.

The southern strategy seemed to the British government to hold great hope for the broader war. "The reduction of the southern provinces must give the death-wound to the rebellion, notwithstanding any assistance the French may be able to give it," Germain wrote to Clinton in May 1781. "And if that were the case, a general peace would soon follow, and this country be delivered from the most burdensome and extensive war it ever was engaged in. As so much, therefore, depends upon our successes in America, you cannot be surprised that the eyes of all the people of England are turned upon you, nor at the anxiety with which the king and all his servants wait for accounts of your movements."

Charles Cornwallis, the current hero of the southern campaign, became the focus of British hopes. "The rapidity of your movements through a country so thinly inhabited and so little cultivated is justly a matter of astonishment to all Europe, as well as to the rebels in America," wrote Germain to Cornwallis. "And although they appear to make every possible exertion to oppose your progress and conduct their enterprises in Carolina with more spirit and skill than they have shown in any other part of America, His Majesty has such confidence in your lordship's great military talents that he entertains no doubt of your fulfilling his utmost expectations in the course of the campaign."

64

When the British had marched out of Philadelphia, Washington sent an order to Benedict Arnold. "You are immediately to proceed to Philadelphia and take the command of the troops there," he said. Arnold remained a favorite with Washington despite friction that had emerged between Arnold and some of his officer comrades. Whatever his rough edges, Washington judged, at least Arnold could fight. When he disregarded orders, it was to get closer to the enemy, as at Saratoga, where he was badly wounded. Arnold was still recuperating when Washington required an experienced officer to assume charge of Philadelphia after nine months of British rule. "You will take every prudent step in your power to preserve tranquillity and order in the city and give security to individuals of every class and description, restraining as far as possible, till the restoration of civil government, every species of persecution, insult or abuse, either from the soldiery to the inhabitants, or among each other." For the year after independence, Philadelphia patriots had ridden high and loyalists lain low. For most of the year after that, the positions were reversed. Now they were flipped again. Many on both sides felt they had scores to settle. Washington wanted Arnold to keep them under control.

Arnold kept them under control, but he didn't keep them happy. As military governor he answered to Washington rather than to the civic leaders in Philadelphia, and they didn't like it. When he ruled against them, they complained to Congress, which ordered Washington to summon a court-martial to investigate Arnold's alleged corruption. Washington let Arnold know he did so reluctantly.

He maintained their personal relationship. "Let me congratulate you on the late happy event," he wrote to Arnold after the birth of his first child with his new wife. "Mrs. Washington joins me in presenting her wishes for Mrs. Arnold on the occasion."

Mrs. Arnold was the former Margaret Shippen, called Peggy, who had been the belle of British-occupied Philadelphia. She had a flock of suitors, including a dashing young British officer named John André. But she chose Arnold, not least because he wooed her so passionately. "Twenty times have I taken up my pen to write you, and as often has my trembling hand refused to obey the dictates of my heart—a heart which, though calm and serene amidst the clashing of arms and all the din and horrors of war, trembles with diffidence and the fear of giving offence when it attempts to address you on a subject so important to its happiness," he wrote. "Dear madam, your charms have lighted up a flame in my bosom which can never be extinguished. Your heavenly image is too deeply impressed ever to be effaced.... On you alone my happiness depends, and will you doom me to languish in despair?"

She didn't doom him. Not at once. They married. She heard his stories of mistreatment by Congress on promotion and by the army in his court-martial. One thing and another delayed his trial, making him feel he was condemned to limbo while other officers pursued glory.

Arnold's disillusionment came to the attention of John André, who while not pursuing Peggy Shippen directed British intelligence operations. She was probably the one who put André in communication with Arnold. The correspondence between the two men was carefully guarded, involving invisible ink and secret codes. André said the British would be interested in any information that came Arnold's way. His remuneration would be commensurate with the value of the intelligence provided.

This value increased dramatically in August 1780 when Arnold received new orders from Washington. "You are to proceed to West Point and take the command of the post and its dependencies," Washington wrote. West Point was the fort that dominated a key passage of the Hudson River forty miles above New York. The British defeat at Saratoga had postponed plans for cutting the United States in two along the Hudson-Champlain line, but it hadn't killed them. A friend of Britain in control of West Point might revive those plans.

In cipher Arnold shared the news with André, describing West Point as "a post in which I can render the most essential services." He insisted that he be rewarded appropriately. "As life and fortune are risked by serving His Majesty, it is necessary that the latter shall be secured, as well as the emoluments I give up, and a compensation for services agreed on and a sum advanced for that purpose." He proposed to deliver more than services from West Point. He would hand over the fort itself, by divulging and weakening its defenses, enabling its seizure by British troops. "Twenty thousand pounds sterling I think will be a cheap purchase for an object of so much importance." But Arnold refused to consummate the treachery without conferring with André or his agent face to face.

André decided to meet Arnold himself, not trusting a subordinate with so delicate and explosive a transaction. He sailed up the Hudson aboard a British sloop, the *Vulture.* Arnold sent a boat for him. They met on the shore. Arnold satisfied himself of André's reliability, and André of Arnold's. They concluded the bargain.

André had planned to return to New York the way he had come, on the *Vulture.* But some patriot militia had spotted the vessel and fired, driving it away.

Arnold told André not to worry. Locals crossed the lines all the time, on business and family matters. Arnold wrote André a pass to show to anyone who stopped him. It was made out to a false name. But he'd have to swap his uniform for civilian clothes.

This was dangerous for André. To be arrested in uniform would make him a prisoner of war. To be arrested out of uniform, especially while traveling under an assumed name, would make him a spy. Spies were hanged.

André took the risk. He set off. On the road he met three militiamen. Thinking them loyalists, he identified himself as a British officer. They turned out to be patriots and took him prisoner. He changed his story. He said he really wasn't a British officer. He had claimed to be only because he thought they were loyalists. He showed them his pass.

They were skeptical and perhaps larcenous. They searched him. In his boots they found papers that looked suspicious. They delivered him to the nearest officer of the Continental army. This fellow was about to send André to the local commandant—Arnold—but changed his mind and sent a message instead.

The message alerted Arnold that the plot had been discovered or was about to be. He fled for British lines. He found the *Vulture,* which carried him away to New York.

En route he wrote a letter to Washington. "Sir," he said, "The heart which is conscious of its own rectitude cannot attempt to palliate a step which the world may censure as wrong. I have ever acted from a principle of love to my country since the commencement of the present unhappy contest between Great Britain and the colonies. The same principle of love to my country actuates my present conduct, however it may appear inconsistent to the world, who very seldom judge right of any man's actions."

Arnold asked no consideration for himself. "I have too often experienced the ingratitude of my country to attempt it." But he did request that no blame fall on his wife. "She is as good and as innocent as an angel and is incapable of doing wrong. I beg she may be permitted to return to her friends in Philadelphia or to come to me as she may choose. From your Excellency I have no fears on her account, but she may suffer from the mistaken fury of her country."

AS IT HAPPENED, Washington and Alexander Hamilton had been planning to meet with Arnold that very day. Washington wanted to see how Arnold was doing in his new post. Word of Arnold's flight intercepted them. They proceeded to the Arnold house, where Peggy Arnold appeared as shocked by her husband's defection as they were.

Her appearance was at least partly for effect. How much she knew of Arnold's particular scheming is unclear. But his disaffection with Congress and the army was clear to her. Yet she manifested the angelic innocence her husband claimed for her. "I saw an amiable woman frantic with distress for the loss of a husband she tenderly loved—a traitor to his country and to his fame, a disgrace to his connections," Hamilton wrote to his fiancée, Elizabeth Schuyler. "It was the most affecting scene I ever was witness to. She for a considerable time entirely lost her senses. The General went up to see her and she upbraided him with being in a plot to murder her child; one moment she raved; another she melted into tears; sometimes she pressed her infant to her bosom and lamented its fate occasioned by the imprudence of its father in a manner that would have pierced insensibility itself. All the sweetness of beauty, all the loveliness of innocence, all the tenderness of a wife and all the fondness of a mother showed themselves in her appearance and conduct. We have every reason to believe she was entirely unacquainted with the plan, and that her first knowledge of it was when Arnold went to tell her he must banish himself from his country and from her forever. She instantly fell into a convulsion and he left her in that situation."

Washington didn't record his reaction to Peggy Arnold's performance. He was relieved that the Arnold-André plot had been discovered before West Point could be delivered to the British. No substantive damage had occurred. But the plot reflected badly on Washington's judgment of men. Until the moment he received word that Arnold had fled to the British, Washington deemed him one of the best of his lieutenants. Washington had devoted months to worrying about Horatio Gates when he should have been watching Arnold.

Though the traitor had escaped, André was in Washington's custody. Arnold learned that André was being treated as a spy. This was mistaken and unjust, Arnold told Washington in another letter. "He came from on board the Vulture at my particular request, by a flag sent on purpose for him." Arnold had promised him safe passage. "Major André came on shore in his uniform (without disguise) which with much reluctance at my particular and pressing instance he exchanged for another coat. I furnished him with a horse and saddle and pointed out the route by which he was to return. And as commanding officer in the department I had an undoubted right to transact all these matters, which if wrong Major André ought by no means to suffer for them."

Arnold appealed to Washington to do the right thing. "Suffer me to entreat your Excellency for your own and the honor of humanity, and the love you have of justice, that you suffer not an unjust sentence to touch the life of Major André."

He closed in an ominous tone. "But if this warning should be disregarded and he should suffer, I call heaven and earth to witness that your Excellency will be justly answerable for the torrent of blood that may be spilt in consequence."

Washington doubtless required all the self-discipline he could summon simply to read Arnold's latest. To be lectured on his duty by a traitor was more than he could stand. And to be threatened with consequences for doing that duty, by that same traitor, surpassed belief. Washington didn't respond to Arnold's letter.

Nor did he respond to a letter from André in captivity. Washington appointed a tribunal that tried André, convicted him of spying and sentenced him to death by hanging. The prisoner resented the characterization. He was not a spy, he said. He was an officer. If he must die, he wished to die like an officer, shot rather than hanged. "Buoyed above the terror of death by the consciousness of a life devoted to honorable pursuits and stained with no action that can give me remorse, I trust the request I make to your Excellency at this serious period, and which is to soften my last moments, will not be rejected. Sympathy towards a soldier will surely induce your Excellency and a military tribunal to adapt the mode of my death to the feelings of a man of honour. Let me hope, sir, that if aught in my character impresses you with esteem towards me, if aught in my misfortunes marks me as the victim of policy and not of resentment, I shall experience the operation of these feelings in your breast by being informed that I am not to die on a gibbet."

Washington wrote to Henry Clinton rather than to André. He summarized the actions of his tribunal. "From these proceedings it is evident Major André was employed in the execution of measures very foreign to the objects of flags of truce and such as they were never meant to authorise." Washington quoted and endorsed the key finding of the board: "That Major André, Adjutant General to the British Army, ought to be considered as a spy from the enemy, and that agreeable to the law and usage of nations it is their opinion he ought to suffer death."

André was executed by hanging on October 2.

65

Treason is never convenient for those betrayed, but Arnold's treachery could not have come at a worse time for Washington. The French were just starting to deliver on the promise of their alliance. French ships had been on the American coast, though they had sailed off to the West Indies. French troops, commanded by the Comte de Rochambeau, had begun to arrive, landing in Rhode Island. Washington hoped to develop a rapport with Rochambeau and win the confidence of the French government. The Arnold affair threw this into jeopardy. If an officer so respected by Washington could go over to the enemy, what faith should France put in the rest of the American army? Or in the judgment, if not the character, of Washington himself?

"A FINE MORNING," wrote Joseph McClellan of the Ninth Pennsylvania regiment in his diary for New Year's Day 1781. "The day spent in quietness." The quiet didn't last. "About 8:00 in the night a number of men in the 11th Regiment began to huzza and continued some time, but it was generally thought it only proceeded from the men drinking, as they had drawn half a pint of liquor this day. A number of the officers collected in order to quiet the men, which was done in a great measure. But in a short time a disturbance began on the right of the division, by the men parading with their arms and firing some scattering shots, which soon became general through the division, notwithstanding every endeavor used by the officers. The men at length seized upon the artillery and began to drag them off on the road. During this time Captain Bitting was shot through the body and soon died. Captain Tolbert was badly wounded. Several shots were fired from the artillery as they kept them moving, the men in general by this time being in arms, huzzaing, and firing their pieces in the air. The 9th and 5th regiments were kept in their parades until they were threatened by others; if they did not move off they would turn the artillery on them, several shots being fired over their heads. At length the greater part of them mixed in with the other regiments and kept the road by General Wayne's quarters." Anthony Wayne was the commanding officer of the Pennsylvania line, as the collection of Pennsylvania regiments was called. "A number returned that night, collected more men and, indeed, forced near one-half the line away. Their first half was at Vealtown, four miles from camp, and they continued there until they collected most of the line."

Anthony Wayne had been expecting trouble for months. He had repeatedly predicted it. His men were underfed, underhoused, underclothed. And they were underworked, which gave them time to dwell on their discontents. They hadn't been paid for years, in some cases. "We are reduced to dry bread and beef for our food, and to cold water for our drink," Wayne had written to Joseph Reed, president of Pennsylvania, in mid-December. "Neither officers or soldiers have received a single drop of spirituous liquors from the public magazines since the 10th of October last, except one gill per man some time in November. This, together with the old worn-out coats and tattered linen overalls, and what was once a poor substitute for a blanket (now divided among three soldiers) is but very wretched living and shelter against the winter's piercing cold, drifting snows and chilling sleets."

Thirty-five miles away the soldiers' British counterparts were snug and warm in New York. The discrepancy was brought to their attention. "In this situation the enemy begin to work upon their passions and have found means to circulate some proclamations among them," Wayne told Reed. The troops remained loyal—so far. "I don't despair of being able to restore harmony and content, and to defeat every machination of the public foe and the more dangerous lurking incendiary, if aided by your Excellency in a timely supply of stores and clothing." No less important was the soldiers' pay. When they were paid at all, it was in Continental currency, which depreciated by the week. "What will insure success is the immediate passing of the act for making good the depreciation," Wayne said. The Pennsylvania legislature had considered such a measure, to no avail thus far. If the state lacked cash, it could pay the soldiers in land. "Give your soldiery a landed property, and I will answer for their bleeding to *death,* drop by drop, to establish the independency of this country. On the contrary, should we neglect rewarding their past services and not do justice to their more than Roman virtue, have we nothing to apprehend from their defection? Believe me, my dear sir, that if something is not immediately done to give them a local attachment to this country and to quiet their minds, we have not yet seen the worst side of the picture."

What Wayne pleaded for wasn't done, and what he warned of was. Two weeks later, on January 1, the Pennsylvania line mutinied, as Joseph McClellan recorded in his diary. The date was significant, for it was when many of the troops thought their terms of enlistment were to end. Their superiors said this was not so. Yes it was, said the soldiers, and they mutinied. They meant business, as evidenced by the shooting of the two officers and the seizing of the artillery. They declared that if efforts were made to restrain them, there would be more bloodshed.

"The most general and unhappy mutiny suddenly took place in the Pennsylvania Line about 9 o'clock last night," Wayne reported to Washington the next morning. "It yet subsists. A great proportion of the troops with some artillery are marching towards Philadelphia." The mutineers seemed to be taking their case to Congress and the Pennsylvania government. "Every exertion has been used by the officers to divide them in their determination to revolt. It has succeeded in a temporary manner with near one half. How long it will last God knows." Wayne understood what was at stake. "I have ordered the Jersey brigade to Chatham, where the militia are also assembling, lest the enemy should take advantage of this alarming crisis. Indeed the alarm guns have been fired and the beacons kindled towards Elizabethtown."

Wayne said he would continue striving to stem the mutiny. "I am this moment with Colonels Butler and Stewart taking horse to try to halt them on their march towards Princeton." If he couldn't stop them, he would try to slow them down. "What their temper may be I cannot tell."

Washington responded with grave concern. "I this day at noon received yours of the 2d in the morning by Major Fishbourn, who has given me a full account of the unhappy and alarming defection of the Pennsylvania line," he wrote to Wayne on January 3. He didn't blame Wayne and he didn't blame the officers of the regiments. "The officers have given convincing proofs that everything possible was done by them to check the mutiny upon its first appearance, and it is to be regretted that some of them have fallen sacrifices to their zeal. I very much approve of the determination of yourself, Colonel Butler and Colonel Stewart to keep with the troops, if they will admit of it, as after the first transports of passion there may be some favorable intervals which may be improved."

Perhaps to Wayne's surprise, Washington told him to move cautiously.

"Opposition, as it did not succeed in the first instance, cannot be effectual while the men remain together, but will keep alive resentment and will tempt them to turn about and go in a body to the enemy, who by their emissaries will use every argument and mean in their power to persuade them that it is their only asylum, which, if they find their passage stopped at the Delaware and hear that the Jersey militia are collecting in their rear, they may think but too probable."

This was Washington's nightmare: that the disaffected among his soldiers might not simply mutiny but defect to the enemy. Mutiny merely subtracted from his forces, while defection subtracted from him *and* added to the enemy, besides conveying intelligence regarding Washington's readiness and mode of operations. Defection had to be prevented at all costs.

Wayne must complement his soldier's skills with those of the diplomat. "Draw from them what they conceive to be their principal grievances and promise to represent faithfully to Congress and to the state the substance of them and to endeavour to obtain a redress," Washington said. "I look upon it that if you can bring them to a negotiation, matters may afterwards be accommodated, but that an attempt to reduce them by force will either drive them to the enemy or dissipate them in such a manner that they will never be recovered."

Washington related that riders had gone to Philadelphia to warn Congress that the mutineers were coming. He hoped the lawmakers wouldn't flee. "The removal of Congress, waiving the indignity, might have a very unhappy influence. The mutineers finding the body before whom they were determined to lay their grievances fled, might take a new turn and wreak their vengeance upon the persons and properties of the citizens, and in a town of the size of Philadelphia there are numbers who would join them in such a business."

Washington said he would ride to meet Wayne as soon as he made sure he wasn't leaving more mutiny behind. "If nothing alarming appears here and I hear nothing further from you, I shall tomorrow morning set out towards Philadelphia."

He changed his mind. His lieutenants told him his calming presence was needed with the army as a whole. Let Wayne and Congress deal with the Pennsylvanians. Washington allowed himself to be persuaded.

. . .

THE ALARM GUNS Wayne mentioned were intended to call out the militia against emergency. They had the side effect of alerting the British of trouble behind the American lines. "I went over to New York and have now returned," an informant wrote to Wayne on January 4. "Yesterday, about 12 o'clock, the British got news of the unhappy disturbance in your camp. Nothing could possibly have given them so much pleasure. Every preparation is making among them to come out to make a descent on Jersey. I think South Amboy is their object. They expect those in mutiny will immediately join them."

Ahead of his troops, Henry Clinton sent secret agents. "January 7th at Pennington," Joseph McClellan wrote in his diary of the mutiny. "A very wet morning. The soldiery at Princeton took up two spies sent into them by Sir Harry Clinton and sent them to Trenton. Soon after brought them back to Princeton, which caused a suspicion that the soldiers had a mind to push towards the enemy."

The British spies conveyed a message from Clinton to the men of the Pennsylvania line. "It having been reported at New York that the Pennsylvania troops and others have been defrauded by Congress of their pay, clothing, and provisions, and assembled for redress of their grievances, and also that notwithstanding the terms of their enlistments are expired, they have been forcibly detained in the service where they have suffered every kind of misery and oppression—they are now offered to be taken under the protection of the British government to have their rights restored, free pardon for all former offenses, and that pay due to them from Congress faithfully paid to them without any expectation of military service, except it may be voluntary, upon laying down their arms and returning to their allegiances," Clinton proclaimed. Succinctly: if the rebel government won't pay you, the British government will. Clinton said anyone inclined to take up his offer should come to Amboy. "They will there be met by people in power to treat with them, and faith shall be pledged for their security."

Clinton's offer backfired. "The troops have rejected with disdain the proposition made by Sir Henry Clinton," Joseph Reed wrote to Congress. Reed had gone to meet the mutineers, who in a show of loyalty to the American cause seized Clinton's agents and held them under guard. The agents were subsequently convicted of spying and executed. The mutineers emphasized that they loved their country, but they had to get paid. Their families were starving.

The rejection of Clinton's invitation to turn coat tempered the crisis. Anthony Wayne and Joseph Reed heard out the mutineers and offered them amnesty as well as a promise of good faith in addressing their complaints. Most appeared as relieved to return to camp as Washington was to learn they were doing so.

Yet Washington took a lesson. He again implored Congress to feed, clothe and pay his men. The mutiny gave his words new meaning. At the same time, he watched his men with greater vigilance than ever. When regiments from New Jersey, observing what seemed the success of the Pennsylvanians, staged a mutiny of their own, Washington reacted at once. "Persuaded that without some decisive effort at all hazards to suppress this dangerous spirit it would speedily infect the whole army, I have ordered as large a detachment as we could spare from these posts to march under Major General Howe"—Robert Howe of Connecticut—"with orders to compel the mutineers to unconditional submission, to listen to no terms while they were in a state of resistance, and on their reduction to execute instantly a few of the most active and most incendiary leaders," Washington wrote in a circular to several governors.

Robert Howe followed orders. He surrounded the New Jersey mutineers and compelled their surrender. He had two of the ringleaders shot. "This has totally quelled the spirit of mutiny, and everything is now quiet," Washington reported.

66

The mutinies formed a background to the evolution of military strategy for what Washington hoped would be the final campaign of the war. He met and corresponded with Rochambeau during the early months of 1781 to plan the best use of their countries' combined forces. "It was agreed that if by the aid of our allies we can have a naval superiority through the next campaign, and an army of thirty thousand men, or double the force of the enemy at New York and its dependencies, early enough in the season to operate in that quarter, we ought to prefer it"—New York—"to every other object, as the most important and decisive," Washington summarized to Henry Knox. "The general idea of the plan of operations is this (if we are able to procure the force we count upon): to make two attacks, one against the works on York Island, and the other against the works of Brooklyn on Long Island."

The recapture of New York would serve the triple purpose of neutralizing the British threat to separate New England from the rest of the country, depriving Britain of the most useful harbor in America and ending the embarrassment of seeing such an important city in enemy hands for so long. Victory in New York bid fair to end the war at a single stroke.

Yet Washington agreed to a fallback. "If we should find ourselves unable to undertake this more capital expedition," he told Knox, "and if we have means equal to it, we shall attempt as a secondary object the reduction of Charlestown." A southern campaign would be less productive than one against New York, but it would be better than nothing.

New York remained the priority into the summer of 1781. Washington rendezvoused with Rochambeau outside Hartford, midway between their headquarters, in late May to firm up details. "All the French troops, except about 200 to be left as a guard over their heavy stores and baggage at Providence, are to march as soon as circumstances will admit, and form a junction with me upon the North River," Washington reported to Congress. "Upon a full consideration of affairs in every point of view, an operation against New York has been deemed preferable to making further detachments to the southward, while they can only be sent by land." The French fleet was still in the Caribbean, leaving the British in control of the American coast. "The principal reasons which induced to this determination are as follow: the difficulty and expence of transportation; the lateness of the season, which would throw the troops into the extremity of the heat of summer; the great waste of men which we have ever experienced in so long a march at the healthiest season; and above all, a strong presumption that the enemy, weakened as they now are by detachment"—of Cornwallis to the south—"must either sacrifice the valuable port of New York and its dependencies, or recall a part of their force from the southward to defend them."

Washington understood that his emphasis on New York wouldn't sit well with the southerners in Congress and America, who might think he was writing off their region to Britain and the loyalists. He denied it. He contended that his northern strategy was also a southern strategy. "The enemy will, I hope, be reduced to the necessity of recalling part of their force from the southward to support New York," he wrote to Thomas Jefferson, "or they will run the most eminent risk of being expelled with a great loss of stores from that port which is to them invaluable while they think of prosecuting the war in America." Overstating his case, Washington asserted, "The prospect of giving relief to the southern states by an operation in this quarter was the principal inducement for undertaking it." Anyway, there wasn't much choice. "We found upon a full consideration of our affairs in every point of view that without the command of the water it would be next to impossible for us to transfer the artillery, baggage and stores of the army to so great a distance, and, besides, that we should lose at least one third of our force by desertion, sickness and the heat of the approaching season even if it could be done."

WASHINGTON'S REASONING TO Jefferson rested on his lack of naval support. He hoped to remedy that before the fighting season ended. But such a shift depended on the French fleet, commanded by the Comte de Grasse. And de Grasse was as elusive at sea as William Howe had been after the siege of Boston and again before the campaign for Philadelphia. In that era a fleet beyond the horizon might as well have been on the far side of the moon, for all those on shore might know of their whereabouts.

Consequently Washington was delighted to hear from de Grasse in a letter relayed from Rochambeau. Crucial parts of the letter were encrypted, but Washington had the key. "It will be by the 15th of July at soonest that I will be on the coast of North America," de Grasse wrote. "It is necessary, by reason of the short time I have to stay in that country, being besides obliged to leave it by reason of the season, that all that can be useful for the success of your projects should be ready, that a moment for action may not be lost."

In his cover letter, Rochambeau explained that de Grasse understood Washington's priorities—more or less. "I have already wrote to the Count de Grasse that your Excellency had desired my marching to the North river to strengthen or even attack New York when the circumstances will admit of it. I have apprised him of the number of the garrison at New York and of the considerable forces which the enemy has sent to Virginia, that the only means which seems practicable to your Excellency is a diversion upon New York, which you propose to do as soon as the circumstances will allow of it." In fact Washington was thinking of New York not as a diversion but as the main objective. It was Rochambeau who wanted it to be the diversion. The French general continued, "I have spoken to him of the enemy's naval forces and told him that by reason of the constant wind, I thought it would be a great stroke to go to Chesapeake Bay in which he can make great things against the naval force that will be there, and then the wind could bring him in two days before New York. That if he could bring us some moveable forces, five or six thousand men more would render our expedition much more probable."

"Your requisitions to the Count Grasse go to everything I could wish," Washington replied to Rochambeau. "You cannot in my opinion too strongly urge the necessity of bringing a body of troops with him, more especially as I am very dubious whether our force can be drawn together by the time he proposes to be here. Now 4000 or 5000 men in addition to what we shall certainly have by that time would, almost beyond a doubt, enable us, with the assistance of the fleet, to carry our object."

Washington regretted that de Grasse couldn't stay long on the American coast. This made an advantage in troops the more important. It also prompted a shift in Washington's thinking, toward Rochambeau's. "Your Excellency will be pleased to recollect that New York was looked upon by us as the only practicable object under present circumstances, but should we be able to secure naval superiority we may perhaps find others more practicable and equally advisable," Washington said. Everything would depend on de Grasse's schedule. "Will it not be best to leave him to judge from the information he may from time to time receive of the situation of the enemy's fleet upon this coast, which will be the most advantageous quarter for him to make his appearance in?"

Rochambeau seized on Washington's new flexibility. The two generals met in July. "Could not the operations be directed against Virginia?" Rochambeau asked, according to notes of the meeting. New York was a tricky harbor to enter under the best of circumstances. Virginia would be easier for de Grasse. Washington's troops and Rochambeau's could converge on Virginia for when de Grasse arrived. "Would not we be then in a condition to undertake with success on Lord Cornwallis?"

Washington wasn't willing to give up New York entirely. "Should the fleet arrive in season, not be limited to a short stay; should it be able to force the harbour of New York; and in addition to all these, should it find the British force in a divided state, I am of opinion that the enterprize against New York and its dependencies should be our primary object," he responded to Rochambeau.

Yet the conditions Washington now placed on an attack against New York all but ruled it out. And when a few weeks later de Grasse indicated he would be on the Virginia coast for a short while in September, the decision was made. "In consequence of the despatches received from your Excellency by the frigate La Concorde, it has been judged expedient to give up for the present the enterprise against New York and turn our attention towards the south," Washington wrote to de Grasse. "For this purpose we have determined to remove the whole of the French army, and as large a detachment of the American as can be spared, to Chesapeake, to meet your Excellency there."

⟶ 67 ⟵

Washington embraced the decision that had been compelled upon him, for it offered hope of a decisive battle. Yet because it contradicted previous policy, it had to be announced—quietly—to responsible officials who might be affected, starting with nearby governors. Washington sent them a letter. "The fleet of the Count de Grasse, with a body of French troops on board, will make its first appearance in the Chesapeake, which, should the time of the fleet's arrival prove favorable, and should the enemy under Lord Cornwallis hold their present position in Virginia, will give us the fairest opportunity to reduce the whole British force in the South and to ruin their boasted expectations in that quarter," he wrote. "To effect this desirable object, it has been judged expedient, taking into consideration our own present circumstances, with the situation of the enemy in New York and at the southward, to abandon the siege of the former and to march a body of troops consisting of a detachment from the American army, with the whole of the French troops, immediately to Virginia. With this detachment, which will be very considerable, I have determined to march myself."

The march began in late August. It carried the allied armies across New Jersey and Pennsylvania to the head of the Chesapeake. Washington expected to receive updates from de Grasse. But he heard nothing. "My dear Marquis," he wrote on September 1 to Lafayette, who had command of a force tasked with preventing Cornwallis's escape to the north by land. "I am distressed beyond expression to know what is become of the Count de Grasse, and for fear the English fleet, by occupying the Chesapeake (towards which my last accounts say they were steering) should frustrate all our flattering prospects."

Washington unburdened himself to Lafayette as to few others, likely because the young man was so clearly devoted to the American cause, and possibly because, being young and a foreigner, he represented no threat to Washington, the way Horatio Gates had. "You see how critically important the present moment is," Washington wrote to Lafayette. "For my own part I am determined still to persist with unremitting ardour in my present plan unless some inevitable and insuperable obstacles are thrown in our way." He closed, "Adieu, my dear Marquis. If you get anything new from any quarter, send it I pray you on the spur of speed, for I am almost all impatience and anxiety."

Washington reached Williamsburg before he learned that de Grasse had been putting his time to good use. "I had the honor to receive your Excellency's letter of the 4th of this month soon after my arrival at this place," he wrote to the admiral on September 15. "I am at a loss to express the pleasure which I have in congratulating your Excellency on your return to your former station in the bay, and the happy circumstance of forming a junction with the squadron of the Count de Barras," who had sailed south from Rhode Island. "I take particular satisfaction in felicitating your Excellency on the glory of having driven the British fleet from the coasts and taking two of their frigates"—in what was called the battle of the Capes, at the mouth of the Chesapeake Bay. "These happy events, and the decided superiority of your fleet, give us the happiest presages of the most complete success in our combined operations."

With de Grasse in command of the sea, Washington closed upon Cornwallis. "I marched from Williamsburg with the whole army on the 28th and approached within about two miles of the enemy at York," he reported to Congress on October 1, referring to Yorktown. Cornwallis initially contested the advance but after a brief artillery battle retired to the town.

The British commander recognized his predicament. Washington and Rochambeau had cut off his line of retreat on land, and de Grasse was doing the same at sea. Yet hope was not lost. Cornwallis knew as well as Washington that de Grasse couldn't remain long in Virginia. Other theaters beckoned, and the autumn weather on this shore put his fleet at risk. Moreover, help was on the way, in the form of a British naval squadron. If Cornwallis could hold out for a month, he might yet slip Washington's noose.

"On the 29th the American troops moved forward and took their ground in front of the enemy's works on their left," Washington continued in his report to Congress. "No opposition, except a few scattered shots." A desultory rifle battle filled the day, with neither side much damaging the other.

"In the morning we discovered that the enemy had evacuated all their exterior line of works and withdrawn themselves to those near the body of the town," Washington wrote of September 30. "By this means we are in possession of very advantageous grounds, which command in a very near advance almost the whole remaining line of their defence." Cornwallis had accepted the siege, hoping to draw it out.

Washington sought to speed things up. "All the expedition that our circumstances will admit is using to bring up our heavy artillery and stores and to open our batteries. This work I hope will be executed in a few days, when our fire will begin with great vigor."

The work proceeded apace. The American and French engineers and the troops under their command toiled at night to avoid detection and enemy fire. On October 6, Washington's men began constructing their first parallel, or fortified line, within six hundred yards of the British works. They completed it during the next two days. "The 9th at three o'clock in the afternoon the French battery on the left, of four twelve-pounders, six mortars and howitzers opened," Washington reported to Congress on October 12. "And at 5 o'clock the American battery on the right, of six eighteen- and twenty-four-pounders, two mortars, and two howitzers opened also." The artillery fire yielded good results. "We could perceive that our shot, which were directed against the enemy's embrasures"—openings through which British cannons fired—"injured them much."

Washington ordered the shelling to intensify. "Two French batteries, one of ten eighteen- and twenty-four pounders, and six mortars and howitzers, the other of four eighteen-pounders, opened, as did two more American batteries, one of four eighteen-pounders, the other of two mortars. The fire now became so excessively heavy that the enemy withdrew their cannon from their embrasures, placed them behind the merlons"—portions of the battlement protecting the guns while not allowing them to fire—"and scarcely fired a shot during the whole day. In the evening the Charon frigate of forty-four guns was set on fire by a hot ball from the French battery on the left, and entirely consumed."

The bombardment continued. "Yesterday morning two of the enemy's transports were fired by hot shot and burnt," Washington wrote. "This has occasioned them to warp their shipping as far over to the Gloucester shore"—across the York River from Yorktown—"as possible. We last night advanced our second parallel within three hundred yards of the enemy's works, with little or no annoyance from them. Only one man was killed, and three or four wounded." It was almost too easy. "I shall think it strange indeed if Lord Cornwallis makes no vigorous exertions in the course of this night, or very soon after."

Cornwallis did as Washington expected. "The enemy last night made a sortie for the first time," Washington wrote of October 15. "They entered one of the French and one of the American batteries on the second parallel which were unfinished. They had only time to thrust the points of their bayonets into four pieces of the French and two of the American artillery and break them off." This was intended to disable the French and American weapons. "But the spikes were easily extracted." Nor did the British hold their position. "They were repulsed the moment the supporting troops came up, leaving behind them seven or eight dead and six prisoners. The French had four officers and twelve privates killed and wounded, and we had one sergeant mortally wounded."

JOSEPH MARTIN, the soldier from Connecticut, had remained in the army after White Plains and made the march to Virginia with Washington. He remembered working on the parallels and the batteries facing Yorktown. "There came a man alone to us, having on a surtout"—a kind of overcoat—"as we conjectured, it being exceeding dark, and inquired for the engineers. We now began to be a little jealous for our safety, being alone and without arms, and within forty rods of the British trenches. The stranger inquired what troops we were, talked familiarly with us a few minutes, when, being informed which way the officers had gone, he went off in the same direction, after strictly charging us, in case we should be taken prisoners, not to discover to the enemy what troops we were. We were obliged to him for his kind advice, but we considered ourselves as standing in no great need of it, for we knew as well as he did that sappers and miners were allowed no quarters, at least were entitled to none by the laws of warfare, and of course should take care, if taken, and the enemy did not find us out, not to betray our own secret."

The engineer officers returned and with them the stranger. "They discoursed together some time, when by the officers often calling him 'Your Excellency,' we discovered that it was General Washington. Had we dared, we might have cautioned him for exposing himself so carelessly to danger at such a time, and doubtless he would have taken it in good part if we had. But nothing ill happened to either him or ourselves."

The construction of the batteries continued. "The French, who were upon our left, had completed their batteries a few hours before us, but were not allowed to discharge their pieces till the American batteries were ready. Our commanding battery was on the near bank of the river and contained ten heavy guns. The next was a bomb-battery of three large mortars, and so on through the whole line."

The flagstaff of Martin's unit was in the ten-gun battery. "I was in the trenches the day that the batteries were to be opened. All were upon the tiptoe of expectation and impatience to see the signal given to open the whole line of batteries, which was to be the hoisting of the American flag in the ten-gun battery. About noon the much wished for signal went up. I confess I felt a secret pride swell my heart when I saw the star-spangled banner waving majestically in the very faces of our implacable adversaries. It appeared like an omen of success to our enterprise."

And so it proved. "A simultaneous discharge of all the guns in the line followed, the French troops accompanying it with 'Huzza for the Americans!' It was said that the first shell sent from our batteries entered an elegant house formerly owned or occupied by the secretary of state under the British government, and burned directly over a table surrounded by a large party of British officers at dinner, killing and wounding a number of them."

Martin received a new assignment. "There were two strong redoubts held by the British, on their left." These were small forts outside the British lines. "It was necessary for us to possess those redoubts, before we could complete our trenches. One afternoon I, with the rest of our corps that had been on duty in the trenches the night but one before, were ordered to the lines." They arrived a bit before sunset. "I saw several officers fixing bayonets on long staves. I then concluded we were about to make a general assault upon the enemy's works. But before dark I was informed of the whole plan, which was to storm the redoubts, the one by the Americans and the other by the French."

Martin and his comrades awaited the signal. "The two brilliant planets, Jupiter and Venus, were in close contact in the western hemisphere, the same direction that the signal was to be made in. When I happened to cast my eyes to that quarter, which was often, and I caught a glance of them, I was ready to spring to my feet, thinking they were the signal for starting. Our watchword was 'Rochambeau,' the commander of the

French forces' name, a good watchword, for being pronounced 'Ro-sham-bow,' it sounded, when pronounced quick, like 'Rush on boys!'"

The signal came: three shells in rapid succession. "We immediately moved silently on toward the redoubt we were to attack, with unloaded muskets," Martin recalled. "Just as we arrived at the abatis"—a defensive work of felled trees—"the enemy discovered us and directly opened a sharp fire upon us. We were now at a place where many of our large shells had burst in the ground, making holes sufficient to bury an ox in. The men, having their eyes fixed upon what was transacting before them, were now every now and then falling into these holes. I thought the British were killing us off at a great rate. At length one of the holes happening to pick me up, I found out the mystery of the huge slaughter."

As Martin and his fellows pushed forward, the British responded with vigor. "A man at my side received a ball in his head and fell under my feet crying out bitterly," Martin wrote. The British hurled hand grenades. "They were so thick that at first I thought them cartridge papers on fire, but was soon undeceived by their cracking." Martin encountered an old comrade. "I knew him by the light of the enemy's musketry, it was so vivid."

The defenders of the redoubt, overwhelmed by the energy of the attackers, finally broke. "I saw a British soldier jump over the walls of the fort next the river and go down the bank, which was almost perpendicular and twenty or thirty feet high," Martin said. "When he came to the beach he made off for the town, and if he did not make good use of his legs I never saw a man that did."

THE CAPTURE OF THE REDOUBTS rendered the British position in Yorktown untenable. Cornwallis, casting a final glance down the river and seeing no British warships, acknowledged as much. "I propose a cessation of hostilities for twenty-four hours," he said in a note to Washington delivered under a flag of truce on October 17. Each side should appoint two officers to settle terms of the surrender of Yorktown and Gloucester.

"An ardent desire to spare the further effusion of blood will readily incline me to listen to such terms for the surrender of your post and garrisons at York and Gloucester as are admissible," Washington replied. But he insisted on moving things along, lest the British ships appear. He agreed to a truce of two hours, not twenty-four.

. . .

ST. GEORGE TUCKER WAS a soldier in Washington's army who happened to have been a resident of Yorktown before the British seized the place. He was struck by the stillness of the truce. "The night was remarkably clear and the sky decorated with ten thousand stars," he wrote. "Numberless meteors gleaming through the atmosphere afforded a pleasing resemblance to the bombs which had exhibited a noble firework the night before, but happily divested of all their horror."

The truce lasted longer than the two hours agreed to by Washington. Tucker and his comrades inferred that a surrender was afoot. "As soon as the sun rose one of the most striking pictures of war was displayed that imagination can paint. From the point of Rock Battery on one side, our lines completely manned and our works crowded with soldiers were exhibited to view. Opposite these at the distance of two hundred yards, you were presented with a sight of the British works, their parapets crowded with officers looking at those who were assembled at the top of our works. The secretary's house, with one of the corners broke off and many large holes through the roof and walls, part of which seemed tottering with their weight, afforded a striking instance of the destruction occasioned by war." It was this destruction that had prompted Cornwallis to sue for terms. After the loss of the redoubts, the British general had no way to prevent much more of the same.

"On the beach of York directly under the eye, hundreds of busy people might be seen moving to and fro," Tucker continued. "At a small distance from the shore were seen ships sunk down to the water's edge. Further out in the channel the masts, yards and even the topgallant masts of some might be seen, without any vestige of the hulls." Cornwallis realized that even if the British squadron had arrived, his escape under the guns of the Americans and French would have been difficult.

Word soon spread through the army that Cornwallis had indeed surrendered. The denouement was formal but moving. "Our army was drawn up in a line on each side of the road extending from our front parallel to the forks of the road at Hudson Allen's—the Americans on the right, the French on the left," Tucker wrote. "Through these lines the whole British army marched, their drums in front beating a slow march, their colors furled and cased." The pride of the British empire had been humbled. "The sight was too pleasing to an American to admit of description."

. . .

GENERAL BENJAMIN LINCOLN ACCEPTED the British surrender in place of Washington. Cornwallis, claiming illness, declined to deliver his sword personally. He left that task to a subordinate. Washington thereupon assigned the reception of the sword to Lincoln.

The first three articles of the surrender agreement specified the details by which the officers and men of Cornwallis's army would become prisoners of war. Article Four dealt with personal property. "Officers and soldiers to keep their private property of every kind," it said. "Any property obviously belonging to the inhabitants of these states, in the possession of the garrison, shall be subject to be reclaimed."

Each article had a line to indicate whether it was granted or rejected by Washington. He granted the first four, and five more that followed.

Article Ten stipulated, "Natives or inhabitants of different parts of this country at present in York or Gloucester are not to be punished on account of having joined the British Army." Washington withheld his initials. "This article cannot be assented to, being altogether of civil resort," he wrote beside it.

There was more to Articles Four and Ten than met the eye. The clause in Article Four about "property obviously belonging to the inhabitants of these states, in the possession of the garrison," referred to American slaves who had gone over to the British side and were at Yorktown at the time of the surrender. Cornwallis and Washington agreed that these persons would not be treated as prisoners of war but would be "subject to be reclaimed"—by their former owners.

Cornwallis's proposal in Article Ten that Americans in the British army not be punished referred to loyalists, white and black. Washington refused to take a position on the loyalists. Congress would deal with them.

"THE GENERAL CONGRATULATES the Army upon the glorious event of yesterday," read the order issued from Washington's headquarters on October 20. Washington congratulated the French as well.

"In order to diffuse the general joy through every breast, the General orders that those men belonging to the Army who may now be in confinement shall be pardoned, released and join their respective corps," the order went on.

"Divine service is to be performed tomorrow in the several brigades or divisions. The Commander in Chief earnestly recommends that the troops not on duty should universally attend with that seriousness of deportment and gratitude of heart which the recognition of such reiterated and astonishing interpositions of Providence demand of us."

Part IX

Cincinnatus

~ 68 ~

During the whole month of November, the concurring accounts which were transmitted to Government, enumerating Lord Cornwallis's embarrassments and the positions taken by the enemy, augmented the anxiety of the Cabinet," recalled Nathaniel Wraxall, a member of Parliament with friends in the ministry of Lord North. He was referring to Washington's siege of Yorktown, news of which crossed the Atlantic slowly. "Lord George Germain in particular, conscious that on the prosperous or adverse termination of that expedition must depend the fate of the American contest, his own stay in office, as well as probably the duration of the Ministry, felt, and even expressed to his friends, the strongest uneasiness on the subject." Parliament was about to meet after a recess, and Germain and North would be called to account.

"On Sunday the 25th about noon, official intelligence of the surrender of the British forces at Yorktown arrived from Falmouth at Lord George Germain's house," Wraxall continued. "Without communicating it to any other person, Lord George, for the purpose of dispatch, immediately got with him into a hackney-coach and drove to Lord Stormont's residence in Portland Place. Having imparted to him the disastrous information and taken him into the carriage, they instantly proceeded to the Chancellor's house in Great Russell Street, Bloomsbury, whom they found at home, when after a short consultation, they determined to lay it themselves in person before Lord North." Germain wanted reinforcements when he delivered the bad news.

North hadn't heard anything. The prime minister was known for unflappability. But not this time, Wraxall related. "I asked Lord George afterwards how he took the communication when made to him. 'As he would have taken a ball in his breast,' replied Lord George. For he opened his arms, exclaiming wildly, as he paced up and down the apartment during a few minutes, 'O God! it is all over!' Words which he repeated many times under emotions of the deepest consternation and distress."

IT WAS INDEED over for North. The prime minister's American policy was judged a failure by Parliament and Britain at large. In more than six years the British army had been unable to suppress the rebellion. A vote of no confidence compelled North's resignation, and a new administration, under the Marquess of Rockingham, assumed the task of liquidating the American war.

The job was complicated by the fact that the American war had become a European war. Britain could settle with America by acknowledging American independence, but it had other issues to work out with France and Spain. Moreover, the treaties among the anti-British powers prevented America from making peace until France and Spain were ready to do so. As a result, peace negotiations dragged on for many months. Not until November 1782 did the American negotiators—Benjamin Franklin, John Adams and John Jay—reach agreement in Paris with their British counterparts on the shape of a peace pact. Not until January 1783 was that agreement drawn up in legal language. And not until September 1783 were the French and Spanish parts of the puzzle added to produce a comprehensive peace treaty.

"WE ARE HELD in a very disagreeable state of suspence," Washington wrote to Jack from Newburgh, on the Hudson River above New York, in January 1783. The war appeared to be over, but until the treaty was signed and the British departed American soil, he had to remain vigilant. He had to keep his soldiers under arms, but that was getting harder by the day. "The army as usual are without pay, and a great part of the soldiery without shirts, and though the patience of them is equally threadbare, it seems to be a matter of small concern to those at a distance"—namely Congress.

Some of the soldiers were reckoning how to present their case to the government. "In the course of a few days Congress will, I expect, receive an address from the army on the subject of their grievances," Washington wrote to Joseph Jones, a Virginia member of Congress. Washington didn't like the idea of soldiers appealing to Congress. There was a chain of command that was supposed to run through him. But an address was innocuous compared with a mutiny, which was a real possibility. "The temper of the army is much soured and has become more irritable than at any period since the commencement of the war." Washington had planned to request a leave of absence to attend to private matters. He'd had no leave since the start of the war. But he decided he couldn't risk being away. "The dissatisfactions of the army had arisen to a great and alarming height, and combinations among the officers to resign in a body at given periods were beginning to take place."

He had managed to talk the malcontents down, for the moment. The question would soon be with Congress. "What that honourable body can or will do in the matter does not belong to me to determine," Washington told Jones. He hoped Congress would treat the soldiers' concerns judiciously. "Policy in my opinion should dictate soothing measures, as it is an uncontrovertible fact that no part of the community has undergone equal hardships and borne them with the same patience and fortitude that the army has done. Hitherto the officers have stood between the lower order of the soldiery and the public, and in more instances than one have quelled, at the hazard of their lives, very dangerous mutinies. But if their discontents should be suffered to rise equally high, I know not what the consequences may be."

Washington got advice on the subject from a familiar source in an unfamiliar position. Alexander Hamilton had resigned from the army after Yorktown, concluding that an army without battles was no place for a young man of ambition. He taught himself law and passed the bar exam. He entered politics, becoming part of New York's delegation in Congress. From his seat in the legislature, he wrote to Washington. "Flattering myself that your knowledge of me will induce you to receive the observations I make as dictated by a regard to the public good, I take the liberty to suggest to you my ideas on some matters of delicacy and importance," Hamilton said. "I view the present juncture as a very interesting one"—in the sense of engaging great interests. "I need not observe how far the temper and situation of the army make it so. The state of our finances was perhaps never more critical. I am under injunctions which will not permit me to disclose some facts that would at once demonstrate this position, but I think it probable you will be possessed of them through another channel. It is however certain that there has scarcely been a period of the revolution which called more for wisdom and decision in Congress. Unfortunately for us we are a body not governed by reason or foresight but by circumstances. It is probable we shall not take the proper measures, and if we do not, a few months may open an embarrassing scene. This will be the case whether we have peace or a continuance of the war."

Hamilton was thinking beyond the army to the country as a whole. His brief time in Congress had confirmed his view of its ineffectiveness and of the need for fundamental reform of government. He hoped to make the army an agent of reform.

"If the war continues," Hamilton told Washington, "it would seem that the army must in June"—when current money would run out—"subsist itself to defend the country. If peace should take place, it will subsist itself to procure justice to itself. It appears to be a prevailing opinion in the army that the disposition to recompence their services will cease with the necessity for them, and that if they once lay down their arms, they will part with the means of obtaining justice."

The army could compel Congress to mend its ways, Hamilton told Washington. "The claims of the army, urged with moderation but with firmness, may operate on those weak minds which are influenced by their apprehensions more than their judgments, so as to produce a concurrence in the measures which the exigencies of affairs demand. They may add weight to the applications of Congress to the several states." The Articles of Confederation, adopted in 1781, allowed Congress to request money from the states but not to demand it. The army's petition would lend credence to a congressional request. Yet the operation must be handled with care. "The difficulty will be to keep a complaining and suffering army within the bounds of moderation."

Here was where Washington came in. "This"—moderation—"Your Excellency's influence must effect," Hamilton told his former boss. He offered pointers. "It will be advisable not to discountenance their endeavours to procure redress, but rather by the intervention of confidential and prudent persons to take the direction of them." Yet Washington's hand must not become visible, lest his patriotic impartiality be questioned. "Your Excellency should preserve the confidence of the army without losing that of the people. This will enable you in case of extremity to guide the torrent and bring order, perhaps even good, out of confusion."

In short, Washington should use the army to pressure Congress, which would employ that pressure to get more money out of the states. Hamilton had concluded, unoriginally, that money was what made government run. The American government needed more power to obtain money. Some would come from the states. Much would come from lenders, whose confidence had to be cultivated. "The great desideratum at present is the establishment of general funds, which alone can do justice to the creditors of the United States (of whom the army forms the most meritorious class), restore public credit and supply the future wants of government. This is the object of all men of sense; in this the influence of the army, properly directed, may cooperate."

Having told Washington how to conduct his affairs, Hamilton pleaded modesty. "The intimations I have thrown out will suffice to give Your Excellency a proper conception of my sentiments. You will judge of their reasonableness or fallacy, but I persuade myself you will do justice to my motives."

Washington refused to be part of Hamilton's plot. "The predicament in which I stand as citizen and soldier is as critical and delicate as can well be conceived," he replied. "It has been the subject of many contemplative hours. The sufferings of a complaining army on one hand, and the inability of Congress and tardiness of the states on the other, are the forebodings of evil and may be productive of events which are more to be deprecated than prevented." But Hamilton was taking an alarmist view of things. Washington would follow the counsel of patience. "I shall pursue the same steady line of conduct which has governed me hitherto."

HIS PATIENCE WAS TESTED. On March 10 an announcement circulated anonymously among the army. "A meeting of the general and field officers is requested at the public building on Tuesday next at 11 o'clock," it read. "A commissioned officer from each company is expected, and a delegate from the medical staff. The object of this convention is to consider the late letter from our representatives in Philadelphia and what measures (if any) should be adopted to obtain that redress of grievances which they seem to have solicited in vain." A petition previously sent to Congress had elicited no satisfactory response.

A second document circulated as well. The author referred to himself in the third person as "a fellow soldier, whose interest and affections bind him strongly to you, whose past sufferings have been as great, and whose future fortune may be as desperate as yours." The unnamed soldier said he had loved private life and had left it with regret. But duty had called, and he had followed it willingly. "He has long shared in your toils and mingled in your dangers. He has felt the cold hand of poverty without a murmur, and has seen the insolence of wealth without a sigh."

He had until recently believed in the justice of his country. "He hoped that, as the clouds of adversity scattered, and as the sunshine of peace and better fortune broke in upon us, the coldness and severity of government would relax, and that, more than justice, that gratitude would blaze forth upon those hands which had upheld her in the darkest stages of her passage from impending servitude to acknowledged independence." His hope had been disappointed. He couldn't go on as before. "Faith has its limits as well as temper, and there are points beyond which neither can be stretched without sinking into cowardice or plunging into credulity."

This soldier, like his comrades, wanted only what had been promised to him, only that which he was owed and had not been paid. They had petitioned and remonstrated, to no avail. "If this, then, be your treatment while the swords you wear are necessary for the defence of America, what have you to expect from peace, when your voice shall sink and your strength dissipate by division? When those very swords, the instruments and companions of your glory, shall be taken from your sides, and no remaining mark of military distinction left but your wants, infirmities and scars?" Would his comrades consent to grow old in poverty, cast upon the charity of others? "If you can, go, and carry with you the jest of tories and scorn of whigs, the ridicule and, what is worse, the pity of the world. Go, starve, and be forgotten! But if your spirit should revolt at this; if you have sense enough to discover, and spirit enough to oppose, tyranny under whatever garb it may assume, whether it be the plain coat of republicanism or the splendid robe of royalty; if you yet learned to discriminate between a people and cause, between men and principles—awake, attend to your situation and redress yourselves. If the present moment be lost, every future effort is in vain."

Washington forwarded copies of these documents to Congress, with a letter averring his "inexpressible concern" at what they signified. Yet he was as puzzled as he was worried. "There is something very mysterious in this business," he wrote to Hamilton. "It appears reports have been propagated in Philadelphia that dangerous combinations were forming in the Army, and this at a time when there was not a syllable of the kind in agitation in camp." The agitation started only after a certain officer sent from Congress under guise of inspector arrived and began telling the soldiers that Congress intended to disband the army, and they had better take measures to get paid before that happened. The anonymous documents appeared at just this time. "From this and a variety of other considerations, it is firmly believed by some the scheme was not only planned but also digested and matured in Philadelphia." Washington told Hamilton he didn't fully accept this reasoning—yet. "My opinion shall be suspended till I have a better ground to found one on." But the circumstances and timing were suggestive. "The matter was managed with great art, for as soon as the minds of the officers were thought to be prepared for the transaction, the anonymous invitations and address to the officers were put in circulation through every state line in the army."

If Washington believed that Hamilton was one of the plotters in Congress, he didn't say so in this letter. Yet he supposed Hamilton knew who the plotters were and could combat their efforts. The best remedy would be for Congress to pay what it owed the soldiers. "Let me beseech you therefore, my good sir, to urge this matter earnestly and without further delay," Washington concluded to Hamilton, who must have read his old commander's words as chastisement. Hamilton had influence with his colleagues in Congress. He should work on them and leave the army alone. "If any disastrous consequences should follow by reason of their delinquency, that they must be answerable to God and their country for the ineffable horrors which may be occasioned thereby."

WASHINGTON DID HIS own part to quell the turmoil. He issued a general order alerting the officers that he knew of the proposed meeting. "Although he is fully persuaded that the good sense of the officers would induce them to pay very little attention to such an irregular invitation," Washington said of himself, "his duty as well as the reputation and true interest of the Army requires his disapprobation of such disorderly proceedings." In place of the irregular meeting, he called a regular one. "General and field officers, with one officer from each company, and a proper representation of the staff of the Army will assemble at 12 o'clock on Saturday next at the New Building to hear the report of the committee of the Army to Congress."

When the officers gathered on Saturday, they didn't know what to expect. Horatio Gates, restored to Washington's staff, prepared to direct the meeting. But at the last moment Washington arrived and took the floor. The officers as a group had never seen him so emotional. "Gentlemen," he said, "by an anonymous summons, an attempt has been made to convene you together. How inconsistent with the rules of propriety!—how unmilitary!—and how subversive of all order and discipline, let the good sense of the Army decide." Nor was that all. "In the moment of this summons, another anonymous production was sent into circulation, addressed more to the feelings and passions than to the reason and judgment of the Army. The author of the piece is entitled to much credit for the goodness of his pen, and I could wish he had as much credit for the rectitude of his heart."

The implication of the anonymous summons and manifesto was that the commander in chief wasn't protecting the interests of his soldiers. Washington resented the very idea. "If my conduct heretofore has not evinced to you that I have been a faithful friend to the Army, my declaration of it at this time would be equally unavailing and improper. But as I was among the first who embarked in the cause of our common country; as I have never left your side one moment but when called from you, on public duty; as I have been the constant companion and witness of your distresses, and not among the last to feel and acknowledge your merits; as I have ever considered my own military reputation as inseparably connected with that of the Army; as my heart has ever expanded with joy when I have heard its praises, and my indignation has arisen when the mouth of detraction has been opened against it—it can scarcely be supposed, at this late stage of the war, that I am indifferent to its interests."

How were the army's interests to be promoted? The anonymous pamphleteer had one answer. "Never sheath your sword, says he, until you have obtained full and ample justice." Washington shook his head in sorrow and dismay. "My God! What can this writer have in view?" *Who* was this writer to recommend such action? "Can he be a friend to the Army? Can he be a friend to this country? Rather, is he not an insidious foe?" Washington knew what to do with the secret troublemaker's advice. "I spurn it, as every man who regards that liberty and reveres that justice for which we contend undoubtedly must."

Washington avowed his faith in Congress to do the right thing regarding the army's pay. "That their endeavors to discover and establish funds for this purpose have been unwearied and will not cease till they have succeeded, I have not a doubt." To be sure, Congress could have moved faster. "Like all other large bodies where there is a variety of different interests to reconcile, their deliberations are slow." Yet slowness was no cause for rash and dangerous moves by officers of the army, which could not but damage their hard-won reputation for fortitude and patriotism. And to what end? "To bring the object we seek for nearer? No! Most certainly, in my opinion, it will cast it at a greater distance."

Washington looked from man to man among the officers. They

had believed in him in the past, he said. They must believe in him now. "A grateful sense of the confidence you have ever placed in me, a recollection of the cheerful assistance and prompt obedience I have experienced from you under every vicissitude of fortune, and the sincere affection I feel for an army I have so long had the honor to command, will oblige me to declare, in this public and solemn manner that, in the attainment of complete justice for all your toils and dangers, and in the gratification of every wish, so far as may be done consistently with the great duty I owe my country and those powers we are bound to respect, you may freely command my services to the utmost of my abilities."

He asked them to look within themselves. "Let me entreat you, gentlemen, on your part not to take any measures which, viewed in the calm light of reason, will lessen the dignity and sully the glory you have hitherto maintained." They must have faith in the republican self-government for which they all had been fighting side by side these eight years. In doing so, they would attain still greater glory. "You will pursue the plain and direct road to the attainment of your wishes. You will defeat the insidious designs of our enemies, who are compelled to resort from open force to secret artifice. You will give one more distinguished proof of unexampled patriotism and patient virtue, rising superior to the pressure of the most complicated sufferings. And you will, by the dignity of your conduct, afford occasion for posterity to say, when speaking of the glorious example you have exhibited to mankind, 'Had this day been wanting, the world had never seen the last stage of perfection to which human nature is capable of attaining.'"

SAMUEL SHAW WAS one of the officers present. In his diary for the day of the meeting, he explained that Washington had prepared his remarks and proceeded to read them. The general got all the way through without incident. But at the end he began to read a letter from a member of Congress corroborating the confidence Washington placed in the legislature's good faith. "This was an exceedingly sensible letter," Shaw wrote. "And while it pointed out the difficulties and embarrassments of Congress, it held up very forcibly the idea that the army should, at all events, be generously dealt with."

Shaw's diary continued: "One circumstance in reading this letter must not be omitted. His Excellency, after reading the first paragraph, made a short pause, took out his spectacles, and begged the indulgence of his audience while he put them on, observing at the same time, that he had grown gray in their service, and now found himself growing blind. There was something so natural, so unaffected, in this appeal, as rendered it superior to the most studied oratory; it forced its way to the heart, and you might see sensibility moisten every eye."

⟶ 69 ⟵

Washington's appeal froze the incipient mutiny. It also lit a fire under Congress, which within days of learning of the general's bravura performance approved a bond sale to pay the soldiers what they were owed.

Relief gave way to joy when word arrived from France of agreement on the terms of the final peace settlement. "The Commander in Chief orders the cessation of hostilities between the United States of America and the King of Great Britain to be publicly proclaimed tomorrow at 12 o'clock at the New Building," Washington announced in general orders. "After which the chaplains with the several brigades will render thanks to almighty God for all his mercies, particularly for his overruling the wrath of man to his own glory, and causing the rage of war to cease amongst the nations."

Washington got personal, or as personal as the format of general orders allowed. "The Commander in Chief, far from endeavouring to stifle the feelings of joy in his own bosom, offers his most cordial congratulations on the occasion to all the officers of every denomination, to all the troops of the United States in general, and in particular to those gallant and persevering men who had resolved to defend the rights of their invaded country so long as the war should continue. For these are the men who ought to be considered as the pride and boast of the American army, and who, crowned with well-earned laurels, may soon withdraw from the field of glory to the more tranquil walks of civil life."

The men of the army had not merely defeated a foe. They had built a nation. "Happy, thrice happy shall they be pronounced hereafter who have contributed anything, who have performed the meanest office in creating this stupendous fabric of freedom and empire on the broad basis of independency, who have assisted in protesting the rights of human nature and establishing an asylum for the poor and oppressed of all nations of religions."

The soldiers had much to be proud of, and much to celebrate. The commander in chief would assist. "An extra ration of liquor to be issued to every man tomorrow, to drink perpetual peace, independence and happiness to the United States of America."

WASHINGTON MADE READY for retirement. He addressed the nation in a circular letter to the governors of the states. "The great object for which I had the honor to hold an appointment in the service of my country being accomplished, I am now preparing to resign it into the hands of Congress and to return to that domestic retirement which it is well known I left with the greatest reluctance, a retirement for which I have never ceased to sigh through a long and painful absence, and in which, remote from the noise and trouble of the world, I meditate to pass the remainder of life in a state of undisturbed repose," he said.

He had a few thoughts to share before he left the scene. Americans were peculiarly blessed. They controlled fertile lands with abundant resources. They had created new governments in an age of enlightenment, when the rights of mankind were better understood than before. They drew on centuries, even millennia, of wisdom of scientists and philosophers. They had won their independence and become their own masters.

Yet with blessing came responsibility. "If their citizens should not be completely free and happy, the fault will be entirely their own," Washington said, referring to the states. "It is in their choice and depends upon their conduct whether they will be respectable and prosperous or contemptible and miserable as a nation. This is the time of their political probation: this is the moment when the eyes of the whole world are turned upon them. This is the moment to establish or ruin their national character forever."

The challenge transcended the states. "This is the favorable moment to give such a tone to our federal government as will enable it to answer the ends of its institution, or this may be the ill-fated moment for relaxing the powers of the Union, annihilating the cement of the Confederation and exposing us to become the sport of European politics, which may play one state against another to prevent their growing importance and to serve their own interested purposes." Much hung on the present. "According to the system of policy the states shall adopt at this moment, they will stand or fall, and by their confirmation or lapse it is yet to be decided whether the revolution must ultimately be considered as a blessing or a curse: a blessing or a curse not to the present age alone, for with our fate will the destiny of unborn millions be involved."

Washington grew specific. "There are four things which I humbly conceive are essential to the well-being, I may even venture to say to the existence, of the United States as an independent power. 1st: An indissoluble union of the states under one federal head. 2ndly: A sacred regard to public justice. 3dly: The adoption of a proper peace establishment. 4thly: The prevalence of that pacific and friendly disposition among the people of the United States which will induce them to forget their local prejudices and policies, to make those mutual concessions which are requisite to the general prosperity, and, in some instances, to sacrifice their individual advantages to the interest of the community."

Washington elaborated. His first and third points, he said, required converting the loose confederation that had fought the war to a proper national government suited to the needs of peace. His second and fourth aimed at the hearts and minds of Americans, urging them to put justice and the common weal above state and individual interests.

"I now make it my earnest prayer," he declared to the governors in closing, "that God would have you and the state over which you preside in his holy protection; that he would incline the hearts of the citizens to cultivate a spirit of subordination and obedience to government, to entertain a brotherly affection and love for one another, for their fellow citizens of the United States at large and particularly for their brethren who have served in the field; and finally that he would most graciously be pleased to dispose us all to do justice, to love mercy and to demean ourselves with that charity, humility and pacific temper of mind which were the characteristics of the divine author of our blessed religion and without an humble imitation of whose example in these things we can never hope to be a happy nation."

IN SEPTEMBER THE FINAL VERSION of the peace treaty was signed in Paris. Upon receiving word, the British army in New York prepared to evacuate, and on November 25 it and a large coterie of loyalists sailed away. On that same day Washington and George Clinton, at the head of a column of Continental army troops, reclaimed the city for the United States of America and the state of New York.

The war was truly over. On December 4, Washington convened his officers for the last time at Fraunces Tavern. "We had been assembled but a few moments when His Excellency entered the room," wrote Benjamin Tallmadge, one of the officers. "His emotion, too strong to be concealed, seemed to be reciprocated by every officer present." Washington poured himself a glass of wine and addressed the group. "With a heart full of love and gratitude, I now take leave of you. I most devoutly wish that your latter days may be as prosperous and happy as your former ones have been glorious and honorable."

He invited each of the officers to come forward and shake his hand. "Gen. Knox, being nearest to him, turned to the Commander-in-Chief, who, suffused in tears, was incapable of utterance, but grasped his hand, when they embraced each other in silence," Tallmadge wrote. "In the same affectionate manner, every officer in the room marched up to, kissed, and parted with his General-in-Chief."

When the last embrace had been given, Washington left the tavern to catch a ferry to New Jersey and the road to home. "We all followed in mournful silence to the wharf, where a prodigious crowd had assembled to witness the departure of the man who, under God, had been the great agent in establishing the glory and independence of these United States. As soon as he was seated, the barge put off into the river, and when out in the stream, our great and beloved General waved his hat and bid us a silent adieu."

HE HAD ONE MORE STOP in his military career. After the mutiny of the Pennsylvania line had caused Congress to flee Philadelphia, the legislature landed at Princeton before drifting south to Annapolis, where it was meeting in December 1783. Washington returned to his civilian superiors the commission he had been given eight and a half years before in Philadelphia. "The great events on which my resignation depended having at length taken place, I have now the honor of offering my sincere congratulations to Congress and of presenting myself before them to surrender into their hands the trust committed to me, and to claim the indulgence of retiring from the service of my country," he said. He praised the army and asked Congress to remember especially the officers of his military family who had remained to the very end. He expressed gratitude to Providence for blessing the American enterprise.

"Having now finished the work assigned me," Washington concluded, "I retire from the great theatre of action, and bidding an affectionate farewell to this august body under whose orders I have so long acted, I here offer my commission and take my leave of all the employments of public life."

→ 70 ←

George III could hardly believe it. During the eight years of the war the king had been forced to acknowledge Washington's capacity as a military commander. Washington had outmaneuvered and outlasted Britain's best generals. He had managed relations with the American Congress and the states, cajoling and shaming them into providing sustenance for his soldiers. He had, by means George didn't entirely understand but assumed involved some kind of moral force, held the army together at Valley Forge, when the ranks of a lesser leader would have melted away. He had flattered and persuaded his French allies in the campaign that produced the final victory at Yorktown. George was as shocked by Cornwallis's surrender as anyone in Britain, yet by then he couldn't be surprised. His generals had lost to a better general.

The surprising thing to George—the astonishing thing—was what Washington did next. At the moment of victory, at the head of a triumphal army, holding the fate of his young country in his hands, Washington stepped aside and became merely a private citizen.

Benjamin West, an artist born in Pennsylvania who found better work painting portraits in England, became acquainted with George during the war. Toward the end, the king asked West what he thought Washington would do after the fighting ceased. West said he thought Washington would retire to his farm.

West later recalled that George was skeptical. "The King said if he did, he would be the greatest man in the world."

And now he had.

LAFAYETTE HAD DEPARTED America not long after Yorktown. He wrote to Washington from Paris, and Washington owed him a letter. Washington recounted his farewell to the army and his return of his commission to Congress. He said it was good to be home at Mount Vernon. Lafayette had invited Washington to come to France, but Washington declined for the moment and perhaps longer. "I see but little prospect of such a voyage," he said. "The deranged situation of my private concerns, occasioned by an absence of almost nine years, and an entire disregard of all private business during that period, will not only suspend but may put it forever out of my power."

Washington had left his private concerns during the war to Lund Washington, who had been the manager of Mount Vernon for a decade beforehand. Lund lacked Washington's attention to detail, as well as the devotion more common in owners than in managers. Yet even had Washington been on premises, his business enterprises would have been challenged. Every contract he made before his departure for Boston was made under the provincial law of colonial Virginia. Though the state government of independent Virginia tried to carry prewar contracts forward, those who wished to get out of obligations were tempted to wait until their creditors sued them before honoring their agreements. Lawsuits were slowed by Virginia's need to create a new system of courts. When the debtors were loyalists, some took that fact as moral justification for not paying patriot creditors like Washington, just as many patriot debtors to loyalist and especially British creditors wrapped themselves in the new American flag in repudiating their debts.

Not all the debts were worth collecting. Price levels in the British empire had been stable for long periods, not least since the British government refused to allow paper money. During the war the Continental Congress, by printing paper money, caused the currency to depreciate rapidly. Nominal debts plunged in real terms. Even creditors who recouped full face value could lose a great part of what they had lent out. The mutineers of 1781 and the near mutineers of 1783, as creditors of the government by virtue of the pay they were owed, pointed this out with bitterness.

Washington explained how the currency equation looked from Mount Vernon on his return. "You very much mistake my circumstances when you suppose me in a condition to advance money," he wrote to a nephew who had asked for a loan. "I made no money from my estate during the nine years I was absent from it, and brought none home with me. Those who owed me, for the most part, took advantage of the depreciation, and paid me off with six pence in the pound." A pound contained 240 pence.

Washington benefited when he was the debtor, but only to American creditors. To British creditors, who didn't accept American currency, he owed more than he could repay. He was not the kind of person to repudiate debts. "Those to whom I was indebted I have yet to pay, without other means, if they will not wait, than selling part of my estate or distressing those who were too honest to take advantage of the tender laws to quit scores with me," Washington wrote to his nephew. Even selling property, which he hated to do, wasn't much help. So many others were in a fix like his that property sold at a sharp discount when it sold at all.

"This relation of my circumstances, which is a true one," he told his nephew, "is alone sufficient (without adding that my living under the best economy I can use must unavoidably be expensive) to convince you of my inability to advance money." Washington offered advice in lieu of money. "I have heard with pleasure that you are industrious. Convince people by your mode of living that you are sober and frugal also, and I persuade myself your creditors will grant you every indulgence they can. It would be no small inducement to me, if it should ever be in my power to assist you."

BEFORE THE WAR, Washington had looked to the west for future profits. He owned title to tens of thousands of acres beyond the mountains. He had been in the process of surveying the land and offering parcels for sale or lease when the troubles with Britain knocked everything over. "After an absence of almost nine years, and nearly a total suspension of all my private concerns, I am at length set down at home and am endeavoring to recover my business from the confusion into which it has run during that period," he wrote to Thomas Lewis, a retired surveyor he had worked with before the war. Land titles were a particular problem. "My papers are so mixed and in such disorder at this time, occasioned by frequent hasty removals of them out of the way of the enemy, that I cannot (it being likely too, that some of them are lost) by the assistance of my memory, come at a thorough knowledge of that business." Washington wondered if Lewis could help him reconstruct what he owned.

He cited a particular transaction. "I have an imperfect recollection that in the year 1774, I sent a young man (of the name of Young, who at that time lived with me) to you on the business of these lands; but not having as yet met with any letter from you or report from him on the subject, I am unable with precision to recollect the particular matters with which he was charged or the result of his journey."

There was also the matter of land he had been promised by the colonial government of Virginia for his command of the militia. Here Washington spied opportunity in the confusion. He had commissioned William Crawford, a captain in the militia, to locate prime land in the Kanawha valley for him in the early 1770s. Crawford had done so, while locating land for himself too. Washington wondered if Crawford had perfected title to the land before dying a gruesome death at the hand of British-allied Indians near the end of the war. If not, could he—Washington—acquire what Crawford hadn't? "I would be understood, however," he said to Lewis, "explicitly to mean that it is not my wish in the smallest degree to injure my much regretted friend Crawford or any person claiming under him by this application, but if the road is open to learn only from you by what mode I am to obtain it, having the above rights for 5000 acres."

Amid the uncertainty regarding titles, settlers took up residence on the land of absentee owners. Washington heard that squatters resided on properties of his in southwestern Pennsylvania. He enlisted an agent, John Lewis, to investigate "whether there is any person living upon a small tract he"—Washington—"holds at the Great Meadows, what sort of an improvement is thereon, of whom the person took it and upon what terms." Washington didn't want someone else collecting rent due him. "And should Mr. Lewis have a favorable opportunity, the General would be obliged to him for informing those settlers upon his tract west of the Monongahela, on the waters of Shurtee's and Raccoon creeks, that he has a patent for the land, dated the 5th day of July 1774, that he will most assuredly assert his right to. But in consideration of their having made improvements thereon ignorantly or under a mistaken belief founded in false assertions that the land did not belong to him, he is willing that they should remain upon it as tenants upon a just and moderate rent such as he and they can agree upon."

Gilbert Simpson managed a tract Washington had purchased south of the Forks of the Ohio. On the property was a gristmill, which Washington hoped would be a reliable moneymaker. "Mr. Simpson," he wrote, "Having closed all my transactions with the public, it now behooves me to look into my own private business, no part of which seems to call louder for attention than my concerns with you. How profitable our partnership has been, you best can tell, and how advantageous my mill has been, none can tell so well as yourself." Simpson had *not* been telling Washington how the mill was doing. Apparently quite well, according to people in the area. "I ought to have a good deal of wealth in your hands arising from the produce of it, because all agree that it is the best mill and has had more custom than any other on the west side the Allegheny Mountains." Washington insisted on a full accounting.

WHILE UNTANGLING THE PAST, Washington looked to the future. The Paris treaty placed America's western boundary at the Mississippi River, confirming the American title to the Ohio valley. Washington revived his dreams of new settlements in the region, to be made possible by improvements in the waterways connecting the Ohio country to the Atlantic seaboard. This would benefit America even as it enhanced the value of Washington's lands there.

He shared his views with Thomas Jefferson, who had similar ideas. "My opinion coincides perfectly with yours respecting the practicability of an easy and short communication between the waters of the Ohio and Potomac," Washington wrote to Jefferson. One impediment was the falls of the Potomac, fifty miles above Mount Vernon. Another was the height of land between the Potomac headwaters and those of the Ohio. Washington and Jefferson imagined canals, locks and improved portages that would allow farmers in the Ohio country to ship their goods to eastern markets cheaply and efficiently. It would be a big project, likely requiring public funding. Virginia and Maryland should collaborate, because both states would benefit. And they should do so soon, lest other states steal a march on them—Pennsylvania by breaching the Alleghenies, or New York linking the Hudson River to Lake Erie.

"But I confess to you freely, I have no expectation that the public will adopt the measure," Washington told Jefferson. Collaboration between states was difficult, because each state judged it was paying more than its share. Moreover, the states, like the country as a whole, were burdened with debts from the war. Retiring the debt would come before authorizing new expenditures.

Yet the idea of the project was sound, and it could build on work begun before the war but set aside during the conflict. "Not a moment ought to be lost in recommencing this business, as I know the Yorkers will delay no time to remove every obstacle in the way of the other communication," Washington told Jefferson. He thought cooperation with Maryland ought to be possible. "The interest and policy of Maryland are proportionably concerned with those of Virginia."

Jefferson at this time was a member of Congress. Washington proposed to let him take the lead, especially since Congress was meeting in Annapolis, the Maryland capital. "You will have frequent opportunities of learning the sentiments of the principal characters of that state respecting this matter," Washington said. For himself he made no commitments. "How far, upon mature consideration, I may depart from the resolution I had formed of living perfectly at my ease, exempt from every kind of responsibility, is more than I can at present absolutely determine." Yet he might find time. "The immense advantages which this country would derive from the measure would be no small stimulus to the undertaking."

The advantages started with the peopling of the western regions by American settlers. In Washington's day, as for all of history before it, national strength correlated with national numbers. The more Americans there were, the stronger America would be and the better able to defend itself in a dangerous world.

A second advantage of a water connection from the Ohio to the Atlantic was that it would strengthen the hold of the United States on the western country. Washington had retired from the army, but he still thought like a general. "I need not remark to you, sir," Washington wrote to Benjamin Harrison, the Virginia governor, "that the flanks and rear of the United States are possessed by other powers, and formidable ones too." Britain controlled Canada. Spain held Florida and Louisiana, the latter construed as the western half of the Mississippi valley. American settlers beyond the mountains would be drawn by gravity toward the Mississippi and especially New Orleans, near that river's mouth. Water flowed downhill, and the Ohio and Mississippi would carry the goods of the western settlers toward New Orleans.

"The western settlers (I speak now from my own observation) stand as it were upon a pivot," Washington wrote to Harrison. He had been on the Ohio and felt the tug of its current. "The touch of a feather would turn them away," he said of the westerners. "They have looked down the Mississippi, until the Spaniards, very impoliticly I think for themselves, threw difficulties in their way." The Spanish government had suspended the right of American shippers to deposit their goods at New Orleans while awaiting oceangoing ships. "And they looked that way for no other reason than because they could glide gently down the stream—without considering, perhaps, the difficulties of the voyage back again and the time necessary to perform it in—and because they have no other means of coming to us but by long land transportations and unimproved roads."

Under present conditions, market links would tie the westerners to the Spanish.

The proposed connection from the Ohio to the tidewater Potomac would reverse the situation. "Smooth the road and make easy the way for them, and then see what an influx of articles will be poured upon us, how amazingly our exports will be increased by them, and how amply we shall be compensated for any trouble and expense we may encounter to effect it," Washington said.

WASHINGTON'S ENTHUSIASM FOR the Potomac project delighted its supporters in the Virginia assembly, who proposed to thank him for his service to his country by awarding him shares in a company chartered to develop the scheme. If the shares made the famous general even more enthusiastic, all the better for the project's future, they silently reckoned.

Washington reckoned differently. In retirement he was more jealous of his reputation than ever. In the past an embarrassment or reverse might be countered by a subsequent victory or success. Yorktown erased the memories of Long Island, Germantown and Benedict Arnold. But there were no Yorktowns ahead of Washington now. Embarrassment might be irreversible. He had told Congress upon his appointment as commanding general that he would accept no compensation beyond expenses. "How would this matter be viewed, then, by the eye of the world, and what would be the opinion of it, when it comes to be related that George Washington exerted himself to effect this work—and George Washington has received twenty thousand dollars and five thousand pounds sterling of the public money as an interest therein?" he asked Benjamin Harrison rhetorically. "One moment's thought of which would give me more pain than I should receive pleasure from the product of all the tolls."

At the same time, Washington didn't wish to appear ungrateful. He was honestly torn. "You may be assured, my dear sir, that my mind is not a little agitated," he told Harrison. "I have no inclination, as I have already observed, to avail myself of the generosity of the country, nor do I wish to appear ostentatiously disinterested (for more than probable my refusal would be ascribed to this motive), or that the country should harbor an idea that I am disposed to set little value on her favors."

For months he wrestled with the matter. "This state did a handsome thing, and in a handsome manner, for me," he wrote to Nathanael Greene, referring to the shares he was offered. "But as it is incompatible with my principles, and contrary to my declarations, I do not mean to accept of them. But how to refuse them without incurring the charge of disrespect to the country, on the one hand, and an ostentatious display of disinterestedness on my part on the other, I am a little at a loss."

— 71 —

Another incident threatened Washington's reputation from a different direction. After Yorktown but before the Paris treaty, loyalist and patriot irregulars had engaged in a tit-for-tat struggle that layered score-settling atop political principle. Patriot militiamen in New Jersey captured a loyalist and executed him for treason. Loyalists based in New York retaliated by seizing from custody a captured Continental army captain named Joshua Huddy and hanging him.

Because Huddy was one of his soldiers, Washington felt obliged to respond. He wrote a letter to Henry Clinton demanding that the executioners be turned over to him. Clinton refused but put the alleged ringleader on trial. The court-martial refused to convict, whereupon Washington threatened reprisal. By lot from a group of thirteen, one British officer, Captain Charles Asgill, was chosen for execution.

Washington delayed giving the order. He didn't want to inflame things between the loyalist and the patriot militias any further. He didn't want to derail the peace talks in Paris. And he didn't want to execute an innocent man.

While Washington hesitated, the Asgill case gained notoriety. Members of Congress split over the issue. In Britain, Parliament protested loudly against the possibility that a British officer might be sacrificed for the actions of irregulars not under the command of the British army.

King Louis of France stepped in. Claiming partial responsibility for Asgill by virtue of his having been taken at Yorktown, where Cornwallis surrendered to the combined armies of America and France, Louis asked Washington to void the sentence. Washington, relieved, assented.

He thought that was the end of the matter. And he thought Asgill should have been grateful. But at Mount Vernon he learned that Asgill in London had lately complained of harsh treatment at Washington's hands while he was a prisoner. "He alleges that a gibbet was erected before his prison window and often pointed to in an insulting manner as good and proper for him to atone for Huddy's death," Washington's informant related. "And many other insults all of which he believes were countenanced by General Washington, who was well inclined to execute the sentence on him but was restrained by the French General Rochambeau."

Washington was outraged. He expected calumny from ignorant scribblers. "But I never before had conceived that such an one as is related could have originated with, or have met the countenance of Captain Asgill, whose situation often filled me with the keenest anguish," he replied to his informant. "My favorable opinion of him, however, is forfeited if being acquainted with these reports, he did not immediately contradict them. That I could not have given countenance to the insults which he says were offered to his person, especially the grovelling one of erecting a gibbet before his prison window, will, I expect, readily be believed when I explicitly declare that I never heard of a single attempt to offer an insult and that I had every reason to be convinced that he was treated by the officers around him with all the tenderness and every civility in their power."

Washington rarely let others read his letters, but in this case he made an exception. He permitted the publication of his correspondence pertaining to the Asgill affair. This took the steam out of the controversy, such controversy as it was. In truth, the only one genuinely exercised about it was Washington himself.

THE WAR HAD MADE republicans out of Americans. Not all of them: the loyalists still preferred being governed by a king. But the end of the war had carried off the most visible loyalists and silenced those the victory by the republican forces hadn't persuaded. To all outward appearances, postwar America was uniformly republican.

The war had simultaneously made emancipationists out of many Americans. The American colonies couldn't have abolished slavery if they wanted to. British law governed the colonies, and it protected the institution. But when, after declaring independence, the new states began making their own laws, Americans considered whether those laws ought to extend slavery's life. Pennsylvanians said no. In 1780 the Pennsylvania assembly approved a law mandating gradual emancipation. Existing slaves remained in bondage, but children born to slave mothers would become free upon majority.

The opponents of slavery cited the contradiction between the equality espoused by the Declaration of Independence and the egregious inequality of slavery. When patriots had condemned the Stamp Act and the Intolerable Acts as attempts to make slaves of the American colonies, the condemnation clanged on the ears even of many of the speakers and writers, more than a few of whom owned slaves.

Escaping the contradiction was easier for the northern states, with comparatively few slaves, than for the southern states, with very many. Yet more than a few Virginians, including some large slaveholders, questioned the future of the institution. Washington was one of these. "Dear sir," he wrote to Robert Morris of Philadelphia, who had been superintendent of finance for Congress during the war. "I give you the trouble of this letter at the instance of Mr. Dalby of Alexandria, who is called to Philadelphia to attend what he conceives to be a vexatious lawsuit respecting a slave of his, which a society of Quakers in the city (formed for such purposes) have attempted to liberate." The Quakers had long opposed slavery, and many of them thought Pennsylvania's emancipation law too slow. "From Mr. Dalby's state of the matter, it should seem that this society is not only acting repugnant to justice, so far as its conduct concerns strangers, but in my opinion extremely impoliticly with respect to the state, the city in particular, and without being able but by acts of tyranny and oppression to accomplish its own ends."

Under British rule and before Pennsylvania passed its emancipation law, slaves were equally slaves in all the colonies and then states. A traveler with a bound servant had no reason to think his ownership of the slave was at risk traveling from Virginia to Pennsylvania, for instance. But now he did, if Dalby's account was true. Pennsylvania's law required annual registration of slaves. Those who weren't registered might sue for their freedom, and they were encouraged to do so by the Quakers Dalby cited.

"He says the conduct of this society is not sanctioned by law," Washington continued. Washington didn't presume to judge the merits of Dalby's case. That was for a Pennsylvania court to determine. But he hoped Morris and other leading men in the state would reflect on the larger consequences of what happened there. "If the practice of this society of which Mr. Dalby speaks is not discountenanced, none of those whose misfortune it is to have slaves as attendants will visit the city if they can possibly avoid it, because by so doing they hazard their property."

Washington explained his own thinking on slavery. "I hope it will not be conceived from these observations that it is my wish to hold the unhappy people who are the subject of this letter in slavery. I can only say that there is not a man living who wishes more sincerely than I do to see a plan adopted for the abolition of it."

But abolition must be by law. "There is only one proper and effectual mode by which it can be accomplished, and that is by legislative authority. And this, as far as my suffrage will go, shall never be wanting."

Anything else was sowing trouble, and not just for Pennsylvania. "When slaves who are happy and contented with their present masters are tampered with and seduced to leave them, when masters are taken unawares by these practices, when a conduct of this sort begets discontent on one side and resentment on the other, and when it happens to fall on a man whose purse will not measure with that of the society"—the Quakers—"and he loses his property for want of means to defend it"—at trial—"it is oppression in such a case and not humanity in any, because it introduces more evils than it can cure."

72

The interstate rift over slavery was incipient. Other divisions were more developed. The sovereignty the individual states had claimed at independence was moderated during the war by the collective need to defeat Britain. Upon peace the moderation melted away. Even more did such deference as the states had shown toward the national government diminish upon the war's end. These trends boded ill, and they distressed none more than Washington, who more than anyone else felt a proprietary, even patriarchal, interest in the country he had led through war to independence.

Washington's worries formed a central theme of his correspondence. "The disinclination of the individual states to yield competent powers to Congress for the federal government, their unreasonable jealousy of that body and of one another, and the disposition, which seems to pervade each, of being all-wise and all-powerful within itself will, if there is not a change in the system, be our downfall as a nation," he wrote to Benjamin Harrison. "This is as clear to me as the A, B, C, and I think we have opposed Great Britain and have arrived at the present state of peace and independency to very little purpose if we cannot conquer our own prejudices. The powers of Europe begin to see this, and our newly acquired friends, the British, are already and professedly acting upon this ground, and wisely too, if we are determined to persevere in our folly." Washington didn't often employ irony, but he indulged himself here. Beginning with the peace treaty, the British had attempted to loosen the Franco-American connection by adopting an amicable attitude toward America. Washington didn't trust them.

"They know that individual opposition to their measures"—the measures of the states—"is futile and boast that we are not sufficiently united as a nation to give a general one!" he continued, regarding the British. The very idea was infuriating, and it ought to spur action. "Is not the indignity alone of this declaration, while we are in the very act of peace-making and conciliation, sufficient to stimulate us to vest more extensive and adequate powers in the sovereign of these United States?"

Though Washington acknowledged the popular feeling against excessive central power, he emphatically didn't share it. "I have no fears arising from this source," he said. "But I have many, and powerful ones indeed, which predict the worst consequences from a half-starved, limping government that appears to be always moving upon crutches and tottering at every step."

ALEXANDER HAMILTON KNEW of Washington's concerns and echoed them. "I congratulate your Excellency on this happy conclusion of your labours," Hamilton wrote at the war's end. "It now only remains to make solid establishments within to perpetuate our union to prevent our being a ball in the hands of European powers bandied against each other at their pleasure—in fine, to make our independence truly a blessing. This, it is to be lamented, will be an arduous work, for to borrow a figure from mechanics, the centrifugal is much stronger than the centripetal force in these states—the seeds of disunion much more numerous than those of union." Hamilton hinted that Washington's work wasn't over. "I will add that your Excellency's exertions are as essential to accomplish this end as they have been to establish independence."

James Madison initially presumed less upon Washington than Hamilton did. Uncertain health had prevented Madison's service in the military during the war. He devoted himself to politics instead, first in Virginia and then in Congress. In both places he made himself useful to Washington, providing insight and perspective on politics in those arenas. It was in Congress that Madison and Hamilton discovered they shared a conviction that the Articles of Confederation were inadequate to the requirements of America's future.

Madison apprised Washington of efforts to ease commercial competition among the states by means of trade compacts or, better, amendment of the Articles to give Congress power over trade. Madison recognized the difficulty of amending the Articles, a process requiring unanimity of the states. The problem would intensify as America expanded, he observed in a letter to Washington. "The difficulty now found in obtaining a unanimous concurrence of the states in any measure whatever must continually increase with every increase of their number and perhaps in a greater ratio as the ultramontane states"—states to be formed out of the territories beyond the mountains—"may either have or suppose they have a less similitude of interests to the Atlantic states than these have to one another." Madison wasn't prepared to say so yet, but he leaned increasingly toward writing a whole new constitution rather than amending the Articles.

To that veiled end, Madison and Hamilton sponsored a meeting at Annapolis in September 1786. The announced agenda highlighted trade, and the proposed process emphasized amendments to the Articles. The meeting fizzled when only five states sent delegates. Madison and Hamilton shrewdly pivoted, characterizing the Annapolis event as simply preliminary to a larger convention to be held in Philadelphia the following May.

To this point Madison had been content to ask merely Washington's blessing on the reform effort. But after his and Hamilton's decision to double down in Philadelphia, he made bold to request Washington's participation. He wrote to Washington explaining how he was working to win the support of the Virginia assembly for the Philadelphia convention. "A bill for the purpose is now pending and in a form which attests the most federal spirit," Madison said. "It has been thought advisable to give this subject a very solemn dress and all the weight which could be derived from a single state. This idea will also be pursued in the selection of characters to represent Virginia in the federal convention. You will infer our earnestness on this point from the liberty which will be used of placing your name at the head of them." Madison hoped he hadn't overstepped. Washington of course would decide for himself whether to attend. Yet Madison hoped Washington would at least let his name be used on behalf of the Philadelphia convention. "It will assist powerfully in marking the zeal of our legislature and its opinion of the magnitude of the occasion."

Washington declined to commit. He had turned down an invitation to attend a meeting in Philadelphia of the Society of the Cincinnati, a group of officers from the war named for the Roman general who, unlike Caesar, retired to civilian life. Washington pleaded rheumatism and a general disinclination to leave the home he'd been away from so long. He told Madison he couldn't well attend Madison's Philadelphia meeting without insulting the veteran officers.

Madison was undeterred. "It was the opinion of every judicious friend whom I consulted that your name could not be spared from the deputation to the meeting in May in Philadelphia," he wrote. The future of the American republic might hang on the success of that meeting. Yet Madison offered a compromise. Washington should announce that he would attend, thereby encouraging other important men to take part. Then, if necessary, he could cancel at the last minute.

ULTIMATELY IT WASN'T Madison who persuaded Washington to attend the Philadelphia convention but Daniel Shays. The end of the war didn't resolve the money problems of America. The national government and the states had borrowed heavily to fund the war effort and now struggled to redeem the bonds they had sold. The war had driven up prices for commodities, including the produce of farms, and the war's end caused those prices to collapse. Creditors dunned debtors, sometimes from hardness of heart but often because the creditors were themselves debtors to others. Various groups wrestled for control of state governments to tilt the field of commerce and taxation in their favor. In this struggle farmers often lost out, being scattered in the countryside rather than concentrated in the cities where the state governments met.

In Massachusetts the tilt favored Boston and the merchants and creditors of the eastern part of the state against the farmers of the west. Daniel Shays was a westerner, a farmer and a debtor. He was also a veteran of the war, a former soldier in Washington's army. He, like many of his comrades in arms, was still owed pay for his service. Yet his creditors insisted that he pay them what *he* owed or lose his farm to default auction. Shays wasn't alone in his predicament. He and his fellows took measures to save their farms and their livelihoods. They intimidated potential buyers at auctions and forcibly closed the courts that declared owners in default. Soon they numbered in the thousands, and reprising their military service, they looked and acted like a rebel army. The governor of Massachusetts called out the militia to suppress the rebels. Something like Lexington and Concord appeared imminent, but with Americans pitted against Americans.

Washington was appalled. "Are your people getting mad?" he wrote to Benjamin Lincoln, his wartime subordinate, who now commanded the Massachusetts militia. Washington meant insane. "Are we to have the goodly fabric that eight years were spent in rearing, pulled over our heads? What is the cause of all these commotions? When and how is it to end?"

Lincoln answered Washington's questions in turn. Were the Shays men mad? "Many of them appear to be absolutely so, if an attempt to annihilate our present constitution and dissolve the present government can be considered as evidences of insanity," Lincoln said.

Was the fabric of republican government to be pulled over the head of the honest people? "There is great danger that it will be so, I think, unless the tottering system shall be supported by arms, and even then a government which has no other basis than the point of the bayonet, should one be suspended thereon, is so totally different from the one established, at least in idea, by the different states that if we must have recourse to the sad experiment of arms it can hardly be said that we have supported 'the goodly fabric.' "

What was the cause of the commotions? Lincoln blamed the debtors mostly. Farmers during the war had been beguiled by the high commodity prices. "People were diverted from their usual industry and economy. A luxuriant mode of living crept into vogue." Ordinary folks borrowed beyond their means. When the bill came due, they reneged on their debts and took up arms to prevent collection.

How would it end? "It is impossible for me to determine," Lincoln said. Much depended on the willingness of the law-abiding men of Massachusetts to face down the rebels. "If these classes of men should not turn out on the broad scale with spirit, and the insurgents should take the field and keep it, our constitution will be overturned and the federal government broken in upon by lopping off one branch essential to the well-being of the whole." Lincoln doubted that the rebellion could be suppressed by the Massachusetts militia alone. He looked to the other states. "They must send force to our aid."

Matters didn't come to this. Lincoln's ranks grew larger, and his leadership proved more adept than that of the rebels, who were outmaneuvered and dispersed with few casualties.

Washington was relieved. "The suppression of those tumults and insurrections with so little bloodshed is an event as happy as it was unexpected," he wrote to Lincoln.

But the Massachusetts troubles alarmed him. "Good God!" he wrote to Henry Knox. "Who besides a tory could have foreseen or a Briton predicted them!" Those enemies of America had predicted that republicanism would fail, that people could not govern themselves. The Shays rebellion made them appear prophets. Nor was Massachusetts unique. "There are combustibles in every state which a spark may set fire to."

America seemed to be going backward. "If three years ago any person had told me that at this day I should see such a formidable rebellion against the laws and constitutions of our own making as now appears," Washington observed to Knox while the Shays army was still in the field, "I should have thought him a bedlamite—a fit subject for a mad house." Washington held his breath for the future. "Our affairs generally seem really to be approaching to some awful crisis. God only knows what the result will be."

— 73 —

"Waited on the president, Doctor Franklin, as soon as I got to town," Washington wrote in his diary on Sunday, May 13, in Philadelphia. Franklin was in his second one-year term as president of Pennsylvania's executive council. "On my arrival, the bells were chimed."

News of Washington's coming had preceded him. A guard of the Pennsylvania militia's cavalry met him at the ferry over the Schuylkill River and escorted his carriage to the center of the city. Officers of the artillery stood at attention and saluted him as he passed.

The meeting of Washington and Franklin recalled the glory days of the revolution, when Washington had led the army and Franklin directed the diplomacy that won America's freedom. Their reunion underscored the crisis that faced the country. Both had expected peaceful retirement, but both returned to public life. Franklin could hardly have avoided reengagement, living mere blocks from where the Pennsylvania government met and where the convention to revise the Articles of Confederation was about to gather. Washington had been persuaded by the Shays rebellion to make the much longer journey from Mount Vernon. His previous reluctance rendered his participation the more significant. A crisis that caused the former general to leave his beloved farm must be dire indeed.

Yet he soon wondered if he'd made the right decision to come. "Monday 14th. This being the day appointed for the convention to meet, such members as were in town assembled at the State House, but only two states being represented, viz. Virginia and Pennsylvania, agreed to attend at the same place at 11 o'clock tomorrow," Washington wrote.

"Tuesday 15th. Repaired at the hour appointed to the State House, but no more states being represented than were yesterday (though several more members had come in) we agreed to meet again tomorrow."

Was this convention going to be a fiasco like the Annapolis meeting of the previous fall? Did the other states not care enough to send delegates? Had Washington wasted his time and energy?

"Wednesday 16th. No more than two states being yet represented, agreed till a quorum of them should be formed to alter the hour of meeting at the State House to one o'clock." No point getting up early just to see a room of empty chairs.

"Thursday 17th. Mr. Rutledge from Charleston and Mr. Charles Pinkney from Congress having arrived gave a representation to South Carolina, and Colonel Mason getting in this evening placed all the delegates from Virginia on the floor of convention." A slight improvement.

"Friday 18th. The representation from New York appeared on the floor today." Four states now, still shy of Annapolis.

"Saturday 19th. No more states represented."

Washington's time wasn't utterly wasted. He renewed acquaintances from the war. He stayed at the home of Robert Morris and dined with Franklin and other notables. He met with the Society of the Cincinnati.

"Monday 21st. Delaware state was represented."

"Tuesday 22d. The representation from North Carolina was completed, which made a representation for five states."

"Wednesday 23d. No more states." Washington took a tour of the city and observed the changes since the war. He ran into a wedding party and drank tea with a group of the women guests.

"Thursday 24th. No more states represented." One of the servants—slaves—Washington had brought along fell ill. Washington summoned a doctor to attend him.

At last the waiting paid off. "Friday 25th. Another delegate coming in from the state of New Jersey gave it a representation and increased the number"—of states—"to seven, which forming a quorum of the thirteen, the members present resolved to organize the body."

THE CONVENTION REQUIRED a president—that is, a presiding officer. Two delegates were the most likely candidates for the post: Franklin and Washington. Franklin deferred on account of failing health and from a sense that the project at hand would benefit from the prestige and popularity of Washington. Robert Morris of Pennsylvania nominated Washington, and John Rutledge of South Carolina seconded.

"General Washington was accordingly unanimously elected by ballot, and conducted to the chair by Mr. R. Morris and Mr. Rutledge," recorded

James Madison, "from which in a very emphatic manner he thanked the convention for the honor they had conferred on him, reminded them of the novelty of the scene of business in which he was to act, lamented his want of better qualifications, and claimed the indulgence of the house towards the involuntary errors which his inexperience might occasion."

The convention appointed a recording secretary, read the credentials of the delegates, selected a rules committee and adjourned until the following Monday.

WILLIAM PIERCE WAS a delegate from Georgia and a student of humanity. In idle moments during the convention he described the delegates, adding what he saw before him to what he had learned from their biographies. "General Washington is well known as the commander in chief of the late American army," Pierce wrote. "Having conducted these states to independence and peace, he now appears to assist in framing a government to make the people happy. Like Gustavus Vasa"—of Sweden—"he may be said to be the deliverer of his country. Like Peter the Great"—of Russia—"he appears as the politician and the statesman. And like Cincinnatus he returned to his farm perfectly contented with being only a plain citizen after enjoying the highest honor of the confederacy, and now only seeks for the approbation of his countrymen by being virtuous and useful."

Washington's usefulness in the convention was chiefly ornamental. As presiding officer he didn't actually preside most days, for the convention typically voted itself a committee of the whole, under the direction of the chairman of that committee.

Nor did Washington participate in the discussions. He recognized that his talents weren't those of the lawyers and orators who filled the room. His mastery of history, philosophy and political precedent was inferior to theirs. Beyond this, he appreciated that silence was his friend. Delegates quickly took the measure of one another, discovering the boundaries of insight and wisdom from the many words they spoke. Washington remained a cipher. It was easy for the delegates to conclude from this, and from the reputation he brought to the convention, that he knew more than he did.

He wasn't always silent. At times he enforced discipline, as William Pierce related. "When the convention first opened at Philadelphia, there were a number of propositions brought forward as great leading principles for the new government to be established for the United States. A copy of these propositions was given to each member with the injunction to keep everything a profound secret. One morning, by accident, one of the members dropped his copy of the propositions, which being luckily picked up by General Mifflin was presented to General Washington, our president, who put it in his pocket. After the debates of the day were over and the question for adjournment was called for, the general arose from his seat and, previous to his putting the question, addressed the convention in the following manner:

"'Gentlemen, I am sorry to find that some one member of this body has been so neglectful of the secrets of the convention as to drop in the State House a copy of their proceedings, which by accident was picked up and delivered to me this morning. I must entreat gentlemen to be more careful, lest our transactions get into the newspapers and disturb the public repose by premature speculations. I know not whose paper it is, but there it is' (throwing it down on the table). 'Let him who owns it take it.'

"At the same time he bowed, picked up his hat, and quitted the room with a dignity so severe that every person seemed alarmed. For my part I was extremely so, for putting my hand in my pocket I missed my copy of the same paper, but advancing up to the table my fears soon dissipated. I found it to be the handwriting of another person. When I went to my lodgings at the Indian Queen"—a hotel where many of the delegates stayed—"I found my copy in a coat pocket which I had pulled off that morning. It is something remarkable that no person ever owned the paper."

THE CONVENTION MOVED SLOWLY. The pace was irksome to many, but to none more than Washington, whose modest experience of political debate had been largely forgotten during his years of military command when he made dozens of decisions per day. The convention went weeks making no decisions at all, merely batting options back and forth. "The business of this convention is as yet too much in embryo to form any opinion of the result," he wrote to Thomas Jefferson at the end of May. "Much is expected from it by some, but little by others, and nothing by a few. That something is necessary, all will agree." All *present,* that is. Rhode Island had chosen no delegates, for fear of the changes the convention might produce. Other skeptics, including Patrick Henry of Virginia, had chosen not to participate. Washington spoke for himself and most of those who had come when he said, "The situation of the general government (if it can be called a government) is shaken to its foundation and liable to be overset by every blast. In a word, it is at an end, and unless a remedy is soon applied, anarchy and confusion will inevitably ensue."

A first question for the delegates was whether to amend the Articles of Confederation or write a fresh constitution from scratch. Their states and Congress had authorized the former, but the delegates chose the latter, albeit provisionally. They would write a new constitution and present it to the states. If nine states ratified it, it would take effect and supersede the Articles for those states. What would become of holdouts was left for time to tell. If the constitution failed to win approval from nine states, it would die and the convention's effort would have been wasted.

A second question was how the federal government would relate to the state governments. A common sentiment among the delegates was that the federal government needed to be strengthened compared with the states. Madison, Hamilton and other extreme federalists wanted the supremacy of the federal government to be clear and unambiguous. Most delegates were willing for the states to retain sovereignty in matters particular to them.

A third question had to do with representation. The Articles granted each state an equal vote in Congress. Delegates from large states thought this unfair, unrealistic and unrepublican, for it gave each citizen of Rhode Island and Delaware several times the voting power of each citizen of Virginia and New York. The Virginia delegation, led by Madison, and the New York delegation, by Hamilton, wanted representation to be by population. The delegates from the small states liked the status quo.

Much of the first month of the convention was devoted to the fight between big states and small states. Washington sided with the big states, and not simply because he was a Virginian. During the war the big states had provided most of the men and material resources, yet they were often stymied by the small states. Washington had resented the provincialism of the small states then, and he did now. "Rhode Island, from our last accounts, still perseveres in that impolitic, unjust and, one might add without much impropriety, scandalous conduct, which seems to have marked all her public councils of late; consequently, no representation is yet here from thence," he wrote to David Stuart, a Virginia doctor and Washington confidant. "New Hampshire, though delegates have been appointed, is also unrepresented. Various causes have been assigned, whether well or ill founded I shall not take upon me to decide. The fact however is that they are not here."

The pledge of silence prevented Washington from saying more about the convention. He hoped for the best. "Happy indeed would it be if the convention shall be able to recommend such a firm and permanent government for this Union as all who live under it may be secure in their lives, liberty and property," he said to Stuart. "Everybody wishes—everybody expects—something from the convention, but what will be the final result of its deliberation, the book of fate must disclose." Washington avowed his federalist views. "The primary cause of all our disorders lies in the different state governments, and in the tenacity of that power which pervades the whole of their systems. Whilst independent sovereignty is so ardently contended for, whilst the local views of each state and separate interests by which they are too much governed will not yield to a more enlarged scale of politics, incompatibility in the laws of different states and disrespect to those of the general government must render the situation of this great country weak, inefficient and disgraceful. It has already done so, almost to the final dissolution of it. Weak at home and disregarded abroad is our present condition, and contemptible enough it is."

Washington's patience wore thin—but not as thin as that of Hamilton, who left Philadelphia in frustration. Washington himself might have left if he hadn't been president of the convention. He reported to Hamilton the continued slow pace of the proceedings. "They are now, if possible, in a worse train than ever," he wrote on July 10. "You will find but little ground on which the hope of a good establishment can be formed. In a word, I almost despair of seeing a favourable issue to the proceedings of the convention, and do therefore repent having had any agency in the business."

The antifederalists were the problem, Washington said. "The men who oppose a strong and energetic government are, in my opinion, narrow minded politicians or are under the influence of local views. The apprehension expressed by them that the people will not accede to the form proposed is the ostensible, not the real cause of the opposition. But admitting that the present sentiment is as they prognosticate, the question ought nevertheless to be: Is it or is it not the best form? If the former, recommend it."

. . .

THE LOGJAM ON representation broke in mid-July with a compromise. The legislature in the new government would consist of two houses. In one, the Senate, equality of states would be preserved. In the other, the House of Representatives, large states would have more weight than small states.

Pleased with this accomplishment, the convention voted itself a brief vacation, during which a select committee would hammer what seemed the views of the body into manageable form. Washington went fishing with Gouverneur Morris, a Pennsylvania delegate. He revisited Valley Forge, where the cabins his men had built were in ruins. He crossed the Delaware to Trenton more easily than he had on that stormy Christmas night eleven years before.

When the delegates regathered on August 6, they seemed revived. The grand compromise on representation made other compromises easier. The question of sovereignty—whether it lay with the federal government or remained with the states—was settled by not being settled. Federal law would trump state law where the laws directly conflicted, as regarding trade and foreign policy, including war. But the delegates assumed that federal law and state law wouldn't often conflict. The federal government could rein in the states. Who would rein in the federal government? That was left unsaid.

The new government would consist of three branches. The draft constitution devoted considerable detail to the legislative branch—Congress. It devoted much less to the executive and judicial branches. Regarding the judicial branch, it was operating in the dark. Heretofore there had been neither federal courts nor federal judges. The delegates surmised that experience would light the way.

As for the executive—the presidency—the delegates took comfort from an assumption that gained force almost without discussion: that the first president would be Washington. When the delegates couldn't agree on what powers should be accorded the president, they looked to the austere figure sitting quietly amid the debates and concluded that they could trust Washington to find the path forward.

"WE HAVE NOW the honor to submit to the consideration of the United States in Congress assembled that constitution which has appeared to us the most advisable," Washington declared on behalf of the convention on September 17. The delegates at length had concluded their work. Not every delegate approved, but when they voted by state delegations, the vote was unanimously in favor. "In all our deliberations on this subject we kept steadily in our view that which appears to us the greatest interest of every true American: the consolidation of our Union, in which is involved our prosperity, felicity, safety, perhaps our national existence." This overriding aim had caused the delegates to submerge their individual differences. "Thus the constitution which we now present is the result of a spirit of amity and of that mutual deference and concession which the peculiarity of our political situation rendered indispensable."

The constitution was being submitted to Congress as a courtesy. It was being submitted to the states for their ratification. "That it will meet the full and entire approbation of every state is not perhaps to be expected," Washington said. "But each will doubtless consider that had her interests been alone consulted, the consequences might have been particularly disagreeable or injurious to others. That it is liable to as few exceptions as could reasonably have been expected, we hope and believe. That it may promote the lasting welfare of that country so dear to us all and secure her freedom and happiness is our most ardent wish."

74

Following the four most tedious months in his life, Washington returned to Mount Vernon and activities better suited to his temperament. "I rid to all the plantations," he wrote in his diary on November 1. "In the Neck, all the plows were putting in rye, and all the hoes employed in taking up potatoes and hoeing in rye between the corn. At Muddy Hole, the plows began to put in rye in field number 3 where the pease grew in hills. The hoe people continued digging the Irish potatoes which they began on Thursday last." On November 10: "At French's. The overseer and one or two other hands were employed in putting in wheat in the bouting rows, in field number 6, especially in that part where the wheat was sown in drills. The other hand and his plows were at the Ferry. At the Ferry, five plows were at work in number 5. Part of the hands were cleaning wheat which had been tread out and part were getting up potatoes. The new barn would nearly if not quite have the rafters up today."

He planned improvements. "Began a survey of the road leading from my Ferry to Cameron and thence along the back road by Mr. Lund Washington's and Mr. Triplett's to my mill, and from thence direct to the Ferry," he wrote on November 13. He enlisted skilled labor when he could. A German neighbor offered to find him a gardener in the old country. Washington accepted the offer, with stipulations. "I requested that it might not exceed the following conditions for him and his wife (if he brings one)—viz.—Ten pounds sterling for the 1st year—eleven for the 2d—twelve for the 3d and so on, a pound increase, till the sum should amount to £15, beyond which not to go. That he would be found a comfortable house, or room in one, with bedding, victuals and drink. But no clothes; these for self and wife to be provided at his own expence. That he is to be a complete kitchen gardener with a competent knowledge of flowers and a green house. And that he is to come under articles"—of indenture—"and firmly bound. His or their passages to be on as low terms as it can be obtained. The wife if one comes is to be a spinner, dairy woman or something of that usefulness."

He returned to his plans to develop the west, for the benefit of the country and the value of his holdings there. Recalling his first mission to Ohio, he corresponded with Jefferson about devising a water route—of navigation and minimal portages—from Lake Erie to the Ohio River.

Western investment had once been a flier for Washington, a low-cost speculation. Now it appeared more essential. His finances had never recovered from the war. "The almost total loss of my crop last year by the drought, which has obliged me to purchase upwards of eight hundred barrels of corn, and my other numerous and necessary demands for cash, when I find it impossible to obtain what is due to me by any means, have caused me more perplexity and given me more uneasiness than I ever experienced before from the want of money," he wrote to Charles Lee in April 1788. "In addition to the disappointments which I have met with from those who are indebted to me, I have in my hands a number of indents and other public securities which I have received from time to time as the interest of some Continental loan-office certificates which are in my possession." When people lacked cash to pay their debts, they offered securities of other sorts.

Washington found these confusing. "As I am so little conversant in public securities of every kind as not to know the use or value of them and hardly the difference of one species from another, I have kept them by me from year to year without having an idea that they would depreciate, as they were drawn for interest, and never doubting but they would be received in payment of taxes at any time, till I have found by the revenue law of the last session that only a particular description of them will pay the taxes of the year 1787."

Every state struggled with what to do about bonds it had sold during the war. "The others pay all arrearages of taxes, and I am informed are not worth more than two shillings and sixpence in the pound," Washington wrote. "The injustice of this measure is too obvious and too glaring to pass unobserved. It is taxing the honest man for his punctuality and rewarding the tardy or dishonest with the sum of seventeen shillings and sixpence in every pound which is due from him for taxes." For his own sake, and for the future of the country, he hoped the debt question could be resolved honorably and fairly. "It is a matter which does not concern me alone but must affect many others," he told Lee.

Things grew worse. "Never till within these two years have I ever experienced the want of money," Washington wrote to Richard Conway, an Alexandria merchant, in early 1789. "Short crops and other causes not entirely within my control make me feel it now very sensibly. To collect money without the intervention of suits (and these are tedious) seems impracticable, and land, which I have offered for sale, will not command cash but at an undervalue, if at all." He felt himself in extremis. "I am inclined to do what I never expected to be driven to, that is, to borrow money on interest. Five hundred pounds would enable me to discharge what I owe in Alexandria, etc."

Washington didn't like to plead, but he found himself pleading now. "Having thus fully and candidly explained myself, permit me to ask if it is in your power to supply me with the above or a smaller sum," he said to Conway. "Any security you may best like I can give, and you may be assured, that it is no more my inclination than it can be yours to let it remain long unpaid."

CONWAY LENT WASHINGTON the money. The merchant thought the general a good bet, not least since the general was about to become the president of the United States.

Ratification of the Philadelphia constitution had proceeded deliberately. Three states ratified within three months. Six more did so in the next six months. Technically this yielded the nine states required to put the new government in motion. But practically it didn't, because the holdouts included Virginia and New York, the two biggest states. Without both of them, the effort would die aborning. In Virginia, James Madison led the charge for ratification. In New York, Alexander Hamilton took the lead. The struggle spilled into the summer of 1788.

Washington observed from a distance. In a letter to Lafayette he described the debates at the Philadelphia convention and his moments of doubt that anything good would come from them. "It appears to me, then, little short of a miracle," he continued, "that the delegates from so many different states (which states you know are also different from each other in their manners, circumstances, and prejudices) should unite in forming a system of national government so little liable to well-founded objections," he said.

It wasn't perfect. Nothing in life was. But two features of the constitution gave it Washington's approval, which he reduced to a formula. "My creed is simply, 1st. That the general government is not invested with more powers than are indispensably necessary to perform the functions of a good government, and consequently that no objection ought to be made against the quantity of power delegated to it. 2ly. That these powers, as the appointment of all rulers will forever arise from, and at short, stated intervals recur to, the free suffrage of the people, are so distributed among the legislative, executive and judicial branches, into which the general government is arranged, that it can never be in danger of degenerating into a monarchy, an oligarchy, an aristocracy, or any other despotic or oppressive form so long as there shall remain any virtue in the body of the people."

Washington elaborated on this final check in a letter to his nephew Bushrod Washington. "The power under the constitution will always be in the people," he said. "It is entrusted for certain defined purposes, and for a certain limited period, to representatives of their own choosing, and whenever it is executed contrary to their interest, or not agreeable to their wishes, their servants can and undoubtedly will be recalled." The opponents of the constitution claimed fear of tyranny. Washington thought the fear unfounded and the claims dishonest. "Whilst many ostensible reasons are assigned to prevent the adoption of it, the real ones are concealed behind the curtains, because they are not of a nature to appear in open day." Fear of power wasn't absurd, but it mustn't be allowed to paralyze. "No man is a warmer advocate for proper restraints and wholesome checks in every department of government than I am. But I have never yet been able to discover the propriety of placing it absolutely out of the power of men to render essential services because a possibility remains of their doing ill."

For similar reasons Washington discouraged efforts to hold ratification hostage to amendments, including a bill of rights. "An attempt to amend the constitution which is submitted would be productive of more heat and greater confusion than can well be conceived," he wrote to Edmund Randolph. Again, he acknowledged that the constitution wasn't perfect. But progress required compromise. "I then did conceive and do now most firmly believe that in the aggregate it is the best constitution that can be obtained at this epoch, and that this or a dissolution of the Union awaits our choice and are the only alternatives before us. Thus believing, I had not, nor have I now, any hesitation in deciding on which to lean."

. . .

THOUGH WASHINGTON DIDN'T take part in the ratification debate, his name came up. Federalists, as the pro-ratification party were calling themselves, countered concerns of the antifederalists, as the opponents were dubbed, that the new government would become a tyranny by saying General Washington would allow no such thing. Without asking his permission, they spoke of him as the obvious choice for first president.

He could have silenced the discussion. But he didn't. He thought it unseemly to decline something that hadn't been offered. "In answer to the observations you make on the probability of my election to the presidency," he wrote to Lafayette, "knowing me as you do, I need only say that it has no enticing charms and no fascinating allurements for me. However, it might not be decent for me to say I would refuse to accept, or even to speak much about, an appointment which may never take place, for in so doing one might possibly incur the application of the moral resulting from that fable in which the fox is represented as inveighing against the sourness of the grapes because he could not reach them. All that it will be necessary to add, my dear Marquis, in order to show my decided predilections is that, at my time of life and under my circumstances, the increasing infirmities of nature and the growing love of retirement do not permit me to entertain a wish beyond that of living and dying an honest man on my own farm. Let those follow the pursuits of ambition and fame who have a keener relish for them or who may have more years in store for the enjoyment."

The allure of home remained a theme with Washington. "I am so wedded to a state of retirement, and find the occupations of a rural life so congenial with my feelings, that to be drawn into public at my advanced age would be a sacrifice that would admit of no compensation," he wrote in April 1788. A few months later he said, "At my age and in my circumstances, what sinister object or personal emolument have I to seek after in this life? The growing infirmities of age, and the increasing love of retirement, daily confirm my decided predilection for domestic life, and the great Searcher of human hearts is my witness that I have no wish which aspires beyond the humble and happy lot of living and dying a private citizen on my own farm."

In June 1788, Madison's efforts succeeded in getting Virginia to ratify the constitution. Hamilton then delivered New York. The government called for by the new charter would be coming into existence. The demands on Washington to let himself be drafted into the office of president increased.

He took up the question more seriously. "On the delicate subject with which you conclude your letter," he replied to Hamilton, who was trying to persuade him, "I can say nothing, because the event alluded to may never happen, and because, in case it should occur, it would be a point of prudence to defer forming one's ultimate and irrevocable decision so long as new data might be afforded for one to act with the greater wisdom and propriety. I would not wish to conceal my prevailing sentiment from you, for you know me well enough, my good sir, to be persuaded that I am not guilty of affectation when I tell you that it is my great and sole desire to live and die in peace and retirement on my own farm." Yet he didn't rule out accepting election.

Hamilton pressed the case. He appreciated Washington's reasons for not wanting to return to public life. But duty called. "Every public and personal consideration will demand from you an acquiescence in what will certainly be the unanimous wish of your country," Hamilton said. "The absolute retreat which you meditated at the close of the late war was natural and proper. Had the government produced by the revolution gone on in a tolerable train, it would have been most advisable to have persisted in that retreat. But I am clearly of opinion that the crisis which brought you again into public view left you no alternative but to comply. And I am equally clear in the opinion that you are by that act pledged to take a part in the execution of the government." Washington had helped create the new government. Now he must get it running. "It cannot be considered as a compliment to say that on your acceptance of the office of President the success of the new government in its commencement may materially depend. Your agency and influence will be not less important in preserving it from the future attacks of its enemies than they have been in recommending it in the first instance to the adoption of the people." The world was watching. "The point of light in which you stand at home and abroad will make an infinite difference in the respectability with which the government will begin its operations." Duty again: "In a matter so essential to the well being of society as the prosperity of a newly instituted government, a citizen of so much consequence as yourself to its success has no option but to lend his services."

Washington still hesitated. He told Henry Lee—"Light-Horse Harry" of Washington's cavalry during the war—that his election wouldn't be automatic. "If the partiality of my fellow citizens conceives it to be a means by which the sinews of the new government would be strengthened, it will of consequence be obnoxious to those who are in opposition to it, many of whom unquestionably will be placed among the electors," Washington said.

As always, he calculated how his action would be viewed by others. This complicated his decision the more. "You are among the small number of those who know my invincible attachment to domestic life, and that my sincerest wish is to continue in the enjoyment of it solely until my final hour," he told Lee. "But the world would be neither so well instructed nor so candidly disposed as to believe me uninfluenced by sinister motives, in case any circumstance should render a deviation from the line of conduct I had prescribed to myself indispensable." If he said he didn't want the job but then was persuaded by friends to take it, he'd seem a fool or a knave. "Might I not, after the declarations I have made (and Heaven knows they were made in the sincerity of my heart), in the judgment of the impartial world and of posterity, be chargeable with levity and inconsistency, if not with rashness and ambition?"

The longer Washington refused to say no, the more likely it appeared he would say yes. He got partway there in another letter to Hamilton. "You will, I am well assured, believe the assertion (though I have little expectation it would gain credit from those who are less acquainted with me) that if I should receive the appointment"—the election—"and if I should be prevailed upon to accept it, the acceptance would be attended with more diffidence and reluctance than I ever experienced before in my life. It would be, however, with a fixed and sole determination of lending whatever assistance might be in my power to promote the public weal, in hopes that at a convenient and early period my services might be dispensed with and that I might be permitted once more to retire to pass an unclouded evening after the stormy day of life in the bosom of domestic tranquility."

HAMILTON NEEDED NO further encouragement. In one of its last acts, the expiring Congress of the Articles of Confederation directed the states to choose electors in January 1789 to select the first president under the Constitution. Hamilton engaged his federalist allies in the various states to put Washington's name forward, and every elector cast a ballot for Washington. Each elector had two ballots, under the original Constitution, and these second ballots were divided among several candidates, of whom John Adams received the most.

Washington accepted his new assignment with a sense of grim responsibility. "My movements to the chair of government will be accompanied by feelings not unlike those of a culprit who is going to the place of his execution," he told Henry Knox.

Part X

New York and Philadelphia

⤚ 75 ⤙

"This is a great, important day," wrote William Maclay on April 30. "Goddess of etiquette, assist me while I describe it."

Maclay was a senator from Pennsylvania, elected in the first class of the upper house of the new bicameral Congress. The Senate and the House of Representatives had commenced their business weeks earlier, in part so they could count the electoral votes for president and confirm the result. Having accomplished that task, they prepared to greet Washington and witness his inauguration.

"The Senate stood adjourned to half after eleven o'clock," Maclay wrote. "About ten dressed in my best clothes; went for Mr. Morris' lodgings, but met his son, who told me that his father would not be in town until Saturday. Turned into the Hall." Congress was meeting in Federal Hall in New York. "The crowd already great. The Senate met. The Vice-President rose in the most solemn manner." John Adams became vice president by virtue of being the runner-up in electoral votes for president. As vice president of the United States, he doubled as president of the Senate. "This son of Adam seemed impressed with deeper gravity, yet what shall I think of him? He often, in the midst of his most important airs—I believe when he is at loss for expressions (and this he often is, wrapped up, I suppose, in the contemplation of his own importance)—suffers an unmeaning kind of vacant laugh to escape him. This was the case today, and really to me bore the air of ridiculing the farce he was acting. 'Gentlemen, I wish for the direction of the Senate. The President will, I suppose, address the Congress. How shall I behave? How shall we receive it? Shall it be standing or sitting?' Here followed a considerable deal of talk from him which I could make nothing of. Mr. Lee"—Richard Henry Lee of Virginia—"began with the House of Commons (as is usual with him), then the House of Lords, then the King, and then back again. The result of his information was, that the Lords sat and the Commons stood on the delivery of the King's speech. Mr. Izard"—Ralph Izard of South Carolina—"got up and told how often he had been in the Houses of Parliament. He said a great deal of what he had seen there. He made, however, this sagacious discovery, that the Commons stood because they had no seats to sit on, being arrived at the bar of the House of Lords. It was discovered after some time that the King sat, too, and had his robes and crown on.

"Mr. Adams got up again and said he had been very often indeed at the Parliament on those occasions, but there always was such a crowd, and ladies along, that for his part he could not say how it was. Mr. Carroll"—Charles Carroll of Maryland—"got up to declare that he thought it of no consequence how it was in Great Britain; they were no rule to us, etc.

"But all at once the secretary, who had been out, whispered to the chair that the clerk from the Representatives was at the door with a communication. 'Gentlemen of the Senate, how shall he be received?' A silly kind of resolution of the committee on that business had been laid on the table some days ago." This being the first session of the first Congress, the responsibility of setting precedent weighed heavily on some members. Less so on Maclay.

"Repeated accounts came that the Speaker and Representatives were at the door." This was to be a joint session. "The Speaker was introduced, followed by the Representatives. Here we sat an hour and ten minutes before the President arrived." The delay was the fault of confusion in Congress, not tardiness on Washington's part.

"The President advanced between the Senate and Representatives, bowing to each. He was placed in the chair by the Vice-President, the Senate with their president on the right, the Speaker and the Representatives on his left. The Vice-President rose and addressed a short sentence to him. The import of it was that he should now take the oath of office as President. He seemed to have forgot half what he was to say, for he made a dead pause and stood for some time, to appearance in a vacant mood. He finished with a formal bow, and the President was conducted out of the middle window into the gallery, and the oath was administered by the Chancellor." Robert Livingston led the New York chancery court.

"Notice that the business done was communicated to the crowd by proclamation, etc., who gave three cheers, and repeated it on the President's bowing to them. As the company returned into the Senate chamber, the President took the chair and the Senators and Representatives their seats. He rose, and all arose also, and addressed them."

The Constitution did not mention an inaugural address, but Washington judged he ought to say something on this momentous occasion. The decision seemed to cause him distress. "This great man was agitated and embarrassed more than ever he was by the leveled cannon or pointed musket," Maclay observed. "He trembled, and several times could scarce make out to read, though it must be supposed he had often read it before. He put part of the fingers of his left hand into the side of what I think the tailors call the fall of the breeches"—where side pockets would later go—"changing the paper into his right hand. After some time he then did the same with some of the fingers of his right hand. When he came to the words 'all the world,' he made a flourish with his right hand, which left rather an ungainly impression. I sincerely, for my part, wished all set ceremony in the hands of the dancing-masters, and that this first of men had read off his address in the plainest manner, without ever taking his eyes from the paper, for I felt hurt that he was not first in everything. He was dressed in deep brown, with metal buttons, with an eagle on them, white stockings, a bag, and sword.

"From the hall there was a grand procession to Saint Paul's Church, where prayers were said by the bishop. The procession was well conducted and without accident, as far as I have heard. The militia were all under arms, lined the street near the church, made a good figure, and behaved well."

The festivities continued in the evening. "There were grand fireworks. The Spanish ambassador's house was adorned with transparent paintings"—a style of art then in vogue. "The French minister's house was illuminated and had some transparent pieces. The Hall was grandly illuminated. And after all this the people went to bed."

THE ADDRESS WASHINGTON struggled to deliver reiterated his disinclination toward public office. In his first words as president he made clear he hadn't sought the power he now assumed. "Among the vicissitudes incident to life no event could have filled me with greater anxieties than that of which the notification was transmitted by your order and received on the 14th day of the present month," he told the senators and representatives, referring to the notice of his election. "I was summoned by my country, whose voice I can never hear but with veneration and love, from a retreat which I had chosen with the fondest predilection, and, in my flattering hopes, with an immutable decision, as the asylum of my declining years." Not only did he not seek the job, but he lacked the capacity to meet its demands. "The magnitude and difficulty of the trust to which the voice of my country called me, being sufficient to awaken in the wisest and most experienced of her citizens a distrustful scrutiny into his qualifications, could not but overwhelm with despondence one who, inheriting inferior endowments from nature and unpracticed in the duties of civil administration, ought to be peculiarly conscious of his own deficiencies." Yet his country had called, and he had answered.

He looked to heaven for help. "It would be peculiarly improper to omit in this first official act my fervent supplications to that Almighty Being who rules over the universe, who presides in the councils of nations, and whose providential aids can supply every human defect, that His benediction may consecrate to the liberties and happiness of the people of the United States a government instituted by themselves for these essential purposes." America already owed much to the Almighty. "No people can be bound to acknowledge and adore the Invisible Hand which conducts the affairs of men more than those of the United States. Every step by which they have advanced to the character of an independent nation seems to have been distinguished by some token of providential agency."

Washington cited his job description. "By the article establishing the executive department it is made the duty of the president 'to recommend to your consideration such measures as he shall judge necessary and expedient,'" he told the senators and representatives. "The circumstances under which I now meet you will acquit me from entering into that subject further than to refer to the great constitutional charter under which you are assembled, and which, in defining your powers, designates the objects to which your attention is to be given." Specific recommendations would follow in due course. Until then, he trusted to the character and honor of the members of Congress. "There is no truth more thoroughly established than that there exists in the economy and course of nature an indissoluble union between virtue and happiness, between duty and advantage, between the genuine maxims of an honest and magnanimous policy and the solid rewards of public prosperity and felicity."

Washington mentioned the demands for a bill of rights during the debate over ratification, which had elicited from the federalists a promise to consider amending the Constitution. "Instead of undertaking particular recommendations on this subject, in which I could be guided by no lights derived from official opportunities, I shall again give way to my entire confidence in your discernment and pursuit of the public good," he said. Yet he cautioned against undoing the good the Constitution accomplished. "Carefully avoid every alteration which might endanger the benefits of an united and effective government, or which ought to await the future lessons of experience."

In keeping with the philosophy that made him refuse a salary as commanding general, Washington said he would take no pay as president. He would merely expect to be reimbursed for expenses incurred in conducting his office and required by the public good.

"Having thus imparted to you my sentiments as they have been awakened by the occasion which brings us together, I shall take my present leave," he perorated. "But not without resorting once more to the benign Parent of the Human Race in humble supplication that since He has been pleased to favor the American people with opportunities for deliberating in perfect tranquility, and dispositions for deciding with unparalleled unanimity on a form of government for the security of their union and the advancement of their happiness, so His divine blessing may be equally conspicuous in the enlarged views, the temperate consultations, and the wise measures on which the success of this government must depend."

76

When Washington had taken up his first military command, he was able to read manuals of military discipline and treatises on tactics and strategy distilling the experience of centuries of commanders at war. When Washington assumed the presidency, no comparable literature existed for him to consult, because no truly comparable office existed elsewhere. The presidents of the Continental Congress had little to teach him, having been creatures of Congress rather than heads of an independent executive. The chief magistrate of the Dutch republic, the stadtholder, could speak knowledgeably to the president of the American republic about leading a republic, but historical and cultural differences caused much to be lost in translation. The chief executives of the thirteen American states—the governors, who as a group stopped using the title president at this point—could weigh in, but the states were unitary while the American republic was federal.

The fact of the matter was that Washington had to figure things out and make them up as he went forward. He took care, knowing posterity was watching. "As the first of everything in our situation will serve to establish a precedent, it is devoutly wished on my part that these precedents may be fixed on true principles," he wrote to James Madison. The Constitution afforded little guidance, its framers having relied on Washington's discretion and good sense. It named him commander in chief of America's armed forces. It charged him with appointing ambassadors and federal judges, subject to Senate approval. He could make treaties with foreign nations, again subject to Senate approval. He could pardon people convicted of federal crimes. He was to report to Congress on the state of the Union. He could make recommendations for laws. He could veto laws he disliked, although a two-thirds majority in Congress could override a veto. Finally, in keeping with his role as head of the executive branch, he should "take care that the laws be faithfully executed."

It helped that he came in on a flood tide of good feeling. The fight over ratification had been vigorous, but in defeat the antifederalists took an attitude of watchful waiting. Some wanted to see the new government fail, while others merely wanted to see *if* it would fail. Few of either persuasion had anything bad to say about Washington, leaving the field to those happy to lionize him. He received testimonials of support from individuals and groups all over the country, including both the Senate and the House of Representatives in their collective capacities. Washington thanked one and all for their support.

Yet the enthusiasm inadvertently increased the pressure he felt. "Unelated by your too favorable appreciation of my past services, I can only pour forth the effusions of a grateful heart to Heaven if I have been made in any degree an instrument of good to my country," he replied to an address from the mayor and aldermen of the city of New York. He hoped he wouldn't disappoint. "I cannot avoid expressing an apprehension that the partiality of my countrymen in my favor has induced them to expect too much from the exertions of an individual." He had lived long enough to know that the one held high today could be cast down tomorrow.

WASHINGTON DEEMED EFFECTIVE communication with Congress essential. Yet the Constitution made the executive branch separate from the legislative. How closely might he consult with the leaders of Congress without infringing their prerogatives or demeaning his own? "To draw such a line for the conduct of the president as will please everybody, I know is impossible," he remarked to Madison, who besides being the father of the Constitution now served in the House of Representatives and was emerging as a de facto leader there. "But to mark out and follow one which, by being consonant with reason, will meet general approbation may be as practicable as it is desirable. The true medium I conceive must lie in pursuing such a course as will allow him time for all the official duties of his station. This should be the primary object. The next, to avoid as much as may be the charge of superciliousness and seclusion from information by too much reserve and too great a withdraw of himself from company on the one hand, and the inconveniences, as well as a reduction of respectability, from too free an intercourse and too much familiarity on the other."

To ascertain this line, Washington sent a series of questions to Madison, John Adams, Alexander Hamilton and a few others. He asked how accessible the president should be to members of Congress and the public. Should he hold regular office hours, for instance, during which petitioners might drop in? How much should he entertain? By receptions? Dinners? Washington thought the presidents of Congress had entertained too much. He proposed "about four great entertainments in a year, on such great occasions as the anniversary of the Declaration of Independence, the alliance with France, the peace with Great Britain, the organization of the general government." Should he pay social calls? "And what, as to the form of doing it, might evince these visits to have been made in his private character so as that they may not be construed into visits from the President of the United States?" When Congress was in recess, might the president tour the country "in order to become better acquainted with their principal characters and internal circumstances, as well as to be more accessible to numbers of well-informed persons who might give him useful information and advice on political subjects"?

John Adams responded by urging a middle path between reserve and accessibility. He supposed time would tell just where this path ran. Adams was a republican by nature, and he recommended avoiding anything that smacked of royalty, such as elaborate entertainments. The president might pay social calls without bringing his office into disrespect so long as he kept social calls separate from official ones. "The president's private life should be at his own discretion, and the world should respectfully acquiesce. But as president he should have no intercourse with society but upon public business or at his levees."

Alexander Hamilton cautioned Washington against allowing the presidency to seem too familiar. "The public good requires as a primary object that the dignity of the office should be supported," he said. "Whatever is essential to this ought to be pursued though at the risk of partial or momentary dissatisfaction. But care will be necessary to avoid extensive disgust or discontent. Men's minds are prepared for a pretty high tone in the demeanour of the Executive, but I doubt whether for so high a tone as in the abstract might be desirable. The notions of equality are yet in my opinion too general and too strong to admit of such a distance being placed between the President and other branches of the government as might even be consistent with a due proportion." Washington should hold a levee once a week for receiving visitors, but nothing more. He should not return visits or accept invitations.

· · ·

AN ISSUE WASHINGTON HADN'T raised caused Congress concern. How should the president be addressed? Royalty rated "Highness." Was this inappropriate for a republic? Governors were often "Excellency." Not distinguished enough for America's president? The Senate created a committee that pondered appellations and recommended "His Highness the President of the United States of America and Protector of the Rights of the Same." An important country should have a leader with an important title.

The House of Representatives spent hours on the matter. Many there objected to the Senate proposal as slavishly imitative of Britain. Antifederalists were on the lookout for signs that the presidency contained the seeds of an American kingship. "Highness" set off their alarms.

Madison thought this fear overwrought. "I do not conceive titles to be so pregnant with danger as some gentlemen apprehend," he told his House colleagues. "I believe a president of the United States, clothed with all the powers given in the constitution, would not be a dangerous person to the liberties of America if you were to load him with all the titles of Europe or Asia." Power came from power, not from words.

Madison objected to the Senate usage for a different reason. "I am not afraid of titles because I fear the danger of any power they could confer," he said. "But I am against them because they are not very reconcilable with the nature of our government or the genius of the people." He thought fancy titles did the opposite of what their advocates claimed. "Instead of increasing they diminish the true dignity and importance of a republic." And of its leader. "If we give titles, we must either borrow or invent them. If we have recourse to the fertile fields of luxuriant fancy and deck out an airy being of our own creation, it is a great chance but its fantastic properties render the empty phantom ridiculous and absurd. If we borrow, the servile imitation will be odious, not to say ridiculous also. We must copy from the pompous sovereigns of the east, or follow the inferior potentates of Europe; in either case, the splendid tinsel or gorgeous robe would disgrace the manly shoulders of our chief."

America should adopt a different approach, Madison said. "The more truly honorable shall we be by shewing a total neglect and disregard to things of this nature. The more simple, the more republican, we are in our manners, the more rational dignity we acquire."

Madison didn't claim to speak for Washington, but he was known to be in regular communication with his fellow Virginian. Members assumed Madison wouldn't be advocating something Washington would dislike. This assumption, with Madison's reasoning, persuaded the House. The Senate motion died for lack of a second. Usage defaulted to "President of the United States" and, on direct address, "Mr. President."

THE CONSTITUTION DESCRIBED the presidency but left to Congress the creation of the departments that would round out the executive branch. In July the House and Senate approved legislation establishing the Department of Foreign Affairs, and Washington signed the measure into law. It was shortly renamed the Department of State. Comparable action produced the Department of the Treasury and the Department of War.

To head the state department, Washington looked to Thomas Jefferson, still American minister to France. "In the selection of characters to fill the important offices of government in the United States, I was naturally led to contemplate the talents and disposition which I knew you to possess and entertain for the service of your country," Washington wrote to Jefferson. "I was determined as well by motives of private regard as a conviction of public propriety to nominate you for the Department of State."

Jefferson professed himself flattered by Washington's offer of the job. "Could any circumstance seduce me to overlook the disproportion between its duties and my talents it would be the encouragement of your choice," he said. The job was indeed challenging. The reason for the name change was that the department Jefferson was being asked to head comprised not merely foreign affairs but much domestic responsibility too. Jefferson was as jealous of his public reputation as Washington was, and no more than Washington did he relish being placed in a position where he was likely to be criticized. "When I contemplate the extent of that office, embracing as it does the principal mass of domestic administration, together with the foreign, I cannot be insensible of my inequality to it," he said. "I cannot but foresee the possibility that this may end disagreeably for one who, having no motive to public service but the public satisfaction, would certainly retire the moment that satisfaction should appear to languish."

Yet if Washington wanted him, Jefferson would take the chance. "It is not for an individual to choose his post. You are to marshal us as may best be for the public good." Jefferson ended with flattery of his own. "My chief comfort will be to work under your eye, my only shelter the authority of your name and the wisdom of measures to be dictated by you."

To head the treasury, Washington turned to Alexander Hamilton, who accepted with no humility, pretended or otherwise. Henry Knox accepted Washington's offer to be secretary of war. Congress created no Department of Justice, which wouldn't be established for eighty years. But Washington named Edmund Randolph his attorney general.

The four made up what came to be called the president's cabinet, following English usage. Washington established a practice that would be common among his successors, of striking geographic balance, with Jefferson and Randolph from Virginia, Hamilton from New York and Knox from Massachusetts.

Vice President Adams was also from Massachusetts, but where he fit in the administration was unclear. Washington hadn't chosen him. He was vice president by virtue of finishing second in the election. And the Constitution made him president of the Senate, so he had one foot in the legislative branch.

→ 77 ←

When Congress recessed in the autumn of 1789, Washington took a trip. As president he felt peculiarly responsible for cultivating nationalist feeling among his compatriots. Attachment to states remained strong. The government that touched American lives the most was state government, and local government beneath that. The federal government was an abstraction. Politics was overwhelmingly state and local. Even when Americans voted for federal officers, they voted by state for the Senate and by district for the House of Representatives. The one federal office on the ballot in every state was the presidency—albeit indirectly, through presidential electors. No other federal official had a claim to represent the United States as a whole the way the president did.

Washington proposed to go east to New England. He queried his cabinet. "Had conversation with Colo. Hamilton on the propriety of my making a tour through the Eastern states during the recess of Congress to acquire knowledge of the face of the country, the growth and agriculture thereof, and the temper and disposition of the inhabitants towards the new government," he wrote in his diary on October 5. "Who thought it a very desirable plan and advised it accordingly." He put the idea to Henry Knox. "Who also recommended it accordingly." He asked Madison. "He saw no impropriety in my proposed trip to the eastward."

He went ahead. "Commenced my journey about 9 o'clock for Boston and a tour through the eastern states," Washington recorded on October 15. "The chief justice Mr. Jay and the secretaries of the treasury and war departments accompanied me some distance out of the city." Washington had nominated and the Senate confirmed John Jay as the first chief justice. "About 10 o'clock it began to rain, and continued to do so till 11, when we arrived at the house of one Hyatt, who keeps a tavern at Kingsbridge, where we—that is, Major Jackson, Mr. Lear and myself, with six servants, which composed my retinue—dined." Washington cut a figure traversing the countryside, riding in a large white coach pulled by a handsome team of horses, assisted by two aides and attended by six slaves.

The last time Washington had traversed this country was during the war, when his eye attended matters of military advantage. Now it had the sight of a farmer. "The road for the greater part, indeed the whole way, was very rough and stony, but the land strong, well covered with grass and a luxuriant crop of Indian corn"—maize—"intermixed with pumpkins, which were yet ungathered in the fields. We met four droves of beef cattle for the New York market (about 30 in a drove), some of which were very fine. Also a flock of sheep for the same place. We scarcely passed a farm house that did not abound in geese. Their cattle seemed to be of a good quality and their hogs large but rather long legged. No dwelling house is seen without a stone or brick chimney and rarely any without a shingled roof. Generally the sides are of shingles also." This contrasted favorably to Virginia, where the houses of small farmers showed less care in construction. "Upon inquiry we find their crops of wheat and rye have been abundant, though of the first they had sown rather sparingly on account of the destruction which had of late years been made of that grain by what is called the Hessian fly." This midge pest was not from Hesse but rather from Asia. Yet it was noticed in America during the Revolutionary War and, perhaps as a tactic of psychological warfare, was said to have arrived in the straw bedding of the German mercenaries. American farmers liked the insect as little as they liked its namesakes.

The next day took Washington's party across Connecticut. They fed the horses at Norwalk. "To the lower end of this town sea vessels come, and at the other end are mills, stores and an Episcopal and Presbyterian church. From hence to Fairfield, where we dined and lodged, is 12 miles, and part of it very rough road, but not equal to that through Horseneck"—later Greenwich. "The superb landscape, however, which is to be seen from the meeting house of the latter is a rich regalia. We found all the farmers busily employed in gathering, grinding and expressing the juice of their apples, the crop of which they say is rather above mediocrity. The average crop of wheat, they add, is about 15 bushels to the acre from their fallow land, often 20 and from that to 25."

What the farmers of Connecticut expected at the approach of Washington's carriage is hard to know. They knew of him as a soldier and a grandee of Virginia. For him to engage them so knowledgeably on their farming practices and yields must have surprised more than a few.

The neighborhood had recovered from the war but not entirely. "The destructive evidences of British cruelty are yet visible both in Norwalk and Fairfield, as there are the chimneys of many burnt houses standing in them yet." The burning of Norwalk and Fairfield by the British had inflamed patriot sentiment. In the shadow of the chimneys, business thrived. "The principal export from Norwalk and Fairfield is horses and cattle—salted beef and pork, lumber and Indian corn to the West Indies—and in a small degree wheat and flour." Before the war, American traders did a thriving business with the British West Indies but not—legally—with the French West Indies. The war had flipped things. The Connecticut merchants, and their commercial colleagues in other parts of the country, hoped to revive their trade with the British West Indies, and many looked hopefully to Washington's administration to arrange it.

He spent the night in Hartford, known for its textile works. "I viewed the woolen manufactory at this place which seems to be going on with spirit," he wrote on October 20. "Their broadcloths are not of the first quality as yet, but they are good, as are their coatings, cashmeres, serges and everlastings. Of the first—that is, broadcloth—I ordered a suit to be sent to me at New York, and of the latter a whole piece to make breeches for my servants." Nothing spoke support like a generous purchase. "All the parts of this business are performed at the manufactory except the spinning. This is done by the country people who are paid by the cut."

At Hartford they turned north to Springfield, Massachusetts. "The distance from Hartford to Springfield is 28 miles, both on Connecticut River. At the latter the river is crossed in scows, set over with poles, and is about 80 rod wide. Between the two places is a fall and ten miles above Springfield is another fall and others above that again—notwithstanding which much use is made of the navigation for transportation in flats of about five tons burthen." Navigation in New England fascinated Washington as much as navigation in Virginia and Ohio did.

He observed an aspect of society on which Massachusetts prided itself. "There is a great equality in the people of this state—few or no opulent men and no poor." The farms were prosperous without being ostentatious. There were no great houses, merely solid, comfortable ones. "A chimney (always of stone or brick) and door in the middle, with a staircase fronting the latter, running up by the side of the former—two flush stories with a very good shew of sash and glass windows. The size generally is from 30 to 50 feet in length and from 20 to 30 in width exclusive of a back shed which seems to be added as the family increases."

In Virginia farmhouses sat alone amid their fields. In Massachusetts they clustered together, with the fields at a distance. "The farms by the contiguity of the houses are small, not averaging more than 100 acres. These are worked chiefly by oxen (which have no other feed than hay), with a horse and sometimes two before them both in plow and cart. In their light lands and in their sleighs they work horses, but find them much more expensive than oxen."

"PROCESSION," ANNOUNCED a broadside circulated around Boston in the days before Washington reached the city. "As this town is shortly to be honored with a visit from the President of the United States: In order that we may pay our respects to him in a manner whereby every inhabitant may see so illustrious and amiable a character, and to prevent the disorder and danger which must ensue from a great assembly of people without order, a committee appointed by a respectable number of inhabitants, met for the purpose, recommend their fellow citizens to arrange themselves in the following order, in a procession."

The birthplace of the American Revolution outdid itself for the hero of the revolution. Washington hadn't seen the city since the British evacuated in the spring of 1776. It was in miserable shape then. He wondered what it looked like now. Boston's town fathers put on their best face. They cleaned up the city and built a triumphal arch, akin to those constructed for Roman caesars. And they turned out the whole city to see him.

The broadside choreographed the procession. "The person who shall be chosen as head of each order of artisans, tradesmen, manufacturers, etc. shall be known by displaying a white flag, with some device thereon expressive of their several callings." Order was emphasized again. "That uniformity may not be wanting, it is desired that the several flagstaffs be 7 feet long, and the flags a yard square." Every group had its place, in the following order: "The selectmen, overseers of the poor, town treasurer, town clerk, magistrates, consuls of France and Holland, the officers of His Most Christian Majesty's squadron"—the squadron of France, with which country America remained allied—"the reverend clergy, physicians, lawyers, merchants and traders, marine society, masters of vessels, revenue officers, strangers who may wish to attend."

The artisans should line up alphabetically, in more than fifty listed groups from "bakers, blacksmiths, block makers" to "upholsters, wharfingers, wheelwrights." The groups would march through the town, with the bakers and blacksmiths deliberately overshooting the center to make room for the wharfingers—wharf keepers—and wheelwrights. Those in the lead would circle back, and the artisans would split into two lines between which the president would pass.

Whether Washington read the broadside, which served as the program for his reception, is unclear. With its listing of all the crafts practiced in Boston, it would have enhanced his economic survey of New England. In the event, he was impressed by the effort that went into the reception. His entourage reached Cambridge at ten on the morning of Saturday, October 24. "At this place the Lieut. Govr. Mr. Samuel Adams, with the Executive Council, met me and preceded my entrance into town, which was in every degree flattering and honorable," Washington recorded. The local dignitaries welcomed him. "We passed through the citizens classed in their different professions and under their own banners till we came to the State House, from which, across the street, an arch was thrown, in the front of which was this inscription—'To the man who unites all hearts' and on the other—'To Columbia's favourite son.'" Already "Columbia" was being used as a synonym for the American republic. "On one side thereof next the State House, in a panel decorated with a trophy composed of the arms of the United States, of the Commonwealth of Massachusetts, and our French allies, crowned with a wreath of laurel, was this inscription—'Boston relieved March 17th, 1776.' This arch was handsomely ornamented, and over the center of it a canopy was erected 20 feet high with the American eagle perched on the top.

"After passing through the arch and entering the State House at the south end and ascending to the upper floor and returning to a balcony at the north end, three cheers was given by a vast concourse of people who by this time had assembled at the arch. Then followed an ode composed in honor of the President, and well sung by a band of select singers. After this three cheers." Then followed the procession of the craftsmen.

The whole city turned out. "The streets, the doors, windows and tops of the houses were crowded with well dressed ladies and gentlemen," Washington observed. People from the neighboring districts had poured into Boston for the great event, till the town could hardly hold them.

At length it ended. "I was conducted to my lodgings at a Widow Ingersolls (which is a very decent and good house) by the Lieut. Govr. and Council, accompanied by the Vice-President"—John Adams's home was in Braintree, outside Boston—"where they took leave of me."

. . .

WASHINGTON WAS PLEASED with the tour. He gained insight into the ways and work of the people of New England, and they had a chance to celebrate the national cause. Shortly a cottage industry developed in commemorating his visit. In some cases it was *literally* a cottage industry, in that nearly every public house that hosted him boasted "Washington slept here" to entice further business. Streets were renamed in his honor. People made mental notes of where they stood as the great man passed by.

Yet not everyone was thrilled. Scores of thousands of loyalists had fled America with the British at the end of the war, for fear of what awaited them once the king's protection was withdrawn. But many stayed put. They didn't boast of their wartime affinities, but neither did they forget them. Most didn't get back property seized during the war, and they resented the injury. Not all hoped for reattachment to Britain, though many were drawn to groups that had commercial or other reasons for restoring some of the old ties. More than a few were skeptical of the idea of republicanism and quietly looked for signs of its failure.

Deborah Barker's father had been a prominent loyalist. She lived not far from Boston and was in the city on the day of Washington's entrance. "The General as President of the United States (or in other words as the King of America) thought proper to visit the northern part of his territories," she recorded sardonically in a letter. "Such a movement could not be performed secretly. It was no sooner announced that he intended visiting Boston than every breast beat with rapture, joy and exultation. The mechanics were employed, some in erecting triumphal arches, some in painting flags expressive of their several branches of business, which the most respectable of the order were to carry forth. . . . All of the superior orders were busy in forming addresses expressive of his transcendent merit and their great love and respect for him. The poets in writing odes and other poems asserted their abilities. . . . Thus after a week's preparation and expectation the great, the important day (in honor of which everything that an infant world could do was to be done for the man that many of them fancied themselves under the greatest obligation to) arrived."

Barker described the procession in mocking detail, noting the greater and lesser orders in the parade, all proceeded by the selectmen—"they, you know, must be first," she said.

She knew her humor would be appreciated. Her letter was to a woman friend named Christian Barnes, who with her husband, Henry Barnes, had lost their property on account of their loyalism. They fled for England, leaving behind painted portraits. Christian's was slashed with a knife. Henry's got a bullet to the chest.

78

As commanding general, Washington had tried to set a moral tone for the army. As president, he attempted the same thing for the country. In the autumn of 1789, he proclaimed a day of national thanksgiving.

Thanksgivings far predated American independence, European civilization, Christianity and even human memory. Hunters and gatherers thanked the deities they believed in for good fortune in hunting and gathering. Agricultural societies gave thanks at the end of the harvest. The Pilgrims had done so and discovered kindred spirits among their Indian neighbors. In 1789 a committee of Congress approached Washington and suggested that the successful launch of the government under the Constitution warranted thanksgiving. He obliged with a proclamation.

Washington's language was assertively global. "It is the duty of all nations to acknowledge the providence of Almighty God, to obey His will, to be grateful for His benefits, and humbly to implore His protection and favor," he said. "Therefore, I do recommend and assign Thursday, the 26th day of November next, to be devoted by the people of these states to the service of that great and glorious Being who is the beneficent author of all the good that was, that is, or that will be."

Washington hoped the thanksgiving would bring Americans together. "We may then all unite in rendering unto Him our sincere and humble thanks for His kind care and protection of the people of this country previous to their becoming a nation; for the signal and manifold mercies and the favorable interpositions of His providence in the course and conclusion of the late war; for the great degree of tranquility, union, and plenty which we have since enjoyed; for the peaceable and rational manner in which we have been enabled to establish constitutions of government for our safety and happiness, and particularly the national one now lately instituted; for the civil and religious liberty with which we are blessed, and the means we have of acquiring and diffusing useful knowledge; and, in general, for all the great and various favors which He has been pleased to confer upon us."

THE CONSTITUTION INSTRUCTS the chief executive to communicate with the legislature: "He shall from time to time give to the Congress information of the state of the Union, and recommend to their consideration such measures as he shall judge necessary and expedient." Washington opened the new year, 1790, and the new session of Congress with what would become an annual institution. On January 7 he met with a committee from both houses, seeking an invitation to address them jointly. They agreed upon the following morning at eleven.

Washington made a production of the event. He rode in his coach the short distance from the house he was leasing on Cherry Street to City Hall, where Congress met. He was preceded by two military aides on white chargers—Washington's own—and was followed by two other aides in his chariot and a third on horseback. Completing the entourage for the two-block journey were the chief justice and the secretaries of the treasury and war.

He was formally greeted at the entrance of City Hall by the doorkeepers of the Senate and the House. They conducted him to the Senate chamber. The members of Congress rose as he entered, and he passed between the senators and the representatives. They remained standing until he took his seat at the front. They sat down. As soon as they did, Washington stood up to deliver his address. They bounced back up, so as not to give offense by being seated while he stood.

The substance of Washington's speech followed the directions of the Constitution. He reported on the state of the Union and recommended legislative improvements. He was pleased to note that North Carolina had belatedly ratified the Constitution. This left only Rhode Island on the outside. Other aspects of American life gave similar cause for optimism. "The rising credit and respectability of our country, the general and increasing good will toward the government of the Union, and the concord, peace, and plenty with which we are blessed are circumstances auspicious in an eminent degree to our national prosperity." Washington praised the lawmakers for their contributions to this happy condition. He hoped they would continue to work in harmony and prudence, with "the cool and deliberate exertion of your patriotism, firmness, and wisdom."

The president moved to the recommending phase of his speech. He called for a stronger army. "To be prepared for war is one of the most effectual means of preserving peace," he asserted, in what would become one of his most famous lines. He elaborated: "A free people ought not only to be armed but disciplined, to which end a uniform and well-digested plan is requisite. And their safety and interest require that they should promote such manufactories as tend to render them independent of others for essential, particularly military, supplies."

Washington saw no reason to expect a war with any foreign power. But preparation was important nonetheless. Conflict with Indian tribes was more likely, though hardly inevitable. The frontier was calm at the moment. Yet especially in the west and south, trouble might arise suddenly. "We ought to be prepared to afford protection to those parts of the Union, and, if necessary, to punish aggressors."

Washington asked for funding for a diplomatic corps, to represent American interests in foreign countries. He requested a law defining a path to citizenship for immigrants. Commerce required a uniform currency and a system of weights and measures. Invention should be encouraged by a patent law. The solvency of the post office must be secured and its efficiency enhanced by improvements in post roads.

Congress should give serious thought to the state of the American mind. "There is nothing which can better deserve your patronage than the promotion of science and literature," Washington told the senators and representatives. "Knowledge is in every country the surest basis of public happiness." He left to the judgment of Congress how the acquisition of knowledge might be facilitated. "Whether this desirable object will be best promoted by affording aids to seminaries of learning already established, by the institution of a national university, or by any other expedients will be well worthy of a place in the deliberations of the legislature."

The Constitution accords primacy to the House of Representatives in matters touching the public purse. Washington turned and spoke to its members directly: "I saw with peculiar pleasure at the close of the last session the resolution entered into by you expressive of your opinion that an adequate provision for the support of the public credit is a matter of high importance to the national honor and prosperity. In this sentiment I entirely concur." He would support all reasonable efforts toward this end.

Addressing himself again to both houses, Washington talked of informational exchange between the executive and the legislature. He offered to be forthcoming, within limits. "I have directed the proper officers to lay before you, respectively, such papers and estimates as regard the affairs particularly recommended to your consideration, and necessary to convey to you that information of the state of the Union which it is my duty to afford."

The two branches had the same goal, he said in closing. "The welfare of our country is the great object to which our cares and efforts ought to be directed. And I shall derive great satisfaction from a cooperation with you in the pleasing though arduous task of insuring to our fellow citizens the blessings which they have a right to expect from a free, efficient and equal government."

WILLIAM MACLAY LIKED Washington's performance better than some of his colleagues did. "All this morning nothing but bustle about the Senate chamber in hauling chairs and removing tables," the Pennsylvania senator recorded. "The President was dressed in a second mourning"—in a dark suit made of the cloth he had purchased in Hartford—"and read his speech well. The Senate, headed by their Vice-President, were on his right. The House of Representatives, with their Speaker, were on his left. His family with the heads of departments attended. The business was soon over and the Senate were left alone. The speech was committed rather too hastily, as Mr. Butler"—Pierce Butler, senator from South Carolina—"thought, who made some remarks on it and was called to order by the chair. He resented the call, and some altercation ensued."

Maclay was less impressed with the performance that followed Washington's. Members of the Senate judged that the president's address to them should be answered by an address by them to him. Maclay thought this silly and unrepublican. "I made an unsuccessful motion when it was proposed that the whole Senate should wait on the president with answer to the speech. First, I wished for delay, that we might see the conduct adopted by the House of Representatives. I thought it likely they would do the business by a committee. In that case, I wished to imitate them; and as a committee with us had done all the business so far, I wished it to continue in their hands, that they might have exclusively all the honors attended on the performance; that I, as a republican, was, however, opposed to the whole business of echoing speeches. It was a stale ministerial trick in Britain to get the Houses of Parliament to chime in with the speech and then consider them as pledged to support any measure which could be grafted on the speech."

Maclay's colleagues didn't share his distrust of ceremony. Both houses voted to make a formal reply to Washington's address. "At eleven o'clock, the Senate attended at the president's to deliver their answer," Maclay wrote on January 14. "At twelve o'clock the House of Representatives attended. It is not worthwhile minuting a word about it. We went in coaches. Got our answer, which was short. Returned in coaches. Sauntered an hour in the Senate chamber and adjourned."

Maclay hoped the wasting of time on formality would die of its own fatuity. "Every error in government will work its own remedy among a free people. I think both senators and representatives are tired of making themselves the gazing stock of the crowd and the subject of remark by the sycophantic circle that surround the president in stringing to his quarters; and I trust the next session will either do without this business altogether or do it by a small committee that need not interrupt the business of either house. I have aimed at this point all along. It is evident from the president's speech that he wishes everything to fall into the British mode of business. 'I have directed the proper officers to lay before you,' etc. Compliments for him and business for them. He is but a man, but really a good one, and we can have nothing to fear from him, but much from the precedents he may establish."

That evening Maclay dined at the president's house. "It was a great dinner—all in the taste of high life. I considered it as a part of my duty as a senator to submit to it, and am glad it is over. The president is a cold, formal man; but I must declare that he treated me with great attention. I was the first person with whom he drank a glass of wine. I was often spoken to by him. Yet he knows how rigid a republican I am. I cannot think that he considers it worthwhile to soften me. It *is* not worth his while."

79

"I was very sorry to hear that you and your family had not escaped the prevailing sickness," Abigail Adams wrote from New York to Cotton Tufts, a Massachusetts cousin and physician, in May 1790. The sickness was a strain of influenza. "The disorder has universally prevailed here. Not a single one of our family except Mr. Adams has escaped."

Nor had Washington escaped. "We have been in very great anxiety for the president," Abigail Adams wrote. "During the state of suspense, it was thought prudent to say very little upon the subject as a general alarm might have proved injurious to the present state of the government." To many Americans, Washington seemed the embodiment of the new government, which remained sufficiently tenuous that if something happened to him, the government might not survive.

"He has been very unwell through all the spring, labouring with a bilious disorder," Abigail Adams continued. Washington had thought time away from work would help. It did, but not for long. "He made a tour upon Long Island of eight or ten days which was a temporary relief, but soon after his return he was seized with a violent pleurisy fever attended with every bad symptom, and just at the crisis was seized with hiccups and rattling in the throat, so that Mrs. Washington left his room thinking him dying."

Despite the prudence of Abigail Adams and others, word spread that Washington was ill, indeed at an end. "Called to see the president," William Maclay recorded on May 15. "Every eye full of tears. His life despaired of." On May 16, Theodore Sedgwick, a congressman from Massachusetts, wrote to his wife, "About five o'clock in the afternoon yesterday, the physicians disclosed that they had no hopes of his recovery." Thomas Jefferson wrote to his daughter, "On Monday last the president was taken with a peripneumonia"—inflammation of the lungs—"of threatening appearance. Yesterday (which was the 5th day) he was thought by the physicians to be dying."

But to the relief of all, Washington rallied. "James powders"—a common nostrum—"had been administered," Abigail Adams wrote, "and they produced a happy effect by a profuse perspiration which relieved his cough and breathing, and he is now happily so far recovered as to ride out daily." The country had survived a close call. "I do not wish to feel again such a state of anxiety as I experienced for several days," she said. "Such a train of fearful apprehensions alarmed me upon the threatening prospect that I shuddered at the view. The weight of empire, particularly circumstanced as ours is, without firmness, without age and experience, without a revenue settled and established, loaded with a debt about which there is little prospect of an agreement, would bow down any man who is not supported by a whole nation and carry him perhaps to an early grave with misery and disgrace."

This last remark was about Abigail Adams's husband, who would have inherited the burden of the presidency had Washington died. But her fears reflected the challenges confronting the nation as a whole. "I saw a hydra head before me—envy, jealousy, ambition and all the baneful passions in league. Do you wonder that I felt distressed at the view? Yet I could not refrain from thinking that even a Washington might esteem himself happy to close his days before any unhappy division or disastrous event had tarnished the luster of his reign."

WASHINGTON'S AFFLICTION THAT season was the worst of his presidency, but it wasn't the only physical challenge he confronted. His age was showing. He rarely felt robust and whole. Before the influenza he suffered from an infected tumor in his left thigh. "It was a case of anthrax, so malignant as for several days to threaten mortification," wrote John McVickar, who learned the diagnosis from Samuel Bard, the physician attending Washington. "During this period, Dr. Bard never quitted him. On one occasion, being left alone with him, General Washington looking steadfastly in his face, desired his candid opinion as to the probable termination of the disease, adding, with that placid firmness which marked his address, 'Do not flatter me with vain hopes. I am not afraid to die, and, therefore, can bear the worst.' Dr. Bard's answer, though it expressed hope, acknowledged his apprehensions. The president replied, 'Whether tonight, or twenty years hence, makes no difference. I know that I am in the hands of a good Providence.'"

Bard called in his father, also a physician, and they cut out the tumor. Washington's condition improved at once. "I have now the pleasure to inform you that my health is restored," Washington wrote to James McHenry, a surgeon from the war who would go on to become secretary of war. "But a feebleness still hangs upon me, and I am yet much incommoded by the incision which was made in a very large and painful tumor on the protuberance of my thigh. This prevents me from walking or sitting." He hoped for continued improvement. "Time and patience only are wanting to remove this evil." Ingenuity helped. "I am able to take exercise in my coach, by having it so contrived as to extend myself the full length of it."

Washington regained strength and resumed most of his usual habits. But then he contracted the influenza, and its virulence made him ponder his mortality anew. "I have already had within less than a year, two *severe* attacks, the last worse than the first," he wrote in June 1790. "A third more than probable will put me to sleep with my fathers. At what distance this may be I know not. Within the last twelve months I have undergone more and severer sickness than thirty preceding years afflicted me with, put it altogether." He was thankful to have recovered, almost. "I still feel the remains of the violent affection of my lungs, the cough, pain in my breast, and shortness in breathing not having entirely left me."

THE FOLLOWING SUMMER brought another affliction, or rather a recurrence of the first. "The President is indisposed with the same blind tumour, and in the same place, which he had the year before last in New York," Jefferson wrote to James Madison in the summer of 1791. "As yet it does not promise either to suppurate or be discussed"—dissipated. "He is obliged to lie constantly on his side and has at times a little fever."

Relief came sooner this time. "The President is much better," Jefferson reported to Madison three days later. "An incision has been made, and a kind suppuration is brought on." Recuperation continued. "The President is got well," Jefferson concluded after another week.

Yet the ailments left a mark. Frances Bassett Washington was Martha Washington's natural niece and George Washington's niece by marriage following her wedding to Washington's nephew George Augustine

Washington. Fanny had known Washington for years and was quite familiar with his appearance. "The President looks better than I expected to see him," she wrote to her father in September 1791, "but still there be traces in his countenance of his two last severe illnesses, which I fear will never wear off."

— 80 —

From the moment the first English settlers landed in Virginia and Massachusetts, the government in London had spent countless hours dealing with problems between the settlers and the Indian tribes upon whom they intruded. Tension was ever present and often gave rise to war.

Upon American independence, Britain's Indian problem became America's Indian problem. In particular, it became Washington's problem. The Constitution made the president both diplomat in chief and commander in chief, responsible for negotiating treaties and waging war.

Washington's Indian problem was complicated by the federal nature of the American system. The essential sovereignty of the states during the period between independence and ratification of the Constitution caused several of them to conclude that the Indian problem was *their* problem rather than the nation's problem. Georgia, for example, made treaties with the Creek and Cherokee tribes. Georgia liked the power and wasn't inclined to yield it to the new federal government.

The Constitution was ambiguous on the subject. Article I gave to Congress, not the states, the authority "to regulate commerce with foreign nations, and among the several states, and with the Indian tribes." The state treaties typically transferred title over land from the tribes to the states, which then sold land to settlers. These transactions looked like commerce to some people but not to others.

A second complication for Washington's Indian policy was strategic. During the Revolutionary War many tribes had sided with the British. After the war some of these tribes and others looked to the British to arm them against Americans encroaching on their lands. Spanish Florida, adjoining Georgia, harbored fugitive slaves from Georgia and other southern states. For such reasons, unsettled relations with the Indian tribes risked unsettling relations with Britain and Spain. To leave Indian policy to the states might be to deliver the fate of the country into the hands of the least responsible state.

A third complication was moral. Americans liked to think of their country as a beacon of enlightenment. If not too costly, they preferred that their government treat the Indians in a just and honorable manner. Yet the salience of this preference varied from state to state. Generally, the farther a state was from territory still contested by Indians, the greater the weight of morality in its judgments of Indian policy. Townsfolk in New England lamented injustice against the Indians, while settlers on the western frontier treated Indians as existential foes.

Washington tried to sort things out during the first months of his presidency. He asked Henry Knox, the secretary of war, to summarize Indian affairs, which in the federal government were the responsibility of the war department. Knox began by describing conditions in Kentucky—the western counties of Virginia that were about to become a state of their own—and the Ohio territory north of the Ohio River. Several settlers had recently been killed in the area, and warriors of the Wabash tribe were thought to be responsible. "It is to be observed that the United States have not formed any treaties with the Wabash Indians," Knox told Washington. "On the contrary, since the conclusion of the war with Great Britain, hostilities have almost constantly existed between the people of Kentucky and the said Indians. The injuries and murders have been so reciprocal that it would be a point of critical investigation to know on which side they have been the greatest." Kentuckians aroused by the recent killings had conducted reprisal raids into Wabash country, which lay north of the Ohio. "Possessing an equal aversion to all bearing the name of Indians, they destroyed a number of peaceable Piankashaws who prided themselves in their attachment to the United States."

Knox feared the violence would spread further. "It is greatly to be apprehended that hostilities may be so far extended as to involve the Indian tribes with whom the United States have recently made treaties. It is well known how strong the passion for war exists in the mind of a young savage and how easily it may be inflamed so as to disregard every precept of the older and wiser part of the tribes who may have a more just opinion of the force of a treaty. Hence it results that unless some decisive measures are immediately adopted to terminate those mutual hostilities, they will probably become general among all the Indians northwest of the Ohio."

Knox asserted that the United States government had two options in dealing with the Indians. "The first of which is by raising an army and extirpating the refractory tribes entirely," he told Washington. "Or secondly, by forming treaties of peace with them, in which their rights and limits should be explicitly defined and the treaties observed on the part of the United States with the most rigid justice by punishing the whites who should violate the same."

The first course raised grave ethical problems. "An enquiry would arise whether under the existing circumstances of affairs, the United States have a clear right, consistently with the principles of justice and the laws of nature, to proceed to the destruction or expulsion of the savages on the Wabash," Knox said. "It is presumable that a nation solicitous of establishing its character on the broad basis of justice would not only hesitate at but reject every proposition to benefit itself by the injury of any neighbouring community, however contemptible and weak it might be either with respect to its manners or power."

Expulsion might seem less drastic than direct destruction. But it really wasn't, Knox said. "When it shall be considered that the Indians derive their subsistence chiefly by hunting, and that according to fixed principles their population is in proportion to the facility with which they procure their food, it would most probably be found that the expulsion or destruction of the Indian tribes have nearly the same effect, for if they are removed from their usual hunting ground they must necessarily encroach on the hunting of another tribe, who will not suffer the encroachment with impunity. Hence they destroy each other."

Ethics aside, a campaign against the Ohio Indians would be a formidable undertaking, Knox told Washington. "By the best and latest information it appears that on the Wabash and its communications there are from 1500 to 2000 warriors. An expedition against them with the view of extirpating them or destroying their towns could not be undertaken with a probability of success with less than an army of 2500 men." The United States didn't have such an army, which would have to be raised, provisioned and paid. Knox projected the cost at $200,000—"a sum far exceeding the ability of the United States to advance consistently with a due regard to other indispensable objects."

Knox conceded that money by itself shouldn't decide policy. "Were the representations of the people of the frontiers, who have imbibed the strongest prejudices against the Indians, perhaps in consequence of the murders of their dearest friends and connections, only to be regarded, the circumstances before stated would not appear conclusive. An expedition, however inadequate, must be undertaken."

But national policy should reflect the views of the whole nation. "When the impartial mind of the public sits in judgment, it is necessary that the cause of the ignorant Indians should be heard as well as those who are more fortunately circumstanced. It well becomes the public to enquire before it punishes—to be influenced by reasons and the nature of things and not by its resentments."

Knox contended that the federal government should reconsider America's Indian policy. "The time has arrived when it is highly expedient that a liberal system of justice should be adopted for the various Indian tribes within the limits of the United States." The government should pursue treaties of peace with the Indians. The worst that could happen was that the effort would fail, and war would follow. But at least Americans would know they had tried.

Knox developed this theme a few weeks later in a report on trouble farther south. Members of the Creek tribe were at war with Georgia over lands claimed by the Indians but invaded by Georgians. Knox feared that the conflict would spread as other tribes joined the Creeks. "It will appear that the interest of all the Indian nations south of the Ohio as far as the same may relate to the whites is so blended together as to render the circumstance highly probable that in case of a war, they may make it one common cause," he told Washington. Indian leaders in the past had tried to forge such alliances, with Pontiac's war of the 1760s being an example that chilled American memories to the present. "Although each nation or tribe may have latent causes of hatred to each other on account of disputes of boundaries and game, yet when they shall be impressed with the idea that their lives and lands are all at hazard, all inferior disputes will be accommodated, and an union as firm as the six northern nations"—the Iroquois confederacy—"may be formed by the southern tribes."

No single state could adequately deal with such a threat. Hence the need for the federal government to take charge. It should prepare for war or press harder for peace. Knox elaborated on the former. "The army ought not to be calculated at less than 5000 men," the war secretary told Washington. Anything smaller would "be utterly inadequate to the object—an useless expence and disgraceful to the nation." The army should expect a campaign of two years. The cost would be three million dollars.

A campaign of peace would entail more than the mere avoidance of war. It would require a thorough reframing of American attitudes toward the Indians—and a comparable adjustment of Indian attitudes toward whites. The president should appoint a commission of three distinguished, disinterested men. "The commissioners should be invested with full powers to decide all differences respecting boundaries between the state of Georgia and the Creek Indians, unconstrained by treaties said to exist between the said parties otherwise than the same may be reciprocally acknowledged," Knox said. "The commissioners also should be invested with powers to examine into the case of the Cherokees and to renew with them the treaty made at Hopewell in November 1785, and report to the President such measures as shall be necessary to protect the said Cherokees in their former boundaries."

Knox here conceded that his peace policy would overlap his war policy. Soldiers would be as essential to the former as to the latter, if in smaller numbers. And they must be federal troops and not state militiamen. "All treaties with the Indian nations, however equal and just they may be in their principles, will not only be nugatory but humiliating to the sovereign"—the federal government—"unless they shall be guaranteed by a body of troops." Knox explained: "The angry passions of the frontier Indians and whites are too easily inflamed by reciprocal injuries and are too violent to be controlled by the feeble authority of the civil power. There can be neither justice or observance of treaties where every man claims to be the sole judge in his own cause and the avenger of his own supposed wrongs."

The violation of the Hopewell treaty between the Cherokees and the United States showed why troops were necessary. The Cherokees had consented to give up land in exchange for payments and promises that what remained to them would be off limits to white settlement. The settlers poured in all the same. "If so direct and manifest contempt of the authority of the United States be suffered with impunity, it will be in vain to attempt to extend the arm of government to the frontiers," Knox told Washington. "The Indian tribes can have no faith in such imbecile promises, and the lawless whites will ridicule a government which shall on paper only make Indian treaties and regulate Indian boundaries."

The Hopewell treaty had been the responsibility of Congress under the Articles of Confederation. The new government under the Constitution had an opportunity to write a new chapter in relations with the Indians, Knox said. "It would reflect honor on the new government and be attended with happy effects were a declarative law to be passed that the Indian tribes possess the right of the soil of all lands within their limits respectively and that they are not to be divested thereof but in consequence of fair and bona fide purchases, made under the authority or with the express approbation of the United States."

States like Georgia might complain. But they had no grounds, Knox said. "The independent nations and tribes of Indians ought to be considered as foreign nations, not as the subjects of any particular state." Within the states, on land clearly under state authority, the state governments would retain the right to make and enforce laws. "But the general sovereignty must possess the right of making all treaties on the execution or violation of which depend peace or war."

Knox called for policy toward the Indians to be informed by "humanity and justice, together with that respect which every nation sacredly owes to its own reputation." This would be a challenge, since it clashed with the self-interest of citizens who wanted to settle on Indian lands. "Although the disposition of the people of the states to emigrate into the Indian country cannot be effectually prevented, it may be restrained and regulated. It may be restrained by postponing new purchases of Indian territory and by prohibiting the citizens from intruding on the Indian lands. It may be regulated by forming colonies under the direction of government and by posting a body of troops to execute their orders."

Without this fundamental change in policy, the future would resemble America's reproachful past. "All the Indian tribes once existing in those states now the best cultivated and most populous have become extinct," Knox said. "If the same causes continue, the same effects will happen, and in a short period the idea of an Indian on this side the Mississippi will only be found in the page of the historian."

Knox looked back to look ahead. "How different would be the sensation of a philosophic mind to reflect that instead of exterminating a part of the human race by our modes of population that we had persevered through all difficulties and at last had imparted our knowledge of cultivation and the arts to the aboriginals of the country by which the source of future life and happiness had been preserved and extended. But it has been conceived to be impracticable to civilize the Indians of North America. This opinion is probably more convenient than just."

Knox proposed precisely such a civilizing agenda. "Missionaries of excellent moral character should be appointed to reside in their nation, who should be well supplied with all the implements of husbandry and the necessary stock for a farm." The missionaries should instruct the Indians how to cultivate the land. They would preach the gospel, of course, but also the merits of private ownership. "Were it possible to introduce among the Indian tribes a love for exclusive property it would be a happy commencement of the business." The missionaries should be conduits for presents from the government. "They should in no degree be concerned in trade or the purchase of lands to rouse the jealousy of the Indians. They should be their friends and fathers."

It wouldn't be easy. "The civilization of the Indians would be an operation of complicated difficulty," Knox told Washington. "It would require the highest knowledge of the human character and a steady perseverance in a wise system for a series of years."

It wouldn't be cheap. "The expense of such a conciliatory system may be considered as a sufficient reason for rejecting it." Yet such reasoning would be wrong. "When this shall be compared with a system of coercion, it would be found the highest economy to adopt it."

WASHINGTON WAS MOVED by Knox's appeal. He appointed the kinds of commissioners the war secretary wanted. Benjamin Lincoln was Washington's lieutenant from the war who subsequently scattered the Shays rebels. Cyrus Griffin had been the last president of the United States before Washington—that is, he was the final president of the Confederation Congress. David Humphreys had been an aide-de-camp to Washington during the war and a diplomat from Congress to Europe afterward.

"The United States consider it as an object of high national importance not only to be at peace with the powerful tribes or nations of Indians south of the Ohio, but if possible by a just and liberal system of policy to conciliate and attach them to the interests of the Union," Washington declared in his instructions to the commissioners. "The first great object of your commission is to negotiate and establish peace between the state of Georgia and the Creek nation. The whole nation must be fully represented and solemnly acknowledged by the Creeks themselves to be so." This remark acknowledged a deficiency in many treaties. Sometimes inadvertently, often knowingly, negotiators on the side of the government dealt with chiefs who didn't represent the whole of a tribe. Not surprisingly, the unrepresented Indians didn't feel obliged to observe the treaties.

Washington stressed that the commissioners were to listen fully and carefully to the Creeks. "The United States do not want the Creek lands. They desire only to be friends and protectors of the Creeks and treat them with humanity and justice." Right in itself, this policy would enhance the authority of the American government. "You will establish the principle, in case of concluding a treaty, that the Creeks who are within the limits of the United States acknowledge themselves to be under the protection of the United States of America, and of no other sovereign whosoever, and also that they are not to hold any treaty with an individual state nor with individuals of any state."

Moving to another part of Knox's recommendation, Washington continued, "You will also endeavour to obtain a stipulation for certain missionaries to reside in the nation"—the Creek nation. "These men to be precluded from trade or attempting to purchase any lands." The missionaries would be honest persons and good patriots. "The object of this establishment would be the happiness of the Indians, teaching them great duties of religion and morality, and to inculcate a friendship and attachment to the United States."

Peace was Washington's goal. But he prepared for the alternative. "If after you have made your communication to the Creeks and you are persuaded that you are fully understood by them, they should refuse to treat and conclude a peace on the terms you propose, it may be concluded that they are decided on a continuance of acts of hostility and that they ought to be guarded against as the determined enemies of the United States. In this case you will report such plans both for defensive and offensive measures so as best to protect the citizens of the United States on the frontiers from any act of injury or hostility of the Creeks."

To this end, the commissioners should gather intelligence. "During your negotiations with the Creeks you will endeavor to ascertain the following points: 1st. The number of warriors in the whole nation including upper and lower Creeks and Seminoles. 2nd. Whether they are armed with common and rifle muskets or in any other manner, and how furnished with ammunition. 3rd. The number of each division of upper Creeks, lower Creeks and Seminoles. 4th. The number of women and children and old men in each district. 5th. The number of towns in each district." And so on, down to "15th. To ascertain with great precision the nature of the connection of the Creeks with the Spaniards, and if practicable to obtain copies of any treaties between them, whether the predominating prejudices of the Creeks are in favor or against the Spaniards, and particularly the state of Mr. McGillivray's mind on this subject." Alexander McGillivray was the principal chief of the Creeks.

Washington added a caution regarding the information he sought. "The accurate knowledge of this subject is of considerable importance, but the enquiries thereto should be circuitously conducted," he said.

⟶ 81 ⟵

The commissioners' work began inauspiciously. "After a fatiguing journey through the deep sands which prevail from Savannah to Augusta, we reached the latter on the evening of the 17th instant," David Humphreys wrote to Washington in late September. "The next day the iron axle tree of our carriage broke at a great distance from any house, which accident occasioned the loss of the whole day. Being determined to arrive at the Rock Landing the following evening, according to our last letter to Mr. McGillivray, General Lincoln and myself took two of the carriage horses, with a guide, and proceeded twenty-five miles that night. Yesterday we reached this place"—Rock Landing—"at dark, after having travelled a long distance before we reached the Ogeechee, and from the Ogeechee to the Oconee (between 30 and 40 miles) through a dreary wilderness in which there was not a single house." McGillivray had yet to arrive. "We have not been here long enough to be assured of the prospects of success or to know the difficulties that may occur." Everything depended on McGillivray, apparently. "McGillivray is desirous of peace," Humphreys said, based on what he'd been told. "And his word is a law to the Creeks."

McGillivray appeared, with several other chiefs. "Much general talk, expressive of a real desire to establish a permanent peace upon equitable terms, took place," Humphreys reported to Washington. "The next day McGillivray dined with us, and although he got very much intoxicated, he seemed to retain his recollection and reason beyond what I had ever seen in a person when in the same condition. At this time I became intimate to a certain degree with him and endeavored to extract his real sentiments and feelings in a conversation alone, confidentially. He declared he was really desirous of a peace, that the local situation of the Creeks required that they should be connected with us rather than with any other people, that, however they had certain advantages in their treaty with

Spain, in respect to a guarantee and trade, which they ought not in justice to themselves to give up without an equivalent." The Creeks received weapons and provisions from Spanish traders in Florida. McGillivray was reminding the commissioners—and through them, Washington—that the Creeks had other suitors.

"Upon his desiring to know what were our intentions, especially as he knew from my character and from my having been long in habits of intimacy with General Washington that I would tell him what he might depend upon, I assured him upon my honour that our policy with respect to his nation was indeed founded upon honesty, magnanimity and mutual advantages," Humphreys continued. "We descended to no particulars farther than my assuring him of our good opinion of his abilities and desire to attach him, upon principles perfectly consistent with the good of his nation, to our interest."

The talk continued but got nowhere. Humphreys inferred that McGillivray was deliberately delaying. "I apprehend that we can never depend upon McGillivray for his firm attachment to the interests of the United States," he wrote to Washington. "If I mistake not his character, his own importance and pecuniary emolument are the objects which will altogether influence his conduct. It was held out in discourse yesterday by John Galphin, a creature of McGillivray, that a pressing invitation has just been sent from the Spaniards (accompanied by a vast quantity of ammunition) for McGillivray to come and treat with them. I fancy he now wavers between Spain and America, for which reason he wishes in all likelihood to postpone the farther negotiation with the latter until the spring." McGillivray was weighing his options. "Probably his hopes have been much elevated lately, insomuch as to induce him to believe that he can obtain better terms for himself from the king than from us."

MCGILLIVRAY'S HOPES STALLED the talks with the commissioners. They came home empty-handed. Yet Washington refused to abandon the idea of a treaty with the Creeks. In early 1790 he dispatched a confidential agent to Georgia to reengage McGillivray. Marinus Willett had run a spy network for Washington during the war, and the president counted on his discretion and resourcefulness. In a private meeting Washington explained Willett's mission, and he gave him a message, written as a speech, to deliver to McGillivray and the other Creek chiefs.

A roundabout journey landed Willett in McGillivray's company in late April. "After delivering him my introductory letter, I had some conversation with him, and after a good supper and most kind entertainment, I went to bed, happy in being under the same roof with the man I have traveled thus far to see," Willett wrote in his journal. First impressions were more favorable than he had expected. "Colonel McGillivray appears to be a man of an open, candid, generous mind, with a good judgment and very tenacious memory."

Gathering the other Creek chiefs required two weeks. "Brothers," Willett addressed them, "I am come to you from our beloved town by order of our beloved chief, George Washington, to invite you to a treaty of peace and friendship at a council fire in our beloved city. Brothers, our beloved chief, who wishes prosperity to the red people as well as to the white, has directed me to advise you that he is very desirous of forming a lasting treaty of peace and amity with your nation. That in order to do this effectually, it is his wish to have his own name, and the name of your beloved chief, fixed to the treaty, that it may be strong and lasting. Brothers, I am very pointedly instructed to inform you that the United States want none of your lands. That effectual measures will be taken to secure them all to you by our beloved chief, who has an arm sufficiently strong to punish all such as may presume to act contrary to any treaty which he, in conjunction with your beloved chief, may make. Brothers, our beloved chief is ready to agree with your beloved chief to secure to you your lands, to promote your trade by affording you means of procuring goods in a cheap and easy way, and to do all such things as will contribute to promote the welfare and happiness of your nation. Brothers, I stand before you a messenger of peace. It is your interest, and it is our interest, that we should live in peace with each other. I promise myself that you will attend to this friendly invitation, and that your beloved chief, with such other of your chiefs and warriors as you may choose for that purpose, will repair with me to the council fire that is kindled in our beloved town, that we may form a treaty which shall be as strong as the hills and lasting as the rivers."

Willett retired to let the Creeks consider the invitation. After an hour he was summoned back. One of the chiefs answered for the group. "Brother, we are glad to see you. You have come a great way, and as soon as we fixed our eyes upon you, we were made glad. We are poor and have not the knowledge of white people. Brother, our fathers have told us, whenever any white people came among us, we should take them by the hand and use them well. We have always followed their advice. Brother, we were invited to a treaty at the Rock Landing. We went there. Nothing was done. We were disappointed and came back with sorrow. Brother, you say you come from your beloved chief, George Washington, to invite our beloved chief to a council fire in your beloved town. The road is very long, and the weather is very hot. But our beloved chief will go with you, and such other chiefs and warriors as shall be appointed for that purpose will go with him. Brother, all that our beloved chief shall do, we will agree to. We wish you may be preserved from every evil. We will count the time our beloved chief is away, and when he comes back, we shall be very glad to see him, with a treaty that shall be as strong as the hills and last as long as the rivers."

THE JOURNEY OF MCGILLIVRAY and his entourage to New York captured the attention of the American people. "On Saturday evening last, Colonel Marinus Willett, with Colonel Alexander McGillivray and twenty-eight chiefs of the Creek nation arrived in this city," reported the Philadelphia correspondent of the *Gazette of the United States* on Friday, July 9. "They will shortly proceed to visit the Congress of the United States in order to conclude treaties which, we hope, will secure peace to our southern brethren. These chiefs were received by our citizens with every mark of attention. The bells were rung; the artillery fired a federal salute and with the light infantry companies escorted the chiefs to the Indian Queen"—the hotel—"where lodgings were prepared for them, and a great number of people assembled to behold the largest body of Indians that has appeared in this metropolis for many years. Yesterday they attended divine service at Christ Church."

Ten days later the party got to New York. "A packet, under the direction of Major Stagg, had been dispatched to Elizabethtown Point by order of the secretary at war, on board of which they embarked at that place in the morning, and landed at Murray's Wharf about 2 o'clock," the *Gazette* observed. "As they passed the Battery, a federal salute was fired, which was repeated at the moment of their landing." Local organizations mustered to welcome the Indian dignitaries. "The Society of St. Tammany, in their proper dresses, accompanied by General Malcolm and a detachment of the city artillery and infantry, awaited their arrival and escorted them to the house of Hon. General Knox, after which they were introduced by the general to the President of the United States. They then waited on his Excellency the Governor and dined at the City Tavern, in company with the secretary of war, the senators and representatives of the state of Georgia, General Malcolm, the military officers on duty, and the officers of the Society of St. Tammany. The public curiosity was greatly excited, and the multitude immense which collected on this occasion. Our visitors appeared to be greatly pleased with their polite and friendly reception and the public demonstration of satisfaction at the occasion of their long journey to the Great Council of the States."

John Trumbull was the son of Jonathan Trumbull, the Connecticut governor during the Revolutionary War. The younger Trumbull had been an aide-de-camp to Washington. After the war he turned to art, making a specialty business of painting heroic scenes from the war. In the summer of 1790 he was working on a painting of Washington reentering New York upon the British evacuation at the war's end. "I represented him in full uniform, standing by a white horse, leaning his arm upon the saddle; in the background, a view of Broadway in ruins, as it then was, the old fort at the termination; British ships and boats leaving the shore, with the last of the officers and troops of the evacuating army, and Staten Island in the distance," Trumbull wrote later.

"At this time, a numerous deputation from the Creek nation of Indians was in New York," he continued, "and when this painting was finished, the president was curious to see the effect it would produce on their untutored minds. He therefore directed me to place the picture in an advantageous light, facing the door of entrance of the room where it was, and having invited several of the principal chiefs to dine with him, he, after dinner, proposed to them a walk. He was dressed in full uniform and led the way to the painting room, and when the door was thrown open, they started at seeing another 'Great Father' standing in the room. One was certainly with them, and they were for a time mute with astonishment. At length one of the chiefs advanced towards the picture, and slowly stretched out his hand to touch it, and was still more astonished to feel, instead of a round object, a flat surface, cold to the touch. He started back with an exclamation of astonishment." Trumbull was pleased at this validation of his artistic skills.

He had wanted to paint some of the chiefs—"who possessed a dignity of manner, form, countenance and expression worthy of Roman senators," he said. "But after this I found it impracticable. They had received the impression that there must be magic in an art which could render a smooth flat surface so like to a real man. I however succeeded in obtaining drawings of several by stealth."

McGillivray and the other chiefs wouldn't have made the long journey if they weren't inclined to conclude a deal. Negotiations occupied several days, with sightseeing and ceremonies interspersed. In early August an agreed-upon treaty was laid before the Senate, which ratified it without controversy.

At noon on August 13, Washington, Knox and members of their staffs met with McGillivray and the other chiefs at Federal Hall. A large crowd attended. A Washington aide read the treaty aloud. "The president then addressed Col. McGillivray, the kings, chiefs, and warriors," recounted the *Gazette*. "He said that he thought the treaty just and equal, and stated the mutual duties of the contracting parties. Which address was communicated sentence after sentence by Mr. Cornell, sworn interpreter, to all of which the Creeks gave an audible assent. The president then signed the treaty, after which he presented a string of beads as a token of perpetual peace, and a paper of tobacco to smoke in remembrance of it."The Creeks had signed earlier, with Henry Knox. "Mr. McGillivray rose, made a short reply to the president, and received the tokens. This was succeeded by the shake of peace, every one of the Creeks passing this friendly salute with the president. A song of peace performed by the Creeks concluded this highly interesting, solemn and dignified transaction."

THERE WAS MORE to the Treaty of New York than the audience at Federal Hall realized. Beyond the fourteen articles of the treaty made public at the time, six were withheld from view. These defined a future trading relationship between the United States and the Creek nation, should the existing Creek relationship with Spain break down. McGillivray didn't wish to double-cross the Spanish openly, but he wanted to have options. The secret articles also put McGillivray's entourage on the American payroll, at $100 per year for the chiefs and $1200 for McGillivray, who was commissioned a brigadier general in the United States army. McGillivray and the other chiefs preferred not to be seen as having divided loyalties.

The public articles were controversial enough. Georgians denounced the treaty as a power grab by the federal government. Washington had put the interests of the Creeks above the interests of the citizens of Georgia, the critics said. Some of the critics were sincere defenders of states' right. Others were speculators and land jobbers who disliked having sweetheart deals snatched away from them.

Washington wasn't surprised. Selfish and narrow-minded people there would always be. He was content with the result of his cultivation of McGillivray. "While I flatter myself that this treaty will be productive of present peace and prosperity to our southern frontier, it is to be expected that it will also, in its consequences, be the means of firmly attaching the Creeks and the neighbouring tribes to the interests of the United States," he told the Senate.

— 82 —

Amid Washington's peace campaign toward the Creeks, Alexander Hamilton laid before Congress a report on the public credit. In doing so, he touched off the first great debate in American politics under the new Constitution—a debate on the purpose and meaning of government, one that divided Americans at the time and has never stopped dividing them.

The precipitating issue was the war debt. The American war effort had been funded by taxes, paper currency and debt. Taxes—levied by the states—had quickly fallen short of the levels required to sustain Washington's army. Paper currency, issued by the federal government and forced upon its vendors, entered a spiral of depreciation. Congress and the states had come to rely on debt, selling bonds for cash, with the bonds to be redeemed at specified later dates, presumably after the war was won.

The war *had* been won, and bondholders were demanding to be paid. The matter was complicated, however, by the fact that the current bondholders were often not the original bondholders, many of whom had been compelled by privation to sell their bonds to speculators for dimes or pennies on the dollar. The bonds would be paid out of current taxes levied on the original bondholders, among others. Unsurprisingly they didn't like this plan. Few wanted to repudiate the debt, but many thought a distinction should be made in repayment between speculators and original bondholders who still held the government debt, with the former receiving amounts proportioned to what they had paid for the bonds.

There was another twist in the discussions. The government debt existed in two forms: the federal debt and the state debts. All agreed that the federal debt was the responsibility of the federal government. Most thought the state debts were the responsibility of the states. But a few people argued that the state debts should be assumed by the federal government because the debts had been incurred as part of the national war effort. This argument would have been more persuasive had the states not redeemed their debts at different speeds since the war. Some states had taxed themselves stringently and paid off their debts. Other states had done little or nothing in that direction. A program of federal assumption would transfer resources from the former to the latter—from the responsible to the profligate, as the former interpreted the matter.

Hamilton's report on the public credit—credit being the accounting inverse of debt—came in response to a request from the House of Representatives, the chamber charged by the Constitution with taking the lead on taxes and expenditures, to the Washington administration to propose a repayment plan. Hamilton gave the House what it asked for, and a great deal more.

He commenced with a triad of what he called "plain and undeniable truths," to wit: "That exigencies are to be expected to occur in the affairs of nations in which there will be a necessity for borrowing. That loans in times of public danger, especially from foreign war, are found an indispensable resource even to the wealthiest of them. And that in a country, which, like this, is possessed of little active wealth, or in other words, little monied capital, the necessity for that resource must in such emergencies be proportionably urgent."

If borrowing must be done, it should be on the best terms possible. Hamilton explained how. "To be able to borrow upon good terms," he said, "it is essential that the credit of a nation should be well established."

The surest guarantee of good credit was repayment of existing debts. Hamilton had considered the argument for discounting debt held by speculators. He appreciated its logic. But he couldn't accept it. "The Secretary," he said of himself, "after the most mature reflection on the force of this argument, is induced to reject the doctrine it contains as equally unjust and impolitic, as highly injurious even to the original holders of public securities, as ruinous to public credit." He explained, "It is inconsistent with justice because, in the first place, it is a breach of contract." The government had agreed to pay in full. The bonds said so on their face. For the government to renege would give it a reputation for faithlessness. Discounting was impolitic because distinguishing between original and derivative bondholders would be impossible. Records were lacking. The bonds operated like cash, payable to the bearer. Discounting was injurious even to the original bondholders because they would share in the harm done to the country by a bad national credit rating. And discounting was ruinous to the public credit because that bad rating would compel the government to pay high interest rates for future borrowing. Hamilton noted that to renege on the debt would be to violate the Constitution, whose Article VI mandated, "All debts contracted and engagements entered into before the adoption of this Constitution shall be as valid against the United States under this Constitution as under the Confederation."

For these reasons, the federal bonds must be redeemed in full, no matter the identity of the current holders of the bonds.

This part of Hamilton's recommendation was no great surprise. As one of the instigators of the replacement of the Articles of Confederation by the Constitution, Hamilton was known to favor energetic government. As a friend of bankers—and himself a banker who founded the Bank of New York—Hamilton could be expected to have the interests of creditors at heart.

What was less expected was Hamilton's decision to sweep federal assumption of state debts into the same argument. He repeated the point that all the war debts were for the same cause—national independence—and therefore entailed the same moral obligation of repayment. He cited efficiency in repayment. Bonds had wandered around the country, leaving holders to return to the states of issue to get their money. Assumption would centralize redemption. He pointed out that the Constitution forbade state tariffs, on which the states had been counting for revenue to redeem the bonds.

He added an argument that even many of the federalists hadn't thought of: that federal debt would serve as cement holding the Union together. If bondholders were to be repaid by the states, their attention and interest would be diffused among the states. The diffusion would cause squabbling among the creditor classes, on whom the nation's future prosperity rested. Assumption would change the reckoning. "If all the public creditors receive their dues from one source, distributed with an equal hand, their interest will be the same," Hamilton said. "And having the same interests, they will unite in the support of the fiscal arrangements of the government."

To prevent this, the government—the federal government—must assume the debts of the states.

— 83 —

Hamilton's proposal for assumption of the state debts produced a fateful crack in the wall of American federalism. Congress accepted Hamilton's argument for full funding of the federal debt, but many members balked at the expansion of federal power entailed by the assumption of state debts. The dissidents were led by none other than James Madison, to this point the moving spirit of the federalist movement.

"It is not without much reluctance that I trouble the committee with any observations on a subject which has been so long under discussion and may be thought to be entirely exhausted," Madison declared in the House. Assumption had been struggling, but Hamilton's allies refused to let it die. "It has been contended that the state debts are in their nature debts of the United States, that they were only from different offices, and have borne a different denomination, but that in justice they are the debts of the United States, and that the individual creditors can of right claim payment of the same from the general government," Madison said. "We have been told, sir, not only that the assumption of the state debts by the United States is a matter of right on the part of the states, and a matter of obligation on the part of the United States, but likewise that it is equitable; nay, that it is a matter of necessity."

Madison thought this position wrong in both premise and conclusion. The state debts were state obligations, and no sophistry could make them federal obligations. No Virginia bondholder in his right mind would appear at the door of the federal treasury and expect as a matter of right to be paid. The idea was ludicrous.

As for the necessity of assumption said to follow from this misguided premise, it was equally wrong. "It has been asserted that it would be politic to assume the state debts, because it would add strength to the national government," Madison said. "There is no man more anxious for the success of the government than I am, and no one who will join more heartily in curing its defects. But I wish these defects to be remedied by additional constitutional powers, if they should be found necessary. This is the only proper, effectual, and permanent remedy."

What Hamilton proposed was unconstitutional, Madison said. Nothing in the Constitution supported such an extension of federal power against the states. Nothing in the discussions at the convention that wrote the Constitution supported it. He knew, as one who had been there. "Was it understood that they were a part of the debt of the United States?" he asked of the state debts. "Was it ever supposed that they were to be thrown into one common mass, and that the states should be called on collectively to provide for them?" No and no. Suppose it had been proposed. "Would it have been considered as consistent with equity? Would it have been thought constitutional?" No and no.

Hamilton and his allies had pushed too far. They were taking federal power beyond what the Constitution warranted. In doing so they were claiming a higher devotion to the welfare of the nation. Madison especially resented this. "I would recommend to them no longer to assume a preeminence over us in the nationality of their motives, and that they would forbear those frequent assertions that if the state debts are not provided for, the federal debts shall also go unprovided for; nay, that if the state debts are not assumed, the union will be endangered. Sir, I am persuaded that if the gentlemen knew the motives that govern us, they would blush at such intemperate as well as inconsistent language."

HAMILTON'S VIEWS ON assumption succeeded, but not on their merits alone. The opponents of assumption, and of the accompanying aggrandizement of the federal government over the states, blocked this part of Hamilton's program for months, until it became entangled with a second vexing issue: the physical location of the federal government. The Constitution's Article I mentioned the possibility of a federal district "not exceeding ten miles square" that would become the seat of government. The matter had come up at the time of the mutiny of the Pennsylvania line, when the governor of Pennsylvania had refused, for reasons of local politics, to call out the Pennsylvania militia to protect Congress. Some members and observers concluded that Congress must not remain beholden to a state government for protection. A federal district would free the government from such dependence.

Yet other issues intruded. The federal district and its location languished—until Hamilton's assumption measure stalled. Thomas Jefferson thought each issue might unlock the other. Jefferson invited Hamilton and Madison to dinner. The three, realizing that the sternest opposition to assumption came from the southern delegations in Congress, reasoned that this opposition might be softened by locating the federal district in the south. An agreement was made that each man would promote this package to his friends in Congress.

They did so, and it worked. Hamilton got assumption of the state debts. Madison and the south got the federal district. Philadelphia, which had hoped to be the permanent seat of government, received the consolation prize of getting the government back from New York and keeping it until the federal district was ready to receive it.

HAMILTON WAS SOON ASKING for more, namely a national bank to oversee assumption and manage the accounts of the federal government. "A national bank is an institution of primary importance to the prosperous administration of the finances, and would be of the greatest utility in the operations connected with the support of the public credit," Hamilton asserted in a second report to the House. The most enlightened countries had national banks, which served those countries well.

Banks of any sort were still a novelty in America. Hamilton felt obliged to explain what they did. They converted dead money into living capital by taking as deposits money from people who did not have immediate use for it and distributing it as loans to people who did. "The money which a merchant keeps in his chest waiting for a favourable opportunity to employ it produces nothing till that opportunity arrives," Hamilton said. "But if instead of locking it up in this manner, he either deposits it in a bank or invests it in the stock of a bank, it yields a profit during the interval." And it created jobs and other opportunities in the economy at large.

A national bank, in addition, lent financial heft to the national government. "The reason is obvious," Hamilton said. "The capitals of a great number of individuals are, by this operation"—the creation of the national bank—"collected to a point and placed under one direction." Instead of myriad individuals squandering their financial power working at myriad and often conflicting purposes, the single entity of the national bank would serve the single national purpose.

A national bank, further, would render more efficient and therefore less expensive the operation of the federal government. At present, federal taxes were collected in the thirteen states and deposited in separate banks there. The funds were then transferred to other banks to pay the government's creditors and vendors. "This is attended with trouble, delay, expense and risk," Hamilton said. A single bank as depository and disburser would improve things immensely.

Hamilton provided details of his desired bank. It would be chartered by the federal government and empowered to operate in every state. The government would own a minority of the shares of the bank, with the majority going to private investors. The bank would be managed by a board of directors, whose president would report on the bank's operations to the secretary of the treasury.

The bank would be run as a business, but it would serve the public interest. "Public utility is more truly the object of public banks than private profit," Hamilton said. "And it is the business of government to constitute them on such principles that while the latter will result in a sufficient degree to afford competent motives to engage in them, the former be not made subservient to it."

As always with Hamilton, bolstering the power of government was crucial. "Such a bank is not a mere matter of private property, but a political machine of the greatest importance to the state," he said.

84

The battle over the bank made the assumption fight seem a skirmish. More clearly than anything yet it revived the fundamental rift between the federalists and the antifederalists in the ratification debate. Hamilton's bank would centralize power over the nation's economy in the hands of a small elite, wealthy and well connected to the national government. The federalists were comfortable with this. Indeed they thought it necessary for the future of the Union, or said they did. The antifederalists distrusted elites, government in general and especially the national government. That the instrument of the power grab was a bank made it the more suspect in the eyes of the antifederalists. Banking was comparatively novel and enduringly mysterious. Bankers made money from the labor of others. They lived in cities at a time when most Americans lived on farms.

There was a larger issue. The Constitution said nothing about banks. It conferred no authority on Congress to create a national bank and none on the president to guide its operation. Justifying the bank required an expansive reading of the Constitution. To the federalists, expansion came naturally. The Constitution gave Congress the authority to coin money. A national bank would create money by lending against its deposits. It was entirely within the spirit of the Constitution, the federalists said.

The Constitution was not a matter of spirit, the antifederalists countered. It was a matter of law. If the Constitution did not expressly confer a particular power on the federal government, the federal government did not possess that power. This was understood by the framers of the Constitution, which was why they spent so much time at Philadelphia enumerating the powers of the government.

The debate over constitutionality hinged—hardly for the last time—on a phrase in Article I which asserted that Congress should have the authority to make all laws "necessary and proper" for putting into execution the enumerated powers. The federalists emphasized "proper," meaning fitting, suitable or even convenient. The antifederalists focused on "necessary," noting also the conjunctive "and," meaning *both* necessary and proper.

" 'AN ACT TO INCORPORATE the Subscribers to the Bank of the United States' is now before me for consideration," Washington wrote to Hamilton in February 1791. Hamilton had done his political work well, marshaling support from federalists in the Senate, where the bank bill passed easily on a voice vote. Senators shouted their yeas and nays, and the former clearly outnumbered the latter. Antifederalists in the House delayed passage of the bill there but ultimately lost by a nearly two-to-one margin. The measure went to Washington for his approval or his veto.

"The constitutionality of it is objected to," the president observed to Hamilton of the bill. "It therefore becomes more particularly my duty to examine the ground on which the objection is built. As a mean of investigation I have called upon the Attorney General of the United States in whose line it seemed more particularly to be for his official examination and opinion. His report is that the Constitution does not warrant the Act. I then applied to the Secretary of State for his sentiments on this subject. These coincide with the Attorney General's, and the reasons for their opinions having been submitted in writing, I now require, in like manner, yours on the validity and propriety of the above recited act."

Edmund Randolph's objection had been succinct and lawyerly. "That the power of creating corporations is not expressly given to Congress is obvious," the attorney general wrote. The proposed bank would be a corporation. "If it can be exercised by them, it must be, 1st because the nature of the federal government implies it, or 2d because it is involved in some of the specified powers of legislation, or 3d because it is necessary and proper to carry into execution some of the specified powers." Randolph remarked the difference between America's new government and nearly all others. "Governments having no written constitution"—the British government sprang to mind, but others were similar—"may perhaps claim a latitude of power not always easy to be determined. Those which have written constitutions are circumscribed by a just interpretation of the words contained in them."

Because the Constitution did not expressly confer incorporating power, advocates of the bank employed inference and the "necessary and proper" clause. "To be necessary is to be incidental, or in other words may be denominated the natural means of executing a power," Randolph said. "The phrase 'and proper,' if it has my meaning, does not enlarge the powers of Congress, but rather restricts them. For no power is to be assumed under the general clause but such as is not only necessary but proper." The bill's advocates had failed to demonstrate necessity. "In every aspect therefore under which the attorney general can view the act, so far as it incorporates the bank, he is bound to declare his opinion to be against its constitutionality."

Jefferson's response was more philosophical. Jefferson had been a federalist during the debate over ratification, albeit from the distance of Paris. He cheered the efforts to strengthen the national government. But his federalism fell short of Hamilton's, and after the Constitution was ratified and he saw what Hamilton's federalism entailed, Jefferson moved in the opposite direction. He drafted a long objection to the national bank and sent it to Washington. "I consider the foundation of the Constitution as laid on this ground that 'all powers not delegated to the U.S. by the Constitution, nor prohibited by it to the states, are reserved to the states or to the people.'" James Madison, following through on the federalists' pledge to add a bill of rights to the Constitution, had drafted a list of reserved rights, which Congress had approved and Washington sent to the states for ratification. Jefferson here was closely paraphrasing what would become the Tenth Amendment. Jefferson added, "To take a single step beyond the boundaries thus specially drawn around the powers of Congress is to take possession of a boundless field of power no longer susceptible of any definition."

The Constitution said nothing about a bank, Jefferson noted. The authority to create one, therefore, was not an enumerated power. Jefferson rejected Hamilton's interpretation of the necessary-and-proper clause. The pertinent enumerated powers—to collect taxes, disburse appropriations—had long been exercised by various governments without national banks, and been exercised by the American government without a national bank. "They can all be carried into execution without a bank. A bank therefore is not necessary, and consequently not authorised by this phrase."

Hamilton had argued that a bank would be convenient for the government. Maybe so, Jefferson allowed. "Yet the constitution allows only the means which are 'necessary' not those which are merely 'convenient' for effecting the enumerated powers. If such a latitude of construction be allowed to this phrase as to gain any non-enumerated power, it will go to every one, for there is no one which ingenuity may not torture into a convenience, in some way or other, to some one of so long a list of enumerated powers." It would draw all power to itself, leaving nothing to the states or the people. Patently this was not what the framers intended.

HAMILTON RESPONDED AT great length to Randolph and Jefferson. But the gist of his defense of the bank's constitutionality was his generous interpretation of the necessary-and-proper clause. He dismissed Jefferson's definition of "necessary" as closed-minded and legalistic. "Necessary often means no more than needful, requisite, incidental, useful, or conducive to," Hamilton said. "It is a common mode of expression to say that it is necessary for a government or a person to do this or that thing, when nothing more is intended or understood than that the interests of the government or person require or will be promoted by the doing of this or that thing. The imagination can be at no loss for exemplifications of the use of the word in this sense."

Such was the sense of the framers. "It is the true one in which it is to be understood as used in the constitution," Hamilton said. "The whole turn of the clause containing it indicates that it was the intent of the convention by that clause to give a liberal latitude to the exercise of the specified powers. The expressions have peculiar comprehensiveness. They are 'to make all laws, necessary and proper for carrying into execution the foregoing powers and all other powers vested by the constitution in the government of the United States, or in any department or officer thereof.' To understand the word as the Secretary of State does would be to depart from its obvious and popular sense and to give it a restrictive operation—an idea never before entertained. It would be to give it the same force as if the word *absolutely* or *indispensably* had been prefixed to it."

Hamilton rejected Jefferson's view, and he thought Washington should too.

WASHINGTON'S POLLING OF his advisers wasn't unusual for him. The councils he held with his generals during the war had been similar exercises, though the opinions had been given orally. The stakes were more immediate then. Soldiers would die in battle the next day. The game was longer in this case. The charter of the proposed bank ran for twenty years. Arguably Washington's decision in this case would have consequences that lasted as long as the republic.

In war councils he had kept his opinions to himself lest he discourage free exchange. He kept his opinion to himself now. He hadn't yet vetoed any legislation, which meant that this decision might set a precedent for this aspect of executive power. The Constitution didn't require a president to deem a bill unconstitutional before vetoing it. He might simply think it inadvisable. But the American colonial experience of vetoes by royal governors made Americans wary of vetoes. Congress had passed the bank bill by strong margins. Washington wouldn't overrule the legislature without firm reason.

"The constitutionality of the national bank was a question on which his mind was greatly perplexed," Madison later wrote of Washington. "His belief in the utility of the establishment and his disposition to favor a liberal construction of the national powers formed a bias on one side. On the other, he had witnessed what passed in the convention which framed the Constitution, and he knew the tenor of the reasonings and explanations under which it had been ratified by the state conventions. His perplexity was increased by the opposite arguments and opinions of his official advisers Mr. Jefferson and Mr. Hamilton. He held several free conversations with me on the subject, in which he listened favorably as I thought to my views of it, but certainly without committing himself in any manner whatever.

"Not long before the expiration of the ten days allowed"—by the Constitution—"for his decision, he desired me to reduce into form the objections to the bill, that he might be prepared, in case he should return it without his signature"—that is, veto it. Madison inferred that Washington was going to veto, although he couldn't be sure.

The president waited until the last moment to make his decision. "The delay had begotten strong suspicions in the zealous friends of the bill that it would be rejected," Madison recalled. "One of its ablest champions, under this impression, told me he had been making an exact computation of the time elapsed, and that the bill would be a law, in spite of its return with objections, in consequence of the failure to make the return within the limited term of ten days." In other words, Washington would miss the deadline. This was no small matter, for the markets in government bonds and bank stocks were sizzling with bets for and against a veto.

There would be political consequences. "I did not doubt that if such had been the case advantage would have been taken of it, and that the disappointed party would have commenced an open opposition to the President, so great was their confidence in the wealth and strength they possessed," Madison wrote.

Madison's interlocutor didn't know Washington, who didn't miss deadlines. Before the ten days expired, the president acceded to the views of Hamilton and the majorities in Congress and signed the bank bill.

85

Tobias Lear was a native of New Hampshire who had entered the Washington household at Mount Vernon on the recommendation of Benjamin Lincoln. "Mr. Lear writes a good hand and has obtained a pretty good knowledge of the most exact method of book-keeping," Lincoln wrote. Washington was looking for a young man to keep accounts. Lincoln's son, Benjamin Jr., knew Lear better than the father did, and he gushed over Lear's qualifications. "He is a young man of sobriety, good sense and learning, possesses an honest heart, a generous, elevated spirit and is such a youth as General Washington will esteem and be happy to patronize," Junior said. "He has been unfortunate in the loss of a very handsome patrimony. But his misfortunes while they drained his purse have enriched his understanding and given him a style of thinking which in my opinion at his time of life is preferable to wealth."

Washington met Lear and liked him. He hired him as secretary and also as tutor to Martha's grandchildren then living at Mount Vernon. Lear thrived on responsibility and soon became Washington's majordomo. He moved with Washington to New York upon Washington's inauguration as president, and then to Philadelphia when the government relocated there in the autumn of 1790.

In April 1791, Lear brought a matter to Washington's attention that had come up during a visit by Edmund Randolph while Washington was away at Mount Vernon. "The attorney general called upon Mrs. Washington today and informed her that three of his Negroes had given him notice that they should tomorrow take advantage of a law of this state, and claim their freedom, and that he had mentioned it to her from an idea that those who were of age in this family might follow the example after a residence of six months should put it in their power. I have therefore communicated it to you that you might, if you thought best, give directions in the matter respecting the blacks in this family."

As part of Pennsylvania's plan to end slavery in the state, the law Randolph cited to Martha Washington decreed that nonresidents of Pennsylvania might bring slaves to the state, but if the slaves remained longer than six months, they were thereby freed.

Washington initially believed the law didn't apply to him. "The attorney general's case and mine I conceive, from a conversation I had with him respecting our slaves, is somewhat different," he answered Lear. "He in order to qualify himself for practice in the courts of Pennsylvania was obliged to take the oaths of citizenship to that state, whilst my residence is incidental as an officer of government only."

Washington realized this might make no difference to abolitionists who encouraged slaves to seek their freedom by any means. "Whether among people who are in the practice of enticing slaves even when there is no colour of law for it, this distinction will avail, I know not." Lear should investigate the matter more closely. "Take the best advice you can on the subject, and in case it shall be found that any of my slaves may, or any for them shall, attempt their freedom at the expiration of six months, it is my wish and desire that you would send the whole, or such part of them as Mrs. Washington may not choose to keep, home"—back to Mount Vernon. "For although I do not think they would be benefitted by the change, yet the idea of freedom might be too great a temptation for them to resist. At any rate it might, if they conceived they had a right to it, make them insolent in a state of slavery."

The situation was complicated for Washington by the fact that several of the slaves in question belonged to Martha's estate from her first husband and were legally pledged to his heirs after she died. "As all except Hercules and Paris are dower negroes"—the term for such slaves—"it behooves me to prevent the emancipation of them, otherwise I shall not only lose the use of them but may have them to pay for."

Sending the slaves back to Mount Vernon would maintain their bondage. Yet this must be done discreetly, lest Hercules, who was a cook, and the others be alerted to Washington's design and break for their freedom, which was much easier to gain in Pennsylvania than in Virginia. "If upon taking good advice it is found expedient to send them back to Virginia, I wish to have it accomplished under pretext that may deceive both them and the public," Washington told Lear. The president preferred that the public see him as an enlightened slaveholder. He proposed a ruse. "None I think would so effectually do this as Mrs. Washington coming to Virginia next month (towards the middle or latter end of it, as she seemed to have a wish to do), if she can accomplish it by any convenient and agreeable means with the assistance of the stage horses etc. This would naturally bring her maid and Austin. And Hercules, under the idea of coming home to cook whilst we remained there, might be sent on in the stage." Washington and Martha would be in Virginia between sessions of Congress. Again, discretion was paramount. "I request that these sentiments and this advice may be known to none but *yourself* and *Mrs. Washington.*"

Lear did the further investigating Washington wanted. "I have had a very full conversation with the attorney general respecting your slaves, without however, letting him know that I had heard from you on the subject; but entered upon it with this introduction that as you were absent and could not return before the expiration of the term which the law of this state specifies for the residence of a slave, I thought it my duty to take such advice and such measures in the business, with the concurrence of Mrs. Washington, as might be proper in the occasion, having a due regard to your public station," Lear wrote to Washington.

"The attorney general made the following observations on the subject. That he found it was a received construction of the law, and one which he thought the words of the law fully warranted, that if a slave is brought into the state and continues therein for the space of six months, he may claim his freedom, let the cause of his being brought be what it may; and that this extends, in its full force, to those slaves who may be brought here by the officers of the general government or by members of Congress. If a man becomes a *citizen* of the state, six months residence of the slave is not necessary for his"—the slave's—"liberation; he is free from the moment his master is a citizen; the term of six months being only intended for the slaves of such as might travel through or sojourn in the state."

The rules were different for minors. Some of Washington's slaves in Philadelphia apparently fit this description. "That those slaves who were under the age of 18 might, after a residence of six months, apply to the overseers of the poor, who had authority to bind them to a master until they should attain the age of 18, when they would become free. That the overseers made it a point to bind the young slaves to their original masters, unless there should be some special reason against it; but after they are so bound they cannot be carried out of the state without their own consent."

Randolph had also commented on the abolitionist movement in Philadelphia, Lear told Washington. "That the society in this city for the abolition of slavery had determined to give no advice and take no measures for liberating those slaves which belonged to the officers of the general government or members of Congress. But notwithstanding this, there were not wanting persons who would not only give them (the slaves) advice, but would use all means to entice them from their masters. This being the case, the attorney general conceived, that after six months residence, your slaves would be upon no better footing than his."

Yet Randolph had a further observation. "That if, before the expiration of six months, they could, upon any pretense whatever, be carried or sent out of the state but for a single day, a new era would commence on their return, from whence the six months must be dated for it requires an *entire* six months for them to claim that right."

Randolph's interpretation of the law prompted Lear to specify a scheme for holding Washington's slaves in bondage. "I think that there will be but little difficulty in it," he told Washington. "For Austin is now at home on a visit to his wife, by Mrs. Washington's permission. This will oblige him to commence a new date for six months from his return, which will be next week. Richmond goes in a vessel that sails tomorrow for Alexandria, and I shall propose to Hercules, as he will be wanted at home in June when you return there, to take an early opportunity of going thither, as his services here can now be very well dispensed with, and by being at home before your arrival he will have it in his power to see his friends and make every necessary preparation in his kitchen."

Mrs. Washington would do her part. "Mrs. Washington proposes in a short time to make an excursion as far as Trenton, and of course she will take with her Oney and Christopher, which will carry them out of the state, so that in this way I think the matter may be managed very well." Lear added, "As Mrs. Washington does not incline to go to Virginia until you return to this place, the foregoing arrangement is the best I can think of to accomplish this business."

Lear was least sure that Hercules would do what was asked. Refusal would be revealing. "If Hercules should decline the offer which will be made him of going home, it will be a pretty strong proof of his intention to take the advantage of the law at the expiration of six months."

AFTER OUTLINING A PLAN whereby Washington could trick or manipulate his slaves into remaining slaves, Lear confessed to qualms of conscience, which he shared with Washington. "You will permit me now, sir, (and I am sure you will pardon me for doing it) to declare that no consideration should induce me to take these steps to prolong the slavery of a human being had I not the fullest confidence that they will at some future period be liberated, and the strongest conviction that their situation with you is far preferable to what they would probably obtain in a state of freedom."

Lear's expression of confidence that Washington's slaves would be freed in the future suggested that Washington had spoken to him to that effect. But Washington would free them, if he did, in his own time and not according to Pennsylvania law or the preferences of his slaves themselves.

Events unfolded much as Lear suggested. The slaves who tended to Martha Washington went with her, either unaware of their options or unwilling to risk Washington's displeasure. Hercules returned to Mount Vernon without making objection.

→ 86 ←

"Major L'Enfant comes on to make such a survey of the grounds in your vicinity as may aid in fixing the site of the federal town and buildings," Washington wrote that same spring to William Deakins and Benjamin Stoddert, merchants and land speculators in Georgetown, Maryland. Pierre Charles L'Enfant was a Frenchman who had traveled to America to fight in the Revolutionary War. He rose to the rank of major of engineers and was on Washington's staff at Valley Forge. He remained in America after the war and developed a successful architectural practice in New York. He landed government work redesigning New York's old city hall as Federal Hall.

L'Enfant had sought additional work in a letter to Washington. "The late determination of Congress to lay the foundation of a city which is to become the capital of this vast empire offers so great an occasion of acquiring reputation to whoever may be appointed to conduct the execution of the business that your Excellency will not be surprised that my ambition and the desire I have of becoming a useful citizen should lead me to wish a share in the undertaking," L'Enfant said. "No nation perhaps had ever before the opportunity offered them of deliberately deciding on the spot where their capital city should be fixed, or of combining every necessary consideration in the choice of situation." He realized Rome hadn't been built in a day, and neither would this capital. "Although the means now within the power of the country are not such as to pursue the design to any great extent, it will be obvious that the plan should be drawn on such a scale as to leave room for that aggrandisement and embellishment which the increase of the wealth of the nation will permit it to pursue at any period however remote."

Washington shelved L'Enfant's offer until Congress decided where the new capital would be. When it did, he offered L'Enfant the job of surveying the ground for the federal district. "The President, having thought Major L'Enfant peculiarly qualified to make such a draught of the ground as will enable himself to fix on the spot for the public buildings, he has been written to for that purpose and will be sent on if he chooses to undertake it," Thomas Jefferson wrote to the commissioners appointed to supervise the federal district. The secretary of state's portfolio included such things in those days.

L'Enfant did choose to undertake the assignment, which had prompted Washington's letter to Deakins and Stoddert. Washington had directed L'Enfant to particular tracts. "His present instructions express those alone which are within the Eastern Branch"—of the Potomac, also called the Anacostia River—"the Potomac, the Tiber"—a creek—"and the road leading from Georgetown to the ferry on the Eastern Branch," Washington told the merchant-speculators. "He is directed to begin at the lower end and work upwards, and nothing further is communicated to him. The purpose of this letter is to desire you will not be yourselves misled by this appearance, nor be diverted from the pursuit of the objects I have recommended to you. I expect that your progress in accomplishing them will be facilitated by the presumption which will arise on seeing this operation begun at the Eastern Branch, and that the proprietors nearer Georgetown who have hitherto refused to accommodate will let themselves down to reasonable terms."

Washington had been in the land business long enough to appreciate that a hint of government interest in any property would cause its owner to hold out for a high price. L'Enfant was starting his survey farthest from Georgetown, to deflate those proprietors' extortionate demands. As in some of Washington's previous land dealings, discretion was essential. "Should there be any difficulties on this subject, I would hope your aid in having them surmounted, though I have not named you to him or anybody else, that no suspicions may be excited of your acting for the public," Washington told Deakins and Stoddert.

"THE NATIONAL GAZETTE SHALL be published on the Monday and Thursday mornings of every week in the city of Philadelphia, and sent to the more distant subscribers by the most ready and regular modes of conveyance. Such persons resident in the city of Philadelphia as incline to become subscribers shall be supplied early on the mornings of publication at their own houses. The price will be three dollars a year." Coverage would be ambitious. "The paper shall contain, among other interesting particulars, the most important foreign intelligence, collected not only from the British, French and Dutch newspapers (a constant and punctual supply of which has been engaged) but also from original communications, letters, and other papers to which the editor may have an opportunity of recurring for the most authentic information relative to the affairs of Europe. The department for domestic news will be rendered as complete and satisfactory as possible by inserting a judicious detail of such occurrences as shall appear worthy the notice of the public. The most respectful attention shall be paid to all decent productions of entertainment in prose or verse that may be sent for insertion, as well as to such political essays as have a tendency to promote the general interests of the Union. There will also be inserted during the sessions of Congress a brief history of the debates and proceedings of the supreme legislature of the United States, executed, it is hoped, in such a manner as to answer the expectations and gratify the curiosity of every reader."

With these words Philip Freneau launched the first opposition newspaper in America. There was more to the paper than first appeared. Freneau was moonlighting as a journalist. His day job was at the state department, where Jefferson had hired him to be a translator. The work wasn't demanding, which was a good thing since Freneau's mastery of foreign languages ended with French. In reality, Jefferson put him on the payroll to argue against the policies of the Washington administration—of which Jefferson of course was a part.

Jefferson was acting in self-defense. Hamilton had been sponsoring a pro-administration paper for some time. John Fenno was an ardent federalist who devoted his *Gazette of the United States* to the fine work Hamilton and the Washington administration were doing for the federalist cause. In exchange Hamilton secured loans and government business for Fenno's paper.

A first task of the administration had been to staff government offices. "The President with his usual prudence and discernment has appointed able men to fill them, who are stimulated by every motive to a diligent and active employment of their eminent talents," the *Gazette* declared. The financial policies of the administration had been especially astute. "The states have been eased of their debts, which would have crushed some of them by their weight," Fenno said of the assumption program. "The revenue of the whole country, under one system of management, will enable the United States to provide for them, almost without feeling the burden." The national bank was an even more brilliant idea. "The bank is an institution which our extensive and wealthy country ought not to be without. It will assist us to extend our intercourse from north to south, and we shall like one another better as we know one another more." Under the wise leadership of President Washington, the country's future couldn't be brighter. "America, which was in the *shade* before, seems now to stand in the *sunshine*. Its prospects are the brightest that any nation on earth enjoys."

Jefferson could stand this cheerleading for only so long. The passage of the bank bill prompted him to hire Freneau to present the opposition viewpoint. Freneau opened the pages of the *National Gazette* to voices critical of Washington and Hamilton. A regular, albeit covert, contributor was Madison, whose conversion to antifederalism was even more striking than Jefferson's, given that Madison was the father of American federalism. Madison anonymously lashed Washington for letting Hamilton hijack the Constitution by such measures as assumption and the bank bill and lead the country away from republicanism toward monarchy. "The Union: who are its real friends?" asked Madison accusingly. "Not those who favor measures which by pampering the spirit of speculation within and without the government disgust the best friends of the Union." Assumption was the prime example. "Not those who promote unnecessary accumulations of the debt of the union instead of the best means of discharging it as fast as possible, thereby increasing the causes of corruption in the government and the pretexts for new taxes under its authority, the former undermining the confidence, the latter alienating the affection of the people." Hamilton's praise of debt, and the policies to which his attitude gave rise, did precisely this. "Not those who study by arbitrary interpretations and insidious precedents to pervert the limited government of the Union into a government of unlimited discretion, contrary to the will and subversive of the authority of the people." Hamilton's radical interpretation of the Constitution, and Washington's acceptance of his interpretation, unmasked their unfriendliness to republicanism.

Madison grew more heated behind his anonymity than he ever did in public. He characterized the country as approaching a divide between republicanism and monarchy. "The real friends to the Union are those who are friends to the authority of the people, the sole foundation on which the Union rests; who are friends to liberty, the great end for which the Union was formed; who are friends to the limited and republican system of government, the means provided by that authority for the attainment of that end; who are enemies to every public measure that might smooth the way to hereditary government, for resisting the tyrannies of which the Union was first planned, and for more effectually excluding which it was put into its present form; who considering a public debt as injurious to the interests of the people and baneful to the virtue of the government, are enemies to every contrivance for unnecessarily increasing its amount, or protracting its duration, or extending its influence." Madison summarized his separation of the sheep from the goats: "In a word, those are the real friends to the Union who are friends to that republican policy throughout which is the only cement for the Union of a republican people, in opposition to a spirit of usurpation and monarchy."

"USURPATION AND MONARCHY"—harsher words could hardly be leveled against the government of a constitutional republic. They became the theme of the *National Gazette,* which found their trace in the unlikeliest events. "It is incumbent on everyone who regards the interest and happiness of his country to take notice of every shoal and rock that have proved fatal to other republics and endeavour to guard against the like mischance in this happy land," warned a writer signing as "Valerius." "Unpleasant as the talk is to publicly censure the conduct of any of my fellow citizens, yet as the public welfare, in my opinion, is involved, I conceive that silence would be criminal."

What was the heinous offense? "The measure I allude to is the celebrating the birthday of the President of the United States by a part of the city militia. It appears by the conduct of some men that we are only republicans in name and not in principle. For surely the customs and manners emanating from, and congenial with, monarchy must be incongruous in a republic. Who will deny that the celebrating of birthdays is not a striking feature of royalty? We hear of no such thing during the republic of Rome. Even Cincinnatus, now consigned to immortal fame, received no adulation of this kind."

Valerius didn't cast aspersions on Washington directly. Or at least he professed not to. "I am as sensible of the services of the president as any man, and think him worthy of the high regard of his country. But surely the office he enjoys is a sufficient testimony of the people's favor, without worshipping him likewise. I believe I may venture to say that such fulsome adulation does not accord with his feelings. If this evil was of no greater extent than merely debasing those who are in the practice of it, I should not feel much concern. But when I consider it as a forerunner of other monarchical vices, and holding up an improper example in this country, and an example of precedent, I cannot but execrate the measure."

The camp followers of the president would cry sedition at such criticism, Valerius predicted. "I trust, however, for the honour of my country that such characters are not as yet numerous here." The tendency was ominous, though. "I appeal then to the good sense of my countrymen whether, by placing one man above all equality and heaping honours upon him, it does not in the same proportion lessen the consequence of every other person. And whether this is not sowing the seeds of distinctions and inequality which will indubitably produce a change in our government."

It might not happen under Washington. But Washington's successor might be a different sort. "He may possess immoderate ambition and a desire of dominion. Dazzled with the splendor of his station and puffed up with the homage that a misguided people have annexed to that office, he will expect other marks of adulation besides celebrating his birthday, attending his levees etc. And his courtiers and sycophants, for there will always be such animals, will conspire with him to produce them. His person must be made inviolable, and placed above all law. Thus by degrees equality, the great foundation of our liberties, will be undermined. The people, having unfortunately suffered habits of servility to gain strength among them, and their minds being of course corrupted, will not see their danger until it is too late to be remedied."

→ 87 ←

As much as Jefferson decried the direction of the country under Washington's presidency, he thought things would get worse if Washington *weren't* president. Jefferson judged Washington a check on the more egregious aspects of Hamilton's federalism, and he did his best to get the president to consent to serve a second term. "I have determined to make the subject of a letter what for some time past has been a subject of inquietude to my mind, without having found a good occasion of disburthening itself to you in conversation during the busy scenes which occupied you here," Jefferson wrote to Washington in the spring of 1792. He was putting his thoughts to paper so that the president could read them when he did have some leisure. "When you first mentioned to me your purpose of retiring from the government, though I felt all the magnitude of the event, I was in a considerable degree silent." Washington had never disguised that he accepted the presidency as an obligation, to be relinquished as soon as he honorably could.

"I knew that to such a mind as yours, persuasion was idle and impertinent: that before forming your decision you had weighed all the reasons for and against the measure, had made up your mind on full view of them, and that there could be little hope of changing the result," Jefferson continued. "Pursuing my reflections too I knew we were some day to try to walk alone, and if the essay should be made while you should be alive and looking on, we should derive confidence from that circumstance, and resource if it failed. The public mind too was then calm and confident, and therefore in a favorable state for making the experiment. Had no change of circumstances supervened, I should not, with any hope of success, have now ventured to propose to you a change of purpose."

But conditions had changed. "The public mind is no longer so confident and serene." Jefferson didn't blame Washington. Yet he did blame Hamilton, who operated with Washington's approval. The treasury secretary and his federalist allies in Congress were collaborating closely with merchants and moneylenders, giving rise to complaints from republicans that American liberty was at stake. Jefferson conveyed to Washington the republican indictment of the federalist program, in case Washington hadn't read it in the *National Gazette.* "That it nourishes in our citizens habits of vice and idleness instead of industry and morality," Jefferson wrote. "That it has furnished effectual means of corrupting such a portion of the legislature as turns the balance between the honest voters whichever way it is directed. That this corrupt squadron, deciding the voice of the legislature, have manifested their dispositions to get rid of the limitations imposed by the constitution on the general legislature—limitations, on the faith of which the states acceded to that instrument. That the ultimate object of all this is to prepare the way for a change from the present republican form of government to that of a monarchy, of which the English constitution is to be the model."

The actions of the federalists were invigorating the republicans, whose number increased by the month, Jefferson said. They might soon be a majority in the country, if they weren't already. The federalists wouldn't yield without a fight. And in such a fight lay the great danger to the Union. "I can scarcely contemplate a more incalculable evil than the breaking of the union into two or more parts," Jefferson said to Washington. Yet this was what the federalist policies portended. "Whenever northern and southern prejudices have come into conflict, the latter have been sacrificed and the former soothed." The southern disadvantage was nowhere sharper than on financial questions. "The owers of the debt are in the southern and the holders of it in the northern division." The more the federalists had their way with policy, the deeper the division between sections grew, with a rupture the likely result.

"This is the event at which I tremble," Jefferson said, "and to prevent which I consider your continuance at the head of affairs as of the last importance." Washington's leadership had been indispensable at the launch of the new government, but it was more indispensable now. "The confidence of the whole union is centered in you. Your being at the helm will be more than an answer to every argument which can be used to alarm and lead the people in any quarter into violence or secession. North and south will hang together if they have you to hang on."

Jefferson appreciated that this wasn't what Washington wanted to hear. "I am perfectly aware of the oppression under which your present office lays your mind, and of the ardor with which you pant for retirement to domestic life." But as he had before, Washington must put the interest of the country, indeed of republicanism at large, above his own. "There is sometimes an eminence of character on which society have such peculiar claims as to control the predilection of the individual for a particular walk of happiness and restrain him to that alone arising from the present and future benedictions of mankind. This seems to be your condition, and the law imposed on you by providence in forming your character and fashioning the events on which it was to operate. And it is to motives like these, and not to personal anxieties of mine or others who have no right to call on you for sacrifices, that I appeal from your former determination and urge a revisal of it on the ground of change in the aspect of things."

Washington needn't serve out a full second term. If the republicans could win a majority in Congress and put the federalists in the minority where they belonged, all might be well. "One or two sessions will determine the crisis," Jefferson said. "I cannot but hope that you can resolve to add one or two more to the many years you have already sacrificed to the good of mankind."

HAMILTON AGREED WITH Jefferson on very little these days. But he concurred that the president mustn't retire yet. "I received the most sincere pleasure at finding in our last conversation that there was some relaxation in the disposition you had before discovered to decline a reelection," Hamilton wrote to Washington just after the president left Philadelphia for Mount Vernon during the summer recess of Congress in July 1792. "Since your departure I have lost no opportunity of sounding the opinions of persons whose opinions were worth knowing on these two points—1st the effect of your declining upon the public affairs and upon your own reputation—2dly. the effect of your continuing, in reference to the declarations you have made of your disinclination to public life." As always, Washington worried about his reputation, Hamilton knew. If Washington left office, would people think him a shirker? If he held on, would they dismiss his disclaimers of ambition?

"The impression is uniform that your declining would be deplored as the greatest evil that could befall the country at the present juncture and as critically hazardous to your own reputation," Hamilton said. "That your continuance will be justified in the mind of every friend to his country by the evident necessity for it. Tis clear, says everyone with whom I have conversed, that the affairs of the national government are not yet firmly established; that its enemies, generally speaking, are as inveterate as ever; that their enmity has been sharpened by its success and by all the resentments which flow from disappointed predictions and mortified vanity; that a general and strenuous effort is making in every state to place the administration of it in the hands of its enemies, as if they were its safest guardians."

Hamilton appended another page of reasons, emphasizing the perfidy of the administration's opponents, before concluding: "That on public and personal accounts, on patriotic and prudential considerations, the clear path to be pursued by you will be again to obey the voice of your country, which it is not doubted will be as earnest and as unanimous as ever."

WASHINGTON MIGHT HAVE wondered if Jefferson and Hamilton were describing two separate countries, so starkly did their diagnoses of American politics differ. He might have wondered, as well, how long two such divergent views could exist within a single administration.

Yet he didn't have to choose between the diagnoses to accept the common prescription: that he remain in office. Before he did, though, he lectured the two cabinet secretaries on how they contributed to the very problem they decried.

Washington wrote to Jefferson regarding certain difficulties the British and Spanish were causing with Indians on America's frontiers. At the end of this discussion he turned to domestic affairs. "How unfortunate, and how much is it to be regretted then, that whilst we are encompassed on all sides with avowed enemies and insidious friends, that internal dissensions should be harrowing and tearing our vitals. The last, to me, is the most serious, the most alarming, and the most afflicting of the two. And without more charity for the opinions and acts of one another in governmental matters, or some more infallible criterion by which the truth of speculative opinions, before they have undergone the test of experience, are to be forejudged than has yet fallen to the lot of fallibility, I believe it will be difficult, if not impracticable, to manage the reins of government or to keep the parts of it together."

Washington didn't object to the vigorous airing of opinions while a decision pended. But once made, a decision ought to be implemented by a united administration. "For if, instead of laying our shoulders to the machine after measures are decided on, one pulls this way and another that, before the utility of the thing is fairly tried, it must inevitably be torn asunder. And in my opinion the fairest prospect of happiness and prosperity that ever was presented to man will be lost, perhaps forever!"

Speaking almost as a father to his son, Washington declared, "My earnest wish and my fondest hope therefore is that instead of wounding suspicions and irritable charges, there may be liberal allowances, mutual forbearances and temporising yieldings on all sides. Under the exercise of these, matters will go on smoothly and if possible more prosperously. Without them everything must rub. The wheels of government will clog. Our enemies will triumph, and by throwing their weight into the disaffected scale may accomplish the ruin of the goodly fabric we have been erecting."

Washington assured Jefferson he wasn't blaming him alone. "I do not mean to apply these observations or this advice to any particular person or character. I have given them in the same general terms to other officers of the government, because the disagreements which have arisen from difference of opinions and the attacks which have been made upon almost all the measures of government and most of its executive officers have for a long time past filled me with painful sensations, and cannot fail, I think, of producing unhappy consequences at home and abroad."

Washington wrote in similar vein to Hamilton. "Differences in political opinions are as unavoidable as, to a certain point, they may perhaps be necessary," he said. But the differences must be kept within bounds. And they mustn't give rise to imputations of evil motives. "I would fain hope that liberal allowances will be made for the political opinions of one another." Washington refused to believe that the obstructions to policy represented anything more than the opinions of individuals. "I cannot prevail on myself to believe that these measures are, as yet, the deliberate acts of a determined party," he told Hamilton. "Melancholy thought!"

Washington sincerely desired that matters not come to that. "My earnest wish is that balsam may be poured into all the wounds which have been given, to prevent them from gangrening, and from those fatal consequences which the community may sustain if it is withheld. The friends of the Union must wish this." Washington certainly did. "And all things I hope will go well."

88

Possibly—just possibly—Washington's plea for forbearance between Hamilton and the federalists, on one hand, and Jefferson and the republicans, on the other, might have borne fruit had the world beyond American shores not taken a swift and violent turn. The French revolution began mere months after Washington's inauguration as president. America joined much of Europe in watching the old regime unravel and a new order take its place. Americans were of two minds about the whole business. Jefferson, who as American minister to France observed at first hand the initial stages of the revolution, was an admirer of most things French. He was also, as author of the Declaration of Independence, an ardent believer in natural rights and the capacity of people to govern themselves. He applauded the overthrow of the monarchy of Louis XVI and the establishment of a republic in its place. He deemed the revolution in France a worthy sequel to America's revolution, with all that this implied for human betterment.

Hamilton reacted quite differently to the French revolution. Where Jefferson was a democrat at heart, esteeming the people above government, Hamilton leaned aristocratic, convinced that people needed to be restrained by government, which ought to reflect the interests of the well educated and well-off. Jefferson hoped for the best from the French revolution. Hamilton expected the worst.

The first few years of the French revolution required no major decisions from the American government. The revolution was an internal affair, for the most part. But the monarchies of Europe judged it a baleful influence upon their own realms and expressed their hostility in various ways, including giving refuge to émigrés who plotted the demise of the revolution and their own restoration to French power. Accurately perceiving a threat, and cynically employing it to stifle their domestic critics, the leaders of the revolution declared war on Austria, then Prussia, then

Britain. The invasion of France by Austria and Prussia triggered a shift in power in Paris to the most extreme group, the Jacobins, who executed Louis and launched a bloody purge of their opponents.

The new violence made the French revolution easier for Hamilton and the federalists to assail and harder for Jefferson and the republicans to justify. Emotions and accusations ran hot. Hamilton's side pointed to the terror in France as what the levelers in America were knowingly or inadvertently attempting to reproduce. Jefferson's backers said the crushing weight of French autocracy had driven the French people to extremes and that foreign autocracy was trying to crush the French people still.

Once Britain joined the war against France, the side-taking in America had direct implications for American policy. The alliance from the Revolutionary War continued to bind America to France, causing some of the Jeffersonians to advocate assistance to the French. At the least it caused the republicans to wish republican France well against its reactionary enemies. The Hamiltonians had never warmed to France, finding greater value in the traditions of Britain, despite the break with Britain over independence. That issue having been resolved, the federalists favored the reestablishment of trade ties and other connections to the erstwhile mother country.

The moral heat of the moment congealed the factions around Hamilton and Jefferson into political parties. The federalists became the Federalists, and the republicans the Republicans, although their opponents called the former monarchists and the latter radical democrats.

"MELANCHOLY THOUGHT!" HAD BEEN Washington's reaction to the idea of parties. It grew more melancholy as the parties took firmer shape. His lectures to Jefferson and Hamilton on forbearance constituted one part of his effort to slow the ominous trend. His refusal to identify with either party constituted another. This was no more successful than his lectures, to which each of the protagonists responded that forbearance was lost on the other.

Washington could present himself as being above party. He could even think of himself as above party, doubtless sincerely. But his support of Hamilton's policies made him look decidedly Federalist.

In one area, though, Washington's impartiality took concretely effective form. His reelection was as predictable as his first election, once he decided not to retire. He again received a vote from every elector. John

Adams again got the most second votes and remained vice president. Washington's second inauguration was unmemorable and his second inaugural address perfunctory. He turned to the business at hand.

Most pressing was the war in Europe. The beleaguered government of France appealed to America for support, citing the treaty that remained in effect and the memory of Franco-American solidarity against British imperialism. If anyone should remember that collaboration, the French government said, it was Washington, who had fought side by side with Rochambeau at Yorktown, under the naval protection of de Grasse.

Yet Washington ignored the treaty and the French appeals, which resonated with Republicans. He similarly shunned efforts by Federalists to align the United States with Britain, on grounds of former affinity and future commerce. Finally, he ignored the letter and spirit of the Constitution that placed decisions on war and peace in the hands of Congress.

In April 1793, Washington issued a proclamation: "Whereas it appears that a state of war exists between Austria, Prussia, Sardinia, Great Britain, and the United Netherlands on the one part and France on the other, and the duty and interest of the United States require that they should with sincerity and good faith adopt and pursue a conduct friendly and impartial toward the belligerent powers, I have therefore thought fit by these presents to declare the disposition of the United States to observe the conduct aforesaid toward those powers respectively, and to exhort and warn the citizens of the United States carefully to avoid all acts and proceedings whatsoever which may in any manner tend to contravene such disposition." In a word, Washington declared neutrality.

Washington wasn't known for political shrewdness. If charged with same, he would have denied it, saying he dealt in principle, not calculation. But never did Washington act more shrewdly in politics, and rarely did any of his presidential successors. By the neutrality proclamation, Washington snatched the issue of the European war out of the hands of the partisan Federalists and Republicans. He couldn't keep them from silently rooting for the side they favored, but by exhorting them to "avoid all acts and proceedings whatsoever which may in any manner tend to contravene" America's "friendly and impartial" policy toward the belligerents, he preemptively positioned violators as disregarding America's national interest.

And he did so in what by any nonpartisan calculation was the best interest of the United States. Washington wasn't Machiavelli, but he understood that material interest rather than emotion ought to guide the affairs of state. He had been delighted to have the assistance of Rochambeau and de Grasse at Yorktown, but he recognized that they were there not for love of America but for love of France. Washington must be equally solicitous of America. Washington was the first president to identify what would be a core interest of the United States for more than a century: neutrality amid the wars of other countries. Europe was far away from America, and Washington was happy for it to remain afar. Most Americans agreed—even, at this point, most who identified as Federalists and Republicans.

There was a bonus in all this for a strong-minded president. The Constitution specified that only Congress could declare war. It said nothing about declarations of non-war—neutrality. Did these lie with Congress too? The question hadn't come up. And before it did, Washington claimed the prerogative for the president.

Objectors could dispute his action on this ground, and some did. But because few disputed the substance of Washington's decision, procedural carping seemed frivolous. Over time, presidents would whittle away the power of Congress and expand their own, until the executive branch would often overshadow the legislative. Washington couldn't see that far ahead. But his proclamation of neutrality was a first step toward getting there.

— 89 —

Mathew Carey was born in Ireland in 1760. He apprenticed in the printing business, where, besides learning to set type and compose pages, he developed a knack for provoking Ireland's British overlords. The authorities threatened prosecution, causing Carey to flee to Paris, where he met another former printer's apprentice and continuing scourge of Britain, Benjamin Franklin. Carey worked in the print shop Franklin established in Paris as a distraction from his diplomatic chores. Eventually Carey emigrated to America. Franklin's recommendation letter helped him start a printing business of his own in Philadelphia.

Carey was in Philadelphia when the national government returned from its New York exile. He described a city full of promise and problems. "The manufactures, trade and commerce of Philadelphia had, for a considerable time, been improving and extending with great rapidity," Carey wrote. "From the period of the adoption of the federal government, at which time we were at the lowest ebb of distress, our situation had progressively become more and more prosperous. Confidence, formerly banished, was universally restored. Property of every kind rose to and in some cases beyond its real value. And a few revolving years exhibited the interesting spectacle of a young country with a new form of government emerging from a state approaching very near to anarchy and acquiring all the stability and nerve of the best toned and oldest nations.

"In this prosperity, which revived the hopes of four millions of people"—the population of the United States—"Philadelphia participated in an eminent degree," Carey continued. "New houses in almost every street, built in a very neat, elegant style, adorned at the same time that they enlarged the city. Its population was extending fast." Growth was good, until it got out of control. Rent rocketed upward. "It was in many cases double and in some cases treble what it had been a year or two before. And as is generally the case when a city is thriving, it went far beyond the real increase of trade. The number of applicants for houses exceeding the number of houses to be let, one bid over another."

Ordinary people suffered the squeeze, but the wealthy flourished. "Luxury, the usual and perhaps inevitable concomitant of prosperity, was gaining ground in a manner very alarming to those who considered how far the virtue, the liberty and the happiness of a nation depend on their temperance and sober manners," Carey said. The simplest things became nearly impossible. "The number of coaches, coachees, chairs etc. lately set up by men in the middle rank of life is hardly credible. And although there had been a very great increase of hackney chairs, yet it was hardly ever possible to procure one on a Sunday, unless it was engaged two or three days before." The sober town of William Penn had all but disappeared. "Extravagance, in various shapes, was gradually eradicating the plain and wholesome habits of the city."

Philadelphia was the banking capital of America, and its financial sector felt the strains. "From November 1792 to the end of last June"—Carey was writing in late 1793—"the difficulties of Philadelphia were extreme. The establishment of the Bank of Pennsylvania, in embryo for the most part of that time, had arrested in the two other banks such a quantity of the circulation species as impaired almost every kind of business." That is, the projected appearance of a new bank disrupted the existing banks. "To this was added the distress arising from the very numerous failures in England which had extremely harassed several of our capital merchants." Philadelphia's merchants and financiers had reestablished some trade with Britain. "During this period, many men experienced as great difficulties as were ever known in this city."

But the crisis eased in July 1793. "The opening in July of the Bank of Pennsylvania, conducted on the most liberal principles, placed business on its former favorable footing. Every man looked forward to this fall as likely to produce a vast extension of trade."

INTO THIS BRIGHTENING PICTURE came a ship sailing under a dark cloud. A revolution in the French West Indian colony of St. Domingue—later Haiti—had sent members of the old regime fleeing for their lives. Hundreds arrived in Philadelphia. At first they were greeted with the traditional Quaker affinity for refugees. Philadelphians took up a collection and within days gathered twelve thousand dollars for their relief.

That some of the refugees were sick occasioned little surprise. The troubles that had sent them into exile, and the sea voyage north, could reasonably account for fevers and the like. But by the end of July residents of the city began to fall ill. A physician's child showed symptoms on the last days of the month and died in early August. A lodger who lived on Water Street became sick on a Friday and died on Sunday. Another lodger in the same house died a day later.

Local experts, such as they were, conjectured causes. One doctor put the blame on a cargo of putrid coffee at the wharf. Benjamin Rush, a prominent physician besides being a signer of the Declaration of Independence and a civic leader, concurred. Yet opinions differed, with many pointing to the craft that brought the refugees from the Caribbean.

What none could deny was the rapid spread of the disease identified as yellow fever. "The mortality began about that part of Water Street where the Mary, the Flora and the Sans Culottes lay," wrote Mathew Carey, referring to three ships. "For some time it was entirely confined to that place and its neighbourhood. Almost every death which occurred in the early stage of the disorder could be without difficulty traced to that street. By degrees it spread, owing to the want of precaution and to communication with the infected. It is said and generally believed that the beds and bedding of those who died of the disorder at first, before the alarm went abroad, were sold and spread it among the buyers.

"Several persons were swept away before any great alarm was excited. The first deaths that attracted public notice and struck terror among the citizens were those of Peter Aston, on the 19th, of Mrs. Lemaigre, on the 20th, and of Thomas Miller, on the 25th of August. About this time began the removals from the city, which were for some weeks so general that almost every hour in the day, carts, wagons, coaches and chairs were to be seen transporting families and furniture to the country in every direction. Business then became extremely dull. Mechanics and artists were unemployed, and the streets wore the appearance of gloom and melancholy."

Government took action in late August. "The mayor of Philadelphia, Matthew Clarkson, Esq., wrote to the city commissioners and, after acquainting them with the state of the city, gave them the most peremptory orders to have the streets properly cleansed and purified by the scavengers and all the filth immediately hauled away," Carey wrote. "These orders were repeated on the 27th, and similar ones given to the clerks of the market. The 29th the governor of the state, in his address to the legislature, acquainted them that a contagious disorder existed in the city, and that he had taken every proper measure to ascertain the origin, nature and extent of it. He likewise assured them that the health officer and physician of the port would take every precaution to allay and remove the public inquietude."

The doctors of Philadelphia's medical school proposed measures to curb the epidemic. "They published an address to the citizens, signed by the president and secretary, recommending to avoid all unnecessary intercourse with the infected, to place marks on the doors or windows where they were, to pay great attention to cleanliness and airing the rooms of the sick, to provide a large and airy hospital in the neighbourhood of the city for their reception, to put a stop to the tolling of the bells"—mourning the dead—"to bury those who died of the disorder in carriages and as privately as possible, to keep the streets and wharves clean, to avoid all fatigue of body and mind in standing or sitting in the sun or in the open air, to accommodate the dress to the weather and to exceed rather in warm than in cool clothing, and to avoid intemperance but to use fermented liquors such as wine, beer and cider with moderation."

Carey and others welcomed especially the order about the bells. "This was a very expedient measure, as they had before been kept pretty constantly going the whole day, so as to terrify those in health and drive the sick as far as the influence of the imagination could produce that effect to their graves."

Nothing worked. The death toll rose inexorably. "The consternation of the people of Philadelphia at that period was carried beyond all bounds. Dismay and affright were visible in almost every person's countenance. Most people who could by any means make it convenient fled from the city. Of those who remained, many shut themselves up in their houses and were afraid to walk the streets. The consumption of gunpowder and nitre in houses as a preventative was inconceivable." The explosions were thought to scatter whatever it was in the air causing the disease. "Many were almost incessantly purifying, scouring and whitewashing their rooms. Those who ventured abroad had handkerchiefs or sponges impregnated with vinegar or camphor at their noses."

People desperately tried to avoid infection. "The corpses of the most respectable citizens, even of those who did not die of the epidemic, were carried to the grave on the shafts of a chair, the horse driven by a negro, unattended by a friend or relation, and without any sort of ceremony," Carey wrote. "People shifted their course at the sight of a hearse coming towards them. Many never walked on the footpath but went into the middle of the streets to avoid being infected in passing by houses wherein people had died. Acquaintances and friends avoided each other in the streets and only signified their regard by a cold nod. The old custom of shaking hands fell into such general disuse that many were affronted at even the offer of the hand. A person with a crape or any appearance of mourning was shunned like a viper. And many valued themselves highly on the skill and address with which they got to windward of every person they met. Indeed it is not probable that London, at the last stage of the plague"—of the 1660s, a benchmark of calamity—"exhibited stronger marks of terror than were to be seen in Philadelphia from the 26th or 27th of August till pretty late in September."

Basic relations broke down. "While affairs were in this deplorable state and people at the lowest ebb of despair," Carey wrote, "we cannot be astonished at the frightful scenes that were acted, which seemed to indicate a total dissolution of the bonds of society in the nearest and dearest connections. Who, without horror, can reflect on a husband deserting his wife, united to him perhaps for twenty years, in the last agony; a wife unfeelingly abandoning her husband on his deathbed; parents forsaking their only children; children ungratefully flying from their parents and resigning them to chance, often without an inquiry after their health or safety; masters hurrying off their faithful servants to Bush Hill"—an ad hoc hospital—"even on suspicion of the fever, and that at a time when like Tartarus it was open to every visitant but never returned any; servants abandoning tender and humane masters who only wanted a little care to restore them to health and usefulness—who, I say, can even now think of these things without horror? Yet such were daily exhibited in every quarter of our city."

MEMBERS OF CONGRESS were largely spared the epidemic. The legislature was not in session when the disease appeared. The executive was on duty, though. Washington watched with dismay. "The city is very sickly and numbers dying daily," the president wrote in late August. He was distressed to hear that Hamilton was showing symptoms. "I hope they are groundless," he said of the fears the symptoms raised. They weren't. Hamilton contracted a stubborn but not lethal case.

Washington and Martha left Philadelphia in September for a scheduled visit to Mount Vernon. He delayed their return in hopes the epidemic would ease. He investigated whether he could direct Congress to meet somewhere other than in Philadelphia. "Have you ever examined with attention, and with an eye to the case, whether the Constitution or laws of the Union give power to the executive to change the place of meeting of the legislature in cases of emergency in the recess?" he wrote to Edmund Randolph, the attorney general. "For example, whether the spreading of the fever which is so fatal in Philadelphia, thereby endangering the lives of the members who might assemble there the first Monday in December next"—when the new session would begin—"is a case that would come under any provision in either. If you have not, I pray you to do it and give me the result of your opinion."

Randolph replied that by his reading of the Constitution and applicable law, the executive had no such power. Article I declared, "Neither house, during the session of Congress, shall, without the consent of the other, adjourn for more than three days, nor to any other place than that in which the two houses shall be sitting." Congress had been sitting in Philadelphia, and because it hadn't voted to regather elsewhere, it had to return there. Moreover, the Residence Act of 1790 made Philadelphia the seat of government for ten years.

Randolph recommended doing nothing. "What harm can be done by leaving things in their usual channel? Perhaps by the first Monday in December next, Philadelphia may be restored to health and freed from infection." If not, Congress could meet briefly and itself adjourn to another place.

Washington accepted the advice and hoped for the best.

"THE DISORDER RAGED with increased violence as the season advanced toward the mild fall months," Mathew Carey reported. "In the month of September, the mortality was much greater than in August, and still greater in October, to the 25th, than in September."

Then things changed. "The 26th may be set down as the day when the virulence of the fever expired. The deaths afterwards were mostly of those long sick. Hardly any persons have since taken it." Carey was writing in mid-November. "The week beginning Sunday the 27th of October proved for the most part cold and raw. Northerly winds generally prevailed."

Philadelphians had been hoping cooler weather would stem the disease. Autumn usually tamped down fevers, for reasons then unknown to medical science. In fact, the tropical mosquitoes that transmitted the yellow fever and had stowed away aboard the ships from the West Indies couldn't abide the chill.

"A visible alteration has already taken place in the state of affairs in the city," Carey continued with relief. "Our friends return in crowds. Every hour, long-absent and welcome faces appear." The city returned to business. "The stores, so long closed, are opening fast. Some of the country merchants, bolder than others, are daily venturing into their old place of supply. Market Street is almost as full of wagons as usual. The custom house, for weeks nearly deserted by our mercantile people, is thronged by citizens entering their vessels and goods. The streets, too long the abode of gloom and despair, have assumed the bustle suitable to the season."

Washington returned at just this time. "The arrival in the city of our beloved president gives us a flattering prospect of the next session of Congress being held here," Carey remarked. And Congress did reconvene in Philadelphia on schedule.

"In fine," said Carey, "as everything in the early stage of the disorder seemed calculated to add to the general consternation, so now, on the contrary, every circumstance has a tendency to revive the courage and hopes of our citizens."

— 90 —

Hamilton's grand scheme for an alliance between government and the class of merchants and bankers had a third element, after assumption and a national bank. In a "Report on the Subject of Manufactures," Hamilton proposed a system of subsidies to American industry, in the form of bounties to encourage domestic production and tariffs to discourage imports. By the time the report was delivered to the House of Representatives, Jefferson and Madison had mobilized the opposition sufficiently to keep Congress from accepting the whole package. They didn't like the larger government it entailed nor its tilt toward industry.

Yet government required revenues to fund its operations, including service of the assumed state debts. Congress approved tariffs, which raised revenue in the process of discouraging imports, and a list of excise taxes. One of the excise taxes was on distilled spirits and was commonly called the whiskey tax.

The whiskey tax invited evasion, especially by small distillers whose profit margins couldn't easily afford the new expense and who could hope to hide their operations from the tax inspectors. In rural parts of the country, Hamilton and the Federalists were unpopular to begin with, and the whiskey tax lost them much of what little support they had. Moreover, many of the tax resisters were old enough to remember that the American Revolution started with a tax revolt, and in regions such as western Pennsylvania they cast their cause in terms of patriotic liberty. When the tax inspectors came calling, the whiskey men insulted them, sabotaged their inspective efforts and sometimes did them bodily violence. More than a few of the whiskey men made specific reference to the violent protests against the Stamp Act.

Washington had no special interest in the whiskey tax. But he had sworn to execute his office and defend the Constitution, which included enforcing the law. He issued a proclamation decrying the "violent and unwarrantable proceedings" against the excise law and calling on Americans "to refrain and desist from all unlawful combinations and proceedings whatsoever" that violated or obstructed enforcement of the law. He enjoined the magistrates and courts in the affected districts to take care to follow the law for "the welfare of their country, the just and due authority of government and the preservation of the public peace."

The proclamation did little to deter the rebels, but it put the prestige and credibility of Washington and of the federal government on the line. Because the tax in question was a federal tax, its enforcement fell in the first instance on the federal government.

Hamilton, who *did* have an investment in the whiskey tax, by being its author, and who appreciated any opportunity to confirm the authority of the federal government, closely monitored the response to the president's declaration. He reported a serious challenge to the excise laws in a region Washington knew well from his early days as a soldier. "The opposition to those laws in the four most western counties of Pennsylvania (Allegheny, Washington, Fayette and Westmoreland) commenced as early as they were known to have been passed," Hamilton wrote. "It has continued with different degrees of violence in the different counties and at different periods. But Washington has uniformly distinguished its resistance by a more excessive spirit than has appeared in the other counties and seems to have been chiefly instrumental in kindling and keeping alive the flame."

The rebels prevented the authorities in the area from bringing the perpetrators to justice, as the federal marshal for the district reported. The marshal had sent out a deputy, who had promptly returned. "He declares that if he had attempted it, he believes he should not have returned alive," the marshal said, in an excerpt Hamilton passed on to Washington. Another deputy, who did go out, "was seized, whipped, tarred and feathered, and after having his money and horse taken from him, was blindfolded and tied in the woods, in which condition he remained for five hours," Hamilton paraphrased.

The miscreants defied not only authority but common decency. Hamilton described the case of a stranger in the area, "manifestly disordered in his intellects," who falsely claimed to be a tax collector. "This man was pursued by a party in disguise, taken out of his bed, carried about five miles back to a smith's shop, stripped of his clothes, which were afterwards burnt, and after having been himself inhumanly burnt in several places with a heated iron, was tarred and feathered, and about day light dismissed naked, wounded and otherwise in a very suffering condition." Hamilton added, "The affair is the more extraordinary as persons of weight and consideration in that county are understood to have been actors in it, and as the symptoms of insanity were during the whole time of inflicting the punishment apparent."

The insurrection spread. "A party of armed men in disguise made an attack in the night upon the house of a collector of the revenue, who resided in Fayette county," Hamilton wrote. "But he happening to be from home, they contented themselves with breaking open his house, threatening, terrifying and abusing his family." Warrants were issued for the arrest of some of the attackers. Yet the warrants went nowhere, for the authorities were either intimidated or actually in league with the rebels. "It is a truth too important to be unnoticed and too injurious not to be lamented that the prevailing spirit of those officers has been either hostile or lukewarm to the execution of those laws."

The authority of the government was in peril, Hamilton concluded to Washington. "The declared object of the foregoing proceedings is to obstruct the execution and compel a repeal of the laws laying duties upon spirits distilled within the United States and upon stills. There is just cause to believe that this is connected with an indisposition too general in that quarter to share in the common burthens of the community, and with a wish among some persons of influence to embarrass the government."

WHILE ALERTING WASHINGTON in private to the peril of the whiskey rebellion, Hamilton was beating the drums in public, though pseudonymously, for stern action against the uprising. In a series of essays signed "Tully," Hamilton warned Americans that the tax resistance was a test of the very principle of self-government. "It has from the first establishment of your present constitution been predicted that every occasion of serious embarrassment which should occur in the affairs of the government, every misfortune which it should experience, whether produced from its own faults or mistakes or from other causes, would be the signal of an attempt to overthrow it, or to lay the foundation of its overthrow, by defeating the exercise of constitutional and necessary authorities. The disturbances which have recently broken out in the western counties of Pennsylvania furnish an occasion of this sort." Government must make its stand. "Every virtuous man, every good citizen, and especially every true republican must fervently pray that the issue may confound and not confirm so ill-omened a prediction."

The foes of order insidiously called for compromise, for hearing out the rebels and accommodating their grievances, Hamilton said. The friends of order must close their ears to such counsel. "You should clearly discern in the present instance the shape in which a design of turning the existing insurrection to the prejudice of the government would naturally assume. Thus guarded, you will more readily discover and more easily shun the artful snare which may be laid to entangle your feelings and your judgment, and will be the less apt to be misled from the path by which alone you can give security and permanency to the blessings you enjoy and can avoid the incalculable mischiefs incident to a subversion of the just and necessary authority of the laws."

Nothing less than the fate of the Union was in the balance. "Virtuous and enlightened citizens of a now happy country! ye could not be the dupes of artifices so detestable, of a scheme so fatal; ye cannot be insensible to the destructive consequences with which it would be pregnant; ye cannot but remember that the government is your own work, that those who administer it are but your temporary agents, that you are called upon not to support their power but your own power. And you will not fail to do what your rights, your best interests, your character as a people, your security as members of society conspire to demand of you."

Hamilton employed the whiskey rebellion as a stick to beat the Republicans with. The rebellion wasn't about whiskey. It wasn't even about taxes. There was a deeper issue. "It is plainly this—Shall the majority govern or be governed?" he said. "Shall the nation rule, or be ruled? Shall the general will prevail, or the will of a faction? Shall there be government, or no government? It is impossible to deny that this is the true and the whole question. No art, no sophistry can involve it in the least obscurity." Honest Americans would know patriots from traitors by how they answered this basic question.

"If there is a man among us who shall affirm that the question is not what it has been stated to be, who shall endeavour to perplex it by ill-timed declamations against excise laws, who shall strive to paralyze the efforts of the community by invectives or insinuations against the government, such a man is not a good citizen," Hamilton said. "Such a man, however he may prate and babble republicanism, is not a republican. He attempts to set up the will of a part against the will of the whole, the will of a faction against the will of the nation." Real republicans would be on their guard. "The occasion may enable you to discriminate the true from pretended republicans, your friends from the friends of faction." Counterfeit republicanism had but one end. "There is no road to despotism more sure or more to be dreaded than that which begins at *anarchy*."

WHETHER WASHINGTON READ Hamilton's Tully essays is unclear. If he did, he might or might not have known Hamilton was their author. Either way, Washington accepted the Tully view that the whiskey rebellion was a test of the Constitution and the government it created. "Many persons in the said western parts of Pennsylvania have at length been hardy enough to perpetrate acts which I am advised amount to treason, being overt acts of levying war against the United States," the president said in a new proclamation on August 7, 1794. The threat compelled the government to bring military force to bear against the uprising. "I have accordingly determined so to do, feeling the deepest regret for the occasion, but withal the most solemn conviction that the essential interests of the Union demand it, that the very existence of government and the fundamental principles of social order are materially involved in the issue, and that the patriotism and firmness of all good citizens are seriously called upon, as occasions may require, to aid in the effectual suppression of so fatal a spirit."

The president issued an ultimatum. "I, George Washington, President of the United States, do hereby command all persons being insurgents as aforesaid, and all others whom it may concern, on or before the 1st day of September next to disperse and retire peaceably to their respective abodes. And I do moreover warn all persons whomsoever against aiding, abetting, or comforting the perpetrators of the aforesaid treasonable acts, and do require all officers and other citizens, according to their respective duties and the laws of the land, to exert their utmost endeavors to prevent and suppress such dangerous proceedings."

THE DEADLINE CAME and went. The rebels did not disperse. Washington issued another proclamation. Time was up, he said. "Government is set at defiance, the contest being whether a small portion of the United States shall dictate to the whole Union and, at the expense of those who desire peace, indulge a desperate ambition." The president informed the public that he had called on the militias of four states, which were already converging on western Pennsylvania. The law was the law, and he would enforce it.

THE SHOW OF FORCE was impressive, which was precisely the idea. Washington gathered nearly thirteen thousand troops, more than the number of Americans at Yorktown. He put on his uniform and personally led the troops toward the place where his career of command had started four decades earlier: the Forks of the Ohio, now occupied by the growing city of Pittsburgh.

He halted at Carlisle for a meeting with a small group of men who came from the insurgents to parley. William Findley had been born in Ireland, emigrated to America as a young man, served in arms during the Revolutionary War and served in politics in Pennsylvania afterward. He was elected to Congress from western Pennsylvania in 1790 and joined the emerging Jeffersonian opposition. He had tried to calm the rebels and now tried to calm Washington.

"About seven o'clock in the morning of the day on which we arrived at Carlisle, we waited on the president," Findley wrote afterward. "We found him alone, and were received and treated with politeness and attention. After a short conversation he informed us that he was just going out about some business relating to the army when he saw us approaching, and that after breakfast he was going to see a division of the army march, that therefore he could not examine the papers at present"—Findley and the others had brought resolutions from the rebels offering a compromise—"but would converse with us on the subject at ten o'clock that morning. When we waited on him at ten, we found him in company with Governor Howell"—Richard Howell of New Jersey, who had accompanied his state's militia—"to whom he introduced us. Colonel Hamilton, then secretary of the treasury, was present all the time, but Governor Howell withdrew before the conversation ended."

Washington took charge of the discussion. "The president opened the conversation with a discourse on the subject of the resolutions, in which he expatiated at considerable length on the evils occasioned by the insurrection and the injury resulting from it to the cause of liberty and the general interests of republican government in the world. He said that the outrages committed against the government and the peace of the citizens in the western counties had agitated the United States from one end to the other like an electrical shock, and disposed them very generally to turn out in support of the violated laws"—that is, in support of the government. "He spoke of the respectability of the army that was then at the places of rendezvous or on their march, and the alacrity with which they left their farms and their merchandise in order to support the government and laws, when called on for that purpose, and said that it was found necessary to send repeated expresses to prevent too great a number from marching from some of the states, particularly New Jersey, and that all the states that had been called on appeared to have sent forward the quota required." Washington wished to make clear that the people of America backed the government, not the rebels.

"He lamented the sacrifices that the farmers and merchants were under the necessity of making, and the great expense that would be incurred to the government by the expedition," Findley continued. Washington expressed surprise that the honest citizens of western Pennsylvania had put the rest of the country to such expense by failing to rein in the rebels themselves. "He concluded his observations on the subject by giving his opinion that the resolutions which we had presented were not sufficiently unequivocal to justify him in dismissing the army now when they were rendezvoused and the greatest proportion of the expenses incurred and the sacrifices of the merchant and farmer already made." The money having been spent, Washington wasn't going to send the soldiers home on flimsy pledges of better behavior. "It would be necessary to obtain further and more ample assurances of submission before he could dismiss the army than perhaps would have been required at an earlier period."

Findley and his fellows asked for more time to talk the rebels down. Washington said he couldn't delay the military operation. "The time the insurrection commenced was not of his choosing, and was too near the winter to enable him to afford the time he wished to have given." The president was determined that the spirit of insurrection not spread. "The flame had been caught in Maryland, and symptoms of it having been discovered in some other places in Pennsylvania rendered it improper to delay the expedition till the spring, lest the flame should spread further."

Washington reverted to the expense of the expedition. "He said there might some good grow out of it to console if not compensate us," Findley said. Washington was referring to Americans in general. "That though we had made a republican form of government and enacted laws under it, yet we had given no testimony to the world of being able or willing to support our government and laws, that this being the first instance of the kind since the commencement of the government, he thought it his duty to bring out such a force as would not only be sufficient to subdue the insurgents, if they made resistance, but to crush to atoms any opposition that might rise in any other corner. That this would operate in favour of humanity by effectually discouraging any that might be otherwise so disposed from provoking bloodshed, and that in the result it might teach the citizens to be more cautious of writing or speaking in such a manner of the measures of government as might have a tendency to inflame the citizens, and would also convince other nations that we could defend ourselves."

Findley and the others had hoped for an offer of amnesty to carry back to the rebels. Washington made no such offer. Yet he assured the emissaries that any rebels arrested would be treated justly and given fair trials. He would authorize the use of no greater force than was required to restore the peace and uphold the law.

The conversation ended, and Findley and the others expected to return to Pittsburgh. "But the president sent his private secretary early next morning to our lodging to ask us to wait on him again before we left town." They went to his tent, only to discover that he was out reviewing the troops. "But as he returned from seeing the last division of the army begin their march, he stopped his horse before the door of our lodging, and calling us to him, conversed some time with us in the street, and appointed us to wait on him again in the evening." They postponed their departure. "We spent that evening conversing in the same manner as we had done the former, and chiefly on the same subjects, until we thought it convenient to retire. We were dismissed as politely as we had been received, and in all the opportunities we had of conversing with the president, we were treated with that candor and politeness which have at all times distinguished his character."

Findley appreciated the art in Washington's method. "I do not pretend that we were treated with attention from any particular attachment to us. Whether that was so or not is a matter of no importance in this case. The attention, however, that he paid to us was the result of sound discretion. He was anxious to prevent bloodshed and at the same time to enforce due submission to the laws with as little trouble as possible, and by encouraging us to procure more explicit assurances, he was accomplishing a principal object of the expedition before the army arrived"—at Pittsburgh.

Washington's approach paid off. Findley and the others related their conversations with the president to the rebels and convinced most of them that if they persisted they would be crushed. Washington proceeded with the army to Bedford, where he delivered command of the troops to Henry Lee, currently governor of Virginia.

The rebels scattered ahead of the arrival of the army. A relative handful were arrested and tried for treason. Two were convicted. Washington pardoned them. He described the denouement in his next address on the state of the Union. "The part of our country which was lately the scene of disorder and insurrection now enjoys the blessings of quiet and order," the president said. "The misled have abandoned their errors and pay the respect to our Constitution and laws which is due from good citizens to the public authorities of the society." Washington explained his pardons. "Though I shall always think it a sacred duty to exercise with firmness and energy the constitutional powers with which I am vested, yet it appears to me no less consistent with the public good than it is with my personal feelings to mingle in the operations of government every degree of moderation and tenderness which the national justice, dignity and safety may permit."

— 91 —

Washington's proclamation of neutrality in the European war wasn't the last word on the subject. It was barely the first word, for neither France nor Britain accepted the American statement, certainly not in the terms Washington intended.

The French acted righteously indignant. "We have been as much astonished as piqued at the forms and tone assumed by the American minister," the French foreign minister declared, referring to Gouverneur Morris, the American representative in Paris. "We expected to find in him dispositions which would manifest the close union which should prevail between two people animated by the same principles of liberty, made to esteem and love one another reciprocally on account of the connections and relations of interest which subsist between them." The French found nothing of the sort. "It has appeared that Mr. Morris is in no wise penetrated with these truths. He has on the contrary demonstrated *humour*"—indisposition—"towards us." The foreign minister instructed his representative in America, Jean-Baptiste de Ternant, to convey the French government's displeasure to Jefferson, who relayed the message to Washington.

The French foreign minister was being diplomatic by blaming Morris. He realized that France's trouble was with Washington, who directed American policy. He didn't want to insult the president, but Morris was fair game. If Washington chose to make a change in policy, he too could blame Morris and replace him.

Besides the "esteem and love" the foreign minister mentioned, the French wanted money. The United States owed France substantial sums borrowed during the Revolutionary War. A timetable had been established for repayment. The French government asked for an acceleration of the schedule in light of the peril to France and the "principles of liberty" in the current war. Ternant requested an immediate payment of three million livres, or somewhat more than half a million dollars. To make it easier for Washington to approve the request, the payment would be applied directly to French purchases of commodities in America, to alleviate war shortages in France.

Jefferson urged Washington to say yes. Hamilton recommended saying no.

Washington approved a stopgap shipment of foodstuffs to France, in the amount of $100,000, while he weighed the larger request.

The president summoned his cabinet. Jefferson took notes. "The President desires the opinions of the heads of the three departments and of the attorney general on the following question, to wit: Mr. Ternant having applied for money equivalent to three millions of livres to be furnished on account of our debt to France at the request of the executive of that country, which sum is to be laid out in provisions within the U.S. to be sent to France, shall the money be furnished?"

Hamilton had concluded from Washington's agreement to the interim payment that a partial no was the best to be hoped for. He retreated. "The Secretary of the Treasury stated it as his opinion that, making a liberal allowance for the depreciation of assignats (no rule of liquidation having been yet fixed), a sum of about 318,000 dollars may not exceed the arrearages equitably due to France to the end of 1792," Jefferson recorded. Assignats were a pseudo-currency issued by the French revolutionary government. Like other such currencies they depreciated. How much was a matter of discussion and negotiation. The arrearages Hamilton spoke of were amounts America was behind in the payment schedule. Hamilton recommended paying that sum rather than what Ternant requested.

Jefferson, Henry Knox and Edmund Randolph opposed Hamilton. They argued that the United States should pay the full amount of the French request.

Washington accepted the recommendation of the majority. Jefferson informed Ternant, "The residue of the three millions can be furnished on account." The secretary of state added, "We have very sincere pleasure in shewing on every possible occasion our earnest desire to serve your nation, and the interest we take in its present situation."

BUT FRANCE WANTED MORE: more money, and American aid beyond money. The French government replaced Ternant with a young envoy enamored of the glory of France and the history-defining character of its revolution. Edmond Charles Genêt's disdain for any regime not as forward as France's had got him kicked out of Russia by Catherine the Great, so the government in Paris gave him a new post, in America. Genêt at once revealed he'd learned nothing from his Russian ejection. The French vessel that brought him to America had to dodge British warships, and thus no one could object to his landing at Charleston instead of Philadelphia. But rather than proceed at once to the American capital to present his credentials to the American government and pay his respects to Washington, Genêt remained in Charleston recruiting support for the French war effort. He'd been correctly informed that the southern states were more Republican and more favorably inclined toward France than New England and New York. Offering money that the French government didn't have but hoped to get from Washington, Genêt contracted for the construction of four ships to serve as privateers against Britain. He enlisted mercenaries to fight on France's behalf in Florida against Spain, a British ally.

Washington monitored Genêt's behavior with annoyance, Jefferson with alarm. The president took offense on behalf of the United States and the neutrality he had proclaimed. Jefferson took fright at the damage Genêt seemed likely to do to the Republican cause, not to mention the cause of France itself. Jefferson told Genêt to cease and desist. President Washington had determined that Genêt's belligerent actions in America were "incompatible with the territorial sovereignty of the United States," Jefferson said. Speaking in Washington's name, Jefferson delineated America's neutral policy. "It is the right of every nation to prohibit acts of sovereignty from being exercised by any other within its limits, and the duty of a neutral nation to prohibit such as would injure one of the warring powers." This applied especially to recruiting. "The granting military commissions within the United States by any other authority than their own is an infringement on their sovereignty and particularly so when granted to their own citizens to lead them to commit acts contrary to the duties they owe their own country."

Genêt declined to take the hint, concluding that Washington and Jefferson weren't true friends of liberty. He appealed to Americans more amenable to French policies than the administration was proving to be. He published some correspondence between himself and Jefferson, inviting Americans to take his side of the argument.

Jefferson addressed him face to face when he finally reached Philadelphia. In their conversation Genêt reported the arrival of French warships in the waters off America. "I took that occasion to observe to him that having such great means in his hands, I thought he ought not to hesitate in abandoning to the orders of the government the little pickeroons"—privateers—"which had been armed here unauthorised by them and which occasioned so much embarrassment and uneasiness," Jefferson recorded. "That certainly their"—the American government's—"good dispositions must be worth more than the trifling services these little vessels could render."

Genêt took Jefferson's point. "He immediately declared that having such a force in his hands, he had abandoned every idea of further armament in our ports, that these small objects were now beneath his notice." Yet he wouldn't give up the vessels already constructed and delivered to the French. "Their honour would not permit them to give them up."

Genêt said he thought the existing treaty between America and France allowed what he had done.

Jefferson disagreed. "I told him the government"—the American government—"was of a different opinion." And because Genêt was in America, he must abide by American law.

JEFFERSON FOR MANY MONTHS had been making excuses for the violent and arbitrary turn of the French revolution. This emotional sunk cost disposed him to tolerate a certain amount of misbehavior in Genêt. In public he held his tongue. But in private he vented his growing anger. "Never, in my opinion, was so calamitous an appointment made as that of the present minister of France here," he wrote to Madison. "Hotheaded, all imagination, no judgment, passionate, disrespectful and even indecent towards the President in his written as well as verbal communications, talking of appeals from him to Congress, from them to the people, urging the most unreasonable and groundless propositions, and in the most dictatorial style." If the American people learned the full story of Genêt's misbehavior, relations with France would never recover.

"He renders my position immensely difficult," Jefferson continued. "He does me justice personally, and, giving him time to vent himself and then cool, I am on a footing to advise him freely, and he respects it. But he breaks out again on the very first occasion, so as to show that he is incapable of correcting himself. To complete our misfortune, we have no channel of our own through which we can correct the irritating representations he may make."

To James Monroe, a senator from Virginia, Jefferson declared Genêt a singular impediment to good relations between the United States and France. "I fear the disgust of France is inevitable," he said. "His conduct is indefensible by the most furious Jacobin. I only wish our countrymen may distinguish between him and his nation."

Genêt was playing into the hands of the American enemies of France. "Hamilton, sensible of the advantage they have got, is urging a full appeal by the government to the people," Jefferson said. "Such an explosion would manifestly endanger a dissolution of the friendship between the two nations and ought therefore to be deprecated by every friend to our liberty, and none but an enemy to it would wish to avail himself of the indiscretions of an individual to compromit"—compromise—"two nations esteeming each other ardently. It will prove that the agents of the two people are either great bunglers or great rascals when they cannot preserve that peace which is the universal wish of both."

Jefferson concluded he had no choice. He recommended that Washington demand the recall of Genêt to France. Washington consulted his cabinet. Their counsel was unanimous. Genêt had to go.

Jefferson notified Gouverneur Morris in Paris. Jefferson forwarded a document delineating Genêt's unacceptable behavior in a manner even French officials couldn't deny. "You will, therefore, be pleased to lay it before them, doing everything which can be done on your part to procure it a friendly and dispassionate reception and consideration. The President would, indeed, think it greatly unfortunate were they to take it in any other light, and therefore charges you very particularly with the care of presenting this proceeding in the most soothing view, and as the result of an unavoidable necessity on his part."

92

Before independence, American merchants and shipowners had been required by British law to conduct their trade within the British empire. The Revolutionary War disrupted this trade even as it opened new markets for the American merchant marine, especially to French ports. The end of the war raised the prospect that American merchants might possess the best of all worlds: the opportunity to trade freely with whomever they chose.

The prospect wasn't quite realized. Britain withheld certain trade privileges, because now it could, the Americans no longer being British. Americans were disappointed, in that the French market didn't match the British. The British government hoped the disappointment would draw America back into the British sphere of influence. Federalists in America were willing. Republicans in America were adamantly opposed. To both groups, though, the idea of free trade was alluring and hard to surrender.

Then came the war between Britain and France. Each country treated the conflict as existential and, in particular, far more important than American notions about free trade. Britain hoped to starve France and to this purpose interdicted American vessels headed for French ports. Besides seizing ships and cargoes, the British sometimes seized sailors. They claimed these men were deserters from the British navy. At times they were. Often they were not. In the latter cases, the affront to American dignity, let alone to the rights of the kidnapped, was extreme. The French did some seizing of their own. But the incidents were fewer. And they left the sailors alone, not least because it was implausible that a sailor who spoke only English, as most did, was a deserter from the French navy.

The American government protested the depredations. The political parties employed the depredations to their partisan benefit. Some Republicans called for war against Britain in defense of American rights, and incidentally in support of Franco-American solidarity.

. . .

"THE PRESENT IS BEYOND question a great, a difficult and a perilous crisis in the affairs of this country," Hamilton wrote to Washington in the spring of 1794. "In such a crisis it is the duty of every man, according to situation, to contribute all in his power towards preventing evil and producing good." Hamilton pleaded this necessity in offering advice beyond the realm of a treasury secretary. "It cannot but be of great importance that the chief magistrate should be informed of the real state of things, and it is not easy for him to have this information but through those principal officers who have most frequent access to him. Hence an obligation on their part to communicate information on occasions like the present." In other words, Washington needed Hamilton to explain the world to him.

"There exist in our councils three considerable parties," Hamilton said. "One decided for preserving peace by every effort which shall in any way consist with the ultimate maintenance of the national honor and rights and disposed to cultivate with all nations a friendly understanding; another decided for war and resolved to bring it about by every expedient which shall not too directly violate the public opinion; a third not absolutely desirous of war but solicitous at all events to excite and keep alive irritation and ill humour between the United States and Great Britain, not unwilling in the pursuit of this object to expose the peace of the country to imminent hazards."

The first group, favoring peace with honor, was the one Hamilton preferred. Its agenda was, or ought to be, to strengthen the army and navy, to vest the president with greater power for national defense and to seek resolution of problems with Britain by negotiation. "If that experiment fails, then and not till then to resort to reprisals and war."

The second group was as wrong as the first was right. Its program: "To say and to do everything which can have a tendency to stir up the passions of the people and beget a disposition favourable to war, to make use of the inflammation which is excited in the community for the purposes of carrying through measures calculated to disgust Great Britain and to render an accommodation impracticable without humiliation to her, which they do not believe will be submitted to." In sum, this second group wanted war without the blame for causing it.

The third group tagged along behind the second. "They weakly hope that they may hector and vapour with success that the pride of

Great Britain will yield to her interest, and that they may accomplish the object of perpetuating animosity between the two countries without involving war."

Hamilton didn't give the parties names. Washington didn't like talk of parties. But Washington knew Hamilton was speaking of Jefferson's Republicans when he described the anti-British groups as being driven by passion rather than reason. "They unite from habitual feeling in an implacable hatred to Great Britain and in a warm attachment to France," Hamilton said. "Their animosity against the former is inflamed by the most violent resentment for recent and unprovoked injuries." These were the British seizures of ships and sailors. "In hostility with Britain they seek the gratification of revenge upon a detested enemy with that of serving a favourite friend and in this the cause of liberty. They anticipate also, what is in their estimation a great political good, a more complete and permanent alienation from Great Britain and a more close approximation to France."

The anti-British Republican party was dangerous and must be defeated, Hamilton said. He proposed a plan: "To nominate a person who will have the confidence of those who think peace still within our reach, and who may be thought qualified for the mission as envoy extraordinary to Great Britain." This person would seek a peaceful resolution of problems with Britain. But to give his mission weight, America should prepare for war.

Hamilton offered such an individual: John Jay, currently chief justice, formerly a negotiator of the treaty with Britain that ended the Revolutionary War. "I think the business would have the best chance possible in his hands," Hamilton told Washington. "And I flatter myself that his mission would issue in a manner that would produce the most important good to the nation."

JOHN JAY WOULDN'T have been Jefferson's first choice. Jay was a founding Federalist, indeed an author, with Hamilton and Madison, of the Federalist essays of the ratification debate. Unlike Madison, he hadn't changed his mind about the direction of federalism and remained on good terms with Hamilton.

But Jefferson had no say in the matter. He had resigned the secretaryship of state at the end of 1793. He would have left sooner if the matter had been wholly up to him. "When you did me the honor of appointing me to the office I now hold, I engaged in it without a view of continuing any length of time," he had written to Washington the previous July. "I pretty early concluded on the close of the first four years of our republic as a proper period for withdrawing." He had told Washington as much. "When the period, however, arrived, circumstances had arisen which, in the opinion of some of my friends, rendered it proper to postpone my purpose for a while." The chief circumstance was the war between France and Britain, which led to the Genêt troubles, among others. "These circumstances have now ceased in such a degree as to leave me free to think again of a day on which I may withdraw, without its exciting disadvantageous opinions or conjectures of any kind." Jefferson assured Washington his decision had nothing to do with dissatisfaction with the president, for whom he had nothing but admiration and gratitude. "No man living more sincerely wishes that your administration could be rendered as pleasant to yourself as it is useful and necessary to our country, nor feels for you a more rational or cordial attachment and respect."

Jefferson wasn't being entirely ingenuous. True, he didn't like the managerial tasks that came with the secretaryship. But what he really didn't like was the way Hamilton was running away with the executive branch, carrying Washington with him. Jefferson while inside the administration had failed to prevent Hamilton's coup. He thought he'd have better luck on the outside, where he could speak his mind more freely.

Washington understood. He envied Jefferson's escape to private life. He persuaded Jefferson to delay his departure for a few months, to the year's end. At that point he selected Edmund Randolph, the attorney general, to head the state department.

WASHINGTON ACCEPTED HAMILTON'S recommendation of John Jay for envoy to Britain. In those days the business of the Supreme Court was limited, and the chief justice could spend a few months abroad without being missed. Washington solicited the views of his cabinet on how Jay should be instructed. What kind of treaty should he seek?

Randolph, as secretary of state, combined the recommendations into Jay's instructions. Jay should vigorously assert American rights against British depredations. Yet he should do so in a way that didn't risk war, which most Americans didn't want and for which America was not prepared. Jay should remedy failures of the treaty with Britain from the end of the Revolutionary War. Britain continued to occupy forts in the American northwest, and it had refused to provide compensation for property carried away at war's end. Such property was understood to include slaves. Jay should seek compensation for vessels and cargoes seized in the current war. If possible, he should negotiate a commercial treaty that would grant American merchants greater access to British markets, including the West Indies.

"Such are the outlines of the conduct which the President wishes you to pursue," Randolph told Jay in summarizing. "He is aware that at this distance and during the present instability of public events, he cannot undertake to prescribe rules which shall be irrevocable." Jay should exercise his best judgment as to what was possible. There were two exceptions, two nonnegotiable points. First: "That as the British ministry will doubtless be solicitous to detach us from France and may probably make some overture of this kind, you will inform them that the government of the United States will not derogate from our treaties and engagements with France." Second: "That no treaty of commerce be concluded or signed contrary to the foregoing prohibition."

WILLIAM GRENVILLE WAS the son of George Grenville, who lived in American memory as the author of the Stamp Act. The younger Grenville was foreign secretary at the time of Jay's arrival in Britain. He was no more charitably inclined toward the Americans than his father had been. And much as his father's perspective on America had been colored by the British war with France then just ended, the son's view was dominated by the conflict with France currently under way. William Grenville engaged Jay only enough to conclude that under its present government America wouldn't enter the war on France's side unless egregiously provoked. Having satisfied himself on that score, Grenville let Jay enjoy the sights in London while he—Grenville—tended to more pressing matters.

Jay apprised Washington of the slow progress. "I shall be disappointed if *no* good should result," he wrote in late June of his talks. "As yet the minister"—Grenville—"stands entirely uncommitted. From some light circumstances I incline to believe that our mercantile injuries will be redressed, but how, or how far, I cannot conjecture." Jay had less confidence that the British would relinquish the northwestern forts. "Dr. Gordon has information, which he relies upon, that the posts will not be surrendered, and he authorizes me to tell you so in confidence." William Gordon was an English clergyman who had emigrated to America. He had written one of the first histories of the American Revolution and knew Washington. "His information does not make so strong an impression on my mind as it does on his," Jay observed. "It merits attention, but in my opinion is not conclusive."

Jay had sounded public opinion on the government Grenville served. "The observations I have hitherto made induce me to believe that the war with France is popular, and that a war with us would be unpopular," he told Washington. America itself was popular. "Your administration is greatly commended," Jay wrote. He hoped this would conduce to the success of the mission.

A month later he sent Washington an update. "Some cabinet councils have lately been held, and it is probable that the manner of settling their differences with us has been among the subjects of their deliberations," Jay wrote. "From the silence and circumspection of Lord Grenville I apprehend that the cabinet has not yet ultimately concluded on their plan. This delay is unpleasant, but I do not think it unnatural."

The slow pace was wearing. "I most heartily wish the business over and myself at home again," Jay said. But he kept his impatience in check. "It would not be prudent to urge and press unceasingly, lest ill humour should result, and ill humour will mar any negotiation. On the other hand, much forbearance and seeming inactivity invite procrastination and neglect. The line between these extremes is delicate. I will endeavour to find and observe it."

The outlook improved in early August. "I am this moment returned from a long conference with Lord Grenville," Jay reported to Washington. "Our prospects become more and more promising as we advance in the business." Jay expected the British to accept the principle of a commission to determine compensation for seized American property. "The question of admitting our vessels into the Islands"—the West Indies—"under certain limitations is under consideration and will soon be decided. A treaty of commerce is on the carpet. All other things being agreed, the posts will be included." The emancipated slaves who left with the British remained a sticking point. "They contend that the article about the Negroes"—in the 1783 treaty—"does not extend to those who came in on their proclamations, to whom (being vested with the property in them by the rights of war) they gave freedom, but only to those who were bona fide the property of Americans when the war ceased." The British were complaining that Americans had not paid debts owed to British merchants. They used this as reason not to accommodate the Americans on compensation and slaves. But Jay thought they might accept a commission to sort things out.

Jay cautioned Washington that he was conveying merely the sense of the talks. "These things have passed in conversation, but no commitments on either side."

He related an exchange with George III. "The King observed to me the other day, 'Well, sir! I imagine you begin to see that your mission will probably be successful.' 'I am happy, may it please your Majesty, to find that you entertain that idea.' 'Well, but don't you perceive that it is like to be so?' 'There are some recent circumstances which induce me to flatter myself that it will be so.'" Jay was referring to a response from Grenville to a position he had put forward. "He nodded with a smile, signifying that it was to those circumstances that he alluded."

"I could fill some sheets with interesting communications, if I had leisure," Jay told Washington. But work pressed. "Whatever may be the issue, nothing in my power to ensure success shall be neglected or delayed."

The work went on. As Jay and Grenville got down to exchanging drafts and debating details, Jay realized he might have been too optimistic. He braced Washington for a treaty that might cause a ruckus on arrival in America. He wasn't surprised, and he didn't want Washington to be surprised either. "That attempts will be made in America to frustrate this negotiation"—to reject the treaty—"I have not the most distant shadow of a doubt," Jay said. He supposed the Republicans would object to anything that didn't force Britain to apologize and pay for everything it had done wrong. They were dreaming, or being willfully perverse.

On the Federalists' part, some wanted a treaty of amity with Britain, like the existing one with France. They weren't going to get it, Jay said. Nor should they. Yet speaking like the Federalist he was, Jay said that rather than add an alliance with Britain, America ought to subtract the one with France. He disliked alliances on principle. "As to a political connection with any country, I hope it will never be judged necessary, for I very much doubt whether it would ultimately be found useful. On the contrary, it would in my opinion introduce foreign influence which I consider as the worst of political plagues."

WASHINGTON WAS REACHING the same conclusion. He would address the subject in due course. Meanwhile, he awaited word that the negotiations had concluded.

They finally did, in November. "As to the treaty," Jay wrote to Washington, "it must speak for itself." To Randolph, Jay said, "My opinion of the treaty is apparent from my having signed it. I have no reason to believe or conjecture that one more favorable to us is attainable." To Hamilton, who had got him into this thankless assignment, Jay wrote, "My task is done, whether *finis coronat opus*"—the end crowns the work—"the President, Senate and public will decide."

→ 93 ←

"When we review the calamities which afflict so many other nations, the present condition of the United States affords much matter of consolation and satisfaction," Washington proclaimed to the nation on January 1, 1795. "Our exemption hitherto from foreign war, an increasing prospect of the continuance of that exemption, the great degree of internal tranquility we have enjoyed, the recent confirmation of that tranquility by the suppression of an insurrection which so wantonly threatened it, the happy course of our public affairs in general, the unexampled prosperity of all classes of our citizens, are circumstances which peculiarly mark our situation with indications of the Divine beneficence toward us."

Washington wasn't insincere in thanking Providence for smiling on America. But his proclamation simultaneously patted his administration on the back. The exemption from foreign war, of course, had been Washington's doing with his constitutionally questionable but not seriously challenged declaration of neutrality. The increasing prospect of the continuation of the exemption came from the treaty with Britain recently concluded by Jay. The internal tranquility had been confirmed by his suppression of the whiskey-tax rebellion in Pennsylvania. The prosperity of the citizenry he could plausibly credit to the operation of the national bank. Washington was a firm believer in the principle that heaven helps those who help themselves.

The president recommended that all religious denominations in America join in observing a special day of thanksgiving and prayer on Thursday, February 19. He suggested appropriate prayers: "for the preservation of our peace, foreign and domestic; for the seasonable control which has been given to a spirit of disorder in the suppression of the late insurrection, and generally, for the prosperous course of our affairs, public and private." At the same time, Americans should beseech the Almighty "to preserve us from the arrogance of prosperity, and from hazarding the advantages we enjoy by delusive pursuits; to dispose us to merit the continuance of His favors by not abusing them, by our gratitude for them, and by a correspondent conduct as citizens and men."

WASHINGTON'S PRAYER LITANY had a special purpose at just this moment. The terms of the Jay treaty had not been released to the public, and the president, following Jay, guessed they would provoke an uproar when they were. By urging prayer for domestic peace and reminding Americans not to abuse their rights as citizens and men, he hoped to keep the criticism within bounds.

The Jay treaty was the first treaty negotiated with a foreign power under the new Constitution. How treaties should be handled by the president was unclear. "He shall have power, by and with the advice and consent of the Senate, to make treaties, provided two thirds of the senators present concur," said Article II. Washington had already violated the first part of the clause. He asked no advice of the Senate in sending Jay to Britain or instructing him regarding the negotiations. He was going to have to ask for Senate consent, in the form of a two-thirds majority of that body. But he hadn't decided on the best method for securing that majority. Should he mount a public campaign for the treaty, putting his own reputation on the line for the treaty? Or should he proceed quietly, so as not to provoke the opposition?

He commenced quietly. "We are still uninformed what is Mr. Jay's treaty," Jefferson wrote to James Monroe in May 1795. Washington had yet to release the terms of the treaty. Once ratified, the treaty would become public law, and it would have to be published then. The Constitution said nothing about publishing it beforehand. Washington proceeded in that spirit of silence.

He had to share it with the Senate, for the senators needed to see what they were voting on. He supposed he could count on the votes of the majority of senators who identified as Federalists. He thought he could rely on their confidentiality.

The Republicans were another matter. They didn't like the treaty and had reason to air what they considered its obnoxious terms. One Republican, Stevens Mason of Virginia, did just that. He shared the contents of the treaty with Benjamin Bache, the editor of the Philadelphia *Aurora*. Bache was a grandson and namesake of Benjamin Franklin and an ardent Republican. "Mr. Bache," Mason wrote, "I have been daily hoping to see in the public prints a copy of the late treaty with Britain. But as such a publication has not been made, I transmit enclosed the heads of that instrument collected from memory after an attentive perusal. There necessarily must be deficiencies in an account of this kind which depends entirely on memory, and for the same reason there may be inaccuracies, but I trust the latter are few." Mason signed himself "A Citizen."

Bache printed the gist of the treaty. The British agreed to evacuate the northwestern forts and to allow American ships limited access to the British West Indies. The former concession was nothing more than a repeat of the promise broken for the last decade, and the latter fell far short of what American exporters had hoped for. The contentious issues of debts from the war and of seizures of ships and sailors remained unresolved.

The publication of the treaty terms set off a ferocious debate. The *Aurora* led the opposition, running numerous attacks on the treaty and on Washington himself. An outraged "Belisarius" contributed an open letter to the president, blaming him for betraying his trust to the American people. "Awakened from their delusive dream of gratitude and roused to action by a general sense of feeling at the accumulated injuries which your Treaty of Amity, Commerce and Navigation with Great Britain has prepared for them, the people of the United States demand with indignant pride whence has proceeded an instrument so deeply subversive of republicanism and destructive to every principle of free representative government; aiming too, with masked subtlety, a deadly blow at that generous struggle for freedom which, in the magnanimous efforts of the French republic, now agitates a contending world."

Washington's sins stretched far back, with the Jay treaty being merely the most recent. Belisarius listed them:

"1st. The odious principle of a distinction between the people and their executive servants, as manifested in the mock pageantry of monarchy and the apish mimicry of kingship." Belisarius didn't like birthday parties.

"2d. The wicked principle of legally sanctioning the rapine and plunder committed by herds of base and unprincipled speculators on those war-worn veterans of the revolution, whose blood was the price of our independence and the purchase of your fame." Nor did he like speculators in the war debt.

"3d. Funded debt, and its twin sister assumption, to the amount of 80 millions of dollars, perpetuated on your fellow citizens through the influence of a base and corrupt maxim of your then prime minister 'that public debt is public blessing,' producing as its natural offspring." Hamilton had followed Jefferson out of the administration.

Numbers four through six harped on the national bank.

"7th. The establishment of a monied aristocracy, whose baneful power has greatly influenced all the principal measures of the government, and begotten

"8th. Servile submission to the restrictions imposed by G. Britain on our commerce and to her palpable infraction of the treaty of peace."

The indictment proceeded in similar vein to:

"17th. The unconstitutional appointment of the Chief Justice of the U.S. as envoy extraordinary to G. Britain.

"18th. The unconstitutional negotiation of a treaty with G. Britain by your authority alone, without the privity and participation of the Senate.

"19th. The present unconstitutional treaty itself, which, if permitted to take effect, totally subverts and changes the federal Constitution, and which equally endangers our domestic tranquility and the continuance of peace with the French republic."

"This, sir," Belisarius concluded, "is an enumeration of some of the measures of your six years administration, which has been trumpeted to the world by your idolatrous worshippers as unequaled in wisdom and unparalleled in the history of nations. Truth, that scourge of tyrants and best monitor of the ambitious, presents a different picture." History would catch up with Washington. "Gratitude may yield a falling tear at the recollection of your military services, but gratitude, sir, is a living virtue, and the stern though unerring of posterity will not fail to render the just sentence of condemnation on the man who has entailed upon his country deep and incurable public evils."

ATTACKS ON THE TREATY and the president were not confined to the newspapers. Republicans gathered in cities and towns around the country to protest. Many sent remonstrances to Washington detailing their objections. One from Boston was more articulate than most. "Resolved, as the sense of the inhabitants of this town, that the aforesaid instrument"—the Jay treaty—"if ratified, will be highly injurious to the commercial interest of the United States, derogatory to their national honor and independence, and may be dangerous to the peace and happiness of their citizens." The treaty was one-sided, the Bostonians said. "The complaints and pretensions of Great Britain are fully provided for, while a part only of those of the United States have been brought into consideration." The treaty failed to indemnify Americans for property taken illegally by the British and for the trade opportunities lost on account of the illegal British occupation of the northwest frontier. The treaty left unresolved the problem of British seizures of American vessels and cargoes. "It concedes a right to the British government to search and detain our vessels in time of war between them and other nations under frivolous and vexatious pretexts." The British promised to evacuate the northwestern forts, but they had promised that a decade ago.

The treaty had no provisions for enforcement, the Bostonians complained. "Although the terms of said treaty purport to be reciprocal in many instances, yet from the local situation and existing circumstances of the United States, and the pacific system of policy they have adopted, that reciprocity is merely nominal, and delusive." The treaty impaired the authority of the Constitution. "It limits the powers of Congress, delegated to them by the Constitution, 'to regulate our commerce with foreign nations,' by prescribing conditions and creating impediments to the exercise of that power." In doing so it set a pernicious precedent. "It exposes the United States and their commerce to similar embarrassments from other commercial nations."

In good faith, the Bostonians said, they sent their objections to the president. "We earnestly hope and confidently rely that his prudence, fortitude and wisdom, which have more than once been eminently instrumental in the salvation of his country, will be equally conspicuous on the present occasion and that the reasons we have assigned will have their influence to induce him to withhold his signature from the ratification of this alarming instrument."

WASHINGTON CERTAINLY WASN'T going to respond to the diatribes in the *Aurora*. But the Boston petition was respectful and merited a reply. "In every act of my administration, I have sought the happiness of my fellow citizens," he wrote. "My system for the attainment of this object has uniformly been to overlook all personal, local and partial considerations, to contemplate the United States as one great whole, to confide that sudden impressions when erroneous would yield to candid reflection, and to consult only the substantial and permanent interests of our country. Nor have I departed from this line of conduct on the occasion which has produced the resolutions contained in your letter." Washington assured the Bostonians that he approached the treaty with an open mind. "I have weighed with attention every argument which has at any time been brought into view." He would similarly weigh the Bostonians' arguments.

Having said this, he reminded them that he was president and they were not. "The Constitution is the guide which I never can abandon. It has assigned to the president the power of making treaties, with the advice and consent of the Senate. It was doubtless supposed that these two branches of government would combine, without passion and with the best means of information, those facts and principles upon which the success of our foreign relations will always depend; that they ought not to substitute for their own conviction the opinions of others." The decision, because it involved the executive branch, was his. He would make it.

WASHINGTON LEFT THE hand-to-hand combat to others. Hamilton was the most energetic defender of the treaty, though his sallies were equally intended as assaults on the Republicans. "It was to have been foreseen that the treaty which Mr. Jay was charged to negotiate with Great Britain, whenever it should appear, would have to contend with many perverse dispositions and some honest prejudices," Hamilton said, writing as "Camillus." "That there was no measure in which the government could engage so little likely to be viewed according to its intrinsic merits so very likely to encounter misconception, jealousy and unreasonable dislike."

Hamilton identified reasons for this wrongheadedness. "It is only to know the vanity and vindictiveness of human nature to be convinced that while this generation lasts, there will always exist among us men irreconcilable to our present national constitution, embittered in their animosity in proportion to the success of its operation and the disappointment of their inauspicious predictions. It is a material inference from this that such men will watch with lynx's eyes for opportunities of discrediting the proceedings of the government and will display a hostile and malignant zeal upon every occasion where they think there are any prepossessions of the community to favor their enterprises. A treaty with Great Britain was too fruitful an occasion not to call forth all their activity."

The haters of America's good government were meanwhile lovers of France's noxious one. "It was not to be mistaken that an enthusiasm for France and her revolution throughout all its wonderful vicissitudes has continued to possess the minds of the great body of the people of this country," Hamilton wrote. "It was well understood that a numerous party among us"—the Republicans, obviously—"though disavowing the design, because the avowal would defeat it, have been steadily endeavouring to make the United States a party in the present European war, by advocating all those measures which would widen the breach between us and Great Britain, and by resisting all those which could tend to close it. And it was morally certain that this party would eagerly improve every circumstance which could serve to render the treaty odious and to frustrate it as the most effectual road to their favorite goal."

Hamilton discerned political ambition of a particular sort in the opposition to the treaty. Some of the attacks centered on Washington, others on Jay. The attackers sought to drive the president from office, if only out of his disgust at what the Republicans were reducing the country to. The chief justice was a likely heir and, being a known Federalist, was unacceptable to the Republicans. To block the treaty would be to embarrass Washington and discredit Jay.

Who would benefit from their discomfiture? "It is remarkable that in the toasts given on the 4th of July, wherever there appears a direct or indirect censure on the treaty, it is pretty uniformly coupled with compliments to Mr. Jefferson," wrote Hamilton. "No one can be blind to the finger of party spirit visible in these and similar transactions."

THE BATTLE RAGED ON. Republicans took to the streets to denounce the treaty, Federalists to denounce the Republicans. To some the tumult recalled the protests that culminated in the American Revolution, to others the turbulence of the French revolution. Jay was said to have joked that he could ride at night from Philadelphia to Boston by the glow from his burning effigies.

Finally the treaty came to a decision in the Senate. Twenty senators voted in favor, ten against. By the absolute minimum it won approval and became law. Washington and the Federalists had won.

Yet the Republicans weren't finished. The treaty had served admirably to solidify the opposition to Washington and the Federalists, and they wouldn't relinquish it lightly. No sooner had Washington declared the treaty in effect than Republicans in the House demanded to see the administration's correspondence with Jay before and during the treaty negotiations. The House would have to approve funds to implement certain terms of the treaty, and Republican members wanted the backstory. Their demand carried the House and went to the president.

Washington refused to deliver the papers. "I trust that no part of my conduct has ever indicated a disposition to withhold any information which the Constitution has enjoined upon the president as a duty to give, or which could be required of him by either house of Congress as a right," he told the House. "And with truth I affirm that it has been, as it will continue to be while I have the honor to preside in the government, my constant endeavor to harmonize with the other branches thereof so far as the trust delegated to me by the people of the United States and my sense of the obligation it imposes to 'preserve, protect, and defend the Constitution' will permit."

But the House had asked too much, and in doing so, it crossed the line separating the prerogatives of the legislative branch from those of the executive. "The nature of foreign negotiations requires caution, and their success must often depend on secrecy; and even when brought to a conclusion a full disclosure of all the measures, demands or eventual concessions which may have been proposed or contemplated would be extremely impolitic," Washington said. "For this might have a pernicious influence on future negotiations or produce immediate inconveniences, perhaps danger and mischief, in relation to other powers." The framers of the Constitution had known what they were doing in reserving responsibility over treaties to the president and the Senate. "The necessity of such caution and secrecy was one cogent reason for vesting the power of making treaties in the president, with the advice and consent of the Senate, the principle on which that body was formed confining it to a small number of members"—namely two for each state. The House was much larger. "To admit, then, a right in the House of Representatives to demand and to have as a matter of course all the papers respecting a negotiation with a foreign power would be to establish a dangerous precedent."

Washington reminded the members of the House that he himself was one of the framers of the Constitution. "Having been a member of the general convention, and knowing the principles on which the Constitution was formed, I have ever entertained but one opinion on this subject, and from the first establishment of the government to this moment my conduct has exemplified that opinion: that the power of making treaties is exclusively vested in the president, by and with the advice and consent of the Senate." The House of Representatives had nothing to do with treaties. This view had never been challenged. "Until the present time not a doubt or suspicion has appeared, to my knowledge, that this construction was not the true one."

Washington added that the journals of the Philadelphia convention sustained his view. "In those journals it will appear that a proposition was made 'that no treaty should be binding on the United States which was not ratified by a law,' and that the proposition was explicitly rejected." A law required approval of both houses. By rejecting the proposition, the convention deliberately excluded the House of Representatives from involvement in treaties.

Each branch and part of government must know its place, Washington told the House members. "As it is essential to the due administration of the government that the boundaries fixed by the Constitution between the different departments should be preserved, a just regard to the Constitution and to the duty of my office, under all the circumstances of this case, forbids a compliance with your request."

JAMES MADISON DISPUTED Washington's recollection of the convention. The proposition Washington referred to was about treaties of peace, not treaties of commerce, he told Jefferson. Madison showed Jefferson the notes he himself had kept of the convention. "You will perceive that the quotation is nothing to the purpose," he said.

But Madison recognized that Washington had him in a difficult spot. The journals of the convention hadn't been published, and no one was supposed to have taken notes. If Madison made a public dispute with Washington, it would be his word against the president's. Even if all the journals and notes were published, it would be his interpretation against Washington's. Madison didn't think he could win that fight.

Nor did he win on the larger issue of the treaty. Federalists in the House moved to endorse the treaty, and Federalists outside Congress mobilized in support. Madison conceded he'd been outmaneuvered. "The people have been everywhere made to believe that the object of the House of Representatives in resisting the treaty was war, and have thence listened to the summons 'to follow where Washington leads,'" he told Jefferson. In a narrow decision the House voted to implement the treaty.

94

Following the Senate's ratification of the Treaty of New York with the Creek Indians, Washington's worries regarding Indian affairs had shifted from the southwest to the northwest. Tribes in the region north of the Ohio River had been restive since the end of the war as settlers sought to make up for time lost during the conflict. Thousands of men, women and children pushed into territory still claimed and occupied by the tribes, with predictably violent results. The British government, from the forts they refused to relinquish, encouraged resistance, imagining that an Indian territory to the west of the United States might restrain the growth of the breakaway republic. Congress made treaties with some of the tribes but more typically with mere factions of tribes. When other members of the tribes attacked the settlers, the latter claimed grievance and demanded protection from the government.

Washington in 1790 sent an expedition to pacify the northwest. It was badly defeated by a coalition of the Ohio tribes. A second expedition, in 1791, fared no better. The president and Congress concluded that the army, which had dwindled nearly to nothing since the end of the war, needed to be rebuilt and reorganized. What was left of the Continental army was reconfigured into the Legion of the United States, a fighting force particularly configured for frontier defense. To head this new army, Washington chose Anthony Wayne, the hero of the western theater in the Revolutionary War.

Wayne prepared his men carefully. The time this took allowed Washington an opportunity to exhaust diplomatic efforts to calm the northwestern frontier. These failed for the dual reason that the settlers weren't willing to leave the homes and farms they had carved from the forest, and the Indians, without being defeated on the battlefield, weren't willing to let them stay.

In the autumn of 1793, Wayne led his legion across the Ohio. He wintered in the western part of what would become the state of Ohio. In the spring of 1794 he started north toward the Miamis River, also called the Maumee, hoping to draw the Indians into battle. He moved slowly, reinforcing positions as he went. The Indians watched and waited for their best chance to defeat the American invaders a third time in a row. They found a likely spot in a tangle of trees that had been blown over in a windstorm some years before. With arms supplied by the British and accompanied by Canadians based at a British fort near Detroit, the Indians fell upon Wayne's army, which itself was accompanied by Kentucky militia. The opening salvos favored the Indians, who pursued the invaders beyond the shelter of the fallen timbers. Wayne counterattacked with decisive effect. "It's with infinite pleasure that I now announce to you the brilliant success of the Federal army under my command in a general action with the combined force of the hostile Indians and a considerable number of the volunteers and militia of Detroit," he reported after the battle. "The loss of the enemy was more than double that of the Federal army. The woods were strewed for a considerable distance with the dead bodies of the Indians and their white auxiliaries, the latter armed with British muskets and bayonets."

The absolute number of Indians killed wasn't great enough to break their will to continue fighting. That result was supplied by two additional factors. The first was the refusal of the British troops at the closest fort to enter the battle on the side of the Indians. The Indian leaders had expected that the British would act as aggressively against the Americans as they had often spoken. But amid their country's war with France, and while John Jay was negotiating his treaty in London, the British had orders to stand aside.

The second factor was the after-battle destruction Wayne wreaked upon the Indian villages and food stores. "We remained three days and nights on the banks of the Miamis in front of the field of battle, during which time all the houses and corn fields were consumed and destroyed for a considerable distance both above and below Fort Miamis"—the British post—"as well as within pistol shot of that garrison, who were compelled to remain tacit speculators of this general devastation and conflagration," Wayne reported from the headquarters he had established some distance away. "The army returned to this place on the 27th by easy marches, laying waste the villages and corn fields for about fifty miles on each side of the Miamis. There remains yet a number of villages and a great quantity of corn to be consumed or destroyed upon Au Glaize and the Miamis above this place, which will be effected in the course of a few days."

Wayne's scorched-earth strategy broke the back of Indian resistance. Without British troops the Ohio tribes couldn't match the Americans on the battlefield, and without food they couldn't sustain themselves, including their wives and children. As wherever Indians confronted the white invasion, the question came down to the simple, sobering one of whether resistance remained feasible or the time had come to accommodate to the new reality.

At Fort Greenville the following August the northwestern tribes resigned themselves to the new reality. Their chiefs accepted a treaty with Wayne ending the war and surrendering most of what would become Ohio and much of what would be Indiana, Illinois and Michigan. The United States government agreed to pay an annuity to the tribes, and it renounced claims to the lands not surrendered.

Washington hailed the outcome of Wayne's campaign. "The termination of the long, expensive and distressing war in which we have been engaged with certain Indians northwest of the Ohio is placed in the option of the United States by a treaty which the commander of our army has concluded provisionally with the hostile tribes in that region," the president announced to Congress. All that remained was for the Senate to ratify the treaty, which it soon did. "In the adjustment of the terms the satisfaction of the Indians was deemed worthy no less of the policy than of the liberality of the United States as the necessary basis of durable tranquility," Washington said. "The object, it is believed, has been fully attained."

He knew he was exaggerating. The Fallen Timbers victory and the Greenville treaty brought one war to an end. But the broader issue remained. Treaties that denied territory to settlers lasted only until population pressure on the frontier caused new settlers to cross the treaty lines, get themselves attacked by Indians defending their reduced lands and cry to Congress for protection.

Washington might hope to be retired at Mount Vernon before another war broke out, but he fully expected there to be another war. Several months later, amid a new land dispute in the southwest, this time with the Cherokees, the president wrote to Timothy Pickering, Edmund Randolph's successor as secretary of state. "It appears to be indispensable that the line between the United States and the Cherokees should be run, and distinctly marked, as soon as possible," Washington said. "The Indians urge this, the law requires it, and it ought to be done. But I believe scarcely anything short of a Chinese Wall or a line of troops will restrain land jobbers and the encroachment of settlers upon the Indian territory."

95

Washington had been hoping for retirement from public life since the 1750s, when he resigned command of the Virginia regiment. He hoped again when he relinquished command of the Continental army in 1783. He hoped during his first term as president that it would be his last.

His hope turned to intention, and his intention to planning, during his second term. He had humored Jefferson and Hamilton by accepting reelection. But they had left office afterward, so why shouldn't he?

He wasn't an old man. He had turned sixty-one shortly before his second inauguration. But longevity hadn't blessed his forebears. His father died at forty-eight. His father's father died at thirty-eight. Especially after the ailments of his first term, Washington felt he was living on borrowed time.

He didn't want to die in office. That would set a bad precedent. At the convention of 1787, Hamilton had endorsed the idea of presidents for life. Washington had shuddered personally, suspecting he might be hearing himself condemned to a life sentence. He objected for the sake of the republic as well. A key to its success would be its ability to transfer power from one chief executive to the next. Washington believed in Providence, but he thought it would presume too much to rely on the Almighty to terminate administrations.

He had hoped that by remaining in office he could help calm the partisan passions indulged by his lieutenants. Nothing of the sort occurred. Indeed, the passions raged higher than ever. And Jefferson and Hamilton having left office, he had less influence over them than ever. They humored him in person and in correspondence, but they proceeded to encourage outrageous behavior in their allies and supporters when they didn't commit it themselves.

Much of the outrage from Jefferson's party was aimed at Washington personally. His whole adult life he had cherished and guarded his honor and reputation. Now, in almost every issue of the detestable *Aurora* and other scandal sheets, his honor was impugned and his reputation savaged. He was said to be clinging to power, when he wanted nothing more than to be freed from the cares of power. All the more reason to get out while he was still breathing.

Early in his second term Washington began thinking seriously about what this final retirement would look like. In young adulthood he had dreamed of building a private empire of land, on the model if perhaps not the scale of Lord Fairfax's. The scouting and surveying of land was labor he enjoyed, and likewise the operating of multiple farms. He would create such an estate as any father would be proud to bequeath his offspring.

But there were no offspring. Martha's son Jack would inherit her estate. There were no obvious heirs for his.

Nor did he get the pleasure he once did from the management of his farms. Too long they had been under the oversight of others. He didn't fault Lund Washington and the others he'd engaged for the purpose, but no farm is ever tended so carefully as by its owner. They had managed operations from day to day, but they were in no position—by inclination or authorization—to make big changes.

And changes were required. The same crops year after year or even in rotation wore out the fields. Washington no longer grew tobacco, the worst offender, but such replacements as corn and oats worked their wearing effect over time.

Markets too had changed. The war had severed trade links with Britain, disrupting arrangements generations old. Trade had rebounded after the war, but then the European conflict disrupted the arrangements again. Washington, far from alone, had hoped the negotiations conducted by John Jay would improve the outlook, but the treaty Jay brought home was a disappointment.

A young man with energy and ambition—a version of his younger self transposed to this last decade of the century—might convert the challenges to opportunity. But Washington wasn't that younger man. He had accomplished enough. Let others take it from here.

ARTHUR YOUNG WAS an English agriculturalist charmed by Washington's decision to retire to farming after the Revolutionary War. He had written to Washington to tell him so. "The spectacle of a great commander retiring in the manner you have done from the head of a victorious army to the amusements of agriculture calls all the feelings of my bosom into play and gives me the strongest inclination, I fear an impotent one, to endeavour in the smallest degree to contribute to the success of so laudable a pleasure," Young wrote. He sent the first four volumes of a scientific study of agriculture he was publishing. "Will you do me the honour of accepting them as a very small mark of my veneration for the character of a man whose private virtues rendered a cause successful and illustrious which I have been solicitous as an Englishman to condemn?" He would send subsequent volumes if Washington found these useful.

"But, sir," he continued, "as my love of agriculture is even stronger than that I feel for any species of military glory, you must permit me to speak to you as a brother farmer, and to beg that if you want men, cattle, tools, seeds or anything else that may add to your rural amusement, favour me with your commands, and believe me I shall take a very sincere pleasure in executing them."

Washington had responded in the same fraternal spirit. "Agriculture has ever been amongst the most favourite amusements of my life, though I never possessed much skill in the art, and nine years total inattention to it has added nothing to a knowledge which is best understood from practice," he wrote. "But with the means you have been so obliging as to furnish me, I shall return to it (though rather late in the day) with hope and confidence." He had just received Young's books.

He availed himself of Young's offer to assist with men and supplies. He requested advice on tools, seeds and terms of employment of farmworkers. "Permit me to ask what a good plowman might be had for." Washington had done some investigating but learned nothing definite. "The writers upon husbandry estimate the hire of labourers so differently in England that it is not easy to discover from them whether one of the class I am speaking of would cost eight or eighteen pounds a year."

The correspondence continued sporadically during the next several years, interrupted on Washington's side by his return to public life as president. But as he looked toward leaving the presidency, he wrote to Young asking advice on a plan he had been weighing for some time. He felt comfortable enough with Young to write in confidence. "Whether, in the opinion of others, there be impropriety, or not, in communicating the object which has given birth to them, is not for me to decide. My own mind reproaches me with none, but if yours should view the subject differently, burn this letter and the draught which accompanies it, and the whole matter will be consigned to oblivion."

Washington got to the point. "All my landed property east of the Appalachian Mountains is under rent, except the estate called Mount Vernon," he said. "This, hitherto, I have kept in my own hands; but from my present situation, from my advanced time of my life, from a wish to live free from care and as much at my ease as possible during the remainder of it, and from other causes which are not necessary to detail, I have, latterly, entertained serious thoughts of letting"—leasing—"this estate also, reserving the Mansion House farm for my own residence, occupation and amusement in agriculture provided I can obtain what is in my own judgment, and in the opinion of others whom I have consulted, the low rent which I shall mention hereafter, and provided also I can settle it with *good* farmers."

Washington described Mount Vernon. "No estate in United America is more pleasantly situated than this. It lies in a high, dry and healthy country, 300 miles by water from the sea, and, as you will see by the plan, on one of the finest rivers in the world." Washington included a map. "Its margin is washed by more than ten miles of tidewater, from the bed of which and the innumerable coves, inlets and small marshes with which it abounds an inexhaustible fund of rich mud may be drawn as a manure, either to be used separately or in a compost." The geographic location of Mount Vernon couldn't be better. "It is situated in a latitude between the extremes of heat and cold, and is the same distance by land and water, with good roads and the best navigation, to and from the Federal City, Alexandria and Georgetown: distant from the first twelve, from the second nine, and from the last sixteen miles. The Federal City in the year 1800 will become the seat of the general government of the United States. It is increasing fast in buildings and rising into consequence, and will, I have no doubt, from the advantages given to it by nature, and its proximity to a rich interior country and the western territory, become the emporium of the United States."

Washington described in detail the four farms of the Mount Vernon estate he wished to lease: Union farm, Dogue Run farm, Muddy Hole farm, River farm. He characterized the soil of each, the crops and the buildings. His map situated them around the Mansion House farm and the common woodland.

He described to Young the tenants he sought and the terms he would offer. "I would let these four farms to four substantial farmers of wealth and strength sufficient to cultivate them, and who would insure to me the regular payment of the rents, and I would give them leases for seven or ten years at the rate of a Spanish milled dollar, or other money current at the time in this country equivalent thereto, for every acre of plowable and mowable ground within the enclosures of the respective farms, as marked in the plan, and would allow the tenants during that period to take fuel and use timber from the woodland to repair the buildings and to keep the fences in order until live fences could be substituted in place of dead ones."

If tenants couldn't be found to take on each farm whole, Washington was willing to subdivide them. But this wasn't his preference, because it would entail more trouble. Minimizing trouble and maximizing security were his goals. "My object is to fix my income (be it what it may) upon a solid basis in the hands of *good* farmers, because I am not inclined to make a medley of it and, above all, because I could not relinquish my present course without a moral certainty of the substitute which is contemplated."

Washington returned to the matter of discretion. "I shall now conclude as I began, with a desire that if you see any impropriety in making these sentiments known to that class of people who might wish to avail themselves of the occasion, that it may be mentioned. By a law or by some regulation of your government, artisans, I am well aware, are laid under restraints." The British government didn't want the country's clever workers absconding abroad with their talents and intellectual property. "And for this reason I have studiously avoided any overtures to mechanics although my occasions called for them. But never having heard that difficulties were thrown in the way of husbandmen by the government is one reason for my bringing this matter to your view. A second is that, having yourself expressed sentiments which shewed that you had cast an eye towards this country and was not inattentive to the welfare of it, I was led to make my intentions known to you, that if you or your friends were disposed to avail yourselves of the knowledge, you might take prompt measures for the execution. And thirdly, I was sure if you had lost sight of the object yourself, I could, nevertheless rely upon such information as you might see fit to give me and upon such characters too as you might be disposed to recommend."

. . .

YOUNG RESPONDED BY first assuring Washington that his legal delicacy was appreciated but unnecessary. "There is nothing in the laws of England or in the practice of her government which can occasion the least hesitation on the subject," he said. Farmers could go to America unhindered.

Laws weren't the problem. The preferences of farmers were. "I made every enquiry that could probably be attended with effect, and I have continued those enquiries to the present time," Young said. He consulted far and wide and received no positive response. "None would listen to *hiring* in America though very many were eager to become proprietors there. The acquisition of land in fee is indeed one of the principal inducements which instigate so many men to remove from this country to America."

There was another reason for the reluctance of English farmers to accept Washington's offer. "I have examined and reflected on the plan of your farms and the description which you have given of them, and they seem to me to have been laid out and distributed with great judgment," Young said. "The only drawback is the stock of negroes, which from motives that ought forever to do honour to your feelings you are so assiduous to keep in their envied situation." From Washington's description it seemed that slaves attached to each farm would be part of the bargain. Young was saying that English farmers didn't want to go to America to become the overseers of slaves.

Washington wasn't surprised about the resistance to leasing. "To acquire land in fee is, I am persuaded, *among* if not the *first* inducement to emigration to the United States, and therefore I never was sanguine in my expectation of obtaining tenants from England," he replied to Young.

Regarding the slaves on the farms, he said he had given the wrong impression. "It was not my meaning (if it was so understood) to make it a condition that they should be annexed as an appendage thereto. I had something better in view for them than that. To accommodate, not to encumber, the farmer was the idea I meant to convey to you. That is, that he might, or might not, as his inclination or interest should dictate, hire them, as he would do any other labourers which his necessities would require him to employ."

Washington didn't specify further to Young what he had in view for the Mount Vernon slaves. His leasing plan languished, and he weighed another means of simplifying his life. He wrote to Tobias Lear, then in England. As background he enclosed a copy of his offer to Young. He then said he was trying to *sell* properties that he owned in western Virginia, including tracts on the Ohio and Kanawha Rivers. "I have no scruple to disclose to you that my motives to these sales (as hath been, in part, expressed to Mr. Young) are to reduce my income, be it more or less, to specialties, that the remainder of my days may thereby be more tranquil and freer from cares, and that I may be enabled (knowing precisely what my dependence is) to do as much good with it as the resource will admit. For although, in the estimation of the world I possess a good and clear estate, yet so unproductive is it that I am oftentimes ashamed to refuse aids which I cannot afford, unless I was to sell part of it to answer the purpose."

At this point in the letter to Lear, Washington inserted an asterisk to indicate a passage on a separate sheet of paper headed "Private." The text there read, "Besides these, I have another motive which makes me earnestly wish for the accomplishment of these things. It is indeed more powerful than all the rest, namely to liberate a certain species of property which I possess very repugnantly to my own feelings, but which imperious necessity compels, until I can substitute some other expedient by which expenses not in my power to avoid (however well disposed I may be to do it) can be defrayed."

Lear understood that Washington was talking about freeing his slaves. He also understood why the passage in the letter was marked "Private." As president Washington would not breathe a word of emancipation plans. Nor should Lear. Southerners were already touchy about retaining slavery while the northern states were rejecting it. By no means was the Union so secure that Washington would give southerners reason to reconsider their attachment to it.

This was why he had been so elliptical in his offer to Young. His plan there had been to convert the enslaved workforce on his farms to a paid workforce. The slaves would be freed and offered employment like other paid workers.

That plan was going nowhere. Washington's new plan was to sell his western properties to subsidize the emancipation of his slaves. Shifting to a paid workforce required cash, which the land sales would have to provide since nothing had come of his offer of land leases.

➛ 96 ➛

In early 1796, while Hamilton was in Philadelphia arguing a case before the Supreme Court, Washington asked him to drop by for a visit. The president explained that he was going to retire for good. He wanted Hamilton's help drafting a farewell address to the American people. He had done something similar in 1792 with James Madison, who was then his literary confidant. Madison had produced a document urging Americans to remember what they had in common. When Washington decided not to retire that year, he had filed away Madison's draft. Madison was now a leader of the opposition to the administration, and Washington wasn't inclined to call him back. So he asked Hamilton for help with a rewrite.

Yet he wanted the whole business closely held. Hamilton obligingly was cautious even in a letter to Washington. "When last in Philadelphia you mentioned to me your wish that I should *re-dress* a certain paper which you had prepared. As it is important that a thing of this kind should be done with great care and much at leisure touched and retouched, I submit a wish that as soon as you have given it the *body* you mean it to have that it may be sent to me."

Hamilton was busy and the rewrite took time. Washington meanwhile couldn't decide when to reveal his decision to the public. "Having from a variety of reasons (among which a disinclination to be longer buffeted in the public prints by a set of infamous scribblers) taken my ultimate determination 'to seek the post of honor in a private station,' I regret exceedingly that I did not publish my valedictory address the day after the adjournment of Congress," Washington wrote to Hamilton in late June from Mount Vernon. Congress had adjourned at the beginning of the month. "This would have preceded the canvassing for electors (which is commencing with warmth in this state). It would have been announcing *publicly* what seems to be very well understood and is industriously propagated *privately*"—that Washington would not be a candidate. The political classes were making assumptions. "It would have removed doubts from the minds of *all,* and left the field clear for *all.* It would, by having preceded any unfavorable change in our foreign relations (if any should happen) render my retreat less difficult and embarrassing. And it might have prevented the remarks which, more than probable, will follow a late annunciation—namely that I delayed it long enough to see that the current was turned against me, before I declared my intention to decline."

By the time Washington published his valedictory in September, his decision to retire was generally taken for granted. But he wanted the American people to hear it officially from him. "The period for a new election of a citizen to administer the Executive Government of the United States being not far distant, and the time actually arrived when your thoughts must be employed in designating the person who is to be clothed with that important trust, it appears to me proper, especially as it may conduce to a more distinct expression of the public voice, that I should now apprise you of the resolution I have formed to decline being considered among the number of those out of whom a choice is to be made," Washington said. His message was first published in a Philadelphia newspaper. It was quickly reprinted in papers around the country.

Washington assured Americans that his decision to withdraw from public life signaled no loss of interest in the fate of the republic. He said he had intended to retire after his first term. "But mature reflection on the then perplexed and critical posture of our affairs with foreign nations and the unanimous advice of persons entitled to my confidence impelled me to abandon the idea." Now, though, the international situation had calmed, and he believed he wouldn't be blamed for indulging his desire for rest. "Every day the increasing weight of years admonishes me more and more that the shade of retirement is as necessary to me as it will be welcome."

Washington thanked his fellow citizens for the honor they had done him by twice making him their president. Their support had been crucial to his efforts on their and the country's behalf, and it filled him with pride. "I shall carry it with me to my grave."

"Here, perhaps, I ought to stop," he said. "But a solicitude for your welfare which cannot end but with my life, and the apprehension of danger natural to that solicitude, urge me on an occasion like the present to offer to your solemn contemplation and to recommend to your frequent review some sentiments which are the result of much reflection, of no inconsiderable observation, and which appear to me all important to the permanency of your felicity as a people." These should be taken as counsels from a departing friend with nothing but good wishes in his heart.

He spoke to the citizens of every section and state. But he wanted them to hear him as citizens of one country. "The name of American, which belongs to you in your national capacity, must always exalt the just pride of patriotism more than any appellation derived from local discriminations," he said. "With slight shades of difference, you have the same religion, manners, habits and political principles. You have in a common cause fought and triumphed together. The independence and liberty you possess are the work of joint councils and joint efforts, of common dangers, sufferings and successes."

America was more than the sum of its sectional parts. "The *North,* in an unrestrained intercourse with the *South,* protected by the equal laws of a common government, finds in the productions of the latter great additional resources of maritime and commercial enterprise and precious materials of manufacturing industry. The *South,* in the same intercourse, benefiting by the same agency of the *North,* sees its agriculture grow and its commerce expand." The population continued to spread across the mountains, creating another line that might divide but shouldn't. "The *East,* in a like intercourse with the *West,* already finds, and in the progressive improvement of interior communications by land and water will more and more find, a valuable vent for the commodities which it brings from abroad or manufactures at home. The *West* derives from the *East* supplies requisite to its growth and comfort." To place country above section would strengthen all. To place section above country would weaken all.

Washington warned of weakness from another cause: "the baneful effects of the spirit of party." Something of this spirit might be unavoidable. Humans had always banded together for protection and the pursuit of mutual interest. Party feeling existed in political systems of most sorts. "But in those of the popular form it is seen in its greatest rankness and is truly their worst enemy."

Parties imperiled liberty. "The alternate domination of one faction over another, sharpened by the spirit of revenge natural to party dissension, which in different ages and countries has perpetrated the most horrid enormities, is itself a frightful despotism," Washington said. "But this leads at length to a more formal and permanent despotism. The disorders and miseries which result gradually incline the minds of men to seek security and repose in the absolute power of an individual, and sooner or later the chief of some prevailing faction, more able or more fortunate than his competitors, turns this disposition to the purposes of his own elevation on the ruins of public liberty."

Party spirit was a danger even short of despotism. "It serves always to distract the public councils and enfeeble the public administration. It agitates the community with ill-founded jealousies and false alarms, kindles the animosity of one part against another, foments occasionally riot and insurrection. It opens the door to foreign influence and corruption, which find a facilitated access to the government itself through the channels of party passion. Thus the policy and the will of one country are subjected to the policy and will of another."

Apologists of parties accounted them checks on government. "This within certain limits is probably true," Washington allowed. In monarchies, for example, party spirit could keep a king within his prerogatives. But popular governments were different. "In governments purely elective, it is a spirit not to be encouraged. From their natural tendency it is certain there will always be enough of that spirit for every salutary purpose; and there being constant danger of excess, the effort ought to be by force of public opinion to mitigate and assuage it. A fire not to be quenched, it demands a uniform vigilance to prevent its bursting into a flame, lest, instead of warming, it should consume."

A third danger to the republic, after sectionalism and partisanship, was excessive involvement in the affairs of other countries. "Observe good faith and justice toward all nations," Washington advised. "Cultivate peace and harmony with all." This was best done at a distance and by modeling good behavior. "It will be worthy of a free, enlightened and at no distant period a great nation to give to mankind the magnanimous and too novel example of a people always guided by an exalted justice and benevolence."

The ocean was wide, and for America's sake it ought to remain so, even in the thoughts and feelings of Americans. "Nothing is more essential than that permanent, inveterate antipathies against particular nations and passionate attachments for others should be excluded, and that in place of them just and amicable feelings toward all should be cultivated. The nation which indulges toward another an habitual hatred or an habitual fondness is in some degree a slave. It is a slave to its animosity or to its affection, either of which is sufficient to lead it astray from its duty and its interest."

Washington endorsed trade with other countries, but little more. "The great rule of conduct for us in regard to foreign nations is: in extending our commercial relations to have with them as little political connection as possible." Without mentioning France by name, Washington acknowledged the political connection that already encumbered America. "So far as we have already formed engagements, let them be fulfilled with perfect good faith." But no new connections. "Here let us stop."

America differed from Europe, to America's advantage. "Europe has a set of primary interests which to us have none or a very remote relation. Hence she must be engaged in frequent controversies, the causes of which are essentially foreign to our concerns." Europe's troubles must not become America's.

Americans had work enough to do at home. "If we remain one people, under an efficient government, the period is not far off when we may defy material injury from external annoyance; when we may take such an attitude as will cause the neutrality we may at any time resolve upon to be scrupulously respected; when belligerent nations, under the impossibility of making acquisitions upon us, will not lightly hazard the giving us provocation; when we may choose peace or war, as our interest, guided by justice, shall counsel."

Why imperil this? "Why forego the advantages of so peculiar a situation? Why quit our own to stand upon foreign ground? Why, by interweaving our destiny with that of any part of Europe, entangle our peace and prosperity in the toils of European ambition, rivalship, interest, humor or caprice?"

Washington summed up this aspect of his advice in a sentence: "It is our true policy to steer clear of permanent alliances with any portion of the foreign world."

WASHINGTON CONCLUDED BY asking forgiveness from heaven and his compatriots. "Though in reviewing the incidents of my administration I am unconscious of intentional error, I am nevertheless too sensible of my defects not to think it probable that I may have committed many errors. Whatever they may be, I fervently beseech the Almighty to avert or mitigate the evils to which they may tend. I shall also carry with me the hope that my country will never cease to view them with indulgence and that, after forty-five years of my life dedicated to its service with an upright zeal, the faults of incompetent abilities will be consigned to oblivion, as myself must soon be to the mansions of rest."

Meanwhile, he looked to an earthly recompense made possible by the efforts of Americans together. "I anticipate with pleasing expectation that retreat in which I promise myself to realize without alloy the sweet enjoyment of partaking in the midst of my fellow-citizens the benign influence of good laws under a free government—the ever-favorite object of my heart and the happy reward, as I trust, of our mutual cares, labors and dangers."

Part XI

Mount Vernon

→ 97 ←

With Washington out of the running, America witnessed its first competitive race for president, which was also the first in which parties played a prominent role. The Federalists favored John Adams, the Republicans Thomas Jefferson. Adams won, with Jefferson a close second. Under the election rules still in force, this put Adams in the uncomfortable position of having his chief rival as vice president.

Nor did Adams find his inauguration reassuring, in contrast to Washington, who did. "Your dearest friend never had a more trying day than yesterday," Adams wrote to Abigail Adams. "A solemn scene it was indeed, and it was made more affecting to me by the presence of the General, whose countenance was as serene and unclouded as the day. He seemed to me to enjoy a triumph over me. Methought I heard him think, 'Ay! I am fairly out and you fairly in! See which of us will be happiest.' When the ceremony was over, he came and made me a visit and cordially congratulated me and wished my administration might be happy, successful and honourable."

RELIEVED TO BE OUT of office, Washington remained upset by the partisanship that infected the country's politics. He grew increasingly angry at the Republicans, the party he judged most to blame. He cut off communications with Jefferson, following a final excoriation. In the last substantive letter he ever wrote to Jefferson, Washington explained that he had held him above reproach as long as possible. "If I had entertained any suspicions before that the queries which have been published in Bache's paper proceeded from you, the assurances you have given of the contrary would have removed them," Washington said of some insinuating questions in the *Aurora* in his last months in office. "But the truth is, I harboured none."

Yet he couldn't ignore the mounting evidence. "It would not be frank, candid or friendly to conceal that your conduct has been represented as derogating from that opinion *I* had conceived you entertained of me. That to your particular friends and connexions, you have described, and they have announced, me as a person under a dangerous influence, and that if I would listen *more* to some *other* opinions all would be well. My answer invariably has been that I had never discovered anything in the conduct of Mr. Jefferson to raise suspicions in my mind of his insincerity, that if he would retrace my public conduct while he was in the administration, abundant proofs would occur to him that truth and right decisions were the *sole* objects of my pursuit, that there were as many instances within his *own* knowledge of my having decided *against* as in *favor of* the opinions of the person evidently alluded to, and moreover that I was no believer in the infallibility of the politics or measures of *any man living*. In short, that I was no party man myself, and the first wish of my heart was, if parties did exist, to reconcile them."

Washington confessed further naivete. "To this I may add, and very truly, that until within the last year or two I had no conception that parties would, or even could, go the length I have been witness to. Nor did I believe until lately that it was within the bounds of probability—hardly within that of possibility—that while I was using my utmost exertions to establish a national character of our own, independent, as far as our obligations and justice would permit, of every nation of the earth, and wished, by steering a steady course, to preserve this country from the horrors of a desolating war, that I should be accused of being the enemy of one nation and subject to the influence of another, and, to prove it, that every act of my administration would be tortured and the grossest and most insidious misrepresentations of them be made by giving one side *only* of a subject and that too in such exaggerated and indecent terms as could scarcely be applied to a Nero, a notorious defaulter or even to a common pickpocket."

Washington stopped himself. "Enough of this. I have already gone farther in the expression of my feelings than I intended." He never wrote to Jefferson again, but for a perfunctory note forwarding some papers.

He wished to leave it all behind. He wrote to Lafayette from Mount Vernon: "I have once more retreated to the shades of my own vine and fig tree, where I shall remain with best vows for the prosperity of that country for whose happiness I have toiled many years, to establish its independence, constitution and laws, and for the good of mankind in general, until the days of my sojournment, which cannot be many, are accomplished."

WASHINGTON MIGHT LEAVE POLITICS, but politics wouldn't leave him. More than ever did visitors to Virginia wish to see Mount Vernon and its master. Despite the strains on his household budget he held the doors open for all respectable persons who graced his doorstep. "The following company dined here," he wrote in his diary on a busy but not uncharacteristic day: "Chief Justice of the U.S. Ellsworth, Mr. & Mrs. Steer Sr., Mr. & Mrs. Steer Jr., Mr. Van Havre, Mr. & Mrs. Ludwell Lee, Mrs. Corbin Washington, Mr. & Mrs. Hodgson & Miss Cora Lee, Mr. & Mrs. Geo. Calvert and a Capt. Hamilton & Lady from the Bahama Islands."

To escape the crowds, he woke early. He wrote letters and handled other paperwork. Soon he was on horseback riding from farm to farm, supervising all that needed doing. Like any farmer he watched the sky and noted its effects on the ground. "The drought has been so excessive on this estate that I have made no oats, and if it continues a few days longer shall make no corn," he recorded during an arid August. "I have cut little or no grass, and my meadows at this time are as bare as the pavements."

He wrestled anew with balancing his books and his conscience. "It is demonstratively clear that on this estate (Mount Vernon), I have more working Negroes by a full moiety"—half—"than can be employed to any advantage in the farming system," he wrote to his nephew Robert Lewis. "To sell the overplus I cannot, because I am principled against this kind of traffic in the human species. To hire them out is almost as bad, because they could not be disposed of in families to any advantage, and to disperse the families I have an aversion. What then is to be done? Something must, or I shall be ruined, for all the money (in addition to what I raise by crops and rents) that have been received for lands sold within the last four years, to the amount of fifty thousand dollars, has scarcely been able to keep me afloat."

He tried novel ventures to increase revenues. "Distillery is a business I am entirely unacquainted with," he wrote to James Anderson, a Scotsman who emigrated to America and became a manager of Washington's farms. "But from your knowledge of it and from the confidence you have in the profit to be derived from the establishment, I am disposed to enter upon one." Anderson had been a distiller in his home country. He knew his spirits, and within two years Washington's whiskey works put out more than ten thousand gallons. Washington took care to pay the whiskey tax.

His sociability had always functioned best within limits. He made a point to stay away from the mansion until shortly before dinner at three o'clock. He could be the good host for a few hours, relating stories from the war and hearing the latest political news and gossip. His informants more often leaned Federalist than Republican, in part because they knew he did. The result was that Federalist policies and actions received a fuller and more sympathetic airing at Washington's table than Republican ones.

During the first two years of Adams's administration, the neutrality Washington had proclaimed during his own administration gave way to a sharply anti-French American posture. Washington had pointed the country down this road by the Jay treaty, which created even more outrage with the French government than among Republicans in America. Both groups, for political purposes, exaggerated the substance of the treaty. The Republicans failed to elect Jefferson president or gain control of Congress. The French government hoped for better luck. French officials interpreted the mere existence of the treaty as a signal that America was taking Britain's side in the Anglo-French war. France intensified its campaign against American shipping and made noises about attacking America itself. And in what came to be known as the XYZ affair, its foreign minister demanded a bribe from an American delegation sent to Paris to smooth things over. The delegates rejected the demand and related the story back to the already-hostile Adams administration, which greeted it with glee. The version circulated to the Federalist press put the rejection dramatically: "Millions for defense but not a penny for tribute."

Adams requested the millions for defense, to fight the French abroad should matters come to that. Meanwhile, he and the Federalists in Congress opened a domestic front against the Republicans. They passed a set of laws called the Alien and Sedition Acts, which made it more difficult for French immigrants—the Federalists called them French spies—to engage in politics in America and which criminalized much criticism of the American government.

"You ask my opinion of these laws," Washington wrote to a correspondent regarding the Alien and Sedition Acts. He noted that Republicans were denouncing the measures as unconstitutional. He urged all Americans to read the laws and the arguments both for and against them.

"And consider to what lengths a certain description of men in our country have already driven and seem resolved further to drive matters, and then ask themselves if it is not time and expedient to resort to protecting laws against aliens (for citizens you certainly know are not affected by that law) who acknowledge *no allegiance* to this country and in many instances are sent among us (as there is the best circumstantial evidence) for the *express purpose* of poisoning the minds of our people and to sow dissensions among them in order to alienate their affections from the government of their choice, thereby endeavouring to dissolve the Union."

Washington overgeneralized here. The Sedition Act—the measure the Republicans arraigned most vigorously—applied to citizens as well as to noncitizens. In fact, its chief target was Washington's tormentor Benjamin Bache, who was one of the first arrested under the Sedition Act. Bache died of yellow fever awaiting trial.

Conflation aside, Washington thought the package of laws an admirable effort to continue the work he had done for most of his adult life: defend America against its enemies foreign and domestic. He dismissed Republican criticism of the laws as evidence of the laws' necessity. "The Alien and Sedition Laws are now the desiderata in the opposition," he wrote to a Maryland Federalist. "But anything else would have done. And something there will always be for them to torture and to disturb the public mind."

THE OTHER HALF of the Adams program—the preparation for war—asked more of Washington than simple assent. Adams was not a humble man, but he had learned from Washington the value of appearing humble when assuming a new office. "My administration will certainly not be easy to myself," he wrote to Washington as tensions with France increased. "The prosperity of it to the country will depend upon Heaven and very little on anything in my power. I have no qualifications for the martial part of it, which is like to be the most essential. If the Constitution and your convenience would admit of my changing places with you, or of my taking my old station as your lieutenant civil, I should have no doubts of the ultimate prosperity and glory of the country."

Washington saw where this was going. "In forming an army, whenever I must come to that extremity, I am at an immense loss whether to call out all the old generals or to appoint a young set," Adams said. The Federalist-controlled Congress had authorized the president to raise an army of ten thousand. "If the French come here, we must learn to march with a quick step and to attack, for in that way only they are said to be vulnerable. I must tap you sometimes for advice. We must have your name, if you in any case will permit us to use it. There will be more efficacy in it than in many an army."

Perhaps Washington took comfort that he was merely being asked for advice and the use of his name, presumably in recruiting officers and men. Or was that all Adams was asking? Washington doubtless remembered when James Madison had asked for the use of his name in recruiting delegates to the Philadelphia convention, and Washington wound up not simply attending the convention but becoming its president. If Adams thought Washington's name was worth many an army, how much must he think Washington himself was worth?

He found out almost at once. Even before Washington answered, Adams nominated him to head the army. The Senate unanimously approved.

"To you, sir, I owe all the apologies I can make," Adams wrote to Washington. But time pressed. Adams explained that he would have come to Mount Vernon himself to make his request if duty hadn't kept him in Philadelphia. "As I said in a former letter, if it had been in my power to nominate you to be President of the United States, I should have done it, with less hesitation and more pleasure." As it was, Adams was sending the secretary of war, James McHenry, a holdover from Washington's administration, to pick the general's brain.

Washington couldn't resist the call of duty. "I cannot express how greatly affected I am at this new proof of public confidence," he wrote to Adams in his acceptance letter. As always he disclaimed ambition. "I must not conceal from you my earnest wish that the choice had fallen upon a man less declined in years and better qualified to encounter the usual vicissitudes of war." Yet if the country went to war, so must he.

Washington thought the French deserved a war. "The conduct of the Directory of France"—as the current government styled itself—"towards our country, their insidious hostility to its government, their various practices to withdraw the affections of the people from it, the evident tendency of their acts and those of their agents to countenance and invigorate opposition, their disregard of solemn treaties and the laws of nations, their war upon our defenceless commerce, their treatment of our ministers of peace and their demands amounting to tribute, could not fail to excite in me corresponding sentiments with those my countrymen have so generally expressed in their affectionate addresses to you," he wrote to Adams, who had shared petitions from Americans advocating war against France. "Believe me, sir, no one can more cordially approve of the wise and prudent measures of your administration."

Washington accepted leadership of the new army on one condition: "that I shall not be called into the field until the army is in a situation to require my presence or it becomes indispensable by the urgency of circumstances."

Washington knew he could have asked anything and Adams would have accepted. Adams did accept. Washington remained at Mount Vernon. He would let others raise the troops, procure the supplies and squabble with the politicians. He would take the field with the army when the army took the field against France. Which it might not do.

IN FACT IT DIDN'T. The bellicose mood of the French had coincided with a pause in the war against Britain. The pause ended before the new American army had mustered, and the French suspended what notions they had of dispatching an invading force against America. They contented themselves with arming privateers against American merchant vessels in the Caribbean and with occasional naval battles against the warships Adams dispatched to protect the civilian ships. The conflict was called the Quasi-War. The preface was apt, for it was never declared by Congress and it never came ashore. And Washington never took the field.

Yet he didn't get a free pass. Alexander Hamilton's public career had stalled. A person can be a wunderkind only so long. And Hamilton's sharp elbows had put off even his fellow Federalists. Adams seized the leadership of the party, leaving Hamilton to plot a comeback. The announcement of the new army provided an opportunity. Hamilton hoped to be made a general. Immediately after the Revolutionary War, he had been pleased to be addressed as Colonel Hamilton. But other veterans of the war, men he considered his inferiors, were called general. He should be a general too.

"I have no scruple about opening myself to you on this point," Hamilton wrote to Washington, in a letter urging him to accept Adams's offer of the army. "If you command, the place in which I should hope to be most useful is that of Inspector General, with a command in the line. This I would accept."

Washington had never been able to say no to Hamilton, and he didn't now. He recommended Hamilton for inspector general, with the rank of major general. Adams approved.

Yet this wasn't enough for Hamilton. He wanted to be second-in-command. He recognized, indeed encouraged, Washington's desire to remain at Mount Vernon until necessity demanded he mount up and join the army in person. Someone would have to give the orders in Washington's absence, and Hamilton thought he was as qualified as any. No less important, at the end of any conflict with France, Washington would retire again to Mount Vernon, leaving the army to his ranking subordinate, who at that point might expect to be made commanding general of the army. *This* was the prize Hamilton hungered for.

He hectored Washington, who humored him. "In the arrangement made by me with the secretary of war, the three major generals stood—Hamilton, Pinckney, Knox," Washington wrote to Adams, referring to Charles Cotesworth Pinckney and Henry Knox, besides Hamilton. "And in this order I expected their commissions would have been dated."

Adams had long distrusted Hamilton and was coming to despise him. He had other ideas about seniority, as Washington discovered on seeing the list from the secretary of war. "You have been pleased to order the last to be first, and the first to be last," Washington remarked to Adams.

Without demanding that Adams restore the order of seniority, Washington emphasized how important it was for a commanding general to have the officers he wanted in the positions he wanted for them.

Adams didn't hate Hamilton enough to pick a fight with Washington. The president acceded to Washington's wish—which was to say, Hamilton's wish.

Yet Hamilton didn't get all he sought. Events played out as Hamilton envisioned. Washington resigned when the possibility of a land war passed. Hamilton became the senior officer by rank. But Adams refused to promote him formally to commanding general of the army.

— 98 —

Washington was glad the war didn't come to America. For his country's sake he valued peace over war. For his own sake, especially at his age and condition of life, he cherished calm over excitement.

Yet he wasn't glad about the effects of the war scare on American politics. Clearly his compatriots hadn't taken his farewell address to heart. Lafayette was one of the few people Washington unburdened himself to, since everyone in America seemed to have chosen sides in the political contest that was tearing the country apart. As before, Washington laid the blame on the Republicans. "To give you a complete view of the politics and situation of things in this country would far exceed the limits of a letter, and to trace effects to their causes would be a work of time," Washington wrote to Lafayette. "But the sum of them may be given in a few words, and it amounts to this. That a party exists in the United States, formed by a combination of causes, who oppose the government in all its measures and are determined (as all their conduct evinces), by clogging its wheels, indirectly to change the nature of it and to subvert the Constitution. To effect this, no means which have a tendency to accomplish their purposes are left unessayed. The friends of government, who are anxious to maintain its neutrality and to preserve the country in peace, and to adopt measures to produce these desirable ends, are charged by them as being monarchists, aristocrats and infractors of the Constitution."

The chance of war had diminished but hadn't disappeared at the time of Washington's writing. The parties pulled in opposite directions on this issue. "There are many amongst us who wish to see this country embroiled on the side of Great Britain, and others who are anxious that we should take part with France against her," Washington told Lafayette. Washington hadn't written to Lafayette in some time and felt obliged to explain his personal actions. "After my valedictory address to the people of the United States, you would, no doubt, be somewhat surprised to hear that I had again consented to gird on the sword. But having struggled eight or nine years against the invasion of our rights by one power, and to establish an independence of it, I could not remain an unconcerned spectator of the attempts of another power to accomplish the same object, though in a different way."

Washington offered Lafayette an update of his valedictory. "On the politics of Europe I shall express no opinion, nor make any enquiry who is right or who is wrong. I wish well to all nations and to all men. My politics are plain and simple. I think every nation has a right to establish that form of government under which it conceives it shall live most happy, provided it infracts no right and is not dangerous to others. And that no governments ought to interfere with the internal concerns of another, except for the security of what is due to themselves."

THE RHYTHM OF LIFE included hints of death. "Mrs. Washington has been exceedingly unwell for more than eight days," Washington wrote in September 1799 to Thomas Peters, the husband of Martha's granddaughter Martha Peters. "Yesterday she was so ill as to keep her bed all day and to occasion my sending for Doctor Craik." James Craik, a Scot, had been a surgeon with Edward Braddock's army in the French and Indian War. He had treated the wounded general until his death. Craik retired to America after the war. Washington, who had met him on the Braddock campaign, recalled him to military service, this time against the British in the Continental army. After Craik's second retirement from the military, Washington encouraged him to establish a medical practice in Alexandria, within easy summons of Mount Vernon.

"Hers has been a kind of ague and fever," Washington said of Martha's illness. Ague-and-fever was malaria. "She is now better, and taking the bark, but low, weak and fatigued." Cinchona bark contained quinine and was a common treatment for malaria. The relief was only symptomatic. "Since writing and sealing this letter," Washington wrote on the outside, "Mrs. Washington's fever has returned with uneasy and restless symptoms." Martha survived but symptoms lingered through the autumn.

"MORNING CLOUDY," Washington wrote on December 12. "Wind at NE and mercury at 33. A large circle round the moon last night. About

1 o'clock it began to snow. Soon after to hail and then turned to a settled cold rain."

Washington never minded bad weather. From his first trip west for Lord Fairfax, he treated it as part of life's adventure. The snow and rain didn't curtail his regular round this day. He arrived home shortly before dinner.

"Morning snowing and about 3 inches deep," he wrote in his diary the next day. The wind was still from the northeast, and the thermometer was just below freezing. The snow tapered off in the early afternoon. "Wind in the same place but not hard. Mercury 28 at night."

This was the last entry in the diary Washington had started keeping as a youth. Tobias Lear picked up the story in his own diary, which overlapped Washington's. "On Thursday Dec. 12th, the general rode out to his farms about ten o'clock, and did not return home till past three," Lear wrote. "Soon after he went out the weather became very bad—rain, hail and snow falling alternately with a cold wind. When he came in, I carried some letters to him to frank, intending to send them to the post office in the evening. He franked the letters, but said the weather was too bad to send a servant to the office that evening. I observed to him that I was afraid he had got wet. He said no, his great coat had kept him dry. But his neck appeared to be wet and the snow was hanging upon his hair. He came to dinner (which had been waiting for him) without changing his dress. In the evening he appeared as well as usual."

For December 13, Lear wrote, "A heavy fall of snow took place on Friday, which prevented the general from riding out as usual. He had taken cold (undoubtedly from being so much exposed the day before) and complained of a sore throat. He however went out in the afternoon into the ground between the house and the river to mark some trees which were to be cut down in the improvement of that spot. He had a hoarseness, which increased in the evening, but he made light of it. In the evening the papers were brought from the post office, and he sat in the parlour with Mrs. Washington and myself reading them till about nine o'clock." Martha went upstairs first, leaving Washington and Lear. "He was very cheerful, and when he met with anything interesting or entertaining, he read it aloud as well as his hoarseness would permit him. He requested me to read him the debates of the Virginia assembly on the election of a senator and a governor, and hearing Mr. Madison's observations respecting Mr. Monroe, he appeared much affected and spoke with some degree of asperity on the subject, which I endeavored to moderate, as I always did on such occasions." Of late Lear worried when Washington got upset. "On his retiring I observed to him that he had better take something to remove his cold. He answered no. 'You know I never take anything for a cold. Let it go as it came.'"

Washington's condition worsened in the night. "Between two and three o'clock on Saturday morning, he awoke Mrs. Washington and told her he was very unwell," Lear wrote. "She observed that he could scarcely speak and breathed with difficulty, and would have got up to call a servant, but he would not permit her lest she should take cold." Martha Washington recounted this conversation to Lear afterward.

"As soon as the day appeared, the woman Caroline went into the room to make a fire, and Mrs. Washington sent her immediately to call me. I got up, put on my clothes as quickly as possible and went to his chambers." This was when Martha Washington described the events of the night. "I found the general breathing with difficulty and hardly able to utter a word intelligibly. He desired that Mr. Rawlins, one of the overseers, might be sent for to bleed him before the doctors could arrive. I dispatched a servant instantly for Rawlins, and another for Dr. Craik, and returned again to the general's chambers, where I found him in the same situation as I had left him."

Washington was administered a concoction of molasses, vinegar and butter. He couldn't swallow it. "Whenever he attempted it, he appeared to be distressed, convulsed and almost suffocated," Lear wrote.

Rawlins arrived and prepared to bleed Washington. If doctors weren't around, the withdrawal of blood by incision was accomplished by practiced nonprofessionals. "When the arm was ready the general, observing that Rawlins appeared to be agitated, said, as well as he could speak, 'Don't be afraid.'"

The cut was made in Washington's arm, and the blood ran out readily. Martha Washington grew worried. "Mrs. Washington, not knowing whether bleeding was proper or not in the general's situation, begged that much might not be taken from him lest it should be injurious." Lear prepared to stop the bleeding. "But when I was about to untie the string, the general put up his hand to prevent it, and as soon as he could speak, said, 'More, more!'"

Martha remained worried. After a bit more blood flowed out, she prevailed on her husband to accept a halt. Half a pint had been drawn off. The effect on his symptoms was nil.

Lear tried swabbing the outside of Washington's throat with an infusion of sage. "Tis very sore," Washington remarked with difficulty. His feet were placed in a warm bath. No relief.

Dr. Craik hadn't arrived. Martha Washington insisted that Lear summon a second doctor, Gustavus Brown. Lear did so.

Craik appeared. He tried blistering Washington's throat to relieve the swelling. He had Washington inhale steam of hot water and vinegar. He gave Washington vinegar and sage tea to gargle. "He was almost suffocated," Lear wrote. Yet when Washington coughed, some phlegm came up. Craik encouraged him to cough again. Washington couldn't.

Craik called for a third doctor, because Brown was slow in coming. When this doctor, Elisha Dick, arrived, he and Craik decided to bleed Washington again. "The blood came very slow, was thick, and did not produce any symptoms of fainting," Lear noted. Brown arrived, and the three doctors spoke among themselves. Washington showed a slight improvement. "The general could now swallow a little."

But Washington wasn't encouraged. "About half past 4 o'clock he desired me to call Mrs. Washington to his bed side, when he requested her to go down into his room and take from his desk two wills which she would find there, and bring them to him." Washington examined the two documents. "He gave her one, which he observed was useless as being superseded by that other, and desired her to burn it, which she did, and took the other and put it into her closet."

While Martha was out of the room, Washington turned to Lear. "I find I am going," he said. "My breath cannot last long. I believed from the first that the disorder would prove fatal."

He instructed Lear to collect his papers and settle his accounts. "You know more about them than anyone else." Lear promised he would. Washington asked Lear if he recalled anything further that needed doing. He felt the end approaching. "I told him I could recollect nothing, but that I hoped he was not so near his end. He observed, smiling, that he certainly was, and that as it was the debt which all must pay, he looked to the event with perfect resignation."

Reaching the end wasn't easy. "He appeared to be in great pain and distress from the difficulty of breathing, and frequently changed his posture in the bed," Lear wrote. Lear tried to help him get comfortable. Washington thanked Lear for his ministrations. "I am afraid I shall fatigue you too much," he said. Lear assured him he wasn't tired. "Well," said Washington, "it is a debt we must pay to each other, and I hope when you want aid of this kind you will find it."

Craik returned to the room about five o'clock. Washington said to him, "Doctor, I die hard, but I am not afraid to go. I believed from my first attack that I should not survive it. My breath could not last long."

Craik was visibly moved. "The doctor pressed his hand but could not utter a word," Lear wrote. "He retired from the bed side and sat by the fire absorbed in grief."

The other doctors came in. "I feel myself going," Washington told them. "I thank you for your attentions, but I pray you to take no more trouble about me. Let me go off quietly. I cannot last long."

He continued uncomfortable and restless. He said nothing. The doctors returned at eight o'clock. They tried blisters again, simply to alleviate the symptoms.

"About 10 o'clock he made several attempts to speak to me before he could effect it," Lear wrote. "At length he said, 'I am just going! Have me decently buried, and do not let my body be put into the vault in less than three days after I am dead.'" Washington had a morbid fear of being buried alive.

"I bowed assent, for I could not speak. He then looked at me again and said, 'Do you understand me?'"

Lear said he did.

"Tis well," Washington said.

He died a short while later.

99

In the name of God, amen. I, George Washington of Mount Vernon, a citizen of the United States and lately President of the same, do make, ordain and declare this instrument, which is written with my own hand and every page thereof subscribed with my name, to be my last will and testament, revoking all others."

Washington spoke from beyond the grave when his will was read. Americans might not have been surprised, but they would have been struck, to learn that Washington identified himself first and only as a citizen of the United States. Virginia was his residence, but America was his country.

The handwritten will was many pages long. In it Washington explained that he hadn't sought legal advice in drawing it up. He apologized for infelicities in wording, then got straight to the substance, starting with what had weighed on him for years. "Upon the decease of my wife, it is my will and desire that all the slaves which I hold in my own right shall receive their freedom." The delay wasn't from concern that Martha needed their labor. "To emancipate them during her life would, though earnestly wished by me, be attended with such insuperable difficulties on account of their intermixture by marriages with the dower Negroes as to excite the most painful sensations, if not disagreeable consequences, from the latter." The dower slaves were the ones beyond the power of either Washington or Martha to free, being held in trust for Jack Custis from Daniel Custis's descendants. To free a husband or a wife while the other spouse remained bound would test marriages perhaps beyond their limits. The problem would arise eventually, when Martha died and Washington's slaves became free. But she wouldn't be the one to have to deal with it.

Washington acknowledged that freedom wasn't an unalloyed gift to the old slaves, the infirm and the very young. Such individuals couldn't be expected to support themselves. He made provision for these three groups. "It is my will and desire that all who come under the first and second description shall be comfortably clothed and fed by my heirs while they live." The children's freedom would be withheld until the age of twenty-five. "The Negroes thus bound are by their masters or mistresses to be taught to read and write, and to be brought up to some useful occupation." To underwrite these commitments, Washington ordered that "a regular and permanent fund" be established from his estate.

He stipulated what he had long practiced. "I do hereby expressly forbid the sale or transportation out of the said Commonwealth"—Virginia—"of any slave I may die possessed of, under any pretense whatsoever. And I do moreover most pointedly and most solemnly enjoin it upon my executors hereafter named, or the survivors of them, to see that this clause respecting slaves, and every part thereof, be religiously fulfilled."

"And to my mulatto man William (calling himself William Lee) I give immediate freedom," Washington wrote. "Or if he should prefer it (on account of the accidents which have befallen him and which have rendered him incapable of walking or of any active employment) to remain in the situation he now is, it shall be optional in him to do so. In either case, however, I allow him an annuity of thirty dollars during his natural life." The annuity would be paid whether or not William Lee remained at Mount Vernon. "This I give him as a testimony of my sense of his attachment to me, and for his faithful services during the Revolutionary War."

Washington provided for others in need. He left four thousand dollars for the support of a free school "for the purpose of educating such orphan children, or the children of such other poor and indigent persons, as are unable to accomplish it with their own means." He bequeathed to the Liberty Hall Academy in Rockbridge County some of the navigation company shares the Virginia legislature had at length prevailed upon him to accept, by refusing to accept his no.

The rest of the shares went to another education project, one with patriotic goals. "It has always been a source of serious regret with me to see the youth of these United States sent to foreign countries for the purpose of education, often before their minds were formed or they had imbibed any adequate ideas of the happiness of their own, contracting too frequently not only habits of dissipation and extravagance but principles unfriendly to republican government and to the true and genuine liberties of mankind," he said. "For these reasons it has been my ardent wish to see a plan devised on a liberal scale which would have a tendency to spread systematic ideas through all parts of this rising empire, thereby to do away local attachments and state prejudices as far as the nature of things would, or indeed ought to, admit from our national councils." To this end he proposed to establish "a university in a central part of the United States to which the youth of fortune and talents from all parts thereof might be sent for the completion of their education." The obvious place for the national university would be the federal District of Columbia. Washington offered the shares on the condition that Congress put its support behind the project.

The bulk of Washington's estate passed to Martha for the rest of her life. Specific personal bequests went to various relatives. He forgave several loans due him. He left his letters and other papers to nephew Bushrod Washington, who had shown the greatest interest in them. He left to Charles Washington, his sole surviving brother, a gold-headed cane bequeathed to him by Benjamin Franklin.

He specified his place of final rest. "The family vault at Mount Vernon requiring repairs and being improperly situated besides, I desire that a new one of brick and upon a larger scale may be built at the foot of what is commonly called the Vineyard Inclosure," he said. "In which my remains, with those of my deceased relatives (now in the old vault) and such others of my family as may choose to be entombed there, may be deposited. And it is my express desire that my corpse may be interred in a private manner, without parade or funeral oration."

—100—

We are all Republicans, we are all Federalists," Thomas Jefferson told the nation on ascending to the office Washington had held, fifteen months after Washington's death. A rematch between Adams and Jefferson had produced a victory for the latter amid a groundswell for the Republicans. Jefferson held out an olive branch, in the party-transcending spirit of Washington's farewell address. "We have called by different names brethren of the same principle," he said.

Jefferson echoed Washington on the need to focus on American affairs. "Kindly separated by nature and a wide ocean from the exterminating havoc of one quarter of the globe, too high-minded to endure the degradations of the others, possessing a chosen country with room enough for our descendants to the thousandth and thousandth generation," he said, "what more is necessary to make us a happy and a prosperous people?" Jefferson edited Washington gracefully—so well that Jefferson's formulation would often be attributed to Washington—in characterizing the attitude his administration would take toward the world: "Peace, commerce and honest friendship with all nations, entangling alliances with none."

THE SPIRIT OF WASHINGTON hovered over the country in the years and decades after his death. Yet the more widely he was honored, the less commonly he was consulted. Jefferson was a wordsmith, able to turn appealing phrases. He was also a party boss, willing to shape the Republican party into a force that, having displaced the Federalists of Hamilton and Adams, governed America for a generation. Jefferson avoided the foreign entanglements Washington advised against, but if he gave a thought after his inaugural address to Washington's anti-party counsel, his actions as president failed to show it.

The Federalists were no less partisan, only less successful. Hamilton fell out with Adams before Jefferson's election and doomed Adams's chance of defeating their common foe. The Federalists became a regional party, pent up in New England, before flirting with secession and imploding amid the second war with Britain, the country they long favored.

Briefly the Republicans had national politics to themselves. But they broke apart, with one wing dubbing themselves Democrats and the other, combining with former Federalists, calling themselves Whigs.

Washington's spirit must have groaned. Yet the great man had complicity in this, though he would have been reluctant to think so. Washington didn't create parties, but he created a country that couldn't exist without them.

Henry Lee eulogized Washington as "first in war, first in peace and first in the hearts of his countrymen." Washington had help with the war and the peace, of course. He and the other rebels of 1776, and the other framers of 1787, fashioned a system of self-government. The rebels of '76 agreed that America must have a government of its own. But they didn't agree on the nature of that government. One or many? The framers of '87 agreed on one government above the others. But they didn't agree on the powers of that government.

Why should they agree? They were strong-minded men. They were independent-minded men. By temperament and experience they had different expectations of government, different distrusts of government. That they should seek allies among those who shared their views could have been predicted. That the alliances would contest sharply for power simply showed their members to be human. The struggle for power is as old as the species.

Washington stood outside the contest. This wasn't because he was more virtuous than Jefferson, Hamilton and the rest. It was because he was beyond ambition of the sort that still drove them. They had reputations to establish and enhance. They weren't the hero of the Revolutionary War, the indomitable executor of American freedom. For Washington the presidency was a victory procession, a reward he had to be prevailed upon to accept. He wasn't posing when he worried, ahead of accepting the office, that political missteps would tarnish his military triumph.

From young adulthood Washington had been a soldier. As a soldier he did something no other American had ever done. He did something no other American would ever do. The birth of a nation comes but once in national life.

What was his secret? What made him so great?

On his first mission to Ohio, Washington had shown himself to be resourceful, diplomatic and brave. In his command of the Virginia regiment, he added decisiveness and diligence to the qualities for which he was known. At the head of the Continental army, he manifested a devotion to duty and an ability to inspire that held the army together when everything else seemed bent on pulling it apart. At the end of the war, he astonished the world and gratified his compatriots by resigning his commission and retiring to civilian life.

As much as Americans admired Washington's accomplishments, they revered his character the more. To them he embodied what they hoped their country would be. Already a second father to his soldiers, he became a patriarch to them all.

Washington's character gave his countrymen confidence he wouldn't abuse the power of the presidency. They reasoned that if he hadn't usurped power when he had an army behind him, when his soldiers and certain members of Congress wanted him to march on the capital, he certainly wouldn't usurp power now. And when he voluntarily returned the presidency to the people, as he had voluntarily returned his military commission to Congress, popular confidence in this American Cincinnatus was confirmed.

Character was the key to Washington's success. Different gifts were required by those who came after him. Foremost was aptitude in what Washington couldn't abide—partisan politics. Washington was the first president, and the last not to head a party. What others had to strive for, Washington received without the asking. The others depended on their parties, which soon gained a monopoly on the recruiting of presidential candidates. Even the celebrated generals who followed Washington into the presidency—Jackson, Grant, Eisenhower—had to choose a party to get there. Henry Lee might more insightfully have said that Washington was first in war, first in peace and last of his kind in America. There was one Washington. There would be no others.

The changing politics that made Washington a relic by the time of his death reflected a changing popular sensibility. The personal style Washington cultivated from youth, marked by polite reserve tending to haughtiness, suited the country he was born in much better than the one he died in. The Virginia gentry deemed themselves a cut above the ordinary men and women of the colony, and the ordinary men and women deferred to them. The revolutionary events of Washington's middle years dealt a blow to this habit of deference. Jefferson's assertion that "all men are created equal" at once reflected and accelerated the change, striking first at monarchy but then at pretensions to superiority in the new republic and finally legitimizing the ethos of democracy. Americans were content to look up to their president while Washington held the office, but before long they insisted on looking their presidents level in the eye. In the age of democracy, a Washingtonian reserve was a liability, an intolerable imputation of others' inferiority.

Washington was offended by the criticisms he read in the *Aurora* and other Republican papers. But he was handled gently compared with his successors. He never would have accepted the presidency had he anticipated being treated the way Adams, Jefferson and the others expected to be treated as a matter of course.

In lamenting partisanship, Washington mourned the passing of an old age and the dawning of a new one. He fit the old age perfectly and, for that reason, the new age not at all. He lived a timely life and died a timely death. In doing so, he gained a timeless reputation.

Sources

CHAPTER 1

3 "They represented . . . primitive innocence": Robert Beverley, *The History and Present State of Virginia* (1705), ed. Susan Scott Parrish (2013), 13–14.

CHAPTER 2

6 John Washington: Martin H. Quitt, "The English Cleric and the Virginia Adventurer: The Washingtons, Father and Son," *Virginia Magazine of History and Biography*, April 1989.

CHAPTER 3

8 "I should be glad": George Washington (GW) to John Augustine Washington, May 28, 1755, Founders Online, founders.archives.gov. Unless otherwise noted, documents below will be from this collection.

CHAPTER 4

13 "Last week": *Pennsylvania Gazette*, Nov. 8, 1739.
13 "On Thursday last": *Pennsylvania Gazette*, Nov. 15, 1739.
13 "On Friday last": *Pennsylvania Gazette*, Nov. 29, 1739.
13 "On Thursday last": *Pennsylvania Gazette*, Dec. 6, 1739.
14 "He had a loud . . . gold and all": Benjamin Franklin, *Autobiography* (1886 ed.), 131–36.
15 "I was sensibly . . . holy religion!": *Pennsylvania Gazette*, April 17, 1740.
17 "There are thousands . . . is enough": Davies to J. F., March 2, 1756, in *Letters from the Rev. Samuel Davies Shewing the State of Religion in Virginia, Particularly Among the Negroes* (1757), 18–21.
18 "Wives are drawn": Eric C. Smith, *John Leland: A Jeffersonian Baptist in Early America* (2022), chap. 2.

CHAPTER 5

19 "Friday March 11th": GW journal, March 1748.
20 "Saturday March 12th . . . concludes my journal": Ibid.

CHAPTER 6

27 "Catched a dolphin . . . 16 pistoles": *The Daily Journal of Major George Washington in 1751–52, Kept While on a Tour from Virginia to the Island of Barbadoes,* ed. J. M. Toner (1892), 24–69.

CHAPTER 7

32 "On Wednesday": GW, "Journey to the French Commandant: Narrative."
33 "The lands upon . . . peaceable departure": Dinwiddie to French commandant, Oct. 31, 1753, in *The Journal of Major George Washington* (1754), 25–26.
34 "He has had extensive": GW to John Robinson, May 30, 1757.
34 "The waters were quite . . . deep still nature": GW, "Journey to the French Commandant."
35 "I gave him . . . with 6 Guns": Ibid.

CHAPTER 8

37 "Fathers . . . own drawing": GW, "Journey to the French Commandant."
37 "Brothers . . . consented to stay": Ibid.
40 "This was a question . . . accompany us up": Ibid.

CHAPTER 9

44 "Friday 7": *Christopher Gist's Journals with Historical, Geographical and Ethnological Notes and Biographies of His Contemporaries,* ed. William M. Darlington (1893), 82–83.
44 "We passed over . . . he had engaged": GW, "Journey to the French Commandant."
44 "We set out . . . for themselves": *Gist's Journals,* 83–84.
47 "He desired I might . . . woods on foot": GW, "Journey to the French Commandant."
47 "Indeed . . . enough to sleep": *Gist's Journals,* 84.
49 "We expected . . . to be satisfied": GW, "Journey to the French Commandant."

CHAPTER 10

51 "You are to use": Dinwiddie to GW, n.d., in *The Official Records of Robert Dinwiddie, Lieutenant-Governor of the Colony of Virginia, 1751–1758* (1883), 1:59.
52 "Everything being ready . . . together again": GW, "Expedition to the Ohio, 1754: Narrative."
53 "I hope . . . can muster": GW to Dinwiddie, April 25, 1754.
54 "It gives me . . . enemy was routed": GW, "Expedition to the Ohio."

CHAPTER 11

57 "We had . . . in the sound": GW to John Augustine Washington, May 31, 1754.
57 "He would not say so": Horace Walpole, *Memoirs of the Reign of King George the Second,* ed. Lord Holland (1847), 1:399–400.
58 "We expect": GW to John Augustine Washington, May 31, 1754.
59 "The English": Francis Parkman, *Montcalm and Wolfe* (1885 ed.), 1:154.
60 "We marched . . . King our Master": Villiers journal, in *A Memorial Containing a Summary View of Facts with Their Authorities in Answer to the Observations Sent by the English Ministry to the Courts of Europe,* translated from the French (1757), 177–79.
61 "About 9 o'clock . . . and baggage": GW and Mackay account of capitulation of Fort

Necessity, from *Virginia Gazette,* July 19, 1754, in Washington Papers. Mackay's signature accompanied Washington's on the capitulation. A very similar version is in Dinwiddie to Lords of Trade, July 24, 1754, in *Official Records of Dinwiddie,* 239–40.

62 "We made the English": Villiers journal, in *Memorial,* 180.

62 "We were obliged": Note to Articles of Capitulation, July 3, 1754, Washington Papers.

63 "L'assasin": Articles of Capitulation.

63 "The next morning": GW and Mackay account.

CHAPTER 12

65 "In our way . . . states and princes": Franklin, *Autobiography,* 166–68.

CHAPTER 13

67 "What facilitated": Walpole, *Memoirs of King George the Second,* 1:396.

68 "These depredations . . . permanent foundations": Dinwiddie message to the Council and Burgesses, Feb. 14, 1754, in *Official Records of Dinwiddie.*

CHAPTER 14

71 "The number killed": GW and Mackay account.

72 "That we were": GW letter, n.d. and without recipient, ca. 1757.

72 "Tanacharisson": Entry for Sept. 3, 1754, Conrad Weiser journal, in *Minutes of the Provincial Council of Pennsylvania* (1851), 6:151–52.

72 "We now open . . . some foundation": Account by James Innes of speech of unnamed Iroquois chief, Nov. 5, 1754, Appendix E in David L. Preston, *Braddock's Defeat: The Battle of the Monongahela and the Road to Revolution* (2015), 351–53.

74 "I wish earnestly": GW to Orme, March 15, 1755.

74 "I herewith send": GW to Orme, April 2, 1755.

74 "The sole motive": GW to Robinson, April 25, 1755.

74 "I have had": GW to Fairfax, April 23, 1755.

CHAPTER 15

75 "We are to halt . . . Shirley etc.": GW to John Carlyle, May 14, 1755.

75 "As to any danger . . . military line": GW to John Augustine Washington, May 14, 1755.

75 "The General . . . every brook": GW to John Augustine Washington, June 28, 1755.

76 "Our scouts . . . the battlefield": French account of the battle of the Monongahela by Michel-Pierre-Augustin-Thomas Le Courtois des Bourbes, Oct. 20, 1755, Appendix F in Preston, *Braddock's Defeat,* 355–56.

78 "We were attacked . . . of the frontiers": GW to Dinwiddie, July 18, 1755.

79 "We have been": GW to John Augustine Washington, July 18, 1755.

CHAPTER 16

80 "I am always ready . . . my expectation": GW to Augustine Washington, Aug. 2, 1755.

80 "Honored Madam": GW to Mary Washington, Aug. 14, 1755.

81 "I have just come": Lewis to GW, Aug. 9, 1755.

81 "I never will . . . in a storm": GW to Lewis, Aug. 14, 1755.

82 "I reposing . . . receive from me": Dinwiddie commission to GW, Aug. 14, 1755.

CHAPTER 17

83 "I have succeeded": Paul A. W. Wallace, *Conrad Weiser* (1945), 385, 395.
83 "Two and forty . . . into ashes": Parkman, *Montcalm and Wolfe,* 342–43.
83 "All burned . . . and kills them": Wallace, *Conrad Weiser,* 403, 410.
84 "Not an hour": GW to Dinwiddie, April 24, 1756.
84 "No officer": GW general instructions for recruiting, Sept. 1, 1755.
85 "You are to lay in": GW to Charles Dick, Sept. 6, 1755.
85 "You are to be": GW to Andrew Lewis, Sept. 6, 1755.
85 "All the shoes . . . their companions": GW to Dinwiddie, Sept. 11, 1755.
86 "You are hereby": GW to Joshua Lewis, Sept. 18, 1755.
86 "If any man": GW orders, Sept. 19, 1755.
86 "As complaint": GW orders, Sept. 19, 1755 (different from previous).
87 "1st . . . answerable for them": GW to Stephen, Sept. 20, 1755.

CHAPTER 18

89 "We are at a loss": GW to Dinwiddie, Oct. 8, 1755.
89 "Matters are": Stephen to GW, Oct. 4, 1755.
89 "I arrived yesterday . . . plantations are destroyed": GW to Dinwiddie, Oct. 11–14, 1755.
92 "You will be": GW to Stephen, Nov. 18, 1755.
92 "I do advise": GW advertisement, Oct. 13, 1755.
92 "Remember": GW address to officers, Jan. 8, 1756.

CHAPTER 19

96 "Last night . . . all dispatch": Dinwiddie to Shirley, Nov. 4, 1755, in *Dinwiddie Papers,* 2:261.
97 "Last week . . . Colonel Washington": *Pennsylvania Gazette,* Feb. 12, 19, 26 and March 11, 1756.
98 "Governor Dinwiddie": Shirley order, March 5, 1756, in *Correspondence of William Shirley,* ed. Charles Henry Lincoln (1912), 2:412–13.

CHAPTER 20

99 "The enemy have returned . . . of the country": GW to Dinwiddie, April 7, 1756.
100 "I was in high hopes . . . two to one": GW to Robinson, April 16, 1756.
101 "First, erecting of forts": GW to Loudoun, Jan. 10, 1757.
101 "I have been posted . . . of this kind": GW to Richard Washington, April 15, 1757.

CHAPTER 21

103 "I shall enter . . . in those parts": Forbes plan of operations, Feb. 1, 1758, in *Writings of General John Forbes Relating to His Service in North America,* ed. Alfred Procter James (1938), 33–37.
104 "My infirmities": Forbes to Loudoun, Feb. 3, 1758, in *Writings of Forbes,* 37.
104 "My damned legs": Forbes to Loudoun, Feb. 5, 1758, in *Writings of Forbes,* 40.
105 "And therefore": Forbes to Denny, March 20, 1758, in *Writings of Forbes,* 58.
105 "He has the character": Forbes to Blair, March 20, 1758, in GW to Forbes, April 23, 1758, n1.
105 "Permit me . . . quarters for them": GW to Forbes, April 23, 1758.
106 "Pardon the liberty . . . continent at least": GW to Forbes, June 19, 1758.

CHAPTER 22

108 "Sundry persons": *Pennsylvania Gazette,* June 1, 1758.
108 "I have lately": Forbes to Abercrombie, June 7, 1758, in *Writings of Forbes,* 109–10.
109 "Mr. Amherst": Forbes to Abercrombie, June 10, 1758, in *Writings of Forbes,* 113–14.
109 "I am in hopes . . . confidence in": Forbes to William Pitt, July 10, 1758, in *Writings of Forbes,* 140–42.
109 "I received some": Forbes to Abercrombie, July 25, 1758, in *Writings of Forbes,* 159.
110 "I have been very much": Forbes to Abercrombie, Aug. 3, 1758, in *Writings of Forbes,* 169.
110 "My men": GW to Bouquet, July 3, 1758.
110 "I have been long": Forbes to Bouquet, June 27, 1758, in *Writings of Forbes,* 125.
111 "It gave me": GW to Bouquet, July 13, 1758.
111 "Several years ago . . . sinister views": GW to Bouquet, Aug. 2, 1758.
113 "I find him fixed . . . assured of": GW to Halkett, Aug. 2, 1758.
113 "A jealousy arising . . . coming this way": Forbes to Abercrombie, Aug. 11, 1758, in *Writings of Forbes,* 173.
114 "The General's orders . . . discharged my duty": GW to Bouquet, Aug. 6, 1758.

CHAPTER 23

115 "We are still . . . remote a distance": GW to Robinson, Sept. 1, 1758.
116 "This is a heavy stroke": GW to Fairfax, Sept. 25, 1758.
116 "The troops were . . . tents much longer": GW to Fauquier, Sept. 28, 1758.
116 "This plan": GW to Forbes, Oct. 8, 1758.
117 "My march . . . my judgment": GW to Fauquier, Oct. 30, 1758.
117 "The General": GW to Fauquier, Nov. 5, 1758.
117 "Do you believe . . . little imprudent": GW to Bouquet, Nov. 6, 1758.
118 "The arguments . . . prudence dictates": Council of war, Nov. 11, 1758, in *The Papers of Henry Bouquet,* ed. S. K. Stevens et al. (1951), 2:600–601.
119 "You may believe . . . killed or missing": Forbes to Abercrombie, Nov. 17, 1758, in *Writings of Forbes,* 255.
119 "We have had": *Pennsylvania Gazette,* Nov. 30, 1758.
120 "three prisoners": GW to Fauquier, Nov. 28, 1758.
120 "During the time": GW remarks for David Humphreys, ca. Aug. 1786, in Orderly book, Nov. 12, 1758, n1, GW Papers.
121 "He asked me": *Niles' Register,* May 9, 1818.
121 "Two detachments": Thomas W. Bullitt, *My Life at Oxmoor,* ed. William Marshall Bullitt (1911), 3–4.
122 "Which if true": Forbes to Abercrombie, Nov. 17, 1758, in *Writings of Forbes,* 255.
122 "The keeping": GW to Forbes, Nov. 16, 1758.
122 "I fear": GW to Forbes, Nov. 18, 1758.
122 "I have the pleasure . . . comfort of life": GW to Fauquier, Nov. 28, 1758.

CHAPTER 24

128 "I would go to law": "John Custis," in *Encyclopedia Virginia,* encyclopediavirginia .org.
129 "*Aged 71 Years*": "Custis Tombs/Arlington Plantation," co.northampton.va.us.
129 "My place of residence": GW to Robin (last name not given), n.d. (1749–50).
129 "Oh ye gods": GW poetry, n.d. (1749–50).
129 "'Tis true": GW to Sarah Cary Fairfax, Sept. 12, 1758.

131 "We your most . . . know and love": Address from the officers of the Virginia regiment, Dec. 31, 1758.
132 "To the Officers": GW to the officers of the Virginia regiment, Jan. 10, 1759.

CHAPTER 25

133 "It is now too apparent": *The Parliamentary History of England from the Earliest Period to the Year 1803* (1812), 12:1035.
133 "Pitt, it was expected": Walpole, *Memoirs of King George the Second,* 3:9.
134 "My Lord": Walter Vernon Anson, *The Life of Admiral Lord Anson* (1912), 139.
134 "Mad is he? . . . them together": Parkman, *Montcalm and Wolfe,* 2:188–91, 206.
135 "The 8th . . . fortifications": "A Journal of the Expedition up the River St. Lawrence," in *Manuscripts Relating to the Early History of Canada,* 2nd ser. (1868), 4–10.
137 "Everything proves . . . *De la Reine*": Parkman, *Montcalm and Wolfe,* 2:275, 280, 286.
137 "I remember": "Le Regiment des Montagnards Ecossais," *Revue canadienne* (1867), 4:856.
138 "The 12th": "Journal of the Expedition," 11–12.
138 "Now, God . . . my friends": Parkman, *Montcalm and Wolfe,* 2:297–98.

CHAPTER 26

139 "No British monarch . . . chosen for him": Walpole, *Memoirs of the Reign of King George the Third* (1844), 1:4–6, 65.
141 "I am the Maker . . . happy and prosperous": Francis Parkman, *The Conspiracy of Pontiac and the Indian War After the Conquest of Canada* (1885 ed.), 1:206–7.
142 "Going instantly . . . have touched me": *Alexander Henry's Travels and Adventures in the Years 1760–1776,* ed. Milo Milton Quaife (1921), 77–84.
144 "Could it not be . . . at present": Parkman, *Conspiracy of Pontiac,* 2:44–47.
145 "grant warrants": George III proclamation, Oct. 7, 1763, Canadian Constitutional Documents, solon.org.

CHAPTER 27

146 "It might . . . void of credit": GW to Cary, Aug. 10, 1764.
147 "Visited my plantations . . . herrings were come": GW journal, Jan. 1 and 9, Feb. 5, 15, 22 and 25, March 5, 15 and 24, April 3, 5 and 10, 1760.
148 "Sir": GW to John Thompson, July 2, 1766.
149 "Sit down": William Wirt, *Sketches of the Life and Character of Patrick Henry* (1817), 45.
150 "Another tempest": GW to Robert Stewart, Aug. 13, 1763.
150 "I can never . . . to accomplish": GW to Crawford, Sept. 21, 1767.

CHAPTER 28

153 "Resolved . . . American freedom": Wirt, *Life of Patrick Henry,* 56–57.
154 "Caesar . . . most of it": Ibid., 65.
154 "I was then": Jefferson notes on Patrick Henry, n.d. (before April 12, 1814), Jefferson Papers.
155 "Peter Green": GW journal, May 30–31, 1765.
155 "Government is set": Fauquier to Halifax, June 14, 1765, in GW to Francis Dandridge, Sept. 20, 1765, n1, in *The Writings of George Washington,* ed. Worthington Chauncey Ford (1889), vol. 2.
155 "The Stamp Act . . . repeal of it": GW to Francis Dandridge, Sept. 20, 1765.

CHAPTER 29

158 "What is your name . . . indeed make one": Franklin examination before committee of the whole of House of Commons, Feb. 13, 1766, Franklin Papers.
159 "An act for": Declaratory Act, March 18, 1766, Avalon Project, avalon.law.yale.edu.

CHAPTER 30

160 "He is a boy . . . horse racer": GW to Boucher, May 30, 1768.
161 "A natural parent . . . his own country": GW to Boucher, May 13, 1770.
162 "Joshua Evans": GW diary, Feb. 16, 1769.
162 "About a fortnight . . . any other relief": GW to John Armstrong, Aug. 18, 1769.
162 "Having once or twice": GW to Ramsay, Jan. 29, 1769.
163 "It is difficult . . . raising the money": GW to Posey, June 24, 1767.
164 "P.S.": GW to Posey, Sept. 24, 1767.
164 "The terms were offered": GW to Botetourt, Dec. 8, 1769.
164 "My old chariot . . . be engraved": GW to Cary, June 6, 1768.
165 "Rid to Muddy Hole . . . which were fine": GW diary, June 1, 4, 5, 22, 25 and 28, 1768.
166 "Rid to see . . . can be cut in": GW diary, July 4, 5, 8, 12 and 25, 1768.

CHAPTER 31

168 "the full enjoyment": Massachusetts circular letter, Feb. 11, 1768, Avalon Project.
168 "equally derogatory . . . in Parliament": Letter to George III and memorial to Parliament, April 14, 1768, in *Journals of the House of Burgesses, 1766–1769,* ed. John Pendleton Kennedy (1906), 165, 169.
169 "At a time . . . be tried here": GW to Mason, April 5, 1769.
170 "A new Association": GW to Fairfax, June 27, 1770.
170 "That there should . . . have too little": GW to Boucher, July 30, 1770.
171 "You will perceive": GW to Cary, Aug. 20, 1770.

CHAPTER 32

172 "Set out about . . . established there": GW journal, Oct. 13, 15, 19, 25, 28 and 29, Nov. 1, 2, 3, 17, 18 and 22, 1770.

CHAPTER 33

178 "IMPORTER . . ." "Horrid Massacre": Hiller B. Zobel, *The Boston Massacre* (1970), 172–74, 182, 195, 211.
179 "Bloody Massacre": "Paul Revere's Engraving of the Boston Massacre, 1770," Gilder Lehrman Institute of American History, gilderlehrman.org.
179 "Feb. 1st": GW account of the weather, Feb. 1771.
179 "Inclination having": GW to Boucher, May 21, 1772.
180 "You may believe": GW to Matthew Campbell, Aug. 7, 1772.
180 "It is an easier . . . ebb of misery": GW to Burwell Bassett, June 20, 1773.
180 "I am now set down . . . at her death": GW to Benedict Calvert, April 3, 1773.
181 On the journey: GW diary, May–June 1773.
182 "The subscriber . . . Great Kanhawa": GW advertisement, July 15, 1773.

CHAPTER 34

187 "When the committee . . . destruction inevitable": Hewes quoted in James Hawkes, *A Retrospect of the Boston Tea-Party* (1834), 38–41.
190 "Are we, sir": *The Parliamentary History of England from the Earliest Period to the Year 1803* (1813), 17:1280.

CHAPTER 35

191 "Things seem to be": GW to George William Fairfax, June 10–15, 1774, n10.
192 "The cause of Boston . . . as at present": GW to Fairfax, June 10–15, 1774.
192 "As to your . . . be just ourselves": GW to Bryan Fairfax, July 4, 1774.
193 "That this Colony . . . slavery and misery": Fairfax County resolutions, July 18, 1774, in *American Archives: Fourth Series* (1833), 1:597–99.
194 "the united wisdom": Association of the Virginia convention, Aug. 1–6, 1774, Avalon Project, avalon.law.yale.edu.

CHAPTER 36

195 "On Friday . . . alarming crisis": Proceedings of the Congress held at Philadelphia, in *American Archives: Fourth Series,* 1:900.
195 "Colonel Washington . . . such an undertaking": Silas Deane to Mrs. Deane, Sept. 10, 1774, in *Letters of Members of the Continental Congress,* ed. Edmund C. Burnett (1921), 1:28.
196 "If you speak": William Wirt, *Sketches of the Life and Character of Patrick Henry* (1860 ed.), 132.
196 "He never spoke": Adams to William Wirt, Jan. 23, 1818, Adams Papers.
196 "The present unhappy . . . adhered to": Proceedings of the Congress, 913–16.
197 "Mr. Atchison": McKenzie to GW, Sept. 13, 1774.
197 "Spent the afternoon": GW diary, Sept. 28, 1774.
197 "Permit me . . . remembrance of": GW to McKenzie, Oct. 9, 1774.

CHAPTER 37

199 "the completest speaker": Deane to Mrs. Deane, Sept. 10, 1774, in *Letters of Members of the Continental Congress,* 1:28–29.
199 "As soon as": John F. Watson, *Annals of Philadelphia and Pennsylvania in the Olden Time* (1857), 1:421–22.
200 "Resolved": William Wirt, *Sketches of the Life and Character of Patrick Henry* (1860 ed.), 135.
200 "No man thinks . . . or give me death!": Ibid., 138–42. Also Henry speech, March 23, 1775, Avalon Project, avalon.law.yale.edu.
203 "Imagine to yourself": Wirt, *Sketches of the Life and Character of Patrick Henry,* 140.
203 "I have promised": GW to John Augustine Washington, March 25, 1775.

CHAPTER 38

204 "The winter . . . some convulsion": Gage to Dartmouth, March 28, 1775, in *The Correspondence of General Thomas Gage with the Secretaries of State, 1763–1775,* ed. Clarence Edwin Carter (1931), 1:394–95.
204 "Having received . . . oppose them": Gage to Dartmouth, April 22, 1775, in *Correspondence of Gage,* 396–97.
205 "You must undoubtedly . . . man hesitate?": GW to Fairfax, May 31, 1775.

CHAPTER 39

207 "Colonel Washington . . . be a soldier": Adams to Abigail Adams, May 29, 1775.
207 "This measure . . . as he lived": Adams autobiography, "In Congress, June and July 1775," Adams Papers.
209 "To George Washington . . . purpose appointed": GW commission, June 19, 1775.
210 "Mr. President . . . all I desire": GW address, June 16, 1775.

CHAPTER 40

213 "My dearest . . . in the fall": GW to Martha Washington, June 18, 1775.
214 "The skirmish . . . Lake Champlain": Gage to Dartmouth, June 12, 1775, in *Correspondence of Gage,* 404.
215 "This action . . . various quarters": Gage to Dartmouth, June 25, 1775 (two letters), in *Correspondence of Gage,* 405–7.

CHAPTER 41

217 "I have this morning . . . common case": Adams to Abigail Adams, June 23, 1775.
217 "Washington, Lee": Thomas Jones, *History of New York During the Revolutionary War,* ed. Edward Floyd de Lancey (1879), 1:55.
218 "The fire . . . this colony": Massachusetts provincial congress to Continental Congress, June 20, 1775, in *The Journals of Each Provincial Congress of Massachusetts in 1774 and 1775* (1838), 365–66.
219 "which I sincerely": GW to Hancock, June 25, 1775.
219 "You are to take": GW to Schuyler, June 25, 1775.
219 "The greatest civility . . . good spirits": *Pennsylvania Gazette,* July 12, 1775.
219 "The Continental Congress . . . in Cambridge": GW general orders, July 4, 1775.
221 "A general court martial": GW general orders, July 5, 1775.
221 "It is with . . . martial severity": GW general orders, July 7, 1775.

CHAPTER 42

222 "It was too strong": Jefferson autobiography, Jan. 6–July 29, 1821.
223 "A Declaration . . . and not before": Declaration, July 6, 1775, in *Journals of the Continental Congress,* 2:140–56.
224 "Most Gracious Sovereign": Petition, July 8, 1775, in *Journals of the Continental Congress,* 158–61.

CHAPTER 43

225 "Dear Brother . . . of the continent": GW to John Augustine Washington, July 27, 1775.
226 "I have directed": GW to Hancock, Aug. 4–5, 1775.
226 "I find": GW to Otis, Aug. 10, 1775.
227 "I understand . . . ever entitled": GW to Gage, Aug. 11, 1775.
228 "To the glory . . . under misfortune": Gage to GW, Aug. 13, 1775.
228 "You affect, sir": GW to Gage, Aug. 19, 1775.

CHAPTER 44

229 "The design . . . this enterprize": GW to Schuyler, Aug. 20, 1775.
230 "You are entrusted . . . interests of America": GW to Arnold, Sept. 14, 1775.
230 "Friends and Brethren . . . able to prevail": GW address to the inhabitants of Canada, Sept. 14, 1775.

CHAPTER 45

233 "The Connecticut . . . absolutely break up": GW to Hancock, Sept. 21, 1775.
234 "There are . . . and contempt": Franklin to Bache, Oct. 19–24, 1775, Franklin Papers.
235 "good firelocks . . . honorable Congress": Minutes of conference, Oct. 18–24, 1775.

CHAPTER 46

237 "We have had": Arnold to GW, Oct. 13, 1775.
237 "I have been much": Arnold to GW, Oct. 27–28, 1775.
237 "I accordingly": Arnold to GW, Nov. 8, 1775.
238 "I received . . . country secure": GW to Arnold, Jan. 27, 1776.
238 "You may be": Arnold to GW, Feb. 27, 1776.

CHAPTER 47

240 "In the following . . . TIME TO PART": Thomas Paine, *Common Sense* (1776).

CHAPTER 48

243 "The small pox": Adams to Cooper, June 9, 1776.
243 "Cruel small pox": Adams to Abigail Adams, June 16, 1776.
243 "The small pox": Adams to Abigail Adams, June 26, 1776.
243 "Our army": Arnold to GW, May 8, 1776.
243 "It will appear": GW to Otis, Dec. 10, 1775.
243 "The small pox is": GW to Hancock, Dec. 15, 1775.
244 "About 150": GW to Hancock, Dec. 14, 1775.
244 "If we escape": GW to Hancock, Dec. 15, 1775.
244 "Should the disorder": GW to William Shippen Jr., Feb. 6, 1777.

CHAPTER 49

245 "On the 9th of November": *The Narrative of Lieut. Gen. Sir William Howe in a Committee of the House of Commons on the 29th of April 1779* (1780), 3.
245 "To harass . . . day or two": GW to Hancock, March 7–9, 1776.
247 "He has no intention": Boston selectmen to GW, March 8, 1776.
247 "There is no possibility": GW to Hancock, March 7–9, 1776.
247 "All officers . . . accordingly": GW proclamation, March 21, 1776.
248 "As the enemy": GW general orders, March 13, 1776.
248 "The hospital": GW general orders, March 25, 1776.
248 "The town has . . . the disappointment": GW to John Augustine Washington, March 31, 1776.

CHAPTER 50

253 "Early in February . . . some in another": Jones, *History of New York During the Revolutionary War*, 1:82–84.
255 "A republican mob . . . 'to do with it'": Ibid., 101–4.
256 "Congress": GW to Hancock, June 28, 1776.
257 "May it not": GW to Hancock, May 11, 1776.
257 "The disaffection": GW to Hancock, July 4, 1776.
257 "The honorable": GW general orders, July 9, 1776.
257 "Agreeable": Webb journal, July 9, 1776, in *Correspondence and Journals of Samuel Blachley Webb*, ed. Worthington Chauncey Ford (1893), 1:153.

258 "Last night": Ibid., July 10, 1776.
258 "Though the General": GW general orders, July 10, 1776.

CHAPTER 51

259 "General Howe's . . . leading to it": GW to Schuyler, July 11, 1776.
259 "As this city": GW to New York committee of safety, July 19, 1776.
260 "As I expect . . . any disturbance": GW to John Augustine Washington, July 22, 1776.
260 "By two deserters . . . takes place": GW to Trumbull, Aug. 7, 1776.
261 "The enemy's whole . . . suitably noticed": GW general orders, Aug. 13, 1776.
262 "It was about . . . below the pass": T. W. Field, *Historic and Antiquarian Scenes of Brooklyn and Its Vicinity* (1868), 63–66.
264 "Good God": James McSherry, *History of Maryland* (1849), 201.
264 "Had the troops . . . even criminal": Howe letter, Sept. 3, 1776, and Howe testimony, April 29, 1779, in *Parliamentary Register* (1802), 9:322–23.
265 "This was the first . . . ferry stairs": "Major Tallmadge's Account of the Battles of Long Island and White Plains," in Henry P. Johnston, *The Campaign of 1776 Around New York and Brooklyn* (1878), part 2, 77–79.

CHAPTER 52

267 "Long did I endeavour": Franklin to Richard Howe, July 20, 1776.
267 "We walked . . . 'mortification'": Adams autobiography, Sept. 17, 1776, Adams Papers.
268 "Our situation . . . profound secret": GW to Hancock, Sept. 2, 1776.
269 "Congress, having": Hancock to GW, Sept. 3, 1776.
269 "It is hardly possible": *Journal of Rear-Admiral Bartholomew James, 1752–1828,* ed. John Knox Laughton (1896), 31.
270 "As soon as I heard . . . blessings of freedom": GW to Hancock, Sept. 16, 1776.
271 "About the time . . . of our troops": GW to Hancock, Sept. 18, 1776.
272 "The fire raged": *New York Mercury,* Sept. 30, 1776, in *Diary of the American Revolution from Newspapers and Original Documents,* comp. Frank Moore (1860), 1:311–12.
272 "I have not been": GW to Hancock, Sept. 22, 1776.
272 "Providence . . . errors of Congress": GW to Lund Washington, Oct. 6, 1776.

CHAPTER 53

274 "If the enemy": GW to Trumbull, Oct. 20, 1776.
274 "We crossed . . . all the evening": Joseph Plumb Martin, *Narrative of Some of the Adventures, Dangers and Sufferings of a Revolutionary Soldier* (1830), 38–41.
276 "If we cannot": GW to Greene, Nov. 8, 1776.
276 "This is a most . . . motions of things": GW to John Augustine Washington, Nov. 6–19, 1776.

CHAPTER 54

278 "Having no idea": GW to Reed, Nov. 30, 1776.
278 "I received . . . accoutred for service": Lee to Reed, Nov. 24, 1776, in *The Lee Papers,* in *Collections of the New-York Historical Society for the Year 1872* (1873), 2:305–6.
279 "I do not mean . . . will be vain": Reed to Lee, Nov. 21, 1776, in *Lee Papers,* 2:293.
280 "We are all . . . total defeat": Reed to GW, Dec. 22, 1776.

281 "The weather": Howe to Germain, Dec. 20, 1776, in *Documents of the American Revolution, 1770–1783* (Colonial Office Series), ed. K. G. Davies (1976), 12:267.
282 "Christmas day . . . push on": GW to Reed, Dec. 23, 1776.

CHAPTER 55

283 "Each brigade . . . five o'clock": GW general orders, Dec. 25, 1776.
283 "Trenton is . . . completely surrounded": Knox to Mrs. Knox, Dec. 28, 1776, in "Life and Correspondence of Major-General Henry Knox," in Francis S. Drake, *Memorials of the Society of the Cincinnati of Massachusetts* (1873), 120–21.
285 "About daylight . . . from the boats": William S. Powell, "A Connecticut Soldier Under Washington: Elisha Bostwick's Memoirs of the First Years of the Revolution," *William and Mary Quarterly* 6, no. 1 (1949): 101–3.
285 "I have the pleasure . . . to the others": GW to Hancock, Dec. 27, 1776.

CHAPTER 56

287 "I am just setting out . . . pursuit at that time": GW to Hancock, Dec. 29, 1776.
287 "Three or four days . . . volunteers": "Diary of Sergeant R—— at Princeton," in *The Pennsylvania-German Society Proceedings and Addresses* (1908), 119–24.
289 "Cornwallis left . . . scene of carnage": Ibid.

CHAPTER 57

293 "My Lord . . . from Rhode Island": Howe to Germain, Jan. 20, 1777, in *Documents of the American Revolution,* 14:33.
293 "In these circumstances . . . the northern army": Howe to Germain, April 2, 1777, in *Documents of the American Revolution,* 64–65.
295 "As yet": GW to Trumbull, April 12, 1777.
295 "The stratagems . . . in that quarter": GW to Hancock, April 18–19, 1777.
295 "I should be happy": GW to Trumbull, May 11, 1777.
296 "I was surprized": GW to Arnold, April 2, 1777.
296 "It is needless": GW to Hancock, May 12, 1777.
296 "My ambition": Hamilton to Edward Stevens, Nov. 11, 1769.
297 "Your letter . . . principal intention": Hamilton to McDougall, March 10, 1777.
299 "I have been . . . to conciliate": GW to Franklin, Aug. 17, 1777.
299 "a young nobleman": Franklin et al. to GW, Aug. or Sept. 1777.
300 "By the motions . . . perplexing": GW to Rutledge, July 5, 1777.
301 "We are told": GW to Trumbull, July 7, 1777.
301 "General Howe": GW to Heath, July 19, 1777.
301 "We have been . . . intelligence": GW to Hancock, July 22, 1777.
302 "The expedition": Howe to Burgoyne (purportedly), July 20, 1777, note to GW to Israel Putnam, July 25, 1777, in *The Writings of George Washington,* ed. Worthington Chauncey Ford (1890), vol. 5.
302 "The complexion . . . destination": GW to Putnam, July 25, 1777.
302 "Since General Howe's . . . of the enemy": GW to John Augustine Washington, Aug. 5, 1777.
302 "I am now": GW to Gates, Aug. 20, 1777.
303 "I this morning": GW to Hancock, Aug. 27, 1777.
303 "The enemy advanced . . . enemy today": GW to Hancock, Sept. 9, 1777.

CHAPTER 58

305 "The war is now": Howe to Germain, July 7, 1777, in *Documents of the American Revolution,* 14:129–30.
305 "He seems to point": Howe to Germain, July 16, 1777, in *Documents of the American Revolution,* 145.
306 "I cannot flatter": Howe to Germain, Aug. 30, 1777, in *Documents of the American Revolution,* 181.
306 "Last night . . . all of his cannon": Friedrich von Muenchhausen, *At General Howe's Side, 1776–1778: The Diary of General William Howe's Aide de Camp* (1974), 31–32.
306 "I am sorry . . . now sustained": GW to Hancock, Sept. 11, 1777.

CHAPTER 59

309 "I have just now": Hancock to GW, Sept. 30, 1777.
309 "Friday morning . . . were engaged": Gates to Hancock, Sept. 22, 1777, in note to ibid.
310 "The divisions . . . being in actions": GW to Hancock, Oct. 5, 1777.
311 "Since I had . . . to circumstances": GW to Hancock, Oct. 7, 1777.
312 "But for a thick . . . stroke of Providence": GW to John Augustine Washington, Oct. 18, 1777.
313 "total defection . . . and permanent": Burgoyne to Germain, Oct. 20, 1777 (two letters), in *Documents of the American Revolution,* 14:228–37.
313 "My lord . . . present possessions": Howe to Germain, Nov. 30, 1777, in *Documents of the American Revolution,* 264–65.

CHAPTER 60

315: "Heaven has been": Conway letter excerpted in GW to Conway, Nov. 5, 1777.
315 "I wrote . . . way of thinking": Conway to GW, Nov. 5, 1777.
316 "The hopes": Conway to GW, Nov. 16, 1777.
316 "It remains": GW to Conway, Nov. 16, 1777.
317 "Your appointment": GW to Conway, Dec. 30, 1777.
317 "I cannot sufficiently . . . moment to conceal": GW to Laurens, Jan. 31, 1778.
318 "My caution": GW to Henry, March 28, 1778.
318 "I do myself . . . have in contemplation": GW to Gates, Oct. 30, 1777.
319 "degeneracy . . . incendiary": Hamilton to Clinton, Feb. 13, 1778.

CHAPTER 61

320 "Prisoners and deserters . . . much esteemed": "Valley Forge, 1777–1778: Diary of Surgeon Albigence Waldo, of the Connecticut Line," *Pennsylvania Magazine of History and Biography* 21, no. 3 (1897): 299–321.
324 "I am perfectly satisfied": GW to Steuben, June 18, 1778.
325 "She could speak": Hannah Till interview, March 1824, in John F. Watson, *Annals of Philadelphia* (1830), 552.
325 "We arrived": Diary entry for April 6, 1778, in *The Diary of Elizabeth Drinker,* ed. Elaine Forman Crane (2010), 75.
327 "Alas": Jeffrey Brace, as told to Benjamin F. Prentiss, *The Blind African Slave* (2004 ed.), 159.
327 "Three or four days . . . clothes or blankets": GW to Laurens, Dec. 22, 1777.
328 "The present situation": GW to Peter Colt, Feb. 7, 1778.

329 "It is with great reluctance . . . mutiny and dispersion": GW to Clinton, Feb. 16, 1778.
329 "To the inhabitants . . . bloody contest": GW proclamation, Feb. 18, 1778.

CHAPTER 62

331 "By death and desertion": GW to John Cadwalader, March 20, 1778.
331 "Last evening . . . were drank": *The Military Journal of George Ewing* (1928), 44–51.
333 "I there assure . . . new conquests": *Narrative of Lieut. Gen. Sir William Howe,* 11–13.

CHAPTER 63

337 "The favorable issue": GW to Lee, May 25, 1778.
337 "That the enemy": GW to Morris, May 29, 1778.
337 "You are to use": GW to Lafayette, June 25, 1778.
338 "Take the most effectual": GW to Morgan, June 23, 1778.
338 "You are immediately": GW to Scott, June 24, 1778.
338 "I have directed": GW to Maxwell, June 24, 1778.
338 "The enemy . . . yet come in": GW to John Augustine Washington, July 4, 1778.
342 "The reduction": Germain to Clinton, May 2, 1781, in *The Campaign in Virginia, 1781,* comp. Benjamin Franklin Stevens (1888), 1:469.
342 "The rapidity": Germain to Cornwallis, June 4, 1781, in *Campaign in Virginia, 1781,* 2:10.

CHAPTER 64

343 "You are immediately": GW to Arnold, June 19, 1778.
343 "Let me congratulate": GW to Arnold, March 28, 1780.
344 "Twenty times": Arnold to Margaret Shippen, Sept. 25, 1778, in "Life of Margaret Shippen, Wife of Benedict Arnold," *Pennsylvania Magazine of History and Biography* 25, no. 1 (1901): 30.
344 "You are to proceed": GW to Arnold, Aug. 3, 1780.
344 "a post in which": Carl Van Doren, *Secret History of the American Revolution* (1941), 463–65.
345 "Sir . . . of her country": Arnold to GW, Sept. 25, 1780.
346 "I saw an amiable": Hamilton to Elizabeth Schuyler, Sept. 25, 1780.
347 "He came from . . . in consequence": Arnold to GW, Oct. 1, 1780.
347 "Buoyed above": André to GW, Oct. 1, 1780.
348 "From these proceedings": GW to Clinton, Sept. 30, 1780.

CHAPTER 65

349 "A fine morning": "The Diary of the Revolt in the Pennsylvania Line, January 1781," *Pennsylvania Archives,* ser. 2, 11:657–59.
350 "We are reduced . . . of the picture": Wayne to Reed, Dec. 16, 1780, in William B. Reed, *Life and Correspondence of Joseph Reed* (1847), 2:315–17.
351 "The most general . . . cannot tell": Wayne to GW, Jan. 2, 1781, in "Diary of the Revolt," 665–66.
353 "I went over": Unknown writer to Wayne, Jan. 4, 1781, in "Diary of the Revolt," 665–66.
353 "January 7th": McClellan diary for Jan. 7, 1781, in "Diary of the Revolt," 675.
353 "It having been": Clinton proposal, Jan. 7, 1781, in "Diary of the Revolt," 678.

353 "The troops have rejected": Reed to Congress, Jan. 7, 1781, in "Diary of the Revolt," 678.
354 "Persuaded that": GW circular letter, Jan. 22, 1781.
354 "This has totally": GW to Nathanael Greene, Feb. 2, 1781.

CHAPTER 66

355 "It was agreed . . . Charlestown": GW to Knox, Feb. 10, 1781.
355 "All the French troops": GW to Samuel Huntington, May 27, 1781.
356 "The enemy will": GW to Jefferson, June 8, 1781.
357 "It will be by": Undated letter from de Grasse enclosed in Rochambeau to GW, June 12, 1781.
357 "I have already": Rochambeau to GW, June 12, 1781.
357 "Your requisitions . . . appearance in": GW to Rochambeau, June 13, 1781.
358 "Could not . . . primary object": Notes of meeting, July 19, 1781.
358 "In consequence": GW to de Grasse, Aug. 17, 1781.

CHAPTER 67

359 "The fleet": GW to Meshech Weare et al., Aug. 21, 1781.
359 "My dear Marquis . . . impatience and anxiety": GW to Lafayette, Sept. 1, 1781.
360 "I had the honor": GW to de Grasse, Sept. 15, 1781.
360 "I marched . . . great vigor": GW to Thomas McKean, Oct. 1, 1781.
361 "The 9th . . . soon after": GW to Thomas McKean, Oct. 12, 1781.
362 "The enemy last night": GW to Thomas McKean, Oct. 16, 1781.
362 "There came a man . . . a man that did": Martin, *Narrative of Some of the Adventures, Dangers and Sufferings of a Revolutionary Soldier,* 167–71.
364 "I propose": Cornwallis to GW, Oct. 17, 1781.
364 "An ardent desire": GW to Cornwallis, Oct. 17, 1781.
365 "The night was . . . admit of description": "St. George Tucker's Journal of the Siege of Yorktown, 1781," ed. Edward M. Riley, *William and Mary Quarterly* 5, no. 3 (1948): 391–93.
366 "Officers and soldiers . . . civil resort": Articles of Capitulation, Oct. 19, 1781.
366 "The General congratulates . . . demand of us": GW general orders, Oct. 20, 1781.

CHAPTER 68

371 "During the whole month . . . consternation and distress": *The Historical and the Posthumous Memoirs of Sir Nathaniel William Wraxall, 1772–1784,* ed. Henry B. Wheatley (1884), 2:137–39.
372 "We are held": GW to John Augustine Washington, Jan. 16, 1783.
372 "In the course . . . consequences may be": GW to Jones, Dec. 14, 1782.
373 "Flattering myself . . . to my motives": Hamilton to GW, Feb. 13, 1783.
375 "The predicament": GW to Hamilton, March 4, 1783.
375 "A meeting of . . . is in vain": Anonymous documents in *Journals of the Continental Congress, 1783,* 294–97.
376 "inexpressible concern": GW to Elias Boudinot, March 12, 1783.
376 "There is something . . . occasioned thereby": GW to Hamilton, March 12, 1783.
377 "Although he is": GW general orders, March 11, 1783.
377 "Gentlemen . . . capable of attaining": GW remarks, March 15, 1783.
379 "This was . . . moisten every eye": *The Journals of Major Samuel Shaw,* ed. Josiah Quincy (1847), 103–4.

CHAPTER 69

381 "The Commander in Chief . . . United States of America": GW general orders, April 18, 1783.
382 "The great object . . . happy nation": GW to governors, June 8, 1783.
384 "We had been assembled . . . silent adieu": *Memoir of Col. Benjamin Tallmadge* (1858), 63–64.
384 "The great events . . . of public life": GW address to Congress, Dec. 23, 1783.

CHAPTER 70

386 "The King said": West quoted in Joseph Farington, *The Farington Diary*, ed. James Grieg (1923), 1:278.
387 "I see but little prospect": GW to Lafayette, Feb. 1, 1784.
387 "You very much . . . to assist you": GW to Fielding Lewis Jr., Feb. 27, 1784.
388 "After an absence . . . for 5000 acres": GW to Lewis, Feb. 1, 1784.
389 "whether there is": GW to Lewis, Feb. 14, 1784.
389 "Mr. Simpson": GW to Simpson, Feb. 13, 1784.
390 "My opinion . . . the undertaking": GW to Jefferson, March 29, 1784.
391 "I need not remark . . . to effect it": GW to Harrison, Oct. 10, 1784.
392 "How would this matter . . . on her favors": GW to Harrison, Jan. 22, 1785.
392 "This state did": GW to Greene, May 20, 1785.

CHAPTER 71

394 "He alleges": James Tilghman to GW, May 26, 1786.
395 "But I never before": GW to Tilghman, June 5, 1786.
396 "Dear sir . . . it can cure": GW to Morris, April 12, 1786.

CHAPTER 72

398 "The disinclination . . . at every step": GW to Harrison, Jan. 18, 1784.
399 "I congratulate": Hamilton to GW, March 24, 1783.
399 "The difficulty": Madison to GW, Dec. 9, 1785.
400 "A bill for the purpose": Madison to GW, Nov. 8, 1786.
400 "It was the opinion": Madison to GW, Dec. 7, 1786.
401 "Are your people": GW to Lincoln, Nov. 7, 1786.
402 "Many of them . . . to our aid": Lincoln to GW, Dec. 4, 1786 (–March 4, 1787).
402 "The suppression": GW to Lincoln, March 7, 1787.
402 "Good God!": GW to Knox, Dec. 26, 1786.
403 "If three years ago": GW to Knox, Feb. 3, 1787.
403 "Our affairs generally": GW to Knox, Feb. 25, 1787.

CHAPTER 73

404 "Waited on the president": GW diary, May 13, 1787.
404 "Monday 14th . . . organize the body": GW diary, May 14–25, 1787.
405 "General Washington was accordingly": Madison notes for May 25, 1787, in *The Records of the Federal Convention of 1787*, ed. Max Farrand (1911), 1:3–4.
406 "General Washington is well known": William Pierce, "Character Sketches of Delegates to the Federal Convention," in *Records of the Federal Convention of 1787*, 3:94.
406 "When the convention . . . owned the paper": Pierce, "Anecdotes," in *Records of the Federal Convention of 1787*, 3:86–87.
407 "The business": GW to Jefferson, May 30, 1787.

408 "Rhode Island . . . enough it is": GW to Stuart, July 1, 1787.
409 "They are now . . . recommend it": GW to Hamilton, July 10, 1787.
410 "We have now . . . most ardent wish": GW to president of Congress, Sept. 17, 1787.

CHAPTER 74

412 "I rid to all . . . that usefulness": GW diary, Nov. 1, 10, 13, 14, 1788.
413 "The almost total loss . . . affect many others": GW to Lee, April 4, 1788.
413 "Never till . . . long unpaid": GW to Conway, March 4, 1789.
414 "It appears to me . . . body of the people": GW to Lafayette, Feb. 7, 1788.
415 "The power": GW to Bushrod Washington, Nov. 10, 1787.
415 "An attempt": GW to Randolph, Jan. 8, 1788.
416 "In answer": GW to Lafayette, April 28, 1788.
416 "I am so wedded": GW to John Armstrong, April 25, 1788.
416 "At my age": GW to Charles Pettit, Aug. 16, 1788.
417 "On the delicate subject": GW to Hamilton, Aug. 28, 1788.
417 "Every public": Hamilton to GW, Sept. (no day), 1788.
417 "If the partiality . . . rashness and ambition": GW to Lee, Sept. 22, 1788.
418 "You will": GW to Hamilton, Oct. 3, 1788.
419 "My movements": GW to Knox, April 1, 1789.

CHAPTER 75

423 "This is a great . . . went to bed": *Journal of William Maclay,* ed. Edgar S. Maclay (1890), 7–10.
425 "Among the vicissitudes . . . government must depend": GW inaugural address, April 30, 1789, American Presidency Project, presidency.ucsb.edu.

CHAPTER 76

428 "As the first": GW to Madison, May 5, 1789.
428 "take care that the laws": Article 2, section 3.
429 "Unelated by your": GW to citizens of New York, May 9, 1789.
429 "To draw such a line . . . political subjects": GW to Madison, with queries, May 12, 1789, in Ford, *Writings of Washington,* vol. 11.
430 "The president's private life": Adams to GW, May 17, 1789.
430 "The public good": Hamilton to GW, May 5, 1789.
431 "I do not conceive . . . dignity we acquire": Madison speech, May 11, 1789.
432 "In the selection": GW to Jefferson, Oct. 13, 1789.
432 "Could any circumstance . . . dictated by you": Jefferson to GW, Dec. 15, 1789.

CHAPTER 77

434 "Had conversation": GW diary, Oct. 5, 6 and 8, 1789.
434 "Commenced my journey . . . Hessian fly": Ibid., Oct. 15, 1789.
435 "To the lower end . . . wheat and flour": Ibid., Oct. 16, 1789.
436 "I viewed": Ibid., Oct. 20, 1789.
436 "The distance . . . than oxen": Ibid., Oct. 21, 1789.
437 "As this town . . . wheelwrights": "Procession," Broadside, Oct. 19, 1789, Massachusetts Historical Society, masshist.org.
438 "At this place . . . leave of me": Ibid., Oct. 24, 1789.
439 "The General as President . . . must be first": Barker to Christian Barnes, n.d., excerpted at Hingham Historical Society, hinghamhistorical.org.

CHAPTER 78

441 "It is the duty . . . upon us": GW proclamation, Oct. 3, 1789.
442 "The rising credit . . . equal government": GW address, Jan. 8, 1790, American Presidency Project.
444 "All this morning": *Journal of Maclay,* 174.
444 "I made an unsuccessful . . . worth his while": Ibid., 175–77.

CHAPTER 79

446 "I was very sorry . . . thinking him dying": Abigail Adams to Tufts, May 30, 1790, Adams Family Correspondence, Massachusetts Historical Society, masshist.org.
446 "Called to see": *Journal of Maclay,* 265.
446 "About five o'clock": Theodore Sedgwick to Pamela Sedgwick, May 16, 1790, excerpted in note to William Jackson to Clement Biddle, May 2, 1790.
446 "On Monday last": Jefferson to Martha Jefferson Randolph, May 16, 1790.
447 "James powders . . . luster of his reign": Abigail Adams to Tufts, May 30, 1790.
447 "It was a case": John McVickar, *A Domestic Narrative of the Life of Samuel Bard* (1822), 136–37.
448 "I have now the pleasure": GW to McHenry, July 3, 1789.
448 "I have already had": GW to David Stuart, June 15, 1790.
448 "The President is indisposed": Jefferson to Madison, July 24, 1791.
448 "The President is much better": Jefferson to Madison, July 27, 1791.
448 "The President is got well": Jefferson to Madison, Aug. 3, 1791.
448 "The President looks better": Frances Washington to John Bassett, Sept. 21, 1791, in A. Hammond to GW, July 8, 1791, n3.

CHAPTER 80

451 "It is to be observed . . . the United States": Enclosure in Knox to GW, June 15, 1789.
453 "It will appear . . . to adopt it": Knox to GW, July 7, 1789.
456 "The United States consider . . . circuitously conducted": GW to commissioners, Aug. 29, 1789.

CHAPTER 81

459 "After a fatiguing journey": Humphreys to GW, Sept. 21, 1789.
459 "Much general talk . . . to our interest": Humphreys to GW, Sept. 26, 1789.
460 "I apprehend that": Humphreys to GW, Sept. 27, 1789.
461 "After delivering him": Willett journal, April 30, 1790, in *A Narrative of the Military Actions of Colonel Marinus Willett, Taken Chiefly from His Own Manuscript,* ed. William M. Willett (1831), 101.
461 "Brothers . . . long as the rivers": Journal entry for May 17, in *Narrative of Willett,* 105–7.
462 "On Saturday evening . . . Great Council of the States": *Gazette of the United States,* July 24, 1790.
463 "I represented him . . . several by stealth": *Autobiography, Reminiscences and Letters of John Trumbull* (1841), 164–65.
464 "The president then addressed": *Gazette of the United States,* Aug. 14, 1790.
465 "While I flatter myself": GW to Senate, Aug. 7, 1790.

CHAPTER 82

467 "plain and undeniable . . . of the government": "Report Relative to a Provision for the Support of Public Credit," Jan. 9, 1790 (transmitted Jan. 14, 1790).

CHAPTER 83

469 "It is not without . . . inconsistent language": Madison speech, April 22, 1790.
471 "A national bank . . . importance to the state": Hamilton report on a national bank, Dec. 13, 1790.

CHAPTER 84

474 "An Act . . . recited act": GW to Hamilton, Feb. 15, 1791.
474 "That the power . . . constitutionality": Randolph memorandum, Feb. 12, 1791.
475 "I consider . . . enumerated powers": Jefferson to GW, Feb. 15, 1791.
476 "Necessary often . . . prefixed to it": Hamilton memorandum, Feb. 23, 1791.
477 "The constitutionality . . . strength they possessed": Madison memorandum, ca. Jan. 31, 1820.

CHAPTER 85

479 "Mr. Lear writes": Lincoln to GW, March 15, 1786.
479 "He is a young man": Lincoln Jr. to Lincoln, Jan. 2, 1786, in Lincoln to GW, Jan. 4, 1786, n1.
479 "The attorney general": Lear to GW, April 5, 1791.
480 "The attorney general's case . . . and *Mrs. Washington*": GW to Lear, April 12, 1791.
481 "I have had a very full . . . state of freedom": Lear to GW, April 24, 1791.

CHAPTER 86

484 "Major L'Enfant": GW to Deakins and Stoddert, March 2, 1791.
484 "The late determination": L'Enfant to GW, Sept. 11, 1789.
484 "The President, having thought": Jefferson to commissioners, Jan. 29, 1791.
485 "His present instructions . . . for the public": GW to Deakins and Stoddert, March 2, 1791.
485 "The National Gazette": *National Gazette,* Oct. 31, 1791.
486 "The President with his usual": *Gazette of the United States,* March 2, 1791.
487 "The Union . . . usurpation and monarchy": *National Gazette,* April 2, 1792.
488 "It is incumbent . . . to be remedied": *National Gazette,* Feb. 27, 1793.

CHAPTER 87

490 "I have determined . . . good of mankind": Jefferson to GW, May 23, 1792.
492 "I received . . . unanimous as ever": Hamilton to GW, July 30–Aug. 3, 1792.
493 "How unfortunate . . . and abroad": GW to Jefferson, Aug. 23, 1792.
494 "Differences in political opinions . . . will go well": GW to Hamilton, Aug. 26, 1792.

CHAPTER 88

497 "Whereas it appears": GW proclamation, April 22, 1793.

CHAPTER 89

499 "The manufactures . . . extension of trade": Mathew Carey, *A Short Account of the Malignant Fever Lately Prevalent in Philadelphia* (1793), 9–13.
501 "The mortality began . . . of our city": Ibid., 20–31.
503 "The city is very sickly": GW to Howell Lewis, Aug. 25, 1793.
503 "I hope they are": GW to Hamilton, Sept. 6, 1793.
503 "Have you ever examined": GW to Randolph, Sept. 30, 1793.
504 "What harm can be done": Randolph to GW, Nov. 2, 1793.
504 "The disorder raged . . . hopes of our citizens": Carey, *Short Account*, 67–72.

CHAPTER 90

506 "violent and unwarrantable": GW proclamation, Sept. 15, 1792.
507 "The opposition . . . embarrass the government": Hamilton to GW, Aug. 5, 1794.
508 "It has from the first . . . demand of you": "Tully No. 1," Aug. 23, 1794.
509 "It is plainly this . . . begins at *anarchy*": "Tully No. 2," Aug. 26, 1794.
510 "Many persons . . . dangerous proceedings": GW proclamation, Aug. 7, 1794, American Presidency Project.
510 "Government is set": GW proclamation, Sept. 25, 1794, American Presidency Project.
511 "About seven o'clock . . . before the army arrived": William Findley, *History of the Insurrection in the Four Western Counties of Pennsylvania in the Year MDCCXCIV* (1796), 169–88.
514 "The part of our country": GW annual message, Dec. 8, 1795.

CHAPTER 91

515 "We have been as much": Jefferson to GW, Feb. 20, 1793.
516 "The President desires . . . end of 1792": Jefferson memorandum, Feb. 23, 1793.
516 "The residue": Jefferson to Ternant, Feb. 25, 1793.
517 "incompatible with": Jefferson to Genêt, June 5, 1793.
518 "I took that occasion . . . different opinion": Jefferson memorandum, July 26, 1793.
518 "Never, in my opinion . . . he may make": Jefferson to Madison, July 7, 1793.
519 "I fear the disgust . . . wish of both": Jefferson to Monroe, July 14, 1793.
519 "You will, therefore": Jefferson to Morris, Aug. 23, 1793.

CHAPTER 92

521 "The present . . . to the nation": Hamilton to GW, April 14, 1794.
522 "When you did me the honor": Jefferson to GW, July 31, 1793.
524 "Such are the outlines": Randolph to Jay, May 6, 1794.
524 "I shall be disappointed . . . greatly commended": Jay to GW, June 23, 1794.
525 "Some cabinet councils . . . find and observe it": Jay to GW, July 21, 1794.
525 "I am this moment . . . neglected or delayed": Jay to GW, Aug. 5, 1794.
526 "That attempts will be made . . . political plagues": Jay to GW, Sept. 13, 1794.
526 "As to the treaty": Jay to GW, Nov. 19, 1794.
527 "My opinion of the treaty": Jay to Randolph, Nov. 19, 1794.
527 "My task is done": Jay to Hamilton, Nov. 19, 1794.

CHAPTER 93

528 "When we review . . . citizens and men": GW proclamation, Jan. 1, 1795.
529 "We are still uninformed": Jefferson to Monroe, May 26, 1795.
529 "Mr. Bache": *Aurora Daily Advertiser*, June 29, 1795.

530 "Awakened from . . . incurable public evils": *Aurora General Advertiser,* Sept. 11, 1795.

530 "Resolved . . . alarming instrument": Boston citizens to GW, July 13, 1795.

532 "In every act . . . opinions of others": GW to Boston selectmen, July 28, 1795.

533 "It was to have been foreseen . . . similar transactions": "The Defence No. 1," July 22, 1795, Hamilton Papers.

535 "I trust that . . . with your request": GW message, March 30, 1796, American Presidency Project.

536 "You will perceive": Madison to Jefferson, April 4, 1796.

536 "The people have been": Madison to Jefferson, May 9, 1796.

CHAPTER 94

538 "It's with infinite pleasure . . . of a few days": Wayne to Henry Knox, Aug. 28, 1794, Papers of the War Department, wardepartmentpapers.org.

539 "The termination": GW annual address, Dec. 8, 1795.

539 "It appears to be indispensable": GW to Pickering, July 1, 1796.

CHAPTER 95

542 "The spectacle . . . in executing them": Young to GW, Jan. 7, 1786.

543 "Agriculture has ever . . . eighteen pounds a year": GW to Young, Aug. 6, 1786.

543 "Whether, in the opinion . . . to recommend": GW to Young, Dec. 12, 1793.

545 "There is nothing in the laws . . . envied situation": Young to GW, June 2, 1794.

546 "To acquire land in fee . . . him to employ": GW to Young, Nov. 9, 1794.

546 "I have no scruple . . . can be defrayed": GW to Lear, May 6, 1794.

CHAPTER 96

548 "When last in Philadelphia": Hamilton to GW, May 10, 1796.

548 "Having from a variety": GW to Hamilton, June 26, 1796.

549 "The period for a new election . . . labors and dangers": GW farewell address, Sept. 17, 1796, American Presidency Project.

CHAPTER 97

557 "Your dearest friend": Adams to Abigail Adams, March 5, 1797.

557 "If I had entertained . . . than I intended": GW to Jefferson, July 6, 1796.

558 "I have once more retreated": GW to Lafayette, Oct. 8, 1797.

559 "The following company dined here": GW diary, June 20, 1799.

559 "The drought has been . . . keep me afloat": GW to Lewis, Aug. 17, 1799.

559 "Distillery is a business": GW to Anderson, June 18, 1797.

560 "You ask my opinion": GW to Alexander Spotswood Jr., Nov. 22, 1798.

561 "The Alien and Sedition Laws": GW to William Vans Murray, Dec. 26, 1798.

561 "My administration . . . many an army": Adams to GW, June 22, 1798.

562 "To you, sir": Adams to GW, July 7, 1798.

562 "I cannot express . . . of circumstances": GW to Adams, July 13, 1798.

563 "I have no scruple": Hamilton to GW, June 2, 1798.

564 "In the arrangement . . . first to be last": GW to Adams, Sept. 25, 1798.

CHAPTER 98

565 "To give you . . . due to themselves": GW to Lafayette, Dec. 25, 1798.

566 "Mrs. Washington . . . restless symptoms": GW to Peters, Sept. 7, 1799.

566 "Morning cloudy": GW diary, Dec. 12, 1799.
567 "Morning snowing": GW diary, Dec. 13, 1799.
567 "On Thursday Dec. 12th . . . Tis well": Lear diary, Dec. 14, 1799.

CHAPTER 99

571 "In the name of God . . . or funeral oration": GW will, July 9, 1799.

CHAPTER 100

574 "We are all Republicans . . . alliances with none": Jefferson inaugural address, March 4, 1801, American Presidency Project.
575 "first in war": Henry Lee, *A Funeral Oration on the Death of General Washington* (1800), 10.

Index

"GW" refers to George Washington

ILLUSTRATION CREDITS

Robert Dinwiddie: Wikimedia Commons
Washington's journal: Library of Congress
Braddock's field: Wikimedia Commons
George III: Wikimedia Commons
Boston Tea Party: Wikimedia Commons
Thomas Gage: Wikimedia Commons
Battle of Lexington: Wikimedia Commons
Washington as commanding general: Wikimedia Commons
Siege of Boston: Wikimedia Commons
William Howe: Wikimedia Commons
Retreat from Long Island: Library of Congress
Crossing the Delaware: Library of Congress
Brandywine: Library of Congress
Valley Forge: Library of Congress
Horatio Gates: Wikimedia Commons
Saratoga: Wikimedia Commons
Benedict Arnold: Library of Congress
John André: Wikimedia Commons
Rochambeau and Washington: Wikimedia Commons
Battle of the Capes: Wikimedia Commons
British surrender at Yorktown: Wikimedia Commons
Washington the hero: National Gallery of Art
James Madison: Wikimedia Commons
Pennsylvania state house (Independence Hall): Library of Congress
Constitutional convention: Wikimedia Commons
Federal Hall: Library of Congress
Thomas Jefferson: Wikimedia Commons
Alexander Hamilton: Wikimedia Commons
Bank of the United States: Wikimedia Commons
Whiskey Rebellion: Wikimedia Commons
John Jay: National Gallery of Art
Mount Vernon: National Gallery of Art
Washington's tomb: Library of Congress

ABOUT THE AUTHOR

H. W. BRANDS holds the Jack S. Blanton Sr. Chair in History at the University of Texas at Austin. He has written biographies and histories that cover most of the American past. Two of his biographies, *The First American* and *Traitor to His Class,* were finalists for the Pulitzer Prize.

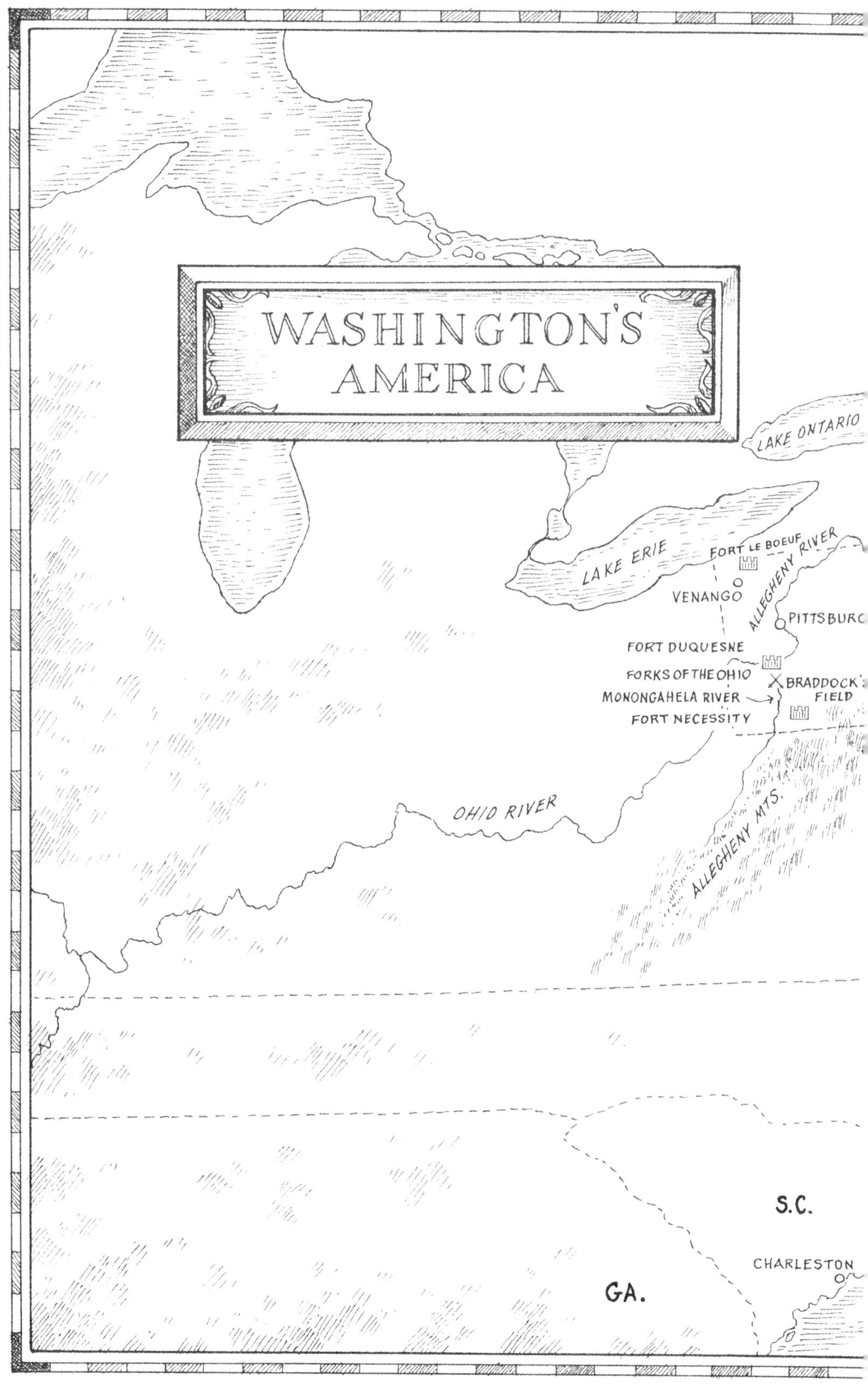
WASHINGTON'S AMERICA
LAKE ONTARIO
LAKE ERIE
FORT LE BOEUF
ALLEGHENY RIVER
VENANGO
PITTSBURG
FORT DUQUESNE
FORKS OF THE OHIO
BRADDOCK'S FIELD
MONONGAHELA RIVER
FORT NECESSITY
OHIO RIVER
ALLEGHENY MTS.
S.C.
CHARLESTON
GA.